Practical Dreamer

Gerrit Smith and the
Crusade for Social Reform

Norman Dann

LOG CABIN BOOKS

LOG CABIN BOOKS
6607 Craine Lake Road
Hamilton, NY 13346
www.logcabinbooks.com

First Paperback Edition: April 2009
10 9 8 7 6 5 4 3 2 1

ISBN 978-0-9755548-7-6

Library of Congress Control Number: 2009925905

The publisher will donate a portion
of the sale of this book to the
National Abolition Hall of Fame & Museum.

Cover Design by Carol Ann Henderson

Cover portrait of Gerrit Smith painted by Daniel Huntington,
a graduate of Hamilton College and
president of the National Academy of Design.
It is believed that this portrait hung over the coffin of Ann Smith at her funeral.
Portrait used Courtesy of the Madison County Historical Society.

Dedication

First, to Leighton and Marion Dann—Dad and Mom—
whose inspiration to persist and to do the best one can has
been eternal

Second, to Dorothy H. Willsey-Dann, Beth Dorrance
Spokowsky, and Donna Dorrance Burdick, three persons
whose infectious spirit for the history of Peterboro, New York
inspired this research

Contents

Foreword

Gerrit Smith deserves first honor among nineteenth-century social reformers because he participated in almost every important effort to transform America into a more just and equalitarian nation. Wealthy enough to provide monetary support for the Temperance movement, Women's Rights, and the Abolitionist crusade, Smith could indulge in his reformist impulses.

But as Norm Dann demonstrates in this landmark biography ten years in the making, Smith's passion for reform welled up from a complex and Olympian-like personality always ready to take up the cause of those left out of the prevailing enclaves of power.

That Smith's reformist zeal should sometimes cause him great public embarrassment, as did his support of John Brown, does not diminish his stature in Norm's superbly researched study of one of our country's most important but under-appreciated historical figures. While in his prime, Gerrit Smith used pen, voice, and purse toward so many good ends that reform became for him not an avocation, but a vocation. When calling for the abolition of slavery or for equal rights for women and in any number of other efforts to create a more perfect community, Smith was preeminently "the reformer"—as if reform defined his whole self.

Nevertheless, as Dann points out, Smith's modest headstone on his grave at the cemetery in Peterboro reads simply, "Gerrit Smith." No epitaph, no judgment of the ages. After reading this new and compelling biography, one wants to chisel "The Reformer" on that stone.

- Dr. Milton C. Sernett
Professor Emeritus of
African American Studies and History
Syracuse University

Introduction

Wind blew strongly from the northwest, moving waves of loose snow across the open meadows behind Gerrit Smith's rural upstate New York mansion. He and Franklin B. Sanborn, a prominent Boston abolitionist, walked there bundled against the cold as the snow drifted in the hedgerows. They used the winter solitude and isolation from other ears to discuss an idea that would soon shake the nation.

Abolitionist John Brown had a plan that was destined to ignite a civil war, and Smith, long frustrated with slow-moving efforts to end slavery, was ready to fund Brown's plan. On this snowy February 23, 1858, in the hamlet of Peterboro, Smith and Sanborn agreed to pay Brown's expenses in his attempt to invade the South and encourage slaves to seek freedom. Their decision could expose them to charges of treason.

Brown was waiting inside Smith's house for the result of the meeting.

Smith's momentous decision at Peterboro was the culmination of a life dedicated to the rights of the oppressed. This biography will tell the story of Gerrit Smith's life by relating the philosophical and institutional trends of his time to his thinking, his actions, and his personal life in Peterboro. The way he lived his life so closely paralleled the intellectual and practical undercurrents of the reform era preceding the Civil War that to study Gerrit Smith's life is to review the philosophies of a generation of thinkers. They believed that a sense of morality inhered in every person. In that case, they could bring that common morality to the fore and spark institutional change that would usher in an era characterized by compassion and altruism.

Gerrit Smith was a rich landowner and philanthropist in central New York, one of the richest men in the country. He used his wealth to support the issues of moral reform that he thought could improve the long-term welfare of the human community. Some remember him as a radical who instigated terrorist activities; others regard him as a fanatic who had to have his way. Yet others knew him as a tender, loving philanthropist, husband, and father dedicated to his family, his community, and to the moral responsibility of all people.

It all made good copy for the newspapers, but which was the real Gerrit Smith? In my view, they are all valid impressions, and to focus on any one of them is brutally unfair to him. Previous biographies by Frothingham, Hammond, and Harlow have claimed him to be insecure, obsessed with public approval, unbalanced, hypochondriacal, fanatical, and absolutist. They have not offered him a careful reading. Although some of his opinions were radical, he usually balanced them with practicality and reason. He often realized that his chances of success were minimal, but that did not dilute his conviction to what he saw as right.

This book is a comprehensive, intimate biography, using the written record left by Smith and his correspondents to gain insight into his life. Gerrit Smith's America was unique in the world, in that the reform movement, with its different philosophical and religious ideas, could flourish in an open society. Smith was free to incorporate Utopian and Transcendentalist ideas into the way he lived his life. He combined this philosophical foundation, his wealth, his family, and his beloved Peterboro into an optimistic, benevolent, and caring personality that provided the balance he needed to be able to accomplish success in business, become one of the leading philanthropists in American history, and to help change the way Americans thought about themselves.

Smith hoped that no one would ever "write his life," because he realized that people tended to see only his radical stands on issues without understanding his thinking. He feared that a biographer who ignored his reasoning would cause people to either idolize him or hate him. Yet as was the habit of prominent people of his day, he saved every piece of correspondence or computation that either entered or left his home or office. Although his complex land business deals justified the need for extensive record keeping, it is interesting to note that most of what he saved had nothing to do with his business. He seems to have had a notion of the historical significance of his work.

He must have agreed with his black abolitionist friend and colleague Frederick Douglass, who said, "Sad, indeed, will be the condition of the living, when they fall so low as to cease to venerate the lives and deeds of the noble dead."[1] The massive collection of papers that Smith left required many hundreds of hours to read, a task made even more difficult due to the poor quality of much of the penmanship—especially Smith's.

In this biography, I will make the case that Gerrit Smith was an important figure in American history, especially as it relates to the abolition of slavery and the beginning of the Civil War. Abolition was the only one of his reform efforts that tipped the usual balance in his life toward violent radicalism. The book will also look at his philanthropy, his work for women's rights and education, both of which became successful reform movements in America; and his work on temperance. By addressing all of these, the book will clarify some misconceptions perpetrated by previous biographers and show him as an astute businessman, a loving husband and family man, a philanthropist on a scale perhaps unprecedented in American history, and an influential participant in America's 19th-century reform movements. For him to have accomplished all of this, the book will describe a personal equilibrium in his life that was, in light of everything that he did, extraordinary.

Because I have used subjective observations to make sensible interpretations of data, some conclusions are undocumented, and I have taken care to state this point when appropriate. It is important for the reader to understand that I have used the facts of Smith's life to search for patterns. When searching for facts only, one finds what some shallow investigations of Gerrit Smith have reported. When searching for patterns, one senses the feelings of the person. Unlike previous biographers, I did not focus only on his extreme behavior—such as his piety or his foolishness—but on the totality of the way he lived. As my professional expertise lies in the arena of interdisciplinary social science, I looked at the interplay of institutional forces in an effort to discern patterns of balance.

I was interested in how and why he did what he did; illustrating one's extremes is easy, but bearing them as one's sole legacy is absurd. In fact, what appears to be outrageous behavior when taken on its own may actually prove one's life balance when observed within the context of a person's values and the way that person lives his life.

As this story plays out, I have given the reader as much of a feel for the times and the people as possible. Original source material allows Gerrit and his family and associates to describe in their own words their actions, habits, feelings, beliefs, motives and inclinations. I retained their original spelling and punctuation.

Part I of the book describes his early development, his style, his values, and his family. Part II relates his perceptions concerning religion, business, and politics. Part III covers his participation in the reform movements of abolition, suffrage, and temperance. Because he was a complex person, Smith was at times a bigoted fanatic, and at other times an unselfish and benevolent champion of the oppressed. Taken alone, neither perception of him is fair and just. Taken together, they help the reader begin to perceive the sources of Smith's personal security, balance, and optimism.

Near the end of a long speech to the New York State legislature on February 6, 1861, Smith, recognizing that the ideas he had just stated on human rights were radical, said, "Let me become, if it is possible, even more than ever the public laughing-stock, because of my fanaticism, which prefers truth to numbers and the right to popularity." And, in a speech in Peterboro on April 14, 1861, he said,

"Life is short. Let us hasten to say what we believe men need to have said, even though we shall be hated for saying it." These statements hardly sound like the efforts of a weak person seeking accolades or public approval, as some writers have suggested.

Smith's obsessions seem incompatible: he spent enormous amounts of time making money, but he was also consumed with moral reform. Yet the press of these seemingly contradictory pursuits stimulated him. He worked hard in the isolation of his beloved Peterboro through 10- to 15-hour days with a personal sense of security and dedication.

His recreation was writing. He recorded his ideas in letters, circulars, newspaper articles, speeches, sermons, and verses. That written record shows he could face the complexities of victories and defeats, successes and frustrations. In the end, he was able to sort out the attending advantages and disadvantages—always practical, and ever the dreamer.

PART I

The Personal Side of Gerrit Smith

- 1 -

The Early Days:
Boyhood, College, and the Era

Peter Smith was born in Rockland County, New York on November 15, 1768.

As a young man, he developed a friendship with John Jacob Astor. They became fur traders doing business with Native Americans from the Oneida, Seneca, Mohawk, and Cayuga tribes in upstate New York. In 1789, Peter moved to what is now Utica and established himself by opening a store in a house that he built on the Bleecker property on Main Street. He acquired furs from the Native Americans in exchange for supplies and sent the furs to Astor for sale in New York City. The two men split a handsome profit, and Peter invested some of his money in land in central New York State.

He became a member of the aristocratic Livingston family of Johnstown, New York when he married Elizabeth Livingston on February 5, 1792.

Gerrit Smith was born in the Main Street house in Utica on March 6, 1797—the same day on which George Washington hosted his presidential farewell dinner. Gerrit was the third of five children born to Peter and Elizabeth. The Livingstons and Astors would prove to be valuable connections for Gerrit Smith later in his life.

Gerrit Smith considered his father, as he wrote in a letter to his mother from college in 1815, to be "cold and repulsive."[1] Their

tragic relationship would later affect Gerrit's relationship with his
own son.

Gerrit's poor relationship with his father probably started in the
early Utica days. After Gerrit's death, Rutger B. Miller, brother-
in-law to Gerrit's daughter Elizabeth, reminisced about Peter and
Gerrit:

> "[Peter] had domestic troubles with his children.
> His sons Peter + Gerrit were unruly scapegraces,
> and levied blackmail on the surrounding village
> for the pocket money denied them by the sordid
> avarice of their father...."[2]

Gerrit recalled in adulthood that his mother "would gladly have
taught me more had I only been more teachable."[3]

In 1806, when Gerrit was nine years old, his father moved his
family west to the Madison County area to be closer to his developing business interests in land speculation. The hamlet Peter
Smith settled became known as Peterboro, and the surrounding
township was called Smithfield.

Gerrit did not appear to be happy in Peterboro. Later, he would
write to his own son, "Yours is a youth of immense advantage.
Mine was not."[4] Until the age of 16, Gerrit spent his Peterboro
days engaged in manual labor at his parents' insistence,[5] probably
with Peter's slaves, one of whom was named Jack. He helped clear
land around the developing estate, providing firewood for two
local glass factories owned by his father. In 1801, Peter may have
had as many as seven slaves.[6]

Gerrit spent some of his time after the age of 12 in Peter's land
office "to assist in his business."[7] Peter was a pious man and a domineering patriarch. He was not well-liked by his family. He wrote
in his diary in the 1820s of his dependence on divine guidance in
managing his life.[8] Peter married twice. Elizabeth died in 1818,
and his second wife, Sarah Pogson, returned to her native England
after a few unhappy years, leaving Peter more bitter than before.[9]

Gerrit did have the advantage of a lively household that welcomed strangers. His father allowed local Native Americans to use his house as a gathering place for councils, at which he would act as "moderator over [their] deliberations.... The kitchen floor at night was often strewn with sleeping Indians, and the council fire often blazed among the trees...."[10]

Gerrit also attended school in Peterboro. One boyhood friend remarked in an 1874 letter, "I suppose, as you do, that we are the only survivors of those who attended school at Peterboro in 1807 and 1808."[11] In 1809 and 1810, he attended the Fairfield Seminary (Herkimer County) with his brother, Peter Sken. A letter to Peter from Gerrit's teacher indicated that Gerrit and Peter Sken were doing well and should return for more schooling.[12]

In the fall of 1814, Gerrit departed Peterboro for Hamilton College in Clinton, New York. This exit from Peterboro must have been at least somewhat pleasant for him, because it removed him from direct contact with his father. Nevertheless, he still found his father's influence to be disagreeable. In a letter to his mother, Gerrit called his father a poor parent and complained of having received a visit in Clinton from him when he (Peter) was sick, thus endangering Gerrit's own health. Gerrit said, "Life to me has been but a scene of trouble." Life's pleasant moments, he wrote, brought only "momentary hope" before "quickly increased dejection."[13]

Throughout his college years, Gerrit complained that his father did not send him enough money to cover his expenses and did not support his desire to become "a scholar and a man worthy of his relatives and friends."[14] Peter did respond positively to Gerrit's request for $100 to pay for a trip to Montreal in order to study the French language,[15] but most of their communications were antagonistic. Rutger Miller accused Peter of "an inordinate Egoism [which] prevented him from being happy or making others so."[16]

Gerrit did well in his collegiate studies. He was not, however, a role model for morality. He enjoyed playing cards, gambling, and drinking. A college friend, F. W. Haight, gave him a book as a gift in which he inscribed, "to his sincere, affectionate, sentimental, poetic, ambitious, superior-minded, noble, generous, honest, honorable, jealous, deceitful, hoaxing, partial, epicurean, gambling Smith, as a token of high esteem. Hamilton College, July 23, 1816."[17]

This paradoxical list of traits presages balance in Gerrit Smith's life. He was a popular figure in college and enjoyed the games and pranks of youth with his colleagues. One of them, Oren Cothin, recalled,

> "Often I have reflected with the greatest delight
> upon the time we passed so pleasantly together
> in our collegiate course.... But those days, which
> perhaps then we might consider as almost void of
> pleasure... I can now receive with greatest delight
> and count them among my happiest days."[18]

Although the Hamilton College catalogs for 1814-1818 contained no indication of the courses of study, the one for 1823 did, and it is unlikely that the standard curriculum of the era in classical letters would have changed much by that date. A survey of the topics and authors Gerrit Smith most likely studied offers a glimpse into the ideas that shaped his adult mind.

Smith's freshman year was probably steeped in the history of Greece and Rome, with much reading and discussion of the writings of Livy. The Roman historian reviewed history in personal and moral terms and encouraged students to trace the process of Roman moral decline to learn lessons for the present. His emphasis was on one's character and the primacy of fairness and modesty as forces producing social change.

During Gerrit's sophomore year, students studied the thoughts and writings of Horace, a Latin poet who attacked social abuses in moralistic verse. Horace's principal concern was individual human conduct, which he believed should exemplify an entire society's values. Horace believed that one achieved wisdom through peaceful serenity and detachment from public life. He considered the pursuit of wealth and social position to be unethical.

In the second half of his college career, Smith read the works of Tacitus, a Roman official of the first century who wrote that the pathology of political tyranny was inherent in the tendency of power to corrupt those who held it. Tacitus emphasized the value of simple virtue in counteracting moral decay. Smith's religious study included Homer's *Iliad*, the thesis of which is the fusion of the divine and the human; and William Paley's ideas on ethics and science. Paley built what he called a natural theology, with God being manifest in nature.

Samuel Butler's ideas on religion attacked the tendency of religious belief systems to be absolute and extreme, leading to pretentiousness, fanaticism, hypocrisy, and intolerance. Gerrit spoke well of his college days, praising several of his professors as "devoted to the improvement of... pupils," "good natured," or "the very ablest."[19]

He also studied the practical sciences of mathematics, chemistry, geography, and surveying, all of which probably taught Smith that pragmatic approaches were best in the pursuit of social change. As will become clear in later chapters, the courses of study at Hamilton College were the intellectual inspiration for Gerrit Smith's evolving view of the world.[20]

Gerrit Smith graduated Hamilton College on August 26, 1818 as valedictorian of his small class of ten students.[21] He was a complex thinker and an excellent scholar who hoped to become a lawyer. He had, even before graduation, received from his Uncle Edward Livingston in Columbus, Ohio an invitation to pursue a legal career there. "As soon as you have completed your studies," his uncle wrote, "it would afford additional satisfaction to see you here on a visit and as your state is already overstocked with professional characters, there might be strong inducements for you to settle in this State...."[22]

Tragedy, however, would put an abrupt halt to his legal aspirations. On August 27, 1818, the day after his graduation from Hamilton College, his mother, Elizabeth Livingston Smith, died of cholera. Gerrit was close to his mother, and her death was a blow to him. It squelched the joy of his graduation and his plans for a career apart from his family.

Gerrit's father turned to him—not his older brother, Peter—for strength in his time of bereavement. Gerrit was trapped in a situation where his father sorely needed his calm and steady personality. He remained in Peterboro with his father for the rest of 1818 while making wedding plans with Wealtha Ann Backus, his college sweetheart and the daughter of the late president of Hamilton College.

Gerrit and Wealtha were married on January 11, 1819 in Rochester, New York, after an engagement of two years. Only seven months later, on August 19, 1819, Wealtha died of what was then called "dropsy of the brain," now recognized as encephalitis.

The death of both his mother and his wife within one year of each other turned Gerrit's thoughts away from his plans to be a lawyer. His father lost interest in his extensive business, and decided to turn it over to Gerrit.

Even at this early stage of his life, Gerrit's generosity was evidenced by a gift to Wealtha's doctor of a deed for land as "consideration for your kind services to my wife during her severe and lingering illness…."[23] On November 1, 1819, Peter Smith sold his land business to Gerrit Smith and Daniel Cady, Gerrit's uncle. Gerrit came to manage most of the practical business affairs. He moved into the Peterboro mansion in November of 1819 while his father was still living there, bringing with him Wealtha Backus' mother as house manager. Gerrit and Wealtha had lived with Mrs. Backus before Wealtha died.

For just over two years, while Gerrit was unmarried and living in his father's house, the relationship between an idle father and a busy and independent son worsened. Gerrit, burdened with hundreds of thousands of dollars of debt from his father's business, felt that he did not need the additional anxiety produced by the presence of his father. Gerrit and Cady's new estate was worth approximately four hundred thousand dollars and was based on many thousands of acres of land.

Smith's career as a lawyer had been dashed by the burdens of an estate that would occupy much of his attention for the rest of his life. An observer of his early life said those "pursuits… most agreeable to his tastes and in consonance with his most ardent desires and fired anticipations" were gone, to be replaced with business cares that "would engross his whole time and require his best energies and would indicate and give direction to his future career and prospects from which he would gladly have been relieved…."[24]

As Gerrit became increasingly independent from his father, he courted Ann Carroll Fitzhugh, a sister to Rebecca Fitzhugh Backus, the wife of the late Wealtha Backus Smith's brother. They married on January 3, 1822 and started family life in the Peterboro mansion built in 1804 by Gerrit's father. Peter then moved to Schenectady, New York, quickly becoming more cynical and reclusive. Gerrit could now carry on the business largely free of his father's anxieties.

Gerrit's business acumen developed quickly as he encouraged "feelings of congeniality which form the basis of lasting esteem…."[25] His real estate clients generally appreciated his goodwill toward them, and his reputation for fair dealing grew. Although his dreams of becoming an attorney were gone, he studied law informally for his own use, and, on occasion, used his knowledge to aid others. In 1865, Adrian College in Michigan would confer upon him the honorary degree of L.L.D.[26]

In his later life, Smith was admitted to the New York State Bar and successfully defended a friend who had been indicted for murder.[27] Regarding that court case, he said to the judge, "To save him from the gallows has been the most painstaking labor of my life."[28]

By the age of 25, Gerrit Smith had set the course he would follow for the rest of his life: he was newly married, successful in business, the owner of a huge estate, and in search of a worthwhile cause. America was ripe for change, and Gerrit Smith was ready to leap into moral reform.

Gerrit took his professional seat in the game of life in 1819 and quickly developed a positive public reputation and a taste for moral change. The 1820s ushered in an era of optimism regarding individual responsibility, as Calvinist notions of fate and predestination were beginning to give way to more inspiring notions of individual accomplishment—even to the point of perfection. College students of Gerrit's generation studied the work of the optimistic French philosopher Condorcet, who believed that the perfectibility of humanity could result in the achievement of equality between nations and classes—including the abolishment of slavery—through the establishment of new rules that would recognize the natural base of freedom and equality.

Religious revivals were sweeping across central New York State, infusing a new enthusiasm and optimism in those wishing to build a morally perfect society. So many preachers, movements, and reformers fired up the emotions of central New Yorkers that the area became known as the "Burned-Over District."

The burning fire of reform was not lost on Smith, who was just beginning to develop as a philanthropist. It was the beginning of his lifelong obsession with social reform in America. He was attracted to efforts to help people understand the inalienable human rights of every person; he became involved in such a bewildering array of reform movements that they taxed the time and resources he could spend on his business and family.

As a budding utopian, Gerrit Smith wanted to see a world free of war, slavery, intemperance, and privilege, where equal rights were available to all—and discrimination against the less fortunate was eliminated. He saw people as self-controlling moral agents who were responsible for their own actions. This philosophy, perhaps naïve in its optimism, nonetheless fueled the reform era.

These were noble and enlightened ideas at a time when self-ishness and acquisitiveness were becoming the motivation for capitalism. In the 1820s, trends toward mechanization, capitalism, entrepreneurship, and the desire for privacy and profit shook the traditional moral foundations of communities and led to increasing problems with social order. Thus the new emphasis on moral reform. While many reformers worked in cities (e.g. Garrison in Boston, Finney, Leavitt, and the Tappans in New York) where the corruption they sought to eradicate prevailed, Smith stayed in rural Peterboro where he could see the success of his efforts. Because of their emphasis on moral perfection, reformers were vulnerable to criticism for imperfections in their own lives. A cliché of the time was that the only item that the reformers were not interested in reforming was themselves. Smith, however, seems to have tried his best not only to change others, but also to practice what he preached.

This was a complex time, both for his home life and for American society. As the culture moved from rural simplicity to urban complexity, people searched for new values, or "higher truths," with which to ground their lives. Visionaries like William Lloyd Garrison, John Greenleaf Whittier, and Gerrit Smith challenged people to stretch beyond the immediate benefits of personal gain and reapply the Revolutionary-era values of justice and liberty for the benefit of the general welfare.

As the Federalist elite eroded before the growing tide of individual power, humanitarian leaders sought to channel the newly found energies of the common man into efforts to improve the lives of all—especially the oppressed. Many people ridiculed and abused these new prophets, speaking out against them instead of the social wrongs against which they fought. In the midst of these ambiguous forces sat rural Peterboro and Gerrit Smith.

As the cities convulsed and powerful individuals took the reins of economic and political power, the moral message that rolled through the countryside emphasized one's responsibility for the well-being of others. As the reform movements and reformers fought against immorality and inequity, they gravitated toward Peterboro for financial support from Gerrit Smith. Frederick Douglass and John Brown fought the frontline battles; Smith dealt out the money.

The reform era before the Civil War spawned two fascinating and interrelated intellectual trends: Jacksonian democracy and transcendentalism. Liberal ideas pervaded American political thinking—especially in Northerners. Equality, individualism, and the desire for self-governance stirred men like Henry David Thoreau, Wendell Phillips, and Gerrit Smith into a brand of radicalism that emphasized morals and conscience.

Andrew Jackson, whose popularity eclipsed all others of his time, brought to his presidential administration a commitment to furthering the fortunes of the middle- and lower-class Americans. Jacksonian democracy was a radical expression of optimism, a militant attack on the elitist status quo and a symbol of faith in the ability of every person to improve morally and to express that improvement institutionally.

Jacksonians did not want to clutter the mind with unnecessary learning. Unlettered people could develop morally through the observation of nature, and with self-reliance. The study of nature, they believed, opened one's eyes to the significance of equality and the balance among diverse species and elements. Virtue came from being close to nature, and people could accomplish moral perfection—or at least progress toward it—through intense determination and will.

Jacksonians believed the role of government to be protection of persons and property, not regulation of people; such regulation only squelched talent and industry. Thus, paradise on earth was achievable, and its pursuit became expressed mainly through religion and communal experiments. Every individual was seen as innocent with a vast potential.[29]

Smith believed in these values and became a transcendentalist. An essential feature of transcendentalism was that people were free and limitless in their powers. The old Calvinist pessimism changed with the transcendentalists into emphasis on self-improvement through reason. Learned moral values took the place of predestination and put people 'on duty' and responsible for the quality of life. Salvation and redemption were no longer required; moral behavior was.

This was a radically optimistic view of human nature—seeing people as inherently worthy and not depraved, collectively capable of implementing a kind of moral group therapy that could lead a whole society to an educational revolution regarding the humane treatment of all citizens. In stressing reform by example, the transcendentalists pulled away from established institutions—which they saw as corrupt—and founded new ones: The Free Church, the Liberty Party, and many communal experiments.

Smith's way of thinking was what transcendentalist Ralph Waldo Emerson referred to as "idealist." Whereas "materialists" depended on history, facts, and biological drives to understand and explain the human condition, idealists looked toward free will based on inspiration and individual interpretation of what was important.[30] In the early 1800s, this was radical thinking.

In 1834, Emerson challenged the new generation of which Gerrit Smith was a part to "Build... your own world." He saw danger in retrospection—building a philosophy of life on tradition rather than on insight—and he predicted that American thought would now become practical.[31] It did, and it produced a new amalgamation of traditionally separate themes that reflected Smith's way of thinking throughout his life. Abolition was integrated with women's rights; religion was combined with nature, and politics with religion. Every person was potentially perceptive and aware of these practical connections and could perceive ways to implement the greatest good for society. Optimism minimized defeatism.

The effects of transcendentalism were not all positive, however.

Their faith in the eventual victory of morality blinded northern social leaders to the psychological benefits of intentional discrimination for those perpetrating it. Southern slave owners, for instance, regarded ownership as a source of prestige and respect, and they aspired to it. Failure to see this side of discrimination doomed the victory of morality for which the optimists worked.

This may explain in part why Smith kept at the reform effort for so long. Transcendentalists—including Gerrit Smith—perceived God and nature as one. So, if one lived by reason and saw diversity and balance operate for the good of all elements in the natural world, surely this reasonable person could transfer that principle to the social world and see what is best and right for people. One could be morally good from within oneself, and not need to depend on rules stated by dogma or by government.

Such practical thought helped people understand the operation of both natural and social systems. This combination of optimistic thinking, utopian ideas, and Transcendentalist motives drove Gerrit Smith's lifelong determination to act in the practical ways with which he might actually implement some of these idealistic goals. Although he did not achieve all of the goals, his persistent effort to find practical ways of implementing them was a success.

This web of radical ideas and political optimism reached Peterboro, where Smith stood poised with his money, his pen, and his voice to offer counsel and support to nearly anyone who would come. The list of those who visited would rival any collection of heroes of American history: William Lloyd Garrison, Frederick Douglass, Elizabeth Cady Stanton, Susan B. Anthony, John Brown, Sojourner Truth, Harriet Tubman, John Greenleaf Whittier, Charles Grandison Finney, Theodore Weld, and Lewis Tappan all made the trip to Peterboro.

Smith was convinced that diversity among people was a healthy sign in society. He was a systemic thinker, seeing all parts of a system—in this case, a social system—as being valuable to the whole.[32] This view enabled him to transcend bias and embrace all

people—blacks, women, Native Americans, poor, and foreign.
His pastor said of his life,

> "Wherever trouble came, there was he with his
> sympathy, prayers and assistance, a father to the
> oppressed and afflicted, a counselor to the erring,
> a helper to the needy, a friend to every one."[33]

The pastor's glowing evaluation begs the question: if Gerrit Smith was such a man as this, why is he largely ignored by historians?

His absence from the history books is not because he was of ordinary means; he was uncommonly rich, and during his life gave away more than $8 million, the equivalent of more than $600 million in 21st-century terms. Nor was it because he wielded an unimposing presence; one acquaintance described him thus:

> "Physically he was of large stature, tall, erect,
> symmetrical with full, fair light visage, slightly
> florid black hair, large black eyes, beaming with
> intelligence and radiant with benignity, and
> tender affection, a placid countenance, endowed
> with a noble and commanding presence, a clear
> sonorous voice, with a pleasing and winning
> address."[34]

Gerrit Smith is probably so poorly represented in the history books because he was adamant during his lifetime about avoiding the limelight. He lived in relative isolation in Peterboro, missing the visibility and contact with other prominent people that he would have enjoyed if he had lived in a city. He avoided politics whenever possible; he served his brief term in the United States Congress reluctantly and considered it an unwelcome interference into his personal and professional affairs. He never became a noted statesman or a policy maker, and was only a self-appointed advisor to politicians. Though he became very wealthy, he was not a nationally known businessman. He confined his land deals mainly to New York State, eschewing the investments like railroads or shipping that would have placed him on the national stage.

He was not a church leader; even though he founded his own church and often spoke from the pulpit, he hired people to be ministers and avoided national denominations and organizations. He was not an 'action' person as were William Lloyd Garrison or John Brown or Susan B. Anthony. He would support them financially, but would not publish a newspaper, or physically fight for slaves, or travel on months-long speaking tours to cities across the nation.

Gerrit Smith was a quiet reformer, and when the public's interest in reform wanes, so does its interest in the reformers who did not get battle-scarred on the front lines of action. Initial or cursory readings of Smith make it easy to see his flaws and obsessions and thereby to minimize his importance as a nationally historic figure. But when the full context of time and events and people are integrated, he emerges as a compassionate, gentle, well-balanced person whose practical ideas and efforts influenced important policy makers.

His frequent speeches and writings kept before the masses a clear perception of their own shortcomings and hypocrisy and set in motion efforts at improvement. Smith knew that the process of reform was a significant undertaking, and that the realization of the goals of reform was often impossible. Women might not obtain their constitutional rights during his lifetime, African-Americans might suffer untoward prejudice well beyond the end of slavery, and people would always find solace in the excessive use of alcohol. But Gerrit Smith would carry on the fight anyway, undaunted.

Smith did make some blunders. In fact, his obsessions and fears at times led him into horrific traps. He made false statements publicly about persons he perceived as rivals. He committed stupid acts that produced trouble for his family, and he broke promises of loyalty to his constituents. In short, he behaved much like the rest of us. However, if it is the stand one takes against injustice that counts for the public welfare, then Gerrit Smith did his part to improve the quality of life for the oppressed. He saw inequity and tried to remedy it. He saw injustice and tried to right it. He saw discrimination and fought against it. He saw poverty and tried to relieve it. He saw ignorance and tried to inform it. He saw greed and tried to reduce it. He saw arrogance and tried to soften it.

The leaders of various reform movements frequently sought Smith as a speaker. He was an effective drawing card, popular and trusted by the public, and his name on a convention program nearly ensured its success. A fair speculation is that he spread his attention among so many reform issues that lack of specialization reduced his influence on any one movement. The fact is, where he saw injustice, he could not stand to do nothing about it, and his moral collection of 'oughts' and 'shoulds' drove him into action.

Smith's energetic expression of reform covered so many bases that he often appeared to be self-contradictory. From 1837 to 1874 he was a member and an officer in the American Peace Society, championing the notion of the peaceful settlement of disputes. By the late 1850s, he had become ready to support war. Although he was attracted to the temperance movement throughout his life, other issues interceded to, at times, dilute the priority of temperance. He favored the religious movement for non-sectarianism; denominations, he thought, supported dogma that prevented free thought. Yet he established a new church based on his own chosen principles.

His stands were clear on the other reform issues swirling throughout the country during his time. He perceived no legal or moral basis for slavery, and he worked intensely for its eradication. He supported dress reform for women as a means of leading to greater respect and freedom in their struggle to acquire the vote. He perceived secret societies to be agencies that reduced public access to information and taught biases, so he opposed them. He favored the Sunday school movement as a technique for starting children out in life the right way, and he aided a variety of institutionalized education efforts from schools for orphans and black youths to colleges.

He advocated prison reform because inmates were unjustly treated, and he opposed capital punishment. Use of tobacco products, he thought, wasted resources and desecrated the body, and helped sustain slave labor. Smith advocated boycotting all products of slave labor, and he became a vegetarian as a way to allow the earth to support more people.

He was especially concerned about several specific categories of people: prostitutes, of course, needed advice, and canal workers drank too much. He believed slave holders were criminals, yet he thought them eligible for what he called compensated emancipation. If they were to lose what they considered their property because of reform, he felt they deserved compensation.

He opposed the oppression of Greeks, Irish, Italians, and other foreign nationals who came under the sword of racial bias on the international scene, and late in his life, he spent thousands fighting what he saw as unjust slavery in Cuba.

Both home and foreign missions received his support, and he fought against public works projects, supporting instead private subscription to stock offers for building canals and roads. In short, any issue that suggested a compromise to the inherent dignity of a human being attracted Gerrit Smith's ire.

Nonetheless, the bulk of his lifelong humanitarian work and support went not to the causes listed above, but to stressed, sick, or poor individuals, many of whom never even appealed for his help. The plights of oppressed individuals who garnered his attention and his resources touched him personally. Because the workings of large reform movements like abolition were not effective through established institutions (guilds, universities, governments), the movements relied on individuals to campaign for change. Smith did this best on the local level. Thus, his radical energy was not institutionalized, but went directly to the public.

This unconnected, unnetworked approach to change, however, was not very effective.

In sum, Smith worked hard to find practical, local outlets for his resources. He funneled his money and his time, his optimism and enthusiasm toward the support of equal justice and human rights. And if his personal, individualized approach to reform did not make him famous, it remained the fundamental force of his life.

- 2 -

Human Rights and Values

In June of 1842, Henry Devan, a Peterboro resident accused by his neighbors of fornication, was pulled from his house by a mob and dragged through the streets, tied to a board. Gerrit Smith protested the mob's behavior, charging that they had ignored Devan's human rights as a citizen.[1]

Smith's fundamental motivation for becoming involved in a reform movement was the breech of human rights, which he believed were grounded in natural law and could therefore not be legitimately violated by any individual or institution. Indeed, he believed even the Constitution of the United States stood below human rights as a source of knowledge or right action.

As he wrote in a letter to Susan B. Anthony, "The Constitution is not the end of the law; …an appeal lies from it as well as from a statute. The appeal from the statute is to the constitution; the appeal from the constitution is to the law of our being...."[2] This natural law was so universal and so obvious, Smith thought, that any person could discern it. Utopian and Transcendentalist philosophers saw natural law as emanating from God, and they defined it as essentially the golden rule—to treat others as you would expect to be treated by them.

Smith agreed that fairness and justice to all human beings was a natural principle guiding all behavior.

"To the right-minded," he wrote, "there are no partition walls between [people].... Every man

is every other man's keeper."[3] All of us, he said,
should "look on every other man as a brother—as,
indeed another self."[4]

Near the end of his life, he stated this principle beautifully in a letter to Nellie W. Dyer: "I would have all men + women of whatever complexion or condition stand equal before the Laws."[5] Smith's compassion for human beings knew no national boundaries. In a letter to a member of the British Parliament, he wrote,

"The doctrine that the conventional lines, which
men have drawn upon the earth's surface, decide
the question for whom we may, + for whom we
may not feel, is utterly repugnant.... To tell me,
that I may not love [a foreigner]... is to tell me
what my nature + the God of my nature flatly
contradict."[6]

Letters between Gerrit Smith and other human rights advocates often refer to this basic principle of nondiscrimination. In writing to his "old abolitionists," he noted that for each of them, including him, "human rights have been a life-long study."[7] And John Green-leaf Whittier wrote in a touching tone to Gerrit, "It is a long time since I have seen thee. We are both getting old; but I trust that our hearts are still warm as ever in the cause of humanity and justice, temperance and peace."[8]

Smith saw human rights as fundamental to the quality of life for everyone. He claimed that to the extent that natural human rights are denied to anyone, we thereby deny ourselves an orderly existence.[9] He even held that if one was biased and realized it, the effect of the bias could be controlled, thereby upholding the rights of another person. In a speech on suffrage to the New York State Legislature in Albany, he put it this way: "Doubtless you participate in the general, the almost universal, prejudice against [the black man]. Nevertheless you are not so swayed and blinded by it, as to be unable to see, that suffrage belongs to men irrespective of their complexion...."[10]

He hoped to free people trapped by the 'them-against-us' thinking so typical of ethnocentric human cultures. The social class divisions he fought had produced elites and legitimized efforts at social control to secure one's position; discrimination was a regular feature of life for most people. Although he saw this inequality as a product of capitalism, it was not capitalism as an economic system that he opposed, but the use of its fruits: it was acceptable to be rich as long as one used his wealth to improve the opportunities of those less well-off. Hoarding wealth for personal use or gain was a sin that contradicted the natural laws of human rights.

Poverty was a major concern of Smith throughout his life. He saw a commonality in the rich and the poor, both searching for self-respect, dignity, and hope. How much money one had was not a true source of identity; how much compassion one had was. "After all," he wrote, "it is comparatively unimportant whether we are rich or poor."[11] Smith was so rich that he had few economic peers. His real peers were poor people who fought oppression: Frederick Douglass, John Brown, Beriah Green. He viewed aristocrats as a cancer on the social body and held that societies cannot prosper until they "get rid of that spirit of aristocracy and caste, which is the disease, of which poverty is but a symptom...."[12]

This deep concern for human rights pervaded all of Gerrit Smith's reform efforts. A previous biographer of Smith wondered how he managed to deal with so many "different and unrelated situations."[13] The answer is simple: Smith's causes were not, in fact, unrelated. They illustrated his consistent and abiding concern for human rights and signaled a balance of thought, perception, and purpose; they were symptoms of a clear notion of one's values.

What Smith searched for in his effort to champion human rights was a way to reconcile the conflicting forces of logic and passion. Logically, he knew that social inequity worked and that most people supported it, but his emotions and the passions of his heart could not rest knowing that the denial of equal rights made some people hurt. Logical reasoning moved him toward practical, obtainable goals designed by authority in order to implement on a social level the natural laws founded in equity and justice. Throughout his life, Smith sought practical means to balance his wealth against an unjust social system through benevolence. That is, with his head, he devised logical ways to bring about the passion of his heart.

His choice of practical techniques involved the use of existing social institutions to implement reform toward "a more perfect union." He did not renounce existing structures, but tried to reform them. In short, he balanced "head and heart," as he called it, with practical dreams. He used tested and proven tools (the current social institutions) to bring about the utopian ideals of justice and equity among people.

Smith was a utopian and a persistent reformer. Frustration and discouragement can come quickly to one who is not optimistic about the chances for eventual success, but Smith had faith in the essential goodness of people. He persisted in the face of setbacks that probably would have caused most people to quit. One of the reasons he did not feel defeated was because the practical techniques he devised to implement changes in thought and behavior brought quick, visible, small-scale benefits. As chronicled later in this book, he preferred such techniques, often giving money to individuals to help them achieve small, measurable goals.

Smith was certain that once people perceived and then experienced a life based on the natural law as stated by God and Jesus Christ, they would opt for it voluntarily.[14] He was optimistic enough to believe that his example and counsel could influence social thought and action in his state and nation,[15] although his brief tenure in the national Congress firmly tested his resolve. He had been a reluctant candidate whose neighbors nevertheless successfully drafted him in 1852.

The conciliatory nature of national politics displeased him; it did not fit his preference for local action and practical solutions. When he failed to convince others of his views, he often felt abused. After serving only half of his term, Smith quit the Congress and returned to Peterboro. He told his constituents,

> "I have, always suffered, very greatly and very unjustly... because the world has... persisted in judging me, by the light of its own, instead of my own, creeds and practices."[16]

At home, away from the politics of Washington, Smith felt powerful and secure. There, his self-definition went relatively unchallenged because he did not depend on others to define his identity. He did not define himself by his wealth, which he gave away; or by aristocratic connections, which he avoided; but as an outsider to upper-class society, a moral persuader and counselor by example. He wanted people to feel strength within themselves, and he tried to create the conditions for people to realize that strength. The role of government, he felt, was not to secure one's position through aid programs, but to protect human rights by ensuring justice. The source of personal security should come from within, not from a public crutch.

Smith was a romantic radical, believing that individuals could develop a just society if they could be helped to perceive the natural principles on which it was grounded. Their beacon would be his example of a life of benevolence. Smith lived plainly in order to set an example and to produce identity with his causes. He enjoyed spending money not for himself, but for the benefit of others. He avoided wearing fancy and expensive clothes, and there was no showy or ornamental character to his property. His house was rather plain for that of a millionaire; its most obvious symbol of ostentation may have been added in the mid-1850s, when he had its facade garnished with columns.

Smith pursued no expensive hobbies or recreation, traveled as little as possible, and ate simply. He did pay for retaining household and yard help, but he treated workers as family members, encouraging them to share in decisions and celebrations. He conserved his resources so that he could spend them to benefit others. Sometimes,

The Gerrit Smith Mansion, looking north from the Peterboro village green. Built by Peter Smith in 1804, the mansion burned in 1936.

From the author's collection

when he believed members of his family had become extravagant, he would admonish them and encourage them to think of the poor and the oppressed. He did not like to buy gifts for others, but would give them money to buy whatever they needed.

Near the middle of his life, he expressed such sentiments in a letter to his wife:

> "I this day complete my 34th year—and may I
> have grace to make it an occasion for renewing my
> gratitude to the [God] of my life, + for entering on
> his service with fresh efforts to glorify Him…. Oh
> that the year on which I have now entered, may
> be the good year… in which I shall act as though
> Heaven + Christ were all + the world + its charms
> nothing."[17]

There is some evidence that his prosaic lifestyle clashed at times with the desires of his family—especially his wife, Ann. But at least in the case of her plans for a portrait of their daughter, Elizabeth, there was no disagreement. "As to your dress for the painting, I am not particular. It may be colored as well as white, but I wish your hair plain and everything plain, as plain will look decent."[18]

He wished to draw attention to the commonality of humanity, not the differences. Accordingly, he chose to avoid the benefits of wealth and caste. He saw the hypocrisy of the elite's conservative approach to maintaining its own privileged status at the expense of others. It was during the mid-1830s that Smith finalized to himself his commitment to social equity, beginning work on abolition and temperance.

Formed in 1816, the American Colonization Society supported the idea of sending black people back to Africa to establish a free black colony. Smith supported it until the early 1830s, when he came to perceive it as a hypocritical organization whose leaders wanted to preserve the position of southern whites by ridding the area of free blacks. He quit the group and turned his support toward the immediate abolition of slavery. At about the same time, he became disaffected with Temperance movement leaders and organizations that advocated gradual progress so as not to threaten their in-group wine drinkers. Smith advocated immediacy in both reforms.

Such hope for expediency required passionate zealots like him to bring the seriousness of the issues into public view.

Schools seemed ineffective to Smith as avenues to reform. As early as 1844, he understood that schools could do little to alleviate social problems as long as attitudes at home did not change:

> "I would not speak disparagingly of schools.
> Nevertheless, they are an inferior agency in
> the work of education…. [The] object—the
> enlightenment of the lower classes—cannot be
> effected until the cord of caste is cut, and… until…
> all classes are permitted to constitute one class….
> Let the barriers of aristocracy… be thrown down,
> and more will be done in five years, toward making

the diffusion of knowledge and the blessing of
education [available to our] whole population,
than can be done in five hundred years if these
barriers remain."[19]

The values of Christianity drove Smith's reform. He was a devout
worshiper and believed that his brand of religion had the right answers. In a speech at the inauguration of the New York State Anti-
Slavery Society in 1835, he said,

"If God made me to be one of his instruments for
carrying forward the salvation of the world, then
is the right of free discussion among my inherent
rights: then may I, must I, speak of sin, any sin,
which it is my duty to search out and to assail."[20]

He counseled individuals and governments on policy toward a
just society, and noted in an address to Congress in 1854, "In this
disordered and misgoverned world there are far more precedents
for the wrong and the false than for the right and the true. Shall we,
therefore, give up the right and the true?"[21]

Although Smith's rhetoric was somewhat haughty and arrogant-
sounding, his behavior was humble. With access to Smith's diary,
Frothingham stated, "The diary is entirely free of self-consciousness,
…abounds in expressions of touching humility."[22] Once, for instance,
while traveling toward Schenectady on a stage, he disapproved of
the behavior of others, but did not offend them. "My four traveling
companions enjoyed their drinking + profaneness + filthy [talk]. I
wrapped myself up in my own thoughts as far as I could."[23]

On the subject of pride, though, Smith was adamant, as he
viewed pride as a sin and humility as a virtue. When a friend wrote
to him asking for a gift of ten dollars, he sent her five dollars, and
counseled,

"Allow me a little freedom with your feelings. You
say: 'I have still pride left, if nothing more.' I am

sorry it is left. It is the most wretched possession
we can have…. Pray God, my friend, that He will
deliver you from it, and make you his humble
brokenhearted child…. That we may both be
stripped of our pride, + be brought to lie low,
'infinitely low,' at Jesus' feet is the prayer of your
friend Gerrit Smith."[24]

To his son, Greene, he once wrote, "I found that you were pick-
ing up the sayings + phrases of vulgar and ill bred people. I hope
you will drop them all. Guard against a doubtful + critical spirit.
Be modest, meek + humble."[25]

Whenever he received compliments for his humility, Gerrit would
meekly respond that he was undeserving of such praise. When Mary
H. C. Booth of Zurich, Switzerland wrote a glowing poem honoring
his good works, his annotation on the poem read, "The grand poetic
Compliment of which I am so unworthy."[26] This combination of
values, compassion, and humility led to a third value that underlies
much of his philanthropy: benevolence.

In spite of many people's sinister motives, Smith saw and wrote
about the love all around him. "Indeed," he said in a speech condemning war in 1854, "society could not be held together, were it not
true, that the generality of men are swayed by love, and confidence,
and generosity, existing either in their own hearts, or accorded by
them to others."[27]

As parents, he and Ann taught their children to put love of
others—*all* others—as the first of their priorities. "Oh, my dear son,"
he wrote to Greene,

"may you ever so behave as to be sure to be well
spoken of! Be sincere, truthful, frank. Desire no
one, love all…. Love all your school fellows. I feel
sure, that you will never hurt any of your school
fellows. You will never… kick, bite or scratch
them. You know how offensive + horrid is all such

brutality in the eyes of your parents. Be tender to
their bodies + be tender to the feelings of their
hearts. Neither act nor speak unkindly. Love, love,
love—love all + love continually."[28]

Smith personally lived by these values. On one occasion, when
a slave was derided as a bad person, Smith paid for his freedom
and invited him to Peterboro to live a life that showed how good
the former slave could be.[29] When Henry Devan was mobbed and
defiled as a fornicator in Peterboro, Smith rose in public defense of
Devan's good side. He could not stand for the selfish tendencies of
some people to put down others to make themselves feel better or
to raise their own status. He wrote,

"Deeply engraved upon the heart of human
nature is equity.... Nature shows that men are
made to love one another.... The deeper they sink
themselves in selfishness, the deeper they sink
themselves in misery. Our nature, if preserved
in its original benevolence, forbids our betaking
ourselves to occupations, in which we cannot
benefit and bless, but in which we rather curse
mankind."[30]

Recent research into the origins of human culture suggests that
Smith was right: according to Leakey and Lewin, it was traits of
altruism and kindness—not those of aggression and selfishness—
that allowed humans to succeed as a species.

Smith's personal perceptions of behavior and his philosophy of
life contradicted then-popular notions of a noble savage surviving
by means of aggression. As he put it, "Life is short—and we have
no time to lose in doing good."[31]

Julia Griffiths, an abolitionist friend, wrote of a visit to Gerrit Smith's home, "His own beautiful spirit seems to me diffused
throughout the members of his household. Love pervades each

look, and word, and action."[32] To exemplify this spirit of love and benevolence and have it diffuse to others and influence their thought and behavior was what Smith dearly hoped for. "Charity" he said in an 1873 speech urging Cuban freedom, "has no home—but is ever on the wing in quest of objects needing her relief and comfort."[33]

Love and benevolence simplified life for Smith into a basic maxim: If oppressed, you hurt; and if you hurt, you needed help. This inspired his giving to the point that he could see opportunity in almost any situation. Traveling on a railroad car, a black woman with a baby had created a commotion that bothered other passengers. The train conductor tried to evict her, but Smith objected, intervened, and gave the woman and child his seat.[34]

Children, in fact, were often the focus of his benevolent attentions. He enjoyed having his grandchildren around, and he invested large amounts of money in the home for destitute children that he established in Peterboro. "I took a basket of apples yesterday to my dear children of the Asylum. They were very happy to get them—and I made my visit fun."[35] The last letter that he ever wrote, on Christmas Day from New York City in 1874, was to Aunt Betsey at his Peterboro homestead, charging her not to neglect the needs of the children at the orphanage while he was away.[36]

Even in his business affairs, he found opportunities to express kindness. One client feared that he had lost five acres of land purchased from Smith because he could not procure enough money to pay for them. Gerrit responded by giving him the land along with a message: "You felt bad, that you had lost these five acres—lost them by your carelessness.... It is, at but a small sacrifice that I make you a present of them.... Learn, then, to pity the poor broken-hearted slave, who has lost his all—+ lost it, too, by no fault of his own."[37]

In another case, an acquaintance who was writing a book on capital punishment knew of Smith's benevolence and wrote asking for his opinions on the issue, saying, "[I] know that your whole life has given evidence of your love for your fellow man, and standing aloof as you do from sect and party, no one... who is familiar with your life and habits, volunteers to attack you."[38]

Gerrit Smith's primary strength was as a businessman. He exhibited an acute sense for practical affairs and profit, and he was well respected for it. Business occupied his attention daily, and he frequently complained that trips and speeches removed him from this primary concern. The important people of the time—statesmen, clergymen, politicians, scientists, scholars, diplomats—were not his peers.

Smith had once been valedictorian at Hamilton College. But because of the press of business on his time, the adult man was not an avid reader, or even a profound thinker or a serious scholar, and he knew it.

> "The influence of my circumstances upon my modes of thought + action + upon my whole character, has, undoubtedly, been very great.... I am exceedingly impatient. Radical, thorough, prompt measures are the only measures I have patience with. I cannot bear a book for I have not the time to read it. Even a newspaper article, if it is more than a column long, is too much for me to wade through."[39]

And again, "...it is almost literally true, that I read no book but the bible—+ that but little—+ that my reading of newspapers might, more properly, be called glancing at them."[40]

The personal library in the Peterboro mansion contained approximately 1,800 volumes, but in the collection there were no works of literature, very little on history, no philosophical works of the classical thinkers, no science books, no treatises on social or political philosophy, no biographies, no foreign books, no travel books, nor works of drama or fiction.[41] One might wonder, what was left to account for the sizable inventory? Religious writings dominated Smith's holdings. He collected them and read mostly in tracts and small organizational journals. Thus, beyond his college experience, he was relatively unschooled and uninformed.

When he established and funded a new library in Oswego, New York in the early 1850s, he said concerning its contents, "As to the character of the library—I have only to say... that no books unfriendly to truth and purity may ever find a place in the library."[42]

Although he could read French, having studied it in Montreal, it contributed little to his scholarly sophistication. In one letter, he mentioned having read Guizot's *History of Civilization*,[43] and late in his life he did try to acquire Mark Twain's "new book."[44] But in sum, his favorite reading was on the subject of religion.

However valid this criticism of Gerrit Smith's intellectual development, it cannot detract from the good done for others through his benevolence. As Harlow suggests, Smith's lack of variety in study left him with "a profound respect for his own conclusions,"[45] but let us not ignore the point that his conclusions led him to a kindhearted philanthropy that left the public with profound respect for him.

- 3 -

Philanthropy

It was a 19th-century standard for strong males to protect the weak, but it did not follow that they should be expected to identify with those they helped. Smith did identify with those he aided, thus adding a dimension to his philanthropy that he regarded as a modeling or manifestation of the life of Christ.

If a person received a gift of land or a home, his self-esteem would rise and he would be more inclined to assert his inherent human rights. This was Smith's thinking, and he gifted thousands of acres of land to the landless and purchased homes for people who did not own them. Charitable help to one's fellows is the essence of philanthropy, and because Smith did not develop positions of leadership inside any large national institutions, he is remembered as a philanthropist. Upon his death, *The New York Herald* would describe him as "entirely philanthropic in disposition.... He was wholly sincere and honest."[1]

For Smith, it was painful not to give; he believed that philanthropy should not support the status quo, but should radically change it. To him, money provided an opportunity to rectify injustice. Smith gave away so much money that he was likely cheated out of it at times, but he claimed that he would rather be cheated than miss an opportunity to help someone who genuinely needed it. Why would he feel so? What were the reasons for his philanthropy?

Certainly religion played a part in his giving, especially early in his adult life. He claimed in his autobiography that his philanthropic tendencies were a result of his love of Christ.[2] Charles Hammond, a Peterboro resident and pastor of Smith's Free Church, believed religion to be the force that led Gerrit "to see in every man a brother, in every woman a sister."[3] According to Peterboro Methodist minister David Koeppel, "Those who knew him best knew that a deep reverence for God lay at the bottom of his philanthropy."[4]

Smith was not a devoutly religious person as a young man. After taking over his father's land business in 1819, he spent a few years searching for personal grounding and an outlet for his developing wealth. Smith's second wife, Ann, was a highly religious person who urged him toward a conversion experience. That influence, plus the waves of religious revivalism sweeping central New York in the early 1820s, must have convinced him that a religious conversion was his calling. In 1826, four years after their marriage, he experienced that conversion and began focusing his philanthropy on moral causes. He began to see himself as the steward of a divine gift of wealth given to him to improve the quality of life for all, but especially for the oppressed.

As a young, romantic visionary, Smith believed that a better world was possible, and that he was in a position to bring it about—and to experience spiritual redemption for himself in the process. Evangelist Charles G. Finney, a major figure in spreading the new theology of this "Second Great Awakening," taught that benevolence was the social manifestation of the long-term effect of salvation.[5] "Disinterested benevolence," as Finney called it, was viewed as an expression of virtue that glorified God. It became an engine of moral reform and a source of pleasure to liberal reformers such as Gerrit Smith as they put into practical form the tenets of their piety.

Smith, however, extended his benevolence not just to the morally depraved, such as drunkards and prostitutes, but also to those who were oppressed: the slaves, the sick, the poor, women, and children. His aim went beyond purifying the few to improving the welfare of an entire society. Smith believed in socialization efforts to develop males as protectors and defenders of the weak using Christ's compassion as a model. Some of his first gifts of money were to churches seeking to build or expand,[6] but as he matured, Smith came to perceive established denominations as the pernicious efforts of narrow-minded people who taught bias and intolerance, and who discriminated against others who held different beliefs. Although his religious faith remained part of the reason he continued his philanthropy, his justifications became increasingly complex.

As Frothingam has put it, "Nature made him a philanthropist."[7] Gerrit Smith did what now seems to be a very simple thing: he observed nature and saw balance among its diverse parts.[8] This is not much of a revelation now, but in the mid-1800s, it was a radical idea—especially to the religious. Most protestant denominations of the time believed that God created everything in a hierarchy of importance, with mankind at the top. Smith saw equality among all elements of "nature," as he called it.

Today, ecologists recognize a dynamic balance among all elements of a natural ecosystem. No single element, living or nonliving, is more important than any other; all species of organisms are equally marvelous and significant in contributing to the overall balance of the system. This is not far from the fundamental ecological principle that Smith clearly embraced: diversity equals stability. Every element is as good as any other, regardless of the role it plays.

Smith reasoned that any person could perceive this natural balance, and that it was but a small step to apply the same notion to social life. That is, diversity among people was also natural, and contributed to social stability. Therefore, every person was of equal value. Smith's integration of religion and nature involved the application of "ecological" thinking as a secular approach that saw balance among all parts and contradicted the traditionally accepted Calvinist theology based on predestination.

His perception of the world in a natural/social balance achieved through diversity allowed him to see good in everyone and to escape the trap of the dualistic 'us-versus-them' thinking that justified the dominance of some over others. His concept of a world in which everything is connected to everything else, where there is unity amid diversity, enabled him to reject traditional notions of social supe-riority/inferiority and to embrace the notion that the significance and value of all elements or persons is equal.

Smith sought no power over others; he looked only for opportuni-ties to use his resources to help others achieve equality. In perceiving diversity as a benefit, he could exercise empathy; and because he did not define himself in accordance with wealth or superior status, he was free to interact with all people as equals. Money did not produce for Smith a competitive advantage over others, but it did provide a tool to advance his vision of a communal society based in natural balance among its diverse social elements.

This philosophical foundation allowed Smith to direct his phi-lanthropy to any individual in need, regardless of who they were. He loved not only his own kind—males, whites, rich, Northerners, tem-perates, neighbors, Christians—but also nonbelievers, drunkards, slaves, foreigners, women, Native Americans, and children. As Smith put it, "If we are ambitious and self-seeking, it is because we have failed of the natural duty to live for others as well as for ourselves; failed, in other words, to identify ourselves with humanity...."[9]

"Humanity" included all classes of people, so his perception of the value of social diversity caused and guided his philanthropy. Though social diversity was the driving force of his philanthropy, there were other causes for it as well.

Guilt was one such cause. Smith felt guilty over having wealth, even though he had purchased his father's business and worked hard to develop it. He acted more on emotion than concern for gain or for winning. Therefore he was susceptible to guilt, and he adopted a personal responsibility for the suffering of others. One author saw his generosity "as a means to mitigate his self-imposed guilt... [as he] struggled with his conscience over the matter of his great wealth."[10]

Perhaps Smith's philanthropy was a defensive reaction formation. That is, he may have felt like a sinner and sought ways to defend against others perceiving him as such. He wrote in a letter to fellow abolitionist Lewis Tappan, "I long to be a good man. Nevertheless, I often fear that I shall die without being one."[11] And in a letter to David Koeppel one month before his death, Smith wrote, "I seem fated to make very slow progress in the Divine life, and yet Heaven knows that I desire to make rapid progress in that life of purity, and love and sweetness."[12]

Even though his wife praised him often for his tender compassion toward her, he still doubted himself and expressed his guilt in verse:

"Malignant the stars which rul'd the sad day
When this porcelain so pure was mixed with this clay!
And Nancy became the wife of a man
Who's failed to do by her the best that he can."[13]

Though guilt played a role in driving Gerrit Smith's philanthropy, it seems that by far the larger source of motivation came from his perception of inequity among people and his determination to do something about it.

Smith's empathy allowed him to feel the pain of others to such an extent that it overrode his own. During the economic panic of 1837, he allowed debtors to defer payments to him while he paid interest rates as high as twenty percent on money he had borrowed to cover his debts. He gave money to people because they were poor, not because they favored him. "If men, whom I have been in the habit of helping, year in and year out… join themselves to the great party against me—I do not say, that I shall cease to help them, (for in helping the poor I stop not to inquire, which of them are for or which are against me)...."[14]

The average annual wage for one who worked in the 1840s near Peterboro was $100, the equivalent of $7,500 in today's currency. Smith noted, "With us, a common laborer does remarkably well, if after having clothed himself, etc., etc., he lays by fifty dollars at the end of the year."[15] Smith believed that having only $50 to invest in items other than necessities left many people locked out of the American promise of equal opportunity. He believed it was his duty to provide remedy. To one who had complimented him on being philanthropic, he replied, "It is true that I own three quarters of a million acres—and yet, paradoxical as it may seem to you, I am an Agrarian, + think it wrong for a man to own more than one farm. I am rich, as the world says—+ yet paradoxical as it may seem to you, I think it a sin to be rich, and would rather live + die poor than live and die rich.

"All I can add is, that I am doing what seems to me to be my duty with my great + incumbered inheretance."[16]

Smith was willing to listen to anyone, making him gullible and susceptible to tales of woe. One problem was that he drew beggars to him, upsetting local people who sometimes complained that they were a detriment to the community. His diary includes many references to destitute people who visited his Peterboro mansion and benefited from his kindness.[17] This was, however, as we have seen, part of his plan. Wealth, to him, was of no value in itself, and acquired significance only through the manner in which one used it.

He lamented that his model of philanthropy did not spread as he would have liked it to. In praise of William Evans, a former Peterboro resident who made a fortune and returned with a gift of ten thousand dollars to aid the poor, he said, "We honor and love you: and this is not because you are rich, but because you know how to use riches. The man of great riches is not uncommon. But the great heart to use great riches is very uncommon." And Smith restated his hope that the proliferation of good works by others would result from his own philanthropy. "Whilst your generosity will bless from age to age the poor of our town, it will incite not a few rich men to make a similar provision for the poor of their native towns."[18]

Smith was often disappointed, though, as he said: "All my life, I have labored to interest them in the best things and the best people; they allow me to do it unassisted.... Yet... they take no interest."[19] It could have been due to the self-centeredness of those he helped that his philanthropic attitude never did spread much, yet he did not view his efforts as wasteful. It was worth it because he was certain that the resources would surely have been wasted if he had spent them on himself.

Obviously, then, Gerrit Smith's feelings about his philanthropic use of money were important to him. It pained him when he became nearly destitute during the economic depression that started in 1837 because "the days of my 'luxury of doing good' are gone by—perhaps never to return. I refer, of course, to the 'doing good' by... giving money."[20]

Upon Smith's death, his friend and sometime adversary William Lloyd Garrison recognized his benevolent use of wealth by noting that Gerrit Smith was "exceptional among millions in what he achieved in the matter of self-conquest over the strongest temptations and the most ample opportunities to lead a luxurious and purely worldly life."[21] Luxuries and worldliness would not have made him feel good, but giving did.

Another partial explanation for Smith's philanthropy rests in the notion of a hierarchy of needs similar to that later developed by Maslow. As basic needs of protection and physical drives are met, one can graduate to meeting needs of acceptance and love. When these are also fulfilled, one can self-actualize, or actually implement that behavior with which one chooses to define oneself. Affluence allowed Smith to self-actualize.

The reasons for Smith's philanthropy, then, were religion, guilt, nature, inequity, and affluence. Philanthropy, he thought, was natural to survival, and people did not need research statistics, counselors, priests, or the Bible to tell them "to do what we already know we should do.... [We know] the wrongs, which nature and common sense call on us to condemn."[22]

Joseph Alden of Williams College saw empathy in Smith's donation. "There was that in your letter that led me... to desire a further acquaintance—there was an expression of feeling fresh + unworn that indicated a power of sympathizing with many feelings that the world has taught me to conceal."[23]

Gerrit did not conceal feelings. His fellow abolitionist Oliver Johnson said of him,

> "You have a place in the hearts of thousands who
> have never looked upon your face, but upon whose
> pathway has fallen the warm sunlight of your
> bounty, and whose lives have been made nobler by
> the inspiration of your words."[24]

While Gerrit Smith's empathy is admirable, the effectiveness of his philanthropy has been widely criticized by historians. If widespread social change was his goal, as he said it was, then his tactics were certainly misplaced. He seldom gave a huge sum to a single agency in order to support a program of which he approved. His donations were generally small, and he spread them widely among individuals and relatively ineffective groups. This is because although his feelings for oppressed or poor individuals were intense, he had little patience for the dynamics of social movements and gradual change. He did not support networking among groups opting for change, and he always tried to stand clear of political processes.

Social change is usually not immediate or revolutionary, as he wanted it to be. The ponderous process of institutional change may require decades and depend upon coalitions of various structured organizations lobbying from a weblike network base of political power. By giving his money to poor individuals, he could see changes take place quickly; and at the same time, he could give each individual his personal and moral counsel.

Often, Smith's gifts of cash would be accompanied by a lecture. When the Leonards wrote to Smith requesting money for clothes for their family, Gerrit sent them $5 and counseled, "Be patterns of piety. Be industrious. Be frugal. Be simple in dress. Be self-denying. Pity the poor, the wronged, the wretched—the slave, the drunken, the heathen." [25] And to Lucius Gilbert, who had asked for both employment and money, Smith offered a job for $8 to distribute Bibles to every family in Peterboro that did not have one. "You may call at my office from time to time for copies of the Bible to carry with you."[26]

In a sense, philanthropy directed toward oppressed individuals was a way of minimizing risk. Hearn recognized that "Gerrit Smith had money and... not much courage."[27] He donated his money quietly, to people or groups that did not make much news nor had little power or influence. Contrast Gerrit Smith's style of giving with that of Benjamin Franklin, who had been a philanthropist a whole generation earlier: Franklin directed his money and inventive talents toward visionary projects that would benefit the public in practical ways, increasing the quality of their everyday lives. He would design a change—a university, a hospital, street lighting, or paving—make an initial donation, then induce the rich to donate toward its completion.[28]

Gerrit Smith wanted to accomplish his dreams immediately—and by himself. Although he wanted to achieve societal change, his tactics offered little hope for widespread social or moral change and little control over the use of his resources; yet the recipients were usually gracious and complimentary, and his reputation as a compassionate man spread widely. Many knew of his soft heart and large purse, and they trekked to the end of the rainbow at Peterboro.

In 1843 when he was struggling to pay his own debts, the wife of Smith's friend, Harris Rich, died. Gerrit sent him $5 "that your future may be happier than your former years...."[29] And when local resident Asa Raymond grieved over the death of a loved one, he received a gift of $50 because, "at a time when you especially need relief and composure, you are sent to extraordinary expenses, which, in your poverty, cannot fail to be somewhat burdensome + distracting."[30]

When a business client was ill, Smith decided to help him. "I... conclude to aid you by giving you the piece of land, which you wish —I send you the Deed therefore."[31] And when a liberal friend had been sick, Gerrit sent him well wishes and $20. His response to Smith: "May Heaven reward you for your great tenderness and regard for the unfortunate in this world...."[32]

By far the most frequent kind of requests Smith received were what he called "begging letters." There are many hundreds of them in his papers, and they made up at times more than half of all incoming letters. Smith actually approved of begging, as long as it took place among private individuals. He believed that wealthy individuals should be responsible for the welfare of the poor, not government.[33]

He assigned the reading and evaluation of most begging letters to Aunt Betsey Kelty, a member of his household staff whose judgment he trusted. These letters were frequently annotated by Smith, "Aunt Betsey will respond." She would attract his attention to those she deemed legitimately needy. A typical begging letter, especially in its opening phrase, read as follows:

> "Though myself a stranger to you, your reputation
> as a lover of truth, and a friend of humanity
> excites corresponding emotions, till I feel that
> congeniality which says, such an individual is no
> stranger to me. May I not hope for pardon for
> what may seem presumption in addressing you... I
> write to ask pecuniary assistance."[34]

Some requestors tried to coddle him with a claimed family tie. Mrs. E. Tannahill wrote that her father and Gerrit's father, Peter, were "intimate friends.... I have written this letter to ask Mr. Smith if he will not, for old time's sake, send me a little assistance."[35]

C.J. Talbot thanked Smith for sending him three dollars and then wrote four pages telling of his family sicknesses and unpaid mortgage. Gerrit's May 1, 1859 annotation on the letter: "I send my dft. for $20.00."[36] Other letters asked for aid for a wide variety of reasons. William Jenks asked for help in establishing his son on a farm.[37] Anne Adams requested funds to help raise the orphaned daughter of William L. Chaplin.[38] William Morton had spent his savings developing ether during the Civil War, and asked for re-imbursement. Smith sent him $80.[39]

Vagrants would occasionally walk up to Smith's Peterboro house and ask for lodging, money, or meals. He seldom refused them. On one occasion a transient had taken advantage of the Smith family's tolerance and grace by overstaying his welcome, so "Mr. Smith one morning in his prayer asked that the friend who was going to leave them that day might have a safe and prosperous journey."[40] The man, having heard the prayer that was intended more for his ears than for God's, got the hint and left.

Sometimes Gerrit became suspicious of those who solicited his aid. Nelson Ruske was a young man who had been inspired by one of Smith's public speeches to go to Kansas as a free-soil immigrant and set up a sawmill to provide lumber for the new settlers there. He was dismayed with Smith's response to his request for aid, which Ruske thought "can not possibly be construed into anything else than a contemptuous insinuation that under pretence of assistance for Kansas, I was seeking to obtain a donation for myself."[41]

The begging for help never ended. On the day Smith died, A.D. Gridley of Hamilton College addressed a letter to him on behalf of the artist who had painted Smith's portrait, which hung at the college, asking for additional compensation, as the artist had expressed his continuing displeasure at having originally done it so cheaply.[42] Smith did not discredit most monetary appeals to him, and at one point concluded that if used for collective benefit, wealth could solve many problems. He wrote, "The longer I live, the more I am persuaded that wealth is what the world most needs for its redemption from ignorance, wickedness and unhappiness."[43]

Aside from the many "beggar letters" he received, a major focus of his philanthropy was education, and that interest fitted nicely into his adamant support of abolition. His interest in education began early, when in 1825 he accepted a position as a trustee at Hamilton College. He invested much time and some money in the institution as it struggled financially, and he stayed on as a trustee until 1837 when he resigned in a dispute over the antislavery cause. The leaders of Hamilton College had refused to take a public stand against slavery, and Smith was infuriated, remaining apart from the college and its mission for many years. Late in his life he must have had a change of heart, as seen in a letter that Henry A. Foster, a trustee of the college, wrote to Smith in March of 1874: "Allow me to express my grateful thanks for the generous and substantial donation of $10,000 which you have made to Hamilton College."[44]

At about the time he resigned as trustee of Hamilton College, he became interested in a new, abolitionist-oriented, evangelical school in Ohio: Oberlin College. He liked its radical stands. In 1839, Smith donated to the college 21,000 acres of land in nearby Virginia (now West Virginia), along with $2,000.[45] President Charles Grandison Finney acknowledged the gift and remarked that he was pleased with the quality of the land.[46]

Smith also donated substantial funds to the racially integrated Oneida Institute at Whitesboro, New York, in the 1830s. Smith's abolitionist friend Beriah Green, a radical committed to interracial equality, managed the institute.[47] When it closed in 1843, Smith turned his interest in interracial education to a new, liberal venture—New York Central College—founded in 1848 in McGrawville, New York. Other financial supporters included Frederick Douglass, Wendell Phillips, William Lloyd Garrison, and Horace Greeley. The college's president was William C. Allen, the first black head of a predominantly white college in the United States. Allen advocated miscegenation and opposed the colonization of blacks and the use of alcohol and tobacco. The New York State legislature attacked Smith for his "amalgamationist" policies, and the *Syracuse Star* condemned the college as a "nigger Institution."[48]

When the college faced bankruptcy in 1858, in an effort to keep the college going, Smith purchased the property and sold it back to the college trustees in 1860. The college still failed, and in 1868, New York Central College merged with the Union School District and ceased operations.[49]

Smith made significant donations to colleges whose policies pleased him. His interest in religion-based institutions prompted a gift of $50 to the theological division of Yale College.[50] Dartmouth College received $100 as a reward for admitting black students.[51] Berea College in Kentucky took a stand against slavery, so Smith sent $20 to aid with starting costs.[52] He later sent them gifts of $1,050, $1,000, and $3,720.[53] Smith was partial to aiding interracial educational institutions because he believed in the ability of the Negro race to improve. He wanted the nation to see that blacks really were fit for freedom.

During the 1860s and 1870s Ezra Cornell and Cornell University's first president, Andrew D. White, encouraged Gerrit Smith to donate to this new, liberal university. He never did.[54] Had he concentrated his many donations on one educational institution, he could have had considerable influence but, as was typical of Smith, he spread them around to several smaller colleges.

In the village of Peterboro, Smith proposed to help build an academy, saying,

> "I have long felt that there should be an Academy
> in Peterboro, [and] that I would have the building
> put up at my own expense.... I propose... that
> if a company shall be organized for building +
> maintaining an Academy here, I will... make
> a donation to such company of the South Half
> of Temperance Park + one thousand dollars in
> money."[55]

Smith chose a spot at the east end of the village green, and after he had formed and fully subscribed the stock company, construction started in mid-1851. In June, Smith wrote to his son, "The basement story of the Academy is built, + it is very pretty."[56] The building was raised on June 26, 1851 and classes commenced that fall. Smith noted, "The Academy makes Peterboro very lively. There are nearly 100 scholars in it."[57] One local resident wrote in October,

"The Seminary erected by a Joint Stock Company at a cost of about 4,000 dollars is to be opened at the end of this month.... This establishment will be a great acquisition to Peterboro and vicinity...."[58]

Smith also dreamed of building a university he would name after himself, but it never materialized. Daniel Cady referred to the plan for the university as being "for the highest education of both sexes and all complexions...."[59] Smith's idea, as reported in *Frederick Douglass' Paper*, was to form

> "a University of the highest class... established on
> the most liberal principles. It is to be surrounded
> with an ample farm, to give the opportunity of
> tillage to such students as may desire to strengthen
> and invigorate themselves by labor and is to make
> suitable provision for cases of struggling merit."

The author suggested that Smith build the university in Rochester, but nothing ever came of the plan.[60]

Other educational institutions to receive Smith's donations included Howard University ($100),[61] American Polytechnic Institute ($100),[62] Hampton Normal and Agricultural Institute ($2,000),[63] the Institution for the Blind in Boston,[64] and the New York Institute for the Instruction of the Deaf and Dumb.[65]

He also paid the college expenses of those he considered to be deserving.[66] One recipient, John W. Adams, actually taught for a brief time in Peterboro before moving to Wilmington, South Carolina. He wrote to Smith from there: "Perhaps it may not be uninteresting to you to learn what has become of at least one of the 'colored' persons who have resided in Peterboro."[67] Adams and Smith stayed in touch until Smith's death in 1874.

When abolitionist Hiram Kellogg founded the interracial Young Ladies Domestic Seminary in Clinton, New York in the late 1830s, Smith agreed to pay one-half of the expenses of black students.[68] Patrick Ford, editor of *Irish World*, also commended Smith for his defense of the right of Roman Catholics to operate independent schools.[69]

One last example of Gerrit Smith's commitment to public education involves the Public Library of Oswego. In 1853, he selected trustees and gave them a charge to which they responded: "You inform us that you have appropriated the sum of $25,000.00 for the purpose of founding a Public Library in the city of Oswego; and you request us to take upon ourselves the charge of expending the money, in procuring a proper site and building, and in establishing the Library."[70] They accepted the charge.

A series of letters from Gerrit Smith's business agent in Oswego, John B. Edwards, chronicled the building of the library. Edwards kept Smith apprised of the progress and expenses and made recommendations for the library's future needs.[71] The library opened in late 1856, and the trustees invited Gerrit to speak at its opening.[72] Subsequently, Smith donated $1,000 to the library in 1862 and $4,000 more in 1868.[73]

Gerrit Smith's legacy in education was more personal than institutional; since his donations were scattered among many schools, they failed to make a lasting impact. But he may have been one of the first Americans of means to invest in the idea of integrated schools—100 years before the landmark Brown vs. Board of Education decision made desegregation the law of the land.

Gerrit Smith directed much of his philanthropy toward people who had suffered loss. For instance, a Mr. Hyde Crocker was robbed during his visit to Syracuse. Hearing of this, Gerrit sent him $2 to sustain his needs as he recovered. Crocker later returned the gift to Smith.[74]

In the fall of 1871, Smith sent $250 "to the fund for relieving the sufferers in [Wisconsin] from the recent brush fires." In the summer of 1874, when the states of Minnesota, Iowa, Kansas, and Nebraska were plagued with grasshoppers and farmers there suffered economic loss, Smith sent his donation of $500 to each state to be distributed to those in need. Governor Carpenter of Iowa responded, "It is a credit to human nature that in this hour of sore affliction to a large number of people in these... states they are not forgotten by the generous... people in more favored localities."[75]

Smith donated $100 to people in Switzerland hurt by a flood,[76] $300 to an institution dedicated to helping blind people,[77] and $500 to the New York Greek Relief Fund.[78] He even spent time visiting Ku Klux Klan prisoners in an Albany jail.[79]

Smith's real estate business (he owned nearly a million acres of land during his lifetime) placed him in a unique position to help the oppressed through the gifting of land. In a deal made with a friend's family, Smith stated his perceptions: "In the distribution of the property, of which God has made me the steward, I wish to do something for your little sons. The above draft [for $100.00] will enable you to buy in their name, eighty acres... which may, by the time they reach manhood, be worth much to them."[80] As one writer has put it, Smith "looked upon [land] holdings as a sacred trust, and that as steward, he should manage the same for the welfare of man."[81]

Daniel Cady was close to Smith both in his business and in land deals, and he wrote of Smith, "He became deeply impressed with a sense of his responsibility to God for the right use of such an immense portion of the earth's surface.... He came to look upon it as a trust committed to him for the benefit of others...." Instead of hoarding land for his own wealth and use, "his constant aim was to see how much good he could do to his fellow men, and as fast as his property became available, he devoted it to purposes of philanthropy."[82]

Although Smith had considered giving land to the poor in the 1830s, the economic depression of 1837 curtailed such plans. In 1844 George Henry Evans, editor of the labor journal *People's Rights*, wrote an article accusing Smith of being a land monopolist who deprived many poor people of the opportunity to own land.[83] This public rebuke may have stimulated Smith to develop a land distribution plan; in 1846, he had 3,000 poor black men chosen from throughout the state to receive gifts of land. They were between the ages of 21 and 60, were landless, and were required to be temperate. He deeded to them 40 or more acres of land each, to be worth at least

$250 when developed. The state as of 1846 required that black men own property worth that much in order to be eligible to vote, so this would make them eligible—and alleviate their poverty.

In a letter to some of his land agents in this deal, Smith said that to counteract discrimination "done to them by their white brethren," blacks could work hard on their new lands to prove their worthiness by developing a strong character. "This character will compel the restoration to them of their now withheld rights."[84]

Smith also perceived this gift of land as a way of finding out what blacks could really make of themselves. "What people of color... are capable of becoming in this nation is an experiment yet to be tried. Hitherto we have seen how far... they can rise under all the dead weights we attach to them."[85] Smith believed land monopoly to be one of the causes of slavery, and he hoped that this land gift would inspire both self-reliance and reliance on neighbors. The new community that developed in northeastern New York State was called 'Timbucto' by Smith's friend, John Brown, and it represented a way to balance ponderous reform efforts with Smith's desire for immediate change. If moral reform toward communal life could not occur fast enough in the nation, at least it could here. Smith's benevolent motives were sincere, but they sometimes were misinterpreted by poorly informed historians.[86]

There were, however, some problems involved with this land deal. One problem was the quality of the land: it was not good farm land. When Beriah Green faulted Smith on this, Smith replied, "You have a just idea of the land question. The soil is thin—+ the climate forbidding." Then Smith revealed to Green a notion that contradicted his previously stated idea that blacks could work there to prove their worth. "I do not wish any of the grantees to go upon their lands. Twenty years hence will be time enough to make settlements so far back in the wilderness. But I wish the grantees to keep their lands, + pay the light taxes on them...."[87]

Some of those blacks who did go there were met and guided by unscrupulous local people who would lead them intentionally to the wrong land plots, then offer to buy their seemingly worthless deeds for a few dollars.[88]

Although people generally believed Smith's motives were honorable, they wrote to him concerning the potential waste. The "reward [of your Timbucto efforts]," wrote one, "may be rather measured by your intentions than by the actual benefits the recipients are likely to secure by it."[89]

It was just a few years later that Smith cooked up a land deal for poor white people. His proposal was to give 1,000 white people 40 acres of land plus $10 each. "These persons must be white inhabitants of the State of New York; must be between the ages of 21 and 60; must be virtuous, landless, and poor; must be entirely clear of the vice of drinking intoxicating liquors. Moreover, they must in each County, be taken from the sexes in equal numbers."[90] But in a January 4, 1850 follow-up letter to the county leaders, he had changed his mind. "I have come to the conclusion, that it is not best for the females to receive land from me.... The five hundred females will each receive fifty dollars." His rationale for this decision was that he did not have enough land for everyone originally chosen, so the females were left out.

One of Smith's programs was an effort to help the poor families of Peterboro own houses. In ten letters written between December 2, 1846 and February 11, 1847, he offered fifty to one hundred fifty dollars to local families for the purpose of buying land and/or building homes.[91] To one local resident, Smith wrote, "I should be glad to help you buy a little house in the name of your children - + I will give you $150.00 towards enabling you to do so. One of the warmest desires of my heart is to see all of the old inhabitants of Peterboro owning their homes."[92] To Neale Eastman he wrote, "I write you this letter + make you this offer in fulfillment of the purpose which I found last fall of helping every poor man then living in Peterboro + intending to live there to get a shelter for himself + family, which they could call their own."[93]

In letters to two local women, he donated money to buy teeth and to paint their house.[94] One business client owed him money on a land purchase. "You owe me $227.63. It is more than you can pay. Hence I give the property to your family—May God bless the gift to you + your wife + children."[95]

His concern for those in need showed readily. "You are the widowed mother of eight small children—and you are a hard working and worthy woman," he wrote to Elizabeth Torry. "I conclude to make a deed for the benefit of yourself and children of the lot next to your father's."[96] Then he offered to pay to have a house built on the property for her.

By 1848, Smith had already helped local resident Asa Raymond and his family struggle through a couple of winters. Now to help him become independent, Gerrit replied to Raymond's request: "I reply Aug. 5, 1848, proposing to help him buy a farm by giving him $250.00, or by lending him $1,000.00, payable in 20 equal annual payments with annual interest."[97] And when someone made a claim of "several dollars" against the estate of Peter Smith following his death, Gerrit, as executor, could not get any of the other nine legal heirs to agree to pay, so he sent a personal check for $20, recognizing the applicant's "poor" status.[98]

As one last example of Smith's concern for fostering equity for the poor, in a letter to fourteen town supervisors in Madison County, he asked them each to choose "seven unmarried poor, landless, worthy, white women..." to whom he could give fifty dollars each for "aiding them to get homes for themselves."[99]

Smith also rewarded friends, sometimes even when there was no stated need. He sent Henry A. Foster, a boyhood friend, $2,500 as a surprise gift. Foster, his schoolmate in Peterboro in 1807 and 1808, replied that he had long watched Smith's business career and his benevolence, and was impressed with how Smith had "resisted the allurements which so strongly tempt those who... are the inheritors of large estates, and have liberally used your worth to benefit your fellow men."[100]

While in Washington, D.C. as a Congressman, Smith was a friend to Thomas C. Connolly, who wrote to Smith in 1855 requesting money to help pay the medical bills of his sick wife. Smith complied.[101]

Gerrit Smith also helped his own family. Relatives sometimes felt cheated while the patriarch gave away what might be theirs, but whenever there was need, he responded. To his mother's sister Catherine Henry, he donated fifty dollars with the promise of future aid because "it has... been a fixed purpose of my heart not to see a brother or sister of my sainted mother want, if in my power to afford relief."[102]

In generous recognition of the value of his daughter and son, he endowed their futures with substantial funds. In a highly personal letter to each on his 50th birthday he wrote, "I am this day fifty years old. With me advancing as I am in life + afflicted with disease, time must be short." He deeded land to each, and promised fifteen thousand dollars to each as soon as his debts from the late depression were paid. Then he advised them:

> "Be industrious—be frugal—give, give, give, freely
> + continually, according to your means. Lend
> money rarely, if ever—and never lend but in small
> sums. Never, never, never indorse—nor in any
> wise [become] security for another."[103]

How would Smith's giving during the antebellum period translate into 'today's dollars'? John Stauffer's latest book, *GIANTS: The Parallel Lives of Frederick Douglass and Abraham Lincoln*, offers a well-formulated explanation of the system for estimating comparable values. He arrived at his calculation using data from the U.S. Census, the U.S. Department of Commerce, and with the help of Stanley Engerman, the John Munro Professor of Economics and Professor of History at the University of Rochester:

> "On converting 1830s money into 2008 currency,
> I multiply antebellum money (1830-1860) by a
> factor of 75. I arrive at this figure by comparing

a skilled laborer's wage of roughly $500 in the
1840s to an average annual family income in 2000
around $37,500...."[104]

By this standard for comparison, Gerrit Smith donated nearly
$650 million in today's money during his lifetime.

Smith's support of people in need and of educational institutions
reflected his optimistic wish to help create a more egalitarian society. His philanthropy provided a model of progressive reform that
contradicted much of the selfishness of emerging industrialism, and
if such efforts never left much of a legacy in established institutions,
they at least eased the pain in life for many oppressed individuals.
Who is to say which end is best? At least in Smith's case, most of his
dollars went directly to the source of need. His feelings for the plight
of many small individuals tell us much about the man's style.

- 4 -

Style

It is difficult to outline a specific style of thought or action for Gerrit Smith. He was a complex person, and his distinctive and characteristic modes both of thought and action changed over time. To label him, as the press often did, was unfair.

At about the middle of his career, Smith said of the press,
> "It does not allow me to speak for myself. And when it speaks concerning me, it is not for the purpose of acquainting its readers with my real character and real conduct, but for the purpose, by means of perversions and caricatures, of exciting, at one time, their mirth, and at another, their indignation."[1]

There were, however, some regularities that typified the man. Gerrit Smith saw himself not as an aristocratic man, not as a white man; not as a rich man, but as a man. To him, personhood was one's most significant and primary characteristic based in natural human rights. This led him to perceive people as equal, and to be perceived by others as deviant. He cannot be fairly presented as an icon or as a fool, but as a mix of both. He could have been rough, but chose to be gentle. He could have been arrogant, but chose to be humble. He could have been a winner, but chose to share. As an outsider to most traditional institutions, he remained a sentimental, romantic reformer. He renounced efforts to acquire power; he did not crave public approval, status, or position. I respectfully disagree with previous biographers Frothingham and Harlow, both of whom claimed that Gerrit Smith sought the legitimation of others. In my opinion, he certainly did not.

As one of his critics noted, he was "too proud to derive... importance and standing from extraneous glitter and costly show and equipage."[2] Smith was a man of easily triggered emotions. His compassion for others ruled his acts because feelings produced facts for him and determined his judgments. What he felt about a situation became his source of legitimate authority.

He was sensitive to the needs of others, tolerant of their eccentricities. He gained their favor and cooperation by complimenting their talents in public while he encouraged them to do the kinds of tasks that best suited them. For instance, Beriah Green, the arrogant and impetuous leader of the Oneida Institute, was encouraged to argue and disagree with Smith while Smith celebrated their differences and found value in Green's ideas. Smith accepted John Brown's aggressiveness as a sign of the times, and although he did not condone it, Smith supported it as an expression of Christian concern for the oppressed. Indeed, as will be seen, Smith supported Brown's militancy in the raid on Harpers Ferry. William Goodell, an abolitionist editor, needed to be heard, so Gerrit called on him for ideas.

This receptive attitude, supported by his ready willingness to donate money to what he saw as worthy causes, gained him respect in the clique of political activists who were influential in founding the Liberty Party—a move that eventually led to the creation of the Republican Party and the election of Abraham Lincoln to the presidency. Respect for others' needs, Smith believed, encouraged them to see themselves as dignified and worthy, thereby developing in them the self-respect that would lead to responsible local citizenship. Such voluntarily adopted responsibility, he thought, would then develop into moral behavior—and establish the foundation for a just and righteous society.

This capacity for empathy led him to see order in freedom instead of its more restrictive opposite, freedom in order. He would model the behavior necessary to create an egalitarian community, yet leave people free to choose it for themselves. He ruled lightly with recognition of the value of diversity.

Persistence was one part of his style that he practiced unfailingly: once he chose an issue on which to focus, he would not give up on it. Temperance, for instance, tapped his resources throughout his adult life. His focus on a goal sometimes became obsessive and earned him the label of "fanatic." He even agreed that his high level of enthusiasm might make him seem fanatical, yet he did not like that perception. In another's eyes, " 'Thundering Jove' could not shake his tenacity of purpose...."[3]

Hope for social peace, he knew, rested in feelings of humility and tolerance, and he did display both. But humility and tolerance did not buy him much success in a competitive world. As he wrote and spoke, he was not shopping for approval, for he knew that his ideas were often unpopular. What he really wanted was to stimulate more effort by people to strive for equity and justice through mutual caring.

As a public speaker, Smith was among the best of his time. He had the gift of a powerful baritone voice. He was eloquent and enthusiastic, and he lived in an era when wealth itself brought a speaker credibility. When Gerrit Smith spoke, people listened. He was a great orator, speaking with persuasiveness and with Biblical references at the tip of his tongue.

He described himself in his autobiography as standing "like Jupiter, thundering and shaking" as he drove home his message. Jupiter in Roman mythology was the god of the heavens whose powers could be used to protect the poor and guard community morals.[4] This was an egotistical self-image, but much of Smith's audience must have agreed.

A rhetorical analysis of Gerrit Smith's speeches and writings class them under the Jeremiad format.[5] There are three parts to a

Jeremiad: 1. A chosen population 2. has "fallen," and 3. prescribed action can restore them. Smith also used logical, Socratic argument as a technique: 'If this, then that.' For instance, if the Negro is a man, then he must possess the right to vote.

Samuel Ringgold Ward, a black abolitionist and friend to Smith, spoke of Smith's "rich, deep, flexible, musical voice... [which] rendered me, and thousands more with me, unable to sit or stand in any quietness during his speech.... To mortal man it is seldom permitted to behold a sight so full of or so radiant with moral power and beauty."[6]

Smith's public speeches often displayed an exuberant, crusading arrogance that was not overly tempered by learned knowledge. Not being a well-read man past his collegiate studies, his naiveté showed. According to one who watched him speak,

> "He talked in a dignified, open, confiding way, in
> the manner of one so full of his purpose, so deeply
> in love with the truth, so profoundly impressed
> with the importance of what he was saying, so
> sure of its power to command the assent of all
> considerate minds, that the extreme boldness
> of his positions gave no shock even to sensitive
> feelings."[7]

A Cazenovia resident, having attended an antislavery convention at which Smith spoke, remarked,

> "A crowd was there and eager listening, bent to
> catch each sound that fell from lips so pure.... Sure
> index of a noble heart—that face. So speaking,
> yet so calm—so firm, yet mild. More souls his eye
> has calmed—more minds illumed... than scores
> of those with sordid minds who cling to glittering
> dusts and trample neath their feet the humble
> poor. He opens his mouth and pleads the rights
> of all. His voice is melody and falls upon the ear

as sweetest perfumes float upon ambient air—as zephyrs fan upon the burning brow and seared cheek. His words sooth aching hearts."[8]

One feature that was lacking in Smith's oratory was humor. According to one newspaper correspondent who heard Smith speak at a Buffalo convention, "He has but little humor, and less wit... for the amusement of a crowd. He can make no appeal, except to the higher and more earnest sentiments of human nature."[9]

The *New York Times* described him at an 1863 speech before a largely hostile Montreal audience as:

"a man of almost heroic proportions, with the flowing, silvery locks of a patriarch, and a countenance expressing benevolence itself.... [He was] a pure and earnest patriot, speaking for the honor and salvation of his country in the midst of a life and death struggle."[10]

And an old friend wrote about having heard Smith speak thirty years before, remembering,

"the silvery eloquence of your voice... when advocating the great reforms of our age.... As a boy, I always admired the bold, uncompromising and self-sacrificing manner in which you stood up for the right.... My present position as a sober man + a total abstinence advocate is to be ascribed to your agency."[11]

Further testimony as to Gerrit Smith's speaking style and influence are offered by a correspondent of the *Philadelphia Register* who, having seen Smith on the floor of the House of Representatives, wrote,

"I never beheld Gerrit Smith until the assembling of the present Congress, and I was then prepared

from what I had heard, to look upon an ascetic
dogmatist and arbitrary man of cranks, and
notions and eccentricities. Never did I realize a
more complete or more gratifying disappointment.
I found in him a man whose identity I would not
exchange for that of any other man upon whom
my eyes have ever looked.... I have never seen a
man whose presence is more impressive: dignity
without austerity; intelligence and genius, without
the seeming consciousness of either; benevolence
and courtesy upon which no shadow ever seems
to fall and a courage so constant and unfailing
that it never needs the fuel of intolerance or anger
to sustain it.... His tall and well developed form
is quite erect, his features are all prominent and
tinged with healthful ruddy glow and his dark
penetrating eyes give him assurance that it is
possible for him at least to be wise as a serpent
though harmless as a dove. His smile, his manner,
and his very gesture are all as natural and gentle as
ever... yet when he speaks none are inattentive to
him. No man can doubt the sincerity of his look,
no man can [ignore] the deep, rich and thrilling
tones of his voice. No man for a moment can fail
to appreciate the thoughts he utters, in language
all simplicity and dignity. Many smile at and some
deride the 'ultraism' of the sentiments he utters;
but these very men are among the foremost to
acknowledge the greatness of his intellectual and
moral nature."[12]

Another observer of Smith's Congressional speaking noted that
he presented "the pleasing and subduing influence of a benevolence,
the genuineness of which no beholder can for a moment doubt....
His intellectual power and the tones that thrill us, may indeed be

resisted; but the attributes of the heart that are mirrored upon the face demand our respect and our [empathy]."[13]

A visitor to Smith's Peterboro home who signed as "G. W. B." spoke of him as

> "an accessible, sociable, pleasant man.... In
> intellect, he ranks with such men as Clay, Calhoun,
> and Benton. His mind is comprehensive and
> well cultivated—his imagination volcanic, but
> controlled by acute judgment. As an orator, he has
> but few superiors.... His manner is deliberate and
> dignified—his matter choice and classical—his
> personal appearance noble and attractive. He
> is about six foot high, and of perfect mould.
> His forehead high and broad, his eyes large and
> expressive—hair brown and cropped close to his
> head.... He never decorates his person with the
> tinselry and jewelry of fashion. He eats plain food,
> ...bathes every day, drinks nothing but cold water,
> walks from four to ten miles a day; frequently
> writes from one to two hundred letters per week,
> ...and frequently preaches on the Sabbath to his
> little flock at Peterboro.... He is remarkable for
> generous simplicity, eloquence, piety, and love of
> the writings of Shakespeare."[14]

When it came to writing, Smith was prolific. His records of household expenses as early as the 1820s and 1830s indicate that he wrote a lot, frequently purchasing pens, pencils, paper, and ink powder. Between the needs of his business records and correspondences, personal letters, and composition of circulars, he wrote a prodigious amount. Hundreds of his letters and circulars were printed and sent to anyone he wanted to influence.

In one case, Smith sent a printed letter to the faculty of Hamilton College, accusing them of being pro-slavery; he mailed a copy of it to his abolitionist friend Lewis Tappan. Tappan had received much of Smith's printed material and responded with some humor,

> "Do you keep a press in your house? Are your
> family all printers? Do you sleep nights? To be
> serious, I rejoice that you have the power—
> intellectual and physical—to do so much, and that
> in general you do so well."[15]

Smith said of himself, "I have no leisure under the constant and crushing burden of my cares, to turn to human counsel, when an occasion calls for the use of my pen. I respond to the occasion—shove aside the business I have at hand—look up for Divine guidance—and write."[16] One person referred to Smith's frequent writings as "An inkshower + pensstorm."[17]

One problem that bothered people in his time—and still burdens people today—was the quality of his penmanship: in short, it was terrible. His own clerks would quip "that he wrote in three distinct hands; one that he and his clerks could read, one that he alone could read and one that he nor nobody else could read."[18]

As the guardian of a great many of Smith's letters, this author did develop the ability to read his handwriting—but only after developing cue cards regarding letters or words represented by certain shapes, and about six months of trial and error. In the early stage of Smith's life—up until about 1835—his handwriting was legible, but after that point, it deteriorated.

Respondents to his correspondences often complained about having difficulty reading it. Sarah Grimké noted, "I have been trying again to decipher your letter...."[19] Even his granddaughter commented on it: "When a letter came from you,..." Elizabeth Smith Miller wrote her father, "Nannie said, 'That's from Grandfather, I know his handwriting.' "[20]

An educator who was having a minor dispute with Smith and expected a written response from him, which he intended to print, made a special request. "It is desirable to me, that your letter... be written in a hand I can read without effort.... Be good enough, therefore, to let a clerk copy your letter in a particularly legible... hand." [21] Smith did have his clerks copy many of his letters into two Letter Books,[22] and when circumstances required it, he could write legibly. On April 3, 1847, Smith wrote a multi-page contract to a client in very legible script.[23]

The quality of the content of his writings differed with the topic being covered. In general, they did not reflect great learning. Smith was not a scholar who did much research into his topics. As he said, he simply looked for divine guidance and wrote. So his long circulars on many topics were not intellectually enlightened analyses of various perspectives on issues or even attempts to synthesize ideas, but ponderous, redundant statements of simple ideas.[24]

He had a habit of securing a point in his argument by saying, "By the way...." This seems to be an assumption that he was right, and that the reader should know it. One of Smith's clients who had received a number of his printed circulars responded,

"I am charmed with these productions of
your mind. They are characterized not merely
by a strong logical form, but [also by] a deep
vein of moral pathos—a pervasive eloquence
which reach[es] at once the moral chambers
of the human mind. And with me, the latter
characteristic constitutes their principal merit."[25]

On issues of legal consequence, Smith was skilled in logical argumentation through the use of metaphor. In his printed speech on the Nebraska Bill before Congress he made many persuasive points, clearly perceiving the legal implications against slavery stated in the United States Constitution.[26] Mostly, however, his thought and writing were not that focused or direct. Often he would choose a subject for writing, then wander about through his collection of moral reform efforts, touching on several points.[27] As a technique of persuasion, many of his letters began with lavish compliments to the recipient that recognized that person's positive traits or accomplishments, then requested his aid, or sought to change her opinion, or asked for his friendship, or even outright attacked her ideas.

Much of the criticism of his speaking and writing involves the claim that he was an absolutist who expected others to conform to what he knew was right. This critique is a result of not reading far enough into his works; on the whole, he exhibited a balance between being absolute and being relative. Like humans in general, he was certain of some things and not so certain about others; if this was inconsistency, then so be it. Inconsistency of ideas or techniques may indicate more honesty than does an attempt to make everything match or coincide.

It was in proclaiming his certainty on some points that Gerrit Smith was seen as a fool. His confidence in being right came from his belief that Christian morality was right, and that with God on his side, he could ignore the relativity of cultural rules because there existed "the everlasting moral code."[28] When critics attacked vagueness in his logic, he attacked them on moral grounds. He did not think he needed to be a conciliator because he was right to begin with; and as a self-appointed purveyor of truth, he had high confidence in the universal rightness of his own beliefs. As he put it, "The longer I live the more I am convinced that men may be very good, and yet do things that I think to be very bad. They do not survey the subject from my standpoint."[29] On another occasion he picked up this same theme: "Multitudes once hostile to my life-long principles, I have lived to see become identified with them. And ere they are aware, those who dissent from my present positions, may have come round to them."[30]

This self-righteousness drove people away from him, and he found that he could seriously discuss issues only with others like himself. He appealed to "reason" to decide matters of social justice, but he did not grant that all reason is relative. This made him at times a moral absolutist. "It is true that the reason of most men is greatly perverted," he said, "reduced to... a compound of passion and prejudice." He wanted people to search for the "right reason."[31]

In its obituary of Smith, the *Oswego Daily Palladium* referred to him gently as "a fearless and bitter denouncer of what he conceived to be wrong, and an intense advocate of the right as he understood it."[32]

Smith's own reaction to such perceptions of him was realistic. At an American Anti-Slavery Society meeting in 1851 he acknowledged in a speech, "I know full well that I am a very odius man...." [33.] He seemed even to understand those who thought him to be a zealot. "It would not be strange if I deserved, in more than small degree, the reproach of fanaticism so freely bestowed upon me...."[34] Even so, he was prone to attack those whose ideas opposed his.

In a long letter to Stephen Phillips, Smith wrote that he was upset and disapproving of others who were not as enthusiastic and as committed as he was to a cause—especially abolition.[35] He felt his perceptions on most matters were correct as a matter of course, and he staunchly believed he could convert other people to them. When he could not persuade them, he tended to become frustrated and incensed that others could not see things the way he did. "God is for instantaneous reformations," he said, and other people should realize that.[36]

Speaking about his tendency toward absolute stands on issues that obsessed him, Smith said, "My reputation for sound understanding [of the majority viewpoint], poor as it was before—and poor as that of every radical and earnest abolitionist must continue to be until abolition shall be in the ascendant—is far poorer now." He admitted himself to be "deficient in common sense."[37]

As Gerrit Smith grew older, he became less absolute. Perhaps a warning from his respected friend, Lewis Tappan, had some influence on him: "You are sometimes rather hard with those who do not come up to your standards.... Is there not some danger that you may repel some who, by patience, might be won over? Is it not best to ask ourselves often, am I sure that I am wholly right, + [the other] wholly wrong? Is it not possible that truth may lie on both sides?"[38]

Smith did become aware of the drawbacks of obsession. "I was brought up to look at only one side—my side. Hence I entered upon my manhood a political and religious bigot. But, for more than the latter half of my life, I have trained myself to look at all sides and to seek knowledge from all sides."[39]

For example, notwithstanding his intense opinions on abolition, he had sympathy for the perspectives of southerners and pitied the slave holder as a victim of delusion who had been brought to commit what Smith considered a criminal act by social institutions that supported slavery. During a speech to the New York State Legislature regarding fugitive slave laws, he insisted, "Think not... that I am opposed to all compromises. I believe in compromises; and I would consent to large concessions in the way of justice and kindness to our Southern brethren."[40]

The realization that different subcultural experiences in life lead to different opinions prompted him to say, "If we are... kind of expressing these views and patient in listening to them, not harm, but on the contrary, great good, will come from our discussions."[41]

Smith's Peterboro friend and former Pastor Charles Hammond claimed that Smith's influence helped Hammond to become more tolerant and less of a fanatic. "I think I grew more reasonable while under your influence."[42]

Smith wished he could have that kind of an effect on everyone; he did show ire toward those who did not share his political views. Of them he said,

> "That you should be thoroughly convinced by your own arguments is a natural and almost necessary consequence of the self-complacency, which uniformly characterizes persons who regard themselves as ne plus ultra [the best] reformers. I wish you could find it in your hearts to reciprocate our liberality, in acknowledging your sincerity, and to admit, that we, who differ from you, are also sincere.... I am deeply grieved

at our superciliousness and intolerance toward
those, who desire to know and do their duty is
no less strong nor pure than your own.... I would
that I could inspire you with some distrust of your
infallibility."[43]

Many would have liked to have said the same of Smith.

Later, when he was a member of Congress, he was even more concerned with the relative rightness of positions. Perhaps it was his long quest to implement absolute morality that had left him with a clearer sense of his own mistakes. "That a life, always so full of errors, before my coming to Congress, was to be entirely empty of them, whilst in Congress, was not be to expected either by my constituents, or by myself."[44]

One of Gerrit Smith's concerns about political life was that all people should be able to exercise free speech—and still experience respect.

"Now I am aware, that a lot of the doctrines,
which I utter in this Hall, are very wrong in
[other Congressmen's] eyes. But should they not
remember, that their counter doctrines are no less
wrong in my eyes? And yet, I appeal to all... that
patience and kindness should be accorded to me,
as by me."[45]

To reinforce the point of open-mindedness for himself, he said, "I am in the habit of freely imputing errors to my fellow men.... But... I do not claim, that I am myself exempt from errors; that I acknowledge, that I abound in them.... I trust... that so long as I shall have the honor to hold a seat in this body, I may be able to keep my spirit in a teachable posture...."[46]

Perhaps the best arena in which to see Smith's tendency to think in relative ways in his later life is, ironically, religion. He did not claim the Bible to be an immutable source of truth, and he often

saw pernicious results from the doctrines taught by Christian denominations. Inconsistency in his thoughts created dissonance that,
while bothersome, he viewed as a healthy sign of growth. He was
impatient with those who expected him to be consistent over time,
and he saw any unchanging theology as an object of suspicion:

> "All who know me, know, that I make no
> pretentions to consistency. I am a man of change.
> All, who live, not to stereotype, but to correct their
> errors, must be men of change. Upon many things
> in my anti-slavery history I look back with regret:
> and I hope, by the Divine help, I shall, hereafter, go
> counter to them."[47]

In recognizing his faults, Smith took responsibility for them
and for personal improvement. "I confess… that I am a bundle of
faults — +that I cannot look back with any degree of complacency
on any past year, or hour, or moment of my life."[48] This recognition
of his own shortcomings kept his attitude humble and positive and
allowed him to deal constructively with inconsistencies that might
have driven a less balanced person to paranoia. He could be, simultaneously, a combination of practical and irrational thought.

> "Do I pray for an increase of my physical or
> spiritual health? If I pray intelligently, it is not that
> God may increase it, but that He may influence
> me to increase it by my improvement of the means
> to that end placed by His providence within my
> reach."[49]

He did not feel fated or controlled, and was responsible for his
own attitude. Such a positive approach to life encouraged him to see
what good was available in any situation, and to accent it.

It also armored him against attacks. Having accused the faculty
of Hamilton College of being pro-slavery, he had a bitter dispute
with a Professor Eaton over the issue, saying,

"I pass over all that you say of myself. I am but
an untitled and odius individual; and, therefore,
whether I am the 'eminently calumnious,' the
'raving,' 'rabid,' 'insane,' 'crazy' man—the 'political
demagogue'—which you call me, cannot be very
material in the public esteem."[50]

Smith was, quite simply, secure enough to let such criticisms
bounce off.

To conclude this coverage of Gerrit Smith's style of thought, what
seem at first to be inconsistencies or contradictions may be signs
of balance and health. He could tolerate dissonance as long as he
felt that he was gaining or learning from it. Whereas the general
public expected its leaders to be consistent, Smith was secure in
the knowledge that he was not. This usually influenced his style of
action in accommodating ways.

There seem to be contradictions when we refer to the action
style of Gerrit Smith. He worked hard, but achieved few goals. He
was constantly in motion, but seldom left Peterboro. He was liberal
to the point of wanting radical change, but not willing to pursue
revolution. Direct, radical actions by Smith were rare, but he supported such actions in others. As an impulsive idealist, he worked
for change at the local level, hoping the example would spread. At
home, he could use a hands-on approach to effect change.

In Peterboro he personally established a Temperance Hotel, a
manual labor school for black men, a home for destitute children,
a nondenominational Free Church, an Underground Railroad stop,
and an academy.

One pattern that appeared in his reform activities was "frustrated
withdrawal." Smith would work inside an institution to reform it,
and when it appeared futile, he would withdraw and pursue his goal
from a different angle. When the local Presbyterian Church would
not conform to his anti-slavery stand, he withdrew and started a new
church. When the Hamilton College Board of Trustees disagreed

with him, he resigned and supported other colleges. When he became frustrated with his inability to get politicians in Congress to
support his positions, he left his seat there and returned to safe and
malleable Peterboro. In short, he didn't give up; he just changed his
focus of action to an arena where he felt he could succeed.

Anger amid disagreements did not characterize Smith's actions.
Only in a couple of instances did he let his composure slip and make
monumental blunders, the details of which will be recounted in later
chapters. He usually tried to be fair; when he and William Lloyd
Garrison disagreed over who was right regarding charges made
against each other, Smith replied, "My reputation for fair dealing is
very dear to me."[51] He normally kept his own anger in check.

One trait that typified Gerrit Smith's style of action throughout
his life was vigor. He was not lethargic, nor did he lack for energy in
seeking some focus of application. George W. Putnam, a Peterboro
intellectual and one-time secretary to Charles Dickens, said, "Mr.
Smith's friends have remarked in him a preternatural brilliancy of
mind. It blazed constantly and in its... vigor it seemed to seek almost
in vain sufficient material to feed its fires."[52]

In a 1856 Christmas poem, Edwin Morton, an in-house tutor at
the time, wrote of the aging Gerrit,
> "Here's Grandfather still fresh and whole
> As when you saw him last—
> The mantle of perpetual youth
> Seems o'er his shoulders cast.
> 'Tis time his beard is growing grey
> And he fain would think he's old;
> But see his stalwart form today
> And lofty bearing bold:
> To him the hardest work is play
> And he's good to last as gold."[53]

At home in Peterboro, Smith could keep his eye on local folks and
guide their behavior. He once said that he did not want to be per-

ceived as "a meddlesome fellow," as that would not be gentlemanly.[54] But meddle, he did. He gave frequent warnings to local churches regarding their doctrines. His admonishments to individual residents kept them defensive, sometimes to the point that they would engage him in public debate. One such debate over proper sermon topics with Asa Rand, a Peterboro minister, prompted Smith's apology. "I can only add, that I am deeply sorry, that I did not tell the truth + that I hope you will believe, that the error was one of inconsideration, not of intention."[55]

Rather than being angry and abusive at Rand's public declaration of him as a liar, Smith wrote, "I have not yet condemned you. I mean to be patient with you.... I will wait for still more full and certain revelations of your character, before I decide upon that character."[56]

In another instance of his monitoring of local behavior, Smith admonished his anti-slavery colleague James C. Fuller for being a "disturbor" of public anti-slavery meetings with his temper. Fuller answered by justifying his actions. Smith's reply: "If I have accused you of what you are not guilty of, I am sorry, very sorry. I did not write to wrong you. I knew that I should wound your feelings—but I hoped that it should not be unprofitable to you."[57]

Such fatherly monitoring of others' morals and behavior was Smith's technique of achieving at least local change. In this case it worked, as Fuller responded by acknowledging value in their continued friendship. Gerrit in turn replied, "Well, we will drop what is past—but let me assure you that, for the future, I shall behave no better." He would still report perceived faults and expect Fuller to do the same, because "I wish you to deal just as faithfully with me—for I have more faults than you have."[58]

Generally, an inflated ego did not characterize Smith. But at times, it did show. In a printed circular, "Gerrit Smith to His Townsmen,"[59] he opened by saying, "I wish to say a few words to you." This sounds like an assumption of superiority, as if he knew something that he assumed his neighbors needed to know. He wrote to dignitaries, from local officials to the president of the United States, to tell them of his disappointment over their policy positions. Although such communications are on one level positive acts in a democracy, Smith's letters reflected pride in knowing what was right regarding slavery, temperance, or politics. They often carried an air of condescending pretentiousness.[60]

He felt justified in expressing himself, although his friend, Susan B. Anthony, counseled that such advice was given "at the hazard of being called... a visionary and a fanatic for holding opinions, which, though they will be entirely welcome to the more enlightened future sense of men, are as entirely repugnant to their present sense...."[61]

When Smith did receive compliments on his actions, he liked to spread the word. Between 1862 and 1865 he received a series of long letters "from my learned + romantic counterpart David Reeder." He annotated the letter of June 24, 1863, "Mr. Calkins, Hammond, Putnam, Barnett + etc. + etc., will perhaps like to read another letter from... David Reeder. There is danger that I shall think myself to be a great man. I certainly shall, if I let Mr. Reeder think for me."[62] Yet, for the most part, Smith's ego was not inflated in his dealings with others.

Perhaps it was the warnings of his friends that helped keep him humble. Charles G. Finney warned him about his tendency to injure people with words. "My precious Br. you will not take it amiss if I touch your elbow + say, 'guard your spirit when your feelings are greatly tried + when you take your pen to reprove or rebuke a brother.' Your rebuke was merited by Br. Blanchard in my apprehension, but I almost found as I read that [your] spirit was a little caustic."[63]

It is admirable that these public figures were on guard to critique one another's performance in an effort to soften blows and protect reputations. Charles Hammond, Smith's laudatory biographer, chastised him for holding a grudge over a former disagreement.

"You [told] me once on the sidewalk in Peterboro
    that it was not best for our intercourse to

continue.... It seems to me that the spirit which
prompts its possessor to do this is not the spirit
of Christ but rather that of selfish love of power +
jealous regard for personal influence + 'dignity,' so
called. I think it is unlike you, exceptional in your
life + spirit thus to punish a man...."[64]

Smith wanted to be a popular and well-liked person so as to establish identity with others and thus influence reform; but he feared that he was disliked. In a debate with Hiram Crozier, a local minister at Smith's Free Church of Peterboro, he noted, "You are a popular man, + I am a hated one—my very neighbors hate me, + run admiringly after you. Indeed, he is popular here who is opposed to me."[65]

Smith may have been a little paranoid about others' opinions of his ideas. The Sherburne, New York postmaster once returned to him some circulars simply because he could not read the addresses Smith had written. Believing that their return was a rejection of his ideas rather than his penmanship, he said, "I am aware, that my sentiments are unwelcome and distasteful to postmasters, as well as to almost all other persons."[66] At one point, he was so concerned that people would not heed him that he wrote to Ann, "Oh how annoyed I am with afflictions for my [ideas], + yours also. It is almost to be hoped that we shall not be eminent persons in the next life."[67]

Gerrit did achieve victory over his guilt for his own wealth by maintaining humility. Perhaps he even carried the tendency too far. After seeing several doctors for what he called his "eye disease," (later determined to be psychosomatic) and obtaining no firm diagnosis other than being told it was a nervous problem, he sought advice at several churches. "Their expressions of love to me were [humbling]. I am so unworthy of them that I am ashamed of myself. I loath myself."[68]

This remark indicated an intent to be introspective and humble, and humility was usually a part of Gerrit Smith's personality. One reporter said of his style of action that he had developed a "utopian scheme of self-disfranchisement."[69]

Smith believed the world was a place where one should give more than one takes, and even when he was in financial trouble, he gave away what he could. "The state of my pecuniary affairs is seriously trying to me. But nevertheless God is good, amazingly good to me, who am so evil and unthankful," he wrote to a friend in the clergy. [70]

In his humble and philanthropic style, Smith was quick to forget a grievance and to relinquish anger. He showed no revenge against those he felt had hurt him. When his local controversy with Asa Rand ended in a stalemate, he declared his love for Rand as a man. "My heart knows no feeling of revenge toward yourself or any other being—and... such a thing as justified revenge... never entered into my conceptions."[71] Years later, after the Civil War had ended, he wrote, "The heart of the whole world would be softened... by... an absence of revenge [against] those who had done so much to provoke revenge."[72]

When others pointed out what they perceived to be Smith's errors, he usually listened and tried to grow from their advice. In response to one who had accused him of having "grossly erred in judgment," he replied, "[That] may well be. I have often done so, and I have no very high respect for my fallible judgment."[73] And to business client David Anderson, who accused Smith of having wronged him, he replied, "If I committed a wrong in the matter, I wish to know it. I wish to repent of it. I wish to make amends for it. I cannot afford to leave any wrong which I have ever done any person unrepented of, unatoned for."[74]

Smith's humility became extensive when he could clearly see his own mistake. "I see my own error, ...[and] admit to you, that it would have been Christian in me to have brought my grievance to your private ear—and that it was unchristian in me to make it public, and especially with the spirit and in the manner I did. I write you this letter to inform you, that I am sensible, I trust penitantly sensible, of the wrong of which I was guilty, both in indulging the feelings I did toward you, and in giving so reprehensible a vent to them."[75]

Smith received good lessons in humility from some of those with whom he interacted. Of Lewis Tappan, he said, "It always gives me pleasure to receive a letter from you + you are a friend with whom it is easy amicably to differ in opinion."[76]

Tappan returned the compliment after chastising Smith for language used in one of his printed circulars. "You have taken my expostulation in good part. I feel that I have done my duty, and can add no more. You have not been wanting in courtesy to me, nor do I take anything you have said or written as a personal reflection."[77]

Such personal strength among correspondents allowed candid communication without fear of reprisal. Even when Smith saw no benefit in exchanging critiques, his action was polite. Accused of being "a rogue" for serving notice to persons whose land he planned to buy for taxes, he replied that the letter contained "gross and utterly causeless + uncalled for impeachments of my integrity.... You will pursue your course in this matter + I mine. Any further correspondance between us would be unavailing."[78] He could be terse, yet still humble enough to be polite.

A challenge to Smith's humility came when he became the target of prejudice. It was received without retaliation, malicious revenge, or a need to defend himself. In a classic response to one who reminded Smith that many people were prejudiced against him, he said, "You refer to the 'strong and deep rooted prejudices' against me. It is true, that there are such.... These prejudices may not hurt me. But they hurt those who cherish them."[79]

Smith realized that judgments of others tell more about those who hold them than they tell about the persons at whom they are aimed, and that as a sign of self-aggrandizement or self-defense, prejudice evidences weakness and delusions of persecution.

The tolerance and accommodation shown toward subcultures by Gerrit Smith, coupled with his repulsion of the prejudice directed toward him, signaled strength of personality and balance of mind.

As he said to Francis Hawley, who had threatened to defame him, do not write of me "as a mean man.... It is not my life."[80]

Smith wanted people at the local level to like him, and thought that if they did not, his influence over them would be minimal. Yet he was close enough to his Peterboro neighbors that their knowledge of him sometimes bred contempt. Perceiving that, he lamented, "So notoriously bad am I... that when a man is to be most effectually stigmatized, he is likened to myself.... [Others are] making me the example and standard of misconduct"[81]

People participating in movements for social change regularly found themselves labeled as radicals or deviants because they opposed established practices. Smith was very susceptible in this sense, and he did understand that this could have a negative influence on his chances for local success in his mission.

Neighbors once accused Smith of damaging the reputation of his attorney, Nehemiah Huntington, because Huntington was not willing to join the Liberty Party. Gerrit replied with the fear that he would have little influence over the townspeople regarding reforms if "the abhorance with which I am now regarded" did not subside.[82]

Peterboro and Smithfield were very important scenes of activity to Smith. Because he wished more than all else to succeed there, he was concerned about what people who knew him thought of him. To James Fuller he commented, "If you care too little to please others with themselves + with you, I err on the other hand—and care too much to have others pleased with themselves + with me."[83] Smith realized that this desire for public approval could weaken his message. He wrote to fellow abolitionist and friend Samuel J. May of his "excessive love of approbation. It is a weakness which I am ashamed of.... I wish to be an humble and self-forgetting man."[84]

One of Smith's biggest blunders regarding his public reputation was his reaction to a statement made by the *Chicago Tribune*. On June 13, 1865, the Tribune published an article about Smith's behavior in connection with John Brown and the Harpers Ferry raid that Smith thought was libelous. He sued the newspaper and eventually settled out of court, but the process took over two years and kept his name and his ire before the public during that time.⁸⁵ He had brought the lawsuit to protect his reputation, or so he thought; still, it backfired. Had he not been so concerned, and just ignored the article, there probably would have been no storm over it. Most of the nation's people had probably not seen it, and those who had would probably have quickly forgotten about it as the newspaper went searching on for some other supposed scandal. By pursuing editor Horace White and the *Chicago Tribune*, Smith injured himself.

In a similar incident, Smith spent a lot of time, ink, and effort assailing the *New York Tribune* for having mistakenly accused him of leaving the floor of Congress and missing the vote on the important Nebraska Bill because the vote came after his self-appointed bedtime. As the *Tribune* itself put it, "There are other spheres of labor in which he can at once render good service to the public, and do credit to his own reputation; in this [exchange with the *Tribune*], he seems rather to waste his time and talents to no purpose whatever."⁸⁶

So Smith did spend some energy seeking self-approval, but there were other evidences of self-assured security that balanced his personality. His wife stated the point in verse:

> "Quoth Gerrit to Nancy 'I'm not of your class,
> Who stop as they pass before each looking glass.
> 'And the reason,' said she, 'is your self admiration
> Is ever too full to admit of inflation.' "⁸⁷

Ann clearly had an opinion of him as self-assured and dignified, and she knew that he did not want to be put on a pedestal. This can be seen in his response to the New York and Hartford Publishing Company's request for a written sketch of his life accompanied by a photograph of him. Their request: "We are about publishing an elegant volume... to consist of sketches of the lives of the Progressive Men of America." Gerrit annotated his response: "Gentlemen, I, this hour, receive the letter with which you honor me. I do not send you my photograph— + I do not send it for the reason that I do not believe my unimportant life to be worthy of a place in your forthcoming splendid volume."[88]

Neither did Smith like public accolades about him. He spoke of having a "great... aversion to vindicating myself before a public assembly,"[89] and when Henry H. Garnet proposed a display of public approval and appreciation of Smith in Buffalo, Smith responded: "It would be particularly painful for me to be made the object of a flattering public notice...."[90]

Despite his personal vigor and strong convictions, Smith knew that his views were radical to others, and he declared himself ready "to express my convictions at whatever expense to my reputation...."[91]

His reputation, however, seemed both positive and secure with many who knew him. As early as 1827, he was selected as an Honorary Member of the New York Historical Society,[92] and his influence was sought after for its public attractiveness. An author of a book on capital punishment requested Smith's opinions. "My book will be a financial success, for, the names of my contributors alone will give it large circulation...."[93]

Lewis Tappan summed up public opinion of Gerrit Smith quite well following Smith's election to a seat in Congress by observing, "Your election astounds me. You once said, 'I expect to live and die a hated man.' It may be so, but your neighbors seem to think well of you."[94]

That pleased Smith; it was, after all, at the local level that he wished to have an effect. Peterboro was his first love.

- 5 -

Peterboro

"This is another heavenly morning! Can it be that there are such mornings anywhere else than in Peterboro?" Gerrit Smith wrote of his beloved home in 1873.[1]

A sense of place can be a highly stabilizing force in one's life. Our identities can become so infused in the places we live that we wonder how or if it could be otherwise. This is what happened between Gerrit Smith and the hamlet of Peterboro: he loved the place so much that he would sacrifice nearly anything for it. The transcendentalists who visited him at Peterboro encountered a man whose relationship with nature and place was as pure as was any literary or literal experiment in utopian philosophy.

Largely because Smith lived there, Peterboro became a Mecca for the oppressed and for social reform as money, people, and movements roiled about in a social boil of activity. The hamlet hosted dignitaries and organizations and hatched plans that would affect the whole country. Money flowed in huge amounts, businesses succeeded and multiplied, social service agencies were established, runaway slaves arrived, radical movements such as abolition, temperance, suffrage, and evangelism found their sponsors, and the people of Peterboro felt proud.

Peter Smith's agent, Jasper Aylesworth, had cleared the two-acre "village green" from woodland, forming the center of the hamlet in 1795. (As a note of interest, Jasper Aylesworth had moved to Peterboro from Foster, RI along with fellow worker John Pray. The author was reared on Pray Hill in Foster, RI, and also moved to Peterboro—without any knowledge of the Rhode Island resident who had come there more than 150 years before.)

Peter Smith chose this spot for the village green because its location was central to his land holdings and because of its proximity to an abundance of hardwood with which to fuel the two glass factories he built there. In 1806, Peter moved his family after having built an office for his business and a house. Young Gerrit became a Peterboro resident for life.

Peterboro was typical of the agrarian hamlets and villages of the early 1800s in New York State. People relied on each other without much help from the outside. They efficiently used the resources found locally with little room for waste, and they solved their own problems with local ingenuity. People developed a sense of personal responsibility for the improvement of their village. Jobs were not transient; life was stable and predictable. They had a strong sense of place and a balance in life.

By the 1870s, at the end of Gerrit Smith's career in Peterboro, the hamlet had become a bustling center of life with a population of approximately 350 people. "We have two [physicians]... one drug store, one grist and saw mill, two dry goods stores, one tin shop, one wagon shop, one tailor shop, one harness shop, one meat market, three shoe shops, two blacksmith shops, a cheese factory and a good hotel. We have an undertaker, three painters, a goodly number of carpenters and a host of teachers.... We have one milliner shop, an unlimited number of dressmakers as well as several tailoresses. We can boast of two schoolhouses [and] three churches...."[2]

Surrounding all of this activity were the farms. Hop growing—which bothered the temperance-minded Smith—was common, and "for several successive days every spring, flocks of sheep are driven through this village for the purpose of being washed."[3]

The diary of one local resident during the 1860s offers some insight into the prevalent lifestyle. Clarissa Brown Bliss and her husband, Joseph, lived on a farm near Peterboro. In 50 entries written between 1865 and 1866, Clarissa mentioned 23 agricultural tasks, 41 home economics tasks—and only eight service visits by agents outside the home. Clearly, households of the period were governed by self-sufficiency.[4]

One reason villages at the time were self-sufficient was the difficulty of travel: a trip of just ten miles could take all day. While traveling with Gerrit on a tour giving anti-slavery speeches, Ann wrote to her daughter, "We came the first four miles in a lumber wagon, then two miles in a scow across the river... then two miles in a canoe rowed by two Indians... then eight miles to Ft. Covington in a lumber wagon, then fifteen miles... in another wagon a little better."[5] One of Gerrit's trips to Schenectady via stage included a long stop in Utica, then an all-night ride east. The stage got stuck ten times, and the passengers had to "pry it out." He had to walk "at least ten miles... in the night in the deep wind... my shoes and stockings were continually soaked."[6]

The Erie Canal made travel a little easier, but it was still slow and only seasonally navigable. On a packet-boat headed east toward home, Smith noted, "The water is still a couple of feet deep on some parts of the tow path. We shall probably reach Syracuse by 7 o'clock this evening."[7] "We did not reach Syracuse until after 8 o'clock, so much of the tow path was overflooded. I got a one horse wagon + boy, + we were at Chittenango at midnight.... Left at 5 o'clock this morning. Got home and found all well. After an hour's scrubbing, I ate one of our good breakfasts."[8]

One of Smith's visitors reported back after his winter trip from Peterboro to Canastota, "On arriving at Clockville [five miles north of Peterboro]... we stopped to warm and I found I had frozen one of my ears quite bad and had considerably frosted one of my cheeks."[9]

Travel was also expensive. Tolls were charged to pay for road maintenance, so a round trip from Peterboro to Morrisville—a distance of about six miles—cost ten cents, the equivalent of $7.50 today. The obvious result was that people did not travel far, and small villages became social and commercial centers of action. In contrast to his fellow villagers, though, Smith was able to afford a trip to Morrisville about twice each week. The one-way toll to Oneida was fifty cents, and to Canastota, fourteen cents. As we shall see, Smith, with his money and ideas, made this village in central New York very special in the early 19th century.

The enormous workload of his land business confined him to Peterboro early in his career. The land office was near the center of his geographic domain, and he had to work in order to pay the many debts he inherited from Peter. He also funded regular pay disbursements—"allowances," as they were called—to other family members. His seclusion in Peterboro allowed him to focus better than he could have in an urban setting; besides, he did not like cities.

Gerrit avoided public life and enjoyed the privacy of his home and family. When required to travel, he would go—reluctantly. Little surprise, then, that he viewed his election to Congress as being "against the strong habits formed in my deeply secluded life."[10]

Except for a few intermittent years residing at "The Grove" one and a quarter miles south of the village, Gerrit Smith lived in his family mansion in the heart of Peterboro for 68 years. It was set back from the road one hundred feet, and the driveway looped in from the left and crossed in front of the house, leaving a lawn between the house and a wrought-iron fence across the front of the property.

To the west of the house, about fifty feet away, stood the land office. A small brick structure, it served as the focal point of his long work days. While the house stood three stories tall, the land office was nestled comfortably under the hugging branches of some large trees. Harriet Tubman, Frederick Douglass, and probably many other notables in American history sat in it with him and discussed the issues of the day. The building still stands.

Behind the house was a stable barn, a laundry, an icehouse, and, down the hill next to the flowing Oneida Creek, the Birdhouse. Greene Smith, Gerrit's son, loved birds, studied them intensely, and built a "museum" to house his collection of personally stuffed and mounted specimens.

The Land Office, where Gerrit Smith spent more than 60 years of work. This modest building hosted the purchase and sale of more than a half-million acres of land. Behind the office to the left is the stable barn, which housed carriages and wagons used to help runaway slaves make it north to freedom—and may have provided a hiding place for slaves as well. In front of the office is a stone marker with Smith's story.

Photo courtesy of the National Abolition Hall of Fame & Museum

Greene mounted the birds behind glass in wall cases with cork lining. The building was centrally heated and sported running water from a lead-lined reservoir on the top floor. Hemlock bark covered the outside, with small birdhouses mounted across its front. It blended into its natural surroundings as if it belonged there.[11] Gerrit also used the Birdhouse for various functions. He mentioned a dance that took place there, and in mid-1873, he hosted a conference for the freedom of Cuba in the Birdhouse. "The gentlemen will spend much of their day in the charming Bird House— + will leave for N York after dinner."[12]

On the north side of the creek stood "The Cottage Across the Brook." Built in 1840, it became part of the Smith estate in 1867 as the home of

Gerrit's newly married grandson, Gerrit Smith Miller, and his wife, Susan Dixwell. Its yard held a dairy barn, apple trees, and grape arbors along the brook. A footbridge connected it with the mansion property.

The expansive yard to the east of the south-facing mansion house was a structured garden. Flowers, flowering trees, and a vegetable and strawberry garden surrounded the fountain in its center. Somewhere near this garden was a small family cemetery, as noted by a visitor: "My mind was carried back to the deeply interesting spot in your garden where were deposited the remains of those formerly taken from you."[13] By 1840, Smith had buried five of his children in this plot. One stone read, "This son and this daughter died too young to have names on earth, but not too young to have names 'written in heaven.'"[14] The cemetery was moved later to the family plot in the cemetery east of the village of Peterboro.

The flora around the estate was beautiful. An unnamed visitor spoke of "jessamine, honey suckle, and Michigan rose vine [twined] around the verandahs of his library and sleeping apartments."[15] Smith occasionally hired workers to do yard work,[16] and the gardens, separated from the backyards of nearby village houses and stores by a high stone wall, were kept up by a hired gardener who lived in the "gardener's cottage" on the east portion of the property.

Once, Smith's "gardener had proposed to have some old canvass to cover tomatoes + mellons to preserve them from the frosts."[17] John B. Edwards, Smith's business agent in Oswego, recommended to Gerrit a "German Gardener" who "understands the cultivation of flowers and grapes." The man arrived at Peterboro with a letter of introduction from Edwards: "The bearer is Mr. Adam Fisher... the German man who comes to undertake to be your gardener."[18]

Gerrit regarded the house and yard staff as members of his family, and on Christmas day, 1848, he referred to "The gardener:"

"For Andrew, then next, your bounty we pray,
He works very well, both by night + by day:
On the road, in the garden, + building up fires,
He does what he can to fulfill our desires."[19]

Top photo: "The Birdhouse," Greene Smith's museum for stuffed birds, which stood on the Gerrit Smith estate. It was a two-story structure with an elegant interior that included a mahogany staircase, birch wall paneling, stained-glass windows, oak floors, and skylights. *Bottom photo*: The Cottage Across the Brook. In his later years, Gerrit would take morning walks out the back door of his mansion, north across a field, and then across a bridge to visit his great-grandchildren in the cottage. It is now home to Norman Kingsford Dann and Dorothy Willsey-Dann.

Photos from the author's collection

Near the gardener's cottage stood a water tower that received water pumped up from the brook. It served the main house with running water by gravity feed.

The house, for Gerrit at least, was a comfortable sanctuary. He lived simply, preferring to avoid conspicuous consumption and ostentatious display because he wished to conserve his money for helping oppressed people. A visitor to his house in 1861 who kept a week-long journal of his experience there described it as "a barrack... in which literary culture and even domestic comfort were sacrificed to a fanatical philanthropy."[20] There were no elegant carpets, no ornate furniture, no mirrors, no drapes, and no rich-looking gold-framed paintings. "The hall dividing the building was sixty feet in length, on one side of which was a large drawing-room opening into a conservatory, on the other, the library and dining room."[21]

Without central heating, the house was cold in the winter. Gerrit wrote to Ann, "I had a cold time of it Monday night. Fire + blankets are, you know, insufficient to keep me warm."[22] When the January temperature outside reached thirty degrees below zero, he had problems: "I forgot the pipes—I find they are frozen in my dressing room + probably in the 2 bathrooms. The pipes are all dripping."[23]

An 1832 receipt from the Howard Insurance Company provides an insight as to the value of the property. The receipt is for $40.12 for insurance "on buildings at Peterboro" valued at $6,800, more than half a million dollars in today's currency.[24] The estate included 30 buildings on 30 acres of land, and most of the buildings—even the house—were simple in their designs.

Smith treated the people hired to help around the house and yard well, and they valued their jobs and their personal relationships with the Smith family. Gerrit did some work in the house himself, but probably not much. "I cleaned in the library this morning. My books + etc., all lie in the middle of the floor yet."[25] He did not sound too enthusiastic about the chore. During the 1830s, his household expense book shows that he paid his hired help between $4 and $8 per week. Because $100 to $200 per year was a fair wage at that time,

A view of the Smith mansion, looking west from the east lawn. The well-sculpted walkways and gardens were a favorite among the family's many visitors.

From the author's collection

this was generous.[26] Interestingly, this expense account book also indicates Smith's grudging release of money to family members, as he noted about his daughter, "Let Mrs. Miller have $5.00." He probably would rather have spent the money on others.

Some of Gerrit's domestic help included Laura Bosworth, affectionately called "Lolly." She was first employed in November of 1819, and worked for thirty years as a nurse and helper to Gerrit and Ann's children while living in her own house on the east side of Peterboro.[27] Elizabeth H. Kelty, known as Aunt Betsey, started work at the Smith mansion in 1828, serving in a variety of roles. She was still working there after Gerrit's death in 1874. Her jobs included housekeeping, counseling Gerrit and the children, and suggesting editorial changes to his writings. She was also responsible for reading Smith's "begging letters" and recommending action on them. Aunt Betsey was a respected and loyal household member who also owned her own home in the village.[28] She was close to all the members of the Smith household, and was trusted with the regular care of the interior of the house. To Ann she wrote, "The sewing society is to meet here this afternoon and I must brush about and make ready."[29]

As late as 1873, Gerrit was still hiring helpers. "We yesterday hired a new cook—a very black maiden 32 years of age—Nettie Phillips is her name—$4.00 a week."[30]

Detailed records of household expenses from the 1820s and 1830s indicate that the family lived comfortably. The Smiths kept an accumulating account with Asa Raymond's general store in Peterboro in the 1820s, which they paid off once per year. Expenses for June 1827 through April 1828 totalled $75.27. By 1836, the storekeeper was John Campbell. Gerrit wrote this note in the expense book: "Mr. Campbell will call for payment of Mr. Smith's account as often as he pleases—monthly or weekly."[31] They went to the store often; purchases during the year 1829 occurred on an average of thirteen days in each month. The record-keeping itself was impressive: every item purchased was noted, along with its price. A few examples:

Eggs - 6 cents	1 doz. fish hooks - 9 cents
1 doz. Quills - 4 cents	1 qt whiskey - 8 cents
8 lb. Sugar - $1.00	1 qt. Brandy - 30 cents
2 lead pencils - 12 cents	1 bottle rum - 11 cents
5 yds. Cloth - 26 cents/yd.	Paper, ink powder - 12 cents
1 tin dipper - 25 cents	1 lb. salt - 6 cents
1 ½ yd muslin - 72 cents	2 lb. mackerel - 10 cents
powder + shot - 6 cents	8 lb. candles - 13 cents/lb.
1 ½ galls Lasses - 75 cents	12 blue plates - $1.08

Someone purchased an alcoholic beverage on average once every other month, probably for use in cooking. Elizabeth was a cook of note, and did use it in her recipes. "From the current receipts I have adopted I do not reject wine nor in many cases, brandy...."[32]

Gerrit's business agent in Oswego, John B. Edwards, also purchased items for the household. His records indicate large amounts spent on food sent to Peterboro. "June 5, 1860—paid for 15 beef tongues sent to you—$5.00. June 6, 1860—Paid Ira Jenkins for 180# hams sent you—$21.60"[33] Edwards also sent "Sea Biscuits," a form of hardtack popular with sailors that was one of Ann's favorites; and frequent shipments of three or four barrels of flour.[34]

Gerrit himself actually purchased items for use on his estate. One list of supplies "for the consumption of my workmen" included fabrics, food, tobacco, nails—all in large amounts. While he was dutiful in his household purchases, Gerrit was annoyed with these distractions from his business obligations. Elizabeth Cady Stanton, a frequent visitor at the Smith home, commented, "I have often heard Cousin Gerrit complain of the time he lost managing the estate."[35]

They purchased flour by the barrel, butter in lots of 28 pounds, and cheese in amounts averaging 27 pounds. Their sugar purchases averaged 45 pounds each, and they used maple sugar often. They regularly bought candy, figs, ginger, spices, turkey, duck, cranberries, oysters, and several different kinds of fish. They bought all of the

A Peterboro Street Scene in 1907, looking north from the village green. Not much had changed since Gerrit Smith's days in the 1800s.

From the author's collection

items mentioned here in the early 1830s. By the late 1830s, purchases of cane sugar and a few other items ceased because of Gerrit's policy of boycotting the products of slave labor.

The Smiths made most of their own clothes. There are many entries in the expense book for thread, needles, scissors, buttons, padding, and even bonnet wire. They used several types of cloth: muslin, flannel, Irish linen, silks, and towel cloth. Accessories included feathers, braid, and ribbon.[36] One Peterboro resident commented about local women, "There is scarcely any of the women here that does any outdoor work but then they are almost all smartly employed indoors at work such as Sewing, Tailoring, Weaving and Spinning."[37]

Repair and maintenance required the purchase of door hardware, screws and nails, tacks, padlocks, paintbrushes, and tools such as brooms, saws, scythes, rope, and a plow. The Smiths bought books infrequently, and then, they chose simple texts: an almanac at six dollars per year, a spelling book, a geography atlas, one testament, a few blank writing books, and a fishing book.[38]

The Smiths also had pets. In the spring of 1861, Gerrit's dog, Frolic, was sick. He wrote a poem to her, in part:

"Farewell, dear babe! for that sweet sound
Does best express my tenderness:
I seldom in my life have found
A babe so charming to caress."[39]

She died on April 29, 1861. By the fall of that same year, Gerrit had a new dog. Gerrit wrote to Greene, "So you would like to see Bob! What an affectionate being he is.... An hour ago I heard poor Bob barking in the barn, I found him tied up. I let him loose + his joy was boundless."[40]

They also kept chickens. "What lovely weather," said Ann. "The hens are scratching in the front yard, and the robins are hopping from tree to tree."[41] Although horses were always around for work and transport, the Smiths did not pay much attention to them. They were probably the charge of the hired help. Gerrit's son-in-law, Charles Dudley Miller, was the 'hoss' man who enjoyed caring for them. Gerrit revealed his attitude toward the horses in a letter to Greene about some new purchases: "I love one of our new horses. The other horse we call 'The Dancer'. I am afraid to drive him."[42]

He also mentioned to Greene a newly plowed and planted pasture, a "handsome garden," and the observation that "The cows have got fat upon the clover."[43] The Smiths' love for nature and for animals was natural in such a pastoral setting as Peterboro, and, in an age of expansion and manifest destiny, Gerrit Smith stayed put in the place that he nurtured and loved. One visitor to Peterboro referred to it as "a resting place of holy laws."[44]

In a discourse delivered in Peterboro, Smith stated his pride:

> "[Peterboro,] probably the only spot in the State to which the Anti-Slavery Society, that was mobbed out of Utica... could retreat in safety—is, in respect to a sound and rational religion, greatly in advance of almost every other place in the land. Our families... dwell together in peace and love; and... there is no little proof that [tobacco use and liquor sales are no longer with us]. When I heard... that our... youth of white faces and black faces had mingled together freely in a public dance... I felt proud of my village."[45]

His use of "my village" is proprietary, and reflects pride. Both Gerrit and Ann were away from their home in the spring of 1836 when he wrote, "A long letter from my dear wife is one of the grander comforts I have in my absence from her. Rite me, my dear as soon as you receive this, + direct to me at Peterboro, at which beloved spot I hope to be about the middle of next week. My increasing attachment to that spot makes me homesick everywhere else."[46]

At the time, Gerrit was in New York City for an anti-slavery meeting. When he traveled, his homesickness made him dream of the beauty and comforts of his home and village. He wrote the following poem as he returned toward Peterboro from a visit to New York City:

> "Once more, my lov'd home, am I cheerful + blest
> With hopes of return to thy dear sacred rest;
> Once more I rejoice that again I shall see
> The spot of all earth that is dearest to me.
> There flow'rs seem more bright + the fields seem more green,
> There streams seem more pure + the skies more serene;
> But far more than this, there all hearts seem to flow
> With such peace, love + joy as sweet homes only know."[47]

Gerrit's love of the natural beauty of Peterboro, like the transcendentalist movement itself, manifested itself in a semi-religious feeling toward nature and its relationship to the individual. How could it be, he wondered, that people could not see beauty in nature? Surely it followed that if natural systems and social systems shared internal dynamics, then seeing beauty in all people was possible. "This is a very sweet morning in the natural world," Smith said. "The sun is bright—there is no wind—the birds are singing + it will... be warm in an hour or two."[48] And even in winter, "It is beautiful winter weather. The sleighing is fine—and never were moons made of brighter silver."[49] Travel by sleigh was common during long winters. Clarissa Bliss noted in her diary that the first buggy to pass her house in the spring of 1873 was on April 11.

Ann shared Gerrit's love for Peterboro. When her son-in-law Charles had taken sick and was coming to town, she noted, "Peterboro air will make him bright and happy."[50] Ann was often away in distant cities seeking medical treatment while Gerrit stayed with his business in Peterboro. He wrote to her about his beloved home. "This is another beautiful morning upon our beautiful hills."[51] One month later he reported, "This is the first day of summer! + a lovlier day than this never spared its likeness upon the earth. Oh that your eye, were here to witness with my eyes the surpassing beauties of this Peterboro morning. The climax of those beauties is the old crabapple tree just East of the Conservatory. It is one broad sheet of shining whiteness...." And the next day, "It is another beautiful morning. Nature puts on her best weather for your eyes—but you... hide your [views] within thick walls. Why, the whole City of N York does not present a view equal to the old crab tree!"[53]

His obsession with and attachment to the place he loved so much kept him optimistic about life. In 1861 an old friend from college days, Judge Haight, visited him in Peterboro. Smith saw an old, fat, white-haired man, and he mused that it must be that staying in Peterboro had kept him vigorous and young.[54] As he wrote to his son and grandson, "The mind is vigorous in this clear + cold weather."[55] He encouraged them to enjoy it.

Peterboro had the same positive effect on visitors. After Edwin Morton left Peterboro for Cambridge, Massachusetts, he remarked, "We're having such a beautiful summer! I often think how fresh and beautiful it is with you—your mornings, + evenings, + nights, + days. And I do not forget all around you, who will add to its beauty."[56]

Smith and his family shared their Peterboro home with incredibly generous, loving, and unbiased hospitality. They built a "community family" that encompassed not only Peterboro, but, one by one or in small groups, the rest of America. In an almost biblical sense, the Smiths considered all of the earth's children to be their own. Gerrit Smith's Peterboro became attractive to thousands of visitors. Whereas most families attract to themselves people of their own class, the Smiths attracted everyone. They cared, especially where they saw inequity or oppression. They installed and lived the communal principle of the utopians, the transcendentalists, and the religious revivalists of the time.

The number and diversity of their visitors were astonishing. They included abolitionists designing antislavery plans, politicians courting Smith's political allegiance, poor people seeking aid, vagrants begging for food, inventors requesting financial support for strange ideas, runaway slaves seeking freedom, Native Americans, suffragettes, and reform-minded persons of all sorts who hoped to enlist Gerrit Smith's influence and money in their causes.

Smith opened his heart and purse; few were turned away empty-handed. George Thomas, a friend who visited in 1859, remarked of the Peterboro hospitality:

> "I... was most courteously received and hospitably entertained. Had I been a duke or dutchess, president or potentate, I could not have expected or desired to have met with more kind attention and regard. I have reason to believe that the... black fugitive slave from the south met with a warmer reception and a more kindly greeting at the home of Mr. Smith than myself or any of the more favored of any race."[57]

Frothingham gave us a rare glimpse at Gerrit Smith's cordial, open-minded way with his visitors. In his diary, Smith listed and commented upon a few of them:

> "A man calling himself George Brown, of Corning, comes here to-night with a very heavy pack on his back. He is accompanied by his wife and child. The child is deaf."

> "Mrs. Crampton, a beggar woman, spent last night with us. Charles Johnson, a fugitive slave from Hagerstown, took tea at our house last evening and breakfasted with us this morning."

> "Mr. William Corning, a wandering pilgrim, as he styles himself, dines with us. He is peddling his own printed productions."

> "Peter Johnson, a colored, illiterate man, calling himself a missionary, arrives this afternoon. He

has been among the colored people in Canada, and is going to Hayti."

"Mrs. Phiak of Port Byron, a poor old Dutch woman, arrives. She leaves after breakfast. A begging blind man, and a begging woman and her son from Cazenovia breakfast at our house."

"Poor Graham, the insane literary colored man, has been with us a day or two."

"William Henry Douglass, of Paterson, New Jersey, Son of Aaron Douglass, comes to our house this morning. Says he is nineteen years old, and ran away from his home a week ago last Saturday. Has been to Buffalo, repents of his folly, and is on his return home. He has no money. I gave him three dollars and some bread and cheese. He breakfasts with us, and starts for home."

"Elder Cook and William Hanes of Oneida depot arrive this evening. Mr. H is a 'medium,' and speaks in unknown tongues."

"Dr. Winmer of Washington City, with five deaf mutes and a blind child take supper and spend the evening with us."

"We find Brother Swift and wife and daughter at our house, where they will remain until they get lodgings. There come this evening an old black man, a young one and his wife and infant. They say that they are fugitives from North Carolina."

"A man... brings his mother, six children and her
half sister, all fugitives from Virginia."

"An Indian and a fugitive slave spent last night
with us. The Indian has gone on, but Tommy
McElligott (very drunk) has come to fill his
place."[58]

The parade to the Smith's house was constant. During the years
1841 and 1842, Elizabeth kept track of visitors daily in a "Common
Place Book" labeled "Arrivals."[59] For these years, the listings read
as follows:

1841

Month	Number Visiting
May	15
June	48 (25th was William Goodell, abolitionist)
July	38
Aug. 2	36 for dinner
Aug.	34 (20th was Theodore Weld, abolitionist)
Sept.	16
Oct.	49 (19th was James G. Birney, former slave owner turned abolitionist)
Nov.	8
Dec. 1st	24 for dinner
Dec.	12

1842

Month	Number Visiting
Jan.	87 (19th was William Goodell)
Feb.	12
March	14
April	22

May	34	
June	20	(included "Two Squaws + a boy")
July	54	(10th was William Chaplin, abolitionist)

The Smiths averaged 33 visitors per month during this time. Ann seems to have concurred with Gerrit on the importance of helping all who came, although at times, they may have taxed her patience. "I wanted to write to you before this, but we have had so many coming and going that I have found no time."[60] She then goes on to list twenty-two people who have visited within three days. And again, "Since last Tuesday we have had twenty visitors. Three staid all night, 15 ate with us + the rest were calls."[61]

The list of visitors included some well-known names: abolitionists Frederick Douglass, William Lloyd Garrison, Henry Highland Garnet, Jermain Loguen, Wendell Phillips, John Greenleaf Whittier, Theodore Dwight Weld, Lewis Tappan, James G. Birney, Beriah Green, Samuel Ringgold Ward, Charles Sumner, Horace Greeley, Salmon P. Chase, and John Brown. Women's rights advocates Susan B. Anthony, Elizabeth Cady Stanton, Lucy Stone, Angelina and Sarah Grimké, Sojourner Truth, and Abby Kelley Foster. Underground Railroad 'conductor' Harriet Tubman depended on Smith's Peterboro "station" for aid on her trips from Maryland to Canada, and even pro-slavery supporter and author George Fitzhugh visited Smith in his effort to understand the abolitionist mind-set.

Abolitionist Julia Griffiths, while visiting Peterboro in October of 1852, commented,

> "Whatever be the season, I think I always breathe more freely in Peterboro, than elsewhere. The moral atmosphere is so clear here.... The spirit of Christian love permeates all words and actions; and almost every hour in the day, while in this sweet home...."[62]

Ann shared her view of love for one's fellow man in a letter to her daughter. They had hosted a dinner at the house at which forty ate at five o'clock, "and a larger party had supper in the evening. I fear the presence of the poor caused the separation.... I feel more and more the necessity + joy of identifying ourselves with the poorest of the poor."[63]

Gerrit wrote to Ann, describing a large dinner party for a variety of local people. "Greene + Henry talked about hunting.... All of us were astonished at the graceful training and very ladylike manners of all. Peterboro's status has risen much."[64]

After leaving Peterboro, Edwin Morton remembered the visitors and the hospitality: "Beside me hangs a daguerre of your house, and I fancy a crowd going through the yard to lunch."[65] Frederick Douglass wrote of comments made to him by Charles Sumner: "Our friend Charles Sumner never wearies of the subject of his visit to you last winter. You must have made him very happy there."[66] Sumner was a U.S. Senator, an avid abolitionist, and a long-time friend of Smith. He gained an unwanted level of notoriety in May of 1856 when South Carolina Congressman Preston Brooks beat him with a cane in the Senate chamber because of Sumner's staunch antislavery stand.

On his arrival home from a trip, Gerrit wrote, "I found a queer religionist... here. He had been at our house some 24 hours. He still sticks. Queer + crazy people always seek for each other. How much we have suffered by my reputation for queerness + insanity!"[67] And on the next day, "We had a pleasant Sunday School yesterday.... We have just had worship. The queer stranger is still with us."[68]

James G. Birney, a Kentucky slave owner-turned-abolitionist and twice the Liberty Party presidential candidate, visited Smith several times and commented favorably about the peacefulness of Peterboro and Smith's good hospitality. Birney's wife spent time with the Smiths in Peterboro battling tuberculosis, and following her death, two of the Birney children lived there for a while in order to relieve James of the pressures of child-rearing.[69]

To all who visited, the Peterboro hospitality was gracious and sincere. Lewis Tappan summed it up well:

> "I have often thought that you + your dear family
> made many sacrifices in living in so large a house,
> but as you have [offered] hospitality to such a
> liberal extent I know it gratified you to act... on
> the principle—it is more blessed to give than to
> receive."[70]

Another friend noted the Smiths' gracious hospitality to any visitor:

> "Not to have visited Gerrit Smith at home, not
> to have received his hearty greeting at the door,
> not to have seen him glowing and beaming at his
> porch, not to have heard his copious table-talk is
> to have missed one of the satisfactions of life."[71]

It is difficult to believe that, while living in such a 'fish bowl', family members could have had much of a private life; yet they did. Gerrit tried to keep order in his daily routine while at home, but given the frequency of overnight visitors, it must have been difficult. "Order and system [were]... observed in his business and life enjoyments. He arose at an early hour, retired at 9 p.m. His meals were taken at regular hours and all his home surroundings were in perfect order. He was scrupulously neat in person...."[72]

In notes to Ann, Gerrit wrote, "I slept well last night—rose, shaved + bathed...."[73] "I have just made my toilet, + am about to go into the dining room to meet the dear members of my family in the praying circle. But before I go, let me say to you, that I have had a night of sweet sleep, + that I am in [good] health. Aunt Betsy, as is her wont, brought dear Florey [Birney's child] to my bed AM 6 o'clock, to annoye me with her chattering."[74]

Smith cared about his appearance, and normally dressed in neat but plain clothing. He remarked in one verse about having "put on fine clothes instead of plain," as he expected the arrival of a visitor. When she failed to appear, "I'll put the plain ones on again."[75] When he did dress up for a special occasion, he wore tailored shirts. "I am concerned darling about your shirts," wrote Ann. "They cannot be made in Peterboro. You will have to come here [New York City] or go to Geneva to be measured."[76] Obviously, his family was concerned about his appearance and his reputation.

Religious devotions started each day and usually ended it, too. The family would pray together and ask blessings on the day, or thanks for it.[77] From Gerrit's diary are notes of evening talk at a family circle where they discussed the day's events.[78] Gerrit spoke of planning to convey some good news from a friend's letter "When I go to dinner."[79]

The voluminous amount of writing between family members reveals the personal side of Gerrit Smith. Because he intentionally isolated himself from the world, people outside of his family did not generally get to know him well; they were often inaccurate when describing his personality. As he told James Fuller, he seldom criticized others' faults because he had few close friends for whom he cared intensely.[80] Smith reserved his greater affections for his family. "For the first time since I came to [Albany], I attended a party last evening.... I remained for a few minutes over an hour. I saw nobody half as handsome as my wife + no other object a hundredth part as interesting as my children."[81]

Ann felt bad when she could not find time to write. "How much I have to say to you. It's a real trial not to write now."[82] Although family members did not like to be apart, they took many trips, especially to visit other family members. Elizabeth Smith Miller wrote to Gerrit: "We reached [Rochester] safely, my dear Father, about 2 o'clock last night.... We remained on deck [on a packet boat] a short time after you left us. Mother sighed.... I must confess that I too felt bad a little on parting with you."[83]

Letters from various family members were chatty. They told of daily events and had lots of news about people—how they were and what they were doing. Affectionate letters were a family habit and served to maintain emotional connections during absence. On a trip to Rochester where her family lived, Ann wrote to her daughter, "I thought I would not write to you again 'till I reached Rochester, but I have such a longing to see you that I must write a little this evening by way of relief. I do indeed desire to see you, my dear, more than I can express."[84] Her daily letters to "Libby" were often three pages long.

Gerrit's letters to his family were frequently "serial letters," written three or four times a day over two or three days. They were a chronicle of daily activities, and Ann loved to receive them: "Your letters create delightful little ripples in the even stream of our... life."[85] If anyone neglected to write, it was considered almost a sin. "It will be two weeks Friday since I had a letter from you," Ann admonished her daughter. "You do not know how disappointed I have been day after day to see the mail come—and no letter from you. I suppose you thought since you began to make ready for home that we did not care to hear from you. That was natural.... But in the future I hope you will act contrary to the nature in this matter."[86]

Another rich source of information about the Smith family and their personal lives is in the poems they wrote to each other. Poems, or "rhymes," as Gerrit called them, were an important way for the family to communicate to each other their feelings and emotions, and they were all good at it. At one point, they collected scattered poems that had been written on bits of paper and made them into a "Verse Book" prefaced by Gerrit. "These rhymes will be prized by our successors because they will reveal one of the ways in which the members of our family sought to interest + gratify each other, + thus one of the ways for enabling them to form opinions of the tastes, habits, + character of our family."[87]

Gerrit seemed concerned about the quality of his rhymes: "I need not say that I am a poet. I occasionally write rhymes...."[88]

"I crawl on earth's surface + lie in its dust
Asham'd that my soul will not soar.

I try to write Stanzas—but oh they are just
Most wretched of rhymes—nothing more."[89]

The way Gerrit Smith lived his life in Peterboro so closely paralleled and so often intersected the phenomenon of the "Burned-Over District" in New York state that he became a living history of the evolution of a whole generation of thinkers. Peterboro provided the natural beauty and the self-sufficient individualism that reinforced Smith's utopian beliefs about diversity and philanthropy.

His philosophy led him to influence one of the greatest conflicts in American history: the Civil War. But understanding the impact of Gerrit Smith on the 19th-century reform movement begins with a better understanding of his relationships with his own family members.

- 6 -

Elizabeth and Greene

"I want to [s]'leep long wi[th] papa," said two-year-old Elizabeth about her Daddy when he was away from home. Gerrit's little daughter Elizabeth enjoyed a close relationship with her father, even occasionally lying in bed with him.[1] Elizabeth Smith's parents taught her sweetness and love; those who knew her spoke of her in glowing terms. She was a joy to Gerrit, and she graced the Smith family for nearly 90 years.

It was on September 20, 1822 that Gerrit first became a father. His college chum, F.M. Haight wrote, "I have heard with gladness that you are a father, for a man of your peculiar feelings and ideas this circumstance will open new and endless sources of enjoyment."[2]

When "Libby" was two years old on a visit to Hampton, Livingston County, New York with her mother, Ann wrote, "As for your little Perfection she is the admiration of the whole country. We find it quite a difficult task to manage her, after being so spoiled by her father."[3] Five years later, also while visiting her grandparents at Hampton, Elizabeth demonstrated her affection for her parents and her home. Said Ann, "I found Libby well and delighted to see me. She has grown tall and slim and I think her somewhat improved in manners. She sends a kiss to Papa, Aunt Betty and Poopoo…."[4]

Ann and Gerrit wanted to develop in their children a set of sophisticated manners that reflected unadorned grace and refinement—coupled with concern for the well-being of others. Elizabeth did well with this charge, but later, Greene became a problem.

In her early teens, Elizabeth went away to school in Clinton, NY, while Ann guided her with conservative counseling from Peterboro. She warned "Lib" about using correct spelling in her letters, and cautioned, "I hope you have mended your… dress. Be particular my dear to keep everything about you in nice order, teeth especially,"[5] "Do take good care of your health. I hope you wear thick shoes and… stockings to school."[6] Both parents were concerned that she keep a pious Christian bearing. Gerrit declared, "I hope our dear Elizabeth will at all times cultivate sound sense and sound piety. Life is too short to justify our fooling away any part of it."[7] They must have been pleased when Libby reported, "I like secret prayer. I have been trying by the help of God this week to do unto others as I would they should do unto me."[8]

Also reflective of her parents' values was Libby's lifelong appreciation for the beauty of nature. Many of her letters contained descriptions of what she perceived as unmatched natural beauty, and in typical Gerrit Smith fashion, she saw beauty in things and people wherever she was. Many years later while in Massachusetts, she wrote to her father,

> "We have had a lovely time this morning—Mother, Dudley, + I in our room looking out on this wonderful ocean which lies like a thing of life with its tidal pulsations. Cloud shadows are chasing over the lawn, + the snowy soils are wonderfully beautiful in the sun light."[9]

One area of disagreement between Gerrit and his wife and daughter may have been the level of sophistication to which one should aspire. Perhaps Ann and Elizabeth preferred a higher standard of living than did Gerrit; he complained sometimes about how much they spent on luxury items. When Elizabeth was twenty-one, her father talked with her about weddings. "She expressed her surprise last evening at my opposition to a fashionable wedding. She will, however… be convinced that it belongs to the class of things which

God hates. It seems to me, that I could never drag my reluctant feet again to a fashionable wedding: and to have one in my own family would be to violate if not make void, my long standing example in behalf of simplicity....”[10]

Gerrit got his way, for the Smith family's long-time domestic employee, Elizabeth Kelty, described Elizabeth's wedding day as “a private wedding” with only “the immediate families” except for two friends of Mr. Miller, the groom. Elizabeth Kelty went on to write, “Lib looked very sweet in her simple white muslin without gold or pearls + nothing on her head save her black glossy hair except a little bunch of white Tu-be-rose + green geranium stuck in her comb.”[11]

Three months later Gerrit counseled Elizabeth, “Be careful, my beloved daughter, to get, + to keep out of your heart all aristocracy. See to it that you sympathize with the masses, rather than with the conspicuous few.... Cast your lot with the despised and trodden down, and count as spurious the Christianity which stands aloof from them.”[12]

As her writings showed, Elizabeth remained concerned about those who did not share the Smiths' privilege. The following poem reflects Gerrit's difficulty in reconciling his distaste for the upper classes with the reality of his own family's place in society; in it, he seems a bit dissatisfied with Elizabeth's low level of sophistication.

“We had hoped our own Lizzie a lady would be
And would grow into love of refined company:
But like her dear Mom she with diffidence chokes
When brought into contact with highly-bred folks.”

Though Gerrit may have felt a little uncomfortable about it, Elizabeth lived the life of the upper-class lady in her thirties and forties. She enjoyed visiting distant cities, and at least talked about buying “plush” clothing to wear there. She invited her father to come to New York City and stay for a while, writing, “I feel almost sure the change would be of service to you. Indeed, I can hardly

understand how you do so well in the dull routine at home. There
are much great advantages here.... I quite long for a city residence
for half the year."[14]

While visiting Hamburg in 1862, she glimpsed royalty. "As Charlie
and I were out riding the last afternoon we met the king—William
1st—who politely returned Charlie's bow." Later, from the window
of their abode, they "received a bow" from the King. "Do you think
we can ever be contented in Peterboro again, after reveling in the
attentions of European Royalty?"[15] She was likely being facetious,
for she did return to remote Peterboro for a while, and spent the
rest of her life in central New York State.

Perhaps the real difference or "struggle" between Elizabeth and
Gerrit involved her desire for seemingly perfect order. In the early
1870s, she wrote a book detailing proper style in preparing and
presenting meals, and included in it many recipes (recipts, as she
called them). She titled the book *In the Kitchen*, and in the book,
she emphasized precision.

> "No silent educator in the household has higher
> rank than the table.... Its impressions sink deep,
> and its influences for good or ill form no mean
> part... of our lives. Its [appearance] give[s]...
> lessons in neatness, order and taste.... Should it
> not, therefore, be one of our highest aims to bring
> our table to perfection in every particular?"[16]

She gave specific descriptions of how things should be. "Knives,
forks and spoons must be in line.... [The table] stands in the center
of the room, and perfectly straight." Regarding the tablecloth, "be
careful to have the point where the folds cross... lie exactly on the
center of the table."

The arrangement of plates, silverware, glasses, and condiments
was strictly specified, but traditional seating patterns were "sometimes waived for convenience' sake."[17] Although this penchant for
perfect order characterized Elizabeth's design, extravagance was

not a part of it. "Even where no table cloth can be afforded, the well-scoured pine table is most welcome…. The china must be of one kind, and neither nicked nor cracked." She did not specify elegant or expensive china, only that "of as choice a quality as can be afforded."[18] She based her notion of "refined taste" on order and cleanliness—not necessarily on expense.

Interestingly, to Elizabeth the most important commodity at the table was not material, but social. It was *time*. A meal must not be rushed, for people needed "time to talk, laugh, and be merry."[19] The order and precision of the table served to foster social grace and compassion.

Perhaps here Gerrit experienced a bit of friction, for the anxiety over proper display of manners could detract from his spontaneity. "My dear wife tells me that I was so ungentlemanly as to pour coffee into my saucer and to put my cup on Mrs. Walter's beautiful table cloth. My dear daughter tells me that I was so ungentlemanly as to throw a cluster of grapes to a guest across the table. I acknowledge the scorn in the following lines—

> My wife and my daughter do both of them say
> That a true gentleman I'm not every day—
> That a true gentleman would never be loth
> To stain with his coffee a fine table cloth—
> That flinging a cluster of grapes cross the table
> Is what no gentleman could ever be able
> To do—+ still be so bold as to hold up his head
> 'mong those who are truly both well-born + bred—
> I ask your forgiveness—I never again
> Will be guilty of this of which you complain.
> I'll scald my poor throat 'eer my coffee I'll cool
> In a way that shall break one Fashion stamp'd rule.
> And if ever again I fling grapes to a guest
> By the stoutest of halters may my neck be press'd
> You may scold me and choke me + ay cause me to die
> 'Eer again I Great Fashion shall dare to defy."[20]

Elizabeth Smith Miller with her daughter, Anne, in about 1860.
From the author's collection

Because she was a supporter of equal rights for women, it seems strange to note that Elizabeth segregated the woman's role so completely. She even scripted cleanup after the meal. Regarding washing dishes, "this is done by the mother or daughter, and such an arrangement has great advantages. [The care of kitchen items is] thus kept under your own supervision."[21] Elizabeth believed that the men of the household should not be trusted with such tasks, even though taking full responsibility for the dinner could lead to problems for women. "Most ladies have but little pleasure in giving dinners, as there must be a constant undercurrent of anxiety about the table and the service."[22] Yet women did find solace in their work. "We must rejoice, however, that the house-work is more healthful than fancy work; that making beds, sweeping, and dusting give strength, and that kneading bread, making biscuits, and canning fruit 'brush the cobwebs from our brains'. "[23]

Elizabeth summed up her efforts to prescribe the woman's proper role: "I have tried to make these directions... so clear that any young person of intelligence, who has never been in the kitchen and therefore has no 'judgment' to help her, can follow them to the letter and be rewarded...."[24]

While Gerrit approved of his daughter's work toward refinement without extravagance, he did have a tendency to admonish her—and others—for what he considered to be excessive spending.

> "That Lillie's a lady + puts on grand airs
> Is proved by her buying two sumptuous chairs
> The one costing thirty—the least twenty-five—
> Who else could spend so + still keep alive?"[25]

This from a millionaire! Yet in spite of his frugal warnings, he gave her $100 to cover the cost of the chairs. Gerrit certainly had enough money most of the time so that everyone in his family would have plenty, but he was reluctant to disburse it. When in 1862 his family toured Europe without him, he wrote,

> "Good bye, good bye, my precious four;
> And as you journey Europe O'er,
> I'll work to meet your drafts on me
> And feel your joy'll my payment be."[26]

But later he complained of their spending too much.

> "Said Gerrit the old
> To his folks far away
> 'Spend money untold
> Be careless + gay,
> But pity your Dad
> And feel very sad

That he sits all in rags
Mid his empty cash bags."[27]

Although Gerrit was responsible for paying his extended family their yearly allowance, he often needed reminders that it was due. Once when Libby was traveling to Peterboro from her new home in Geneva for a visit, Ann asked her to bring a list of things: "Ice pitcher, gloves, …12 yds. Calico, piece of boiled chicken. I have no money to send for these things. If you have none you need not get them."[28] That statement seems strange, but Gerrit wanted to hold the money for his philanthropic goals, even though he was proud to be able to help his family. "One of the greatest joys of my life," he said, "has been to supply my wife and children with the means for making things… comfortable."[29] He just did not want them to be *too* comfortable.

When Elizabeth and Ann were traveling on the east coast of America, they implored, "Keep writing + give us plenty of money. That's all we ask."[30]

In July of 1869, Gerrit acquiesced to Elizabeth's aristocratic desires when he gave her and Charles a huge estate on the shore of Seneca Lake near Geneva, New York. They had been living in Peterboro since their marriage in 1843, and were seeking a more elegant lifestyle. "As I do not any longer doubt that you will… be invested with a home that should content a King + Queen I have them make the deed directly to you. I send it herewith. I send also the Policy of Insurance…."[31] Elizabeth felt good in finally having left Peterboro for something more refined, but she found that her annual $8,000 allowance was no longer sufficient. Being still reluctant to simply ask him for more money, she wrote to him, asking for advice as to what she should do.[32]

Elizabeth showed a high level of devotion to her parents. Part of her long-term plan in developing Lochland—the Geneva estate—was to have it become a home for them in their old age. "We hope to make it a happy home for ourselves—our children—+ our dear

Mother + Father," she wrote to Gerrit.[33] While in their mid-seventies, Gerrit and Ann received the call: "[The family] all say you + Mother should live here + give us the privilege of caring for you in your old age…. No one [is] more earnest about it than Charlie."[34] The chances that Libby was going to be able to get Gerrit to leave his beloved Peterboro were slim. Because he never retired, his land business kept him busy at work throughout his life. A letter from Elizabeth's son, William Fitzhugh Miller, announced the decision that the Smiths had made. "Mother received your letter + we are all sorry to hear you could not be induced to live in Geneva."[35]

Elizabeth now had to content herself with being a counselor to her parents rather than a caretaker, although she admitted to her mother that she did not feel comfortable at it because she was not well-educated or well-read. An undated letter from Ann to Libby acknowledged her daughter's help. "How I thank you for all your earnest solicitude for me. I do feel <u>free</u> my darling, to call on you for any service I may need. It would be strange if I did not after all your unselfish devotion to me."[36]

Libby also was close to Gerrit as he aged. As he worried about death, she counseled, "From…the bright, happy spirit of your letters, we think you are entitled to more birthdays. Instead of saying 'I am too old for this + that'—you must now begin to think 'am I old enough?' "[37] She tried to keep his spirits up as the end neared. Little more than two years before his death, she wrote, "[I] wish you all the health, happiness + length of days possible to mortal man. And… congratulate you… on your present fine physical, mental + moral condition…."[38]

Elizabeth and Gerrit had a loving, warm, and mutually supportive relationship. It was quite different with Gerrit's son Greene, his only other child to live to adulthood. Greene's rebellious nature caused Gerrit much stress. She tried, but Ann could not deter her husband from trying to mold Greene into what he wanted him to be.

When Greene Smith was born on April 14, 1842, it must have been a day of mixed emotions for Ann and Gerrit Smith. In all, they had at least seven children. The deaths of "Nanny" (Ann) at age six in 1835, and of Fitzhugh at age twelve in 1836, were devastating blows to loving parents. Having another child in 1842 must have made Gerrit and Ann wonder if they were setting themselves up for another heartbreak. In a way they were, but it would not come through the child's death.

Gerrit's dissatisfaction with Greene's moral development, and the guilt he felt at having failed as a counselor for his son, did not begin to surface until Greene was eight or nine years old and displayed some behavioral problems. As a little boy, he had brought his parents joy and fueled their hope for his future. The Smith family housekeeper described "little 'Green' with his pranks + his chatter aids very much in helping to do without Lissy (Elizabeth had moved to Cazenovia). He is a great talker + very smart."[39]

When Gerrit was in Philadelphia for medical treatment for piles, he had high anticipation of seeing "Beeny" (Greene's nickname).

"Our Beeny is coming, hurrah! Hurrah!
Our Beeny is coming, hurrah!
He'll make good our praises of all his sweet ways,
For he is a beautiful boy."[40]

By the time Greene was eight years old, he showed signs of becoming an outdoorsman. A brook ran through the Smith property in Peterboro, and Greene loved to fish. His father, however, saw fishing as a waste of time and effort; in pure business fashion, he wrote a contract between them to make Greene stop what he enjoyed doing.

"It is agreed between Gerrit Smith + Greene Smith-

1ˢᵗ   Gerrit is convinced that boys fishing is a bad practice, that it leads to idleness + vice + loss of health—that it is cruel + hardens the heart—Hence, Greene will give up the practice of fishing.

2nd   Instead of wasting his time in fishing,
Greene will have a garden, + work skillfully in it.

3rd   To encourage Greene to be a gardener, his
father Gerrit Smith agrees, provided Greene gives
up fishing, to give him for what he shall grow… the
following prices…."[41]

This must have been devastating to a young boy who was not a
sedentary gardener. His father subverted the desires of his son and
conditioned his love on Greene's compliance with his own set of
expectations. It was clear at this early point in Greene's life that he
would experience a great deal of personal anguish in trying to live up
to his father's standards, and cause Gerrit much pain in the process.
By his ninth birthday, this tragedy had become more obvious.

"This, my dear boy, is your Birthday. The Lord
has spared you to us for nine years. How good +
how patient he is. Do love + praise + thank Him.
Remember too, that the Lord has spared you all
this time, not withstanding your forgetfulness of
Him, and your frequent + wicked disobedience of
Him."[42]

Enclosed with the letter was the following poem, replete with
Gerrit's warnings to Greene to give up what pleased him in order
to become what pleased Gerrit:

"Nine years this day did Heaven give
To Ma + me our precious boy:
Dear boy, dear boy, may you so live
As, aye, to be our hope + joy!
"Be just + true—without deceit -
Be pure in deed, + thought, + word;
And let your heart with kindness beat
Tow'rd man + beast, + fish + bird.

"Love God the Father of us all,
And Jesus Christ, his only son;
Hark to the Bible's Heavenly call,
And in its ways delight to run.
"Then Pa + Ma will happy be
In all your years they live to see;
And when they're dead, your years shall be
An Honor to their memory."

In 1851 at the age of nine, Greene was sent to a private school in Belleville, New Jersey operated by his parents' friends and fellow abolitionists Theodore and Angelina Grimké Weld. (Starting in 1854, the Welds became noted for their operation of the Eagleswood School, which was part of the Raritan Bay Union Cooperative Community in New Jersey managed by wealthy utopian reformer Marcus Spring. Greene's participation in the Belleville school predated this communal school.)[43] Gerrit gave his son instructions as to how to improve his moral development at school: "Be a good + lovely boy. Tell Mr. Weld + Mrs. Weld + Aunt Sarah [Angelina's sister] your thoughts. Lay open your heart to them. Never be guilty of the least deceit or falsehood."[44] After visiting him there in June, they seemed more optimistic. "We feel that our dear Greene is a good boy—+ that he is + will be, a great blessing to us."[45]

The Welds' philosophy of education was positive and optimistic, grounded in a decade of revival and reform activity. Their belief was that each child was essentially good, and with love, patience, and example, would turn out right.[46] During 1852, hope reigned, as Angelina wrote of Greene's progress. "I am glad to hear that you think Greene so much improved. It seems to us that he has begun a new course of life—that is—he now begins to realize that he has a character to form for future manhood, + that life is not given merely to make fun for himself…."[47] By August, she reported to the Smiths, "Green's behavior has been good…. He is obedient, industrious, obliging, generous, considerate. In the main governs his temper, and though he is sometimes deceitful, generally otherwise. Has a <u>strong will</u>... needs care respecting his appetite—and <u>great care</u> about his personal habits. With Greene everything depends on his contact and surroundings. If these are pure + elevating, he will be a noble character, but bad associates would make in it terrific inroads."[48]

As time passed, Gerrit attempted to reinforce the improvements. "You must be a good, truthful, candid, unselfish, gentle boy."[49] And a month later, "Do you remember that the meanest + basest of all vices is lying. Oh, never again be guilty of any kind or extent of deception or artfulness."[50]

Greene's rebelliousness, however, resurfaced in early 1853. He had been accused of lying at school, of hurting a fellow student, and had even begun playing cards. Gerrit warned him that if he continued to lie, he had better be prepared to die. "Do you remember how near you came being killed by the ox?"[51] He told Greene to apologize and to repent, and to give up card playing:

> "In my youth, I played cards—+ became so fond
> of cards as to be well nigh ruined. My card playing
> made deep wounds in my soul, the scars of which
> no length of time will renew. I beg you never to
> play cards again.... I am frightened at the sight of
> playing cards."[52]

When Weld reported to Gerrit that Greene—now eleven years old—was a nuisance by being rebellious and disruptive during classes, his father reprimanded him, saying, "[I hope] you have given up your sinful practice of making disturbance in the Recitations. It is sinful to waste your own time. It is no less sinful to waste the time of others."[53]

The difficult relationship that developed between Greene and Gerrit should have reminded Gerrit of his father, Peter, who had built a similar relationship with him. While away at college, Gerrit had been rebellious in his own right. He played cards, drank and gambled, and generally did not meet his father's expectations. Now that relationship had come full circle. Like his father, Gerrit was intolerant; yet he clung to the hope that Greene would become a model Christian. "Are you making progress in the ways of truth and goodness? I trust, that you are. Do, oh do, my dear child, strive hard to conquer all your sinful habits. Heavenly Father will help you."[54] Gerrit felt helpless, and he passed on the responsibility for Greene's moral development to God and the Welds.

The Welds did their part, and reported,

> "Greene is <u>upward</u> in all things! In study he
> has <u>never</u> done so well as he is now doing. His
> outrageous conduct at recitation has given place
> to civility, docility and manliness. His proclivity to
> falsehood and boasting he is keeping under <u>check</u>
> and in all respects he nears an improving aspect."[55]

As Gerrit and the Welds molded Greene, how did he feel about his parents sending him away for what amounted to moral training? Greene said, "With sorrow in my heart I had to go away to the school that I did hate…. I'de rather be at home again, where everything's so pleasing…. But if ever I get home, I'll n'ere go back again."[56]

Greene's desires were irrelevant to Gerrit. When Greene did come home, he brought with him his father's list of expectations of what Gerrit hoped to see in Greene:

"1st Good <u>moral</u> health—truth, candor, unselfish love -

2nd Good <u>bodily</u> health—erect body, strong + active limbs

3rd Good <u>intellectual</u> health—An increase of kindness + wisdom.

The 1st is infinitely most important."[57]

Good bodily health became a problem for Greene. At thirteen he was stricken with sickness, the course of which Gerrit and his Oswego business agent John B. Edwards talked about in a series of letters. Edwards wrote in February 1855, "It is [an] affliction to us that your son is sick with the painful disease of Inflamatory Rheumatism."[58] Greene seemed to be recovering a couple of days later, but a relapse sent him to New York City for treatment.[59] By late April, Edwards cheerfully noted, "I am happy to hear that your son has entirely regained his health."[60]

To be sure, physical health for Greene was not the only problem that concerned Gerrit. His continuing anxiety about his son's moral development reinforced Greene's rebelliousness. In characteristic fashion, Gerrit poured his heartfelt emotion into "rhymes." The poems are long, and they often reflect the enmity between them. In one poem titled "The reasonable boy," he laments:

> "If with a teacher qualified
> To fit him quick for College joy,
> He'd rather dance, + hunt + ride -
> He's not a reasonable boy."[61]

Gerrit had trouble acknowledging throughout his life that there might be more than one definition of 'reasonable'. When it came to morals based on the Golden Rule, he could not understand why everyone did not see his 'Right Way'; to him, it was simply unreasonable to believe or do anything else. This was a constant source of anxiety for him, especially when it occurred within his family. He could accept diversity in beliefs and behavior outside of his family much more readily.

On Greene's seventeenth birthday, his father anguished over what paths he would take in the future.

> "Oft looms the question in our sight:
> Where, when we're gone, our son's career?
> In paths of wrong or paths of right?'
> This question wakes our hopes + fears."[62]

There were some signs of hope that as Greene matured he would please his father more; but overall, Gerrit remained frustrated. While on a hunting trip with his friend Louis Jarnacque, Greene made positive impressions on his friend, who said, "Your loving son conducts himself very well. He has given up smoking altogether—it

Greene Smith (right), at age 25, with hunting buddy Hiram C. Wilson, in an 1867 photo. A constant disappointment to his father, Greene favored hunting and fishing to the business world from which his father and grandfather had secured their family fortune.

From the collection of Peterboro Area Historical Society, Peterboro, NY.

took pains, but he did it."[63] And in January of 1861 from Jarnacque, "Greene behaves like a gentleman. He has just given up the quid, and I hope forever. It seems to me that he is ashamed of chewing in society, that is, in company with women, where it is absolutely necessary to heed… urbanity.…"[64]

Gerrit saw Greene's habit of spending large amounts of money as a deficiency in moral development. When Greene spent time in Europe traveling with other family members, Gerrit warned him, "I wish you to be as economical as you can well be, and yet be comfortable."[65] But following Greene's request from Paris for more money, Gerrit accused him of "vices or crimes" that wasted money.

Greene admitted to the vices, but added, "I don't know why you should suspect me of being guilty of crime." He wrote of having gambled while in college at Cambridge, "for the sake of getting money for which I need not account to my parents." And he admitted to having cheated his opponents in order to win. Still, he was angry with Gerrit for having accused him of gambling in Europe. "I have not played for money, nor will I."

He was angry with himself for causing his father pain. "I sometimes think from the pain I so frequently give to you and mother that perhaps my whole heart and head is wrong. Were it not a wicked wish, I would wish that I had never been born.… I will go on and do my best to come out right."[66] Later, on the day after his father's birthday, perhaps to assuage his own guilt and at the same time soothe Gerrit's anxiety, Greene wrote, "I see now that I did wrong and acted very foolishly in my expenditure of so much money. I hope I shall never give you cause for such anxiety again.…"[67]

Gerrit's pain never did subside much. He worried until his death that Greene was a poor reflection of his family.

> "[That Greene] is throwing himself away is a very
> sad spectacle. Often in my heavy toils in the Office
> + Library I think what a relief + comfort + joy it
> would be to me had I a son to work with me + to
> share in my burden. But alas of all the [people]

he is the one who works against me—+ he is himself my burden. All my… burdens… are light compared with what he has been to me."[68]

Evidence of Greene's defiance of his father's wishes can be read in a comment that Gerrit made to Elizabeth when Greene was 21: "Greene left us last evening for a fortnight on a fishing excursion in the North Woods."[69]

The huge irony in the relationship between Gerrit and Greene is that Gerrit, who so sensitively and morally shaped the character of other people—including many children—devastated his own son by setting for him unrealistic and unfair expectations. Greene was blamed for causing his parents distress, and even adopted a view of himself as an ungrateful rebel. It may be that only the tender, consistent, and understanding love of his mother salvaged his sanity.

Fortunately for Greene, his mother was his ally in this long dispute. She defended his right to different opinions while Gerrit criticized him. She appealed to Gerrit to wait for Greene's conscience to work on him. But Gerrit constantly badgered his son with efforts at persuasion. There was a closeness between Greene and Ann that escaped Gerrit. In an early, undated note to Greene, she wrote:
"The Mother's heart within me reaches forth
With all intensity of earnestness
To thee my Father, for Thy rich blessings on my child:
Strong in joyous youth—'Things that are seen
and temporal' fill his heart's whole circle.
His spirit is fast linked to mine. O let
The telegraphic line, which my faith forms
Up to thee, bring countless blessings down
To him—influences divine—which shall
Purify him + transform him into thine
Own image—So that through eternal years
Where Thou art, he may also be."

By the time Greene was 19, Ann was actively countering Gerrit's attacks on him. "Greene will never do nor be anything under compulsion. Leave him to his own free will...."[71] She wanted to help Greene by helping to pay some of his debts, but Gerrit opposed the move. Ann wrote to her husband, "You say he does not deserve it. Perhaps not. But this kindness + great relief to his spirit at this time will do more for his heart than giving him his deserts."[72]

Ann did accept some responsibility for what they considered to be Greene's errant ways, but she exhibited much less guilt over it than did her husband. "We must expect that it will take large sums to work him out of our mistakes concerning him.... We can help him only by love and kindness...."[73] When he was with his mother, Greene had the freedom to be himself and feel good; her love for him was less conditional than was Gerrit's. While the family (minus Gerrit) was traveling in Europe, his mother allowed Greene enough slack to pursue his own interests and to contribute in positive ways to the family's experiences. Ann wrote to Gerrit,

> "[I write] chiefly to tell you how well Greene behaves + how hard he works at his birds. He has prepared 25 and still goes to the market every day in search of new ones." (Greene stuffed and collected birds.) "He has not written to you yet that I know of, but never mind that. Let him alone. 'Laissez-faire.' All will work around right in the way that we have marked out for him. The part of wisdom for us in this case is never to refer to his past. We have said enough. He knows our whole mind. The more silent we are the sooner conscience will do its work on him."[74]

Ann was witnessing during the European trip what a slackening of parental control would allow Greene to become.

> "It made Greene quite happy to have the entire charge of us, and I saw so plainly that all he needs

is intense occupation in the line of his tastes. I
trust something will open up for him when we
reach home. One thing is certain, he must be left
to choose in entire freedom. His heart-wish was
to join the Army, but he came to Europe because
he thought it was our wish. His fortune has been
constantly on my mind. I hope the Lord will grant
us to see eye to eye concerning him. But remember
darling to receive him cheerfully, as you would
receive the son… of your best friend who had
erred as our dear boy has."[75]

Gerrit seemed both surprised and pleased at Ann's reaction to
Greene's presence on their journey, as he had previously thought that
Greene would be a hardship on them.[76] After their return home,
Greene did serve in the Army for a while. By 1866, Gerrit was still
trying to reform him while Ann remained optimistic and tried to
calm her husband.

"I am sure we shall be blessed together in our dear
boy. Only wait in patient hope + let us not lose
the blessing intended for us in the present state of
things. Let us rejoice in this tribulation knowing
that order must come out of disorder…. Darling,
our child knows our opinion + wishes concerning
his use of strong drink + his extravagance. Now
I hope Our Father will give us patience + self
control enough to hold our peace."[77]

Ann continued her pleas to Gerrit, "We must let him alone that
he may develop from within…. We all the time strengthening +
making him 'great through our gentleness.'"[78]

Gentleness and patience were traits that Gerrit found in short
supply when it came to his son. He mostly saw Greene's faults, and
demanded change. As Ann put it, "We do not understand him. In

the distance we see only the faults. The pleasant things are hidden. We must get nearer + tolerate his faults before we can do him good. We must put away all antagonisms that he may perceive from us...."[79] Yet the antagonisms on Gerrit's part continued into the last years of his life. He could not settle for the notion that his son was less than he wanted him to be. Ann warned: "Be patient, my precious one, with our dear boy's wrong opinions.... Respect his <u>right</u> of opinion, + wait till it becomes what it should be, holding him all the time to your heart as Our Father holds us. Let him <u>feel</u> your sunshine + the rain of your love."[80]

His father's constant hectoring may have been the cause of Greene's stuttering. His problems with pronunciation first surfaced as a problem in an 1848 letter from Gerrit to Ann,[81] and evidently was manifest throughout his childhood. It was not until 1857—when Greene was 14—that his parents sought help to correct it. In February of that year, Ann and Greene left Peterboro for New York City and a visit to Doctor Laveruer, who might cure "stammering." As they left, Gerrit remarked:

"My dear Laveruer have the art
To cure the stammering of my son;
Then, dear Laveruer, will my heart
Bless thee for his delivered tongue."[82]

It may have been the expertise of the doctor, or Greene's absence from his father's tormenting demands; but whatever the cause, the effect was positive. "Dear Father," said Greene, "I have not stammered or mumbled today and never intend so again."[83]

Another interesting facet of Greene's personality was that the handwriting in his letters to Gerrit varied so much in style from letter to letter that one might think they were written by different people. Perhaps Greene's mood varied with different thoughts about home. Also, Greene continued to have difficulty reading Gerrit's letters because of his poor penmanship. Earlier, while away at school, he needed to have the schoolmaster read them to him; he found that to be quite embarrassing, so he stopped reading them altogether.[84]

Greene was usually unsure of what direction his life should take. His parents sent him away to Weld's school, but he did not want to go. Gerrit's hired educator, Edwin Morton, tutored him at home. But when it came time for college, he could not apply his talents to the work. Greene attended Harvard University, evidently under some duress from home. While there, he could not focus on academia. He wrote to his mother that he wanted her to send him his pistol for protection. Also, "I mean to bring my deer horns and some of my pictures here.... My room would be very handsome with some such things about the walls."[85]

In the spring of 1860, he quit Harvard and went home. Gerrit had recently returned to Peterboro after a brief stay at a hospital for emotional instability caused in part by his financial support of John Brown's raid on Harpers Ferry. His doctor was pleased to see that he was managing well under the stress of Greene's return. According to Gerrit's doctor, John P. Gray,

> "[Greene] is very young and his character is yet all unformed, and his excessive physical activity and the energy and elements in his constitution which have led him astray may under cultivation and control be so directed as to lead him into paths of usefulness."[86]

Gray was worried that any stress on Smith's mind might again destabilize him, and he was trying to lessen the shock.

Edwin Morton was less gentle: as the tutor who had worked hard to prepare Greene for college, he showed disappointment.

> "I now hear from Cambridge that Greene has returned home, and I much regret it, for I thought he would keep the... end in view.... But the time allotted, I hear, was too short for one who made study + college 'secondary matters'.... I still wish that he would be determined to go through College."[87]

Greene was not so determined. About a year later, he left for Europe on a lengthy tour of several countries with his mother, sister, and brother-in-law. The European tour took Greene out of the United Sates as the Civil War was starting, but his adventurous spirit attracted him to the excitement of the war, and he wanted to be a part of it. He went on the trip to satisfy his mother's wishes for him to accompany them, and he wrote to his father from London in September of 1861, inquiring, "Have the Peterboro soldiers been in an engagement yet? I do not see the American papers very often."[88]

Shortly after he returned home, he enlisted in the Army and was commissioned as a second lieutenant in the 14th New York Heavy Artillery.[89] Gerrit was proud that his son had joined the Union forces to support the cause of the abolition of slavery. He paid for having Greene outfitted as a soldier, but refused to allow him to draw pay. "Once his son drew (pay) + his father sent Drft. $409.14 May 23, 1865 to repay it."[90]

Greene wrote from Baltimore that he was "mustered in" for three years and headed for battle. Heavy artillery units usually did not fight battles on the front lines, but because northern infantry units had been so decimated by previous fighting, General Grant called for heavy artillery units to make up that difference during the Cold Harbor battle near Richmond, Virginia in May of 1864. They were still on such duty during the siege of Petersburg just south of Richmond in July of 1864. His mailing address was:

> Lieut. Greene Smith
> Acting Aide de Camp
> 2nd Brigade, 1st Division, 9th Corps
> Washington, D.C.[91]

In a series of letters written to his parents between July 30 and August 19, 1864, Greene told of his first taste of battle as part of the force under General Grant in the siege of Petersburg, Virginia. Grant's goal was to seal off supply routes to the Confederate capital of Richmond and thereby cause its surrender. As of July 30, although

Greene had "expected to be frightened in the first fire," he found himself "under fire now and don't mind it much."

The Battle of the Crater resulted from the Union effort to blow a hole in the Confederate defenses around Petersburg. Having tunneled under the confederate line, Union forces exploded gunpowder, causing a breech in the line. Then they attempted to cross through the crater to a position behind enemy lines. Greene Smith's brigade

"formed the first line, and at the explosion... made a splendid charge on the enemy.... The fire of musketry was incessant for we were not more than 20 yds. from the Rebs. We were soon in the pit of the blown up front where we had great trouble to rally our men for they were falling constantly.... There must be a Providence in my not being hit for men fell so thickly around me that we had to walk on the dead."

The next day, August 1,

"a flag of truce was out at 5 this morning and will be out until 9 to bury the dead. This is the first time since I came that a minute has passed without firing."

On August 7, Greene reported that the siege continued because the Union effort had failed. Random firing was common. At one point, a bullet entered Greene's tent and landed on his pillow. On August 9, he reported that "our Brig[ade] which should number 5,600 men has now but 800 fit for service." By August 14, Greene had contracted a respiratory disease and was too ill to fight.[92]

As it was for many Civil War soldiers, Greene's sickness made it difficult for him to carry out his duties.

"Being so blind, I have to depend on my clerk + orderly sergeant for all the writing. I only sign the papers. Mother, I can't keep things straight for my

head is so weak everything is mixed up. I can't see
to write…. I am too weak to walk more than a mile
+ if we get into a fight I must go to the rear or fall
down + stay where I fall, thus exposing myself to
the charge of cowardice."[93]

He had previously told his mother, "I hope we will do no more
fighting for I cannot walk over two miles without falling."[94]

Ann grieved over her son's poor physical condition and wrote to
her daughter Elizabeth, "Our dear Greene grows rather worse than
better…. He has command of Co. F. the largest in the regiment +
is responsible for the arms, rations, clothing, ammunition + camp
equipage."[95]

In a rare letter to his father, Greene pleaded with him to use
his connections to Greene's favor. "I don't know what to do. Please
father find out what can be done and advise me. I certainly can't
stand it here very long."[96] Whatever was done, it worked; Greene
was expected home by early January of 1865.

"Poor Greene!" said Gerrit. "The supply of all his letters comes
today. His brain is in very bad condition. We hope to get him out
of the army + to get him home."[97]

By January 20, 1865, Greene was in New York City recovering from "a cough,"[98] and was subsequently sent to an Annapolis,
Maryland hospital to recover from his illness. He was discharged
from the Army on May 12, 1865, and returned to Peterboro.[99] His
doctor had told him "not to write, read, or think much for a year.
He must live outdoors as much as possible + be kept cheerful with
pleasant company."[100]

In 1863, while he was still in the Army, Greene had a "Birdhouse"
built on the Peterboro estate as a museum in which to house his
collection of stuffed birds. He had developed new techniques of
preservation for stuffed birds, and he would eventually donate over
400 specimens to Cornell University.[101] When Greene was only two
years old, Gerrit noticed that he was fascinated with a bird that was

building "her nest on one of the pillars of the piazza of the Library,"[102] and as early as 1858, Aunt Betsey took note of his hobby:
"The day that our 'Beenie' was born,
Aunt Betsey was baking cookies.
But little thought she what a Lad he would be,
To drive the poor birds from their 'Nookies.'
"Well, go ahead, go ahead, my dear Boy,
And use up the Steam as you can,
But remember the [birds] must come 'n play too,
To perfect the life of a man."[103]

Six months after his discharge from the Army, Greene was recovering well and had moved to a small farm near Geneva. Gerrit felt good about his son's physical recovery, but he must have harbored feelings of failure about their personal relationship. This giant of philanthropy and universal love had stumbled when it came to being emotionally close to his son. He wrote to Ambrose Burnside (Greene's commanding general) as if he were detached from Greene: "His health is good, save that he is still occasionally afflicted with dizziness + double vision in consequence of his sun-stroke in the... battle before Petersburg. He is at work on his beautiful farm adjoining the village of Geneva + will soon be married."[104]

Gerrit helped fund Greene's farm at Geneva, where he kept deer in a "deer park," and also raised "about three hundred quail."[105]

In 1870, just ten years before his early death, Greene was still making additions to his collection of birds.[106] He had lectured at Cornell University on the subject of birds on June 14, 16, and 21 that year,[107] in spite of the fact that he was convinced that he could not do a good job of lecturing.[108]

With some humor, President White of Cornell University had earlier responded that he would "never believe that a son of [Gerrit Smith] couldn't talk."[109]

Greene did eventually realize what his parents had called the errors of his youthful ways, and he decided to change his behavior. In

July 1869 at a public speech in Geneva, he referred to himself as "a reformed farmer."[110] But the most revealing and touching evidence of his intent to reform himself is seen in an 1863 poem written, of course, to his mother.

> "When sorrow and remorse their dark shrouds cast
> Around my gloomy thoughts of misspent years,
> I will remember through the sinful past
> Thy gentle warnings + thy bitter tears.
> "Oh! Lovely one! I heeded not thy prayers,
> Although my hardened heart beat warm for thee.
> In wine and play I tried to drown my cares
> And to forget thy tender love for me.
> But no, that love can ne'er forgotten be—
> Thy soul hath still its resting-place in mine.
> My heart shall never turn again from thee,
> Nor seek to drown its cares in play or wine."[111]

Greene and his mother were emotionally close to one another. They shared a high degree of tender, common identity. Gerrit was the outsider, alienated from his son by his own bias toward what he viewed as right. His obsession with moral perfection conditioned his love for his son, the one person whom he perceived as most reflecting himself. And when that mirror did not show him what he wanted to see, he reproached Greene. The "tender love" and "gentle warnings" that came from Ann overmatched the bitter reproaches from Gerrit, and Greene's affection turned toward his mother.

Greene's death came only five years after both of his parents had died. Greene had moved back into the family house in Peterboro after their deaths, and in 1878 he contracted tuberculosis, then called "consumption." Following two years of unsuccessful treatments, he spent his last days in The Birdhouse at his request, and died there in July of 1880. He was 38.[112]

Gerrit's close relationship with his granddaughter—Elizabeth's child—may have compensated somewhat for the lost love of his son.

Other Relationships

"Dear Nannie is as sweet as ever.... She so delights in her being upon my lap.... I never knew so lovely a child as she," said Gerrit to Ann.[1] Gerrit's relationships with his grandchildren reflected those he had with his own children: he was much closer emotionally to his granddaughter than to his grandsons. While Smith helped his grandsons financially and worried over their health, he became deeply and emotionally attached to his only granddaughter.

Greene Smith had no children, so all of Gerrit's grandchildren were in Elizabeth's family. Her son, Charles Dudley Miller, Jr., does not surface in the records of Gerrit's life until 1868, when he had reached the age of twenty-one. Their relationship at that time was built more on respect than on emotion.

Charles wrote Gerrit a laudatory letter on Gerrit's seventy-first birthday, congratulating him on his "spotless reputation," referring to Smith as "a model of honesty + benevolence, an honor to your country, your family, and all who have the happiness of your acquaintance."[2] The letter was cold, as if he wrote to his boss instead of to his grandfather. The main tone was not love, but admiration, as it was in another of Miller's letters. Gerrit had in typical fashion reprimanded Charles, Jr. for having caused his mother pain. Miller responded very respectfully, "I am very thankful to you grandfather for the very good and reproving advice which you gave me in your last letter. I agree entirely with you, and can account for the sentiments expressed in my letter to mother in no other way except by a want of due consideration of the subject before expressing my thoughts to others."[3] This chilly respect was reserved for Gerrit. In short verse, Miller indicated tender emotions for both his mother and grandmother:

"Thou cam'st like a dove
And brought with thee mine,
A Mother of love
And daughter of thine."[4]

The respect Charles showed Gerrit may have paid off: by 1870, Charles was trying to start a lumber business in Oswego when Gerrit deeded him some land to help him get financially established. The business finally settled at Otter Lake, employing as many as 80 men.[5] Miller complained to Gerrit about the necessary exactness in business bookkeeping, something his grandfather was very good at. "As yet my carelessness or inexperience in being obliged to be accurate has caused me a great deal of anxiety and trouble."[6]

By mid-1873 his lumber business had failed, and Miller was in the New York City area operating a stone quarry for which Gerrit had loaned him six thousand dollars to get started.[7] Their relationship continued to be one of financial support coupled with respect. In March of 1872, Miller wrote Gerrit a congratulatory note regarding his 75th birthday. "It is doubtless owing to your temperate habits, and is a good example for everybody to follow."[8]

Charles Dudley Miller, Jr. was Gerrit's second grandson. Gerrit Smith Miller was the first—"Gatty," as he was called. Strangely, Gerrit Smith Miller is nearly absent from Smith's records until Gerrit's death, at which time "Gat" takes over some of the operations of the land business. The third grandson, William Fitzhugh Miller, was born in 1850, and he surfaces in the records in 1863 because he became sick. Concerned about Willie's health, Gerrit wrote:

"God help little Willie! + free him from pain,
And raise him to health + to vigor again:

God bless little Willie! and make him to grow
In patience + kindness + goodness also."[9]

By 1873, a series of letters between William F. Miller and Gerrit
Smith indicate that Gerrit had financially supported his grandson's
orchard near Geneva.[10] Gerrit's fourth grandchild was Ann Fitzhugh
Miller, born in 1856.

"Nannie" was the apple of granddaddy's eye. He loved having her
with him and showered her with loving emotions. He wrote about
her frequently. As a tot, she loved the strawberries Gerrit grew in
his garden, and he wrote her a long and touching poem about the
"Bobbinies," as she called them.[11] In several letters, he delighted at
how Nannie loved to sit on his lap. He lauded her personality and
intelligence.

While his family toured Europe in the early 1860s, Gerrit kept
the grandchildren at home, writing often of Nannie but only hinting
of the presence of other children. "Dear Nannie came to me this
morning for 3 cents more, another of her mother's weekly allowances to her. She is buying Christmas presents."[12] On Christmas day
of 1861, he chronicled significant events: "6PM Finished our good
dinner (a pair of geese) half an hour ago. Dear Nannie went to bed
after I had comforted her on my lap."[13]

A week later, he continued the theme. At family worship, "Dear
Nannie as ever on my lap filling me as I read + sing." "Nannie was
on my lap during the whole service of worship."[14]

The other grandchildren did not "fill" him with what he needed
as much as "Dear Nannie" did. When she was 12 years old, Gerrit
had sent her some loving lines on her birthday, and she responded:
"Thank you for your very pretty lines to me on my birthday.... I
bought... a doll! ...So you see you have me as your baby still, and
you shall have me so as long as you like."[15]

This emotion-based attention directed toward the female grandchild appears also to have been directed toward Susan Dixwell, Gerrit Smith Miller's wife. Gerrit Smith called her his "granddaughter,"

and treated her as more special than her husband, "Gat":

> "Again my dear Sue in all honor of you
> I've dress'd up myself in my very best clothes
> I'm old it is true but I would in your view
> Surpass e'en the beautiful lilly and rose.
> You wonder, dear Sue, that I who am old
> Should spare so much time my fair toilet to make
> The reason is plain + it's very quick told
> 'Tis all for my new and sweet grandaughter's sake."[16]

Sue and Gat had two sons before Gerrit Smith died—Gerrit Smith Miller, Jr. (1869) and Basil Dixwell Miller (1873). Although nothing appears about a relationship between Gerrit Smith Miller, Jr. and Gerrit Smith, there is at least a comment about Basil. "I go daily across the creek [to the Cottage Across the Brook] to see my 2nd great grandson, who is a beauty. Sue is very comfortable."[17]

In concluding coverage of Gerrit Smith's relationships with his immediate family, it is important to note that the only close, personal relationship that developed was between Gerrit and his only daughter, Elizabeth. It may not be surprising, therefore, that at the celebration of their 50th wedding anniversary in January of 1872, none of Ann and Gerrit's children or grandchildren were present.[18]

Another aspect of what Gerrit would call his "family" relationships involved those of his extended household family—the hired help. Not much is known about most of them. Elizabeth Kelty and Laura Bosworth were both loyal, long-term "family" workers who cared for the house and the children and were provided with a quarterly stipend by Gerrit even after they left his service. A woman named Ellen was remembered in a Christmas poem as a tutor:

> "Forget not our School marm—our dear noble Ellen—
> Whose teaching the youngsters in readin'+spellin'. "[19]

Edwin Morton was employed for a few years in the 1850s as a tutor for Greene Smith. His application to Gerrit for employment came when Morton was twenty-three and about to graduate from Harvard University. "I aspire to a generous liberality of thought and discussion, in religion, philosophy and politics. In the latter I am Antislavery." He was able to teach music and had "six years experience as an organist."[20] Gerrit hired him and paid him $125 quarterly—a handsome salary for the times. Morton was present at a crucial meeting with Gerrit and John Brown in 1858, and after Brown's capture at Harpers Ferry, Morton fled to England out of fear of indictment.

By far the most important and influential house servant at Peterboro was Elizabeth Hebbard Kelty. "Aunt Betsey" started working at the Smith residence in 1828, and she worked there until her death in 1880. Much is known about her, because she kept a journal of her experiences and relationships. It is not a diary with regular entries, but a "special occasions notebook" in which she recorded much feeling and emotion. As such, it is a rich source for viewing the personal side of life in the Smith household.

Elizabeth Kelty's father, John, was born in Cork, Ireland and migrated to Pennsylvania in his youth. He married Margaret Conner on December 17, 1780, and they had eight children. The family moved to Peterboro in 1811. John got a job in the local glass factory owned by the elder Peter Smith. Betsey was then 20 years old. At the age of five, she had an accident that partially disabled her left shoulder. "I never could raise [the arm]... either from the shoulder or elbow. But with what little strength has been in the hand, have always managed to do some work, not only to be independent myself but to aid some others of my kindred. I have received many benefits, ...+ one of the greatest comforts of my life has been the pleasure of doing a little for the comfort of others."[21]

Her work for the Smiths involved a wide variety of tasks from cleaning the house to managing some of the affairs of the land business. She was well-liked and trusted, and she attended to Gerrit's "begging letters" by reading them and making recommendations to him. She reviewed his articles before they were sent to press, and

administered the Evans Charity Fund, choosing benefactors among the
Peterboro poor each year. The Smith family felt close to her.

"A dear one is she—there's no such other Miss
Outside of the circle of conjugal bliss."[22]

They treated her as a confidant, and she reflected the generally
optimistic Smith family ethos. She saw beauty in nature and people,
and tried to help folks think well of themselves.

Betsey tendered love to each family member, and they responded
in kind. When Ann was not feeling well, she wrote, "I do not know
what I should do without Aunt B. K. She is so full of cheerful wit
and a word of comfort always ready."[23]

Gerrit seems to have had deep feelings for Aunt Betsey. He wrote nearly
nothing about the male hired help, but often told Betsey how he felt.

"My dear Betsey Kelty, these youngsters think they
Full justice do to you in what their rhymes say:
But I who have known you, when young and when old
Declare that these rhymes have not half your worth told."[24]

Betsey once gifted Gerrit "with a bookmark wrought with my hair."

"This little momento I weave,
With a thread of my whitening hair,
Tis a token of friendship, believe,
And a union to Christians so dear."[25]

Her attitude toward life and toward others shone with benevolence. On her 76th birthday, she noted, "I thank God for what
strength remains + that memory, + reason hold out… that I can do
a little for the poorest."[26] Then on her next birthday, she revealed
some particulars about her relationship with the Smiths.

"I am… comfortably housed through the cold
months by these dear Friends, and not only a
warm room, but the warmth of their hearts is
shown in kind words + smiling faces. I bless God +

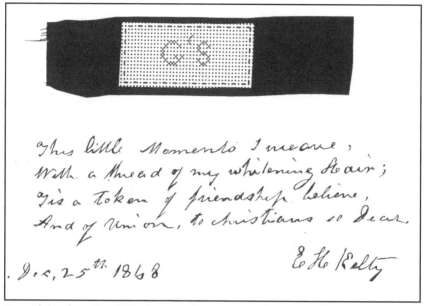

Betsey's bookmark, which she wove from her own hair as a gift to Gerrit.
From the SU collection

bless them for all the sweet mercies so comforting
to an aged heart."[27]

Gerrit felt the warmth, too, and returned love to her in verse.
    "This dear Aunt Betsey—Aunt of all
    Our village holds—both great and small—
    When she shall bid our world 'good night,'
    That village will have lost its light.
    And my poor house especially
    Will then so dark and dreary be,
    When she our saint for fifty years,
    Shall leave us to our gloom + tears."[28]

Both this technique of communicating and the words themselves must have been touching to receive. Gerrit continued to be emotionally close to the females in his family.

> "This day dear Aunt Betsey is just Eighty-two:
> So many long years Heaven giveth to few:
> Yet where is there one, though but fifty years old,
> So ceaseless as she 'mong the hungry + cold?
> Keep on dear Aunt Betsey, your work of sweet love!
> The work of sweet love is the sole work above.
> Hence they who do most of this love-work below,
> Are thereby best fitted to Heaven to go."[29]

It was Elizabeth Smith Miller who expressed the most tender emotions toward Betsey Kelty. Elizabeth had grown up with Betsey as her household guardian and companion, and she well remembered some touching moments. "One joy I can never forget... was lying in the back of your bed, enjoying the most satisfying quiet + sense of security, as I feasted my eyes on the dear old 'Anchor' who sat by the fireside darning Stockings."[30]

Betsey's presence at the Peterboro mansion seemed to underwrite a warranty for the mental health of others, and she was dearly loved. Elizabeth wrote, "From early childhood, when from my little place in her bed—I watched her from night to night reading the Bible.... From that time until now, when she frolics with my grandchild, her love, her care, her wise counsel, have been beyond all praise."[31]

With such touchable love within easy reach, the poems to Aunt Betsey flowed.

> "Such wisdom, Love, + gentleness
> Blessing all with their sweet influence
> Will leave a light behind them
> Which neither time, nor sin can darken."[32]

This was Betsey's 66th birthday, and birthdays in the Smith family were a time for social gifts. People knew and felt what others thought

of them before the epitaph.
"What gift can I bring that's worthy of thee,
My dear Aunt Bettie at seventy-three?
Both tissue of silk + gold of the mine,
Are paltry compared with such merit as thine."[33]

One of Elizabeth Smith Miller's favorite symbols was the Christmas Rose, a white flower that blooms under the snow in the winter season, thus symbolizing the hidden beauty in everything and in everyone. To Betsey she wrote:
"The winters numbering eighty-three
Have left many a record there,
Like 'Christmas Rose' beneath the snows
Her spirit blooms in beauty there."[34]

Aunt Betsey was grateful for the love of her "family."
"Dear Elizabeth Smith Miller is one of the best
women that I have ever knew. Her activity keeps
pace with the kindness of her heart. She has
written me more than one sweet piece of poetry.
God is so good in giving me so many Dear,
precious friends."[35]

The "gift" was certainly not undeserved. Such mutual appreciation as reflected in these poems revealed a family spirit of which Gerrit Smith was proud. It flowed among people in the Smith family like a soothing elixir—except for the sad relationship between Greene and Gerrit.

But Greene was not incapable of feeling and exhibiting love. As it was with his mother, he also loved Aunt Betsey, and said of her,
"Her lovely spirit can never grow old,
Tho thirty score years shall pass o'er it.
Aunt Bettie's dear soul is of heavenly mould
And who can e'rr help but adore it."[36]

There is much more of Aunt Betsey's "journal" that contains thoughts randomly recorded and poems carefully composed to other family members, including Charles Dudley Miller, Gerrit Smith Miller, and even local friends. They in turn responded with lines of love toward her. Once, when Betsey had received the gift of a new dress from a local friend, Martha Gray, in 1849, she wrote in response a long poem of thanks that ended with:

"One thought for thee, Dear M, is pressed,
Above all others in my breast,
When you shall reach that last great day,
And all things here have passed away,
May you be found in richest Dress
The Robes of Jesus' Righteousness."[37]

Betsey's attitude toward others was aided by Gerrit's example; she wanted to help those less well-off than herself. She typically sent a basket of flowers to the Town Fair each year to be distributed among children there. Gerrit's feelings for her showed in his will: When he died in 1874, he bequeathed her $200 a year for the rest of her life. On her death in February of 1880, the obituary read,

"Compitent. Industrious. True. This good woman had no children to call her Mother. But 'Aunt Betsey Kelty' was a mother to the poor, a joy to the young, a ready helper to those who had none to help them, a counselor to the great. She lived for others and was blessed alike by five generations. For more than half a century, Miss Kelty was one of the family of the late Gerrit Smith."[38]

Gerrit Smith's family extended to both the Smith and Fitzhugh relatives, and he expressed an open-hearted and generous nature with them that went far beyond finances. In 1825, Gerrit's sister Cornelia died at the age of 33, leaving eight young children for someone to care for. The habit of the day was not for men to care for

Betsey Kelty – *From the collection of Peterboro Area Historical Society.*

children, and her husband, Walter Cochrane, sought relief from that task while he recovered from his grief. The newly married Smiths agreed to care for the children in Peterboro. Ann wrote to Gerrit while on a visit with her family in Hampton,

> "I suppose by this time the children … are with you. Those children will be a great care to us my dear G., but as it appears to be so plainly our duty to take them, I trust that with the Lord's help we will go through it cheerfully."[39]

The children stayed at the Peterboro home for nearly three years. On their departure, Gerrit and Ann wrote a joint letter to "John,

James, Ellen, Peter, Gertrude, Mary, Cornelia + Catherine, Our dear Nephews and Nieces." "Now that your father is about to resume housekeeping and to take you again under his own care, we wish to say a few things to you…." The Smiths spoke of their strict rearing practices and assured the children that it was for their own good. Their "parting advice: Fear God and keep his commandments; for this is the whole duty of man."[40]

This episode reflected Smith's benevolent attitude toward his family, which he backed up with some of his financial resources. There are scores of letters in Smith's papers from his relatives requesting money for payment of taxes, business or living expenses, school bills, and the like. Normally, he did not refuse to help, and his help was not offered grudgingly. Nannie Livingston, a cousin, remarked, "To attempt to express my gratitude for your benevolence…would be impossible. Suffice it to say, I shall always feel indebted, + if ever in my power to do you a favor, I am with pleasure at your service." She then offered repayment of his former gift, and concluded, "Although I may never repay the kindness, you have my warmest affections + most earnest desire that the blessings of Heaven may rest upon you."[41] The significance of this letter rests in her appreciation for his attitude of kindness. It was the best reimbursement of all.

In other letters remote relatives seemed to beg, as they preyed on Smith's benevolence and resources. His responses usually catered to their needs, sometimes even beyond what was requested. He was especially generous with those nieces and nephews who spent childhood time in Peterboro. Ellen's family received continuing financial help,[42] as did Catherine's family,[43] and Gerrit stayed in close contact with John Cochrane. It was on a visit to John's residence in New York City that Gerrit died in late 1874.

On the Fitzhugh side of the family, Gerrit also expressed an early willingness to help. In a September 12, 1825 letter to his brother-in-law, Henry Fitzhugh, he wrote, "You will probably be able to take up your residence with me by the 1st Dec.—+ I hope it may be a happy and permanent residence. Probably I can, after a few years, connect you in my business...."[44] Henry eventually bought land in Oswego, settled there, and worked for a while for Smith.[45]

The Fitzhugh family was also a relatively large one, Ann being one of five sisters. When all five were together at the Peterboro mansion in 1856, Gerrit wrote a long poem to them praising the virtues of each.[46] In it, he called his wife "Pale Flower, ... the name which Wahoo, an Indian in the Spirit Land, gives to my wife." In a later supposedly humorous poem, he referred to "The Five Fat Sisters."

"The sisters Fitzhugh, again are together;
They're healthy + fat in all kinds of weather;
Their joint weight is now about nine hundred pounds;
How butchers would joy to get hold of such rounds."[47]

When Rebecca, one of Ann's sisters, was in recovery from a trauma, the Smiths offered their home as a therapeutic sanctuary.

"Our house with its comforts we tender to you
And what's very much more our warmest heart too.
Here eat and here drink and here get blessed sleep
And here may you have no occasion to weep."[48]

Rebecca later remarked, "Oh! How rich I feel in all the love you have manifested toward me. I look back on my earliest childhood and I can recollect no angry word that has ever separated us...."[49]

There are other family members who figure into Smith's relationships. Charles Dudley Miller became Elizabeth Smith's husband on October 18, 1843. Gerrit's relationship with him over the years was characteristically cool. On their wedding day, he warned them to stay out of debt, as it would produce much unhappiness. Using himself as an example, he noted that because of his own debt "have my happiness + usefulness been thereby diminished."[50] At that time, Smith was still recovering from the effects of the 1837 market crash.

Perhaps some of the coolness between Charles Miller and Smith came from Charles' orientation toward religion. Ann admonished the newlyweds, "My children, my heart longs after you with tears, that Charlie may be 'born again' + that Lizzie may come under a fresh baptism of the Holy Ghost...."[51]

Charles worked for Gerrit at business duties and home projects during the 1840s, yet his letters to Gerrit are short and factual, with little emotion or chattiness about family and events.[52]

For his part, Gerrit continued the pattern of maintaining cold relationships with the males in his family. As shown in Gerrit's poem, Charles had some interests that did not match Gerrit's ("Hoss" refers to horses, which Charles fancied):

"There's Charlie, that lover of all that is hoss,
Give him something to suit him, oh dear Santa Claus!
Or, if you have nothing that's hoss-like for him,
Have you not what is swamp-like, to suit his swamp whim?"[53]

One Smith-Miller connection that must have irked Charles at times involved the $8,000-per-year "allowance" promised by Gerrit as their income. Smith was often late in disbursing their due, and as the Miller accounts became overdrawn, they wrote reminders to him.[54]

One of the strange relationships in Gerrit Smith's family involved his older brother, Peter Skenandoah Smith. When their father Peter decided to retire in 1819, he had sold most of his estate in land to a partnership between his son, Gerrit, and Gerrit's uncle, Daniel Cady. Gerrit's sister, Cornelia, and brother, Peter Skenandoah, were granted annual stipends for their support. As the eldest son, Peter Skenandoah probably should have received responsibility for his father's business; his father deemed him too irresponsible to handle it, so he turned to his college-educated son, Gerrit. Cady eventually (1835) surrendered his side of the partnership to Gerrit. From an early age, Peter Skenandoah had exhibited traits of instability that rendered him incapable of managing complex affairs. This problem also extended to his family.

Peter Skenandoah's first child, Gerrit Henry Smith, was born in 1831, and almost immediately became the charge of Ann and Gerrit. Ann wrote, "Kiss for me the dear children which God hath graciously given us—and I was going to say little Gerrit—but I have a distressing fear that his cheek is cold."[55] Their rearing of "Little Gerrit" occurred intermittently over the ensuing twelve years. He appeared at the Smith home in Peterboro again in 1841, and brought with him some distressing habits evidently picked up from his own family.

"[He] came to live with me nearly a year ago," said Gerrit. "He came with the bad habit of lying—and even with that of pilfering. We think he is much improved…."[56] A year later, Gerrit noted, "Little Gerrit is very well. My clerk, Mr. Calkins, has this moment finished cutting his hair."[57] Interestingly, Gerrit Smith's business clerks also had domestic responsibilities as part of the family.

Gerrit's concern over the quality of his brother's life started early. In 1836, Gerrit told his father that he was willing to pay all of Peter Skenandoah's debts, and he encouraged Peter to move south to a warmer climate.[58] While "Sken" was in Alabama for the winter of 1835, Gerrit wrote to one of Sken's creditors, "I have no doubt that you + I will be able to arrange the matter. Altho I have paid 10% of 1,000 upon tens of thousands for my dear brother, I am not yet so tired of paying for him, as to refuse to make some reasonable adjustment or compromise of his matter with you."[59]

As Peter Skenandoah continued to mistreat his family and spend short periods of time in jail,[60] Gerrit started to reprimand him for misbehaving. This pattern is reminiscent of the way he treated his son, Greene, and it occurred at about the same time. Sken told Gerrit, "You are at times very severe upon me and partly it is deserved tho not to the extent of your rebukes…."[61] Alcohol abuse was one of Peter Sken's problems that piqued Gerrit's long-term and intense advocacy of temperance. When Gerrit accused him of having contracted delirium tremens, Sken responded, "…the charge against me…is false—totally so if referred to drunkenness or ardent spirits as the cause of my illness…."[62] "I protest that I am not and have not been a drunkard nor have I ever had delirium tremens."[63]

Sken became upset with his brother's admonitions and even

blamed Gerrit for some of his own problems. "Since… the children have been treated talked and corresponded with as the inheritors of estates… I have found myself more and more in their estimation, 'of no account.'"[64] He asked for Gerrit's help and advice in getting his seventeen-year-old son, Gerrit Henry Smith, established in some stable, income-producing endeavor. The lad eventually attended an agricultural institute in preparation for farming.[65]

As noted previously, one of the irksome habits Gerrit had was neglecting to send family members their financial allowances when they were due. This happened with Peter Skenandoah also. In 1848 he wrote his younger brother, "As much depends in our residence on the prompt payment of rent, please remit for the quarter ending with this month."[66] He also made regular requests of Gerrit for additional money to meet debts.[67] Sken did appreciate his brother's help—in spite of the fact that Gerrit continued to chastise him. "I thank you from my heart for all your generous purposes and kindness toward me under all circumstances, and with God's help I will better manifest its worth in the future."[68]

Perhaps Gerrit's moral influence did, over time, have some impact on his errant brother; by mid-1851, Sken was expressing penitence in his letters.

> "What hath sin wrought? …I acknowledge my
> transgression, and my sin is ever before me….
> By God's grace strengthening me, I am resolved
> in mind body soul and strength never under
> any circumstances, to touch taste or handle
> the unclean thing, henceforth + forever. I most
> fervently hope my dear brother that… you have
> been unable to answer the personal summons of
> my… wife. It spares you inconvenience… on my
> account [for] I fervently wish it were all upon me
> to bear without reflecting it upon others. I feel that
> the correction of error tests…me, while I shall be
> most happy to receive and cherish your brotherly

counsel + admonition upon paper whenever you
are so disposed."[69]

A week later, Sken wrote to Gerrit after having lost his bid for a
political appointment in his home city of Philadelphia. "Here I desire
to remain and exhibit the fruits of an upright manly + temperate
walk among my fellow men without shadow of turning from such
a course. If I fail in this thing, I am ready to go anywhere—to adopt
any expediency that you may suggest or advise.... I shall make no
more protestations...."

Sken's wife, Ann, added, "Help me Brother, Sister beloved—for
I am very weak, very sorrowful... yet not helpless.... It is best for
him that I nourish hope. I need to do that, for I suffer more than
you can understand."[70]

The tone of these letters was both penitent and despondent. Sken
and his wife were reaching out in the direction of family for help, and
in spite of his disgust with his brother's former choices in life, Gerrit
responded with characteristic benevolence. He and his own wife,
Ann, traveled to Philadelphia to visit Peter and reinforce his attempt
at personal reform. After the loving visit, Sken wrote to them,

> "I thank you both, nay, I am grateful to God for
> all your kind solicitude, for your anxiety, for your
> help, for your reproof, for your visits; and my most
> earnest desire now is for time and the fruit of
> well-doing.... Let the future test my sincerity + the
> genuineness of the reformation."[71]

Two months later, he stated his continuing resolve.

> "That I shall under God's gracious providence
> continue to abstain from [intoxicating drinks]
> to the end of my natural life I have no [more]
> reason to doubt than I have the simple fact of my
> existence as I write it."[72]

Although he was not mentioned during much of the remainder of Gerrit's life, his brother Peter Skenandoah Smith became for Gerrit an example of the success of his moral reform efforts. Peter died in 1858, but shortly before his death, he wrote in his last letter to Gerrit of the glories of salvation. He lavishly praised Gerrit for his example and for his unending efforts to help him recover from a life of sin. "Brother Smith, why do you talk so much about Christ? You are a better man than he ever was!" And in looking back, he praised their mother. "Oh, how beautiful in holiness is our mother's images + face clothed in the brightness + light of her high attainment...." He did not so praise his father. He ended this last letter with a comment about himself. "I preach humbly the religion of which Jesus Christ was, + is, and ever will be, the Great Exemplar."[73]

It is instructive to examine the relationships Gerrit had with those of his children who did not survive to become adults. These were Fitzhugh Smith (October 18, 1824—July 10, 1836) and Ann ("Nanny") Smith (July 17, 1830—April 21, 1835).

Probably because of Gerrit's patriarchal desires for a male heir, there is more written material available about Fitzhugh than there is on Nanny. She remained a relatively obscure family figure, even though she lived for nearly five years. Gerrit mentioned her briefly in an 1832 letter to his wife, and then turned his attentions to Ann.

> "I have this moment put down the dear baby,
> after pacing the room with her, and...receiving
> her kisses—and now I turn to another of my dear
> babies, and none the less dear because she is the
> biggest of them all. I must occupy a few minutes of
> this sacred [Sabbath] evening to write you...."[74]

Nanny suffered early in life from a convulsive disease. Ann wrote, "I am greatly grieved to hear that our dear Ann has had another fit. I did not expect it so soon, however, I know that God does not afflict us unwillingly and that there is a needs be for all that He sends to us.... There is a darkness over my mind concerning spiritual things."[75] Ann had negative thoughts about the way life was turning out for her compared to her hopes for it, and was trying to resolve this dissonance spiritually.

Nanny died suddenly on April 21, 1835, probably of convulsive complications.[76]

Fitzhugh Smith lived to be 12 years old. Before his death, he had begun to exhibit what his parents considered to be behavior problems that presaged those Greene would demonstrate a few years later. Both Smith parents were away from home frequently—sometimes simultaneously—and at those times, it was the hired help at the Peterboro mansion who had the child-rearing responsibilities. On returning home from one of his trips while Ann was still visiting her parents in Livingston County, Gerrit remarked: "Fitzhugh is getting quite fat, and most of the time is swinging to his heart's delight, in a basket that the girls have suspended to a beam in the kitchen. He rejoiced to see me on my return—and I had scarcely got into the house before Lib began to exclaim—'what have you brought us, Pa?'"[77]

"Lib" was three years old at the time. A few years later, on his 34th birthday, Gerrit indicated concern over lack of attention to their growing children.

> "God grant, my dear Nancy, that you + I may both
> lead better lives than we have done—that we may
> do far more than we have done in exciting each
> other to faithfulness in the Christian life... and may
> we take a juster and deeper interest in our dear
> children...."[78]

Gerrit worried over his commitment to his family; his time spent away from them and his philanthropy toward others diluted what he believed inside himself to be his parental obligations. After having been away for a while, Gerrit lamented that "my dear boy says 'he can't remember how Pa looks'—I hope he + Libby will both see something of their Pa in the picture I send you—and what they see of me in that picture is the best part of me—my outside being the best."[79]

By the time Fitzhugh was about 10 years old, he was becoming a problem for Gerrit. He was selfish and was not much interested in pious matters, so his parents sent him to a school for moral training in Utica run by Lewis Bailey. Fitzhugh had previously expressed his difficulty in accepting Christianity. On a blank page of a Bible given to him by his father he had written, "Oh! That my soul could find peace in the Lord," and to his sister in the spring of 1834, "Dear Elizabeth—Do pray for me. I am a sinner before God. I have broken his holy commandments.... Do pray for me for I am cursed, and shall go down to perdition unless something is done. Remember your only brother."

Those who knew Fitzhugh claimed that although he "expressed his hope in the Savior, ... it was... not very strong." They recognized "his occasional disobedience of the divine commands."[80]

While Fitzhugh was at Bailey's school, Bailey reported to Gerrit that the boy was "unmannerly" and unwilling to attempt interest in religious studies. His preference was to "entertain himself in other diversions" rather than attend services on the Sabbath, or read the Bible.[81] Bailey also reported that Fitzhugh was cynical about Bailey's religious teachings, and "did not see the use of being so strict." Fitzhugh's lack of piety was deeply ingrained, and the boy claimed "he learnt [it] of the kitchen folks at home."[82] He had become a self-centered rebel who scorned discipline. Gerrit knew that some influence in this direction had come from home and was possibly due to his own lack of attention to Fitzhugh. The fact weighed heavily on Gerrit's shoulders. What he could not have known was that there would be no time for redemption.

In June of 1836, Gerrit was summoned to Utica because Fitzhugh had become ill. On June 17, after eating, he had started vomiting, and had then contracted "a painful disease of the bowels." He was attended to by doctors, his Peterboro nurse Laura Bosworth, and his parents.[83]

When Gerrit arrived at Utica, he noted, "I found him very sick, and he was so still, but [the doctor] thinks that his symptoms are decidedly improved. His disease is disordered bowels. He was attacked last Friday, + has taken no nourishment since. He is very weak and much emaciated."[84] Gerrit wrote these letters regarding his son's health to his father, Peter, rather than to his wife. It appears that the potential loss of the male child was a serious patriarchal concern.

In the 1830s, sudden deaths of children were not uncommon, but the effect did devastate families. Fitzhugh's death on July 10 sent Gerrit reeling into depressive grief. "God mercifully gives me [relief] of my bereavement—but much of the time my sense of it almost overpowers me."[85] He spent days just sitting and brooding over his loss. Five months later, he wrote to Ann, "My poor heart bleeds almost continually under our bereavement."[86]

Through letters, friends tried to console him through his piety. Lewis Tappan counseled, "I give you increasing faith that this solemn providence was not only for dear Fitzhugh's welfare but yours also."[87] John B. Edwards consoled, "I expect and believe that this event will be sanctified to you and be a means of drawing and keeping you near the savior. Oh the blessings of the religion of Jesus."[88]

Libby mourned her brother's premature death: "Dear boy, how little he thought last year at this time that before that year closed he would be praising God in a world that never ends."[89]

When their bereavement eased, Ann and Gerrit commissioned the writing of a book to commemorate their son. They financed the printing of 1,500 copies of *A Tribute to the Memory of Fitzhugh Smith*. It is nearly 300 pages long and has almost nothing to do with Fitzhugh. It is an ethnocentric, gender-biased recipe for properly raising "manly" children who are honorable, noble, and benevolent.

No such tribute was made to Nanny soon after her death. Her tribute came 10 years later:

"Ten years, this day, have rolled away
Since our dear Nanny's spirit fled;
Ten years this day, have rolled away,

Since she was numbered with the dead.
Within that time our only son,
Father + brother of us each
And other kindred too, have gone
Beyond time's ever shortening reach.
The next ten years! What freights their wing
Of joy or woe, we cannot tell;
Enough to know what e're they bring,
The friends of God can say—'Tis well.'"[90]

Gerrit's sorrow included the loss of at least two other children, either at birth or during infancy. The gravestones of "Little Katy" and "Henry" bear no dates. Evidently one of them died in late 1823; a friend wrote to Gerrit, "I [am] sincerely sympathetic in the loss of your child. Having endured the same misfortune, I can easily imagine the severity of your affliction."[91]

Throughout all the heartaches and joys of family relationships stood the stalwart figure of Ann Carroll Smith. As Gerrit's lifelong partner, she reflected his inner self.

- 8 -

Ann Smith

William Lloyd Garrison once wrote of Gerrit Smith and his second wife Ann, "If ever two souls were perfectly mated, it was surely so with them."[1]

Smith met his future wife, Ann Carroll Fitzhugh, in January of 1819. It was in that very month that he married Wealtha Ann Backus, daughter of the late Azel Backus, first president of Hamilton College, from which Gerrit had recently graduated. Little is known of Wealtha, who died seven months after their marriage.

A college friend of Smith who believed that marriage robbed a man of his freedom did say that in Wealtha and Gerrit's case, he had approved of their union.[2] Tragically, Wealtha died of encephalitis. One of the first of Gerrit's "rhymes" to appear in his Verse Book was written on August 4, 1819, "During my first wife's last illness."

"Then fare thee well, Maria dear,
A happier world is yet to come;
A world from every sorrow clear
The saints eternal only home."[3]

Gerrit went into deep depression after Wealtha's death. His friend, Thomas Beekman, wrote to Gerrit soon after Wealtha died,

"Under this sudden and awful bereavement, how
can you sustain yourself? What can I say to you to
quell the anguish of the wound inflicted on your
heart? I will not attempt it."[4]

The intensity of Gerrit's feelings can be gauged by a poem he wrote
to his beloved Wealtha a few months later, prefaced with,
"Sunday afternoon 20th March, 1820. I absent
myself from church for I am too much occupied
with my sorrows to receive either knowledge or
consolation. I am sitting before the portrait of my
wife! It fills me with recollections, with sorrows,
+ even with emotions of pleasure which I cannot
suppress."

In the poem, he longs for his lost wife:
"Ah Wealtha, since the happy hour
We last on Time's unfriendly shore
Communed together—peace has forsook me—
Of all the chores that sting this breast
Not one has kindly sounded rest
Each strives to swell the notes of misery.
Methinks already, I can see,
That cherub form so dear to me
Hov'ring in light around the Eternal throne.
Thy golden harp is ne're unstrung—
Redeeming Love is ne're unsung—
What, what are Heaven's joys! They're all thy own."[5]

Although Gerrit's grief over the loss of his beloved Wealtha
waned, he never forgot her, marking the time of her death throughout his life in quarter centuries: "24 years this day since Wealtha
died—How rapid is the flight of time!" "It is 51 years today since
dear Wealtha passed on to the higher life."[6]

While Gerrit and Wealtha were married, Gerrit became acquainted with Wealtha's brother, Frederick Backus, who was married to a former Maryland slave-owner's daughter named Rebecca
Fitzhugh. Rebecca's younger sister, Ann Carroll Fitzhugh, would
become Gerrit's second wife.

The widowed Gerrit remained single for more than two years before he married the young Ann, whom he called "Nancy," on January 3, 1822. Forty-four years later, he would reminisce:

"This month the years are forty seven
Since Nancy Fitzhugh met my eye:
But then my Wealtha was in Heaven
And so I passed sweet Nancy by.
Tis four and forty years today
Since that dear marriage knot was tied
The warmest thanks to Heaven I pay
Are thanks that she's still by my side."[7]

Ann was a supportive and optimistic partner. Although they did have disagreements, Ann usually shored up Gerrit's efforts with consensus and wise counsel. She knew that Gerrit was keenly focused on his work on human rights, moral reform, and his business concerns; she did not want to cause him undue stress. Submissiveness was the rule for most women of the day, and although Ann did not always conform, she seldom upset the balance in their relationship.

When she did have thoughts of self-pity, she checked them. While away from home, she wrote:

"Here I am (thought I) without a husband,
daughter or son—without a sister or brother. I
blacken my own boots + keep mending + mending
my tattered under garments—I have to write every
letter myself…. My darling, this lasted only a few
moments. I soon looked on the brightest side of
my happy lot, + I am happy."[8]

Her attitude was modest as she attended to the feelings of others and worked to support them. She advised her daughter, "complaining does no good—let it pass."[9] While on an extended stay in Philadelphia with Libby, she rented a piano for their own entertainment and was told by the owner of the boarding house that they could not place it in the parlor. In a letter to Gerrit, she said, "We have consented, thinking it right to deny ourselves to save the feelings of others."[10] This "Golden Rule" attitude did rub off on others—especially Gerrit, whom she advised, "Be happy, the dear spirits always say."[11] He did attribute his own happiness and his opportunity to pursue reform work to Ann's efforts to understand and support him. Just before one of their many reunions after travel, she wrote to Gerrit, "I trust the pain has entirely left you + I shall find you feeling bright + happy—but you are always happy."[12]

Ann's faith in Gerrit was not, as biographer Frothingham mistakenly maintained, unwavering. Frothingham painted Ann Smith in such saintly colors as to obscure all blemishes by calling her "sympathetic," "affectionate," "cooperative," "cheerful," and "delicate."[13] She was all of these, but she could also be as much a fool as her husband. The fact that they could be candid with one another was probably part of the balance that held them together in spite of some discord.

Those who knew only Ann's front-stage presentation thought her to be, as Susan B. Anthony said, "a most splendid woman...."[14] And Gerrit also admired her positive attitude toward life.

"A happy woman is my wife
(For this how little's due to me!)
She's happy in her Christian life;
Her soul from guilt has Heaven set free."[15]

Although Gerrit had a loving attitude toward Ann, it could also be possessive and condescending. Most of his letters from her were annotated, "My Wife." When upset with her, he sternly addressed her as "Mrs. Smith." His reference to her as "My Wife" emphasized her role in their marriage rather than her significance as a person. In her letters, he corrected her spelling and underlined what he saw as important. He once complained about her lack of generosity toward him,[16] and suggested that he expected her to be supportive and deferential—if not at least mildly submissive. Ann maintained a dutiful commitment: on one occasion when he traveled to Albany to consult with doctors regarding a health problem, she followed. "Nancy was at Rochester with Greene but hearing I had gone to Albany she scooted on after me—a true wife!"[17]

Although Gerrit's posture toward Ann might seem cold and lacking in affection, that was not the case. It was probably more a reflection of 19th-century social rules for males than an expression of his lack of affection or respect for her. From the time of his courtship of this young Maryland girl—whose slaveholding family had moved to the Genesee Valley—until his death, his display of overt affection for Ann was clear. When she was 16 years old in 1821, Gerrit wrote of his respect for her. "God grant that I may ever feel able + disposed to return a full measure of comfort into the bosom which shall be my own supplying fountain."[18]

He treasured her presence and her partnership, and valued her input into his philanthropy and reform endeavors.

"In obedience with suggestion in your letter, (Even
your suggestion, you know, is law with me) I took
onion soup on going to bed. I never slept sounder...."[19]

He admired her as a personal counselor, social thinker, mother, community worker, and as a specimen of physical beauty. As time passed, said Gerrit, "I... try in vain to find one change in thee, that mars thy growing lovliness."[20] In the 1848 Christmas family poem, he wrote:

"And now, dearest Clause, our plea is for one,
Who as Mother or Wife, can ne'er be outdone.
Give to dear Madam Smith the best of your treasure,
Compared with her worth, t'will be a small measure."[21]

In later years, Gerrit wrote to his teenage son, Greene, "You have a mother who is precious. I hope, you will never forget."[22]

Gerrit's land business was the only part of his life in which Ann was seldom involved. Gerrit was a superb businessman. He administered, clerked, calculated, and communicated for long hours daily—resting only on Sundays. "This is our quiet + sweet Sabbath. Wearied and exhausted by my labors on the days of the week, I do greatly welcome the return of this day. And, then, this is the day, in which dear Ma + I can talk and read + pray together, as we have not opportunity to do on the days of the week."[23]

He regretted that his work kept him from Ann. Looking back on his life two months before he died, he wrote, "How many days I have seen you sitting alone.... I punish myself for not having stopped all to talk more with you + to read with you. Often I accuse myself of being a husband quite unworthy of such a wife."[24] When they were apart he worried over Ann's health and safety,[25] and admonished her, "I am very glad you could walk out. But I hope you will be out only in broad daylight. Your safety requires this."[26]

He even quipped about her health and beauty. "I am very glad to...learn... of your high health and spirits. Your old husband will think himself very fortunate if you do not run off with some younger man."[27]

As Ann and Gerrit aged and became overweight and infirm, his admiration of her still grew. In the winter of his last year, having fallen in the snow, he said, "How blind + clumsy I am. Can I be the same person who married you 53 years ago? You are the person I married—lovely then + lovely now."[28] Their partnership reflected mutual admiration. It was balanced with a clear perception of obligations and responsibilities. As he wrote in 1871 on a visit to the Fitzhugh family in Rochester, where they were married:

"Of all homes to my soul, none dearer can be
It was here my dear Nancy took pity on me
And bound my glad heart in that same blessed chain
Which I still wear with joy, unmingled with pain."[29]

Gerrit valued Ann in their partnership not only for her "charms," but also for her mind; he often sought her evaluation and criticism of his ideas. On one occasion James C. Fuller, a fellow abolitionist whom Smith had reproved for disruptive behavior at local anti-slavery meetings, wanted Ann to evaluate their controversy and advise Gerrit's course of action. Gerrit responded, "And since you desire it, my wife shall also see [our letters]—albeit I know, that, from her... fondness to criticize me, her judgment will be very like to incline to your side.

"P.S. My wife has just got through with the correspondence. It is as I apprehended—she pronounces you right + me wrong."[30]

Still, in spite of his seeming ire, Smith did value her input.

> "I thank the Father that he gave
> His Christ a vivid world to save:
> I thank Him that He's bless'd my life
> By giving me a Christ-like wife.
>
> A wife who one + forty years,
> In sorrow's nights has dried my tears:
> And by whose wise and watchful care
> Has sav'd my feet from frequent snare.
>
> Who, more than all the world beside,
> Has been my teacher + my guide;
> And by her lips + life each day
> Has helped me in the Heavenly way."[31]

As can be seen from the many poems, writing was an important part of their relationship. When they were apart they wrote many letters, and when they failed to write each other, it hurt. "Disappointed again!" Gerrit wrote to Ann in 1862: "No letter from you tonight!"[32]

More than just a way to relay news, letters were a technique of showing affection, building and cementing love, and conveying feelings. As frequent and emotion-laden missives, they performed a cathartic and therapeutic function and helped to maintain closeness between them. As early as 1831, Ann wrote to Gerrit,

"I finished a letter to you last evening, and
began another today—for, I believe, you love to
receive letters from me, almost as well as I love
to receive them from you. I think, if you were
fully persuaded of my great comfort + pleasure
in getting letters from you, you would tax your
industry to send me more of them."[33]

Gerrit's early letters to Ann were chatty, long and frequent, often several pages in length written over two or three days, chronicling events from the start to the finish of each day. With much detail he told her of what he ate, who he spoke with and what they talked about, where he went, or how he felt. He told her of the weather, who had visited, who had dined, who had gone to church, what the sermon was about, what business transactions he was working on, and what the children were doing. His thoughts jumped from one subject to another in a stream-of-consciousness type of thinking as if she were there, talking with him.

The letters were a symptom of their desire to talk with each other—a kind of foreplay grounding the relationship in love. One example of Gerrit's serial writings in a letter starts on "Friday evening" and progresses through paragraphs he added one by one throughout the weekend:

"10 AM Saturday"
"Saty evening, almost 11 o'clock"
"Sabbath morning"
"Sabbath noon"
"after church"
"after Sabbath"
"9 o'clock"
"Monday morning"

What Ann read was a running account of life in Peterboro—as if she were there to experience it. The letters attest to Gerrit's constant thoughts of her, and how much he missed her participation in daily life with him when she was away from Peterboro.

Although Gerrit and Ann often remarked in letters how much they disliked being away from each other, they were apart often for long periods of time. While in Albany, Gerrit wrote on March 10, 1831: "I fear my dear wife, that I shall not be able to leave here until 1st to 5th Apl. Oh! What a long time to add to that which already parted us."[34] In 1836 the affection between them was clear. "I was never, my dear wife, more desirous for our reunion, and it seems to me, that we must not let small causes separate us again."[35] And three days later, "For a youth of 18 to spring from his bed at 6 o'clock to write an epistle to his beloved would not be so very strange a thing— but for a middle aged gentleman, whose looks and wrinkles show, that some forty years have travelled over him, to be this romantic + love-like is not a little surprising."[36] "I get along pretty well—but my heart aches for your return."[37]

Their long separations were due mostly to Ann's need to seek medical treatment. Although Gerrit did travel around the northeast to attend a variety of social reform meetings or conventions, he was generally gone for only a week or two. Ann's health concerns, however, took her away for months at a time. The reasons for her travel were curious; certainly, their affluence allowed travel and extended stays away from home, but there is a question as to whether they were necessary for reasons of physical health alone. Previous authors have mistakenly described Gerrit as a hypochondriac.[38] He was generally optimistic about life, and although he did have some chronic health problems, he did not usually allow them to interfere with his normal routine of home and business. In fact, his wife was the real hypochondriac in the Smith family.

Ann Smith was prone to the faddish cures that grew popular in the second half of the 19th century, such as "water cure" and "movement cure" therapies. Movement cure therapy referred to a variety of exercise programs thought to be beneficial to health, and water cure was a type of hydrotherapy that included the use of water, internally and externally—at any temperature and in any form—to improve one's health. Mineral waters were not necessary, but could be used.[39] An advertisement for a water cure business indicated its assumed potential:

> "Among the complaints which are here successfully treated are, Headache... cold extremities, general and nervous debility, Bronchitis, Pulmonary Affections, Liver Complaint, Jaundice, acute and chronic inflammation of the bowels, Piles, Dyspepsia, nervous and spinal affections, Inflammatory and Chronic Rheumatism, Neuralgia, Sciatica, Lame Limbs, Paralysis, Fevers, Salt Rheum, Scrofulous and Erysipelas Humors."

The cost was nine dollars per week, at the Northhampton Water Cure.[40]

Ann did have some legitimate physiological concerns, and her hope was that these miracle cures would make her feel better. To pursue them, she traveled to New York City, New Jersey, Philadelphia, Pennsylvania, Clifton Springs, New York and other places, often boarding there for months at a time. The frequency and length of her periods of time away from Peterboro increased as she aged. During the first three decades of Ann's married life, she was away from home for an average of more than a month each year. The reasons varied and included some family visits to the Rochester area. In the next decade, roughly from 1853 to 1862, her time away increased to an average of 2.2 months per year, and most of these visits were health-related. By the last decade of her life, she was away from Peterboro for an average of 3.3 months per year, about 90 percent of which was health-related. These time periods are those which can be documented from letters, and they are less than the actual amount of time Ann spent away from Peterboro—and Gerrit.

Gerrit was left working at his land business in Peterboro and feeling lonely. He wrote her, "You are very good, my dear Nancy, in expressing your desire to visit me in my actual loneliness."[41] He told Ann of cold winter nights, of having ailments with no one there to comfort him.[42] Yet he wanted her to stay wherever she was long enough to get well. The resulting mix of emotions plagued him. "Stay longer at Plymouth if your health requires it. Come home if it does not…. I deeply desire your health + happiness—+ yet—I cannot live without you."[43] Even though Gerrit was not sure that she really needed to be there, he prized her feelings enough to support her freedom to do what she thought was necessary. "Not a word from you yet. Of course, I am uneasy about you, + am reproaching myself for letting you travel alone at your advanced age + with your [declining] health. Would that, like me, you felt that home is the only place for persons as aged and infirm as we are."[44]

Perhaps because Ann felt worse as winter approached, or because she was looking for a way out of Peterboro, her absences usually spanned the winter months. Few physiological ailments can be cured only by exercise or water use, yet she usually improved enough to return home when spring arrived. Gerrit lamented in late December of 1871 that even Christmas was not enough of a force to keep her home. "A bright and beautiful morning—but still windy. I slept well, beloved. I am doing as well as I can without you. I live, as I do whenever you leave me, on the hope that you will not leave me again."[45] One can get a sense of the intensity of Gerrit's inner feelings of missing Ann from what he writes.

> "I had a good night's sleep, but
> Whenever I awake, I cry out for Ma—
> The voice that comes back says 'she is not here'
> I turn over then, poor desolate Pa!
> And try to get sleep, while quaking with fear."[46]

When she did come home, Gerrit became almost giddy with excitement, as the poem "Ma's Coming!" shows:

> "Make way for dear Ma, ye wonder-struck crowd!
> She comes like the wind! She's as fleet as a hound!

'Tis not strange that the crowd shouts long + shouts loud
To see her climb fences at one single bound!"[47]

The irony in Gerrit's concern over Ann's aging and poor health is that he might better have been more concerned about his own. Her last time away from him was October through December of 1874, when she went to New York City for treatment of an eye problem. As Gerrit neared death, Ann expressed doubts about the wisdom of being away from him. He responded,

"I... fear that your eye is not to be restored under your present treatment. So you exclaim on hearing my letter: 'I want to go to him!' God grant you may come to me + never more have occasion to leave me."[48]

He also expressed disappointment that she had gone away in the first place. "Your long + unexpected absence from me + your intense sufferings in that absence have made that absence the pre-eminently sad [period] in my life."[49] Although Gerrit was sad when Ann was away, he tried to make the best of it. He suggested, "Let us improve this season of our painful separation from each other in studying the bible, in prayer, in holy living. It may be the most profitable season of our lives."[50] Gerrit's letters to Ann revealed his affectionate feelings for her, and although he wanted to have a continual partnership with her, he could not, due to her frequent long absences. When she was home, he was happy. "Dear Ma returned home last evening.... We are glad to have her home. Home is good even without her, but it is very good with her."[51]

Her feelings toward him were similarly revealed in her letters. Ann often expressed loving gratitude to Gerrit because he wrote to her every day. "Your letters come every morning, my precious Gerrit, and make me very glad."[52] "It is so pleasant a thing to know that I shall hear from you every day while we are absent from each other."[53] "I cannot tell you how good it is to get your sweet letters every day."[54]

She knew that Gerrit's business communications took much of his time and that his effort to write to her daily said much about the high quality of their relationship. "You are very good, my dear husband, to write me so often. I should feel more lonely than I do, if it were not for your good long letters."[55] She liked his affectionate attention, and urged, "Always write me so darling."[56] Letters were reread many times "with increasing pleasure," as their mutual household friend Betsey Kelty remarked.[57]

Ann wrote often, too, but found it difficult to keep pace with Gerrit. "I am really ashamed of myself my dear Husband for suffering your second letter to reach me before I have answered your first."[58] If Gerrit's letters were often a chronicle of daily events, her letters were often full of news about other people. Ann wrote of connections or visits with others, of what others were doing and how they felt, and she often ended with a list of people back home in Peterboro to whom she sent "best wishes," and "lots of love." Ann's relationships did not focus on just Gerrit, but spread out among others close by. Even Gerrit was surprised at her desire to write to and about all of her friends, commenting on the length of her letters so full of news. He wrote her, "I never knew you half so good a correspondent—never knew you write letters so frequently or of so good length. I thank you, my dear wife, for this kind attention to my happiness."[59]

One thing that is vivid in reading Ann's letters to Gerrit is that while they were apart, she missed him, and she frequently said so in emotional terms. Ann wrote,

> "Write me a good letter from the bottom of your
> heart to take the place of your arms about me
> while you are absent…. Twice I have been in your
> dressing room. Your drab pants hanging there
> looked more like you than anything else there—I
> kissed them almost involuntarily."[60]

Ann seemed to express as much loneliness as did Gerrit during their separations, and she apparently felt this emptiness as early as

1826. "Every day seems a week while I am absent from you...."[61] More than just wanting to be with Gerrit as a friend, she seemed to need him to fulfill her sense of self. Her salutations reveal incompleteness without him. "Your attached wife;"[62] "Your own as ever;" "Yours in strongest bonds." She frequently wrote that she never wanted to be apart from him again, yet Gerrit evidently enjoyed some of his "free" time; Ann wrote to him,

> "We have been separated a very long time, and
> I now think that I never will be absent from you
> again, at least not for so long a time. I have received
> letters from you regularly,... and am very glad to
> find that you have enjoyed yourself so much."[63]

Gerrit was clearly optimistic about life; even without his "beloved," he could have fun. His life was balanced among business, reform, and family activities in a way that left no holes of need, although he did miss talking with his confidante and she missed him as well. "I miss you, beloved, more than ever," he said. "We have read so much together of late + interchanged thoughts that I feel very much the loss of your presence."[64]

Ann was pleased with what she felt was Gerrit's willingness to listen to her. "You have always been so patient in hearing my troubles that I do not fear to carry them to you."[65] "I... prise more fully... the happiness which we have in one another. You have had great patience with me, dear Gerrit, in all my faults, and it has made me love you the more."[66]

Ann fancied herself a sympathetic listener also, and she was disturbed if Gerrit did not confide in her. She called herself the "sympathiseress,"[67] and assured others that she knew his inner thoughts well enough to evaluate rumors concerning what he believed.[68] The closeness of their relationship was publicly known, and it could have been a model for others. While Ann traveled in Europe, her niece wrote to Gerrit of her, "Dear Aunt must be now enjoying the delightful climate of Italy, but I daresay that she longs to be at home with you on the snowy hills of Peterboro."[69] Indeed, Ann did love to be with Gerrit. Following his visit to her in New York City in April of 1873, she noted, "These rooms are a different place to me since you have ate + slept + thought + talked in them. I cannot thank you enough for coming. God bless you, darling, for all that you are + have been to me."[70]

"[My indebtedness] to you increases every moment. My debt of loving kindness + tender care go far beyond my ability to meet. I can only rest under it—grateful, peaceful + happy."[71] Given Ann's abiding anxiety over her presumed poor state of health, she needed someone who would listen without trivializing her concerns. This Gerrit did, and without him present, she did not feel whole.

Ann wanted to believe that the reason she should be home was that Gerrit needed her. "Your last letter (10 July) makes me hurry home to you…. I shall soon have the happiness of being with you, to rejoice with you or to sooth and comfort you…."[72] But the real reason probably could be found in her own needs. Ann wrote, "I feel quite weak this AM. Let me explain. I was woken up at 11 last night by a rapping at the front door. I went to the window in a… fright expecting news of your death."[73] "Darling as soon as I can bear the journey I will return to you, + I think I will never leave you again. When I cannot get well without leaving you, then Providence teaches me, that the time has come for me to 'pass on.'"[74]

The irony of her condition was that she still believed that she had to leave Peterboro to get well: even in their early years of marriage, Ann left Gerrit behind in her quest to feel better. In 1824 she wrote, "My health has improved very rapidly since I left you, and I am growing so fat and strong, that I am sure, unless you come for me soon, you will be afraid to take me home, on account of my superior strength."[75]

By the 1830s, Ann was spending winter months away from home "dreaming" of Gerrit and wishing that she did not need to be absent for so long. "This long separation is very very hard to bear. If I felt strong and well I would not mind it so much."[76] When Gerrit suspected there was a psychosomatic basis to her hypochondria and became cynical about it, Ann responded, "You do not know me if you think I prefer New York [City] + feebleness to home + health."[77] Her guilt about being away from Gerrit, and perhaps about her self-presumed "feebleness," caused self-denigration. "I flatter myself that you miss this helpless + almost useless one somewhat."[78] "What sweet letters you have written to your... runaway wife."[79] In a moment of candor, she even hinted at her desire to escape Peterboro winters. "In spite of my many absences I love home almost as well as you do...."[80]

What Ann Smith did while she was at home is obscure. Except for a brief period in the early 1840s, she seldom helped in the land business. She read little except for the Bible, and probably did minimal amounts of housework because of their hired help. During the summer she did enjoy gardening. They bought new seeds each spring, and she sent "seeds and cuttings" to the Douglasses for their gardens in Rochester.[81] Ann loved the strawberries that they grew at home, and while away from home, she advised Gerrit, "Please... have our strawberries mulched. That is to surround every plant with fresh cut grass, so as to protect it entirely from the earth around. Beside keeping the fruit clean, this keeps the ground moist. Do not forget."[82] Sewing was also a common home-based task, and Ann and Elizabeth made some of the family's clothes. In 1858 she wrote to Gerrit, "I am busy making my baby's shirts...."[83]

One issue that commanded a lot of her thoughts was religion. When Ann and Gerrit were married in 1822, she was a devoutly religious person and Gerrit was not. His secular attitude lingered from his college days, as Ann tried to persuade him to seek salvation. By 1826 she had succeeded, and she remained a major influence in Gerrit's growth in religion throughout their partnership—even though they had some significant differences in beliefs. Gerrit often praised her for keeping him attuned to the principles of Christianity, from which he felt that he frequently strayed. He said of Ann,

"Dear God! I ask for my poor sake,

Thy blessing on this gift from Thee:
Oh let this angel presence make
All angel—good to grow in me!"[84]

Ann liked the revivals that periodically swept through the Peterboro area, and she spoke of one as she proselytized her father-
in-law.

"The power of God was manifest in the conversion
of sinners, but especially in the reclaiming of
backsliders.... These meetings seem greatly blessed
of late. Hundreds are coming to the waters.... And
will you, dear father, stay away and perish?"[85]

As late as 1860, she was exhorting Gerrit to grow in piety. "I trust
you sleep well and that your spirit grows more and more passive in
the hands of our... Father. I am sure that submission + patience are
the two things that will bring all things right...."[86]

Gerrit was not quite as "passive" in his religion as his wife. As
an activist, he found submission and patience to be rare traits in
himself, and he became more worldly as Ann became more spiritual.
He wrote about it:

"Sept. 28, '63—G.S. + wife are on the Erie Railway
returning from N York to their home. He wonders
at the ignorance... her questions betray. He pencils
the following:
'A.C.S.' [said]
'I'm studying the map of the sweet Summer land
Where I hope soon to join the blest Spirit land;
And this is my reason for knowing no more
Of distance + course on the earth-side shore.
'I wish, my dear husband, that you'd look with me
At things which the angels desire us to see:
Much better 'Twould be had you less earthly love
And of Heavenly wisdom a far greater store.'

'G.S.' [said]
'I own, my dear wife, that I foolish have been
In looking so much at the things which are seen:
Of those great things unseen + eternal may I
Have far clearer sight ere I enter the sky.'"[87]

She was abstract, spiritual, and inductive; he was practical, empirical, and deductive. Their differences in styles of thinking led to troubles between them, and one of the troublesome areas was religion. When Spiritualism developed in the United States in 1848, Ann was attracted to the belief that the spirit of a person survived after death and could communicate with the living. Spiritualism attracted mostly women, perhaps because it afforded them a sense of power denied them by the gender-based institutional structure of mid-19th-century society. It offered a different outlook by challenging the authoritative views of reality that had normally been defined by clergy and church doctrine. Spiritualism needed no middle-level interpreter, so it offered a style of believing that was especially attractive to women who might be interested in avoiding male domination. The fact that Ann was drawn to this belief system irked Gerrit. In June of 1852, Ann recorded in a diary that she was hearing "raps" from her dead son, Fitzhugh, that spelled out words conveying messages of his love for her.[88]

Gerrit was compassionate enough to tolerate Ann's spiritualism, but he saw no validity in it. As she sought out the services of mediums and fortune-tellers, his suspicion and cynicism of both her new religious beliefs and her hypochondria showed through.
"You will soon outgrow this nonsense,…
And with your [own] strong sense
Find yourself entirely well."[89]

This was part of his anniversary poem to Ann which he annotated: "Tho' half a Spiritualist myself, I nevertheless was in the habit of making fun of the earnest Spiritualism of my dear wife."

This condescending attitude was also revealed in an undated poem regarding her beliefs.

"Mind you your Bible, not the Raps,
The first is true—the last perhaps....
"The ticks you hear are cracking frost,
Not spirits sav'd, or spirits lost:
The wondrous sounds which keep you wake
The scamping rats + mice do make."[90]

A few days later on her birthday, he noted:

"She's crazy be sure, on one or two themes—
But her goodness of heart full recompense brings.
For all that is foolish + mad in her brain:
Moreover, I b'lieve, that she yet will be sane.
"The Fishes + Foxes she'll quit by + by;...
The old orthodox creed will yet win her back...."[91]

"Fishes" and "Foxes" were the last names of people who advocated Spiritualist ideas. Although one splinter group of Quakers—the "Progressive Friends"—did believe in Spiritualism, it is inaccurate to label Ann Smith as a Quaker because of her similar belief. She even believed fortune teller Caprell, who told her that Gerrit would soon meet and marry a young woman, so she made an effort to make herself look young again.[92] Gerrit thought the effort was silly, and he responded:

"Your Gerrit is willin', that fifty years more
Should stretch between you + eternity's shore:
He is not impatient to get his child-wife
The old lady will do to the end of his life."[93]

His humor might have helped to soften the blow of her superstitions. And despite his ire over her Spiritualist leanings, Gerrit stayed loyal with his support of her.

"Of course we'll let grandmother call Spirits to her side

Her spirits unlike tother, Are Spirits true + tried....
Despite her superstitions She's our chief earthly love
How happy our position If near to her's above."[94]

As Gerrit aged, he became much more of a practical thinker than did Ann, and as her interest in Spiritualism developed, discord appeared between them. Their marital troubles were mild and probably did not threaten to dissolve the relationship, but it is unfair to the overall balance in Gerrit Smith's life to ignore them and paint his relationship with Ann with a smooth stroke. The best way to trace their minor difficulties is chronologically through their poetry.

In the late 1840s, there was no sign of distance between them in Ann's birthday poem to Gerrit.

"Think not the day can pass unheeded,
Best loved of all below,
The frosts of time have not impeded
My warm love in its flow.

O no! While frosts of time are flinging
O'er weak love chills + blight—
To mine they are forever bringing
Sweetness + new delight."[95]

By the early 1850s her interest in the occult perhaps had fueled her hypochondria, and she spent increasing amounts of time away from home in pursuit of mysterious cures. In a woeful poem, Gerrit expressed dejection at her absence.

"When journeying homeward hitherto,
My heart has longed my home to view;
But coming toward my home last night,
My sad, sad heart would not be light.

The sweetest solace of that home—

The brightest joy within that dome—
She who's my own good guiding star—
I knew did not await me there.

And when at home with weary feet,
I met her not I used to meet;
I felt how lone and drear is life
Without my wife, my precious wife."[96]

    Within the next year, Ann had tried two water cures and home-
opathy in attempts to cure unnamed ills, and had listened for hours
at a time to spirit raps. Gerrit wrote:
    "The husband of this 'odd fish' wife
Of course must lead a sorry life:
But he'll not murmer—no, not he
He took her risking what she'd be."[97]

But the "risks" were getting greater, and he did more than murmur.
    "I think as how I'de like to see
The woman whom I call my wife:
She + myself do well agree
Save in our times of marital strife."[98]

    It was sometime during the year 1852 that Gerrit's cousin and fre-
quent Peterboro visitor, Elizabeth Cady Stanton, became concerned
about what she saw as a deteriorating relationship between Ann and
Gerrit, and she wrote about it. She blamed Ann for their troubles due
to what Stanton perceived as Ann's growing dissatisfaction with her
home, and her tendency to roam for long periods. Stanton's scathing
poem was titled, "How Art Thou Fallen O! Nancy!"
    "I wrote some lines in years gone by—
(As I think of that time my heart heaves a sigh)
And I praised in rhymes
Two cousins of mine

For their Love + devotion
And harmonious motion.
They were a pattern man + wife
And led a happy, loving life.

The wife thought not then of running from home
And leaving her husband sad + alone
Wherever he went
She went too
Whatever he did
That did she do,
But now, 'they say,' Nancy's growing capricious
And Gerrit, dear soul, is quite unsuspicious....

And to Saginaw! Now she has gone, + alone!!
Oh! Rib of his rib! + bone of his bone!
Gerrit pours forth his love
To her every day
In tender love missives
Sent by lake + railway.
What she will do next, no one can tell
Tho' we'll hope for the best—fallen Nancy!
Farewell!"[99]

Clearly, Stanton was worried that "Nancy's" new wanderlust had alienated Gerrit, who became cynical as Ann drifted into mysterious territory. "It was... in the year 1852 that my wife was sitting one evening by my side.... She was very desirous to have a spirit write with her hand, + hence she sat for perhaps half an hour with a pen in it....

Here by my side my poor wife sits,
Waiting the spirit's mighty shove:
Oh, 'tis enough to give me fits,
To see my wife 'a silly love'."[100]

As her "silliness" progressed and she left home again in search of
better feelings, Gerrit mused that his love might be growing cold.
> "And must we part my precious wife
> Upon our Wedding Day?
> This day the sweetest of our life,
> I'de gladly with thee stay....
>
> And eight days hence, I'll not forget
> You're forty-eight years old;
> And thank our God we're too young yet
> To let our love grow cold."[101]

By early 1854, Gerrit was reminiscing of better days.
> "This day makes two and thirty years
> Since I this wondrous woman wed:
> 'Tis proved by my briney tears
> I'de better kept my single bed."[102]

Ann also expressed her dampening love. She wrote:
> "A nation now doth sing thy praise [in Congress]
> Still thou wilt not forget the lays
> Wherewith in quiet humbler days
> I sought to make thee glad.
>
> And thou wilt welcome once again
> My offering poor, in which I'de fain
> Express my love, but all in vain—
> The future makes me sad."[103]

In response, Gerrit admitted of his need for love "Anew."
> "This timely warning—may it raise
> My heart above all flatt'ring praise;
> And bind that loving heart anew
> To god, my children, + to you."[104]

These concerns Gerrit and Ann had about their cooling love were somehow worked out over the next few years; they remained committed to one another. By the time of their thirty-seventh anniversary in 1859, Gerrit was again singing marital praises.

"The years are thirty-seven, my Fraw,
Since Parson Cummings clasp'd our hands;
And I did gladly thee endow
With all my cash, + stocks, + lands.

But though so many they have been,
Each year has prov'd a precious boon
Our married life the world has seen
To be a lifelong honeymoon."[105]

But lest one get the notion that Gerrit viewed married life as a dream come true, one need only read how he felt three years later:

"The wife I have lov'd with for forty long years—
I find has made my life 'a valley of tears.'
I'de bear with her still be it forty years more
And repeat the sad case full many times o'er."[106]

Regardless of how good he felt about their relationship, he always harbored feelings of being trapped—of not being able to fully express and actualize himself because of his dependence on Ann. By 1865 he complained,

"Such dependence me ties always close to her side
While other men go + return as they please."[107]

Even their son, Greene, felt the sting of his parents' cool love as he grew up at home in the 1850s, and later he wrote a note about it to his mother. He had been speaking in this letter of how nature lies in repose under winter's blanket of snow awaiting the warmth of spring to regenerate.

"Not so with the heart when by sorrow 'tis wasted;
No music e're lulls its deep throbs to repose;
Naught e're can awaken the pleasures once tasted,
Or ever remove the dark mantle of woes"[108]

For Ann and Gerrit, by the early 1860s the "mantle of woes" had lifted, and they moved on to other concerns and new challenges. The knowledge that they had one spot where the foundations of their relationship trembled reveals them as fallible. Even in the pastoral splendor of a horse-drawn world, life's complexities and their contrasting personalities had produced disappointment and tears.

One result of their "mid-life crisis" was an increased level of assertiveness in Ann. She had become tired of being submissive to her husband, and she started to flex her independent muscles. His response to her newly-felt power was cynical:

"My husband, says Nancy, I firmly now state
That for what is my own I'll no longer wait:
Of all of my wealth let me now be possest
That I may its income make haste to invest....

A cypher's poor Gerrit—a prime Number One
Is this woman who'll show how things should be done:
It's right when the husband has lost all his force,
That the wife, whip in hand, should drive round the course."[109]

A few days later, Gerrit spoke of Ann's new-found sense of power:

"This twentieth day of October I find
Mrs. Smith to be still in her new state of mind:
Another newspaper she'll buy of the lad
If he'll take for his pay the one that she's had."[110]

Gerrit was clearly displeased with Ann's new self-centered, non-benevolent posture, and he composed a soliloquy for her to recite. "Scene—The Library at the Peterboro Mansion—Mrs. Ann C. Smith

is sitting on the sofa with both fists doubled, + determination in
her eyes…

> "My diffidence I now cast off
> Self abnigation fare thee well!
> Benevolence is now my scoff
> Against my nature I rebel.
>
> For Number One I henceforth go:
> For all the world I've done enough
> My sympathies now inward flow:
> This care for others is poor stuff…"[111]

Ann's assertiveness was getting on Gerrit's nerves, and his cynicism probably acted as a way to compensate for it. When he criticized
her, she accused him now of a lack of tenderness.

> "My Nancy complains that I lack tenderness—
> How ingracious in her such thought to express!
> For if true that my heart's all bankrupt and poor,
> 'Tis because it has spent its treasures on her."[112]

In fact, his cynical "lack of tenderness" extended to even seemingly minor areas. He had a tendency when walking with Ann to stay
a little ahead of her. Now that she had developed the self-confidence
to call him on it, he cynically replied:

> "Oh no, my dear Nancy, Oh no, nevermore,
> Will I leave your sweet self and walk on before!
> I will stop with your stops, and stick to your side,
> Whatever misfortune or slowness betide…."[113]

There is some irony in Gerrit's conservative response to Ann's
assertiveness: he supported women's rights ideas and contributed his
resources to those who pursued that movement. Maybe it was just at
home that his conservatism surfaced. One area where it was evident
was in his disbursement of money within his immediate family.

With the exception of a brief period in the late 1830s and early 1840s, Gerrit Smith had so much money at his disposal that he could support any cause he wished; yet his wife constantly needed to beg him for funds. He paid little attention to her financial needs when she was away, thereby necessitating her pleas. "After I pay the present… week's board, I shall have but about three dollars left," she wrote him in 1836.[114] By the mid-1850s, Ann seemed disgusted with her lack of financial independence, and she requested her own account:

> "I do seriously desire to have $1,000.00 to use
> according to the dictates of my own head +
> heart…. I may not give it the way that you would,
> but if I do no wrong and satisfy my own heart in
> the disposal of it, you will not object I am sure."[115]

Gerrit *did* object. He held a tight rein on the purse strings of his family, and Ann and Elizabeth had to grovel for what they needed to live comfortably. While they were on a stay in New York City, Libby had asked her father for two hundred dollars. "We have bills that should be paid now," she wrote.[116] Ann added, "Please send her another hundred. She will never waste anything. She is constantly contriving some way to make money so as not to apply to you so much, and so as to have more than she can ever have the face to ask you for."[117]

Gerrit was a miser with his family, and his niggardliness was a source of aggravation to them. Ann even tried to go around him. "I told Charlie [Miller] to ask you to send me $200.00. He thinks it will suit you… for him to give me the drafts."[118]

When his family traveled to Europe in late 1861, he relaxed his thrift a bit, but their expectation of his warnings of extravagance led to some misunderstandings. Ann scolded him for criticizing their overseas spending, prompting his response that they could spend what they wished. She then felt bad about her assertiveness.

> "My repentings are kindled within me. I am full
> of reproaches. How could I have been so little

and narrow souled as to allow your few words of
caution as to expenditure to cover over us with
a thick cloud all your previous nobleness and
self denial in sending us for this delightful tour!
Reproach me and forgive me darling. I shall be
much better satisfied than for you to carry this
your burden of spirit one moment longer. Give me
your hand. 'I will be good'."[119]

A few years later, she was still pleading for money. While in New
York City for health treatments in 1867, she wrote, "Please send
me $150.00…. I will not waste."[120] Her concern for "waste" made
it sound as if her health was less important than Gerrit's philanthropy. As Ann aged, she gave up asking Gerrit for money and got
her own bank account against which she could write checks. Seven
years later, Smith's Oswego business clerk, John B. Edwards, noted
in his account ledger, "Deposited in Oswego County Savings Bank
to credit of Mrs. Smith $1500.00."[121]

Although the money issue irritated Ann at times, her health was
her greatest concern. She was nearly always dissatisfied with how
she felt, and she was vulnerable to anyone claiming that they had
a cure. Her lifelong interest in religion was a symptom of this; her
faith promised a better life and rationalized discomfort as divinely
ordained. Ann felt uncomfortable wherever she was. Early in life
she called herself "Nanny the grunter," and she was frequently
plagued by headaches and numbness.[122] These symptoms could
have been psychosomatic. When in Peterboro, she thought she
would feel better if only she could be in New York City. When in
the city, she was convinced she would feel better if only she were
back in Peterboro.

At one point, she stated clearly what was probably the real source
of much of her health problem. It was January of 1866 and Ann was
on an extended stay in New York City, undergoing exercise training
and treatment in the "movement cure" process. "Yes, dear Gerrit, I

Gerrit and Ann Smith, in a carte de visite, from the 1870s. Cartes de visite were small albumen prints that were mounted on 2 1/2 x 4-inch cards. They replaced ambrotypes and Daguerreotypes as an easy means of sending photographs through the mail and exchanging them with friends to be posted in their photo albums.

From the author's collection

---

am happy chiefly because this treatment… is working 'the maggots out of my brain.' I am not uselessly depressed as when a[t] home."[123] Even Ann realized that it was depression that caused her symptoms, and flight was a temporary defense against it. Once she felt better, she would write for Gerrit to come and visit her. "If you should come down [to New York City] Ellie has a nice room for you."[124]

Gerrit viewed Ann's cure-seeking with contempt. "I trust we shall hear tomorrow that you have entered upon some curative process—+ that you will be in a few weeks… 'all right'," he wrote her in 1867.[125] Gerrit thought that except for the "maggots in her brain," she had been alright all along.

Ann herself said, "Darling, do not feel anxious about my health. I do not suffer more than I can bear. I am only 'comfortably sick'…."[126]

In her efforts to become less "comfortably sick," Ann became the "runaway wife." She spent many months and dollars trying exercise programs and water cures, and even became enamored of the use of something new: electricity. "We are more + more impressed with the wonders of electricity," Elizabeth wrote to her father. "One current coagulates, another thins the blood. It cures cancers."[127] Of course, none of these "cures" alleviated the source of Ann's depression, and she seemed to realize that. Her sister, Elizabeth Birney, told Gerrit, "I do not think she has much faith in the water cure with regard to herself."[128] But she kept trying.

To be sure, Ann did have some actual physiological problems, and psychological and physiological therapies were primitive in the mid-19th century. Even being "comfortably sick" could be life-threatening. Over the years, Ann experienced a few relatively minor ailments: teeth that had to be pulled and frequent bowel problems.[129] But the physical issue that plagued her for years was a problem in one of her eyes.

When her symptoms first appeared in early 1861, she went to New York City for treatment. The symptoms included pain and "smarting" when she moved her eye, which made reading difficult;[130] and "inflamation" and "hot tears" that ran from the eye.[131] These symptoms matched the disease 'iritis', in which eye tissues "become sensitized to a protein…, usually bacterial in the body. Attacks occur… when the toxic agent comes in contact with the sensitized iris tissue…. The eyeball is tender to touch and movement…. Pain in and around the eye is sometimes exquisite."[132]

Whatever the syndrome was, it flared up periodically, causing Ann much pain and aggravation. While undergoing eye treatments in March of 1861, she also got the mumps,[133] but she felt well enough by the end of March to think about returning home.[134]

Her daughter Elizabeth was eternally concerned about the state of her mother's mental and physical health, and she stayed with Ann through the winter in the city. Years later she wrote to Gerrit about Ann:

> "Always sick and weak, [mother] has not for years
> been able to say for an hour, 'I have no pain"…+

with her physical suffering is the trial of being
separated from you + knowing… how you mourn
her absence. The great expense also pains her…."[135]

In fact, Ann's last extended trip away from home and Gerrit was
for treatment of her eye. She visited her niece, Ellen Walter, in New
York City on October 16, 1874. Ellen wrote, "Aunt slept very well +
after lunch we took a carriage + searched for Dr. Knapp—finding
him at his office at last on 26 W 24th St."[136] Ellen wrote to Gerrit
regarding Ann's health nearly every day for the rest of October, and
less frequently during November and December.

"Aunt longs to get better that she may go home to
you…. She feels that if she had 2 weeks more it
would make a favorable change in her eye…. As
soon as her eye is free from pain she will act on the
reasonable suggestion of your head + heart."[137]

By November it was clear to Ann that she would need to stay
much longer. She wrote to Gerrit, "The necessity of remaining longer
from you gives me more pain than my eye."[138] Gerrit was feeling
physically well at home in Peterboro and he challenged Ann: "I…
fear that your eye is not to be restored under your present treatment."[139] When he suggested that she change doctors, Ellen warned
him that such remarks only upset Ann's mental state and retarded
her improvement.[140] Just before Christmas, Gerrit traveled to New
York City to be with Ann for the holidays. He died of a stroke there
on Dec. 28, 1874.

The effect of Gerrit's death on Ann shows a great deal about their
religious beliefs, and about the intensity of their relationship. Less
than three months later, on March 11, 1875, the *Oneida Democratic
Union* printed the following piece of news:

"Mrs. Gerrit Smith died at the family mansion in
Peterboro, on Saturday morning last…. Her death,
though sudden, was not unexpected. She has

survived her husband but a short time and finally
died upon the day which would have been her
husband's 78th birthday had he lived."[141]

This news item, and other elements of research, have produced
an interpretation from this author that former writers on the Smith
family either never had, or at least never wrote about. Although what
follows is partly undocumented speculation, it seems relatively clear
that Ann Carroll Fitzhugh Smith committed suicide.

Her death is officially recorded in the 1875 census of the Town
of Smithfield Deaths as follows: "Ann L. [probably a misread 'F.']
Smith age 70F., widow, March 6, [born in] Maryland, Peritonitis."
The speculation of suicide can be supported by a number of hints in
the news article quoted above. First, her death was "sudden," indicating that she was not ill from any disease that posed an immediate
threat to her life. She died "at the family mansion in Peterboro,"
not in a hospital where treatments might have been administered.
Death occurred in the "morning," as if something might have been
planned during the previous day or night. And, most importantly,
she died on her husband's 78th birthday. Perhaps after a life spent so
often apart from him, she gave to her beloved husband the ultimate
birthday present: she went to meet him.

The beliefs of Ann and Gerrit regarding death are important to
survey here, and they lend support to the speculation of suicide.
These beliefs appear in the family's poetry, which is wonderfully
expressive of mutual emotion. Ann spoke of her love for Gerrit as
possessing
> "A deathlessness, which not the things to come—
> Nor past nor present—neither time nor space
> Can take away—because it is of Grace."[142]

Gerrit worried over Ann's readiness to die.
> "Yes, now I am sure that you do wish to die,
> Since you keep no account of your years, as they fly;

You even forget, that, on this very day,
Fifty years of your life, for aye, fled away."
"My dear wife is not only always willing, but sometimes impatient to die."[143]

Ann showed no fear of death, as did Gerrit. He wondered whether there was even an afterlife, but she did not. For most of their lives, however, their Christian beliefs supported the notion that they could plan on an eternity together in Heaven. As Gerrit said,
"But short or long, or swift or slow,
The life we're living here below,
No difference makes to those who have
A hope of life beyond the grave."[144]

As they aged, their thoughts about life after death became more frequent. For their 25th anniversary, Gerrit wrote,
"Oh yes, we must die—but our love will not die—
Of what is so heavenly, death's not the doom:
The love that now joins us, will join us on high,
Increasing in vigor—immortal in bloom"[145]

Their frequent and prolonged separations were a source of anguish for both Ann and Gerrit, but they knew that after death, they could not be parted.
"We may not here in earth, my love,
Much longer walk together;
But when we reach the goal above,
We'll then be parted never."[146]

And to Gerrit, "life" might even be better there.
"But far more pleasant will it be
Upon that shore that ever shineth
By no weak love now twined are we
But stronger love in Heaven twineth."[147]

So they did, indeed, look forward to even a better life, one in which they would live forever in loving peace, and would also be reunited with loved ones who had died earlier.

"But the thought that we soon shall meet them on high
Makes our sorrows but light, makes it pleasant to die."[149]

They expected to do it together. Their relationship had been a close one for decades, and they saw no reason why that should change.

"Oh abreast may we live! And abreast may we die:
Abreast may we enter the mansions on high."[150]

Ann made their deaths as close to "abreast" as she could, but she had some business to take care of as she planned ahead for that very special day. In February of 1875, she wrote inquiries to two publications received by Gerrit regarding unpaid charges due. They both responded that there were none.[151] Ann paid to Gerrit's nephew John Cochrane $2620.75 to close past debts.[152] To Hamilton College she paid one hundred fifty dollars due, which Gerrit had pledged on a portrait of President Backus.[153] By early March, Ann had tied the loose ends of life and was ready to meet Gerrit. As a last jolt, she had probably read the poem that Gerrit had left behind for her on what would have been their fifty-third anniversary:

"Fifty-three years today
The parson did say
To fast yoke me with Ann....
A prise fell to me then
That doth rare fall to men,
In long ages of time.
'Twas a woman in face
But an angel in grace
And in wisdom sublime.

Ann! I beg you stay here
For many a blest year,

If your husband remain.
For whene're you shall die,
You will go up so high,
He'll ne're see you again."[154]

She knew, of course, that Gerrit's instructions to stay "if your husband remain" did not apply, as he had gone first; so she felt free and ready to go. The question now becomes, how did she do it?

The speculation is that during the evening of March 5, 1875, Ann consumed a large dose of arsenic that would, within 24 hours, produce symptoms of peritonitis. The setting would have been nearly perfect: the family and the hired help had retired early. It was March, with darkness arriving by 7 p.m. After retreating to her bedroom, she probably prayed, talked with Gerrit, and took the poison.

The night would have been one of excruciating pain, with death coming probably by noon on March 6, Gerrit's birthday.

Arsenic was available around most houses and barns in 1875. It was useful in veterinary medicine for treatment of large animals, "(1) to expel worms in the horse, with action also as a digestive tonic by stimulating the muscles of the alimentary canal; (2) as a nerve tonic in asthma, chorea, and epilepsy;...(4) in combination with salts of iron in anemia and general debility.... Arsenic is sometimes given to horses in the hope that it will improve their condition...."[155] It probably improved the condition of horses by killing trypanosomes, a blood parasite that caused sleeping sickness.[156]

Arsenic also was, in the mid-19th century, a common element used in small doses in many households. In compounds, its highly acidic and poisonous action killed bacteria. It was used in a "green salve" form for the cleansing of external wounds, and in a saturated solution as a cure for fever.[157] It was consumed internally as "Fowler's Solution" for a stimulant effect on the nervous system, and was thought to improve appetite and digestion.[158]

They used arsenic then as we today use antibiotics. It killed life forms, and in small doses might kill disease organisms. There are also reports of people using it in large doses in order to commit suicide.[159] When used according to prescription, it probably had beneficial effects, but it was well-documented even then that "arsenic at high doses kills cells immediately...."[160]

The list of arsenic use in humans is long. In the past, it was considered useful in the treatment of asthma, actinomycosis (an inflammatory disease), aspengillosis (disease caused by mold fungus), chlorosis (iron deficiency anemia), Hodgkin's disease (inflammation of lymph nodes), Kala-anemias, trypanosomiosis (sleeping sickness), and tuberculosis.[161]

Interestingly, arsenic is finding new uses in the twenty-first century as treatment for acute myelogenous leukemia. As one journal put it, "The drug seems to act by telling cancerous cells to commit suicide." Clinical trials are also underway to test arsenic as a therapeutic agent in other blood-related cancers.[162]

Symptoms of arsenic use would have included diarrhea, kidney failure, elevated liver function, swelling of the extremities, "violent purging, ...and death in a variable time when a large amount has been taken, ...[depending] on the presence or otherwise of food in the digestive system."[163] Ann could easily have planned the timing of her death.

The diagnosis of peritonitis as the cause of Ann's death was probably accurate. Peritonitis produces a visible inflammation of the abdominal area due to infection and fluid accumulation. The direct cause is the transfer of bacteria from the intestinal tract to the abdominal cavity, infecting the serous lining of that cavity—the peritoneum. The acidic shock of a large dose of arsenic would rupture the digestive system, releasing bacteria into the peritoneal area. The most common causes of it are appendicitis and diverticulitis—outpockets on the intestinal wall that burst. Ann most likely developed Diffuse Septic Peritonitis, "described as massive contamination of the peritoneal cavity,"[164] and died in a matter of a few hours.

Before modern research into the bacterial causes of disease (1860-present), physicians dreaded the diagnosis of abdominal infections because of the certainty of death. Previous to 1895, the fatality rate for perforation of the intestine was one hundred percent. The germ theory of infections was not understood until 1863, and conclusive evidence of the action of bacteria in causing and compounding infections was not published until 1878. Initial investigations of the workings of the peritoneal cavity were begun in 1863, with understandings of its physiology being published in 1876.[165] Successful operations on patients with a perforated ulcer or colon were not performed until 1880, and it was not until 1893 that it was understood that "peritonitis was a multimicrobial infection and that anaerobic bacteria played a pivotal role."

In fact, the exact bacteriology of peritonitis was first reported in 1922.[166] Steeb reported that "the most common organisms responsible for the production of peritonitis have been identified as Escherichia coli and Bacteroides species.... We now understand that when bacteria are released into the peritoneal cavity, complement activation occurs."[167]

Various bacteria interact synergistically, and, as they die, release toxins that dissolve body cells, thereby releasing histamine. The histamine reduces blood pressure and stimulates gastric secretions that abnormally enlarge fluid ducts, thereby allowing fluids normally confined within duct walls to shift into the peritoneal cavity. "In addition to synergism, the infectious potential of bacteria is enhanced by feces...." Once this invasion occurs, "positive blood cultures can be demonstrated in less than 12 minutes.... If the contamination was massive or if the contamination was ongoing, then the host mechanisms [for defense] within the peritoneal cavity can be overcome and the septic [infective] state ensues."[168]

Probably the reason that this speculation—that Ann committed suicide—has not surfaced before is because of the stigma against a person or family inherent in the notion of suicide. It is likely that people close to Ann—Betsey Kelty and Elizabeth Smith Miller— knew what she had done, but did not want it to become public information. Elizabeth, after all, had worked to purge notions of treason relative to the Harpers Ferry incident from Frothingham's first edition of her father's biography. In her mother's case, she found the diagnosis of peritonitis to be socially acceptable—and a welcome alternative to the truth.

Gerrit Smith's family relationships were good. He was beloved as a husband, father, uncle, and grandfather. His attitude toward his family was kind and accommodating, and even when it hurt, he usually let them pursue their own desires. Perhaps the Smith family legacy was best summed up by Gerrit's sometime adversary and friend William Lloyd Garrison, as he wrote to Elizabeth Smith Miller shortly after Ann's death:

> "The one being called away, the other could not
> remain behind. What delightful remembrances
> they awaken. Such a home as they presented, with
> its glowing affection and unstinted hospitality,
> has been seldom seen on earth. I know of none
> comparable to it. The spot will ever be a hallowed
> one."[169]

- 9 -

Friendship, Recreation, Health, and Balance

A look at the personal side of Gerrit Smith would not be complete without a look at his relationships with a wide variety of friends. Although many prominent social reformers visited his home, he chose friends who were humble. Pompous dignitaries, statesmen, and powerful executives attracted less interest from Gerrit than did humble working people.

Ira Hills, a farmer in Vernon Center, New York, admired Smith's benevolence for years, and wrote him a letter recognizing his defense of a runaway slave. Gerrit annotated the letter, "I shall always regard the writer as one of the best of men. He is a plain farmer, + is 80 years old.... God give me many friends like this friend."[1] Several years later, Gerrit still maintained affection for Hills, even though he was "sinning." He annotated an 1868 letter,

> "There are few men on the earth whom I so much
> esteem + love. He is about 89 years old. His wife
> is living, tho' he is carrying on a sort of courtship
> with Nellie who is 86. His letter to me... before
> this gently... reproved me for voting for Grant."[2]

After friends moved from Peterboro, they often still fondly remembered Smith. Neale Eastman had once had a small business in a shop almost in front of Gerrit's house. In 1869, he wrote from Missouri:

> "It is high time for us old men who have lived and
> struggled through good report and bad report,

who have been slandered and maligned, battered
and… resented, on whom ignorance and prejudice
have visited their [power], to enjoy ourselves, to
comfort one another, to lay aside our Dignity and
become little children…."

Eastman deplored divisions created between people by money,
and he praised Smith for working to create equality across social
and economic barriers.[3]

Edwin Morton, who had tutored Greene Smith in Peterboro in
the 1850s, spoke of Gerrit in an 1866 letter.

"Many happy returns of yr March birthday. I do
not think the month seems quite so bleak and
forbidding when we associate yr hearty and genial
presence with it. I think yr friends hold you a good
offset to March."[4]

One of Gerrit's wonderful qualities was that even when friends
turned against him, he would often react gently and avoid confrontation. John Curtis, for instance, had accused Gerrit of firing his
business clerks because they differed with him on moral questions.
The real reason was economic, so Smith counseled Curtis,

"Believing… that you will come to see, that the evil
things, which are now said of me, are slanders, I
entreat you, because I love you… not to increase
the part, which you have had in giving circulation
to the evil reports in question."[5]

A person's opinions did not matter to Gerrit when it came to
friendship. He could disagree with another on an issue, try to change
the opposing opinion, get into active arguments about it, and still
perceive and treat that other person as a friend. In 1844, he wrote
to B. B. Stewart, "I beseech you to examine this new doctrine of
ours—that a man cannot be the friend of those in whose view he

sees, or thinks he sees, errors."[6]

A good example of Smith's tolerance was a dispute that developed with his friend, Beriah Green, in early 1850. Green was an abolitionist who operated a Christian school near Utica that received Gerrit's enthusiastic moral and financial support.[7] Smith admired Green so much that he had named his son, Greene, after him. Beriah Green valued their friendship highly, saying,

> "I speak as a friend to a friend. And if I say some
> things which may seem unduly frank + unguarded,
> I think I shall find indulgence in your candor +
> charity."[8]

Ten years later, they had a strong political disagreement. The issue was whether the general public could effect the greatest good. Smith trusted in the masses, while Green believed that an enlightened aristocracy should rule. Green rejected not only Smith's idea, but their friendship as well, saying, "A 'genuine friendship' between us cannot exist." Smith responded:

> "I have just received your honest, faithful +
> therefore welcome letter. I love you not the less
> but the more for it. I have done wrong, and you
> manfully tell me so…. I never loved + confided
> in you more than I do at this moment—never felt
> more like honoring you before the world for the
> soundness of your head and heart."[9]

When Green continued to protest their friendship, Gerrit told him, "You may cast me off, but I shall never cast you off."[10] In his effort to maintain their friendship, Smith invited Green to his home in Peterboro and to the Anti-Fugitive Slave Law Convention in Cazenovia in August of 1850—even though Green had told him that he wished to cut off all correspondence. Smith wrote,

> "I eagerly seize upon an occasion to assure you
> that I still love and honor you, and that no ill

opinions you form of me shall have the effect, to change the good opinions of you, which I expect to carry with me into eternity."[11]

Smith was loyal to his friends in the face of rejection because he was less concerned with what they thought of him than he was with what he thought of them.

As stated in earlier chapters, Gerrit's best friend was his wife, Ann. In a touching statement about the quality of their relationship, he talked of both liking her and loving her. He wrote in 1832,

"I love to be employed in communicating my thoughts and feelings to one who is interested in my thoughts and feelings—to the dearest friend with whose earthly destinies God has so kindly linked my own, that dearest friend with whom I have spent ten peaceful, happy, blessed years, + from whom, I hope, not even death shall separate me."[12]

Smith did not have much leisure time. His "recreation" was usually solitary, and it often involved business-like activities such as writing. He spent so much of his time on business and reform that he had little available for fun; he spent what leisure time he could muster on a wide variety of activities with no focus on any one in particular. He once wrote to a minister, "You wish me, when I have 'a leisure hour,' to give you my views on certain subjects. But, my dear Sir, 'a leisure hour' is such a thing, as I do not have."[13]

Smith spent hours daily answering his business mail. As his daughter commented: "We fancy you so busy with your pen that you are quite independent of your surroundings."[14]

Yet he did consider writing to his family to be a type of recreation. To Ann he wrote, "I impose a little leisure to go on with my letter."[15]

One leisure activity for the Smiths was the entertaining of guests at home. As a part of both their business and their philanthropy, they had frequent dinner parties. Gerrit wrote in a letter about one large dinner party for which the guest list numbered 68.[16] While living in Washington, D.C. for about a year, Gerrit did much home-based entertaining. "I believe according to Lizzie's list, about 300 have eaten in our house—99 of them members of Congress."[17]

Back in Peterboro, one of Gerrit's major avocations was the welfare of those in need. His leisure activity involved seeking ways to aid orphans, runaway slaves, the poor, and the sick. He donated money, land, and even houses to local people, prompting the comment by one resident, "He rides and walks every pleasant day, and is round the village, ministering, as usual, to the wants of the sick and poor."[18] Even Smith's business clerk commented, "The poor + middling classes of the people love to deal with me for the reason that you have dealt very kindly with them + they think I will be somewhat so."[19]

Unless they had something to do with reform, Smith was not attracted to community activities. He does mention, on one occasion, watching a dance.

> "Last evening, there was a very happy dance in the Bird House. I witnessed it for 20 minutes. Mr. Dixwell saw the whole of it, + even went so far as to shuffle his own aged feet…. Nannie's cup of joy was full…. Little Gatty [was] prettily dressed."[20]

Because Ann loved the opera, she would occasionally get Gerrit to go. "Ma + I have finished Fantasia. When we go to [the city] next week I will try to see… Les Miserables."[21]

Gerrit did enjoy some recreation on his estate. It had gravel paths leading from the house to the garden, the Bird House, and the brook, and he enjoyed walks around the property. Near the house was a croquet court where he "daily during the summer months, was accustomed to play a game or two."[22]

Because he hired workers to keep up the estate, it is unclear how much gardening he did, but when he took time for it, he enjoyed it.

The household expense records indicate the purchase of garden seeds
and tools every spring, and he did report to Ann on working at it.

> "It is a beautiful day, + I have improved it in
> diligent labor in the garden. Neither the eggplant
> nor [pepper?] seeds came up. I think we shall have
> an abundance of cauliflower + tomatoes + celery
> …+ cabbages. The grape tomato looks very well.
> The gooseberries… are bearing well. The winter
> was too hard for the raspberries—tho, I trust, they
> will yield many quarts."[23]

He was proud of his gardening work. "It is cold weather. Our
garden is very backward—tho, now since I have taken it in hand, it
may come on better."[24]

In all, the time Smith spent on recreation was minimal. He never
developed a love for a particular sport or game, such as hunting or
fishing, and was never a member of an organized team. He did enjoy
riding, but he depended on others to care for the horses. Ann told her
daughter in 1864, "Father keeps up his riding. He + Willie have just
started on the white horses."[25] His main interests in life were work
and philanthropy, the one employed to support the other.

The most regular exercise he got was his daily walks. "I believe,"
he wrote in 1839 "that I have not failed to take my mile + a half
walk every day…."[26] Sometimes he used his walking time to visit
the sick. "I have just taken my daily walk. The measled children are
all doing well."[27]

Even winter weather did not stop his routine. "I found my mile +
a half walk this afternoon thru deep snow drifts + against the wind
quite fatiguing. Even my long boots failed to keep out the snow."[28]
While living at The Grove, Smith walked the one and one quarter
miles to and from his land office daily.[29] He noted later in his last
few months of life that he still took daily walks.[30]

It was difficult to maintain good health in the 1800s. If you were
fortunate, good health would roll your way; the odds, however, were

against it. So it was in Peterboro: many letters of the era spoke of health problems, and the infant/childhood mortality rate was quite high. In 1824, Ann expressed to Gerrit her deep concern over the local epidemic of smallpox.[31] Measles were also common. Gerrit wrote to Ann in 1839,

> "The measles are very prevalent in our village. 7 of
> Mr. Davis' children are now sick with the disease.
> I was in there a couple of hours ago. His house is
> like a hospital."[32]

Scarlet fever caused the deaths of a number of children in Peterboro and may have been the reason 5-year-old Nannie Smith died in 1835. Beriah Green wrote to Gerrit in 1841, "We have had the scarlet fever to contend with in our family. Iona, Charles + Mary are getting thru; Ruth is now sick with it."[33]

People frequently suffered from "disordered bowels," probably from drinking unclean water. John B. Edwards warned Gerrit to beware as he prepared for a trip: "I hope the Lord will preserve you in your Journey. It is somewhat perrilous to travel in this colera time."[34]

Peterboro resident Henry Campbell wrote to his sister, "There has been a deal of sickness from Typhus Fever and a number of people have died this winter." Also, the diary of an unknown Peterboro resident between March and October 1863 documents the deaths of seven children from diphtheria, and three other persons from consumption (now known as tuberculosis).[35]

Questions have arisen about Gerrit Smith's mental health, but there is no conclusive evidence of mental instability over the long term. The public, and some historians, often considered radical reformers to be mad. The reformers' visions of reality were often different from the norm, and because they believed in the need for immediate change—as Smith did—people more readily interpreted their radicalism as imbalance. Perhaps some were afraid to see what the reformers saw, because they were the beneficiaries of social injustice. In that case, they might well consider those who would take away those benefits to be abnormal. On another level, the reformers' dreams of spiritualism and communalism, for which they fought through political and social change, made them seem "out of touch." The establishment defended itself by labeling the reformers as psychotics.

Smith's wealth added fuel to this fire. Many thought that only a fool would sacrifice such a high amount of his own resources to help blacks, or women, or the poor. Gerrit Smith must, therefore, have had psychological problems. For the most part this was untrue; still, he did experience some physiological problems that are worthy of mention.

Smith had a rational attitude toward physical disease. He wrote, "Diseases of the body are good for us if we but allow them to remind us that we are mortal, + must soon leave this world."[36] In October of 1857 he traveled to New York City in an attempt to borrow money to help him through a recession. While there, he contracted typhoid fever.[37] After one month of treatment, he appeared to be getting well, but had a "severe relapse" that required another month of treatment before he could return home.[38] This illness probably made him susceptible to some other diseases that followed, such as "dropsy" (congestive heart failure), "dyspepsia" (indigestion), and a "heart complaint."[39]

Colds were also a problem for him, especially in the spring.[40] Although they were frustrating and taxed his energy, he kept on working. He wrote to Greene in 1853, "My health has been quite broken for the last month by colds.... I am sick and very weak all this time, though I go daily to the office."[41] And in 1868 he reported to Ann, "I have been quite sick today [with a] heavy cold.... I slept 4 hours last night. I had hardly strength enough to leave my bed. After breakfast I went to Morrisville to read proof sheets."[42]

John B. Edwards noted in 1854 that Smith tended to heal rapidly. "I... hope that you will soon get over the effects of the heavy cold that you have taken. You generally soon recover from the effects of a cold."[43]

One problem that bothered Smith as he grew old was his frequent nosebleeds and occasional sudden attacks of headache followed by forgetfulness.[44] These symptoms might have been precursors to a stroke, and he worried that he would someday die of one.

Back pain also annoyed him periodically. One episode occurred in November of 1839. "I... stepped into a hole + hurt my back very much," he wrote Ann.[45] Three days later, "My back has felt very well... today. No pain, except [when] I assume an unusual position." And by November 30, "My back feels very comfortably."[46] This sounds like lordosis, the problem many people have stemming from curvature of the lower spine. Flare-ups of pain generally last only a few days.

Smith frequently complained of a "disordered bowel," for which his brother, Peter Skenandoah, had a unique remedy.

> "It is this: to pass my hand in rapid 'friction passes' over the extreme lower section of the 'spinal column'— say from a little above the fundamental orifice to the height of 6 inches above it or thereabouts. This artificial excitability has often relieved me without recourse to... medicinal remedies."[47]

It probably would have been better to drink clean water.

Hemorrhoids also afflicted Gerrit for most of his adult life. In 1835, he told his daughter, "I... have been confined to my bed room nearly all the time since you left us with my old complaint of Piles."[48] The associated pain made it difficult for him to sit, so he stayed in bed.

Smith underwent an operation for the affliction in Albany on February 18, 1836. Ann stayed there with him for two weeks while he recovered. She wrote, "Gerrit suffers much pain, but still, he is as comfortable as could be expected."[49] Evidently, the operation was not very successful; the complaint continued off and on for two decades.[50]

Friends made some novel suggestions for remedy. When going to the toilet, wrote one, "Take... a mug, or pot, of hot water, dip a tallow candle into it, so as to melt the candle somewhat, and then insert the candle; this repeated effects a cure."[51]

Or, suggested another, "make a strong decoction of Mullen and Flax seed and take about three wine glass full each day and every other day an injection of the same and every few days a few pills of Burgundy pitch."[52] Gerrit did purchase a "self injecting instrument," so maybe he actually tried some of these ideas.[53]

Probably no cure worked, because over the next two decades, he mentioned the same "local ailment" in a series of letters.[54] John B. Edwards wrote in 1853, "I am sorry that you are again afflicted with piles." "I hope that surgical operation that you are to undergo this day will be successful in relieving you the ailment."[55] By August of that year, Edwards could say, "I am glad to learn that you are in good health again."[56]

Perhaps Angelina Grimké Weld suggested the most interesting remedy for piles. "Does the Horse chestnut tree grow in your region," she asked, " + have you ever heard that simply carrying one in your pocket will cure you of that disease which has distressed you so long?"[57] The tree search may have commenced immediately, but the ailment persisted.

Another persistent ailment that caused Smith much anxiety was a problem with his eyes. In late 1842, he first noticed "mists and specks before my eyes" that impaired his vision.[58] He received his first diagnosis from an "Oculist [who] is sure that the disease is inflammatory rheumatism—and he is quite confident, that I shall regain my sight perfectly."[59] Smith feared that he had cataracts and would go blind, so he sought a second opinion from another ophthalmologist. "I went to see Dr. Wallace, a distinguished oculist.... He examined my eye with magnifying glasses... + pronounced it entirely free from all tendencies to cataract."

But Dr. Wallace did believe that Gerrit had some form of eye disease.

"He came to my room...+ took from my temple
a large tumbler entirely full of blood. Tonight, a

large blister is to be applied immediately above the
eye. He thinks I shall be cured, because the disease
is taken in an early stage."[60]

The next day Dr. Wallace applied more blistering compound and
recommended that Gerrit consult another doctor.[61] A year later, as
the problem persisted, Smith received another professional opinion.
"Dr. W[arner] examined my eyes very carefully, and saw no defect
in them. He pronounced the disease purely nervous...."[62]

It is possible that hysteria induced the eye "disease." The years
1842 and 1843 were ones in which Smith was fearful of going into
bankruptcy. He had borrowed heavily at high interest during a severe
depression, and he felt guilty that he had to abate his philanthropy.
As he became more anxious, he experienced physiological symptoms
for which physicians could find no organic cause.

Smith saw two more doctors—Cox and Delafield—both of whom
thought that he would not get well with the use of medicines.[63] For
the next few years, the symptoms of his eye disease came and went
intermittently. On one occasion, he admitted that his eyesight problem was "much affected by a nervous affliction."[64] After the economic
depression passed and profits from his land business improved, so
did his eyesight.

Smith had two occasions in his life when stress induced physiological symptoms of illness. One was the eye problem in the early
1840s caused by financial stress; the other was a brief psychotic
episode that occurred in late 1859 after he had played a pivotal role
in John Brown's raid on Harpers Ferry. In both cases, he was temporarily under severe stress and later emerged in a healthy state.

Previous biographers have tended to judge Gerrit's overall mental
health on these serious, but brief, periods of stress. This, of course,
is unfair; by such a standard, most of us might be labeled as psychotic. Those who knew Smith intimately said that, although he was
occasionally sick, he usually disregarded the effects of the illness so
that he could continue his work.[65] Stress was not the cause of most

of Gerrit Smith's health problems. In early 1840, he contracted a urinary tract infection that was painful and debilitating. He wrote to his abolitionist friend, Lewis Tappan: "I have been confined for upwards of five weeks by a serious disease in the bladder and ure-thra + consequent swelling in the scrotum."[66] Ann noted, "He has lost flesh a good deal, and suffers much from want of exercise.... He stays in the parlor all day sitting in the rocking chair and lying on the sofa."[67]

The infection persisted through the summer,[68] and in the fall, he underwent surgery in Philadelphia. "I returned home last evening, having been confined several weeks in Philadelphia by a surgical operation, which promises to be entirely successful."[69]

In November 1840, he returned to Philadelphia for a follow-up operation. These operations appear not to have been completely successful, as he went again to Philadelphia in February and March of 1841 for further treatment. "My local ailments have become such that... I must give up the transaction of business until I get relief."[70] Apparently he finally was relieved of this infection. Nothing more appears in his correspondences until late 1846 and early 1847, and this could have been the continuing problem with piles.[71]

Smith's biographers have portrayed him as a nervous hypochon-driac. When he was sick, he did express intense concerns about his illness—and legitimately so. Even minor infections could be life-threatening in the 1800s, so such concerns did not reflect un-due anxiety. Even in the case of his eye "disease," he mused, "Why, heavens, should I fear? If I love God, the disease is a mercy + will work for my good."[72] This does not sound like high-anxiety-based hypochondria.

Later in Smith's life, some of the chronic health problems as-sociated with aging appeared. His personal physician, Dr. John P. Gray, advised him in 1869 to work less and rest more, and to "use the anodyne... at night as may be necessary" to sooth the mind.[73] Fatigue was common for both Gerrit and Ann, for which Dr. Gray advised them, "Brace up on some good leaf tea with a little good brandy in it."[74] On November 27, 1873, Dr. Gray sent Gerrit two bottles of brandy to relieve his fatigue. For problems with digestion, Gray prescribed lactic acid combined with wine, and suggested that Gerrit eat more meat and fewer vegetables.[75]

Gerrit experienced other aging problems. In 1873 he noted, "My failing sight makes me too tired to travel. 'Stay home!' is my... motto."[76] As the winter of 1873 approached, Ann wanted to leave Peterboro, but she felt trapped by her ailing husband. "That spare bed room! My flesh + heart long to repose there for a little time at least," she wrote to Greene's wife. "But dear father cannot be left at home + cannot go from home so there it ends."[77]

Perhaps the most telling of the symptoms of aging was the occasional episode of vertigo, the sensation of dizziness. In 1873, a friend named David Plumb wrote to Gerrit that having received a complex letter from him "gave evidence that your vertigo had at least abated."[78] But by January 4, 1874, Plumb wrote, "I was grieved to hear by Miss Kelty's letter that you had been and was still suffering from that distressing sensation of vertigo. I hope it is not a precursor of anything worse." It probably was; before the year ended, Gerrit Smith would die of a stroke.

In his later years, Gerrit showed some measure of satisfaction and accomplishment. In an address to the New York State Anti-Secret Society Convention in Syracuse on November 16, 1870, he spoke of an emerging new age of humanity as social "wrongs" were righted. Slavery had been abolished and a women's rights movement was underway. He saw his life as a "testimony against such wrongs as imprisonment for debt, slavery, dramselling, land monopoly, war, secret societies, and the injustice done to woman." He felt the urge to continue the reforms, but he was tired. "I have ever been interested in reforms," he said, "but I must not allow my interest... to extend so far, as to impose additional burdens upon my old age."[79]

"By the way," he said in late 1872, "are there not a few persons left to revive the Anti-Dramshop Party...? But the work to this end must be performed by younger persons."[80]

Smith's cousin, Elizabeth Cady Stanton, noticed one bothersome change in his habits in old age. Having visited friends, she said,

> "I told them all about the kins of Peterboro, all
> the charming points in your character, your
> purity, innocence, + etc., but said nothing of your
> profanity which was too painful for me to hear
> without ever repeating. Alas! Alas! That in the
> mature age of seventy six you should have fallen
> into such a vice. May your…angel help you to
> retrace your steps, to the chaste, polished diction
> of your earlier years when I used to look up to you
> with awe + worship as the noblest man God ever
> made."[81]

Gerrit Smith was no saint. Although he did much good, he also made some horrible blunders that hurt other people. Some of these we have seen—for instance, his relationship with his two sons; some others are yet to be covered. And although he was mentally stable, on at least two occasions he experienced neurotic or psychotic problems. The point is, overall he was a balanced person, and that balance deserves attention.

'Balance' here refers to a mental state in which seeming opposites are reconciled. For balance to be achieved within an individual, that individual must be able to know opposing sides of the self, and eliminate potential dissonance by finding a harmonious counterpoise of forces. With the potential clash of opposites thus controlled, stability results, allowing adjustment to nearly any contingency. For one person to perceive another's balance, that first individual must see all sides of the other person—or risk making judgments based on incomplete information.

Newspaper reports and, later, some biographies created Smith's public image based on only one side of him. People came to believe he was a bigoted fanatic or a loving philanthropist—with no clear notion that he was actually both. Reporters and interviewers were most interested in relaying their *knowledge* of a person rather than their *feelings* about a person. Because feelings about a person develop slowly over time as one sees all sides, fragmented knowledge relayed in brief reports can only show one side of that person.

Smith's poor reputation, therefore, grew from what people read. They perceived hypocrisy because they thought that Smith should be different—more complex—than he appeared to be. Smith was complex, but seeing only one side of him bred perceptions of imbalance. Only seeing both sides of the whole can lead to compassion and feelings of understanding of oneself or of others.

The person who knows both sides of the self and can accept both as real can be stable with low anxiety, because nothing contradicts what one believes should be. When this internal balance exists, self-love is inevitable, and love of others—all others—becomes possible. Love grows out of seeing both sides and sensing their integration in a yin-and-yang type of equilibrium in which opposites can complement rather than contradict one another.

If one cannot resolve the opposites in oneself, then one cannot love oneself. One feels unbalanced, guilty, anxious, and angry, and needs to create enemies who can be lashed out at and blamed for the dissonance. Scapegoating is a defense mechanism that saves face, but not health. It obscures understanding and produces an unenlightened rationalization of prejudice.

One can legitimately describe the balanced person, as perceived within oneself or in others, in terms of opposites. Gerrit Smith was indeed a benevolent fool, a bigoted philanthropist, a belligerent pacifist, and a loving absolutist. As an uncommon common man, he lived in elegant simplicity and practiced pious consumption. He was a simply complicated wise fool who became, in some cases, a benevolent despot.

This description of Smith does not besmirch his character, but fully recognizes his wholeness. His long-time abolitionist friend, Samuel Ringgold Ward, recognized this dichotomy when he recommended in 1848 that persons interested in fostering change in interracial attitudes vote for that "unpractical and truly practical philanthropist Gerrit Smith."[82] Smith perceived these qualities in himself, and, therefore, believed that they—or something like them—existed in others. That projection allowed him to love anyone, regardless of which small piece of them he actually knew. He was emancipated from bias and suspicion, could be tolerant of divergent opinions, and was quick to let go of anger. When a client accused him of bribery but then recanted, Smith responded, "I have no more complaint to make of your charges that I sought to... bribe you. Let all that pass away forever."[83] He could feel good in spite of accusations against him because his armor of self-perceived balance protected him. When his business clerk, Federal Dana, accused him of being insensitive and intolerant in releasing him, Smith replied, "The responsibility of this belief is wholly yours... +... I refuse to take any blame to it for myself."[84]

Many aspects of Gerrit Smith's life reflected this balance. As a nonlinear thinker, he could deal well with the nebulous ideas of freedom, justice, and religion, and see how they might be interlinked. A friend wrote to him,

"How true it is that the virtues are all kindred....
While laboring to break the chains of slavery...
we are at the same time unconsciously breaking
the equally galling chains of religious intolerance
which bind our own minds + hearts."[85]

Alternately, as a linear thinker, Smith could calculate pennies and record business transactions in detail. When a friend had helped him with some business affairs without compensation, Gerrit asked him to submit a bill anyway: "As you are aware, I am a man of business habits."[86] His outgoing mail was evidence of this balance among styles of thought: letters on moral reform and anti-slavery issues mixed daily with business letters bearing the specifics of dollars and cents.

As evidence of balance in other areas, he could be a member of the American Peace Society, yet advocate and fund violence in Kansas.

He advocated land reform to achieve equity, yet he never completely divested himself of his huge land holdings. He favored women's rights, yet procrastinated in supporting women's suffrage.

While observers interpreted these paradoxes, or seeming inconsistencies, as weakness or vacillation in position, they actually reflected the complex balance of the real Gerrit Smith. Perceiving his own balance helped him maintain both low anger and high optimism. When times were rough, Smith dipped into his reservoir of strength, saying,

"Unto Thy feet, O Savior divine,
I come with my troubled life;
I am so weak, so weary with all
The constant tumult and strife.

Teach me to smile when the way is rough,
And sing when the day grows sad;
Into my heart Thy sunshine put
And make thy tired one glad.

Fill me so full of Thy own pure life
That each day may be lived for Thee;
Then neither the strife, nor the woes of life
Can darken the days for me."[87]

Smith's ability to balance opposites led him to a lifelong interest in moral reform. But, understanding Smith's participation in reform movements requires a careful look at three areas that profoundly influenced his perceptions of reality and his thought patterns: religion, business, and politics.

PART II

Religion, Business, and Politics

The Impact of Religion

Gerrit Smith pointed to the founding of the non-denominational Free Church of Peterboro in 1843 as one of the crowning accomplishments of his life.

He had begun to appreciate the value of religion after a series of stressful events as a young adult. In 1818, at age 21, Gerrit had just obtained his four-year degree from Hamilton College and was considering several career choices when his beloved mother died—just one day after his graduation. His father, who had long rejected and criticized him, now suddenly burdened him with the concerns of a complex business and an estate.

At about the same time, Gerrit married his college sweetheart, only to watch her physically deteriorate and die within seven months. Searching for meaning and love, he remarried—this time to a young woman only 16 years old. All of this happened to Gerrit in a span of three years between late 1818 and early 1822, at a time when he was also feeling the intense concerns that most young men feel as they search for identity and purpose in life. As complex and seemingly unsolvable problems burdened him, along came a simple, easy-to-understand answer that promised relief: religion.

The first three decades of the 19th century were tough times in central New York State. It was still frontier territory, and hardships were common. People hacked out meager livings while facing life-threatening dangers from ill health and native peoples who were often hostile to the transplanted Europeans who had taken over much of their ancestral land. Work consisted of hard labor on farms, canals, railroads, docks and in woodlands, crude factories, and salt mines. The work was strenuous, dangerous, and long, and it spawned some unsavory recreation. Saloons, houses of prostitution, prize fighting rings, and gambling dens catered to the secular attitudes of fun-seeking workers.[1] This lifestyle made fertile ground for the radical Christian revivalists and moral reformers moving westward through the Mohawk Valley between 1800 and 1840. The evangelistic agitation caused many people—Smith included—to worry about their own moral health.

By 1827, Charles Grandison Finney had stirred up central New York with his anti-Calvinist ideas, which meshed well with the culture's developing infatuation with individual power and self-sufficiency. Such new thinking spurred a wave of optimism; the belief that the individual could aspire to altruism replaced the pessimistic concept of predestination. It inspired self-reliance and dependence on pragmatism and reason rather than submission to authority and fate.

As one source put it, those who embraced the radical religion of the time seldom exhibited "profound understanding or trespass[ed] upon the threshold of critical thought."[2] As an easy solution to complex problems, faith in God rooted well in Smith's mind and became a lifelong guide. He was a 'feelings'-oriented person, and without the benefit of psychotherapy, religion became the counsel of choice.

Finney's advice that "All sin consists in selfishness; and all holiness or virtue, in disinterested benevolence" probably guided Smith's attitude concerning what to do with his developing wealth.[3] Evangelistic religion had been part of Smith's early life in his parents' home; Peter loved religious revivals, and as early as 1816, was vice-president of the Madison County Bible Society.[4] Gerrit probably knew Charles Finney by the mid-1820s, and he became a vice-president of the newly formed New York State Tract Society in February of 1824. Long, intense, and emotional revivals were frequent in Peterboro in the 1820s and 1830s, and Gerrit wrote about them in his diary.

There were other reasons he embraced religion. The revivalist movements sweeping New York State kept religion in the forefront of people's thinking. As early as 1824, Gerrit had done a favor for a friend who had thanked him and added,

> "Permit me to express to you on this occasion a
> secret hope that I have long indulged that the time
> is not far distant now when you will see it in your
> way to make a public Dedication of yourself + your
> very useful talents to the service of Christ...."[5]

The greatest pressure put on Smith to declare salvation was from his wife. Throughout 1825, Ann hoped that he would have a conversion experience. As she told her sister,

> "I think it is the wish nearest my heart at present,
> to partake of the 'Lord's supper' in some church...,
> but I am waiting for my dear husband, who I
> hope will before long connect himself with some
> church...."[6]

As Gerrit grew closer to making that commitment, he wrote of the good in his life.

> "I returned home on Saturday morning, and found
> our dear children + all the family in perfect health.
> The great and good Being in whom we trust, and
> to whose Providence we command ourselves +
> ours, had suffered no evil to befal them."[7]

Six months later, on his 29th birthday, Ann told him, "I wish you many happy returns of this day, my dear husband, but with how much more joy would I celebrate it, if it were the anniversary of your spiritual birth."[8]

What Gerrit was about to become caught up in has been labeled the Second Great Awakening, a massive public surge of interest in religion. By 1830, the revival spirit had increased membership in Methodist churches seven times and in Presbyterian churches fourfold. In Baptist and Congregationalist churches, congregations doubled.[9]

This development of religion was in part a response to hard times. The primitive state of medical technology could not counteract the harsh environmental conditions, and epidemics raged. Scalding cloths were the common treatment for pneumonia. Mercury was the prescription for treating fever. Laudanum—a solution of opium in alcohol—was given to headache sufferers.[10] Small wonder that as people searched for meaning and answers, they turned toward religion.

Gerrit gave in to Ann soon after his birthday, and on March 17, 1826, they joined the Presbyterian Church in Peterboro.[11] The Smiths were determined to raise their children as devout Christians, so they practiced a rigorous and pious regimen of home worship. Daily family prayer sessions came near mealtime. Bible reading, Sunday school, and attendance at church were required.[12] They kept records of sermons preached and lessons learned.

Gerrit and Ann had more success with Elizabeth than with Greene in all of this, but for these two young parents, it was a lifelong commitment. Through their faith, they developed a capacity to feel loved and to love others. A sign that said "God is Love" hung over a door in the house, and they taught those around them that if love was what you felt inside of yourself, then you would have a pool of it to give to others.[13] Their religion provided them with solace in times of tragedy and a sense of unity when they were apart.[14]

While religion helped Gerrit understand some of life's complexities, it also gave him a great sense of guilt for his sins: "This Friday evening, my dear wife and I, under a sense of our sins, resolved to spend the following day in fasting and prayer and searchings of heart!" A journal entry for May 7, 1843 read, "I know I'm guilty.... There is no part of my life...on which I look back with complacency.... My sins are already so numerous and aggravated [that] I should not add another to them."

Even near the end of his life, on March 6, 1873, his diary entry read, "I this day complete my seventy-sixth year, and yet, as I feel, my heart is not right in the sight of God." And on May 19, 1874, "[Last] Friday night, my sins pressed heavily upon my conscience, and I got very little sleep."[15] Whether his sins were real or imagined, his pervasive guilt robbed him of some of the enjoyment of life, yet religion also helped him better understand the complexities of both nature and society.

A word about Gerrit's diary, which is quoted often in this text: Its fate is an area of heavy speculation. We know that it was "4[00] to 500 pages" long in 1839,[16] and that he maintained it until his death. Housekeeper Betsey Kelty mentioned that, "The last note in his diary was, 'my dear daughter leaves me today.'"[17] Frothingham used Smith's diary as a resource in the three years following Smith's death. Ralph Harlow knew Gerrit Smith Miller in the 1930s, and he stated that Miller "knew nothing of it."[18] By 1874, it could have involved as much as a thousand pages of manuscript, and it strains credulity to suggest that it would have disappeared without a trace. My guess is that family members destroyed it after Frothingham's research because it contained potentially incriminating evidence concerning the Harpers Ferry affair. It is also possible that Gerrit Smith Miller had it secreted away in his personal possessions, and that it was destroyed when the mansion burned in 1936.

Although his religious values became deeply ingrained, Gerrit Smith did not have a positive regard for established Christian institutions. He deplored the Crusades, the Inquisition, the witch trials, and the concept of Hell. He was disillusioned with sects and denominations because of their immutable positions. He searched for a way to reconcile what he saw as the valuable and secular practical forces of reason and science with the equally valuable and sacred power of religion. It is a tribute to the balance of his mind that he was able to do it.

A number of influences may have guided his path toward rational secularism. While in college he was probably exposed to William

Paley's natural theology, which encouraged the perception of God in nature. He likely studied Samuel Butler's relativist ideas, which advocated moving away from absolute positions. The rationalist philosophers saw human reason as the chief source and test of knowledge. They encouraged people to use their practical and observant intellect to perceive fundamental patterns of relationships that were common to the elements of all systems. In this way, one could see connections between natural and social systems and, through reason, determine how to encourage social peace and order.

Other philosophers contemporary with Smith, such as David Strauss and Ernst Renan, had challenged the Bible as an unsatisfactory source of revelation of truth or history because of its internal inconsistencies. Smith was suspicious of Christianity, but he had no such reservations about the human mind as a source of knowledge. He believed that one's cognitive powers were sufficient to lead one's reason toward the existence of God, thereby voiding the need for inspired persons or writings.

Whether Smith borrowed this process of synthesizing religion and science from other thinkers or discovered it anew is not clear, but because of his post-college tendency to avoid books, it is likely that his active mind figured out his "Religion of Reason" all by itself. He discovered a point where the reason of the secular world could intersect with the sacred fantasies of religion in a way that tempered the extremes of both. In his typically paradoxical fashion, he combined a sense of duty toward moral reform with humility, high social status with empathy, and egotism with compassion. And his inspiration for the integration of these ideas was nature.

If Gerrit Smith were alive today, he would probably be an ecologist. He not only loved natural beauty, but he perceived in it a complex balance among diverse, equal parts that delivered messages about human social life. In June 1848 he composed a poem in praise of the beauty of the Saginaw River.[19] Many of his letters to family members opened with a recognition of natural beauty. "This is a lovely morning!—and all creation is shouting that God is good…."[20]

Here is a poem he wrote about a winter frost scene. "I never saw nature so beautifully dressed as she has been for several days. It is not snow but chrystalized mist upon the branches.

Thou dear fairy land! My memory still yields
Some glimpses of thy rich forests + fields,
Thy flowers, fruits, green banks + bright streams
As they gilded + blest my childhood's sweet dreams.
But here in old age my dreams are come true,
No fairy land equals the land I now view:
Yet how simple the cause of Pageant so grand!
God's moisture + cold make god's fairy land.
'Tis His finger decks from His own silver store
This Temple of Beauty in which I now stand:
I see all I dreamed, + a thousand fold more
Of the charms + enchantments of dear fairy land...."[21]

Smith believed that one could—and should—learn about religion from studying nature. He wrote to his friend, Albert Barnes, "Surely, God has not left us to get our religion from a source so uncertain and so corrupt as history."[22] Albert Barnes was a student at Hamilton College shortly after Smith graduated. He had become a Presbyterian minister. Barnes commented to Smith, "…your name was more frequently referred to than that of anyone who had graduated at that Institution."[23] Their letters fueled Smith's developing secular attitude, which grew increasingly opposed to what he saw as Barnes' sanctimonious positions.

Smith saw in the observation and study of natural ecosystems an avenue toward understanding what humans needed in order to produce peace and order. "The scientific study of nature, in her earth, sea, and sky, should be our chief mental employment; for then should we be kept … from confounding fancies with facts, and fictions with certainties."[24]

Smith first published his ideas about religion and nature in 1858, so reviewing them at this point jumps a bit ahead in his life.

Still, it is helpful to understand them before tracing the evolution of his development of ideas about religion. Smith viewed nature as a model for balance among different but equal parts. This was the same goal that religion—for him, Christianity—strived for in society. The balance in nature was created by God, so if natural balance was possible, he reasoned, then so was social balance. The fact that social balance did not exist was because people sinned against their fellows, thus upsetting that balance.

To illustrate the perfect balance created by God, Smith reasoned in a public speech that nature was "sufficient to teach and illustrate religion…. All that religion [and social balance] requires of us is obedience to the laws of nature."[25] In another speech titled "Miracles," he had previously argued, "Religion consists in nothing more or less than the knowledge and observance of the laws of nature."[26]

When people do things to upset the natural balance, Smith reasoned, nature becomes polluted or disordered. When people do selfish things that thwart justice and upset social equity, society also becomes disordered or unbalanced. The idea, for Smith, was simple: "It [would be] madness for [people] to assume the mastery of the elements of the physical world."[27] That is, humans cannot selfishly dominate nature and benefit from it in the long run.

Smith argued that the same must be true in social life: people cannot dominate others and benefit from it in the long run. Religion proposed a set of natural rules to accomplish balance. For Smith, balance in nature was used as an analogy for what the vehicle of religion could produce in people if they would only follow the rules. He viewed scientific research as a technique of clarifying the rules of natural balance. He believed that once those rules were more clearly understood, people would readily apply them to social life, thereby making it sin-free; thus the marriage between nature and religion.

"Doubtless the day is coming when there will be
comparatively little sin on earth. Science… hastens
the coming of this day. For we may reasonably
hope that, when science shall have more fully

revealed to men the laws of their being, obedience
to these laws will be in greater proportion to the
knowledge of them than it now is."[28]

But established churches fought against Smith's ideas, perhaps
fearing that he would usurp their monopoly on righteous teaching.
Speaking of the Christian church, Smith said,
"She claims to be, by force of her infallible
traditions, her infallible Bible and its infallible
interpretations, the infallible teacher of mankind.
And yet she is busy in shutting out from her
dark inclosures the constantly and every-where
breaking light of natural science."[29]

Smith was especially enthralled with the findings of astronomers
regarding the place of earth in the solar system and in the universe.
He was dismayed by traditional Christian teachings of geocentrism.
"How much longer must this theological trash be allowed to abuse
our patience?"[30] He accepted Darwin's idea of natural selection regarding the origin of the human species, thereby arranging humans
as only one of many equal species in natural systems.[31]

This contradicted established church doctrines. Miracles such as
the virgin birth and the resurrection of Christ could not have happened, Smith said, because they would contradict the laws of nature.
He concluded "that the miracles connected with [Christ's] birth,
life, and death are mere fictions" that should inspire not uncritical
acceptance of divine intervention, but reasoned research into the
function of natural systems.[32] "In every branch of knowledge, study
and toil,… not ignorant, indolent receptiveness, is the condition
of needful progress."[33] Such research would, he thought, inevitably
illuminate the validity of the Golden Rule.

Smith called his system of thought "moral reasoning," and he
made a practical distinction between religion and theology. Theology, he said, legitimized through its dogmatic doctrines the existing

state of things, whereas religion—based in practical, moral judgments—led to optimism regarding moral change and improvement. It avoided the stagnation resulting from belief in absolutes. Smith's brand of religion, based in practical moralism without theological doctrine, led one toward relativity in thought. "One thing [lost]," he wrote to William Lloyd Garrison, "is the certainty of the objects of your faith…. Now we find ourselves remitted to all the conscious uncertainty of human reasonings."[34]

Smith was, therefore, an iconoclast—one who smashes old idols—not a pagan. He was always deeply religious, but he was not attached to old patterns of thought. His ideas focused on collective humanity rather than on the 'self'; he perceived a universality in human nature founded on one ethical rule: "All know how they would be done by: and hence all know what to do to others."[35] He also assumed that all people could have common emotions based on their common instinct for survival, so cooperation among people should come naturally, as it does among elements in nature.

All analogies are inherently fallible to some degree, and perhaps what Smith failed to note was that elements of nature are balanced because they have no choice, as do people. Human nature could be self-centered, thwarting what he thought would be the inevitable growth of a sinless society. Gerrit Smith focused on oneness and similarities among people, but most others focused on creating and maintaining differences because they could personally benefit from those differences. To Smith, personal gain meant collective loss; Society became more corrupt as self-interest grew, and more moral as collective interest grew. He thought a humane sense of justice would grow out of a clear comprehension of balance in nature, and he assumed people would choose it over selfish gain.

Such was the fallacy of thought of a person steeped in the philosophy of the reform movement: what Smith thought was common sense was not at all common. Dignity, for some, accrued from hoarding instead of giving. A major fault in reform movement theology is its presumption of altruism as a dominating motive of enlightened human action.

Given the caveat of this critique, it is still remarkable that Smith was able to perceive the similarities in balance for both the natural and social worlds, and to invent a type of religion to accomplish that balance on a social level. "My own religion is very simple," he said. "It consists in the aim to deal impartially and justly with all men."[36] The irony of his theology was that while he decried the doctrinaire, scripted authority of sectarian denominations, he approved of a universal script for morality as dictated by God and perceived through human reason—with the arguably false premise that human nature is benevolent. "The great duty of life is to be natural…. God has made us right."[37] Such assumptions regarding the universality of human nature left Smith at odds with groups that believed differently.

Smith did help the Roman Catholic denomination with donations of money, even though he did not approve of their doctrine. "I should indeed greatly prefer, that they would worship with their Protestant brethren—but if they will not, …I cannot find it in my heart to refuse to assist them."[38] He also supported the idea of separate schools for Catholic children, and he received two highly complimentary letters from Roman Catholic institutions late in his life, praising his support.[39] But his understanding and tolerance of other perspectives on religion was not as liberal.

Of Eastern religions, he commented,

> "Mohammedans, Hindoos[sic], and other Eastern peoples, are more earnest and devout worshipers than Christians. This is the natural result of their being less enlightened. For being so, they are the more ready subjects of authority, and the more implicit believers in the dogmas which that authority imposes upon them."[40]

A few miles from Peterboro, the Oneida Community based its concept of "complex marriage" on the theological ideas of John Humphrey Noyes. The community's 'sharing of mates' irked Smith as an immoral practice, and he referred to their effort at communal life as a "Disgraceful... cause!"[41] Other letters also refer to Smith's public disapproval of their practices.[42] But his most vehement bias against another set of religious beliefs was aimed at the Jewish community.

He disliked what he called "the vindictive and bloodthirsty spirit of the Jewish theology,"[43] and he spoke of Jewish people as "a people in whom... the pride of race was controlling, contemptuous and cruel.... The Jewish part of our religion authorized us to make... property of [the black man], and to strip him as bare of rights as is any kind of property."[44] This intolerance of others' beliefs appeared in Smith's life mainly with regard to religion, and the arena in which it produced the most thought and activity was that of sectarianism within Christianity. His anti-sectarian stand lasted throughout his life, but its most intense expression occurred in the time period between 1835 and 1855. The mid-1850s represented a turning point in Smith's thinking about religion, marking his switch from absolute values to more relative views.

Gerrit Smith's anti-sectarian position can be viewed as a typical stand for reform-minded activists: a symbolic revolt against established institutions. He detested the authority of denominational doctrine, and wondered,

"How many ages more must pass away ere
ignorance and superstition and bigotry will be so
far dispelled as to permit men to see that these
churches are in effect, the worst enemies of Christ
and that the progress of his cause over the earth
will be measured by their disappearance from it!"[45]

Divisions among denominations, Smith believed, diluted the power of Christianity and corrupted Christ's message. In an address to the Christian Union Convention in 1838, he said:

"No person, acquainted with the words and the
heart of Jesus Christ, believes, that it is His choice

to have His disciples separated from each other
by party lines—wearing badges and contending
with each other about the peculiarities, of their
respective sects."[46]

The issue that sparked Smith's anti-sectarianism was abolition.
He was a member of the Peterboro Presbyterian Church, and by the
mid-1830s, he considered the Presbyterian General Assembly to be
pro-slavery. His identification with immediate abolition began in
1835, coinciding with his anti-sectarian thrust. In 1837, the Presbyterian Church split into Old and New School factions with the
Old School group being less evangelistic, southern-oriented, and
pro-slavery.[47] Smith encouraged the local Onondaga Presbytery to
secede from the Constitutional General Assembly of the Presbyterian Church,[48] and when it declined, he started considering other
avenues of opposition.

Smith viewed most of the major Christian denominations as
pro-slavery. "The Presbyterian and Baptist Churches of Peterboro
would discipline one of their members who should vote for a sheep
thief—but not if he should vote for a man thief."[49] Such doctrine,
Smith said, shut out reason by power of authority and convinced
most adherents to believe that they were deficient and depraved.
Denominations thus denied "to men the ability, and therefore the
right, to judge for themselves.... It is by this overriding them with
authority... that they are so largely characterized by a sense of ir-
responsibility...."[50] Smith saw human nature as being essentially
good, and therefore not in need of being saved by a priesthood
looking for work.

In fact, he viewed denominational religion as a hindrance to
reform. "The great mass of Christians still remain bound hand and
foot by Denominational and Sectarian cords: and not until they are
released by the spirit of Christian Union, will our Benevolent enter-
prises prosper."[51] Smith believed the confrontation and controversy
among denominations was sapping the strength of potential reform;

people became so attached to doctrinal disagreements, he argued, that they ignored societal improvement. He warned a friend, "Do not bow your neck to the base yoke of Sectarianism."[52] The notion that people within a denomination should be required to think alike in upholding a doctrine was deplorable to Smith. He felt it impeded one's search for guiding principles of conduct relevant to one's own life. People "should no more be required to adopt a common religious creed, than to shorten or stretch out their bodies to a common length," he said.[53]

Doctrinal uniformity in belief, he claimed, was prejudicial and intolerant, and it led believers into pride in sect and moral indifference. The cure for this ailment of mind, Smith thought, was the establishment of a new, doctrine-free church.

Although Smith had been attending the Presbyterian Church in Peterboro since the mid-1820s, he maintained that he did not know what denomination he belonged to.[54] As his opposition to sectarianism in general and the pro-slavery stance of the Presbyterian Church in particular grew, he attended, and probably organized, "Christian Union Meetings" in Peterboro to discuss the possibility of uniting all of the local denominations into one "Free Church." In 1839, he had been instrumental in establishing a free church in Oswego. He wanted to see the same thing happen in Peterboro.[55]

From the January 29, 1841 Christian Union meeting in Peterboro came the following resolutions, which were sent to the Methodist, Presbyterian, and Baptist churches in Peterboro:

"1. The division of Christians into rival sects or parties, is anti-Scriptural and wicked.

2. The ecclesiastical [group] which excludes from or refuses to receive into its fellowship any person [is not considered to be a church].

3. [We should establish] a common Christianity and a common Church."[56]

When the Peterboro denominations did not agree to merge, Smith decided to go ahead with the Free Church project himself. He and Abishai Scofield, a local Presbyterian minister and abolitionist, organized a nonsectarian Church of Peterboro in 1843, with Smith as its pastor.[57] The church invited anyone to attend, as long as doing so "would not make war upon his own convictions...."[58]

The fact that Smith thought people would flock to his new church in order to escape authoritarianism reflected his optimism. He did not get the point that many people found roots and identity in their own denominations that they might not find elsewhere. Although the Free Church movement did spread, it never became the helpmate of reform that its sponsors hoped for.[59] Smith supported the movement even after his Peterboro church disintegrated,[60] but in so doing, he found himself the target of scorn by local residents.

The Free Church movement throughout New York State grew out of the disappointment of abolitionists that existing moral-based institutions had failed to bring about their great expectations of social equality. Some turned inward toward personal religious fads like Spiritualism and Perfectionism; Smith looked to the establishment of a new institution that was "free" of doctrinal constraints that legitimated slavery. He implemented a secular type of evangelism through a politically oriented antislavery crusade. For Smith, liberty and equality did battle with the altar, which by its refusal to condemn slavery was seen as a symptom of the enslavement of the human mind. The Free Church movement attempted to replace spiritual despotism with spiritual democracy, as creeds were cast aside for commitment to social reform—and people had the option of choosing whether they preferred a society based on obedience or one based on justice.

The peculiar feature of the Free Church movement was its union of religion and politics. In attempting to minimize doctrine and unify all churches, the Union movement—as it was also called—connected perfectionist philosophy with political action through the Liberty Party, accepting one's antislavery vote as a sign of secular, yet evangelical salvation.

Smith's support of the Free Church identifies him as an "ecclesiastical abolitionist," one who is nonsectarian, opposes hierarchical authority, encourages social diversity in membership, and links the church to political activity.[61]

Before the Free Church of Peterboro built its own meeting house, meetings were held in "the assembly room in the Temperance Hotel." People from other Peterboro churches tried to stigmatize Smith's church meetings as nonreligious. They called him a dangerous man and warned others to stay away from him.[62] On Dec. 7, 1842, Smith had written to the elders of the Presbyterian Church of Peterboro to request that his name be removed from the membership roll.[63] The Presbyterian Church records list 27 "seceders" among whom, from the Smith household, were Laura Bosworth, Elizabeth H. Kelty, and Gerrit and Ann Smith.[64] These four people were issued a written summons "by order of the Session" of the Presbyterian Church:

> "You are hereby cited to…appear before the
> Session of the Presbyterian Church in Smithfield,
> of which you are members… on the 28th day of
> May… at 9 o'clock, A.M., to answer to the charge…
> of seceding from the worship and communion
> of said church, and your breach of covenant
> obligations with said church…."[65]

The Peterboro churches, having invested in members, did not want to lose them; still, they did lose them to the Free Church of Peterboro. One 1867 report indicated that "the Baptist congregation has left the town and closed the house. The Presbyterian church… appears like a wreck…. The small Methodist chapel…keeps alive the worship of the savior…."[66] During the period of formation of the Church of Peterboro, a "Committee on Plan" began to meet. Comprising Peterboro residents, the committee discussed the wisdom of Smith's proposal.

The lengthy minority report of that committee has only recently been found. It is a curiosity because its author appears to speak for

The Church of Peterboro, which Gerrit Smith founded in 1843, first met in the Temperance Hotel near Gerrit's Land Office on the northwest corner of the village green. In 1847 it moved to this building on the northeast corner, which Gerrit built for the church. Part of the Free Church movement of the mid-19th century, it operated for more than three decades.   *From the author's collection*

both sides. Composed by Roger Maddock of the Peterboro Baptist Church, this report, now in the possession of the author, will be donated to the Peterboro Historical Society.

On the side of those opposing the new church, Maddock wrote, "The formless plan of Union—this creedless attempt to embody all who Unionists may think have been the subjects of the renovating power of God… is but the carrying out of the notion of open communion." He reported that the opponents of union perceived any church as a 'body of Christ'.

> "This body is represented as compact as a building,
> the parts mutually depending upon and indispensible
> to each other… very unlike the proposed union
> ch[urch], so incoherent in all its parts."[67]

Maddock compared Smith's Free Church proposal to "cats, dogs, bears + lions caged together, with an injunction to keep the peace," and called it "a Kennel [or] an asylum." Then, seemingly on the approving side of the issue, Maddock cited the "impenitent" of the village who were indifferent to religion, but found themselves repelled by sectarian squabbles. He recognized that the unionists "sympathize with the impenitent so [much] that they are willing to sacrifice all the peculiarities of their own views of doctrine or practice, so far as to present the disciples of Christ in harmonious aspect." Of the sectarians, he said, "I can scarce find an individual…who can pretend to give any satisfactory reason for their practice.… The reading of God's word by those who are not bound by prejudice gives light. But shaded by the force of authority… it becomes darkness."

Maddock proposed as a conclusion to his report that the Presbyterians and Methodists "let go of the supreme power" that limited them. Also, as the older Baptists died, the Baptists, too, would be ready to join unionism. "I am not pertinacious in holding our denomination—but should be glad to resign it for the general appelation of Christian."

The vacillation in this original report is unimportant. What is significant is that it reveals the thoughts of a committee of Peterboro citizens who did feel some dissatisfaction with the state of local affairs among Christian denominations. As Maddock said,

> "There are antagonistic elements in sectarian constitution, at war with each other.… A restless spirit of insubordination is gradually subverting rule and order, in the different denominations of Christians. There is a growing disposition to yeald to feelings and impulses, rather than principals.… The prevailing evil is that we refuse to let God reign over us; we do that which is right in our own eyes as tho their was no King in Israel."[68]

Regardless of the local controversy, the Church of Peterboro was established, and its members practiced non-denominational religion for three decades in Peterboro; at least, that is what they claimed.

Their own beliefs about non-sectarianism could, themselves, be viewed as sectarian. Although it looks to some like the same play with slight variations in the script, to Gerrit Smith, it was a dream come true. Perhaps like the colony at Timbucto, if he could not reform society as a whole, he could at least influence Peterboro and hope that the model would spread.

By 1858 Smith could boast,

> "I must think, that this little village is, in respect to
> a sound and rational religion, greatly in advance of
> almost every other place in the land. [Our glory]
> is to be found in the breaking up of our sectarian
> churches and in the general and growing dislike
> to sectarianism.... God hasten the day when...
> Christians...shall...be deeply ashamed to be called
> Methodists, Baptists, Presbyterians, or to pass
> under any other religious party name."[69]

The small Church of Peterboro, built in 1847 on the corner of the village green, drew many well-known speakers, among whom were John Brown, Frederick Douglass, John Greenleaf Whittier, and, of course, Gerrit Smith. Of the sermons preached there, one person commented,

> "...those I hear practice what they preach and
> [their] deeds are evidence of what they are. This
> last I may not be able to attain but asuredly it will
> not be the fault of the doctrines preached in the
> Church of Peterboro."[70]

The church was a haven for abolitionists who, having spoken there, remembered it well. William H. Fish of Cortland had to turn down Gerrit's invitation to address the congregation, but reflected, "I shall think of you, however, + your friends assembled with you in that ever-to-be memorable little Church of Peterboro + rejoice with them in spirit whilst they 'look up + are fed.'"[71]

Smith loved the free church and was pleased with its development.
> "I love the Church of Peterboro dearly. I can
> almost say, that I live in its life—If I have done any
> good things in my life, they are, all put together, of
> far less value than the part I have had in gathering
> + maintaining the Church of Peterboro… on the
> one…distinctive principle, that the Christians of a
> place are the Church of such place."[72]

Smith felt one of his own shortcomings was that he was unsuccessful in getting all of the residents of Peterboro to attend the free church.[73] With the end of abolition after the Civil War, the church's significance waned, and it went out of existence altogether in the early 1870s. Gerrit would later attend the local Methodist Church, even becoming its Sunday School superintendent, but it must have galled him somewhat to be labeled as "one of those." Smith's former church, the Presbyterian Church of Peterboro, had disintegrated in 1862 when it had only thirty-one remaining members.

During the time period leading up to the mid-1850s, Smith's strong convictions about religion tended to get him into social trouble. He took immutable stands on issues that developed into lengthy, public, verbal battles that consumed a great deal of time and energy. These arguments illustrated well his penchant for making blunders, the magnitude of which damaged his reputation. One such episode involved a dispute with Asa Rand, the pastor of the Presbyterian Church of Peterboro. This dispute is worth covering at length because it reveals the pitfalls of absolute thought—and some important details of Smith's personality.

On July 15, 1845, Smith issued an open letter to "Those Ministers in the County of Madison who refuse to preach politics." He viewed religion and politics as intertwined, and he often used the pulpit for anti-slavery speeches. The letter read,
> "It is again to entreat you to preach politics, that I
> come to you. My conviction [is] that the continued

enslavement of millions in this Nation, is because
its religious teachers will not preach politics…."[74]

This challenge to the clergy was met by Asa Rand, a Peterboro
resident and abolitionist who did not object to sermons that applied
God's word to the issue of slavery, but did object to "electioneering" from the pulpit. Electioneering, to Rand, meant efforts to gain
recruits to a political party, or votes at the ballot box, or attempts to
influence the outcome of an election.[75] Smith admitted, "I warmly
hope and fully intend, that my Sunday meetings shall aid the Liberty
Party."[76] Rand saw this as profaning the Sabbath, and he said so in
public discussions and printed articles. Smith took offense at this
and penned the following complaints:

"1st That he, Mr Rand, has in a public discussion in
Sept 1845 and subsequently in various written and
printed communications falsely and slanderously
represented him, Mr. Smith, to be crooked,
dictatorial, sly, deceptive, unfair, dishonest, false,
lying, railing, slanderous, + meriting punishment
at the hands of a legal tribunal.

2nd That he, Mr. Rand, has trifled with truth and
with the deep wounds which he has inflicted on
his, Mr. Smith's, feelings + reputation by declaring
in written and printed communications, that
he, Mr. Rand, has said and done nothing, which
calls in question his, Mr. Smith's, veracity—
nothing which impeaches his, Mr. Smith's, moral
character."[77]

The complaints went on and on. The essence of them was that
Smith was aggrieved that Rand had called him a liar, and he reacted
by posting some derogatory comments about Rand in a store in
Peterboro. Having read these comments, Rand responded to Smith,

"Let us…have an investigation… before unfounded prejudices become fixed in the minds of the community against you or me."[78]

In a privately held document in which he kept track of his own perception of the religious identity of Peterboro residents, Smith questioned the quality of Rand's Christianity. "Asa Rand, is perhaps, in spite of his obstinacy + temporising, a christian."[79] Smith thus seemed biased against Rand before the public controversy even started. This, and his obsession with anti-slavery goals, sent him off on a childish display of temper against Rand.

In public discussions under the supervision of a moderator who enforced mutually agreed-upon rules, Rand and Smith attempted to settle their dispute. Smith did a fine job of making a public fool of himself through emotional displays and unfounded accusations against Rand. After one episode, Rand stayed behind in fear of what Smith might do to him.

> "[I] stayed at the church on Monday evening after
> the close of our discussion, for I perceived that
> you were highly excited, and feared that your
> impetuosity would betray you into something you
> would have occasion to regret."[80]

Smith wrote to Rand, apologizing for "grievous accusations" made during their public discussion, and said that he was "deeply sorry," and that his error was one of "misconsideration and not of intention." Rand asked him "to make your retraction known, as publicly as your accusations were made; and as soon as practicable."[81]

Rand was clearly the more level-headed and rational person in these "discussions." He saw that Smith intended to keep arguing and charging him, so he suggested arbitration.

> "Let us, when convenient for both, select a few
> mutual friends in Smithfield, lay before them our
> several grievances… and take their counsel on the
> whole matter. Explanation and friendly counsel
> may lead us to results very desirable to us both…."[82]

Smith agreed to this proposal, but the dispute dragged on while they tried to solicit arbiters. In June of 1847, Smith remarked, "I regard Mr Rand as bent upon the destruction of my reputation for truth…." Then he accused Rand of abandoning the cause of abolition. "It is true that I did resolve Mr. Rand's outrage on my reputation into apostasy from the Antislavery cause. I cast about for an explanation of the outrage and (though perhaps with much more egotism than wisdom) came to that conclusion…."[83] In his continuing arrogance, Smith also informed Rand that he, Rand, needed more advice in his decision-making. Rand rejected the suggestion and reminded Smith of their mutual willingness to submit the matter to arbitration.[84]

Smith again reacted irrationally with the following annotation to Rand's letter:

It reads:

> "This letter wrongs me in holding me up to myself
> as unwilling to make confesions for any wrongs I
> had done Mr R. [Then refer to my promptness to
> confess errors 1st. The first use I made of my pen
> was to write him a retraction of my own Sept 22
> 1845. So too in case of the errors I confessed in
> June 1847 through the Albany Patriot."

Smith wrongly assumed Rand had attacked him, failing to see that Rand was simply trying to move the controversy forward to arbitration.

One week later, Rand again reminded Smith of their agreement to arbitration, "to have a judgment passed on our several charges, from which there shall be no appeal."[85] When Smith worried he might not approve of the arbiters' judgment, Rand explained,

"to 'acquiesce in the judgment' does not mean
to 'approve of it.' It does not even mean that we
shall 'be content with it,'.... It does mean that we
shall submit to it, abide by it, and desist from all
agitation of these personal matters before the
people by pen or tongue."[86]

The final decision of the arbiters was signed on September 3, 1847, and read in full as follows:

"Resolved, by the Arbitration, that the mutual charges and
defenses of the parties, together with the whole controversy,
are so involved in misunderstandings and lack of definiteness
and clearness, that we decline pressing upon them in whole
or in part by definite verdicts; But wish to render our decision
in the following form. To wit. We are led in view of the whole
case, as far as it was made clear to us, to conclude, that the
manner of prosecuting said controversy should be viewed in
a light which does not involve moral turpitude in either party.
The arbitration makc[s] much allowance for the influence
which such misunderstandings must have upon any minds in
controversy; and further we agree that Mr. Rand's employing
definitions and making implications which could not fail
to be offensive and to endanger an odius construction, and
Mr. Smith's employing unguarded, unqualified and most
obnoxious terms against his opponent was in both cases
unhappy, unfortunate and reprehensible.

Sept. 3, 1847   C. Stebbins
                                       Beriah Green
                                       E. J. Gillette
                                       Thos Castleton
                                       Wm Goodell"[87]

Charles Stebbins was a lawyer in Cazenovia whose counsel was acceptable to both Smith and Rand. Beriah Green and William Goodell were chosen by Smith, and E. J. Gillette and Thomas Castleton were chosen by Rand.

In essence, what the arbiters did was slap the wrists of two immature boys. Although Rand had been the more reasonable of the two, both had been publicly irresponsible. To show how foolish Gerrit Smith could be when obsessed, he rejected the arbiters' decision and asked for a reopening of the controversy with a second arbitration. Rand wisely rejected that request, but agreed to ask the arbiters for written responses to their charges against both him and Smith "for the sake of peace."[88]

Rand was both conciliatory and polite to the end, asking Smith:
> "Reflect on…the conduct you have manifested
> throughout this whole affair,…a spirit of
> retaliation and revenge…for alleged injuries
> which were never given, which your own friends
> on the arbitration are convinced never existed….
> When I shall have done my duty respecting the
> adjustment, I am ready to pass by all that you have
> done…as though it had never been; to forgive,
> unasked, and to treat you in future as I would treat
> any other neighbor, according to your conduct
> from day to day."[89]

In the end Rand was a gentleman, and Smith a fool. The whole affair occurred because of Smith's fear for his reputation. Ironically, in the long run, he damaged it more than did Rand. Smith was vengeful, malicious, spiteful, and unrelenting. Compared to his benevolence toward most people, this was an anomaly. Rand had been right all along about Smith's "electioneering" from the pulpit. Smith denied it, then could not support his denial.

Smith had long before maintained that politics and religion were intertwined. "As to my own politics, …they are part of my religion."[90] "I have no scruples in spending the whole of [the Sabbath] in pleading with my fellow men to give their votes to the poor bleeding slave."[91]

In subsequent years, Smith developed this point of preaching politics into an argument against the separation of church and state. "Let American Christianity, not only cease from her opposition to, and contempt of, bible politics, but identify herself with them; and, on the Sabbath and from the pulpit, and in season and out of season, preach them...."[92]

On another occasion, he wrote:

"Christians are educated to draw a line between religion and politics, and to regard religion as one thing, and politics as another. They are educated to look upon the civil government as a thing distinct and different from the Divine government, instead of being but a department of that government.... Urge the duty of making civil government religious and holy, and the great mass of christians will pronounce you foolish, fanatical, mad."[93]

Smith viewed Christian principles as a worthy basis for political policy, and he believed that ministers should be controversial public figures as they vigorously pursued specific political goals from the pulpit.[94]

One might think that because of the mess Gerrit Smith got himself into with Asa Rand, and the wasted energy, wasted time and loss of face, he would have at least learned the lesson of avoiding public debates involving his church. He did no such thing. In February of 1849, Hiram P. Crozier, the pastor of the Free Church of Peterboro, was working on weekdays as a clerk in a store in Peterboro that sold liquor. Even though Crozier did not directly sell any liquor, Smith accused him of guilt by association, and in his own personal notes, Smith recorded: "Feb. 20, 1849 Tuesday—Church this day applied the 2 Resolutions disolving the pastoral relation of Mr. Crozier. Mr.

Crozier then resigned." After church "members"—defined as anyone in the community—reversed the vote to dismiss Crozier on March 5, Smith decided on his own that Crozier was finished as pastor.[95]

Crozier responded: "Our convictions are not to be laid at the feet of age, eloquence, wealth, or power.... If you cannot give us this, you must expect that your peace will be disturbed, your reputation (for liberality) assailed, and your influence impaired."[96] At this point, their disagreement was focused less on religious matters than on personal differences.

Crozier was an eloquent, liberal young man who noted Smith's hypocrisy in supporting human rights while demanding certain behaviors from his parishioners. He had printed a circular criticizing Smith: "Your...method of procedure, with myself, has convinced [me], that while you are a man of many transcendent virtues, you are also a man of some transcendent faults, and blunders!"[97]

Smith had again stumbled over principles of religion, and he was in the process of compounding the injury to himself as a public role model. Crozier pointed out Smith's hypocrisy with an apt analogy. "Most of the land of Madison County is adopted to barley and hops. You sold that land. Most of the farmers in your region feed the brewery and distillery from the proceeds of their farms. They bring the money to your office to apply on their land contracts. You receive it. Are you hence responsible for their morality in selling grain to the brewer and distiller?"[98]

Likewise, Crozier noted that Peter Smith had "amassed an immense fortune by land speculation. You use the most of that fortune as though it were honestly acquired."[99] The reference here was to Gerrit's father's dealings with Native Americans in the late 1700s, (Details of the Peter Smith land deal are covered in Chapter 11) when the Smiths' land was acquired illegally. And Crozier knew it.

Crozier's circular went on to point out a list of Gerrit's shortcomings. He noted Smith's "zeal to condemn" based on "taken for granted things that need to be proved." He cited Smith for having "injured my feelings" via "assumptions, and guess-work, that altogether fail you," and for basing his judgments upon "the strength of a morality generated in your own mind," founded on "deduction of universal reason." Crozier eloquently accused Smith of moral duplicity that was so clear and accurate that in the end, Smith could do nothing better than apologize.[100] Crozier acknowledged Smith's apology and requested no public display of it. He graciously stated that Smith's Peterboro neighbors already knew that in the heat of a controversy, folks say things that are unsubstantiated, saying, "All excited discussions of a personal climate rouse up passions that darken reason, prevent conscience, and give great bias to judgment and prejudice on both sides."

Crozier was being courteous and benign where he could legitimately have punished Smith for having been such a fool. Throughout the disagreement, Crozier remained compassionate, calm, and respectful toward Smith, and he terminated their debate with a spirit of tenderness that approached pity. "I desire to erect no barriers to commerce of hearts, or to keep up any that you may suppose I have erected. I shall at any time be happy to meet with you…to converse more fully than we can write."[101]

Although Smith did subsequently describe Crozier as "an intelligent + respectable gentleman," he was not able to admit that he, Gerrit, had a habit of allowing his passions and stubbornness to obstruct his fair treatment of people.[102]

An interesting sideline to this dispute involved Smith's business clerk, Caleb Calkins, who had previously disagreed with Smith over the principles of establishment for the Church of Peterboro. Calkins thought the church to be just another sect, and he refused to join.[103] In the Crozier-Smith dispute, Calkins tried to moderate their exchanges. Calkins was close to Gerrit Smith and knew his shortcomings. He claimed Smith regarded as "enemies" those who opposed his ideas on religion. He wrote Smith a note requesting a private meeting with him.[104] They talked on April 9, 1852, the very day on which Smith apologized to Crozier. Calkins told Gerrit that he believed Gerrit was wrong in his perceptions of Crozier, and he later told Crozier, "I do not think Mr. Smith ever indulged malicious feelings toward you. He thinks he is doing God's service. I regard him as upright."[105]

This obsession with rightness does not characterize Smith's views throughout his life; any attempt to categorize Gerrit Smith as a specific type of thinker will result in confusion. His mind matured over time as he became enlightened about secular and scientific issues, and that enlightenment led him to think very differently about religion during different segments of his life. He wrote in 1866,

"I was brought up to look only at one side—my side. Hence I entered upon my manhood a political and religious bigot. But, for more than the later half of my life, I have trained myself to look at all sides and to seek knowledge from all sides."[106]

As an absolutist in the early stage of his adult life, Smith accepted uncritically the moral stance of Presbyterianism, and he promoted it. As a wealthy potential aristocrat who embraced evangelism, Smith was an anomaly because the upper social classes generally avoided the revival mentality.[107]

Before 1840, the reform effort was carried on mainly through institutions of religion; yet by the mid-1830s, Smith had already become disillusioned with Christian denominations that battled one another over immutable doctrines and creeds. He believed a person should have a creed to guide his behavior, but he should develop it individually, not have it forced on him. Such stirrings of relativistic thought led him to question his own denominational loyalties[108] and to propose the establishment of his non-sectarian Free Church of Peterboro.

During the three decades in which the Church of Peterboro functioned, Gerrit Smith ruled over it like a petty dictator. He invited speakers to preach there as long as they would preach on the themes Smith wanted his flock to hear. To one he wrote,

"You… would call on your hearers to take out of the way of the Lord the stumbling blocks

> + obstacles. You would specify, among these,
> Rum-drinking—Carrying grain to the Distiller +
> Brewer—Voting for oppressors of God's poor…
> [and] division of the people of God into Sects."[109]

Although Smith's thinking had, by the early 1840s, graduated into some relativism, he was still on the absolutist side of the continuum. He wanted to enlighten others concerning truth, and he was condescending toward those who did not see the same truth he did. He had little patience with variety in ideas, and intended to help others choose the "right principles," which, of course, he knew.[110] "The bible—…that is the book we need to understand:—and the earlier we are imbued with its spirit and grounded in its principles, the more wisdom shall we evince in temporal, as well as spiritual things."[111] In the Church of Peterboro's founding principles, Smith wrote: "We learn from the Holy Scriptures, which are the only infallible guide in all questions of morality…."[112]

It was also during this pre-1850s period of thought that Smith supported missionary activity both at home and abroad. Trapped by his narrow vision, he hoped that the whole world would be converted to Christianity through missionaries, who "although destined to labor in small portions of it, are laboring, nevertheless, for the great end of bringing the whole world to the Savior."[113] Local missionary activities, through the newly formed American Bethel Society, were aimed at the moral actions of canal workers. Smith supported this with his name as one of its directors, and with his money.[114] Revivals were also a form of local "missionary" activity designed to kindle passion and guide belief.

In October of 1842 Smith noted:

> "Religion is truly at a low ebb in Peterboro. Our Temperance House is turned into a drunkard-making House. Mob violence is preferred to sacred law—and the professed followers of Jesus Christ are busy in making legislators and rulers of those who buy and sell God's poor."[115]

Time for a revival! Ann Smith wrote of the one that occurred in the summer of 1843 in Peterboro. "An army of defenders of the Sabbath has suddenly sprung up in this county...."[116]

> "The religious revival in this community is
> becoming more intense + is fast spreading over the
> whole County. Indeed, nearly the whole part of the
> proslavery + vicious part of our population have
> already become the subjects of it."[117]

A curious episode of this period of Smith's thought was his identification with the Millerites. The cult that followed William Miller prophesied an end to the world, and Smith believed them and allowed them to use "the Tabarnacle" in Oswego rent-free.[118] His connection with them probably occurred due to their anti-slavery stand and their support of the Liberty Party. Smith saw their beliefs as a practical expression of the anticipated perfectionist society, and for a time, he became caught up in their movement.

He wrote to Ann,

> "We have just had family worship—perhaps for the
> last time.... How my eyes have flowed at the welcome
> thought that we shall meet our dear Fitzhugh and
> Nanny! Oh, the treasures of religion!"[119]

Indeed, if religion could help one balance the sufferings of death with reality, then a treasure it was. Gerrit Smith's thought pattern was in flux at this time, and the changes to come in the decade from 1845 to 1855 would produce an actual revolution in his beliefs.

What forces could bring down the power of absolute certainty? Gerrit Smith's belief moved from divinely ordained knowledge to personal religious skepticism, to genuine secular doubt. The key to understanding this revolution in his thought lies in understanding the pressures he faced during this decade.

Other authors have labeled him—wrongly—as a lifelong absolutist. Hammond claimed,

"Every question, public or private, was decided by
him in the light of absolute right.... He abhored
every compromise of principle, but he was ever
ready and willing to come to an agreement with
his fellow men in matters involving no sacrifice of
his convictions of right."[120]

If one had examined Smith's life only up to about 1845, this
could be an accurate conclusion. Even Harlow, who did much more
extensive research, was cynical about Smith's judgment: "[His] capacity for certitude developed early and stayed with him as long as
he lived."[121] A thorough study of his life shows this to be false. But
what factors led him to believe that he should switch to relativism
rather than fight for absolute principles?

To be able to perceive the validity of various perspectives, one
must first come to the point of doubting one's own certainties. The
anchors of personal security that certified the value of Smith's life
in his eyes were, mainly, his family and his church. During the early
years of his marriage to Ann, things went well as their common
beliefs and their love for each other grew. Financial security seemed
certain. Their children, Elizabeth, Fitzhugh, and Nanny, were "precious," loved, and growing. Religious principles that guided their
behavior seemed immutable and universal, and Smith's philanthropy
made him feel good. In short, several groundings made for a stable
lifestyle until around 1840.

Then, the icons contributing to both national security and good
personal feelings began to fall. The national economy had plunged
into depression in the late 1830s, and the Smith family purse emptied
nearly to the point of bankruptcy. Gerrit borrowed heavily to stay
afloat, wondering if he could ever again afford to be philanthropic.
His family had fallen to illness, with two beloved children dead, his
father dead, and both he and Ann beginning to experience chronic
health problems. His growing son, Greene, dealt a serious blow to
Gerrit's confidence in a just and gracious Creator. Born in 1842,

Greene developed into a rebel against Smith's values, threatening Gerrit's reputation and influence.

While all this was going on, Smith became alarmed at the slow pace of progress toward the abolition of slavery. He blamed this on opposition from churches and from government. He reluctantly agreed to serve in the U.S. Congress when elected, fully intending to get his "immediate abolition" views heard there. But when he saw the stagnant quality of policy making amid the influence of vested interests that were profiting from slavery, he resigned before his term was completed. As his faith in his idols—established Christianity, Constitutional government, his family, the economy—waned, he looked more toward his "beloved Peterboro" with his home and his wife for support. But here, too, there were problems.

Ann was spending more and more time away from home for various reasons. She thought she had persistent ailments that mystical "cures" alone could alleviate, and she was periodically depressed in Peterboro—especially during winter. Gerrit and Ann seemed to question their love for one another during this "mid-life crisis," as their poems and letters to each other indicate. Even Gerrit's cousin, Elizabeth Cady Stanton, wrote about their mutual alienation ("How art thou fallen, O! Nancy!")[122] And, as if these issues were not enough to challenge their relationship, Ann developed an intense interest in Spiritualism, a religious belief system Gerrit thought to be ludicrous.

So here stood Gerrit Smith in the early 1850s: He and his wife increasingly alienated, health issues threatening, family members dead, the economy destabilized, his son rebelling, his faith in Christian principles declining, the government corrupted, and the church uninterested in moral reform. He must have wondered what was next.

His response to such circumstances was to alter his beliefs to accommodate those circumstances, thereby maintaining what he perceived to be balance. He did not lose his idols to worship; he just developed new ones.

Nature became Smith's new idol. He saw in its operational balance the lessons that were essential for social equity. The Bible, religious doctrines, creeds, and certainties took a back seat to the observation and study of natural ecosystems. Having once perceived the Bible to be the supreme source for moral teaching, Smith now found it to be pernicious. He wrote to his cousin, Elizabeth Cady Stanton:

> "[People] run to the Bible...to be taught their duty
> in matters where their very instincts...teach them
> their duty.... They run to the Bible, not to learn the
> truth, but to make the Bible the minister of folly
> and sin.... They run from the teachings of their
> nature and the remonstrances of their conscience
> to find something more palatable."[123]

The Bible, Smith said, "is made the cover of slavery...and the authority for degrading woman. In short, it is made to be the worst book in the world. The satanic and current interpretations put upon it make it the mightiest of all hindrances to the progress of civilization...."[124]

He also lost respect for established religion in the form of its buildings, its spokespersons, and its beliefs. Regarding the opulence of church structures, he penned years later,

> "Seldom do I look at a magnificent church or
> cathedral without thinking that the cost of them...
> was wrung from the toiling poor—and that their
> sad return for what they could so ill spare from
> their penury was but to be sunk deeper in poverty
> and superstition, and to be more enslaved to the
> priesthood."[125]

Churches, Smith believed, should be

> "plain halls... suitable... for lectures on natural
> science—for the geologist and the astronomer.
> These lectures will be immeasurably useful in

clearing the rubbish which ignorance has put in
the way of religion…. They will go farther than
all things else to save religion from sinking into
superstition, sectarianism, and bigotry."[126]

He cynically viewed belief in theologies as the life-blood of the
churches. "The superstitious keep up the dread; and the dread keeps
up the churches."[127] Albert Barnes was writing to Smith because of
his own confusion on matters of religion. Smith advised Barnes
that his anxiety emanated "from the violence which your theological creed does to your reason, and from your not daring to let your
reason condemn your creed." The devout fell into this trap, Smith
reasoned, because "the more arbitrary and inexplicable a theology
of authority, the more suitable…because the more submissive [are]
the superstitious disciples."[128]

The perpetrators of this delusion were ministers, priests, and
other teachers of religion whom Smith perceived as "pernicious."
"Their assumption of an exclusive right to teach
religion makes the teachers conceited, dogmatic,
arrogant, tyrannical; and their hearers lazy in
mind and slavish in spirit…. The religion taught by
Jesus is not a letter but a life. So simple is it that the
unlearned can both understand it and teach it…. A
theological seminary is a mistake."[129]

All this secular skepticism led to what Smith called "The Religion of Reason." He published a series of writings under that title
in 1858 and 1859, stating his new ideas. They set forth what he
considered to be every person's ability to reason against the authority of established religious doctrine. Smith was trying to reestablish
belief in a principle once held by ancient Greek culture—that the
gods did not create the universe, but the universe created the gods.
Christianity had reversed this idea and adopted Hebrew myths of
creation, thereby confirming the power and authority of the gods—

or God—over people, and alienating them from their own power of reason. Gerrit Smith's ideas were aimed at verifying and securing human reason as the foundation for understanding the world and motivating moral behavior.

Gerrit Smith's Religion of Reason had a dual purpose. First, it was designed to disaffirm the value of immutable ideas and expose their corruptive power. Second, it was meant to to affirm the value of human rationality for all people in comprehending their world. Smith now viewed a creed—a set of guiding principles—as necessary and proper. Smith explained the importance of a creed in a sermon at the Church of Peterboro on Feb. 21, 1858:

> "Every man should have one. But a church creed is improper. Fifty or a hundred people in Peterboro or Cazenovia, however much alike in their views and spirit, should [not] be required to adopt a common religious creed.... Jesus no more thought of providing for a sectarian church than for a political party."[130]

Sectarian doctrines were the vehicle for teaching on the church creed, and Smith saw this as backwards. A person's creed, he thought, should be taught to the church after one has verified that his beliefs produce a just and equitable life for all. Jesus, he noted, did not "teach that if a man does not understand and receive [doctrines] he shall perish. He taught that at the close of this earthly drama men are to be judged by their lives. The great decisive question then will be—not what were your doctrines, but what were your deeds?"[131] If sectarian doctrine was a solution to human problems, he reasoned, then the problems would no longer exist.

> "Christianity...has proved false by... failure to overcome the great crimes and abominations. War, slavery, drunkenness, and the various oppressions of women still abound. Give... reason its full play... and these...would fast disappear."[132]

One piece of Christian doctrine Smith saw as particularly dangerous was the concept of Hell: it was necessary, he thought, only because sectarian rulers needed some place to send people who would not obey their authority. Because Smith's version of religion let the people establish their creed and the church doctrine, Hell was unnecessary. There was no rival to a loving God on which one could blame unjust behavior. Such doctrinal beliefs as Hell, the Devil, the immaculate conception, and man's fall into sin were seen as "not only destitute of proof but at war with nature and reason."[133]

Smith thought doctrinal religion was incapable of helping people to reform, because it created guilt for nonbelievers. People spent too much effort trying to understand and believe the doctrines and too little time doing good deeds.[134] Moreover, the various sectarian doctrines were often difficult to comprehend. "Every one of the theologies is obviously but a weaving of fiction and fancy, in which the silver threads of truth are emphatically few and far between."[135] For example, Smith could find no evidence for, and therefore no reason for anyone to believe, that Methuselah lived 969 years, that Lot's wife became a pillar of salt, and that the sun stood still. These events were certainly not natural, and to the degree that one believed them, one became unnatural.[136]

A wonderful quote from a letter he wrote to Albert Barnes summed up Smith's comparison of the old religion of his earlier life with his new religion. He spoke of doctrinaire Christianity as an "Authority religion" that removed choice from people.

"This authority religion! this book-religion! this religion based on history and tradition! Alas, how it has cursed mankind in all ages, and all around the world! It claims to be the salt and savor of the world—but is its destroyer." The merciless spirit of this "authority religion [sleeps], and nothing short of the progress of science can keep the bloody monster from waking.... A religion of authority, ...inasmuch as it renders its disciples entirely

> sure that they are entirely right, makes them
> always intolerant toward dissent, and bloodily
> so…. The religion of reason, on the contrary, is
> tolerant and patient, because men are conscious
> that reason, mixed up as it is in the human breast
> with ignorance, prejudice, and passion, is not to be
> relied on as an entirely infallible guide. Imperfect
> human reason, sensible that it may misjudge
> others, is not in haste to condemn and punish
> them."[137]

None of these ideas were new or original, but at the time, it was a radical move to promulgate them as he did. Following the printing of his discourse on The Religion of Reason in the *New York Tribune* in early June of 1859, Smith received a flood of letters, most of them supportive. One requested a thousand copies to be spread among homes in Binghamton, New York.[138] Smith also received several invitations to public speaking engagements to tell of his ideas.[139] But not all of the reactions to his ideas were positive.

Horace Greeley of the *New York Tribune* received a critical letter from Reverend E. C. Taylor regarding the *Tribune's* publication of Gerrit Smith's "Religion of Reason."

> "In your issue of the 28th…I find another of these
> abominable discourses from Garrett Smith: in
> which the 'sacred book' (the Bible) is put down
> as having no authority in religion…. Some have
> already talked of having an indignation meeting
> here, and of stopping their paper, which you may
> depend will be done… unless you cease to publish
> such poisonous matter to the world."[140]

The next day Greeley, in a liberal and enlightened posture, wrote the following to Smith: "I hope you will write him a… letter calculated to effect on him the miracle of opening the eyes of the blind."[141]

Smith did question the long-held, unchallenged assumptions of nonanalytical Christians. His future biographer, Charles Hammond, acknowledged, "I confess that your discourse has... modified my views somewhat [and] staggered... my faith in the religious views in which I have been educated...."[142]

Smith had made some bothersome conclusions in his discourses. Not many people considered themselves to be just one equal element in a complex natural system, and to contemplate that could be threatening to one's presumed superiority. Traditional Christianity encouraged people to "have dominion" over the earth, and Smith argued that this was a foolish recipe for disaster.

His business agent in Rochester, Thomas C. Montgomery, challenged his ideas. "I cannot refrain...from asking whether you really think that all pain + suffering come from the violation of Nature's Laws—and that Science will reveal the secret, by which all pain + suffering may be avoided?" He cited natural processes of predation as causing pain, and advised Smith: "No—no—My dear Sir—that Great Problem—the Origin of Evil—is not so easily solved."[143]

One reader who worried about no longer having an infallible guide for behavior wrote from Copenhagen,

"...you regard the Bible... as imperfect; and...
human reason is imperfect, as you also admit;
yet reason with whatever imperfection may hang
upon and overshadow it, may be safely trusted....
If true, man has no perfect and infallible guide in
religion; and can have none unless he shall be able
to mature and perfect reason.... I think human
reason an imperfect and therefore unsafe guide in
matters of religion; and must look to the Bible as
higher and better counsil."[144]

What this criticism overlooked, and what Smith was trying to teach, was that human reason had been the source of religion in the first place. As a social institution, religion was created by people to help explain life before the advent of scientific investigation. But Smith saw the understanding of life coming from rational, methodical, inductive investigation rather than from authority.

> "Reason must ever be left free to revise and repeal
> its own decisions.... We may, and we should, have
> respect to the wise judgments which abound both
> within and without the Bible. Nevertheless, the
> final and decisive judgment is that which we are
> ourselves to form."[145]

Smith's connection of the Religion of Reason to science looked ahead toward change instead of backward toward authority. "Whilst the true religion [of reason] obeys the law of progress, the theological religion prides itself in its unchangableness; and...whilst the one lives in the present, the other burrows in the past."[146]

These relativistic and enlightened ideas about religion led Smith along the path toward developing a secular world view. By the mid-1860s, he viewed most Christian theology as "belief in the unrivaled fish story,"[147] and as his cynicism grew, he began to pity Christian believers. "Sadder than all is it, that they should recognize as religion what is so largely and glaringly a compound of superstition, fraud, cruelty, and curses."[148] When reason was stifled by authority, Smith believed, people lost the basis of their humanity. Doctrinal authority did

> "more than all things else to darken life, to shut
> out sweet sunshine from the soul, to fill it with
> trembling apprehension, and to sink it in agony
> and despair.... What can more debase and shrivel
> the soul, as well as distress it, than this fearful
> looking for judgment.... Nothing of these hideous
> structures which have for so many centuries cast
> their baleful shadows over the whole earth, should
> be left standing."[149]

One focus of Smith's secular attack on authority-based, or doc-trine-filled, religion was the Bible. He called it "the best of books" when read "with discrimination," but "the worst of books when read under authority, and with no liberty to call any of its words in question."[150] When misinterpreted, the Bible was "obstructing the progress of civilization and...filling the world with ignorance and superstition.... The clergy make the bible supreme authority. But our reason is... the final judge in all questions.... Reason must sit in judgment upon the bible...."[151] Smith viewed the Bible as a history book "written in unscientific and superstitious ages, and stuffed with grotesque and absurd myths and legends!"[152]

Such stories, Smith thought, were attempts to spice up otherwise dull ideas so that bored people would read it. "The gospels would have been dry and dull reading to those for whom they were writ-ten, had they not been...enlivened with miracles."[153]

Those who believed that Smith had become a heretic were invited to present their opposing views from the pulpit of the Free Church of Peterboro. Discussions followed regarding both views, so attendees had the benefit of reasoning out their own conclusions. Opposing views might have been aired, for instance, about the Biblical account of Jesus' resurrection. The secular Gerrit Smith would have argued, "But little evidence is necessary to prove that a man has died. That his breathless body went straightway into the sky could hardly be believed on any amount of evidence."[154]

There must have been some spirited discussions. Regarding quotes attributed to Jesus, Smith said,

> "...the laws of evidence require me to doubt whether pages written, no one knows when, nor where, nor by whom, and abounding in declarations extravagant and unnatural, contain, in any instance, the exact utterance of Jesus.... And why should I believe that the words of Jesus, not written until after they had floated for many years in uncertain and disagreeing memories [are accurate]?"[155]

If people did need a behavioral guide to hold as a "'Sacred Book'—how much more rational to let the advanced physical and moral science of modern times furnish it! How irrational to turn our back upon the great light of the present, and to keep our face toward the thick darkness of the past."[156]

Smith found it difficult to believe that well-educated people of his time could still believe religious doctrines. He had become secular and open-minded; he thought that anyone else who exercised their own reasoning would come to believe as he did. Because his mind had become open to change, he did not get the point that reason could also lead one to believe in absolutes. "My religion has no sacred… boundaries, which stop my reason, and forbid it to cross into other and unexplored fields."[157] As his explorations of thought processes and ideas progressed, he became more and more secular.

Most Christian doctrines consider Jesus Christ to be divinely conceived—to be the Son of God, or even a god himself. Smith considered him to be just a man.

> "On the suposition that he is God, his words and deeds…excite in us comparatively little interest and no wonder. But that they are the words and deeds of a mere man awakens all our admiration, and encourages us with the hope that we too, if we shall earnestly endeavor to live the Christ-life, will be enabled…. That they are merely human words and human deeds proves what possibilities of wisdom and goodness lie infolded in human nature; and that these possibilities were so developed in the life of one man is an example to inspire their development in the life of every other man."[158]

Smith did not believe in the virgin birth of Christ, claiming that the story was just a scheme by the Catholic Church to attract attention to the high moral quality of Jesus' life.[159]

He was fascinated with the expanding use of the scientific method of inquiry, and he believed it to be a reasonable source of authoritative knowledge. "Modern science, sweeping aside ignorance and superstition, makes room for studying the laws of evidence. A superstitious people… delight in the marvellous. Indeed, the more marvellous a thing is, the more eager are they to let their credulity be abused by it. Science stops all this; and causes facts, instead of fancies, to rule men."[160]

One interesting coincidence of science and religion Smith saw was in the social world. Everlasting life, he claimed, was not possible biologically, but was possible socially. Evolutionists saw altruism as a survival technique for an individual organism because of its fostering of group protection. "Humanity, should be living so emphatically for others, …as to be able to rejoice in the thought that the living forever of the race infinitely overbalances the perishing of the individual."[161]

Probably the most highly anti-doctrinal and secular perspective that Gerrit Smith adopted during this late stage of his thinking was that, in their pursuit of knowledge, humans can only approximate truth or certainty. Even the most exact sciences agree with this principle—that we can only know anything within limits of tolerance. He wrote,

> "Great stress is laid on the importance of having our knowledge…attain to certainty. But the mistake which lies at the bottom of all this is the underrating of human powers and human dignity. It is not man, but beings of an inferior grade, that need certainty in their knowledge…. But man's high faculties supercede the necessity…of instinctive [or] of revealed certainty…. Enough for him is it that, by means of those faculties, he can be ever approaching certainty…. It is the pursuit more than the possession of truth which enables and glorifies man."[162]

Smith thought that those who claimed to know certainties by means of doctrine revealed by authority were poachers of human reason, and would acquire only false pride.

These ideas met with approval among some clergy. Reverend George F. Post of Meredith in Delaware County, New York liked the notion that through scientific measurement there could be documentable evidence of near certainties. "Your reasonable religion must be true for an unmeasurable one cannot be true."[163] A.V. Bentley responded, "How can the Religion of God, + the Religion of Nature disagree? Whatever is scientifically + naturally true, can not be religiously or theologically false."[164]

Mary Quiney, an acquaintance from Boston, liked the tact with which Smith delivered his message. This is a significant point, because Smith's early teaching tactics when he was enamored of absolutes were more coercive.

> "You have the gift not too common of enforcing your teachings with a tender deference for your... brother which must go far towards making them acceptable." "You are doing more than any one in the country to reunite reason + religion, whose divorce is so complete in most minds that any attempt to interpret one by the other is considered sacreligious...."[165]

A summary of Smith's mature ideas on religion can be stated very simply: He equated reason with religion. If there was anything in life to be worshiped, it was human reason—with its power to discern balance in nature, and to use it as a model for social behavior. This put responsibility for the creation of the institution of religion squarely on the shoulders of people.

Smith's most potent statement about this belief came in a letter to Barnes: "Every people resembles its God."[166] Put another way, people made their gods. The story of creation was true, Smith reasoned, but it had been reversed: God did not create people; people created

God. The people were "created," or evolved, "from the original and eternal laws of nature."[167] Having evolved, man created God in his image.

"We know that man's moral nature is good, and therefore that God's is."[168] The liability for good or evil in the world rested not with God, but with people. For instance, regarding prayer, people "should pray about nothing which is entirely beyond the reach of human agency... for human agency has to do with their receiving it. Whether they shall receive it, depends upon themselves."[169]

In Smith's thinking, there were no scapegoats; one could not blame God or fate for anything. The Religion of Reason made rational people accountable for their circumstances, comprehending both their causes and their consequences.

In his old age, Smith reconciled his lifelong piety with his secular opinions by viewing the balance in nature on one side and the human powers of reason on the other as the real gods to be worshiped. He did not remove a Divine God from his perceptions of reality; he simply relocated it from heaven to earth. Divine order resided in nature, and divine power resided in the human ability to reason. Both factors—an ordered natural ecosystem and human reasoning power—were Divine gifts, yet they were not immutable.

The perception of an ever-changing, flexible natural balance depended upon the powers of human reasoning. When properly guided, those reasoning powers could not only discern natural balance among equally valuable parts of an ecosystem, but could also transfer those rules to the social system for the achievement of balance and order in human social life, thereby establishing justice and equity among people.

Gerrit Smith's Religion of Reason set a new course for the vessel of faith. In true optimistic fashion, he taught that people could have faith in themselves—in their abilities to reason and to comprehend both the natural and social worlds that they were a part of—without submitting to the presumed authority of the clergy. The laymen were, in his view, the real priests. This message was radical, liberal, and liberating. The traditional world of the common people had previously developed around the authoritative institutions of religion that trapped their minds. Now, they could be free.

- 11 -

Business Endeavors

"A'nt I smart!" quipped Gerrit's wife Ann after having performed the work of a business clerk in Gerrit's office in 1844. Why would Ann, who did not like business and was not trained for it, need to work for her husband? The answer illustrates the pressure under which Gerrit Smith worked on a daily basis.

Because he was so successful as a land speculator, Gerrit Smith was able to be an abolitionist, a philanthropist, a politician, a minister, a traveler, a public speaker, a lawyer, a temperance leader, a women's suffragist, and an at-home father and husband. The irony is that he did not like being a businessman. As early as 1835, he wrote, "I am exceedingly desirous... to retire from business."[1] Details and numerical calculations bored him.[2] He had little enthusiasm for the daily routine of legal jargon, deed writing, correspondence through the mail, and record-keeping. He would rather have spent his time thinking, preaching, and philosophizing about social equality and justice and the relationship between nature and religion. As a thinker, he preferred those non-linear, subjective topics; but at work, he had to calculate interest rates, acreages, payment schedules, and account details.

It is likely, though, that this is what helped to keep him balanced amid crushing pressures. He could not obsess about anything for long, so his enthusiasm for any endeavor would not carry him far beyond practical realities. As his mind dreamed of a morally better world, he worked daily with the practical needs of business, the one tempering the other.

In Smith's personally sanctioned *Tribute* to his dead son Fitzhugh, the author wrote, "The mart of commerce hath a part… as important as the pulpit in training men for heaven. In the latter, we listen to the theory of the process through which we are to pass; in the former, we try our hand at its practical bearings."[3] "We look upon the great world of human business as a mighty system of means by which man receives both teaching and testing…. Christianity can no more do without her aid, than can the true work of commerce be performed without the spirit of religion to animate it."[4]

In Smith's work, balance sheets and profit schedules relinquished their priority to the poor, the slaves, and the sick; in fact, the needs of these latter groups drove the engine of land sales. He worked hard at the details of practical tasks so that he could implement his utopian dreams, and the businesslike technique he used to fund those dreams occurred within the existing institutional structure of society. Business institutions could aid the poor, churches could oppose oppression, government could abolish slavery, education could help to equalize opportunity, and families could encourage morality. Rather than drop out, Smith chose to stay in—to use the workable, operative practices and customs with which people were already familiar to install reform. Because he pursued practical ways to implement his utopian ideas, he was, indeed, a *practical dreamer*.

Historians have generally overlooked this operational side of Gerrit Smith. Researchers have covered *what* he did, *how* he did it, and *when* he did it, but they have avoided analyzing the influence of business on his personal balance and his work in humanitarian reform. He had the business savvy and the social skills to make great amounts of money while increasing his vast network of contacts, all to achieve social reform. His wealth lent credence to his ideas, legitimacy to his authority, and boldness to his thrust. In its obituary, the *New York Times* described Gerrit Smith as "a business man of extraordinary capacity and foresight."[5] Maybe so, but that is not how he wanted to be remembered. Humanitarian work was his chosen life-purpose, and he used his personal resources and business profits to achieve it. It is true that some of his philanthropic efforts failed, but more than most people, at least he tried.

Smith's business career had started when his father, Peter, retired and handed over to him the management of his land business. As a young man in his 20s, Peter Smith had made lots of money by dealing with Native Americans in central New York State in the fur trade. He became interested in the land occupied by his Native American trading partners. In March of 1784, when Peter was a teenager, the Continental Congress, which made little effort to protect native land rights, appointed a three-member commission that had as part of its charge "extinguishing [Native American] claims and settling boundaries between them and the citizens of the United States."[6]

These "citizens," moving into the frontier territory of New York State, were generally of Northwestern European heritage. Their culture of acquisition, private ownership, and hoarding were alien to Native Americans, who naively wondered how anyone could 'own' land. Their question would have been, "How can someone steal something that is not owned by anyone else?"

The Native Americans saw their native lands as a communal trust for the benefit of all, not subject to private ownership. In the midst of this clash of cultures—one ready to share or lease for public welfare, the other ready to grab—Peter Smith grabbed.

In January 1788, the New York Genesee Company—a group of land speculators led by John Livingston—concluded an agreement with some Oneidas that would lease their land for nine-hundred-ninety-nine years at $1,000 per year. The State of New York intercepted this lease agreement, and on September 22, 1788, signed an "instrument of cession" that leased 5.5 million acres from Native Americans for an annual rental fee, under the guise of protecting it from greedy land speculators.[7]

New York State, however, considered the deal to be a sale, and deeded some of the land to speculators.[8] This action took place *after*

New York State had joined the union by ratifying the United States Constitution, which made it illegal for a state to buy land from Native Americans. This prohibition of land purchase was certified by the Indian Nonintercourse Act of 1790, which forbade land to be acquired from Native Americans "except by a treaty ratified by the U.S. Senate. Moreover, a party cannot even negotiate to acquire Indian land without the presence of a U.S. Commissioner."[9]

Because the land deal of 1788 was a lease, not a sale, the 1790 Nonintercourse Act protected the title of the Oneidas to their land. Subsequent federal legal action reaffirmed the validity of the 1790 Nonintercourse Act.[10]

Enter Peter Smith. His interest in land speculation had begun in 1793, when he leased approximately 50,000 acres of land from the Oneidas. He was on friendly terms with the Oneidas because of his relationship with them through his fur trading business.

The Oneidas were split internally over the lease of their land to Smith. The "Christian" faction, led by Smith's friend Skenandoah, sided with him; the "pagan" faction did not. The latter attempted to disrupt the lease deal by attacking Peter's surveying party. Mr. Annin, the surveyor, and his party of workers were camped on the north side of the brook at Peterboro when they were attacked, and they fled, postponing their survey for a year.[11]

In 1795, New York State Governor George Clinton called the Oneidas, Onondagas, and Cayugas to meet with representatives of the state to establish more treaties. Israel Chapin, Jr., the United States agent for the Iroquois Nations, was suspicious of New York State's intentions. He obtained an opinion from United States Attorney General William Bradford that the state could not extinguish title to Native American land by purchasing it from them. Chapin informed New York State of this and encouraged the Native Americans to refrain from giving "aid or countenance to the [state's] measure [to purchase land]."[12] But the Oneidas did not heed his advice, and they sold to New York State over one hundred thousand acres of land. Following this illegal state purchase, Peter Smith bought from

New York State 22,300 acres with what appeared to be clear title to it. Then, he started to build his fortune by selling it.

It is fair to speculate that Gerrit Smith was aware from the start that his father had purchased land that the state had acquired illegally. Gerrit stated in a speech before Congress on the Nebraska Bill on April 6, 1854,

"The Constitution prescribes limits to the State quite too narrow for the play of sovereignty. It denies the State many specific powers, each of which is vital to sovereignty. For instance, it restrains it from entering into a treaty...."[13]

He knew that his father had purchased much of his original land holdings following the 1795 treaty. By 1871, the Oneidas were trading written communications with Gerrit regarding land claims.[14]

Gerrit had assumed the management of his father's land business in 1818, and the first business letters addressed to him appeared on November 7 of that year. He also assumed some sizeable obligations. He wasn't able to pay off the large tax debt on the land until 1845.[15]

The formal sale of Peter's land business to a partnership of Gerrit Smith and Gerrit's uncle, Daniel Cady, took place on November 1, 1819. The sale contract called for a price of $225,000 to be paid in five annual installments of $25,000 with no interest, followed by ten annual installments of $10,000 with interest. If they paid up the contract as scheduled by 1834, the estate would be divided between Gerrit Smith and Daniel Cady with one half, including the mansion and grounds, going to Gerrit. The other half would belong to both Cady and Gerrit to hold as trustees for the rest of Peter Smith's heirs.

Before and after Peter's death, the trust was obliged to maintain the financial security of Peter's family via monthly payments from the profits of the land business.[16] However, when the contract debt was not paid by 1834, Cady, who had done nothing to help Gerrit manage the property during the intervening fifteen years, relinquished his share of the trusteeship to Gerrit, thereby putting Gerrit in complete control of the estate. Cady probably made this move to avoid impending debt and family squabbles, and because he had not been involved in the business. Also, Cady was opposed to the concentration of wealth, especially through the accumulation of land holdings. "Should it be permitted," he said, "the great mass of mankind would become slaves."[17]

Gerrit Smith's first land deal was an 1818 purchase of 18,000 acres near Florence, New York. Although he had some difficulty meeting payments due on this transaction, he did manage to hold it.[18] One of Smith's favorite techniques for acquiring land, which he probably learned from his father, was to purchase it for unpaid back taxes at state tax sales. Gerrit's business records for the year 1831 include 19 pages of tax purchases of 519 parcels for back taxes of $435.50.[19]

In Albany, Smith's clerk, Federal Dana, negotiated a large tax sale purchase of land in 1843. Dana spent several days in June bidding on available land and sending daily reports to Smith. His final bid total was $17,468.89. A partial list of purchases follows:

June 9–1,450 acres in Chemung County.
June 14–600 acres in Essex County.
June 15–12,000 acres in Franklin and Fulton Counties.
June 16–23,040 acres in Greene and Hamilton Counties.
June 17–5,000 acres in Herkimer and Jefferson Counties.
June 20–3,500 acres in Onondaga, Orange and Oneida Counties.
June 26–2,000 acres in Sullivan, Tioga, and Tompkins Counties.
June 27–500 acres in Ulster County.[20]

Tax sales were an inexpensive source of large tracts of land for Gerrit Smith. He was so pleased with Dana's efforts at this sale that he presented him with a $50 bonus for his work.[21] Dana was worried during the sale that he was spending too much. He wrote to his boss, "I hope you may be able (but I don't know where) to get money to pay for your purchases."[22]

Smith was facing possible bankruptcy brought on from the economic depression that had started with the "Panic of 1837." He had agreed with Dana that this land purchase would be Dana's last official duty before he was released from service.

Smith's business files of the 1840s and 1850s are full of certificates of public sale of land to him for taxes, much of it handled by his Oswego-based agent, John B. Edwards.[23] Exactly how much land Smith owned, even he could only estimate. In the 1840s, he acknowledged holding 800,000 acres.[24] He said, "I can hardly call either 2 or 3,000 acres of northern land a large quantity."[25]

The foundation for Gerrit's wealth, power, and philanthropy was the ownership of land, and he believed that all people "have a natural and equal right to the soil."[26] Yet even with all of his property, he still believed that the possession of too much land could give unscrupulous landowners control over others, even to the point of slavery. He favored the Homestead Bill because "This bill…is an acknowledgment, that the public lands belong, not to the government, but to the landless."[27] He advocated that to alleviate poverty, laws should be passed limiting the amount of land any one person could own.

In the mid-1840s, Smith demonstrated his commitment to this idea by giving away some of his land to poor people.

"Is there a spare home in the great common
inheritance of the human family? Who should
have it if not the homeless? I repeat it, we should
make public lands free to the poor."[28]

Thus could society, if it really wanted to, achieve social equity.

Smith did not seriously diversify his investments outside of his land dealing, because the accumulation of money and personal financial security were not his main goals. Rather than accumulate wealth, he wanted to divest himself of it by distributing it among people less well-off. For instance, although speculation in oil development was gaining attention in the 1860s, Smith showed little interest.

He did dabble in a few local, small, and generally not-too-profitable businesses. He gained small amounts of income from the sale of wood from his lands. He owned a grist mill in Florence, NY that burned in 1835.[29] He bartered with farmers Joshua and Arumah Burdick for returns from one-half of their produce.[30] He owned a struggling hotel in Oswego. Insurance records indicate ownership of a sawmill in Pennsylvania.[31]

In Florence, he had a business relationship with James S. T. Stranahan for the sale of general merchandise and tanning services that lasted five years in the 1830s. And with his brother-in-law, Henry Fitzhugh, he owned a flour milling operation in Oswego.

In April 1852, a fascinating investment opportunity came his way; but, like the later opportunity in oil, he avoided it. He wrote to his "boys" (son Greene and grandson "Gatty") about the wisdom of investing in a "Flying Ship" proposed by Rufus Porter. "What do you think of it? Had I better advance half the money for building it, + own half of it? ...Do you think I had better quit my office + engage in this new business?"[32] Had he invested here, he probably would have lost his money; the Wright brothers did not fly successfully until 1903.

When Smith took over his father's business in 1818, he also assumed ownership of Peter's two glass factories. One was at the east edge of Peterboro, the other two miles east of that. On November 3, 1819, Gerrit listed one glass factory, two furnaces alternately in blast and repairs, $10,000 in invested capital, $7,500 per year in labor costs, $1,000 per year in "contingent expenses," and a monthly production of 32,000 feet of window glass. Smith's comment on this report was that his second glass factory "is in all respects similar to the other."[33]

Smith was in charge of personnel—hiring and firing people to cut wood for the furnaces, perform masonry work, and do general factory work.[34] He hired John Pike in accordance with the following agreement: "Said Pike agrees to work for said Smith at his glass factory, in the capacity of Master Stoker...while the Furnace in said factory is in blast." Pike's pay was twenty-four dollars per month. One third would be paid in cash, and two thirds "in goods of the store of said Smith," including glass, wheat, and corn. "The said Smith reserves to himself the privilege of disciplining said Pike when dissatisfied with his management."[35]

The last recorded transaction for glass from Smith's factories was on November 2, 1826. As a note of interest, remnants from the waste piles of the glass factory nearest to the hamlet of Peterboro make beautiful contemporary jewelry crafted by the author.

In 1827, Smith invested $14,000 in mostly waterfront property along the east side of the river that enters Lake Ontario at Oswego. He then invested in the Oswego Canal Company, eventually owning ninety-one percent of its stock.[36] This property became a major source of income, and it served as collateral on large loans during his brush with bankruptcy. Smith's commitment to the city of Oswego was evident in his $1,000 donation to a relief fund for those burned out by a large fire in July of 1853.[37]

As of 1855, his investments in Oswego were worth $900,000.[38] The Oswego Canal connected Lake Ontario with the Erie Canal to the south and opened the northern city of Oswego to commerce with growing urban centers of central and southern New York State. After the canal was completed in 1828, commerce developed quickly in Oswego. Between 1830 and 1836, its population rose from 2,000 to 5,000, and the number of vessels arriving in port rose from 546 to 2,004.[39]

Smith remained interested in expanding the capacity of the Erie Canal for the rest of his life,[40] but he also became attracted to the railroads, even as they were taking business away from the canals. He subscribed to $1,000 of stock in the Northern Railroad, whose directors asked him to solicit stock purchases by other northern landowners because the railroad would "greatly enhance the value of their lands...."[41]

Years later, because of his property in Oswego, he became interested in the Lake Ontario Shore Railroad. He saved an article from the *Auburn Morning News* of March 30, 1869 that hailed the railroad as "the great invention of the present century…. It has revolutionized the commercial world and the value of property…. It is of vastly greater utility than a canal." People viewed the canals as too slow; besides, they were too often closed due to poor weather.[42] Although Smith and his agent, George J. Post, were optimistic about the future of the railroad, they pulled out of this project because residents along its proposed route would not invest in it.[43]

Gerrit Smith was no different from many others as he experienced America's first great depression. In the end, he made it through the "Panic of 1837," but he faced some worrisome hard times. One of his clerks, Caleb Calkins, thought that Smith overreacted to the crisis. "[Smith] had the hallucination that he was reduced to bankruptcy…. He was not a bankrupt, but a person of large property, in no wise precarious in condition…."[44] John B. Edwards pointed out to Smith in 1846, "You have nearly ¾ of a million acres of land."[45]

Although Smith was in considerable debt himself throughout the period, he was also concerned about the debt owed him and the ability of his debtors to pay. True to his benevolence, he allowed his debtors as much leniency as possible. To accomplish this, he wrote for help from long time family friend, John Jacob Astor.

Smith wrote to Astor on July 21, 1837, requesting a $200,000 to $300,000 long-term loan (the equivalent of between $1.5 million and $2.25 million today). Astor agreed to $200,000, based on the security of Smith's Oswego property. Astor paid most of it to Smith—before the security of a mortgage to Astor on Smith's property was filed.[46] This reveals much about Astor's confidence in Smith's commitment to repay the loan. Smith wrote on August 10, 1837 in his diary,

"The money will enable me to rid myself of
pecuniary embarrassments, and to extend
important assistance to others, and especially
to extend indulgence to those who owe me…. It
relieves my mind of a great burden of anxiety."[47]

This loan was subject to the very high interest rate of 20 percent,[48] and by December of 1839, Smith had to request of Astor the postponement of an interest payment of $7,000.[49] As the value of his property decreased during the depression, Astor required that Smith provide additional security for the loan.[50] Smith was eventually able to pay off the loan, but the 10 years between 1837 and 1846 were difficult for him.

He was not only contending with the beginning of the depression, but during the same year, on April 13, 1837, his father died. Gerrit was saddled with debts from Peter Smith's estate just as his own debtors were indicating their inability to meet their financial obligations. Peter Smith's will required that his land holdings of 556,000 acres be sold and the proceeds divided among Gerrit, his brother Peter Skenandoah, and his sister's eight children. Gerrit, with the consent of the other parties, held the land in return for payment of $6,000 "in hand," $8,000 per year to Peter Skenandoah, and $120,000 to Cornelia's eight children, collectively. He also provided Peter's wife, Sarah Pogson Smith, with $1,200 per year for life instead of the $700 dollars per year specified in the will by her husband.[51] Peter Skenandoah was allowed a grace period of four months in which he could alter the agreement, but he ultimately accepted the proposed terms.[52]

Although Gerrit was not legally required to do any more financially for his nieces and nephews after the 1837 settlement, 23 years later, he did. Because of the ultimate success of the land business, he distributed to them $120,000 in 1860, and again in 1862, and $80,000 in 1864.[53]

Settling his estate was difficult not only in light of the depression, but because his debtors were also having such a hard time. A client wrote of his own insolvency, "the only reason is that I cannot git it, money is not to be had.... I have money due from the best men in our town who was to pay me the first of June but I cannot git one dollar."[54]

Another client was having a "hard time in the woods that year," rendering him unable to pay his debt to Smith. But he indicated that he expected a good summer garden, saying, "I think after getting a going there I can make money if you will not require more than what I can do."[55]

Still another was unable to pay for land purchased, but had built a "small fraimed hous and moved on to the lot and maid som improvement...."[56]

Henry L. Hilyas could not pay Smith "for my helth is very poor at preasant.... I thought best to wright stateing the sircumstances."[57]

Smith's tolerant attitude toward his clients who could not pay their debts was typical of his benevolence, yet it led him deeper into financial trouble. In December 1837 he compiled, in his own handwriting, a list of his largest debts. The top 20 entries amounted to $506,062.28. The list continued for smaller debts covering 66 pages of an account book with an additional total of over $82,000.[57]

As the depression persisted, so did Smith's debt load. "Ever since the failure of friends, whom I had assisted, swelled my indebtedness to upwards of $600,000, and thereby threatened my own failure, I have been struggling to escape bankruptcy.... The amount of my present debt is nearly $700,000."[58]

Even Ann Smith was concerned over her husband's tolerant attitude in hard times. "My husband has so greatly embarrassed himself by helping his friends, that to pay his [interest] debts is as much as he can do," she wrote.[59]

Smith dealt with all of this in a number of ways. In early 1843, he decided to release his clerks and have his wife and daughter do the office work. When clerk Federal Dana learned of it, he had mixed emotions. "If it would be any relief to you, in your desire to lessen your expenses, I would cheerfully resign my situation.... The idea of making clerks of Mrs. S. + your daughter is too absurd to be entertained for a moment. You have, I am confident, no creditor who would be willing to see them thus employed...."[60]

Smith saw the situation differently. "I thought it due to my creditors... to dismiss my clerks—give up my recreations—cease to go from home except on urgent business— + make office laborers of my wife and daughter....”[61] He had written to Federal Dana and Nehemiah Huntington three days earlier: “I cannot pay your salaries; and I, therefore, owe it to myself + my creditors to dispense with your services.”[62]

Although Dana had earlier agreed to resign, he took his dismissal with rancor, claiming that Smith had dismissed him due to a disagreement on moral grounds.[63] Whatever the cause, Gerrit’s “office labor,” as he called it, became distributed among his family members. Elizabeth copied letters and kept records, and Ann did “business work,” although she did not enjoy it. “I have had business enough today: Copied a letter— filled out two Contracts + copied one statement.” “I copied seven letters last evening. A’nt I smart!”[64]

Her housekeeper noted, “Mrs. Smith goes to the office almost every morning and stays ‘till 4 o’clock.”[65] Gerrit even spent time copying some business letters into his Letter Copy Book (knowing, perhaps, that his poor penmanship would make the author’s research into his life much more difficult!).

As the depression lingered into the 1840s, Smith decided to sell his Peterboro house. Knowing how much he loved the spot, the decision must have been difficult to make. He wrote to his brother, “I have advertised my house for sale [and] am preparing to move... into a small house 1¼ miles from the village...”[66] That small house was another one that he owned called “The Grove.”

Ann was away from home when the move took place. Gerrit wrote to her, “We are about to eat our last meal in the old mansion.... The furniture has nearly all gone to The Grove— + we are to follow in an hour or two.”[67] While living at The Grove, he walked daily to and from his Peterboro Land Office.[68] He was still able to use his office; although the mansion house was for sale, he never found a buyer for it. The Smiths were at The Grove intermittently until 1853, when they moved back to the Peterboro mansion permanently.

It was during this stay at The Grove that Smith tried to get a second loan from John Jacob Astor. He told a friend,

> “The truth is (tho’ I wish it + this letter kept to
> yourself) that I have been laboring, for a month

or two, to induce my highly esteemed friend
John Jacob Astor, Esq. to lift me again out of my
difficulties."[69]

Happily, though, this second loan did not become necessary as
Smith's land sales began to increase the next year.

Smith was angry that these "difficulties" had caused his lands to
lose so much value. "I could not sell [my] lands…at one half what
I gave for them to say nothing of my loss of interest."[70]

Henry Campbell, a Peterboro farmer, echoed Smith's exaspera-
tion: "Farm produce has [here] been falling… so that sheep, swine
and cattle can be got now for 1/3, Land for 1/2 to 1/3 below what
they were [in 1839]."[71]

Smith responded to a debtor who was anxious over his inability
to pay, "I will be as tender toward you as I can be. But… you will
not expect my tenderness to be boundless."[72]

He was "tender" towards many who owed him money. In 1841,
he had "twelve or fifteen hundred" debtors, some of whom could
not even make a down payment.[73] At one point, he admitted that
he had "lost totally + irretrievably by…endorsements for friends +
loans to them $200,000."[74]

The only creditors with whom Smith was not lenient were those
he deemed able to pay. When Hamilton College, for instance, delayed payment to Smith, he blamed them for helping cause his near
bankruptcy and told them, "My need of money is so painfully great,
+ your delinquency… is so very great also, that I must insist on payment being made. The whole amount is nearly all due. I beg you not
to neglect this matter any longer." And four months later, "I most
earnestly hope you will be able to send me the Principle soon."[75]

Throughout the depression, Smith continually feared bankruptcy,
and he viewed it not as a route out of trouble, but as a smear on
his reputation. He even tried selling his assets at a loss just to develop cash flow.[76] He largely curtailed his philanthropy during this
period.[77]

It was not until 1844 when land sales began to pick up that Smith recovered from his financial woes. He realized, however, that the short-term need for cash necessitated the sale of his land at very low prices.[78] By April 1845, he was in sufficient financial shape to move temporarily back to the Peterboro mansion, dismiss his wife and daughter from their responsibilities in his office, and hire two clerks.[79]

By the fall of 1846, Smith had regained financial security and optimism. He noted, "More than two fifths of the six hundred thousand dollars, which I owed in the year 1842 are paid; and... in all probability the remainder will be paid... in a few years." His debt had fallen to less than a half-million dollars, and he held auctions to sell land quickly. He felt so good regarding this accomplishment that he gifted five of his former business clerks with $500 each in appreciation of their services.[80]

Smith was not the only person who was happy. His friend, Lewis Tappan, wrote, "I am right glad to hear from you, of your successful sales, of the reduction of the great load."[81]

The greatest part of that load—the huge loan from Astor—was paid in full just before Astor died in 1848. Smith wrote to Astor's son, "You have lost an affectionate father. I have lost a... friend... who had the ability, as well as the disposition to render me very important services."[82]

He felt good that he could reestablish his composure and his philanthropy.

> "Within the past few years God has greatly blessed
> my efforts to recover my affairs from threatened
> bankruptcy. I have enough left to pay my debts
> with, + something to give away."[83]

Gerrit Smith's business style was in keeping with his benevolent personality. "I am no friend to suing," he wrote a client in 1840.[84] Not only did he rarely sue others, but others did not often sue him. He felt that lawsuits were a waste of resources and reflected a lack of mutual trust and a selfish disposition. "They who are acquainted with the great amount of my labors in my Land Office, will not wonder to hear me say, that I have neither time nor taste for controversy."[85]

When he did sue, it was only based on what he felt was overwhelming evidence and a just cause. In 1866, Smith sued the Rome and Oswego Railroad Company for devaluing his property in Oswego, and he was awarded $9,500.[86] He was also troubled with the rustling of timber from his northern lands, so he hired a person to establish lawsuits against the perpetrators.[87] Yet even when actively suing a business client, he wanted to be fair. "I wish to do in this matter what is just and right, not barely what is legal, but what is equitable also."[88]

Smith always tried to keep his clients happy, and when they complained about his treatment of them, he wrote to them personally, attempting to clear up misunderstandings. He would sometimes release buyers from their signed obligations to purchase if they became dissatisfied with their deals.[89] Yet when he felt justified, he would stand his ground. When a client challenged Smith's title to land, Gerrit annotated the letter, "Calkins will write him that it is my business to defend my title."[90]

If he tried to treat others well in spite of their ire, he expected the same in return. Having received a letter accusing him of "avarice," he responded by asking for a more "civil letter" before investigating the issue.[91] His self-defense even went so far as to cut off all further interaction.

When a client complained of unfairness and requested reimbursement of 31 cents, Smith replied, "Your insulting letter is before me. I wish to have no further correspondence with you."[92]

In many cases, Smith let his clerk handle the letters of complaint, which are annotated, "Calkins will answer," or "Calkins will do as he pleases."[93] If the complaint was justified, Smith would respond directly.

For the most part, clients were satisfied with his treatment of them. Some who had formerly complained even wrote back to apologize,[94] and those who were happy often sent notes of thanks. "You will please tender my very best thanks to Mr. Smith... for what he has so kindly done for me. Everything is all right + to my entire satisfaction...."[95]

One lesson that Smith learned from the Panic of 1837 was never to loan money. "I am a borrower—not a lender—of money. The money I receive I either <u>give</u> <u>away</u>, or pay on the debts I owe."[96]

When people did request loans, he would often respond by just giving them the money.

Smith was kind even when he had reason to be angry. In 1843 he was having trouble paying his land tax bills because Thomas Farrington, treasurer of the State of New York, would not accept his checks. Smith wrote,

> "Your predecessors never hinted to me, that I put them to unreasonable trouble in sending them my dfts. Perhaps, however, their spirit of accomadation was excessive, and... yours is of the true standard. But this is certain, that, so long as I believe they were no more accomodating than they should be... that the spirit you evince toward me is less obliging than it should be. You, doubtless, think your course a correct one—And I cheerfully accord to you all the credit of good intentions."[97]

Smith was smooth with words and could jab people gently, making them feel apologetic. He was so accommodating of his customers that he sometimes let them set their own prices for land,[98] and when debtors could not meet agreed-upon prices, he often extended the terms of payment. "I shall cheerfully wait upon you for payment.... My own pecuniary straits... have the proper effect of teaching me to be sympathetic with others who are under pecuniary embarrassments."

"I cheerfully comply with your request to extend the time of paying the $1,000 beyond 1st July."[99]

He advised one corporate client, "I hope you will never think of paying the balance, until it is perfectly convenient for you to do so."[100]

These accommodations came in the middle of the depression.

Smith's tolerance regarding the account of Elizabeth Bunner is particularly illustrative of his kindhearted patience. He did not want to foreclose a mortgage on her property for fear that she would lose it, so he wrote to her in 1858, "let the inconvenience of [my] paying it be what it will… I have advanced you + paid for you some $5,500."[101] By April 13, 1861, she had still not paid him. "The amount of my advance to you is [now] $7,481.14…. Of this I am willing to lose $1,000 + to give you a credit of ten yearly payments with interest for the balance…. Now I submit whether this is not the full share of assistance due from me."[102]

Evidently, it was not. As of March 3, 1869, Bunner owed Smith $14,000. He offered to cancel $5,000 of that debt if she would pay the rest.[103]

Losing money was not something that Smith worried about, because he did not want it for his personal consumption anyway. In an exchange over how much money was still due on a debt owed to Smith by client D.S. Jones, he commented, "If you should persist in refusing to return the sum to me, I will consent to lose the $163.00…. I would far rather lose it than have a clamor with you about it."[104] Jones did eventually pay the bill.

Further evidence of Smith's benevolence appeared in his offers to clients who had experienced some tragedy. Henry Nattine's farm buildings had burned, so Smith cancelled further payments.[105] William Birney was the victim of theft, so Smith sent him $50 to help him stabilize his financial affairs.[106] Issac Forbes was in debt to many creditors, so Smith allowed him to postpone payment.[107] And the list goes on.

Smith was touchingly sensitive to the plights of others, even when he had financial problems of his own. He obliged potential clients with poor credit by allowing others to co-sign the contract with them,[108] and he agreed to pay a bill even though he was unsure he owed it.[109]

In a glowing stroke of honesty, he wrote to W. W. Treadway,

Deputy Comptroller of New York State, to indicate a computational error committed by the State in tax sale bills. "We find in them several important mistakes against the State—amounting in all to nearly $1,200.00…. Mr. Dana… will make a full statement, which will show the precise balance I still owe…."[110] He eventually paid to the state an additional $1,021.75 to make up for the state's own error.[111]

One last example is that of Dr. A. Doubleday. The doctor had complained to Smith about Smith's unpaid debts. Gerrit wrote that, according to his records, he had paid all of his debt to Doubleday, but if Doubleday still disagreed, Smith would deduct the amount due from Doubleday's debts owed to him.[112]

Smith's attention to detail was probably the most significant quality in his approach to business—and the most difficult for him. "I have to work in the Office + at details too. It comes quite hard to me."[113] This explains how he was able to maintain personal balance amid staggering complexities and pressures. He 'micro-managed' and had a part in all aspects of his business, keeping detailed, daily records of transactions in his own handwriting. His records include millions of numbers and calculations regarding dates, receipts, lot numbers, payments due, interest rates, acreages, amounts of timber standing on specific lots, soil quality, surveyed location of lots, checks written, suits filed, supplies purchased, debts paid, and more.

To a linear thinker, his records are a vision of beauty. To a non-linear thinker, they are a nightmarish headache. The genius of Gerrit Smith was that he could handle both sides effectively. In today's terms, he stood in the middle between those who love or hate math. He could use math effectively, but he also enjoyed a beautiful sunrise and thoughts of God just as much—and in the same day.

The filing system in Gerrit Smith's business office was superb. He and his clerks kept track of every detail of a transaction and, importantly, could *find* them years later. In many cases, one sheet of paper tracked a sale, interest calculations, payments made, and personal notes about the client over decades of time. An example:

on one small sheet of torn scrap paper are records regarding a debt of $300 incurred by a pair of clients in April of 1835. Due probably to the depression of the late 1830s, the first payment was not made until September 1842, and it was recorded in a clerk's handwriting. The following two payments made in 1843 and 1844 were recorded in Smith's handwriting, as those were the years in which his business clerks had been dismissed. Payments received in 1846 and 1847 are recorded by clerks, and the final, yet incomplete payment in 1848 was again recorded by Smith. A fair speculation is that Smith forgave the remainder of the debt.

The case of Mrs. E.L.V. Johnson is also illustrative of Smith's meticulous bookkeeping. She made a monetary claim against Smith in 1849 to settle what she believed to be a long-standing issue from before her husband's death. Smith referred to his account books from back in 1821 to show that the claim had been settled.[114]

"Day Books" kept by office clerks indicate land purchases, payments made on each land lot over many years, interest due, and notes about the account. Smith made many entries himself, and most business records show his annotations and comments, indicating that he checked over those accounts that he had not recorded himself. This style of record-keeping and double-checking involved thousands of ledger pages and hundreds of thousands of entries. The work consumed enormous amounts of time and reflected a high commitment to accuracy. For both legal and business reasons, such work was a necessity, and Smith showed a personal dedication to it.

Record books regarding debts due on land sales covering the period 1845 until Smith's death in 1874 contain 466 pages, and 10,252 entries, with approximately 85 percent of all entries written in Smith's handwriting. In a separate book that he titled "Notes + Judgments," he recorded—all in his handwriting—accounts due with judgments against them, and notes about action to be taken. Some examples:

Account #180, 1859: "Rix Robinson debt— I
must by summer of 1859 write to A. Lloyd asking

if his Brother…has left any one to attend to the business."

Account #201, 1859: "Dr. Marrin – This matter of the island must be seen to."

Account #179, 1859: "Hiram Matteson – Sue now."

Account #91, 1859: "Hiram Brown – get possession as soon as possible."

Account #139, 1860: "C. Winslow – Title disputed."

Account #311, 1860: "Alanson Port – Eject now."[115]

Smith even kept a separate book for "Account of monies taken from the Office to the House." This money was either "for the House," "for the [fugitive] slaves," or distributed to specific people.

As another example of his micro-management style, Smith kept detailed and accurate bank account books that recorded every check written and a running account of the balance. These books generally covered 4- to 5-year periods, and they were designed not by the bank, but by Smith. The ledger book for 1860–1864 is 64 pages long, all in his handwriting, on 12-inch pages.

He kept separate account books for his rental properties in Oswego because his land there was a major source of income. As of January 1, 1856, the Oswego Pier & Dock Co. owed him $81,845.96, and in 1860, the "Littlefield property" at Oswego brought in $31,108.84 in rent.[116] Smith's Oswego business records, generally kept by J. B. Edwards, Smith's clerk there, include thousands of entries for rent due or collected, work scheduled or completed on buildings or dock property, and supplies purchased.

A note of interest to the author from these records is a check received from "Thos. Kingsford on account of Michael Butler's rent for W. part of Despard Farm— $20.00." Thomas Kingsford owned a cornstarch mill in Oswego. He was the seventh cousin of Norman Kingsford Dann. In 1848, Kingsford's mill produced 25 million pounds of starch from one million bushels of corn.[117] Smith and Kingsford were also involved in property sales deals.[118]

Edwards kept detailed lists of every nail, paint brush, pickaxe, board, and stamp purchased as a part of Smith's business. Some examples:

"Stamps— 66¢; envelopes 22¢"
"Pd a boy for towing timber— 12¢"
"Pd a man for ½ day labor— 50¢"
"Paid John Gillon for 3¾ days labor— $3.28"
"Round trip travel cost Oswego to Peterboro— $4.00"
"Paid J. B. Edwards salary the past year— $500.00"
(Edwards deducted his salary from the business profits.)"[119]

Smith also maintained financial relationships with members of his extended family, as he was responsible for their income through his business. He displayed the same concern for accuracy and detail here. When a check to Mary Cochran, a niece, was lost, he wrote the following note, which Mary signed:

"Whereas Gerrit Smith did at my request enclose to my address in New York March 29, 1843 his dft. For $100.00.... And whereas said dft. failed of coming to hand. In consideration thereof said Smith now gives me his other dft. For $100.00— And in consideration of his so doing, I do hereby agree to indemnify him against the first mentioned dft. July 1, 1843."[120]

Family also turned to Smith for financial advice. His cousin, Elizabeth Cady Stanton, requested through her husband in 1861 that Gerrit invest for her $3,295.72 because they had been unable to locate a profitable place to invest it.[121]

A constant problem for business during most of Smith's life was the lack of a national monetary standard. Until the passage of the National Banking Act in 1864, banks issued and backed their own money. Over 8,000 banks printed monetary notes redeemable only at the institutions that issued them. This diversity in types of money and standards of value left little faith in the public mind concerning the security of money, so checks were sometimes refused. Smith's business records contain an extensive exchange of detailed letters between September 14, 1840 and January 7, 1842, transferring his accounts from Utica Bank to the New York State Bank at Albany. The move was probably due in part to avoid problems with creditors.[122] All of this added to his daily workload.

Historians have faulted Gerrit Smith for his inherited wealth, but a look at his normal workday proves he earned most of what he had. On an average day, he spent 13 to 15 hours working on business, with about 10 hours spent in his Land Office and the rest in the mansion during the evening. "The amount of property in my hands makes me a man of toil—toil by day + night."[123] When his daughter asked him to visit her in Cazenovia, he responded, "I... should love to see Charles + you... but the claims of my Office are upon me, and forbid my making even as short a ride as Ma is.... I am in bondage to the business of my Office."[124] It is interesting that Smith capitalized the word "office," perhaps indicating his opinion of its importance.

His work schedule remained full throughout his life. Having returned to Peterboro from a trip in 1840, he wrote to D. Jones, "I went straight to work in my Office—and as I drink no wine, and therefore want no repose... after dinner, I am pretty nearly through."[125]

In 1845 as he struggled out of the depression, "My private business always presses on all my time. But, of late, this pressure has been greater than ever before."[126]

As late as 1866, when he was 69 years old, he chronicled his demanding schedule:

"I reached home yesterday between 2 + 3 PM.... I
went right to work finding a great many letters....
[I] went to the Office with Charles [Miller]— +
there we worked until nearly 9. I came in much
exhausted, but I got 5 to 6 hours sleep by 4. At 5 I
was up + soon began to work again.... I must work
until 8 or 9 with my pen + then try the power of
sleep to revive me."[127]

If Smith ever took any "vacations" from his work, they were never
recorded as such. His travels away from Peterboro were usually for
either business or reform work. He even worked during the holidays.
When Ann wanted him to travel to New York City to visit her for
Christmas in 1865, he responded, "But how can I leave home...for
then Calkins will be away + I must be in the Office?"[128]

On Christmas Day of 1861 while Ann was travelling in Europe,
Gerrit spent the time at work: "I went to the Office immediately after
breakfast + have stuck to my work there until now (1/2 past 4)."[129]

He did worry that lack of physical exercise made him susceptible to illness[130] and was the cause of his making mistakes in accounting.[131] The office schedule also included daily conversations
with persons who would simply drop in to conduct business. One
observer noted that this could amount to as many as two dozen
persons per day.[132]

Probably the most valid indicator of the volume of Smith's business was his daily mail. Smith received an average of twenty to thirty
letters per day, read all of them, and responded personally to nearly
all of them. He turned "begging letters" over to Aunt Betsey Kelty
for evaluation, and some business issues received the annotation,
"Calkins will respond." But for the most part, he answered them.

As he mentioned to Ann, "The mail brought me a burdensom
quantity of letters." "My mails are heavy— + I work incessantly from
morning to night." "Your and Libby's letters...came last night—
along with 38 other letters."[133] And to his friend Beriah Green, he

wrote, "On my return home after an absence of 8 days…I find your letter among a hundred on my table."[134]

Realizing what Smith's workload was like, Lewis Tappan warned him, "This over-working is killing a good many. We must be less prodigal of our strength, intellectual + physical."[135]

The letter-reading chores were themselves even more difficult because Smith made land deals with people who were either totally or functionally illiterate. Some people had others do the writing for them and signed with an "X," but most just wrote as best they could, with gross errors in spelling, grammar, and punctuation making the content difficult to follow. Smith's first name was frequently misspelled, but this did not bother him. His annotations on folded letters indicated his filing system: "Put in bundle for 1846," or "Put in his bundle," or "give to Calkins." Many letters were annotated "In G. C.," referring to "General Correspondence." He saved *all* letters he received.

Smith used the services of the post office so much that he decided he should have some influence over its operation. In 1842, he wrote to the Postmaster General Charles A. Wickliffe in an attempt to influence the appointment of a new postmaster in Peterboro,[136] and in 1844 he recommended the continued tenure of Peterboro's current postmaster, Harvey Williams. "I should be well pleased to have him continued in Office—and my testimony in his favor should pass for something, inasmuch as I pay more than half of the postage paid at the Office."[137]

Smith often paid the postage on letters that he received. Before 1847 in the U.S., either the sender or the recipient could pay the postage. He depended on the mail so much for the efficient operation of his land business that he became aggravated when he could not receive daily mail delivery because snowdrifts plugged the roads in winter.[138] He was also dismayed when letters addressed to Peterboro frequently went to Petersburgh, New York, a community east of Albany. This, according to Smith's reports, happened often.[139]

Overall, there were few areas where Smith's business operated inefficiently. One of his best management skills was his ability to direct his employees. He was fussy about who he hired as his clerks. As his representatives, they had to be not only skilled at correspondence and calculation, but also display the proper moral characteristics. "For many years, I have refused to employ as an agent or clerk (+ I keep five agents or clerks) any man, who drinks intoxicating liquor."[140]

Clerks were loyal and respectful of Smith, and some remained employed with him for long periods. Smith hired John B. Edwards in 1831 as his business agent and based him in Oswego because Smith owned so much property there that he needed someone full-time. Edwards was business savvy, was a good judge of property value, and interacted fairly and effectively with the locals. Smith allowed him a great deal of independence, and there was little friction between them during the 43 years in which they worked together. Edward's letters to Smith averaged three pages long and arrived every other day, detailing every transaction conducted. Each letter is addressed to "Dear Friend," and was signed, "Your Friend."

Smith trusted Edwards to handle all the money in his Oswego business and to deposit any surplus in Smith's bank account. Edwards kept detailed records of all transactions, accounting for all monies spent and collected. He worked out land sales and property rentals. A fellow abolitionist, Edwards advised Smith on both personal and reform issues and acted as his Oswego connection on the Underground Railroad as fugitive slaves moved north. He supported Smith throughout his life, even campaigning for him during Smith's 1852 Congressional bid.[141] As late as July 17, 1884, ten years after Gerrit Smith's death, the Smith family still employed Edwards in Oswego.[142]

Caleb Calkins became Gerrit Smith's clerk in Peterboro in 1838, and, like Edwards, he remained so employed even after Smith's death. Calkins' aggressive abolitionism as a student at Hamilton College in 1835 attracted Smith's attention. When Smith offered him a job, Calkins responded,

"I should like your business, if I were competent

to engage in it. But I have my fears on this point. I am unaccustomed to business of the kind + consequently should not be able to handle it with dispatch at first."[143]

Smith must have felt confident in Calkins' ability, as he hired him two weeks later.[144] One of Calkins' early responsibilities was to travel and inspect the lands that Smith owned, but never saw. As evidenced in his notes to Smith, he learned quickly how to evaluate and sell property. "The 49a in Lot 8… about which…you inquire, I sold to Alanson Cornish, who lives upon the lot adjoining, at $4.00 per acre—received $71.00 in hand. Was this right? Four dollars, I considered a fair price for the land."[145]

Smith soon trusted him to make land deals on his own, even when they involved lowering Smith's suggested price.[146] Smith kept Calkins on during the depression of the 1830s and 1840s, during which Calkins offered to work for no salary.[147] When the depression ended and Smith hired his son-in-law Charles D. Miller as a clerk, Calkins feared that he would lose his position. He asked Smith how soon he would need to sell his house in Peterboro.[148]

Smith still needed his clerk's services, and he increased Calkins' salary from $500 to $1,000 annually and gifted his family with $2,500, saying, "The office work will seldom be burdensome— tho' there will still be a great many [issues] to take care of."[149] Smith considered the services of the two clerks, Calkins and Edwards, to be indispensable—even during times of economic difficulty.

Smith offered Federal Dana employment as a clerk in 1831, but Dana declined the offer unless it came with a salary of $400 per year. Smith responded, "I write him Nov. 12, 1831, that I receipt his proposal…. If he removes his family here, he is to have… Home + rent free. Also the keeping of two Cows. Also his firewood delivered at his home."[150]

Dana accepted the offer, and did survey work in the field, maintained land office duties, and also proof-read Smith's writings before they were sent out to be printed.[151] When the depression taxed Smith's resources in the early 1840s, Smith released Dana. The clerk became angry because he thought Smith had fired him due to his stand on moral issues.[152] He wrote Smith, "I deeply regret to have arrived at any condition respecting the subject of my dismissal from your employment, which you should stamp with ungenerousness, injustice, + a cruel want of sympathy."[153] Dana moved away from Peterboro, but 26 years later, he was still in contact with Smith. He wrote, "We often think of old times and old friends, whom we are never more to see on earth, but many of whom we hope through grace to see in Heaven."[154]

Nehemiah Huntington was Smith's very first clerk in the Land Office. Gerrit was looking for a way out of the tedious detail of record-keeping, and he offered Huntington the job. It appears by Huntington's initial response that he did not want to give up the freedom of his own hours: "I fear that the constant + long continued confinement your office business must necessarily require may be prejudicial to my health…. My judgment does not tell me that my 'dignity' would be in the least [compromised] by the change, yet one of my…indolent habits…must require some sacrifice of feeling to be forced into a situation in which I cannot say 'my time is my own."[155]

He took the job anyway, and served as Smith's office clerk and lawyer until his release in February of 1843. Then on May 2, 1843, Smith offered him re-employment as his attorney, a position that Huntington accepted as part of his independent law practice.[156]

Others worked as Smith's clerks for shorter periods. Loring Fowler was employed during the early 1840s, after which he became a lawyer in Canastota and handled some of Smith's legal affairs during the 1850s and 1860s.[157] Near the end of his life, Smith hired his grandson, Gerrit Smith Miller, to do office work, which he carried on after his grandfather's death. For a couple of years in the mid-1860s, George W. Putnam performed clerk services for Smith. He appears to have been somewhat of a pest, inventing odd gadgets and asking Smith for money to market them.

Smith also employed agents in other cities. Thomas Montgomery was Smith's business agent in Rochester, NY, negotiating land deals, collecting rents, and keeping records, which he sent regularly to Smith at Peterboro. George W. Bissell acted as Smith's agent in Michigan, managing land sales and dock property in the Detroit area. At one point, Smith offered him a 10-percent bonus on a $60,000 land sale.[158]

Smith allowed his clerks to use monies collected to pay for their business-related travel expenses, as long as they returned unused amounts to his profit sheets.[159]

While Smith allowed his clerks a fair amount of independence, he demanded reports so that he would know what was going on. His style was to delegate to subordinates but to maintain oversight of the business, which assured him control over both the process and the profits. He may, indeed, have been self-centered in his approach to business, but most of his life was oriented toward the general welfare, and even the proceeds of his business were used toward that end.

- 12 -

Politics

Congressman Gerrit Smith worked hard in Washington, D.C. in 1853, advocating legislation that supported equality and justice. Because Smith wanted to work with the established institutional structure instead of against it, he favored politics over rebellion. And he viewed as ineffective those who would seek change outside of the political process.

The irony for Smith was that he had never wanted to enter politics himself. Small-town life in Peterboro had monopolized his energies, and he tried to avoid political spotlights. "I still live in this secluded place," he wrote in 1846. "I have never been in public life—and have no ambition—no disposition, whatever, to be in it."[1] In his letter accepting the nomination of the "People's State Ticket" Party for governor of New York State in 1858, he warned, "My years have been spent in seclusion. My habits are all formed to private life. It is emphatically true that public employments are not to my taste."[2]

Whenever he did accept a political nomination, he did so reluctantly—and without having sought it. "It will be long, before I consent to be, and <u>very</u> long, before I ask to be a candidate for a civil office...."[3] Once, when asked by a Hamilton College official if he had ever held a civic or honorary office, he replied, "I am no favorite with this...."[4] Seven years later, he would be elected to the United State Congress.

Even when the Liberty Party of which he was a founder indicated interest in his candidacy, Smith wrote,

> "I have taken pains to inform them, that I
> have never held a civil office—that there is no
> probability that I shall ever consent to hold
> one—and that there are abundant reasons for my
> declining to hold one."[5]

The main reason he refused public office, he claimed, was business. With all of the time he spent with his business calculating, thinking, and corresponding, he considered himself unfit for public life.

> "So absorbed have I been with the cares of
> property, and so seldom have my thoughts been
> allowed to travel beyond the range of these cares,
> that the information, which I have picked up is
> quite too scanty and piecemeal to serve me in
> situations, which call for the systematic studies
> and extensive knowledge of the statesman....
> [My habits are too engrained] to overcome their
> repugnance to public life, [or] to admit of my
> being at all contented, or at all useful in it."[6]

Another reason that Smith avoided politics was probably that he perceived politicians themselves as a sorry lot. He was dedicated early in his life to the principles of equality and justice, and he believed that the electoral process compelled those who participated in it to dilute their principles. He appreciated American democracy, but he disdained the attempts by politicians to appeal to everyone, sacrificing their own values in the process. "Politicians," he wrote, "are apt to die poor—especially such of them as espouse principle."[7]

Smith believed that politics diluted the moral quality of abolitionism; men who scrambled for higher office forfeited their principled goals, and once elected, they maneuvered in ways that inhibited one another, thereby slowing the chance for progress or for policy change. "In the breasts of politicians... ambition, the greed of gain and the lust of place and power have... much play," he wrote in 1864.[8]

He did not worry about the effects of this political criticism, as he didn't seek the favor of those within his party or the elective office they might help him win. The fact was that Smith saw his work on the two major reform movements that he was interested in—abolition and temperance—as being inhibited by the actions of politicians and clergy: politicians were loyal to political parties and clergy were loyal to ecclesiastical denominations, both of which either supported the unacceptable status quo or battled with one another to the extent that reasoned change became nearly impossible.

Smith's visionary idealism prevented most conciliatory activities (politics), and it fueled his hopes that he might achieve some of his reform goals by himself. But his dedication to the reform movement and his own personal optimism had convinced him that eventually the real world of politicians and clergy would embrace his ideals. As his enthusiasm grew, he became more and more alienated by the frustrating process of political compromise. He came to view 'parties', be they political or ecclesiastical, as supporters of the status quo.

Smith had a unique perception of the proper function of government that fueled his frustration with politics. While the government through the first half of the nineteenth century accepted more and more responsibility for providing public service, Smith favored a much more limited role. The *only* proper function of government, he claimed, was to *protect* universal, divinely ordained human rights; no government had any legitimate power to *distribute* those rights.

> "No constitution... is to be an acknowledged authority in determining essential human rights. The right to our manhood... is not derived from the constitution. It comes from a source infinitely more sacred and authoritative... from the law of human nature and of God."[9]

Smith saw in this governmental control a sort of meddling with more sophisticated, intrinsic privilege:

> "Too long have people consented to receive as
> franchises, or government-conferred privileges,
> what is inherent and God-given. Resolving natural
> rights into privileges has, in every age of the world,
> been a trick of tyrants."[10]

The idea that natural law had authority over human law contributed much energy to the 19th-century reform movement, but it was not new. It can be traced to St. Thomas Aquinas, Aristotle, and Sophocles. William Blackstone, an English common law theorist, declared in 1765 that the "law of nature... dictated by God himself, is of course superior in obligation to any other.... No human laws are of any validity, if contrary to this."

John Mayhew, a Boston clergyman, wrote in 1750 that "all commands running counter to the declared will of the supreme legislator of heaven and earth, are null and void: and therefore disobedience to them is a duty, not a crime."

These ideas are included in the state constitutions of Virginia, Massachusetts, and New Hampshire, all written in the late 1700s,[11] and it is likely that Gerrit Smith was aware of them. The idea that human law should override natural law ran counter to these assumptions, and it did not gain popularity until after the American Revolution.

The Declaration of Independence also contained the basic, inalienable rights of which Smith spoke. He acknowledged this, but added in an 1854 speech on the Nebraska Bill that those rights "are not conventional rights which... Government may give, or take away at pleasure. But these are natural, inherent, essential rights which Government has nothing to do with but to protect."[12] Smith believed that government had no right to interfere with the morals of a person, or with how one lived one's private life.

"Government is not the custodian of the people's morals," he said in a speech on temperance that same year.

"[It] is not to do the work of the people. It
is, simply to protect the people in doing it.
Government is but the great watch-dog of the
people's house. It is ever to keep watch outside of
that house: but it is never to come into it."[13]

This is an important position, and it eventually became the
foundation for Smith's endorsement of violence as a means to end
slavery. Smith felt that slavery resulted when the government had
illegitimately condoned the rights of some people to control others. He reasoned that if a government supported slavery, it was
interfering with fundamental human rights and, therefore, should
be subverted. As Smith put it,

"When [government] undertakes to... invade the
essential manhood of any portion of the human
family and curtail its inborn and God-given rights,
it then breaks out of its sphere, makes war upon the
divine will and divine arrangements, and becomes
no law.... The equal rights of all men make 'equality
before the law' the right of every man."[14]

Smith had revealed this belief in the effects of a misguided federal government almost 30 years earlier when he wrote to friend
Asa Rand,

"This perversion of Government from its Heaven-
assigned end of protecting human rights +
especially the rights of those, who are too poor and
helpless to protect themselves is a chief reason,
why Millions of our Countrymen are in Slavery."[15]

A dozen years later, after he had served his brief term in Congress,
he said in a Milwaukee speech:

"Despotisms will continue to cover the earth
as long as the people consent to surrender

their natural rights in exchange for grants from
Government; and despotisms will disappear…
as soon as people shall insist on confining
Government to its… narrow limits."[16]

These "narrow limits" could be perceived by only a few chosen leaders, Smith thought; and those leaders, not surprisingly, were non-sectarian Christians. In a classic statement of naïve bias, Smith proclaimed in 1860 that

"…religious men only are fit to bear civil rule,
and…therefore none other should be chosen for
it.… None but a religious man can have the broad,
undeviating justice, the honest, comprehensive
care for others, the quick, tender and thorough
sympathy with the poor, helpless and trodden-
down, which should ever characterize the civil
ruler."[17]

If this were ever carried out, it would obviously limit to a biased few the operation of government, as would his recommendation against electing patriots. In his "Final Letter to His Constituents" published in August of 1854, Smith wrote, "Patriotism is not a virtue, but a vice," aiding leaders to legitimate what exists, and thwarting reform.[18]

Strangely, Smith also advocated a World Government, based on his advocacy of a universal natural law, to deal with nations that infringed on human rights.[19] One wonders where the foreign rep-resentatives to such a government would come from—if the only ones fit to rule were non-sectarian Christians.

So given these political ideas, was Smith a liberal or conservative political thinker? There are some hints in his Seven Principles of a good government:

"That it acknowledges no law… for slavery."

"The right to the soil is as natural, absolute, and equal as the right to the light and air."

"That political rights are not conventional, but natural, inhering in all persons...."

"That the doctrine of 'free trade' is the necessary outgrowth of the doctrine of human brotherhood...."

"War should be prohibited."

"That the province of the Government is but to protect persons and property...."

All public officials "should be elected directly by the people."[20]

These positions are both liberal *and* conservative, but Smith's overall philosophy was a liberal one. Although a cursory reading of his political views may make him appear to have been self-contradictory, he was not. As a political philosopher, Smith was conservative. He believed that government should interfere as little as possible with a citizen's opportunity to plan and execute his own lifestyle. With human rights, he saw every individual as deserving of an equal share of all available resources, and in need of aid if discriminatory social practices had caused an individual to be, in his words, "downtrodden." This is a liberal attitude by today's standards.

The aid, however, was not to come from the government, but from enlightened and prosperous citizens who saw the welfare and happiness of every citizen as a benefit to the whole social system. This political ethos made Smith, in current terminology, a "compassionate conservative" in that, while caring deeply about less fortunate and oppressed people, he did not see it as the responsibility of the government to provide compensation.

He wrote specifically,

> "We do not ask the Government of this State
> to furnish banks and roads and canals for its
> subjects; but, only to protect them, as it now
> does, from frauds therein. We do not ask it to
> furnish its subjects with good books; but, only to
> protect them, as it now does, from the circulation
> of obscene books. We do not ask it to supply its
> subjects with physicians; but to afford them, as it
> now does, the protection of quarantine and health-
> laws."

Smith saw the political stance of "the true man" as being characterized by "sympathies [which] go out in all directions—toward every class of wronged and suffering ones." He believed that government should act morally—even if its actions did not reflect the popular will.[21]

The 'Achilles' heel' of Smith's reasoning was his abounding faith in the ability of the individual to do what was best for the general welfare. This reflected the optimism of the reform movement, which maintained that people really cared about each other, and that if only they were led in the right direction, reform must be the result. Perhaps Smith's love of small-town life in Peterboro grounded his faith in this optimism.

One can use the term "voluntarism" to describe Smith's preference for political action on the local level. It was based on the notion that individuals could have the most influence among people they knew. Free and reasonable people would act communally due to their perception of the common interest, and their actions would create a mutual benefit. As has been noted by past writers, this confidence in local action turned leaders like Gerrit Smith against centrally controlled government programs.[22] Consequently, Smith opposed government aid that sought to achieve changes that he saw as the people's responsibility. He viewed the growing central government as insensitive to issues involving human rights; state and national centralized policy-makers were more concerned with budgets and re-election than with people's feelings, and they were not trustworthy concerning community welfare.

As noted earlier, one movement brought on by voluntarism was the "Free Church" movement. Non-sectarian churches, symbols of a breaking away from central control, were common in small central New York State communities in the mid-1800s. Free Churches, centers for social and political guidance led by those who worked for moral change at the local level, experienced a fair degree of success. But while moral reforms succeeded in rural communities such as Peterboro and the township of Smithfield, they usually did not transfer—as the leadership had hoped they would—to the national scene. Smith bucked the rising tide of centralized power and was happy about what was happening in Peterboro, but he remained disappointed with the nation as a whole.

Smith was intent on ensuring that individuals at the local level were free from federal interference in making decisions for their own good. For instance, in what today would be a conservative political stance, he was inclined to oppose the use of public funds for building projects, because he felt private businesses could do a better job. "I object to such work in the hands of the Government, if only because such work tends to centralization, and to undue Federal power." Yet in a hypocritical stance, when his own business interests were at stake, he would sometimes sanction government spending. Smith owned much property on the waterfront in Oswego, and he advocated adding $50,000 to a Federal appropriations bill for developing the Oswego Harbor because of "very great and very rapidly growing business demands."[23]

There was an obvious conflict of interest in this, especially since in general, he opposed government support for the building of roads or canals or of railroad development. In a speech regarding the proposed construction of a water supply for the city of Washington, D.C., he said, "This work can be done, and kept in repair, by individual enterprise, at one half the expense it would be to Government."[24]

Smith had great faith in private enterprise working for the public good, and he did not want to see government expand its role beyond the protection of human rights.[25]

Smith even opposed taxation for the support of schools,[26] or any interference by government with what was taught in schools. He wrote, "One of the great errors of our times is leaving others to do what we should do ourselves."[27] He wanted government to stay out of public service and to allow people to freely design the institutions that would serve them.[28]

Smith further believed that it was not government's role to provide financial aid to the poor. "Government has no gifts to make—even to the most needy…."[29] But here also, his faith in human compassion was deep. As far as Smith was concerned, the rich should voluntarily assume the needs of the poor.

Such thought was noble if naïve, and, for his part, he actually did practice what he preached. He wrote, "I have…come to feel it to be my duty to use the property in my hands chiefly for the… sustenance + comfort of the bodies of the poor."[30] It was also true, though, that his feeling of "duty" to the poor did not exist in most of those who were rich.

Curiously, while Smith nurtured a belief in the role of the wealthy to aid the poor, he also voiced a much more conservative idea akin to social Darwinism: he suggested that if people cannot make it on their own, then they were not fit to survive. In 1869 he said,

> "Government can never do more for its people
> than to protect their persons and property. If
> thus protected, they cannot prosper, then all the
> Governments on earth cannot suffice to make
> the imbeciles prosper. Having done this much for
> them, Government is to leave them to work out for

themselves salvation, if they be wise and virtuous; destruction if they be foolish and vicious."[31]

Smith had stated a similar belief years earlier in 1854, while he served in Congress:

"Wherever there is a people, who…cannot, or will not, do their own work, and take care of their own interests, both material and moral, there is a people,…that must perish."[32]

Smith was arguing that those who would not prosper—even when they were offered enlightenment through the verbal and financial aid of caring fellow citizens—should be left to languish. He believed that the debt that people owed each other was love, and he expressed it most beautifully in the case of what he called the "Peterboro mob."

On June 20, 1842, Henry Devan, a Peterboro resident, was accused of fornication, defined back then as voluntary sexual intercourse between two people who were not married. Devan was attacked by a Peterboro mob that broke into his private home, "dragged him out, and rode him through the village on a board; and the worst of all is that I find scarce any individual who sympathizes with me in the indignation with which this outrage inflames me," wrote Smith in his diary. Smith stood alone in the village in condemning the actions of the mob as a disgraceful infringement of human rights. Accused by neighbors of sanctioning Devan's vices, Smith replied, "To identify myself with Devan in the affair of this mob is what I desire…. How far I am the friend and patron of vice, my life—not my lips—must say."

Smith even worried that he would become the focus of the next mob action. "They who can strike down the rights of the meanest and poorest man have no principle to restrain them from trampling under their feet the rights of any other man."[5] Whatever Devan's offense might have been, Smith argued, he did not deserve the social or physical abuse inflicted by the mob. Smith was also hurt by this stain on his vision of Peterboro as a moral community. He wrote in his diary, "I am not pained about Peterboro, because I think it worse than other places—but because I find that it is no *better* than other places."[34]

Smith followed up by posting a public notice inviting the citizens of Peterboro to a July 2, 1842 meeting in the Presbyterian church "for a friendly consultation respecting the mob by which their village has recently been disgraced...."[35] This early event symbolizes well Smith's thought and action regarding social issues, and it highlights his deep concern for inherent human rights.

Such rights, he claimed, no government can grant, but can only recognize and protect, with the noblest human right being one's ability to choose without coercion. People are not condemned by fate to anything, he said, including sin and poverty.[36] And he perceived freedom of speech and assembly to be essential to human dignity, believing that the entire society must protect the rights of the minority to access of such rights.

Smith wrote in 1852, "My political party in Peterboro consists of all, who honestly aim to go for all the political rights of all subjects of the Government—black and white, male and female."[37] His reference here was to the Liberty Party, but as a rule, Smith found it difficult to identify with any political party because he saw them as vehicles of discrimination for their own benefit.

There are many examples of Smith's compassionate political stands. In the last public letter he would pen before his death, he wrote of the expulsion of black children from a school in Indiana:

"I ask what is the excuse for this crushing of
hearts, and blasting of... hopes of even innocent
children? Is it that the laws require it? Not his,
surely, who is 'no respecter of persons,' and 'hath
made of one blood all the nations of the earth?' "[38]

Smith believed that patriotism was most often used to justify discrimination, and that political parties encouraged it. Misguided patriotism excluded foreigners from American life, thus thwarting their equal rights.[39] "Patriotism," he wrote upon leaving Congress, "is... nothing, even in its most attractive phases, but modifications of selfishness."[40] In any country, Smith argued, patriotism was ethnic bias in disguise.

Smith also stood against the institutional sanctioning of discrimination against those with disabilities. He noted in 1851, "It was greatly to the dishonor of Kentucky to punish as a criminal an insane man."[41]

As noted, Smith opposed the expansion of governmental power, fearing that eventually it would endanger privacy.[42] In fact, in a speech on the Mexican Treaty and the Monroe Doctrine while in Congress, he argued that such expansion would also cause the United States to become arrogant in its dealings with other countries.[43]

One of Smith's most liberal positions was his support of international free trade—the bane of protectionists and isolationists. Tariffs, he believed, were a way of interfering with the right of every person to benefit as much as possible from nature's bounty. Prices should be kept as low as possible in order to enable the poor to share equally in the earth's resources and be part of a kind-hearted international brotherhood.[44]

Smith also held liberal positions relating to the abolition of slavery and the development of women's suffrage. To summarize his ideas and actions on the liberal-conservative continuum requires a bit of juggling; he was liberal concerning his social goals and actions—and conservative about the role government should play in achieving them. This paradox traces to the characteristic optimism of the era toward the reasonableness and responsibility of the people— and Smith's faith in people's commitment to a common good. Smith trusted that the masses would arrive at the right policies with minimal guidance. His attitude regarding the people and their government was to limit the government, but not human rights.

It seems ironic that although Smith avoided politics and disapproved of political parties, he still used established political institutions to pursue social change. His disgust with the existing political parties only motivated him to form new ones. Hints at Smith's ire at both politicians and political parties emerged early in his career, in a speech he gave in Madison County in 1824:

> "Office-hunters and demagogues…whose whole living depend upon their unwearied labors to keep alive the worn out names of 'Republican' and 'Federalist'… make their noisy <u>patriotic</u> boasts of the one, and their jeering and angry denunciations of the other…. [Political parties have become] selfish and illiberal opponents. The earnestness in the cause of truth and for the public good, which characterized their beginning, soon degenerated into an infatuating zeal for the destruction of one another…. [A] temporary diversity of political opinion should not be tortured and spun out into a lasting distinction…dividing a nation into two bands of mutual spies, watching the conduct of one another with all those jealous and malignant dispositions…which so strikingly mark the selfishness of politics."[45]

Smith viewed the exclusive and combative attitude of political parties toward one another as harmful to human rights and to national unity, and especially so during times of emergency.[46] But the one issue that raised his hackles the most was the unwillingness of the major political parties to take a stand against slavery. As Smith's advocacy of immediate abolition intensified in the late 1830s, he increasingly saw both major parties—Whig and Democrat—as being "proslavery and anti-republican—utterly contemptuous of the great foundation doctrine of our Republic, 'that all men are created equal.' "[47]

Poet and fellow abolitionist John Greenleaf Whittier wrote to Smith of his own disappointment with the proslavery stance of the political parties: "It is awful to see this <u>rushing</u> of anti-slavery professors to the party standards." Whittier was delighted to know that Smith and his followers in New York State were "striving nobly against the evil spirit of party politics,"[48] and he spoke on abolition at the Church of Peterboro.

When Smith wrote to Frederick Douglass on the issue of political party loyalties, he declared that in order to have any influence on the abolition of slavery, a person would first need to sever all party connections.[49] Gerrit Smith's most consistent and focused attacks against what he perceived as a proslavery political party were against the Democratic Party during and after the Civil War. By 1864, he was calling it "our infamously Pro-Slavery and traitorous Democratic Party...."[50] After the war, the party advocated continued suppression of blacks with a policy that Smith called "Kukluxism." As late as 1872, he wrote,

> "The only condition on which the Democratic
> Party will consent to be reconciled to the negro is
> that the negro shall surrender all his rights, and
> accept in their stead such gifts and privileges as the
> white man shall please to dole out to him."[51]

Smith continued such criticism until the very end. Just one month before his death, in a circular titled "To Thyself be True," he lashed out at Democrats for supporting the Ku Klux Klan, and at Republicans for not having the guts to overthrow the Democrats.[52]

During the antebellum era, political parties reflected serious, culturally based sectional divisions, making the individuals who ran as candidates relatively unimportant. A survey of the presidents of the era—Tyler, Polk, Taylor, Fillmore, Pierce, Buchanan, Lincoln— reveals a collection of nonentities who were largely unknown to the public; their personal details were unimportant because the party had defined them with its biases and prejudices. Before the war, the dominant slave power elected all of the above-named men—except Lincoln—because they approved of slavery. The political contests of the era were symptoms of a deep-seated moral dilemma in which aspects of slavery and liberty confronted one another.

As has been noted, in the late 1820s, Smith identified with the Democratic Party. Near the end of his life, in the late 1860s, he sided with the Republican Party. But he never became a wholehearted supporter of either. Smith's son-in-law Charles D. Miller, in writing to the New York Vigilant Association in 1860, commented, "[Gerrit Smith] confesses that he has no sympathy with the Republican Party.... Mr. Smith is an Abolitionist, and not, as you would have it believed, a Republican."[53]

During Smith's brief tenure in Congress, he was proud to be independent. "I rejoiced," he said in one House of Representatives speech, "that I stand alone upon this floor; that I am a party by myself, and in myself; that I am in a greatly and gloriously independent minority of one...."[54]

In a speech at the Loyal League Convention in Utica in 1863, he declared himself "a Democrat of Democrats. Not a sham, spurious Democrat; but a man going for the equal rights of all men."[55] Here, of course, he meant "democrat" in a generic sense. It was because Smith could not identify with any of the major political parties that he tried three times to establish a viable third party.

In both 1842 and 1869, he tried to establish a political party whose sole issue was temperance. Both attempts were largely failures. Smith realized that building a third party was futile, but because he believed in working within the political system instead of rebelling against it, he chose the third party to advance his cause. At least it served to keep his pet issues before the public. But he knew that third parties only absorbed the interest and activity of a few people for a brief time; eventually, followers went back to their "old" parties.[56] He did earn a gold star, however, with his work building the anti-slavery Liberty Party.

Two forces led Gerrit Smith into political activism. First was his belief in the ability of the public to rationally conclude what was right and to express its opinion through voting. Second was his predisposition toward organized activity. His strict anti-slavery stance alienated him from organized politics, but his life in the "Burned-Over District" of central New York showed him what reform-oriented people could accomplish when they were sufficiently motivated. In the late 1830s, evangelical revivalism had become less effective at mobilizing the masses for social welfare while local, secular anti-slavery societies multiplied rapidly, taking the place of revivalism for voters. Smith's leanings toward support of a new, anti-slavery political party were encouraged by these developments and by several other events.

In 1835 he had helped form the New York State Anti-Slavery Society, which advocated immediate abolition. In 1836, a central New York lawyer and friend of Smith suggested that consolidation of abolitionist power was a necessary step toward success.[57] So in October 1837, the New York State Anti-Slavery Society—with Smith as its president—resolved to forbid its members to vote for pro-slavery candidates and established a formal system of questioning for nominees. If, after being screened or "questioned," regarding his stand on abolition, no major party candidate was deemed to be satisfactory, then antislavery people would simply refuse to vote.

The responses of candidates were often misleading, as they promised more than they were willing to perform. Some abolitionist leaders became unsatisfied with the voluntary disenfranchisement of antislavery voters. They realized that if antislavery voters could not elect someone from their own party, they might at least hold the balance of power and draw one of the major parties to their stand. James Caleb Jackson, a local Smithfield abolitionist and close friend to Smith, wrote in late 1838 that he would "favor a distinct political organization" for anti-slavery purposes.[58]

Although Smith was friendly with William Lloyd Garrison, the influential Boston abolitionist, he did not see the benefits of Garrison's "moral suasion" approach. Smith was leaning more toward establishing an independent, anti-slavery political party. The first serious action in that direction was manifested in an Oswego

County convention at New Haven on October 4, 1839, as abolition-ists nominated a third-party ticket of local candidates for the state legislature.[59]

In January of 1840, while at an anti-slavery convention in Arcade, New York, Smith heard abolitionists Myron Holley and William Chaplin call for the nomination of anti-slavery candidates for pub-lic office—independent of the major political parties. By the next month, Smith was calling for the establishment of what he called a "Liberty Party."[60] He met with William Goodell and James G. Birney "around the fire in the Smith home at Peterboro in February" and convinced them that political action should take the form of an independent third party.[61]

Smith and Holley put out the call for the first Liberty Party Convention to meet in Albany on April 1, 1840.[62] Smith's thinking over the years on the state of the major political parties culminated in this convention. Two weeks before the meeting, he wrote, "We cannot trust the abolitionism of any candidates offered by the pro-slavery parties.... [In order] to have candidates for whom we can reasonably vote we must nominate them ourselves. To me it seems perfectly plain, that we are driven to the necessity of 'independent nominations.'"[63]

Smith knew that his opinion was coincident with that of other notable public figures. Charles Grandison Finney had written to him that his "disgust at the course which the politics of this nation have taken has prevented my voting altogether. If a party shall arise who will take consistent ground I shall go to the polls."[64] Henry B. Stanton had also declared the election of antislavery candidates to be the only viable route to abolition.[65]

Smith was convinced that it would take uncommon and radical enthusiasm for the new party to remain committed to its original goals and not backslide into a general appeal for support as the major parties do. Just days before the convention, he asked in a letter to Beriah Green, "How [can we] maintain...a Human Rights [party] without investing ourselves in the same evils as now stare so frightfully upon us from the ranks of the existing parties [?]"[66] After the convention, Smith warned Lewis Tappan that if he, too, did not support the new party, the public would stick with their old loyalties.

This new political party integrated politics with religion in a political crusade for a slavery-free society. Unfortunately, his Liberty Party would soon split over issues of internal disagreement; but in its early days, the new party offered its adherents reason for hope. The men of the original Liberty Party were already tried and true reformers—moral athletes ready to jump the political hurdles that would thrust them and their concerns before the national conscience. It was the first effort by reformers to achieve moral change by means of a political party, and there was sufficient reason for its members to believe that they could have a significant influence on the outcome of elections.

Between 1840 and 1860, voter turnout for local, state, and national elections ranged from 71 percent to 83.6 percent. These incredibly high numbers reflected the Jacksonian era of politics, during which individuals felt empowered to produce reform. It was a time before radio and television, when competing ideas that spread through widely-read newspapers were exceedingly popular. People didn't read newspapers hastily and toss them aside; they read them seriously, respectfully, and deliberately. The papers didn't separate the stories by subject or section; it was expected that the readers would pay close attention to all the print. Editors fashioned their papers into documents of moral instruction as they blasted one another week after week, in battles their readers often followed like a modern-day soap opera.

The editors' writing was called "slang-whanging," and it was intensely partisan.[67] People attended local speeches and meetings as a means of sharing ideas and improving their lives. According to one report in Madison County,

"...for weeks before the election, the county was
one immense cauldron of abolitionism—state

> conventions, county conventions, town meetings, and district meetings…. We had processions with banners and devices, and the [county] resounded with Abolition sentiment."[68]

By introducing slavery into this political arena, the Liberty Party formalized the abolitionists' protests against an amoral labor system and the institutions that defended it. They stated their goals clearly in four general beliefs:

Government should protect natural, equal rights.

The United States Constitution was an antislavery document.

Expansion of slavery was opposed.

Maintenance of the union was supported.[69]

Their emphasis on slavery was a radical stand for a political party to take. They refused to compromise on the need for immediate abolition, stressing the cruel and unjust treatment of the slave. They were proud to be called agitators for focusing public attention on slavery in the south as the cause of the "Panic [economic depression] of 1837." Northern merchants, they claimed, had invested in southern cotton production, and slaveholders could not pay their debts.

Joshua Leavitt, editor of the abolitionist broadsheet newspaper *The Emancipator*, called slavery "a vampire which is drinking up the life blood of free industry…. It is a bottomless gulf of extravagance and thriftlessness."[70]

When the time arrived for the first Liberty Party nominating convention on April 1, 1840, Gerrit Smith had become ill and could not travel. He did not want to be nominated for public office anyway, so his illness might have been an excuse not to show. Elizur Wright, a fellow abolitionist, wrote to Smith after the convention expressing disappointment that Smith was not there, and stated a classic truth: "You are probably well fitted for public life just in proportion as you prefer domestic…."[71] Simply stated, Wright was arguing that political power should rest with those who did not want it. Because Smith was disgusted with what many politicians did with power, he understood this principle also; but he did not let it change his mind about becoming a candidate himself.

The convention nominated as its first candidate for president James G. Birney, a former slaveholder-turned-abolitionist from Kentucky. Birney was not an enthusiastic campaigner; he spent May through November of 1840 in England, attending the World Antislavery Convention and delivering lectures. He received only a little over 7,000 votes in the election, which was won by William H. Harrison (Whig) over Martin Van Buren (Democrat).[72]

In a "Report from the County of Madison to Abolitionists," Smith noted that the Liberty Party's outspoken opponent, William Lloyd Garrison had called the conventioneers "April fools." Garrison was convinced that politics was a wasted effort; it could change only laws, not minds. In response, Smith announced with pride that his Madison County town of Smithfield was carried by abolitionist votes, "and that instance of success was worth more to the American antislavery cause than a donation of fifty thousand dollars…. It taught abolitionists what they can do in their respective communities…."[73] In fact, Liberty Party candidates carried the Town of Smithfield in bids for state office in every election between 1843 and 1847.[74]

Just after the election of 1843, Smith wrote an open letter to abolitionists, which the *Liberty Herald* printed. In it, he congratulated them for having worked "earnestly, strenuously, untiringly" for antislavery candidates, and he noted that Smithfield had set an example for the nation. In fact, the Liberty Party vote in Smithfield between 1842 and 1847 averaged 44.3 percent, compared to the Madison County average of 14.4 percent.[75]

Smith also made special note of the connection between antislavery churches and politics, a concept he had fostered. "My meetings were held in the open air, and were, generally, very large. In one of them, four thousand persons were present. In others... between two and three thousand." He suspected that Madison County, which included Smithfield, would soon be antislavery in its voting, which "would be the knocking of a stone out of the arch of American slavery...." Others would follow, and "but a few years would pass away ere American slavery would be no more. Such is my hope of the rapid progress of the antislavery cause."[76]

In spite of this local success, Smith was disappointed by the state and national results, and he worked harder to generate support for Liberty Party candidates. He even made an effort to get Abigail Kelley, a Garrisonian 'persuasionist', to join his cause. She replied,

> "You either have no knowledge of my character, or...
> you do not realize what you ask.... It is nothing less
> than to identify myself with the 'Liberty Party'...
> which is in deadly hostility to those whom I believe
> to be the slave's best friends [and] whose policy I
> believe to be one of the greatest obstacles to the
> speedy triumph of our cause."[77]

Kelley then prayed that he would be cured of the folly of political action.

In October of 1840, Smith drafted three resolutions for consideration at the upcoming meeting of the Madison County Anti-Slavery Society. First, the major parties could not be trusted regarding the abolition of slavery; second, abolitionists should nominate their own candidates; and third, "in view of the foregoing Resolutions, 'The Liberty Party'... is a measure of necessity... not to be abandoned...."[78]

The party became the vehicle for Gerrit Smith's peaceful crusade, and he used it to pursue the promised land of justice and equity, saying,

"The Civil Governments of this land, being the
instruments of the most terrible and wicked
oppression, the Liberty Party was organized to
reform their character, by getting them out of the
hands of slaveholders and their allies."[79]

The main issue for the Liberty Party was slavery. During its brief
history, the party pressed the national legislature to pass anti-slavery
measures. It opposed the three-fifths clause of the Constitution, the
extension of slavery into new states, and the 1850 Fugitive Slave
Law. As a major spokesperson for the Liberty Party, Smith garnered
support from western abolitionists who saw it as a workable vehicle,
as Salmon Chase termed it in a letter to Smith, "to accomplish the
proper aims of Christianized Democracy."[80]

Smith described party loyalists as "principled and impartial lovers of Liberty."[81] He wrote a four-page list of thirteen "Principles of
the Liberty Party" that ended with,

"Resolved, that amid all which obstructs and
discourages our endeavors after a righteous
Civil Government, we…shall be blest with a
Government whose principles shall be truth +
justice, whose 'officers' shall be peace, and whose
'executors' shall be 'righteousness.'"[82]

Gerrit Smith closely linked the Liberty Party to religion. He
called it a party that "is emphatically a religious Party…. The Bible
is its supreme Constitution…."[83] The party's connections to religion
were reflected in its major aim: the perfection of society, especially
through the abolition of the sin of slavery. Party leaders held a
general convention of ecclesiastical abolitionists in Syracuse in
1843, during which they attempted to unite many splinter religious
bodies behind them. William Goodell called the party a "political
millennium," and he saw hope that there might be a peaceful end
to slavery.[84]

Others claimed that such optimism among Liberty Party men made their gatherings "a synthesis of political rally and church supper."[85] Although Smith stated that "the wisest and best members of the Liberty Party admit, that it was organized for no other purpose than the overthrow of slavery,"[86] he also viewed it as a vehicle for other moral reforms. "The object of this Party is to...secure to the human family the blessings of impartial and righteous civil government...[where] there will be no landless,...no dram shops,... no slaves,...no war,...and...justice will be done to both man and woman."[87] He viewed any political party that did not strive for such goals as "counterfeit," and therefore working to ruin the notion of democracy.[88]

Actually, the efforts of Birney, Smith, and Leavitt to pursue practical politics was a concession of their moral principles and a repudiation of what they knew to be the ideological necessity of a Garrisonian type of moral revolution. But over time, the noble goals of the Liberty Party and the practical dreams of Gerrit Smith would be dashed—by internal dissent.

As early as 1843, Smith had become aggravated at the Liberty Party because many of its adherents were voting for proslavery candidates. When asked by Connecticut Abolitionist newspaper editor Charles C. Burleigh, "Do you expect the [Liberty Party] ever to elect its candidates?" Smith responded in the negative, saying, "We are content... with realizing the true idea of a righteous Civil Government in our own action and example.... I can exercise a moral influence in my political action...."[89] He refused to travel only ten miles to Canastota to support the party, claiming, "It is when I see men voting against the poor, helpless, bleeding slave, that my sorrow and indignation know no bounds."[90]

Even though Smith had received letters of support for the Liberty Party from black New York City residents, he proclaimed in 1846 "That the Liberty Party of Madison County is in ruins.... Its pre-eminently distinctive principles... have been trampled on, and dishonored, by a large share of its members."[91]

By the end of 1846, Smith was so disillusioned with the party that he referred to it as "a poor, erring, halfhearted party."[92] The result was that by the summer of 1847, Smith, Frederick Douglass, and other former Liberty Party loyalists broke off and formed the Liberty League. Part of their effort was to expand from a single-issue party to become more nationally oriented.[93] This was the more radical wing of the Liberty Party, and it eventually became the Radical Abolition Party in the mid-1850s.

The Liberty League grew as the old Liberty Party began to realize that its successes at the local level were not influencing the national political picture. As of 1847, the Liberty Party had not gleaned more than four and one-half percent of the New York State vote, and its most significant successes had been limited to the three central New York counties of Madison, Oneida, and Oswego. The township of Smithfield, where Gerrit Smith lived, cast nearly forty percent of its votes for abolitionist candidates in the early 1840s, but even Smithfield elected few of them.[94] Smith even made the comment— probably more cynical than serious—that he wished to be elected president so that he could influence the direction of "this guilty, perishing nation."[95]

Liberty Party leaders like Smith, Douglass, and Beriah Green were practical enough to realize the futility of their local efforts, and as they faced the growing centralization of politics in Washington, D.C., they concluded that their influence was minimal. At the national level where success demanded broad coalitions, they were ineffective; their missionary tactics and idealistic visions could not penetrate the tough hide of national indifference to inequity.

Their response was to reach out for more support. They formed a coalition with "downstate" abolitionists led by Lewis Tappan, and at a convention held in Syracuse on June 26–28, 1855, the Radical Abolition Party was formed.[96] Dr. James McCune Smith, a black abolitionist from downstate New York, chaired the event, making this the first time in United States history that an African-American had chaired a political convention. When Gerrit Smith was nominated as its presidential candidate, a debate arose over his approval of the use of violence in the pursuit of abolition. Those present even took up a collection to support John Brown in his "Kansas work."[97] William Goodell commented that people should use the ballot box instead of the cartridge box.[98]

Present at this convention were such social radicals as Frederick Douglass and James McCune Smith—two black men who identified with white liberals—and John Brown and Gerrit Smith, two white men who identified with black radicals. John Stauffer provides an extensive review of the historical significance of the relationships among these four men in his book, *The Black Hearts of Men*.

While this new party was being organized, the more conservative, less radical faction of the Liberty Party merged with some antislavery Whigs and Democrats in 1848 to become the Free Soil Party, opposed to extending slavery in the new territories. Smith made it clear that he could not follow them because they opposed only the *extension* of slavery instead of its immediate abolition.[99] He was concerned that this emphasis reflected more selfish concern for the white man than empathic concern for the oppressed black man.

His beloved Liberty Party's absorption into the Free Soil Party signaled to Smith its lack of commitment to universal human rights—a goal which he could not abandon in favor of a broader appeal for votes. As Smith stated the issue, whereas the Free-Soilers supported only the non-extension of slavery, the more radical abolitionists advocated the extension of freedom. By the mid-1850s the Free Soilers became the formative roots for the Republican Party of Abraham Lincoln, thereby lending credence to the claim that the current Republican Party experienced its birth, at least in part, in the mind of Gerrit Smith—with his Liberty Party, in the tiny central New York hamlet of Peterboro.

Smith was disappointed that his political efforts could not convince voters that the Constitution was an antislavery document; such an argument challenged the racial prejudice of his time.[100] The death knell for all of the abolitionist parties was, of course, the Civil

War. So, having seen the end of slavery, in what political direction did Gerrit Smith move after that?

The anti-slavery coalition that formed the Free Soil Party in 1848 was a mildly liberal force, and both Smith and Frederick Douglass perceived the Republican Party that emerged from this coalition in 1854 as a potential savior of the country because of its anti-slavery stand. This new party's biggest attraction was its advocacy of racial change. Blacks and others with human rights interests began to drop their demands for perfection in order to support the political avenue with the greatest promise for change, "regardless," said black abolitionist Henry Highland Garnet, "of the unkind things uttered by some of the Republican leaders."

Even Gerrit Smith could foresee "great good" coming from the election of Lincoln.[101] Smith seemed less convinced than Douglass that the Republican Party deserved his unqualified support, but he did financially support *Frederick Douglass' Paper*, which advocated abolitionist support of the Republicans.[102]

The new Republican Party nominated John C. Fremont for president in 1856 because of his ability to unite anti-slavery party factions in the North. Douglass worked for his election.[103] A young Abraham Lincoln had gained public recognition campaigning for Fremont. When the Republicans nominated Lincoln for President in 1860, Gerrit Smith refused to vote for him because of what he perceived as Lincoln's lukewarm anti-slavery position.[104] Still, he did see Lincoln as "a pure Democrat [whose] sympathies were ever with the common people...."[105]

By 1864, Smith was actively urging Democrats to abandon their party and vote for Lincoln, which reflected the thoughts of many northerners. As the northern economy diversified toward a manufacturing base, it needed southern markets for its goods. The North found the stagnating effects of slavery were hurting profits. It was primarily for this reason that northerners became sympathetic to the cause of abolition, providing an electoral base for the Republican Party.[106] Also contributing to growing Republican credibility regarding the immorality of slave power were the burning of Lawrence, Kansas by proslavery forces and the caning of abolitionist Senator Charles Sumner by proslavery Congressman Preston Brooks on the floor of the United States Senate. Both took place on May 21, 1856.

When in 1857 the newly elected President James Buchanan denounced abolitionist agitation and the United States Supreme Court declared that blacks were not citizens in the Dred Scott case, it was clear to abolitionists that, as Garrison had said, the issue of slavery pitted "conscience against organized injustice." By 1864, the Republican Party platform declared for the first time in national history that slavery was incompatible with a government founded upon principles of democracy and freedom.[107] Subsequently, in both 1868 and 1872, Smith supported the election of Ulysses S. Grant as president, and he even headed the Madison County delegation to the Republican Party National Convention in Philadelphia in 1872.[108]

Smith's support of the Republican Party during and after the Civil War seems antithetical to his previous political life, but there is a simple explanation: Smith was *tired*. The Liberty Party he had worked so hard to establish had failed to unite the various anti-slavery factions. The Liberty League and the Radical Abolitionist Party had burned out, and the war had sapped the nation's strength. Smith feared that the Democratic Party would bring back to the nation its "political wickedness," but he did not have the energy or the commitment to the political process necessary to inaugurate another new party. As a result, he reluctantly joined up with the Republicans, who at least seemed as if they were serious about implementing equitable human rights.

But Gerrit Smith's life would end in political limbo. He never achieved the influence he felt he deserved, and in spite of his identity with the Republican Party, he remained a maverick. Shortly before his death, he remarked,

"The Republican Party has disappointed us. It has failed to redeem some solemnly-made pledges.

> What can we do?—we who are black men and
> we white men, who are their friends? I wish we
> could quit this party for a time, and thus punish
> and improve it. But we cannot quit it even for a
> single year, with safety to the country. For the
> Democratic Party is still eager to be restored to
> power...."[109]

One of the ironies of Smith's political life was that in spite of his constant efforts to avoid public life, his supporters kept placing him in nomination as a candidate. Shortly after his graduation from Hamilton College, Smith had composed an open letter to the "Electors of the County of Madison" in which he condemned political parties and nominating conventions as unnecessary tools of divisive political machines. Candidates, he said, should simply place themselves in nomination in a public campaign, as he did in 1825 as a candidate for the New York State Assembly. He lost that election—the only time he actively sought public office.[110]

Two years later in 1827, he allowed an anti-Masonic party to place his name in nomination as a candidate for State Senator. Again, he lost. It was probably this experience that convinced him that running for public office was not something that made him happy.[111] Years later, he succinctly stated the attitude that characterized his entire life beyond 1827 in a letter to Syracuse abolitionist Samuel J. May: "I hate office. I shrink from public life."[112]

Despite this attitude, Gerrit Smith garnered respect in political circles, and he was nominated for president of the United States in four consecutive presidential elections. In 1848 both the Liberty Party, and its splinter group the Liberty League, nominated him for the highest office. Also in 1848, labor leader George Henry Evans' organization, the Industrial Congress, placed Smith's name in nomination for president.[113]

The only one of these nominations that Smith took seriously was that of the Liberty League, the faction that he had encouraged as an effort to revitalize the Liberty Party.[114] He refused the nomination of the Industrial Congress,[115] and asked the Liberty Party to refrain from considering him.

> "As I am not fit for [this] office, and inasmuch as the Liberty Party can unite upon any one of the dozen noble men, who are fit for it—it follows that it would be neither kindness to myself, nor justice and advantage to its course, for the Liberty Party to put me in nomination."[116]

Lewis Tappan, still a loyal Liberty Party adherent, politely asked Smith to be less "vituperative" in his public criticism of the struggling Liberty Party.[117] Smith was realistic about his poor chance to win, but did say, "if elected, I will serve...."[118]

As if to seal its own fate, the Liberty Party again nominated Smith for president in 1852.

Both the Radical Abolition Party and the Land Reformers Party nominated Smith for President in 1856,[119] and the Radical Abolitionists did so again in 1860.[120] Although central New York people were enthusiastic about these nominations,[121] Smith was not, and he did no campaigning except for a few speeches on pet issues which he probably would have made anyway.[122]

Smith was also nominated three times for New York State Governor. The Liberty Party did so in 1840, and in 1842 at the Liberty Party Convention in Peterboro, and the People's State Ticket nominated him on August 4, 1858.[123] He did some active campaigning after the 1858 nomination, but not because he wanted to be elected; he saw it as an opportunity to spread his personal views. He wrote to Samuel May, "I could use the office to some effect in behalf of temperance and freedom."[124]

Frothingham noted that during the campaign, Smith actually "attended fifty-three meetings, travelled some four thousand miles, and spent between four and five thousand dollars, paying...all expenses from his private purse."[125]

As an independent candidate nominated by "The People," he believed that his campaign "time and labor would be well spent whether he were elected or not...." He traveled through 40 counties,[126] delivering speeches that averaged two and a half hours in length. At the end of the campaign he wrote three letters to persons who had worked for his election, reimbursing them with $20, $25, and $100 for their donated services.[127]

His graciousness and moral advocacy during this campaign won for him a sterling reputation as a sincere reformer, but he remained cynical about government and politics. After the elections of 1860, he commented, "We have again passed through the great quadrennial Demoralization...which puts falsehood for truth and darkness for light, and makes ten appeals to passion and prejudice where it makes one to reason."[128] Perhaps his most intense frustration with politics rested in his own house, for he had difficulty persuading his family to vote as he wished. A note in his verse book recalls: "The whole family of C.D. Miller decided against the course of G.S. at the polls + even the wife of G.S. did not confess her agreement with him."[129]

By far Gerrit Smith's most important political nomination occurred in 1852 as candidate on an independent ticket to represent the 22nd Congressional district, which included the counties of Oswego and Madison. Business people in the city of Oswego pressured him to accept the nomination because they were hoping to influence the federal government to negotiate reciprocity agreements with Canada.[130] Smith called his Oswego business clerk John B. Edwards' desire to have him elected "an evil wish,"[131] but he reluctantly accepted the nomination, and in the fall of 1852, he won the election. Smith had made almost no effort to campaign as a candidate for the U.S. Congress. His campaign manager, John Snow of Canastota, advised him to stay out of public view and to say nothing that might be controversial.[132]

Smith spent much of late 1852 preparing the business for his absence in case he won the election. Abolitionists saw Smith's candidacy as a unique opportunity to infiltrate the Washington establishment with their ideas. Frederick Douglass pledged to work for Smith's election,[133] and Senator Henry Wilson of Massachusetts wrote that "the cause of Liberty would gain more by your election than by the election of any man in the country."[134]

Smith was visible and well-known in Madison and Oswego counties, where he had spent two decades speaking and writing on issues of moral reform with notable success in influencing minds regarding the abolition of slavery. With voters thus primed, he pulled enough votes away from the Whig and Democrat Parties to win the election. The Whig candidate received 5,620 votes, the Democrat 6,206 votes, and Smith, as an Independent, 8,049 votes.[135]

George Thomas, of Utica, New York, wrote of Smith, "When a candidate for Congress (to which he never aspired), he received from Smithfield every vote but two. Such an expression demonstrates the feelings and sentiments of his neighbors and townsmen and their estimate of his character, capacity and fitness for the position...."[136] It mattered not what Gerrit Smith wanted for his own life, or how frequently and clearly he articulated it to the public; in spite of his well-stated abhorrence of politics, the voters sent him to Washington. His election resulted in a flurry of letters of surprise and approval from his admirers. Frederick Douglass wrote,

"You go to Congress, not by the grace of a party caucus, bestowed as a reward for party services; not by concealment, bargain, or Compromise, but by the unbought suffrages of your fellow citizens, acting independently of, and in defiance of party! ...You go to Congress, not from quiet nor seclusion—Shut out from the eye of the world—where your thoughts and feelings had to be imagined—but you go from the very whirlwind of agitation, from "rescue trials," from Womans' rights Conventions and from "Jerry Celebrations," where your lightest words were caught up and

perverted to your hurt. You go to Congress a Free
Man."[137]

Joseph Hawley wrote from Hartford of "the joy your triumphant
election gives us. You have...a field for being a 'practical' man.... Madison County has done herself more honor than she has done you."[138]

A.V. Bentley wrote from DeRuyter, New York, "My joy is...deep
– unfeigned – profoundly sincere. I have no words to express it....
The people have trimphed...."[139]

Even Garrison, in *The Liberator*, editorialized, "The election of
Gerrit Smith as a Representative to Congress...is among the most
extraordinary political events of this...age."[140] William Jay of Bed-
ford, Massachusetts expressed his elation over the fact that the nation
should allow Smith to violate federal law by aiding fugitive slaves
and then send him "not to the gallows, but to Congress."[141]

There was deep irony in Gerrit Smith's presence in the national
legislature. As Frothingham saw it,

"The man of prayer is sent down to the metropolis
of profanity; the free soul to the stronghold of
slavery; the child of the spirit to the arena of
gladiators. The people wondered; editors smiled
good-naturedly or sarcastically; the politicians
derided; the high-minded rejoiced."[142]

Smith's own reaction to his election was anything but enthusias-
tic. Out of respect for the expression of public confidence in him,
Smith responded to his election with politeness and good intentions,
yet it was clear that he did not want to leave his beloved Peterboro.
The Congressional session to which he was elected convened in
December of 1853,[143] so he left home in November.[144] Enroute to
Washington, he kept track of every penny spent, and submitted a
bill for reimbursement.[145]

When he reached Philadelphia, problems with headaches caused
a delay, and he wondered whether he should attempt to carry out

his Congressional duties at all. "I do not intend to resign my office immediately," he wrote to a friend soon after. "I presume that my constituents would prefer my holding it for a month or two...."[146]

Clearly, Smith had intended to resign his seat in Congress even before he arrived there. He had said to his loyal business agent, John Edwards, that he was sure that God had no work for him to do in Congress.[147] He had insisted that he did not want the office due to his advanced age and the pressure of his business in Peterboro, and he told Garrison that his election to Congress was "an event as little anticipated...as my going to the moon."[148] Still, his commitment to the job appeared to be sincere, as he wrote in a letter to his constituents: "...my whole heart is moved to gratitude...and that, God helping me, I will so discharge [my] duties as neither to dishonor myself nor you."[149]

He bought a house in Washington in January of 1853, had it renovated to his liking, sent a servant ahead to prepare the place for his arrival, and purchased a new coach for his transportation while there. During his brief stay in the Capital, he lived elegantly enough to impress his peers, spending ten times more than he earned.[150]

Smith was not impressed with the politics of the House of Representatives. At the organizational level, he saw political parties as having full control of the minds of individuals. Some Congressmen did oppose slavery, but because their party did not, they could not risk alienating themselves from their party. "Their individual influence against slavery is as nothing compared with their party influence for it," Smith wrote. Influential southern Congressmen who disapproved of slavery would do nothing to quell it, because they "regard the evil as too formidable for their little courage to grapple with."

Smith certainly would have agreed with North Carolina Whig Congressman David Outlaw, who called Washington, D.C. a city of "hollow hearted and ambitious men."[151] Smith saw it as his obligation to give these licentious public servants some lessons in moral discipline. He told Frederick Douglass, "Congress... needs to witness the achievements of the Temperance reformation, and the Tobacco reformation, and the religion of Jesus Christ."[152] The spirit of conciliation and compromise that was demanded by democratic politics did not come easily to Smith. He said that "the wisest of men... entreated me... not to persevere in... singularity.... I was immovable. How could I be moved, when it was my convictions, that fastened me to my position?"[153]

Few people in Congress would ever claim any close association with Gerrit Smith, probably because he spent so much time telling them how they ought to behave and because he owed no allegiance to either major party. He feared that if he stayed in Congress too long, "I may yet become the dignified, heartless, frigid, conventional sort of being, that makes up the accepted and current idea of a statesman.... Congress is a capital place for getting rid of all sentiment, and sympathy, and conscience."[154]

Smith delivered many speeches on the floor of Congress during his short tenure there. His first on December 20, 1853, titled "Speech on the Reference of the President's Message," lamented the non-Christian nature of the Franklin Pierce administration— claiming that it had violated Biblical law—and railed against its proslavery stance.[155] It was a fitting introduction to his fellow Congressmen by a non-statesman destined to possess little influence.

As a reformer, not a politician, Smith treated the floor of Congress as a platform for his causes, and his New York constituents initially praised his effort.[156] His reputation, however, soured, and he did not stamp any important policy with his name. He delivered long, boring monologues on morality that usually had only weak connections to the bills in question, and although he expected others to be sensitive to his opinions, his colleagues considered him to be insensitive to the opinions of others. They often interrupted him with questions of order and viewed him as a cranky, opinionated, rich, unpleasant nuisance.

It came as no surprise to some—and probably as a relief to many—that Gerrit Smith resigned his seat in Congress on August 7, 1854 at the end of the first year of his term. According to a statement by Henry B. Stanton, who knew Gerrit Smith well, he resigned because "he preferred to work for the public good in his own way, unrestricted by the trammels of public position."[157] This was a very perceptive comment; as a reformer in Congress, Smith was a fish out of water. Although he claimed that he resigned due to the pressures of his private business,[158] he really could not stand the tedious, frustrating process of political policy formation and implementation.

Smith wanted to work for the public good, but he wanted to see change take place quickly. This he could accomplish by giving money to individuals rather than time to policies. Short-term, visible change for one person or family made him feel good. Long-term, nebulous change for the general welfare frustrated him—especially if the process wasn't going his way.

Some people were disappointed that Smith resigned.[159] Solomon G. Haven, a colleague from the Buffalo area who had first come to Congress in 1850, wrote,

"I assure you that amongst my greatest regrets is the fact that you are not to be with us in the House…. Your presence in the House was always of value and your influence + example I think of much service. I shall miss you much."[160]

Abolitionist Angelina Grimké Weld asked,
"Dear Brother why is this—The impression you have made in Congress has been admirable. I know the slave has other friends there, but not one who can exert the benign moral influence you have on this vital question."[161]

Abolitionist Theodore Dwight Weld also wrote to Smith, asking him to reconsider his resignation: "You are the slaves' tongue and have the nation's ear…. This is true of no other man in this generation."[161]

Smith knew, however, that after the passage of the Nebraska Bill allowing slavery an opportunity to spread, his influence on the slavery issue would be minimal.

Others were more understanding of Smith's resignation. Samuel J. May remarked,

> "I learn that you felt constrained to resign your seat in Congress. I most heartily rejoice that you have come back to live amongst us—and infuse into this community more of your spirit of reform…. I venture to conjecture that you have found Congress a hateful place, and can hardly blame you for wishing to get out of it."[162]

Frederick Douglass noted that whereas resignation "would have been lauded as highly democratic and magnanimous in others, [it was seen] as treachery and meanness in you."[163]

And John B. Edwards commented,

> "Slavery seems more + more to reign + rule. I had rather thought that it was your duty to remain in Congress + to be reelected—but with [the] present aspect of the nation I cannot find any fault with your desiring to get out from the national Councils."[164]

Whatever the reasons for and consequences of Gerrit Smith's resignation from Congress, he did what he felt he had to do. He stated his position regarding personal balance and public office well in an annotation on a letter received from Elizabeth Cady Stanton:

> "I… informed her that I, the…Candidate for the Presidency of the Nation was reduced to the small dimensions of a [Peterboro] schoolmaster having only Willie + Nannie for my pupils."[165]

And there, in Peterboro, he was content.

PART III

Social Reform

- 13 -

Temperance

Gerrit Smith lived during what was probably the richest reform era in United States history, especially in the northern states. New York State in particular was primed for reform in the 1820s by an evangelical religious fervor that focused on morality.

"We have a great work to do in our unhappy country," Smith wrote in 1845.[1]

The South, however, held values that were less morally oriented and more static. Materialism and fiscal aggressiveness ran high in the South, interest in social equity was low, and the belief in predestination—and the class conflict it engendered—eclipsed notions of achieving moral perfection.[2] The institution of slavery fostered these values, and attempts to justify it poisoned the social brew with pessimism and violence.

Smith came to believe early in his life that social justice and equity were achievable national goals, and he dedicated himself to their implementation. According to one of his friends,

> "From about the year 1830 to the close of his life he appears to have had but one great object, one end in view, which was that of reformation, amelioration, and salvation of his race. For this he labored and prayed. To this end he contributed his pen, his voice and his means."[3]

By the mid-1830s, abolitionists like Lewis Tappan and Beriah Green recognized Gerrit Smith as a radical reformer. He had embraced immediate abolition. He declared political parties and religious denominations to be supporters of criminal practices that fostered injustice. He attacked established institutions as nothing more than safe havens for those who were already financially comfortable and socially connected.

The economic depression of 1837 gave Smith the national audience he had lacked. As masses of people lost jobs, social position, income, and security, their faith in the old rules waned. Society was ripe for change, and when Smith plunged into public view with optimistic messages of change, they fell on receptive ears.

The public often used religion to integrate reform into their lives, and new systems of belief that offered quick solutions to complex problems became attractive. Smith was dismayed when communities of Shakers, Mormons, Perfectionists, and Spiritualists became popular, because their people withdrew from the larger society. He believed they sustained, in their new cliques, biases that lessened the chances of social equity.

Smith believed the responsibility for moral change lay with the individual in existing society, not with groups that withdrew from society to test their ideas for social reform. He drew comfort from his belief that reform work was a kind of practical holiness that integrated one into the community—instead of drawing one out of it.

Reformers were good at keeping social issues before the public eye. Most of them were personally and economically secure in stable communities, either in or near important cities or close to transportation routes like the Erie Canal. They were not on the frontier fighting for survival, so they could afford to spend their resources on optimistic schemes they hoped would lead toward a new national identity. They worked especially hard in establishing local institutions such as schools, churches, and political organizations that they trusted would stand as beacons to the nation.[4]

Reformers bombarded the masses with local meetings, state and national conventions, newspaper and journal articles, and sermons speaking to the issues of slavery and drinking. As Smith said, "There are not only three millions of slaves to deliver—but more than half a million drunkards."[5] He was a font of ideas for reform, and, in the words of historian Anna Wells, "one of the most picturesque of the... reformers.... Failure neither disillusioned him nor taught him."[6]

Smith's vision of a more equitable social world drove him on in the face of public apathy and frustration. He thought that by his own example, he could rouse public interest in equity. Disheartened by slow change but dedicated to reform, he plodded on, using the one influential tool he had: money. He saw it as a divine gift that he should use for the common good.

Although people looked at many of the 19th-century reformers as nuisances, they considered reform itself a tolerable pursuit. For the most part, reformers were perceived as non-threatening; they were, in general, not subversive, and they embraced the dominant values of the time as they worked within the established institutional system. In the opening half of the century, the wave of Protestant perfectionism that swept across New York State encouraged reformers to believe that immediate moral change was possible. All it would take to succeed would be enough energy.

Smith's belief in the balance found in nature as a model for society led him directly into reform. He saw that although the basic components of nature were sound, they were always in flux in the process of maintaining balance. Nothing was static, or right, or permanent; change occurred by means of succession, with violence sometimes being a normal dynamic in the maintenance of that balance. Smith saw his role as that of a guiding light in the process of succession in social ideas and institutions. It was time, he said, for equality to succeed discrimination, and he would oil the machinery of change with his money.

The fact that he was often a lone siren in a heavy wind did not bother him. He wrote, "It is my fate to be in the minorities."[7] It fueled his passion to work by example, and the example he set on a local level did have an effect. Peterboro, the town of Smithfield, and even Madison County at times, followed his lead as the public voted for programs of abolition and temperance.

Smith wanted to subvert what he saw as a culture of political and religious despotism that had led to a crisis of authority, suppressing individual freedoms. People long held in bondage to ignorance and superstition were finding new leaders in Andrew Jackson and Charles G. Finney, who encouraged them to develop their own natural virtues and to take control of social institutions. Smith joined with them in the reform movement that he hoped would bring equitable treatment of all people through the elimination of such evils as slavery, discrimination, and the consumption of alcohol.

One of Gerrit Smith's major passions was his lifelong determination to minimize the unwise consumption of alcohol. Smith viewed the drinking of liquor as pernicious, calling the dram shop "the great manufactory of incendiaries, madmen and murderers."[8] (A "dram," which today refers to a pharmacist's unit of fluid measure, was back then a small amount of liquor, what we might call a 'shot'. It was typically the unit by which alcohol was sold one drink at a time, such as in a tavern.)

Smith questioned the wisdom of drinking alcohol in a speech before Congress during his two-year term,

"Is it claimed, that there is an overbalance of good in it? There is no good at all in it. It is only evil continually…. It has not one redeeming feature. There is nothing in it to mitigate its immigatable wickedness:—nothing to set over against its unmixed mischief."[9]

It is curious that Smith spent so much energy, time, and resources on such a futile effort as temperance, but perhaps this seems so only after having witnessed the ineffectual federal attempt to legislate prohibition in the 20th century. In the early 1800s when Smith took up the cause, it appeared to him as an honorable duty—a way to save the nation from the evil work of the Devil. He had experienced the effects of alcohol first-hand while he was a student at Hamilton College, and he later resolved to campaign against its use. He wrote in 1841, "I formerly drank intoxicating liquors; and several times I got drunk. But a merciful God showed me my sin in this respect...."[10]

Smith was mainly concerned with the change in behavior brought on by intoxication. While they were drunk, people committed acts that would not characterize their sober states. This produced such imbalance in relationships that families and communities could not be safe, because people who drank could not be trusted. Smith believed that people in general desired a better life, and that by appealing to their morals, he could motivate them to achieve it. The optimism of the reform movement to which he subscribed fueled his faith in the individual's ability to change in response to moral persuasion, so he set for himself the goal of being that source of inspiration leading the public toward communal happiness.

In Smith's mind, temperance provided the perfect movement for the blend of moral social rules and religious teaching. He saw temperance as the way toward the golden age of family and community peace. He was convinced that every person, armed with the power of reason and buoyed by faith in God, could also see this fact—and would opt for temperance immediately if so counseled. He claimed, "To drink after we have been taught in the course of the Savior's providence, that it poisons and kills, is to incur the Divine displeasure."[11]

To Smith, change was just a matter of learning the right moral behavior. All one needed, he thought, was to see logical arguments against the use of intoxicating liquors, and the game would be won. He dealt with it as if the issue of drinking were separate from all the other areas of one's life, and, as such, could easily be 'treated'.

Smith's idea was to deal with temperance in two ways: personal abstinence and ministering to others. He wrote,

> "A man cannot do his whole duty to the cause
> of temperance by abstaining himself from the
> drinking of intoxicating liquors. He must labor in
> various ways to rescue his fellow men who have

fallen victims to intemperance; and to save the
sober from becoming drunken."[12]

He did not, and perhaps at that time *could* not, understand the
physiological and psychological dynamics of addiction. His was a
simple-minded belief: people could easily change once they were
properly informed. He became so passionate that people came to
regard him as an obsessed eccentric and, in a letter to William Lloyd
Garrison and Wendell Phillips in 1865, Smith acknowledged that
many had stopped listening to him.[13]

Gerrit Smith took up the cause of temperance early in his career.
When he returned to Peterboro from college in 1819, he found it
to be, at least in his mind, overrun with "drunkards." He noted six
liquor sale shops in the hamlet and seven distilleries in the Town
of Smithfield.[14] With his firm belief in the morality of the Bible, he
took up the cause in earnest, claiming to have delivered the first
speech on temperance in the New York State Capitol at Albany in
1824. He also boasted of having "spent fifty days in the year lecturing on that subject."[15]

Smith joined the newly formed American Temperance Society
in 1826 and the New York State Temperance Society in 1829. He
was thrilled that local temperance organizations multiplied rapidly
and attracted many members.[16] In the late 1820s he corresponded
frequently with Nathaniel Hewit, editor of the temperance-oriented
Journal of Humanity in Andover, Massachusetts about their shared
belief that alcohol use was the chief cause of crime, poverty, disease, and death.[17] Smith believed that people were motivated to
start drinking after observing the 'safe', or moderate, drinker who
appeared to be a model for the acceptable consumption of alcohol.
These moderate drinkers, he claimed, were the primary target of
reform, as they set a bad example for others who were led to believe
that they also could be "sober drinkers."[18]

During the 1820s, Smith concentrated his efforts on his home
town of Smithfield—especially the hamlet of Peterboro. He per-

suaded the owners of some local establishments that sold liquor to discontinue sales, and he encouraged people who used alcohol to sign pledges of abstention. To a large degree, this effort worked to dry out Smithfield,[19] as did his efforts to control liquor consumption in the City of Oswego, where he had extensive business interests.[20]

It was in the early 1830s that Smith first advocated legal force in combination with moral persuasion as an effective way to achieve temperance. Speaking at several local, state, and national temperance society conventions between 1831 and 1833, he encouraged municipalities large and small to enact legislation prohibiting the sale of liquor by the drink.[21] He fervently worked for temperance during the decade of the 1830s, basing his opposition to alcohol on morality. The Bible, he said, forbade its use on three grounds:

> "First. The bible enjoins self preservation and commands that we do ourselves no harm. 2nd. Scientific, Medical, and other observation on this point of late years has made it clear, that such a beverage is injurious to men's moral, intellectual, + physical constitution. 3rd. The conclusion therefore is, that to indulge in such beverage is to go counter to the Bible, and to violate some of its principles."[22]

Smith's work in temperance conditioned his perception of various social groups. The elite class, he noted, was not targeted for its alcohol use, in part because temperance societies did not include wine on their list of prohibited beverages. As he put it, the societies "passed by the rich man's decanters and demijohns, to quarrel with the poor man's jugs and bottles." Smith believed that people should be treated equally relative to alcohol use—not allowed privileges because they were "refined and polite."[23]

The Irish became a target of Smith's prejudice, however. He and his fellow temperance advocate Edward Delevan concocted a plan to warn Irish immigrants of the sins of their intemperance even before they reached the United States. He wrote to Delevan in 1838,

"How lamentable, that, whilst capable of being
the <u>best</u>, their debasing indulgence in intoxicating
drinks, should render the Irish the <u>worst</u>
constituent in our population!"[24]

During the 1840s and 1850s, Smith's activity in the temperance movement dropped off markedly: as the number of letters in the Smith papers referring to temperance decreased in the early 1840s, the frequency of those referring to abolition increased. Only some local temperance activity in Peterboro drew his interest as the issue of slavery heated up prior to the war. He noted that "Temperance… is a small cause compared with that of 2 ½ millions of slaves…."[25]

His election to Congress in 1852 further muted his interest in temperance, and he became more aware that even those who favored temperance voted for candidates who were drinkers or who supported policies that favored liquor sales. In a letter to Frederick Douglass, Smith lamented,

"The cause of temperance is prostrate…. [People]
are ever proclaiming that the dramshop is the
greatest of all curses:—and yet they are ever voting
to maintain it. Is this their matchless infatuation or
their amazing hypocrisy?"[26]

In spite of his frustration, Smith kept active in the temperance movement when it was convenient. He delivered an address at the July 1858 semi-annual meeting of the Madison County Temperance Union in Peterboro that combined messages about antislavery and temperance.[27]

The end of the Civil War in 1865 offered an opportunity for the old temperance crusaders to mount once again their righteous steeds and charge forth into the moral abyss. Smith had long before admitted, "On the subject of temperance… I carry my notions to what many temperance men regard as an objectionable extremity…." He hoped that others would praise rather than ridicule him for such devotion.[28] Now, with the war over and emancipation of slaves in place, Smith could refocus his eternal energy for moral reform.

Letters from Edwin Morton, Smith's old intellectual mentor, began to reflect less concern for abolition and reminiscences of John Brown, and more concern for temperance.[29] Smith let loose his temperance fervor on his business agent in Detroit, George Bissell, over the issue of a wet or dry business establishment that Smith owned there. Bisell wanted to sell liquor on the premises, but Smith replied,

> "NO! Let no intoxicating drinks be sold there.... I am such an extreme Temperance man that I would not...sell even cider or ale."[30]

By 1869, Gerrit Smith's name was once again of national prominence in temperance circles. He contributed generously to the New York State Temperance Society, even accepting an invitation to attend and speak at the National Temperance Convention in Chicago in 1869.[31] The purpose of the Chicago convention was to organize a National Prohibition Party, the goal of which was legal suppression of the dram shop.

In December of 1869, Syracuse was the location for the convention of the New York State Temperance Society. Smith attended and played an important part in the formation of the New York State Anti-Dramshop Party, and its new journal, *The Anti-Dram Shop*, which Smith supported in part with his contributions.[32] By the early 1870s, he had returned to the dram shop as the focus of his temperance work. He believed that an Anti-Dramshop Party could successfully push for legal suppression of the sale of liquor by the drink.

In an address to the Anti-Dramshop Party, he said,

> "Although this great delay in organizing a political party against dramselling has given time to the matchless and hoary evil to strike its roots so deep and wide, as to embolden it to defy extirpation, we nevertheless do not despair of success...."[33]

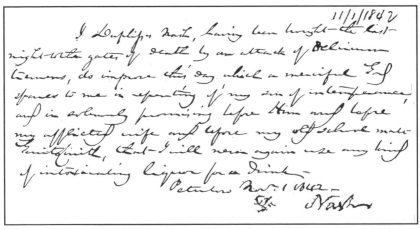

This pledge, written by Gerrit Smith and signed by a friend named Duplissis Nash, represents the kind of personal work Smith did in temperance. It reads,

"I, Duplissis Nash, having been brought—the last night—to the gates of death by an attack of delirium tremens, do improve this day which a merciful God spares to me in repenting of my sin of intemperance, and in solemnly promising before Him and before my afflicted wife and before my old school mate Gerrit Smith, that I will never again use any kind of intoxicating liquor for a drink.

Peterboro Nov. 1 1842 —

D Nash"

Although he had some sense of the futility and inconsequential nature of his temperance effort, calling it "a dead cause," he characteristically continued to plod on, seeing his success in Peterboro as a model for the world.[34]

After Smith's initial success with temperance reform in Peterboro in the early 1830s, some backsliding occurred, and a new effort to close all "tippling places" was launched in 1840.[35] Smith was overjoyed that some former drinkers established the "Washington Reformed Drunkards' Society of the Town of Smithfield."[36] Although he had some hope that existing political forces could legally close dram shops, he still relied mainly on moral persuasion to change minds. He worked on local people, trying to influence them not to vote for officials who would license dram-selling, and complimenting them publicly when they did so.[37] Peterboro residents were encouraged to sign pledges of abstinence, and if that did not work, Smith wrote counseling letters (see opposite page) to his friends and neighbors regarding their drinking behavior.[38]

Although historians sometimes refer to Smith as a prohibitionist, he was not; he focused his opposition to drinking intoxicating liquor on that which took place in bars. Smith never recommended that the government enact laws of total prohibition. "I would not have the Legislature enact laws to restrain the traffic in intoxicating drinks…. All that I would ask of the Legislature in the matter of temperance is that it… set a clean example…."[39] That example could be set, he maintained, by preventing the sale of liquor licenses by local boards of excise. He encouraged people to pressure their local commissioners of excise to refrain from issuing licenses to taverns.

In a speech titled "Vindication of the Chicago Temperance Convention," he said,

> "Does our party mean to prohibit the importation
> of intoxicating liquors, or the manufacture of
> them, or the use of them in families? No! But our
> enemies will say that we mean to prohibit them all.
> It is dramselling only that it means to prohibit…."[40]

One problem with Smith's emphasis on taverns and bars was that the public saw it as class bias: middle- or upper-class people could afford to purchase large volumes of liquor for consumption at home, whereas poor people could afford only a few drinks at a time. Greene Smith criticized his father as he wrote about an upcoming temperance meeting in Morrisville. "I hope you will have a good meeting… and do good without perhaps achieving what you desire." Greene's cynicism echoed the public's perception of Gerrit's position:

> "The distinction which you draw between the evils
> of the dram-shop and the evils of the wholesale
> liquor store where a man may buy a barrel of rum
> to drink in <u>his</u> <u>own</u> <u>house</u>, is simply a distinction
> between the poor and the rich."[41]

Greene's drinking posed an interesting problem for Gerrit, as did his challenge to Gerrit's stand against dram shops. To quote Greene at length,

> "Many a man…is driven by an ill mannered wife to the dramshop, she refusing to allow liquor in the house…. [And] the rich man, who can afford it, drinks at home while the poor man, who only has a small amount of money at a time, has to resort to the dramshop."

Greene challenged his father's claim that dram shop drunkards were a worse threat than those produced at home.

> "What difference does it make if a man drink a pint of rum in a dram shop, at home, at sea, in a church or in a gaming house? The liquor is the same…. There seem to me to be several reasons for the dram shop drinking appearing to be worse, tho' I cannot see that it is worse."[42]

It is likely that Greene was, in part, defending his own behavior, which was a painful anomaly for Gerrit to see in his own family.

Gerrit realized that the closing of the dram shops would be a form of discrimination against the poor, but he rationalized it by claiming that it was what the poor needed. In a letter to Vice President Schuyler Colfax in 1870, he wrote, "But let the poor rejoice that their poverty disables them from sharing in this power. Let them prefer being poor to being liquor drinkers…."[43] He also blamed "colored people" for helping to keep the dram shop alive, noting "the frightful progress of intemperance amongst the emancipated slaves." He admonished them that the physical suffering experienced by blacks before emancipation was "nothing as compared with the drunkard's enslavement of both body and soul."[44]

Smith's arguably class-based prejudice against dram shops produced an obsession that caused him to ignore principles of equal rights as he lashed out at poor people who frequented bars and the owners who operated them. He wrote,

> "If our concern for this cause is not enough to
> induce us to plead earnestly and frequently with
> the dram-seller to relinquish an occupation which
> beggars families and breaks hearts, and kills bodies
> and kills souls—he will be likely to continue in the
> occupation of blood-red guiltiness."[45]

He also accused what he called "temperate drinkers" for setting a bad example for others—even though he used some alcoholic beverages in his own home.[46] In fact, wine and beer were not included in what he considered as "intoxicating beverages." In an 1825 letter to his wife, Gerrit mentioned plans for a large party at his house during which "we shall…drink up all the wine."[47] In spite of recommendations from friends to give up wine,[48] he kept it as part of his household stock for the rest of his life.

It may be that Smith himself did not often drink it, but its consumption was a regular part of life for others there. An old college friend, Fletcher N. Haight, helped Gerrit replenish his stock. "I have ordered to Charles Miller a case of assorted California wine. I intend this for your wife, but you being so long and consistently a temperance man I do not send to your address…. Tell your wife she must drink my health… as I will not ask you to imbibe."[49]

Smith also served wine to guests who visited his Peterboro mansion. Although Gerrit may not have touched it, he did approve of others' social, or "sober," use of it. After a visit to his home by Mrs. Ball, Mrs. Ledyard, and Mrs. Linklaen, he implied in a verse to them that he had, indeed, partaken:

> "We thank you that you came this way
> To cheer our hearts this chilly day.
> We lack not wine when you are nigh:
> We'll drink your words + so 'get high'!"[50]

What *is* clear is that Ann appreciated wine. Her daughter Elizabeth wrote that after a trip to her doctor during one of her winter stays in New York City, she and her mother had returned to their abode and "lunched on soup, bread...+ currants. Mother wound up with a [glass] of her Rhein wine."[51] Ann evidently abandoned her regular use of wine during her trip to Europe: Greene wrote that his mother was sick with diarrhea. With a little humor, when Greene told their hotel courier that Ann was drinking water instead of wine, the courier exclaimed, "Mon Dieu! Mon Dieu! Ils boivent de l'eau? Ils seront <u>tous</u> malade...." [My God! My God! They drink water? They will <u>all</u> be sick....][52]

Smith's detractors used the drinking of wine in his home against him. Also, the fact that he had once participated in the distillery business was fodder for his opponents. Although he wrote several disclaimers about his involvement in the liquor trade, in the early 1820s he had "thousands of bushels" of grain from farms he owned sent to distilleries to be manufactured into whiskey; and, for a brief time, he owned two distilleries. "They fell into my hands on account of liens I had on the ground where they were built," Smith wrote to a friend as explanation. Eventually, he had both distilleries destroyed.[53]

Despite his brief foray into the liquor business and his enjoyment of wine at home, Smith was faithful to his pledge to abstain from hard liquors—and loyal to the effort to get liquor traffic suppressed.

Government, Smith believed, was the agency that should shut down dram shops. He saw two reasons for this recommendation. First, a sober public was necessary to support a government based on popular sovereignty; second, protection of person and property was, in Smith's mind, the legitimate role of government. And, he reasoned, both persons and property needed protection against the rampages of drunkards.[54]

Believing total prohibition to be beyond the scope of any government, though, he focused his efforts on closing down bars that sold liquor by the "dram," prophesying that if the public was unsuccessful in accomplishing this goal on a local level, then the whole nation was in peril. Even in his later years he appealed to voters to "vote right," claiming that, "They see not that the question up is whether it is the dramshop or the nation that shall die."[55]

The local effects of Smith's campaign were profound. Peterboro resident Henry Campbell noted in 1851, "We are completely Totalists in Smithfield as there is not a license granted or a drop sold for anything I know except for medicinal purposes any where in town and our... Tavern is shut... and the late Landlord gone to another town."[56]

Smith demonstrated his own commitment by threatening to sue Peterboro tavern owner Ephraim Woodworth when he continued to sell liquor after the board of excise denied him a license to do so. He wrote the bar owner:

> "I am myself entirely in earnest in my efforts
> to get temptation out of the way of our guilty,
> wretched drunkards. Whatever I can lawfully and
> properly do for their deliverance and reformation,
> I feel myself bound by the high consideration of
> humanity + religion to do."[57]

Smith bore no personal malice for Woodworth; in fact, when his liquor license was denied, Smith offered to pay him the profits he would have had. "I am ready to manifest my sympathy for you in a form that will prove its sincerity."[58] Smith also offered this type of financial consideration to others in the temperance movement. Having invited temperance speaker John G. Stower to travel to Madison County for a series of speaking engagements, Smith added in a letter,

> "You will, of course, be at no expense whilst in our
> County—for there are hundreds of us who will
> be right glad to have you at our houses.... [and
> please] allow the friends of temperance to hand
> you fifty or sixty dollars to compensate you for the

damage your private business has suffered by your
absence from it."[59]

Gerrit's habit was to be intensely committed to the temperance
movement—as long as some other more important issue did not
distract him. Another interesting facet of his temperance work was
his combination of optimism and pessimism. He held the faith that
most reasonable people had the ability to opt for the implementation
of sound moral principles once the principles were pointed out to
them, but he also saw the lack of widespread success of temperance
as a sign of its futility.

Those who could see a more diverse moral mix among the public
than was apparent to Smith criticized his early optimism that voters
could move political parties to oppose dramselling. A friend, local
attorney Artemus V. Bentley of DeRuyter, warned Smith:

> "Permit me to say, you have more confidence
> in the integrity of a majority of the voters of
> [Madison] County than I have. The idea of
> bringing the ballot box to bear on the question
> + voting down rum-selling + rum-drinking is
> [futile]."[60]

Smith seemed to know this, but he simply could not give up the
fight. By the late 1850s, he noted that the cause of temperance was
"prostrate" or "dead," yet he continued to work at it.[61] Even though
he was disgusted with the lack of fervor of temperance workers and
with the failure of voters to vote for temperance candidates, he toiled
on with "the sublime mission of Temperance."[62]

Between June 3 and July 2 of 1870, the Anti-Dramshop Party
held rallies in fourteen locations in Madison County to encourage
a large public attendance at the upcoming July 20 nominating convention at Morrisville. At the age of 73, Gerrit participated in all of
these meetings.[63] Madison County usually responded with a greater
temperance vote than most other areas, and Smith knew this. Local

Unionist pastor David Plumb reminded him in a letter, "You are doing well with Temperance in your town, but the cause elsewhere is not so hopeful, indeed, is distressingly discouraging."[64]

Gerrit Smith saw clearly in his own mind the connection between religion, social morals, and temperance. He was incensed over the failure of Christians to support the Anti-Dramshop Party, especially ministers who would not encourage political action. In an open letter to "The Thoughtful and Candid of the County of Madison," he wrote,

> "One temperance sermon…from a Doctor of
> Divinity, who condemns…political action against
> dramselling, will suffice to make those who hear it
> self-satisfied…in their rum-party connexions."[65]

And when some people criticized Smith's attempt to make the connection between Christianity and temperance by pointing out to him that even Jesus had drunk wine, he simply claimed that people in Jesus' era did not know of the danger of intoxicating drinks. He wrote to friend Edward Delevan, "We are not to go to [the Bible] for scientific instruction."[66] More up-to-date information, he thought, combined with the supposedly obvious moral prohibition of drinking, should be enough to cure "drunkards."

Interestingly, Smith seemed to believe that all people who became intoxicated were males. He asked, "What mother, what wife, would shed one tear [if dramshops were closed]? What sister would have one sigh the more, because of it?"[67] He believed women were more oriented to proper morality than were men. One of his major concerns was that the males of his family should not consume liquor. On a visit to the Fitzhugh family, he told their three boys that he hoped they would "slake their thirst from wells and cows," and he wrote them a rhyme:

> "Believing it to be a sin,
> To drink rum, brandy, wine, or gin,
> Or even cider, if fermented
> Or beet, if strong, or with hops scented—

We do resolve with all our heart
From all these drinks five years to part.
And pray that God us grace may give,
Pure lives of temperance to live."[68]

And to his son and grandson, he wrote, "Oh, what an awfully wicked thing it is to drink intoxicating liquors! People get drunk, + swear, + lie, + steal + murder."[69]

People who knew they needed help with their drinking looked to Gerrit as a role model. Friends with family members in trouble from alcohol even asked if Gerrit would shelter them therapeutically at his home in Peterboro.[70] Gerrit's own brother, Peter, having acknowledged his alcoholism, begged Gerrit for help.

"My eyes, I trust, are now open. I pray God it
may not be too late. I feel remorse and shame. My
longing desire now is to see your face my Brother,
and to accompany you immediately to the Utica
Asylum [for treatment]."[71]

Smith's temperance crusade even led him to go after the farmers who grew the produce used in the production of intoxicating drinks. He wanted people of the churches to work against all participants in the drinking trade. "Set your face like a flint against all forms of oppression—against the whole partnership in intemperance of farmers, distillers, vendors + drinkers...."[72]

Having recruited Francis Hawley to deliver a series of temperance speeches and to distribute Bibles in churches throughout Madison County, Smith advised him: "I should like you to tell your hearers, that the Bible forbids their growing of hops for the brewer, and grain for the distiller...."[73]

His suggested ban on hop growing is curious, given that until the end of his life, he was not sure that beer was an intoxicating beverage.[74] His extreme proclamations against people who were part of the trade bothered some. About hop and grain farmers, he said, "in addition to casting their votes on the side of the dram-shop, [they] yield up the products of their fields to the demands of that devourer and murderer."[75]

It should be noted that Madison County was a leader in hops production for much of the 19th century, at one time being marked as the largest hops-producing county in the largest hops-producing state in the union. Smith's niece wondered how the little girls and boys in Sunday school felt "whose fathers raised hops when you put your trying questions to them."[76] Undaunted, Smith pressed his hopes for temperance on anyone within listening range.

One technique Smith adopted to ensure the temperance option for residents in his beloved Peterboro was his establishment of a temperance hotel. In the mid-1820s, there existed at the east end of the hamlet a hotel/tavern which Smith felt "was not conducted on temperance principles."[77] Opposed to such an establishment and encouraged by his wealthy New York City friend Arthur Tappan, Gerrit built another hotel at the west end of the hamlet as a temperance facility in 1827.[78]

He received advice at the time against attempting to run a temperance hotel because it would be a waste of money better used for other Christian goals.[79] And he was encouraged to convince current tavern operators to stop selling liquor.[80]

In 1841, Smith attempted to buy the local tavern owned by Nathan Harvey that sold liquor. When the sale did not go through, he offered Harvey $60 per year as incentive to operate his business as a temperance house. Harvey's refusal prompted a second offer of $75 per year.[81]

At this same time, Smith's "temperance hotel" was sold to a Mr. Messinger with the understanding that it would be operated on the principles of temperance. Messinger then purchased the "old tavern" at the east end of Peterboro, closed it, and started selling liquor at his new tavern. "The new tavern was but a few feet from Mr. Smith's office, and he was daily pained to see his idol house desecrated by the votaries of Bacchus, and to have his ears saluted with the vulgar slang of the bar-room. He could not endure it for long, …[so he] bought it back, losing considerable money in the trade."

Smith tried then to operate it once again as a temperance facility.[82] To do so, Smith hired E. C. Hyde,[83] who posted the following notice of hotel rules:

PETERBORO HOTEL

Cleanliness; Quiet; Comfort

1. No intoxicating liquors.

2. Persons, so unfortunate, as to use tobacco, are requested to observe the spit-boxes.

3. The traveller is assured, that he shall not be disturbed by dancing parties; and that this House shall not, like many a village tavern, be the resort of ungoverned and idle boys.

4. The Office is closed on Sunday.

This Hotel, which has been recently purchased Remodelled by Gerrit Smith, is kept by E. C. Hyde

June, 1845.[84]

Smith kept the hotel in operation for a few more years, but it was unprofitable and he finally closed it. The hotel was eventually torn down, and Smith "annexed the land to his spacious park grounds."[85] Thus, Smith's experiment with what came to be known as the "Hyde Hotel" was over.[86]

Whereas Smith's efforts at temperance in Peterboro have been accurately interpreted as a struggle between Smith and local residents based on his attempt to impose morals on them,[87] the greater value in its study is that it served as an example of the futility of Smith's temperance activities—a great many resources expended for little real gain. Yet what is important is not that Smith failed to achieve temperance, but that he did not quit trying. In fact, because of his influence so long ago, the town of Smithfield remains a 'dry town' today.

Persistence in attempting to achieve what he thought was right while facing adversity was a lifelong trait for Gerrit Smith.

- 14 -

Women's Rights

The women's rights movement fit well into Smith's outlook on life, because women faced discrimination and deserved the opportunity to exercise their natural rights as much as did any other oppressed group.

Yet with this reform movement, Smith equivocated. His inconsistent attitude toward women is difficult to explain. He would speak of the equality of women and men, and then just as easily, he would degrade women. He seemed to be unaware of the contradictions in his thoughts and actions; he claimed to be a liberal and progressive thinker on the issue. But some women—especially Elizabeth Cady Stanton—called him on it.

Stanton wrote to her cousin in 1856 about what she considered to be his lukewarm support of women's rights. "I fear you have not been faithful in holding up our side of the questions," she charged.[1]

After the American Revolution, states started making their own laws. Many were based on the harsh English view that women were the property of men. The notion of equal rights did not apply to women; lawmakers assumed that if men were treated equally, they would in turn take care of the needs of women. As British philosopher and biologist Herbert Spencer put it, "Our laws are based on the...sufficiency of man's rights, and society exists today for women only in so far as she is in the keeping of some man."[2]

During this period, a woman lost her identity at marriage; legal rights, her name, her property, her earnings, and her right to enter into contracts were all forfeited at the altar. These social degradations had a deleterious effect on women and their self-conceptions, causing them to acquiesce to their inferior status. Even after the first women's rights convention in Seneca Falls, New York in 1848, public opinion was against them. One Philadelphia newspaper printed at that time,

> "A woman is nobody. A wife is everything…. The ladies of Philadelphia… are resolved to maintain their rights as Wives, Belles, Virgins, and Mothers, and not as Women."[3]

Smith rejected these ideas and worked for the advancement of women's rights. He had an interesting personal connection to the movement in his cousin, Elizabeth Cady. As a teenager, she had visited him in Peterboro for extended summer stays. She credited her weeks-long visits to Peterboro in the 1830s with instilling in her the significance of individual human rights.

The bright, young Elizabeth enjoyed the philosophical discussions that routinely took place in the Smith household. They talked passionately of abolition, religion, temperance, women's rights, and other issues of the day. She interacted there with people who would mold her mind and inspire her to work for social reform. Her sense of equal rights and justice motivated her lifelong commitment to action.[4]

At Peterboro, runaway slaves told Cady of the horrors of punishment and discrimination. Native Americans related tales of poverty. Reformers who visited Smith helped Cady to understand that social and economic injustices were causes worth fighting for. She saw how these forces played on her as a woman. The arguments she heard, especially from "Cousin Gerrit," were liberal, and they encouraged her to strike out against injustices to women.

Writing to Amelia Bloomer in 1852, Susan B. Anthony, Cady's friend and fellow suffragette, lamented, "Oh! I am sick and tired of the senseless, hopeless work that man points out for woman to do."[5] Yet Anthony knew that one man, Gerrit Smith, was sensitive to this issue, and she sought his help. She wrote him in 1856,

"Mrs. Stanton and I are…in earnest that your voice
shall be heard [at the sixth annual woman's rights
convention] because you take the view of the
oneness of the sexes…. The men are very few, who
identify themselves with us."[6]

Smith believed that men and women were social equals. He wrote,
"It is for… barbarous, not for civilized, to stamp woman with inferiority, and to thrust her away from duties, to which she is as well
adapted by her nature, as man is by his."[7] He saw that "the natural
powers of woman to produce the means of subsistence are as great
as those of man,"[8] and he regarded as dangerous the opinion that
men and women were mentally different from each other. "I regard
this doctrine as very false and very pernicious: and I believe that
the wrongs of women will never be righted until this doctrine that
there is sex in mind is exploded."[9]

The only real differences between men and women, Smith believed, were those related to biological sex. Males and females could
be legitimately separated where matters of procreation were concerned, but in all other respects, "man is woman, and woman is man."
This led to the conclusion that "man and woman are one in their
rights, in their responsibilities, in their duties, dignity and destiny."[10]
Smith made a proper distinction between *sex* on the biological level,
and *gender* on the cultural level. And he believed that one did not
control the other. Whereas 'sex' referred to unalterable biological
functions, 'gender' referred to learned roles, which some believed
to be restricted to one sex or the other. Smith maintained that men
and women should share their culturally stereotyped roles.

To those who regarded women as beautiful and men as strong,
he replied,

"Why would he [God] not have each become
both beautiful and strong? Beauty is as desirable
and attainable an element in male character as in
'female character'; and so is strength as desirable

and attainable an element in 'female character' as
in male character.... And why should he not be as
much concerned to have man modest and delicate
as woman?"[11]

Smith believed in the equality of men and women throughout his
life. In a letter written to Susan B. Anthony in 1873, he recognized
that people considered men stronger and rougher than women, and
that men were not treating women justly. "Such things go somewhat
toward making me ashamed of being a man."[12]

Elizabeth Kelty admiringly recorded in her journal a quote from
Smith:

"Heaven speed the day when...the whole world
shall demand the same mental and moral
character, the same mental and moral strength,
beauty and delicacy for woman as for man, for
man as for woman. There is but one standard of
modesty and delicacy for both men and women;
and so long as different standards are tolerated,
both sexes will be perverse and corrupt."

Writing to Elizabeth Cady Stanton, Smith commented on the
similarity of the sexes relative to potential gender roles. "Believing
man and woman to have the same nature.... I would subject them
to a common standard of morals and manners."[13] To his daughter,
Elizabeth, he wrote, "A man should be able to choose to knit or
sew—and a woman to choose to fell trees or to be a blacksmith."[14]
And when it came to political and legal rights, Smith advocated
equal treatment of the sexes. In the last year of his life, he wrote, "I
would have all men + women...stand equal before the laws."[15]

An important source of Smith's radically progressive views on
women probably was the influence early in his life of the local Native
American Iroquois culture. During Gerrit's youth in Peterboro, his
father, Peter Smith, was on friendly terms with the Oneidas. Gerrit

knew them, talked with them, and knew the value patterns of their matriarchal culture. Later, in his own home, he received the Oneidas and introduced them to Elizabeth Cady.

The social prestige afforded women in the Oneida culture most likely influenced both Smith and Cady. They observed women who were not the legal charges of men, and had rights to property and decision-making that far exceeded those of American women. The Iroquois traced their lineage through the female, and they considered it unthinkable that males should be domineering. Women nominated male chiefs to represent their clan in the Grand Council, and if the males became abusive, the women could remove them from power. Matilda Jocelyn Gage, a suffragist and friend of Smith and Cady who lived with and wrote about the Iroquois culture, noted,

> "The family relation among the Iroquois
> demonstrated woman's superiority in power. When
> an Indian husband brought the products of the
> chase to the wigwam, his control over it ceased.
> In the home, the wife was absolute; the sale of the
> skins was regulated by her, and the price was paid
> to her."[16]

The proximity and influence of this culture primed these central New York social activists for work in the woman's rights movement. As Wagner put it, "They caught a glimpse of the possibility of freedom because they knew women who lived liberated lives, women who had always possessed rights beyond their wildest imagination...."[17]

Elizabeth Cady met abolitionist Henry B. Stanton at Gerrit Smith's house in Peterboro. When she became Elizabeth Cady Stanton on May 1, 1840, she felt ready to commit her life to a cause to which Cousin Gerrit had introduced her. In her old age, she spoke about that time, reflecting on the values that Smith and the Iroquois helped to instill in her.

> "Half a century ago the women of America were
> bond slaves.... They were shut out of the schools
> and colleges, the trades and professions... and
> denied everywhere the necessary opportunities for
> their best development. Worse still, women had
> no proper appreciation of themselves as factors
> in civilization. Believing self-denial a higher
> virtue than self-development, they ignorantly
> made ladders of themselves by which fathers,
> husbands, brothers, and sons reached their highest
> ambitions...."

She concluded this reminiscence with a powerful shot: "The humiliations of spirit are as real as the visible badges of servitude."[18]

Stanton stayed in contact with Gerrit Smith throughout his life, although she became somewhat cool toward what she considered his weak support of activities related to women's rights. Stanton saw her role as that of "stirring up the women generally to <u>rebellion</u>,"[19] whereas Smith, especially following the Civil War, advised women to wait their turn to acquire rights.

Smith blamed the institution of Christianity for "making women guilty of the first sin," and for having "gone far to justify man in stamping her with inferiority and in playing the tyrant over her."[20] Just as he was disillusioned with the neutral positions most churches took regarding slavery, so also was he disillusioned with their positions on women's rights. Yet it was the women themselves, especially Smith's friends Matilda Jocelyn Gage and Stanton, who best stated the feelings of women about this issue.

Both saw the power of institutional discrimination by the church. Women, Gage said, "must be aware of the historical fact that the prevailing religious idea in regard to women has been the base of all their restrictions and degradation. It underlies the political, legal, educational, industrial, and social disabilities of whatever character and nature." She saw the church as "the enemy of liberty and progress and the chief means of enslaving woman's conscience and reason...."[21]

Stanton agreed:

> "I now see more clearly than ever, that the arch enemy to woman's freedom sulks behind the altar.... To rouse woman to a sense of her degradation under the canon law and church discipline is the work that interests me most..."[22]

Church law, she said, made marriage "a condition of bondage, maternity a period of suffering and anguish, and in silence and subjection she was to play the role of a dependent on man's bounty for all her material wants...."[23]

Gerrit Smith also saw these forces at work in the degradation of women, and, at least in the latter part of his life, he perceived the solution to be the empowerment of women through the vote. In his early reform work, Smith had advocated allowing women equal rights with men in expression and decision making in antislavery meetings,[24] but he hesitated in supporting women's suffrage until after black males had achieved it. Abolition, to Smith, was a much more demanding issue than was women's rights.

By the 1870s, though, he was supporting women's suffrage. He subscribed to *The Woman's Journal* and donated funds to women's suffrage associations.[25] Writing to Susan B. Anthony in February of 1873, he acknowledged that women have an "equal right with man's to participate in choosing the guardians of the rights of person and property...." Smith even lamented his fate that he was male and, therefore, was identified with those who take "barbaric pride in their stronger and rougher sex...."[26] Later in 1873, he wrote Anthony again with his belief that the nation "is guilty of the folly and the sin of clothing man with all political power and reducing woman to a political cipher."[27]

There was still in Smith, however, some insensitivity to the depth to which women felt degraded. When Susan B. Anthony was arrested for voting in 1872, Smith sent to her $100 to pay her fine. Anthony took this as a slight to the women's movement that she should just pay the fine and be done with it. She curtly wrote back,

> "I surely shall not recognize the right of government to prosecute me by paying the fine. To the contrary, I shall sacredly appropriate my every dollar and every word to the education of the people to ignore all such government assumption over the rights of women."[28]

Even though Smith did hold back on his approval of women's suffrage, women still appealed to his liberal image for support of their causes. As a major administrator of the affairs of the women's rights movement, one of Susan B. Anthony's constant concerns was money. She appealed to Smith to be generous, and to encourage others of means to donate to their cause. She even tweaked his vanity with her requests. "You will hear…my appeals to you, Mr. Smith, I know—for your love for the principle of equal rights to all is never failing."[29]

Women's rights leaders frequently requested that Smith participate in their conventions. Lucy Stone enlisted Samuel J. May's help in getting Smith to attend an 1852 convention: "You know that we want to make it tell gloriously for the cause of human freedom—and to this end we want the best helpers on that occasion. We want Gerrit Smith."[30] In 1856 Stone, Antoinette Brown, and Elizabeth Cady Stanton "expressed a strong wish… that you should be present by pen or tongue in all our conventions. In future history we wish you identified with this movement…."[31] In 1865, Smith received an Equal Rights Convention call signed by Lucretia Coffin Mott and Susan B. Anthony with a letter of encouragement to attend from Elizabeth Cady Stanton. The call announced their intention "to secure the right of suffrage to all citizens, without distinction of race or sex."[32]

Matilda Gage sought Smith's help by requesting from him a list of former Liberty Party members who supported women's suffrage and might attend a New York State convention at Saratoga in July of 1869 "for the purpose of effecting an organization of the state."[33]

Lucy Stone invited Smith to attend the American Woman Suffrage Association convention in Cleveland, Ohio in 1869, and in New York City the following year.[34] Julia Ward Howe and Stone wrote, asking him to attend a St. Louis women's convention in 1872,[35] and there were many other similar invitations. If he chose not to attend a convention, he would usually send a letter of support for their cause.

As new reform organizations established themselves, they sought Smith's endorsement to add prestige to their movements.[36] It is curious why so many prominent women sought Smith's endorsement, when for decades he had not fully supported their demand for the vote. In fact, as late as 1868, Smith refused to sign a petition that proposed, relative to suffrage, that there be no differences between men and women. He felt that the national mood at the time was too conservative to allow women to vote, but it was ready to enfranchise the black male.

Smith wrote to Susan B. Anthony, "The removal of the political disabilities of race is my first desire, of sex, my second."[37] To another he wrote, "Very desirous am I that justice be done to woman.... But my first duty is to my colored brothers and sisters."[38] His stand favoring the enfranchisement of black males went back over twenty years before the letter he wrote to Anthony. In 1846, when the newly developed New York State Constitution did not allow for black suffrage, Smith was enraged. In a printed circular, he sent his reprimand "To the Voters of the State of New York." This message applied to black males, and not to women:

> "To be guilty, under a representative...
> Government, of shutting out a part of the people
> from a representation in the Government, is to be
> guilty of a partiality for which there is, certainly,
> no excuse.... It is, simply, a triumph of the strong
> over the weak.... The denial of the right [to vote]

degrades them, both in their own esteem and in the esteem of others...."[39]

Ironically, such strong language did not acknowledge the importance of empowering women; it did not even place them among the "part of the people" Smith felt was being so mistreated.

Later, in 1854, Smith voiced his opposition to the Nebraska Bill because "it insults colored men...by limiting suffrage to white men.... To shut them out from governing their territories, would be to deny and dishonor the doctrine of 'popular sovereignty'...."[40] Elizabeth Cady Stanton saw the contradiction between Smith's comments about black men and his stand on women's suffrage. She accused him of trivializing the interests of women, reminding him, "The cause of woman is, as you admit...a question...of human rights." She claimed that those who advocated one issue at a time were missing the point of universal suffrage.

In 1868 she wrote, "...it is infinitely more important at this hour to secure the rights of 15,000,000 women, black and white... than to bring 2,000,000 more men to the polls."[41]

Smith claimed that the reforms demanded by women were too extensive, and that their reform movement was not sufficiently sophisticated to succeed. Stanton was insulted. She retorted, "The mass of women are developed at least to the point of discontent, [and] the steps between discontent and action are few and short indeed." She reminded Smith of his claim that women and men were equal, and asked him to imagine himself as a woman. Would he consent to "silent indignation?"[42]

This question is telling, because if Smith could, as he claimed, imagine himself as a black man, why could he not also imagine himself as a woman? Was it because he did *not* perceive all people to be equal? Was it because his prejudices against women prevented such a self-conception? He voiced his own indignation toward Stanton and her view that women in bad marriages should escape their "dreadful duress" in a poem written to her in which he called her a "match breaker."

"For this dangerous woman does e'en confess
That she more joyful + thankful feels
When wives escape from their dreadful duress
Than when the poor slaves take safe to their heels."[43]

If Smith did harbor biases against women, what were they, and how did he express them? Most people considered males to be dominant in the American culture of the mid-19th century, and in spite of his comments about the equality of the sexes, Smith was not immune from this perception. Elizabeth Cady Stanton pointed out tersely that he had addressed his correspondence to her as "E.C. Stanton," failing to recognize her maiden name. "E.C. is no name. Suppose I should write to you... G.S. Fitzhugh. You see my dear cousin you have not taken in the whole idea."[44]

Ann, whom he often called "Mrs. Smith," or "my wife," complained frequently in letters to him of his attitude of masculine superiority and his tendency to be critical of her thoughts and actions.[45] Her son Greene was not immune to a superior attitude toward women, attempting to console his mother when she was sick by cheering her on to "be a man":

"Dear Mother, my father has told you the news
So I will not try my talents to use.
But hurry, get well, as fast as you can,
Dance polkas, buy houses, once more be a man."[46]

A clear indication of Smith's attitude of prejudice toward women emerged in a poem written to his friend, Alida Littlejohn, in 1865. He had a model in mind to which he wished women would adhere, disregarding their individuality, as if there were a "Standard Woman."

"The Standard Woman
To be a woman, noble, good,
Is what indeed each woman would:

To be 'The Standard Woman!' Oh!
Who's so ambitious that you know?
I know but one, Alida she
Who dares 'The Standard Woman' be
We hear her say 'by me' 'by me'
'Shall every woman measured be'!"

Littlejohn answered him derisively as follows:
"In those we love best we are often deceived
And even last night I could scarce have believed
That friend Gerrit who talks of 'Woman's right'
Could slander woman before it was light….
So wearily he tossed on his sleepless bed
Till slanderous rhymes came into his head
Then calmly he slept till morning light
Then rose and girded himself for the fight
No more will I wrestle for woman's right
But down with her! Down! With all man's might!
Now all who may these simple lines see
I ask can Gerrit an honest man be
No! Hard and dishonest I'll proclaim him now
And forever and ever I will keep this vow!"[47]

Clearly, she was not happy with his stereotyping. Men—including Gerrit—subscribed to the notion that the moral standards for women ought to be higher than the standards set for men. It followed that because men's standards were lower, they should be less accountable for their sins than were women. Smith also had the impression that women could not carry out successful reform work. He penned one poem to the Boston Female Anti-Slavery Society in which he seems to equate their interests in charitable donations to those of children who might use the money for refreshment:
"My dear Mrs. Chapman bids me send
A few lines for the 'Fair.'

I have ten dollars I wish to spend,
Suppose I spend it there!

So take the money I here convey   .
And spend it for a cake,
Or for a drink, if my lady may
A drink prefer to take."[48]

At one point, Smith declared to Elizabeth Cady Stanton that the women's movement "is not in the proper hands...." He believed that the social realities of the age made it impossible for women to succeed in acquiring equal rights when men had not been successful at attaining their goals of temperance and abolition.[49]

For her part, Stanton wondered why it was worthwhile for men to pursue their obsession with reform, but not worthwhile for women. In a speech, she lashed out at men who lacked confidence in women's abilities:

"Woman herself must do this work—for woman
alone can understand the height, and the depth, and
the length and the breadth of her own degradation
and woe. Man cannot speak for us—because he has
been educated to believe that we differ from him
so materially that he cannot judge of our thoughts,
feelings, and opinions on his own."[50]

Those who were not slaves or women, she said years later, "can never conceive the feelings of those who are born to contempt, to inferiority, to degradation."[51]

Smith felt that it was a bad time just after the Civil War for women to seek the right to vote. As his friend Wendell Phillips put it, "This is the negro's hour." Stanton shot back at him, "Do you believe the African race is composed entirely of males?"[52]

Smith eventually supported immediate women's suffrage in accordance with what he had said before the war:

"Many and mighty are the influences needed
to redeem great popular Elections from the
coarseness and corruption which characterizes
them. Preëminent among these influences is the
presence and part of woman. The conduct and
character of men as voters will become far better
after the advancing stages of civilization shall have
brought up woman to vote by their side."[53]

The leaders of the woman's rights movement were bothered by
Smith's post-war identification with the Republican Party. They saw
Lincoln's position on women's rights as weak, Johnson's as hostile,
and Grant's as apathetic; so Stanton admonished her cousin: "I
shall… make an occasional missionary visit [to Peterboro] in the
hope of lifting you safe one step beyond the Republican Party."[54]

Smith had also decided not to give women land as a part of his
effort to help poor people. He claimed that he had given all of his
good land to men, and that what was left was not worth much, so
he gave the five hundred females chosen by his agents $50 each,
hoping that they would "expend it in the purchase of…land."[55] One
can see hints of Smith's latent sexism in the way he spoke about the
proper role of government. Ignoring any notion of female authority,
he said, "The people choose their ruler not only…for the purpose
of having him protect them. Their leading object, in choosing him,
is to have him direct… their affairs…."[56]

When it came to Christianity, his references to God made it clear
that he had not come into the notion that power could be feminine.
God, he said, 'is our Friend and Father; …He is never angry with
even the worst of us…. He curses none, and blesses all who will
let Him bless them." At least he also considered the power of the
Devil to be masculine. "Is the Devil one of the facts on which the
true religion rests? He is not. He is a mere myth."[57] Even late in his
life, Smith did not seem to realize the power game being played by
referring to God as "Father" or as "He."[58]

Perhaps the most blatant of Smith's positions of gender bias was that related to marriage. He said, "In no case should there be divorce." He believed divorce to be a breach of contract, yet he placed much of the burden of maintaining the marriage on the wife.

> "My crime may be such as to make it incompatible with her self-respect...to continue to live with me. But she is never to cease from her efforts for my reformation, and she is never to put herself in such circumstances as would disable her from receiving me, should I return to her in penitence...."[59]

He did not speak of the man's duties or responsibilities to the woman, and Elizabeth Cady Stanton chided him for such an opinion. "Tyranny on a southern plantation is far more easily seen by white men... than the wrongs [to] women in their own households...."[60]

Boston abolitionist Lydia Maria Child also tried to counsel Smith.

> "I do not agree with all you say on the indissolubility of marriage.... I see so much matrimonial unhappiness 'round me...that I cannot but think it would be well for all parties to have the right to separate.... [Marriages] are formed in the early, unreflecting, and inexperienced period of life," and can, therefore, be flawed.[61]

Although Smith's prejudice against women was typical of his time, one discriminatory aspect of American culture that he fought against was the restrictive style of women's clothing. Dress in the mid-1800s included corsets, wide hoops, petticoats, and long dresses which, according to Gerrit Smith, inhibited women's progress toward equal rights. Smith saw the clothing as a symbol of the oppression women faced, and their wearing of it as evidence of acquiescence in that oppression.

The wearing of such clothing, he said, was a self-imposed handicap equivalent to cutting off one hand. Long dresses, he said, left women with "less than half their personal power of self-subsistence and use-fulness.... [It is] voluntary imprisonment and...self-degradation.... Wearing a dress... both marks and makes their impotence...." He compared the wearing of a long, hooped dress with foot-binding for Chinese women,[62] and he favored dress reform as a route toward greater female independence. Women, he felt, dressed in order to please men rather than for practicality, simply because they were dependent on males for financial support and social status. While traveling with his daughter by train, Smith remarked in a letter to his wife, "Dear Lizzie! It is pretty hard for her with her harness, to get in + out of the Cars."[63]

Susan B. Anthony also noted that the physical restrictiveness of bulky dresses made women unable to compete with men for equal status. She wrote to Smith about "the terrible bondage of these long skirts...."[64]

Enter Gerrit Smith's daughter, Elizabeth Smith Miller, and the innovation that made Peterboro a small but important footnote of fashion history: the invention of 'bloomers'. When Elizabeth appeared at a public event in Hagerstown, Maryland in 1854 "attired in a full Bloomer costume, [she] attracted some attention." The editors of *The National Era* went on to say,

> "The eccentricity of enlarged benevolence, extensive information, fine abilities, and a life of unsullied purity, is a universally-admitted attribute of Gerrit Smith; and we presume a daughter eminently worthy of such a parent, however arrayed, could not fail , in Hagerstown or elsewhere, to attract some attention."[65]

Elizabeth Smith Miller moved dress reform along with her invention of "bloomers," but her father thought that even bloomers were too restrictive. "Whilst the 'Bloomer dress' is...better than the common dress, it…affords not half the freedom [to] which woman is entitled…."[66]

Smith was upset with the women's rights movement for not pushing harder for dress reform, and he withheld contributions of money to the cause.[67] Even women inside the movement, he claimed, were not committed to change; had they been, they would not "hamper [their] person with an absurd dress, and… trick it off with jewelry and gewgaws…."

This opinion he followed with his own accusatory bias:

> "The great change which is indispensable in order
> to get and enjoy what they demand, is a change
> in themselves…. They are [so] content in their
> helplessness…and destitution of rights…as to
> believe that all this belongs to their natural and
> unavoidable lot."[68]

Obviously, Smith was insensitive to the inner feelings of women. He saw their dress as a symbol of oppression, and he naively thought that different clothing styles would alter societal discrimination against women. He lacked confidence in the ability of women to sustain the intellectual level of the women's rights issue. Elizabeth Cady Stanton, as was her habit, scolded Smith, claiming that dress styles had little to do with human rights.

> "We have no reason to hope that [pants] would do
> more for us than they have done for man himself. The
> Negro slave enjoys the most unlimited freedom in his
> attire…yet in spite of his dress…he is still a slave."[69]

Francis D. Gage criticized Smith in a published letter to *Frederick Douglass' Paper*. She had read Smith's long letter of December 1, 1855, to Elizabeth Cady Stanton, and she made the following remarks about the cause of discrimination against women:

> "[Regarding] our present mode of dress,…bad as
> it is, and cumbersome, and annoying, I still feel

that we can wear it, and yet be lovers of liberty,
speaking out our deep feeling, portraying our
accumulated wrongs, saving ourselves…from
that antagonism which we must inevitably meet
when we don the semi-male attire. We must own
ourselves, under the law, first, own our bodies,
our earnings, our genius and our consciences;
then we will turn to the lesser matter of what shall
be the garniture of the body…. Was Christ less
a Christian in his vesture… than he would have
been in the suit of a Broadway Dandy?"[70]

Even Smith knew of the public criticism women faced when they
wore the bloomers. As Ann told him, "Poor Lissies [bloomer] dress un-
dergoes all sorts of criticisms. Even those who approve suggest various
improvements. Those who disapprove look solemn and pained."[71]

Elizabeth Cady Stanton stated the issue succinctly at the 1890
founding convention of the National American Woman Suffrage
Association:

"Men tell us we must be patient and…womanly….
What is a man's idea of womanly? It is to have
a manner that pleases him, quiet, deferential,
submissive…. He wants no self-assertion on our
part, no defiance, no vehement arraigning of him
as a robber and a criminal."[72]

Eventually, many of the women who had championed the
bloomer style went back to long dresses as a way of avoiding societal
disapproval. Some even believed that the change to bloomers ham-
pered their movement for equal rights. Susan B. Anthony reverted
to long dresses reluctantly, saying that she doubted her own courage to implement reform. "I own that the want of moral courage,
caused me to return to [long skirts]—and I can but doubt my own
strength…."[73]

After the Civil War, Gerrit Smith lost interest in dress reform, perhaps reflecting some of his pessimism about the women's rights movement in general. Stanton recognized his pessimism as resulting from the fact that he was only a man, but appreciated his mostly feeble efforts to help. In a poem to Smith, she wrote:

"Ah! Noble cousin, you'll ne'er scorn
The griefs that make me rave—
The crown of <u>Manhood</u> you have worn
But I, was born <u>a slave</u>.

To you the world gives rank + fame
Its welcomes + its cheers—
Throws wide its gates, + all you claim
You take—+ meet no sneers.

But I, alas, my right must <u>prove</u>
To all I dare + do—
The rough paths for myself make smooth
Though <u>help</u> I've had from you."[74]

Perhaps Gerrit was justified in his pessimism about the potential success of the women's rights movement in his day, but given the effort he threw into abolition, it was unfortunate that he did not believe that women deserved the same quality of effort after the war.

The push for suffrage went on for another half-century after Smith's death. In their waning years, his friends Susan B. Anthony, Elizabeth Smith Miller, Ella Wright Garrison, and Harriet Tubman met in late December of 1902 at the home of Eliza Wright Osborne in Auburn, New York to discuss strategies for pursuing the women's movement. In 1911, shortly before their deaths, Elizabeth Smith Miller asked Harriet Tubman during an interview designed to convince Tubman to join the Geneva Club, which advocated women's suffrage, "Do you really believe that women should vote?" Tubman replied, "I suffered enough to believe it."[75]

Gerrit Smith understood the suffering faced by women, but he could not get past the notion that changing their clothes would earn them equal rights. He prided himself with being able to think like a slave, a poor person, or a child. But he had obvious difficulty in thinking like a woman—even though he shared common interests with them on important issues.

One of those issues was the abolition of slavery, and it is primarily as an abolitionist that Gerrit Smith is remembered.

- 15 -

Abolitionists

On the cold, rainy night of October 21, 1835, over 100 men rode in an open packet boat on the Erie Canal from Utica to Canastota and then walked ten miles uphill to Peterboro. They endured this arduous journey at the invitation of Gerrit Smith to gather in the Peterboro Presbyterian Church for the inaugural meeting of the New York State Anti-Slavery Society.

The abolition of slavery was probably the most important reform movement in United States history. Both southerners *and* northerners perceived it as dangerous: it challenged the status quo racially, morally, politically, and socially. The benefits of slavery were institutionally ingrained to the point that nearly everyone felt threatened by abolition.

As a movement for change, abolition combined three major intellectual trends: Rationalism, which emphasized order, practicality, and individualism; Evangelism, which encouraged optimism and the denial of the concept of preordained fate; and Revolution, which enabled people to express their ideals and emotions in political realities.[1]

Integrating these three themes, abolitionists saw their work as a compact between God and man that had originated with the American Revolution. As George W. Putnam, an abolitionist, one-time Peterboro resident, and friend of Gerrit Smith, said poetically:

"When the Briton's hand was on us,
When earth trembled at his tread,

Did our fathers crouch to wear the chain?
Go, ask the martyr'd dead!
The blood-stained plains of Lexington
Can tell the tale;—neath Bunker's sod
They sleep, whose war-cry once was, 'On!
For Freedom and for God!'
And has their proud blood in our veins
Grown still and cold?
Say, shall we stoop to wear the chains
They spurned of old?"

The difference between the political revolutionaries of the 1770s and the social revolutionaries of the 1830s was that the former fought for their *own* liberty with military weapons, whereas the abolitionists fought for the liberty of others with moral weapons. They were a handful of determined men and women who molded national opinion against the sinfulness and brutality of slavery. They dedicated their well-being, their fortunes, and in some cases, their lives to the freedom of people whom they did not even know.

It was an exquisite issue for reformers. Tailored to their need to stir up emotions, slavery slapped the faces of democratic principle and Christian virtue. Its injustice touched several levels: moral, economic, practical, social, philosophical, political, and personal. With the exception of woman's suffrage, no other social movement has focused singly on the way one easily recognizable group of people treated another.

As a symbol of the struggle against oppression, abolition was a noble effort. The concerns of abolitionists defined the intellectual transition from the conservative attachment to the privileges of class, caste, race, and sex to the more liberal and equity-based goals of the post-Civil War era and beyond. Their work highlighted with distinct emphasis and clarity the notion that some people would no longer be accepted as being "more equal" than others. They articulated new social goals through both their words and their deeds, and they often dedicated their lives as examples of a new moral sensibility.

The abolition movement occurred at a time when traditional social structures were changing. The advent of independence in social and political thought was overturning an old and well-established order. New, revivalist sects were challenging traditional religious authority. Territorial expansion to the American frontier following the War of 1812 had encouraged rugged individualism. The political aristocracy of the Federalists' governing class was giving way to new political initiatives. Capitalistic entrepreneurs were challenging the traditional wealth and power of heredity, and self-reliance was supplanting the importance of community.

In such a context, slavery became evil personified—an offense against humanity that was seen as a social crime. Yet even with social structures quaking under the strain of change, the institution of slavery remained intact. Abolitionists, then, as budding transcendentalists, stepped in as the opposition to political and religious institutions that supported slavery—and took on the fight as a personal moral obligation. They stood on moral principles that they would not compromise, even in the face of physical and social abuse. With unswerving confidence in their absolute rightness and a relentless faith in the power of ideas to win over the selfishness of profit, they strove toward the transformation of the fundamental political, religious, and economic institutions of a whole society. In the end, they would succeed in purging a social evil that contaminated the lives of every United States citizen. They helped to end the greatest crime against humanity—the sin of all sins, as they called it—by dedicating their lives to the cause.

To sustain themselves in the tough fight against the culture of slavery, they developed within their clique a form of group therapy. In their meetings, newspapers, and letters to one another, they perceived themselves as prescient leaders of a reform community that was guiding a nation toward more pure ways of thinking and acting. Through these media they sustained a sense of optimism and purpose, and in homes such as Gerrit Smith's, they gathered for visits that became more than merely planning sessions for the movement. They used these sessions to recharge their commitment, reaffirm their stance, dress their wounds, and renew their reformers' will to face the hostile world.

Although Gerrit Smith frequently noted his reluctance to be an historic figure, he knew he was playing a role in a drama that would forge a nation. The framers of the Constitution had intentionally postponed the settlement of the issue of slavery, and Smith viewed it as the responsibility of his generation to take on the cause. He posed for the portraits and saved the correspondences because he knew we would be watching. Other abolitionists—white, black, male, and female—consecrated their lives to the pursuit of justice for all. If we of the modern age could ever recover the emotions that surged through their hearts, we could change the world again. For these abolitionists, the fire did not just burn; it *raged* in a storm of indignation. Their names will echo forever among the mountains of the American landscape:

> Frederick Douglass
> Harriet Tubman
> William Lloyd Garrison
> Elizabeth Cady Stanton
> John Greenleaf Whittier
> Sojourner Truth
> Charles Sumner
> Angelina Grimké
> Theodore Weld
> Charles Grandison Finney
> James G. Birney
> Beriah Green
> Susan B. Anthony
> Henry Highland Garnet
> Jermain Loguen
> John Brown

Although this list is not exhaustive, there is something significant about it: at one time or another, *all* of these persons, whose names have inspired students of American history from elementary school through old age, visited Gerrit Smith at Peterboro. They sought him out for his liberal views, his dedication to the cause, his oratory, and his money.

Smith's Peterboro estate was a sanctuary for abolitionists—a retreat where society's abused victims could seek in-group support. Frederick Douglass claimed that the mentorship of Smith was important in his own orientation toward abolition. He noted that Smith "has educated a [Jermain Wesley] Loguen, a [Samuel Ringgold] Ward, a [Henry Highland] Garnet; he has supported the papers established by them, and for them, and has shown that he has a heart for practical benevolence...."[2]

Peterboro was a hotbed of abolitionist sentiment in the 1840s. Said one resident in 1842, "We are to have a great State [abolition] convention on the 19th and 20th of this month at Peterboro and all the vicinity are put in requisition for their hospitality. We have agreed to lodge a Team and 2 people."[3] Abolition was the topic of sermons, meetings, writings, conventions, and visiting dignitaries. This was unusual even at that time, for most northerners were indifferent to the cause of abolition, and either despised or, at least, opposed abolitionists.

Powerful professionals and merchants openly discriminated against northern blacks. They feared the compromise of their social positions by an invasion of free blacks.[4] Although the nation claimed to provide liberty and justice for all, many politicians, clergymen, businessmen, and Christians generally did not see it that way.

Smith believed that the journalists of the North gave the abolitionists a bad rap. In a letter of over four thousand words to slaveholder John H. Cocke of Virginia, Smith said,

> "Our political + religious papers have felt it to be
> their interest to misrepresent us to you; + for the
> most part, they have consented to sacrifice truth
> and humanity to their interest.... But if you would
> know, who, at the North, love God, and the slave,

<u>and</u> <u>the slaveholders</u> <u>too</u>, it is the abolitionists preeminently."[5]

Cocke was a slaveholder who was troubled by slavery and searched for advice regarding God's intentions. He tried to treat his slaves well and considered his plantation to be a self-management experience for slaves and a training ground for their freedom.[6] He eventually freed his slaves on the condition that they emigrate to Liberia.[7]

Abolitionists were plagued by media-driven public notions that they were irrational fanatics. To them, the double standard was clear: To risk one's life and honor for the cause of liberty made Washington and Jefferson respected leaders, but it made a slave or an abolitionist a fanatic. As abolitionist Wendell Phillips remarked, it had become "hard to tell who's mad."[8]

Although many abolitionists stated their willingness to die for the cause,[9] Gerrit Smith provided for them a more practical list of duties:

Pray for the welfare of the slaveholder and the slave.

Refuse to attend proslavery churches.

Refuse to support proslavery ministers.

Refuse to vote for proslavery political candidates.

Refuse to support proslavery organizations.

Refuse to consume the products of slave labor.

Disconnect from proslavery denominations and political parties.[10]

Smith lived by these duties to the point of obsession, and, as with any obsession, it may have caused temporary imbalance. As the years passed, his indignation over the lack of progress toward the abolition of slavery was more than mere disappointment; it was rooted in utopian social ideology, which justified the moral principles by which he was obsessed. He once likened slavery to a wolf devouring sheep, and asked, would the farmer compromise with the wolf, or kill it?[11]

Others noted Smith's anti-slavery obsession. His daughter remembered it in a poem:

> "I often think of words he spoke,
> Which in our youthful bosoms woke
> A fadeless love of Liberty—
> A deathless hate of Slavery."[12]

Henry Highland Garnet, a radical black abolitionist who lived with Smith for a short time in 1848 and 1849 while he worked nearby, quipped, "There are yet two places where slaveholders cannot come—Heaven and Peterboro."[13]

Gerrit Smith based his opposition to slavery on the principle that no person could be the property of another person. He harbored no doubts about the rightness of his goals. He appealed to humanity on its own foundational grounds of humaneness and preached to the public that the time was right for the abolition of slavery. In an 1851 letter, he conjured the founding fathers to make his point:

> "[Slavery] at the hearth of Franklin! No! No!!
> No!!!— Slavery in such a country! Can there
> be any incongruity more monstrous?… Liberty
> bearing a chain! Blasphemy echoing from the altar!
> The collar of the negro chained to the pedestal of
> Washington…. It is impossible…. The light of the
> Nineteenth Century is alone enough to destroy it."[14]

In an 1861 speech in Peterboro, his resolve was the same:

> "The dark thing can not live in the strong
> light of this age. The foolish thing is shamed
> by the wisdom of this age. The wicked thing is
> condemned by the better ethics which are coming
> to prevail in this age…. The organizing of a nation
> at such a time as this on the basis of slavery is an
> unendurable defiance of the moral sense of the
> civilized world."[15]

Confident that they eventually would win, the crusading abolitionists marched on. If they felt any guilt, it was legal, not moral. Moral guilt would be manifest only if they did *nothing* to end slavery, and they assured the world that they had the right advice for it. According to Smith,

> "The counsels of the abolitionists...can alone...see our appallingly imperiled nation. Every step taken by her in accordance with these counsels is a step [toward] her salvation; and her every step to the contrary is [toward] her destruction."[16]

Smith's colleagues saw him as a wise man, and they often sought his counsel. "I wish you lived here," said Lewis Tappan in New York City. "We have so many important subjects of consideration that we need your advice."[17]

Because slavery offended their moral sense of justice, many abolitionists focused on the immorality of the slaveholder, a tactic that tended to force the opposition into a defensive position. Southerners argued the genetic inferiority of blacks, the necessity of slave labor to the Southern economy, and the advantages of civilizing a barbarous people. These arguments revealed the fact that, to southerners, slavery really dealt with the intoxicating effect of *power*. And while their arguments allowed southerners to deny the moral implications of the issue, they fueled the moral passions of northern abolitionists. Imagine the indignation boiling inside Gerrit Smith when he read a colleague's remarks about the attitude of a slave owner concerning the sale of a slave woman: "With the feelings of the poor woman when parting with her family and friends he appeared no more affected than [was] his horse."[18]

When up for sale, a slave was referred to as a commodity, being worth "about $4 or $5 per pound."[19] Even at this early point, the sabres of the North and the South were rattling. How could it be that brothers were so angry at each other? What history led the two major sections of the supposedly 'United' States to a standoff?

The political history of the world includes chapters about empires, monarchies, dynasties, and despotisms. Individual freedom has been rare. The recalcitrant American colonists defied centuries of tradition and the most powerful military force on earth to declare independence and the primacy of democracy. In the face of treason and death, they revolted and forged a government built on individual sovereignty—a notion nearly unheard of before.

There seems to be no more powerful force in world history than the spirit of democracy. It felled the monarchies of the 19th century, and the tyrannies of the 20th, by offering the masses popular consultation, popular sovereignty, and majority rule with minority rights.

The horrible irony is that it took so long and so much blood for the American people, who in current times champion and illustrate democracy, to implement it at home. By resorting to war to emancipate slaves, they countered the histories of France, Spain, England, Portugal, Cuba, and other nations that achieved emancipation via compromise. Americans faced a different institutional reality than did the citizens of these other countries—with business, government, and religion supporting slave owners.

The American Revolution left a legacy of freedom for a budding democracy to build upon, but it left intact one glaring exception: slavery. While institutions based on private property, government protection and individual rights blossomed, slavery continued unrestrained; America tolerated it like the family's closeted secret. Although democracy was the foundation of the new nation, there appeared to be no clear mandate concerning what to do about slavery.

Amid this ambiguity, some states made their own moves. The habitual rebels of Rhode Island were the first to move toward freedom for blacks by granting it to any child born to a black woman starting in 1775.[20] State constitutions made slavery illegal in Vermont in 1777 and in New Hampshire in 1779, and a Massachusetts State Supreme Court decision declared it unconstitutional in 1783.

Connecticut proposed a gradual emancipation plan in 1784, and nearly as its final act, the Confederation Congress passed in July of 1787 the Northwest Ordinance, forbidding slavery north of the Ohio River and east of the Mississippi River.

In 1785, the New York [State] Manumission Society was established to rally support for an emancipation bill proposed by Alexander Hamilton and introduced into the New York State Legislature by Aaron Burr. It failed by a vote of 33 to 13.[21] Because of its large population of slaves in 1790, New York State hesitated to address the abolition issue, proposing only gradual abolition starting in 1799.[22]

The significance of the Northwest Ordinance loomed large: as a compromise measure, it absolved the framers of the Constitution of the United States from having to deal with the slavery issue. Although it left slavery intact, it was probably a fortunate move at the time; had it been resolved either in favor of or against abolition, the Constitution would likely not have been ratified. Southern states entered the union under the Constitutional agreement that the government of the United States could do nothing about slavery for a period of 20 years. But while this temporarily settled the issue *legally*, it did not settle it *morally*.

During the first session of the new Congress, Quaker delegations from Pennsylvania and New York presented petitions to the House of Representatives that called for the federal government to end the slave trade immediately. This move enraged the South, and southern Congressional representatives opposed the petitions and assailed the Quakers for having sat out the Revolutionary War.[23] In the Congressional debate on March 16 and 17, 1790, the Quakers were vilified as utopian dreamers trying to heal the wounds of a struggling new nation with the salve of their own eccentric morality.

Slavery was an integral part of Southern life, but the North was challenging the understanding that the new national government could do nothing to prevent it. The result was a divided nation, as both sides squared off against one another. The Northern "1776ers" saw a revolutionary mandate to abolish slavery, and the Southern "1787ers" saw a compromise agreement that had permitted it. Before this 1790 Congressional debate, slavery was an economic issue. After that time, it became a racial issue. Arguments of inferiority and superiority fueled the fire, and threats of freedom, intermixing, and equality surfaced as racist fears.

It was into this cauldron of racial sentiments that Gerrit Smith was born. A previous generation of far-sighted visionaries had shrewdly left the issue of slavery for future generations to solve; some people born at the close of the 18th century became the visionaries of the 19th century, spurred on to greatness by a lingering human-rights issue. Hoping for a better future they knew they might never see, they committed their energy, their resources, and their lives to accomplishing the goal of freedom for people who would never even know them. These were the abolitionists.

Although their strategies and tactics differed, their moral stance did not. Seething with indignation over the legal denial of freedom to a segment of the population of a republic, they lashed out both at institutions and individuals, demanding justice and equity. They extended George Washington's 1796 farewell message, in which he had challenged the nation to develop unity in spite of sectional differences, into a half-century-long crusade for "liberty and justice for all."

The irony in the work of the abolitionists was that they knew that in order to complete the promise of the American Revolution, slavery would have to be abolished; yet they perceived that the pursuit of that goal would, in all likelihood, seriously divide the nation. Their early optimism—that they could persuade people of the value of abolition—faded into apprehensions of violence. Even during the Constitutional debate, some framers feared violence if the slavery question was not settled.[24] By the early 1830s, slave revolts in the South were proving them correct.

Many abolitionists, including Smith, had predicted the coming of war. In a speech on the Nebraska Bill in 1854 while in Congress, he said, "We all know enough of freedom and slavery to know that they cannot live together permanently. One must conquer the other."[25] Most abolitionists did not encourage civil war; they instead used the cultural popularity of human rights as their weapon to free slaves.

Gerrit Smith's commitment to the implementation of natural human rights was intense. In 1841 he described his call as "laboring in the cause of impartial and universal liberty,"[26] a perspective that had developed even earlier in his life. Peter Smith, Gerrit's father, had owned slaves, and young Gerrit had worked with them. As Thomas has noted,

> "They were very poor and seemed to be friendless, which at the time excited his pity for them and made an impression upon his mind which only strengthened in the years to come. He was young, but he said it was then and there he first learned to hate slavery, and sympathize with the poor slave."[27]

Gerrit spoke of that early experience in later work. In 1854, he spoke out against a bill that would have limited land grants to white people:

> "Born and bred, as I was, among negroes and Indians as well as whites, and respecting and loving all equally well, this insane prejudice [against them] is well-nigh incomprehensible to me."[28]

Smith based his opinions on human rights on the principle of their universal natural origin. He spoke of a world brotherhood in which "all men are made of one blood.... The human race...is a unit.... Every man is every other man's keeper."[29] He liked to quote the poetry of Robert Burns because it identified with the poor and oppressed, and in a letter to his friend and colleague, black abolitionist Dr. James McCune Smith, he quoted a few lines from a Burns poem:

> "For a'that, and a'that,
> Its comin yet for a'that

That man to man, the world a'oer,
Shall brothers be for a'that."[30]

Common people worldwide, Smith thought, were capable of comprehending the natural condition of universal equity as it was taught by abolitionists. Achievement in formal education was not necessary to help one perceive gross social inequity, he believed. Smith had faith that informed masses could cause social change, so in his speeches and writings, he related some of the first-hand stories about treatment of slaves that had enraged him.

Ezekiel Birdseye, an abolitionist friend who had traveled in the South, described to Smith what he had seen. In Mississippi, some slave owners "followed a slave who had committed some misdemeanor and run away. They caught him, chained him to a tree and burnt him alive."[31] In Tennessee, Birdseye described the whipping of a

> "colored woman... stripped to her waist and whipped with a heavy cow skin... about 200 stripes.... Her back was cut to pieces. The blood ran freely down her person and was on him. Her screams were heard all over the village. Her only crime was having made some severe remarks because of the whipping of her husband a few days before by the same man."

In the same letter, Birdseye described the sale of slaves.
> "There were parents and children bound together by all their ties which could be supposed to exist in that situation, then to be separated forever.... All these poor slaves were in tears. The women embraced their husbands in the anguish of their hearts. The husband in quiet grief sustained his weeping wife. The child frantic with screams clung to the bosom of its mother.... Slavery in its best

PRACTICAL DREAMER

estate is a bitter cup, but who can describe a scene
like this—of unutterable woe."[32]

Smith himself described a slave sale in an open letter "to the
abolitionists of the County of Madison" so that all readers could
feel the brutality in emotional terms.[33] Knowledge of such events
reinforced Smith's commitment to the democratic ideal of equality
before the law, and he freely expressed his indignation at a country
whose government professed that ideal, but did not implement it.
Of the United States, he said, "There is no Government on the face
of the earth so quick as our own, to dread, and to oppose popular
movements in behalf of liberty...."[34]

In a speech about the Mexican Treaty and the Monroe Doctrine,
he said in Congress, "That we are a nation for liberty is among our
wildest conceits.... Liberty...belongs to all—to the high and the low;
the rich and the poor; the black and the white...."[35]

Smith's perception of human rights as natural and inalienable
led him to see slavery as "a war upon nature" that removed legal
protection from the slave, and thereby gave the slave owner absolute
power. No such law, he claimed, should contradict nature. "Law is
for the protection—not for the destruction—of rights," he said in
1854.[36] Smith claimed that the Constitution did not support slavery,
and that, therefore, the nation upheld slavery not because of, but in
defiance of, fundamental law.

Some people, however, believed that the Constitution did support
slavery. Of them, Smith wrote,

"How shameless the hypocrisy of our countrymen!
Whilst glorying in the historical fact that our
fathers were ready to take up arms against laws
imposing petty taxes on tea and paper, they
nevertheless roll up the whites of their eyes in holy
horror at refusals to obey laws, if laws they can
be called, which sink innocent men, women and
children in the hell of slavery."[37]

Slaveholders, of course, were among those who believed that slavery was a legal institution. Gerrit Smith's opinion of the slaveholder was not what one might think; he pitied the slaveholder more than he did the slave. In his eyes, those who owned slaves had been brainwashed by a subculture that legitimized slavery. The slave owners were, themselves, victims of a terrible delusion. When Smith attended the Wisconsin State Anti-Slavery Convention in June of 1857, he defended the slave owner as a virtuous person who had no knowledge of the sin being committed. "We must dismiss our prejudices against the slaveholder.... Unconscious of his wrong explains the possibility of his goodness."[38]

In response to a proslavery book by Rev. James Smylie, Clerk of the Presbytery of Mississippi, Smith wrote a 66-page letter containing many anti-slavery arguments. The letter concluded with, "You have come forth, the unblushing advocate of a system under which... man... is more unfeelingly and cruelly dealt with, than the brute."[39] Yet in this lengthy letter, he did not condemn Smylie as a criminal. He viewed the slaveholder as an abolitionist in disguise, "aggravated... by his own consciousness of the truth of abolition and of the preciousness of personal liberty."

This was so, Smith claimed, because of "the self-application mode of reasoning." That is, slaveholders would never agree to be slaves themselves, and they "never testify so strongly against slavery, as when they tell us, that their slaves are light hearted and happy."[40]

Abolitionists noted one glaring rationalization among the claims of slaveholders. Smith wrote, "The consciences of Southern slaveholders can be pacified by nothing short of the plea, that their slaves, if emancipated, would fare worse than if continued in slavery." Smith defended his opposition to this notion with a sound argument:

"In the free States, we refuse to the colored man
the right of suffrage—the right of a respectable seat
in our churches, our private houses, our cars and
steamboats.... We studiously close upon him the
avenues to respectability... and happiness;—and,

in short, we tax our ingenuity to make him feel,
that he is an outcast from society; and that his
appropriate place is in the deepest debasement....
[Yet], sure I am, that the case is yet to be known,
where a free person of color in one of the free States
sighs for a return to the prison house of slavery."[41]

An interesting feature of Gerrit Smith's abolitionism was his intense identity with blacks, to the extent that he claimed that he was able to conceive of himself as black. He viewed the concept of race as singular instead of dichotomous, yet he knew he was in a very small minority. "Distorted as our minds are by prejudice, and shriveled as are our souls by the spirit of caste, [the] essential equality of the varieties of the human family may not be apparent to us all," he said in a speech in 1854.[42] "Manifestly, the rights of men can no more turn on the color of the skin than on the color of the eye."[43] "That one portion of the human family is essentially inferior to another is… nothing better than a prejudice."[44]

Ethnic rivalries appalled him, and he cited those in Ireland, Spain, and Greece to make his point that such rivalries had a history of impoverishing entire nations. He wished people to "know each other as [people]" rather than as racial or ethnic beings. Even after the war in 1868, he hoped that President Grant's new administration would concentrate on the "recognition of the equal rights of all races of men…."[45]

Black people evidently felt Smith's empathy toward them; they wrote to him often, perhaps more often than to any other white abolitionist.[46] They realized that he saw the discrimination against them and was trying to do something about it. Smith considered blacks to be "the most deeply wronged class of our citizens [who face]…cruel, killing, Heaven-defying prejudice…which…has closed against them the avenues to riches and respectability…."[47]

While he had long advocated peaceful discourse and logical argument as tools of change, Smith became more and more convinced there would be little change without violence. During his famous speech before Congress on the Nebraska Bill in 1854, he said,

> "The American people are, as yet, in no state 'to hear with their ears, and understand with their heart'.... This is a nation of oppressors... of strong and successful oppressors; and, hence, there is but little room to hope that she will listen and repent...."[48]

The responsibility for this prejudice, Smith believed, rested largely with the North. Much of the cause of Northern opposition to abolition rested with business interests that were profiting from trade with southern states. In the mid-1840s, the Whig Party informally divided into "Cotton" and "Conscience" Whigs. The "Conscience" Whigs mildly supported abolition, while textile manufacturers in the North who did not want their commercial connections disrupted by abolition led the "Cotton" Whigs. Transcendentalist philosopher Ralph Waldo Emerson quipped, "Cotton thread holds the Union together."[49]

Businessmen frequently disrupted antislavery meetings and defiled the work of abolitionists, partly because they viewed abolition as a threat to the sanctity of private property which was the source of most of their wealth. Myron Holley, a friend of Smith and a fellow abolitionist, attended an antislavery convention in Utica. He wrote to Smith of "timid men [who] shrink from barely sustaining [abolition]. Men under the highest obligations to obey the laws of God for the prosperity with which he has blessed them, stand aloof... through fear of persecution...."[50]

In a letter to Smith's abolitionist friend Samuel J. May, one businessman put the point clearly: "It is not a matter of principles with us. It is a matter of business necessity. We mean, sir, to put you abolitionists down, by fair means if we can, by foul means if we must."[51] In the same vein, several thousand New York City businessmen attending an October 23, 1850 convention there formed the Union Safety Committee for the purpose of preserving the stability of the

Union—and thereby their future profits—by opposing the work of abolitionists.[52]

Smith was disgusted with the lukewarm stand of Northern opinion-leaders on abolition; in fact, he resigned his seat in Congress in 1854 in part because of that ambivalence. He expressed his feelings in a letter to Frederick Douglass just after his resignation, claiming that it was the "duty" of the North

> "to confess her shame and sorrow, that her political, ecclesiastical, and commercial influence has gone to uphold slavery, and to deceive the… South into the belief, that slavery is right, or, at least, excusable…. Do the people of the North believe, that they would honor and obey slavery, as law, should it ever lay claim to their own necks? If they do not, then they are dishonest, in acknowledging it to be law, when others are its victims."[53]

It had long been Smith's belief that slavery was strong in the South because the North gave it moral credence. Seven years before he joined Congress, he had written that the North should declare "that…humanity + decency give us no right to make civil rulers of baby stealers, and women whippers…."[54]

When Smith's indignation was fired up, his pen seemed to write in blood. In his old age, six months before he died, he wrote,

> "Nay, the laws… by which the free people of color in the Northern States, are vexed, hampered, outraged, crushed, constitute so…wantonly wicked a chiming with the slaveholding policy of the South, and so indispensable a prop of this policy, as to make them not less guilty than her bloodiest slave codes."[55]

He knew that northern bias was selectively prejudicial against blacks, and it countered the good sense of both reason and education.

When an 1847 aid program for Irish people garnered some local support, Smith wrote an open letter "To the People of the County of Madison," chastising them. "For the sufferings and outrages endured by the Irish you are not responsible:— but for those endured by the slaves you are."[56]

Smith held educational institutions in the North responsible for perpetuating attitudes that supported slavery. He termed this a "corrupting" influence. "Slavery is upheld at the South in accordance with education. At the North in the face of education…."[57]

He even wrote of this to President Abraham Lincoln:

> "Slavery has made the whole North servile. I doubt whether even a single abolitionist has entirely recovered from the servility to slavery in which we were all educated."[58]

Even in Waterville, New York, just 10 miles from Peterboro, public meetings gave citizens an opportunity to oppose the actions of abolitionists.[59] Northern opposition to abolition often took the form of threats to the abolitionists themselves. Smith told Douglass of an encounter he had with a proslavery man in Potsdam, New York who said that both he and Douglass should be hanged. "He said that the present deplorable condition of the country was due to just such men as yourself."[60]

Smith was often threatened, and at times, was barely able to escape physical harm. One opponent wrote,

> "You mean contemptible fawning hypocritical apostate. We can see through you as easy as we can through an old sieve. You are marked— and will be attended to wherever you go."[61]

The press sometimes fed the extremists' ire: as antislavery societies organized throughout the North in the 1830s and 40s, the *New York Daily News* referred to their conventions as "a kraal of howling maniacs."[62] Northern opposition to abolition even took the form of unruly mobs. Douglass suffered a broken wrist at the hands of an angry crowd in Indiana,[63] and Garrison was dragged through the streets of Boston by a mob of "aristocrats and businessmen" when he attended a meeting of women abolitionists. The Boston press then attacked those women for instigating the violence.[64]

Smith was also the target of mobs. At an antislavery meeting in Newburg, New York, "some sixty persons...gathered around [the meeting house]. They threw stones...into the house through the glass." This account, written by Ann Smith to her daughter, continued,

> "Your father, of course, was the object of their
> wrath. When he left the house he was pursued
> closely by the most violent, who called out, 'that is
> the man.... Sieze him.' They turned into a private
> yard to escape the mob."[65]

And a few days later, Ann wrote, "Have you heard that the meeting which your father had in New Haven...was broken up by a mob...? They tried to get possession of his person, but through the mercy of God he escaped."[66]

Proslavery mobs also attacked institutions. A mob destroyed the office of James G. Birney's antislavery paper in Cincinnati, Ohio in 1836. Abolitionist editor Elijah Lovejoy was murdered in Alton, Illinois in 1837. The Second Antislavery Convention of American Women in Philadelphia in 1838 was disrupted by a mob that burned the building in which they were meeting.[67]

Even colleges opposed abolition efforts. Smith had a long-standing disagreement with Hamilton College in Clinton, New York over its refusal to allow students to establish an antislavery society on campus. Madison University (later named Colgate) in Hamilton, New York expelled student George Gavin Richie after he published an antislavery article. It also dissolved student antislavery organizations in 1834, 1837, and 1841.[68]

All of this Northern opposition to abolition contributed to a strengthening of slavery in the South. It also fed the development

A Daguerreotype of Gerrit Smith in 1845, when he was
48 years old.   *From the author's collection*

of opposing camps that would eventually lead to violence. Although
the abolitionists tried to settle the issue through persuasion, many
people simply would not be persuaded to see the essential unity in
mankind. Abolitionists had put out a call for the recognition of the
universality of inalienable human rights, protected through policies
based on equality. Opposition to this call gained momentum during
the period between 1830 and 1860.

It must be noted that Gerrit Smith's earliest ideas did not take the
side of abolition. As a young man, he supported the idea that the
solution to the slavery problem was the colonization of America's
blacks in Africa. And although he became an "immediate abolitionist," traces of his support of colonization stayed with him.

From Colonization to Politics

"Slavery," Gerrit Smith said in 1847, "is clearly and utterly un-constitutional."[1] This opinion, which had been uncommon in the early days of abolition, eventually led Smith to political action. Given that he avoided politics whenever possible, it underscores the strength of his conviction that slavery was a breech of human rights, unsupported by U.S. values and laws. However, the political route was yet to come; in his early adulthood, Smith actually supported colonization.

Virginia Congressman Charles Fenton Mercer founded the American Colonization Society on January 1, 1817, to send free blacks to Africa "to spread the lights of civilization and Christianity among the fifty millions who inhabit those dark regions."[2] Mercer viewed colonization as "a drain for pauperism," and he hoped that poor, free blacks would leave the country.[3]

Gerrit Smith would graduate from Hamilton College one year later in 1818, long before the North started demanding immediate abolition. Colonization looked like a solution to slavery, and the idea found support in its early days among many who would later change their minds about it and support immediate abolition: Samuel J. May, Theodore Dwight Weld, Arthur and Lewis Tappan, James G. Birney, and Beriah Green.[4]

Smith joined this group and made donations from 1828 to 1835 amounting to about $10,000.[5] He was committed to abolition early in his career, and he saw colonization as a "great and holy cause."[6]

Smith's early opinions of blacks revealed a latent racism. In 1831 he commented,

> "They are incapable of freedom on our soil. They cannot rise in our esteem above the level of the moral state of the land of their origin, which is their appropriate, their only home. It is of first importance as regards our character abroad, that we should hasten to clear our land of our black population."[7]

His early prejudice against blacks is clear here as he spoke of "*our* soil" and "*our* blacks" and deprecated the "moral state" of Africa.

Although this prejudice may have remained with Smith throughout his lifetime, it is important to note that he was able to control its negative effects as he pursued policies of equity and justice for all humans. His delusions as a young man regarding the potential success of colonization grew from his belief that free blacks could Christianize Africa. He received encouragement for this idea from Ralph Randolph Gurley, the secretary of the American Colonization Society, who wrote to him frequently. In 1827, when Smith was considering establishing a seminary for blacks, Gurley called it a bad idea, and suggested that Smith contribute his money to the colonization effort. "Liberia, after all, opens the fairest and most encouraging field for charitable efforts to improve the minds of the coloured race," Gurley wrote.[8]

Smith did contribute to the ACS, and he tried to secure a financial appropriation from New York State in support of colonization.[9]

Smith also had the idea of starting a seminary to train black ministers to Christianize Africa. By the early 1830s he had established in Peterboro a school for black males that would give them a classical education designed to enable them to educate other free blacks.[10] He wrote to colonizationist Leonard Bacon of his hope that some of the graduates "will go to Africa with a sound education of head and heart."[11]

Even though local opposition had forced others to abandon similar plans for black schools—Simeon Jocelyn in 1831, and Prudence Crandall in 1833, both in Connecticut—Smith displayed no fear in establishing this school for blacks.[12]

As preparations for the school progressed in Peterboro, Elizabeth Smith wrote to her grandfather, Peter, "They have all been preparing things for the black School which is to be held in this place."[13] This was a segregated school for black males. Smith had not yet fully embraced the idea of gender-based equity, and he hoped that blacks who succeeded at his Peterboro school would train other blacks in similar skills and eventually build a colony somewhere.[14] Beriah Green protested the unisex nature of the school, saying that "colored brothers and sisters" should be educated together.[15]

The Peterboro Manual Labor School opened on May 1, 1834 with 15 students. By the following year, it had received more applications than it could handle. One journal reported that

> "The School is established in the belief that it is
> the duty of the whites to elevate the condition and
> character of the colored people…. Mr. Smith provides,
> at his own expense, instructors, books, stationery,
> rooms, bedding, fuel, lights, and boarding…. The
> student is expected to labor four hours daily, in some
> agricultural or mechanical employment."[16]

William Lloyd Garrison opposed the school on the grounds that it had been established to support colonization. He claimed that he would do all he could to "nip it in the bud" so that "it cannot succeed." A student at the school who also opposed colonization wrote to Garrison in support of Smith's efforts, saying that Smith "established the school… to raise up… a useful class of public spirited and pious young men, who will go forth and take an active part in the great work of moral reform…in this or any other country." He told Garrison that Beriah Green had visited Peterboro to speak against colonization. The student hoped that Green's appeals "will make an impression upon our excellent friend [Smith] and convince him of the fallacy and wickedness of that abominable [Colonization] Society."[17]

It is unclear why the school closed in the summer of 1836, but it probably had something to do with economic pressures that became manifest in the Panic of 1837—combined with the fact that by 1836, Smith had changed his ideas from support of colonization to support for immediate abolition.

Smith's enthusiasm for colonization waned as the antislavery movement developed in the early 1830s. Having founded Liberia in 1821, the American Colonization Society eventually sent approximately 12,000 blacks there.[18] But by 1833, Smith had begun to recognize the inherent racism within the organization. One colonization society in Pennsylvania had clearly stated its purpose as being to "remove sundry free persons of color [from our society due to] the desire to rid ourselves of a population injurious to us...."[19] The American Colonization Society refused to condemn chattel bondage—the concept that slaves were the personal property of their owners—thereby allowing slaveholders to avoid guilt.

It appeared to Smith, who lived among free blacks in Peterboro, that the American Colonization Society had refused to listen to some free blacks who were saying that they did not want to leave the United States, thereby ignoring their free choice and humanity. As Smith's empathy for free blacks grew he began to see them as people with feelings and allegiances like his own, and he saw the folly of the idea of colonization in Liberia. As early as 1817, more than 3,000 free black Americans had met at a convention in Philadelphia to protest the recently organized ACS on the grounds that it ignored the interests of blacks in the United States and legitimized the continued practice of slavery.[20] Similar meetings occurred in Philadelphia in 1818 and 1819, and by the early 1830s, blacks in 22 northern cities had held protest meetings to condemn colonization.[21]

There were several forces at work that reinforced Gerrit Smith's empathy for blacks. Young evangelical ministers such as Joshua

Leavitt and Samuel J. May were channeling their piety into abolition rather than the traditional Christian campaigns favoring temperance, opposing profanity, and promoting Sunday worship. A new class of religious liberals was beckoning Smith to join them.

In 1831 William Lloyd Garrison started publishing *The Liberator.* Lewis Tappan and Theodore Weld planned to organize a national antislavery organization and wanted Smith's help.[22] James G. Birney, a slaveholder-turned-abolitionist, wrote to Smith to encourage him to leave the ACS and become an anti-slavery abolitionist. Birney charged that the undisturbed conscience of the slaveholder was a result of colonization efforts.[23]

In 1832, Smith watched the call for immediate abolition take hold among the students at Beriah Green's Oneida Institute in nearby Whitesboro. In 1834, he saw the local establishment of, but did not join, the "Smithfield Society," a group of abolitionists in his own home town.[24] Smith had probably read *David Walker's Appeal* of late 1829, in which colonization was denounced as a tool of slaveholders designed to maintain the "ignorance and wretchedness" of blacks. Walker appealed to blacks to revolt against authoritative whites who "have always been an unjust, jealous, unmerciful, avaricious and blood-thirsty set of beings, always seeking after power and authority."[25]

Americans of white European heritage had already tried to eliminate ethnic variety in the "new world" by exterminating native peoples; the colonization move was perceived as just another ethnic cleansing to make the growing United States into a white persons' club. Supporters of colonization believed in biological inequality and racial inferiority, and they were not interested in emancipation or the betterment of free blacks. So they restricted the education and employment of free blacks in order to force them out of the country.[26]

Smith was beginning to see colonization as a hypocritical denial of the immorality of slavery that pacified the guilty conscience of Americans who were fearful of racial revolt. Whereas colonization asked for only money and lukewarm support of emancipation, abolition required a change in attitude and a daring confrontation of the moral sins of slavery. Realizing his errors, Gerrit Smith said in 1834,

> "[The American Colonization Society] has wronged us greatly…. It has, unhappily, thought the destruction of our society indispensable to the establishment of its own."[27]

Smith saw that the ACS's antislavery stance was "indirect,"[28] and because he began to view it as a racist organization trying to preserve the *status quo* for slavery, he began to look for something more reform-oriented. He wrote to William Goodell in 1833,

> "I am not so welded to the Colonization Society as to remain its advocate one moment after I shall see that it stands in the way of the speedy abolition of slavery."[29]

By August of 1834, Smith described the managers of the ACS as "marked with inconsistencies, and…wicked prejudice against the poor negro…."[30] Within a year, he had become angered by the equivocal stand of the Colonization Society regarding the rights of black people and its moral perception of slavery.[31] He later referred to the ACS as "that exceedingly corrupt and awfully wicked institution…."[32] A month earlier, he had even offered $300 as a contribution to support the expenses of blacks who had been sent to Liberia, but who preferred to return to the United States.[33]

Why did it take him so long to heed the call to immediate abolition? It could be due in part to psychological dissonance: he had contributed $10,000[34] to the ACS as an investment in support of the abolition of slavery, a move that prompted one of his business agents, John B. Edwards, to remark, "What a pity that you threw away $10,000 in colonization. With the interest it would now be $40,000. A fortune."[35] Edwards called colonization a "rotten cause."

Even when Smith could see no tangible return, there must have been an intense motivation to hold on, hoping for the eventual success of colonization. In his own words, Smith later blamed his indecision on selfishness and greed. He claimed, "my religious principles were weak, + my heart was worldly + aspiring."[36] Eventually, his empathy overcame his selfishness, and he wrote,

> "As soon as I came to commune with him… to make myself a colored man—I saw how crushing and murderous to all the hopes and happiness of our colored brothers is the policy of expelling [him] from this country."[37]

In 1835 Smith received a letter from Ephraim Titler, one of the blacks who had moved from the United States to the colony in Monrovia, Liberia. Titler was upset because the blacks being sent there by the Colonization Society were generally old or sick and were not able to contribute to the health of the colony.[38] Smith had been concerned that the Colonization Society was just trying to get rid of undesirable people, so this first-hand information probably helped him to decide to withdraw his support. Also, by the mid-1830s, reports were beginning to reach the United States that free blacks who had moved to Liberia were forcing local natives to work on their new farms as slaves.[39]

In the following years, Smith frequently stated his dissatisfaction with the concept of colonization. In a September 7, 1837 letter to Dr. Joseph Speed, a slave owner from Virginia who had relocated with seven slaves to Tompkins County in New York's southern tier, Smith spoke of having "recently escaped from the Colonization delusion."[40] And to The Rev. Samuel S. Schmuker, president of a seminary in Gettysburg, he commented, "my confidence in the usefullness of the colonization of our colored brethren…on the coast of Africa… has undergone a great, exceedingly great diminution."[41] Reflecting on his experience, he wrote Abby Kelley in 1843,

> "Unhappily, I became connected with the Colonization Society, a year or two after I began

to have thoughts of kindness toward my colored brethren. That connection wasted ten thousand dollars of my property + a considerable part of my years."[42]

He told Frederick Douglass in 1854 that colonization was an "absurdity." Two years later, he told the public in a speech to the New York State Legislature that a source of "prejudice against the black man is the American Colonization Society.... When the abolitionists fell upon the Colonization Society, it could no longer disguise itself. It stood revealed in all its grim ugliness."[43] Even late in his life, Smith looked back with shame on that early time when "my abolition heart was misled by the plausibilities of the Colonization scheme."[44]

In spite of Smith's clear apprehensions about colonizing Liberia, he nonetheless concocted an odd scheme to build a black community in northern New York State. His idea was to give land to blacks in the Essex County town of North Elba, in the Adirondacks. James McCune Smith, the black physician in New York City who was one of Smith's land agents in this deal, originally reacted negatively to it because he feared Smith was a fool, but he eventually supported it.[45]

Others also saw some latent colonialism in Smith. William Ellery Channing tried to enlist Smith's help in establishing a black colony in Tennessee in 1841,[46] and in 1866, a Texas resident suggested that Smith buy his land there to start a black community.[47] Smith actually supported a bill in Congress in the late 1850s and early 1860s that would have allowed a federal subsidy for voluntary relocation of blacks to Central America.[48] Although this idea may not have been a form of colonization, it did look a lot like a segregationist solution to racial problems. After 1850, Smith supported the emigration of blacks to Canada; but even then, he did not perceive it as a form of colonization.

However Smith's opinions evolved in the years after 1835, it is certain that he heartily supported what came to be known as the "immediate abolition" of slavery. "Immediatism" worried Southern-ers, who feared that it would turn slaves loose and encourage them to seek revenge. To the abolitionists, it meant immediate achieve-ment of equal protection of the laws, and it reflected an optimistic faith in progress toward social perfection by rejecting people and institutions that supported conservative, gradual emancipation. Sup-port of immediate abolition provided its supporters with a morally self-satisfying conversion and repentant experience.[49]

Before 1830, organizations that opposed slavery advocated either colonization or gradual abolition. Because there is scant evidence that supporters of colonization were seriously interested in aboli-tion, it is not surprising that Smith switched his interests to those of the immediate abolitionists. The early "abolition societies" differed from the movement later on in three ways: They were state-oriented, they favored gradual abolition, and they opted for legal rather than political action.[50]

One of the first writings on immediate abolition appeared in London in 1824 when Elizabeth Heyrick, a Quaker, wrote *Immedi-ate, not Gradual Abolition*, in which she made the point that gradual emancipation only brought gradual indifference. Slaveholders, she claimed, knew that "the most effectual way of crushing a great and virtuous enterprise" was to gain time to defer it to a more convenient season.[51] When her work was reprinted in New York City in 1825, William Lloyd Garrison read it and became a convert.[52] A growing cadre of "immediatists" added to the cause the power of legal prec-edent as established by the English court case of Somerset versus Stewart (1772), which implied that slavery could not exist except under sanction of specific law.

Armed with these principles, Garrison, Samuel J. May, David Lee Child, and a few other New England-based "immediate abolitionists" established the New England Anti-Slavery Society in 1832. Their idea was that slavery was illegal in the United States and could be abolished by state legislatures.[53] The establishment of the New York City Anti-Slavery Society by Arthur and Lewis Tappan and others in early 1833 echoed "moderate immediatism," and so did the establishment of the American Anti-Slavery Society in Philadelphia later that year under the leadership of Garrison.[54] "Moderate immediatism" held that the states should abolish slavery because they could act before the federal government would.

The American Anti-Slavery Society's inaugural meeting took place December 4 to 6, 1833 in Philadelphia, a city that was at that time biased and unfriendly toward a rising black middle class. When the radical central New Yorker Beriah Green was elected as its chairman, Philadelphians denounced the meeting as an "amalgamationist conclave." The 63 delegates from 10 states proved their dedication to the cause with their extraordinary effort to get to Philadelphia in wintry weather. It took Garrison six days to travel from Boston via stagecoach and packet boat. In the meeting's declaration, Garrison compared the group's campaign for the freedom of slaves to the American revolutionaries' quest for freedom 57 years earlier. But, he added, the grievances of blacks were more intense, because "our fathers were never slaves."

Smith was not yet as radical. His position as a moderate immediatist is clear in this letter of January 1836 to New York State Governor William Marcy: "The federal constitution... leaves 'the right to abolish slavery where only it could be safely left; with the respective states, wherein slavery existed.' We are glad, that this right belongs exclusively to those states...."[55] Some immediate abolitionists were challenging this moderate stance with the "radical immediatist" notion that the federal government had the legal power, based in its Constitution, to abolish slavery nationwide. Alvan Stewart proclaimed the idea in his speech to the second annual meeting of the New York State Anti-Slavery Society on September 20, 1837.[56]

By the 1840s Smith's position had changed, and he adopted the "radical immediatist" position, adding to it the notion that the "natural law" of equal rights for all humans required such legal action. Smith based his argument on the 1st, 9th, and 10th amendments to the Constitution, which empowered the federal government to check any anti-republican tendencies in states and to uphold the general welfare.[57]

His adoption of the "radical immediatist" point of view was a real conversion in Smith's life. He began to advocate change through more practical means, such as politics and voting, instead of just moralizing. Personal commitment to the abolition of slavery became his "evangelical" expression of a life dedicated to reform toward a less sinful society.

A series of events beginning in 1831 reinforced Smith's change in thinking to the "radical immediatist" view. In the fall of that year, a meeting of "friends of the slave" was called at the Baptist Church on West Genesee Street in Syracuse, New York. Gerrit Smith was part of a group of people who, as they approached the church for the meeting, were pelted with rotten eggs by a mob of proslavery protestors. The abolitionist group dispersed in fear and met later in nearby Fayetteville.[58] This event secured Smith's commitment to abolition on two grounds: the moral principle of equity and the social principle of free speech. In 1833 Britain emancipated all slaves in the British colonies, proving the feasibility of abolition. It was in that same year that 10 states sent representatives to Philadelphia to establish the American Anti-Slavery Society.[59]

As Smith's support of colonization waned, he received several letters from prominent abolitionists seeking his support in the budding antislavery movement.[60] Probably the most influential of these letters came from Beriah Green, Smith's friend and a respected leader and abolitionist in the Utica area. In August of 1835, Green primed Smith for action. "What a struggle awaits us! What designs are avowed—what acts perpetrated! What infatuation! The nation marching headlong upon its own ruin! The storm must come."[61] On September 24, Green informed Smith of a key meeting coming up soon.

> "I suppose that you may have heard of the design
> of some of the friends of human nature in this
> state, to meet at Utica in convention the 21st of

next month (Oct.) to take into consideration the
[wisdom] of forming a State A.S. Society. Circulars
are, or will soon be issued. I hope, in the mercy of
God, that something may then be done for downtrodden humanity.... I feel a confidence, which my
heart refuses to let go, that you will, 'some time or
other,' give us your heart + your hand. May God in
mercy hasten the longed for hour."[62]

When the meeting day arrived, Smith had no idea of the significance of the event in which he was about to participate.

A recently surfaced document relates a personal account of the
events of October 21 and 22, 1835 as recorded by James Caleb Jackson, an abolitionist who lived in the Oswego area. Jackson would
eventually come to reside in Peterboro and become a close friend
of Smith.[63] For the trip from Oswego to Utica, Jackson boarded a
packet boat to ride on the Oswego Canal to Syracuse, then on the
Erie Canal to Utica. On the boat he met Smith, who was en route
to Peterboro after having attended to some business matters in Oswego. Jackson had seen Smith speak several years before, and he
had admired him as a role model ever since, but this was their first
meeting. The younger Jackson was awed by Smith: "I felt as if I stood
in the presence of a very great man."[64] Smith was also planning to
attend the Utica meeting.

At Syracuse Beriah Green boarded the boat, and the three of
them discussed antislavery matters as the packet boat crawled
along at four miles per hour. This ride from Syracuse to Canastota,
where Smith's carriage was waiting to take him to Peterboro, was a
chance meeting of future central New York abolitionist giants. The
magnitude of the issues they discussed would, a few years hence,
tear apart a nation.

The Utica convention was called for the purpose of establishing
a New York State Anti-Slavery Society as a local arm of the American Anti-Slavery Society. The Utica Common Council had granted

the group permission to hold the meeting in the local courthouse, but due to public objection, it was moved to the Bleecker Street Presbyterian Church.[65] It was expected that about 50 people would attend the meeting; between 400 and 600 showed up.[66] The meeting probably started in the mid-morning of Wednesday, October 21, and when the names of delegates were called, the total amounted to over 400.

After leaders and committees were chosen, according to Jackson,
"...there came into the church a dozen men
[who] walked down the aisles headed by a very
distinguished looking Samuel Beardsley, an
attorney, a member of Congress, and a close
personal friend of President Andrew Jackson, who
addressed the Chairman asking to be heard."

This group had met at 9 a.m. the same morning in the Utica Court House, then went to the convention of the abolitionists to "read to the delegates the resolutions of the meeting of citizens, and to enforce them...."[67]

Beardsley announced that he and his group represented "the citizens of Utica" who had, in a public meeting arranged by him, decided that the antislavery meeting was dangerous to the professional and commercial interests of Utica because
"...the disgrace of having an Abolition Convention
held in the city is a deeper one than that of twenty
mobs and that it would be better to have Utica
razed to its foundations, or to have it destroyed
like Sodom and Gommorah, than to have the
convention meet here."[68]

Beardsley predicted that if the meeting did not disperse, there would be "violence and confusion." He added that the abolitionists, knowing this, were "morally bound to have called their convention in another place... of smaller size where they had no reason to expect disturbance."[69] He suggested that if the delegates would disburse peacefully, there would be no violence.

The chair then recognized Gerrit Smith's request to speak. According to Jackson, Smith said,

> "It seems from what appears here this morning,
> that it [is] a crime not only to be black, but to be
> a friend of the black man. It is not wise for us to
> [meet here]. Let us accept their proposition and
> leave the city.... I cordially invite this convention
> to meet in the village of Peterboro... tomorrow
> morning at eleven o'clock in the forenoon. I will
> guarantee a peaceful meeting."[70]

The committee on organization then held a brief meeting and reported to the whole with a constitution and officers. These were quickly adopted amid the "howlings" of a mob of about "a thousand men" who had gathered in the street outside the church. Then, Jackson reported, "The mob backed out, and we passed out of the church to get to Peterboro the best way we could."[71] The *Oneida Whig* newspaper editorialized that the abolitionists had caused the disruption by calling their meeting in Utica in order "to produce disturbance and confusion," adding that "There is no other construction to be put upon it, than that the convention tended to alarm and injury."[72]

James Caleb Jackson's first-hand account of the trip from Utica to Peterboro is worth quoting at length because of its clarity in showing the dedication of abolitionists.

> "A dozen plans were gotten up, carriages were
> hired, some strong fellows determined to go
> over on foot, for all it were a walk of thirty miles.
> A young man by the name of Wm. M. Clark of
> Syracuse and myself hailed a boat on the canal;
> and for a wonder, the man was going home empty.
> We asked if he could take out his midships and in a

little [time] fix it so he could carry a large number
of men as far west as Canastota. He said he would
be glad of the freight as he called us. We stipulated
for price, and in less than two hours, one hundred
and four men went into that boat. Of course there
were no cabins; but he got some boards and laid
down, and into the boat we went. We had to sit
on the bottom which these boards covered. About
three o'clock in the afternoon, we went out of the
city of Utica; and a more jovial, hilarious, joyous
set of fellows I never saw. Four men were old white
headed men; one an old minister, quite feeble,
must have been as much as eighty years old. We
sang, and we prayed, and laughed, and cried,
and swore eternal hostility to slavery, and vowed
eternal fidelity to liberty, and so on we went....
I never saw such patience, such forbearance,
such courage, such faith, such abnegation of
selfishness, such promises and pledges to truth
and right and God, and the enslaved as I witnessed
that night. I have never seen it exceeded since.
A little after three o'clock the next morning, the
captain announced our arrival at Canastota. It
was raining, a soft drizzly soaking rain.... There
were one hundred four of us emptied right out
on the brink of the canal. We were in a strange
place, not knowing even where there was a hotel,
but our presence there made a noise, a[nd] soon a
light struck up in a house close by the canal; and
it turned out to be kept by a man by the name of
Montross. There we hired a team to take up the
four old white headed men. From Canastota to
Peterboro is ten miles; and to climb the hills is
like going up Jack the giant killer's ladder. To get
up at all, one had to go up a succession of hills

one after the other. Peterboro must be at least a
thousand feet above Canastota. Having booked our
patriarchs, who, notwithstanding their age, bore
their hardships bravely, some of us boys taking off
their overcoats and spreading them down on the
boards and making beds for the grand old men, we
started a hundred strong on the way to Peterboro.
Wm. M. Clark and myself led the crowd; and as
we went by the farm houses at the dawn of day,
singing and shouting, and laughing and praying,
we startled the house dwellers along the way, and
here would be a bare head and there a nightcapped
head sticking out of a window or door; and when
daylight came here would be a farmer going to
his barn to milk, and there would be a milkmaid
coming in from milking; here a shoemaker who
would look out, and there a joiner and carpenter
on his way to work; and such an astonishment as
we gave everyone who saw us I cannot describe.
In numbers of instances however, men said: 'What
is the matter; is war declared?' Our answer was:
'Yes; war to the death against slavery. We have
been mobbed out of the city of Utica; and we are
going to Peterboro to hold a convention. Come,
put on a clean shirt and come along with us. We
have begun the grandest revolution the world has
ever seen: and if we do not die, we mean to see that
revolution accomplished, and our land free from
the tread and fetter of the slave."[73]

When the group of 100 reached Peterboro shortly after dawn,
Jackson inquired at Smith's house what was to be done about breakfast for such a large, hungry group. Smith's house servants contacted
village residents, who took in small groups of people until all were

fed. At around 10 o'clock in the morning, carriages began arriving carrying those people who had stayed overnight in Utica and intended to be at the Peterboro meeting.

Smith had arrived in Peterboro at 10 p.m. on October 21, and had instructed his household help to begin preparations to feed a large number at breakfast the next morning. Smith stayed up most of that night, writing a speech to be delivered at the Peterboro meeting on October 22. While the speech had a definite antislavery tone, its theme was freedom of speech. He was outraged that a public meeting of free citizens was not allowed freedom of assembly or speech on the previous day in Utica. He defended free speech as a divine right, the denial of which he saw as a form of oppression that could not be sanctioned. If its denial were to stand unchallenged, he claimed, then everyone would be a slave.[74]

This speech could be a classic in American political history. In it, Smith charged that the purpose of the proslavery mob in Utica was "that the oppressed may be more passive at the feet of the oppressor." Perhaps as many as 300 people were gathered in the Presbyterian Church in Peterboro to attend this first meeting of the New York State Anti-Slavery Society, during which the building was guarded by armed men in case any persons from the Utica mob arrived to disrupt it. In a very early example of his readiness to use violence against pro-slavery interests, Smith wrote of the use of "fire arms to surround the church and to shoot down the Utica mob....."[75]

That night, some of the attendees stayed at Smith's house. Many years later, James Caleb Jackson reminisced over their

> "...meeting in Utica in '35 and our flight to
> Peterboro. I remember just where I slept on the
> floor in your old large house and how wonderfully
> you had possession of my heart when you came
> into the room after my comrades and myself had
> gone to bed and looked down upon us, holding
> a lighted candle in your hand and giving us your
> pleasant good night."[76]

One major effect of Gerrit Smith's experience with the Utica/ Peterboro antislavery meeting was that it convinced him to join the formally organized antislavery effort. On November 12, 1835, he joined the American Anti-Slavery Society to the accolades of his colleagues.[77] John Tappan of Boston praised Smith for joining the society, claiming "they greatly need cool, judicious men to guide them in these troublesome times."[78] James McCune Smith, a black abolitionist in New York City, wrote to Smith of his pleasure in Gerrit's new membership in the Society. McCune Smith perceived prejudice against blacks among some of the society's members, and he hoped that Smith's empathic stance would counteract it.[79] Samuel Mills, a former pastor of the Peterboro Presbyterian Church, wrote, "Your formal coming over to the A.S. Society, tho' far from unexpected, was a moment which I greatly rejoice in...."[80]

Clearly, the people of Peterboro supported Smith's antislavery efforts. Beriah Green acknowledged having been under "your hospitable roof.... I rejoice to know that your thoughts + heart are so much with the oppressed.... What a work lies before us!"[81]

Five years later, Smith wrote of the effect of the 1835 event: "It is true... that the outrages on the right of petition, assembling, etc. have multiplied abolitionists. And although it is probable in view of my ethics and temperament that even had these outrages been wanting, I should at no distant day have connected myself with the American Anti-Slavery Soc., I nevertheless cheerfully admit that their occurrence hastened the connection."[82]

On December 5, 1835, Gerrit Smith received a letter from the Washington, D.C. office of the American Colonization Society acknowledging receipt of his 1834 pledge of $3,000 and his intent to withdraw from participation in further efforts at colonization.[83] After this point, Smith's antislavery efforts and reputation expanded quickly. In April of 1836, Lewis Tappan invited him to address the first annual meeting of the New York State Anti-Slavery Society in Utica. He did attend this meeting, and he was elected to the position of president of the Society. He declined the honor, claiming

A postcard of the former Evans Academy. Built in 1820 as a Presbyterian Church, this building hosted the New York Anti-Slavery Society meeting that was chased from a Utica meeting place in October 1835. Still located on the southwest side of Peterboro, the building now serves as the Smithfield Community Center and temporary home of the National Abolition Hall of Fame & Museum.

From the author's collection

that he was too young and lived too far from Utica to be an effective office-holder. He was subsequently appointed to a committee charged with drafting a petition to be sent to Congress, requesting the immediate abolition of slavery in the District of Columbia.[84] Smith also attended a gathering at the Baptist Church in Syracuse that established the Onondaga County Anti-Slavery Society, and he was referred to by Syracuse abolitionist Jermain W. Loguen as one of the "illustrious agitators in attendance."[85]

Smith was also present on "the 25ᵗʰ [of May]—the day of the meeting in Cazenovia to form a [Madison] County Anti-Slavery Society." By mid-July, the Executive Committee of the American Anti-Slavery Society "appointed and commissioned" Smith as their "Agent, for the space of one year commencing with the seventeenth day of July 1836." This appointment was followed by the Society's statement of purpose: "The Society was formed for the purpose of awakening the attention of our whole community to the character of American Slavery, and presenting the claims and urging the rights of the colored people of the United States; so as to promote, in the most efficient manner, the immediate abolition of Slavery, and the restoration to our colored brethren of their inalienable rights."[86]

In the ensuing four years, the American Anti-Slavery Society worked through over 60 selected agents who spoke effectively for antislavery all over the country. Antislavery societies in general depended on individuals to carry forth their message. They realized that as self-righteous organizations, they would have little effect in a land of popular sovereignty, and would need exemplary agents to promulgate the moral message of a natural right to equality.

Smith declined the itinerant speaker role, but he did contribute his name and his money to the national society's purpose, and he worked actively for his local county anti-slavery organization. In November of 1837, *The Liberator* recognized the Madison County Anti-Slavery Society for its efforts at "Genuine Abolition." Two resolutions—almost certainly written by Smith—were passed, condemning the slaveholder as a "manstealer" and reprimanding the U.S. Congress for failing to abolish slavery in the District of Columbia.[87]

In the next few years Gerrit Smith received many invitations to speak at antislavery meetings, as the movement aggressively sought his resources. In 1838, William L. Chaplin wrote to Smith, outlining a program of action for "the moral and political regeneration of this great state [of New York]" and soliciting funds for an annual New York State Anti-Slavery Society budget of $20,000. In this effort, he pressed Smith's guilt button:

> "Understanding that you hold in trust a large
> fund left by your deceased father for charitable
> uses, [we] submit to you whether you can select a
> more appropriate spot than your own native state
> to which to make a large appropriation from that
> fund...."

Chaplin claimed in his appeal that Smith's donation could be "the largest benevolence in behalf of fellow men + fellow citizens crushed + dumb, of husbands torn + mangled by the brutality + lust of the lawless despot,...and orphans... made so by the infernal spirit of slavery." This technique for appealing to the potential guilt of philanthropists regarding their support of human rights was common.[88]

Smith did donate generously to the cause, and as his reputation grew, other activists visited him and requested his help in building the strength of antislavery organizations.[89] By 1840, the membership of antislavery societies in the North was estimated to be 150,000 people,[90] and Smith's leadership in the movement was considered to be important in this growth. His followers viewed him as humane, dependable, and reliable, and they called him "captain."[91]

Gerrit Smith emerged here in his most important life's work to be an empathic person capable of joining diverse groups of people and various forces in the effort to build a power base opposing slavery. His personal opinion was that this power could best be used at a local level to change attitudes, but he did not shrink from the larger scene of state and national political action. William Ellery Channing recognized Smith's value to the antislavery cause and encouraged him to go on in spite of frustrations. "You must expect the zeal of many who expected an easy victory, to grow cool. Still a great work has been done in many minds, + it will go on."[92]

In order to move forward the antislavery movement needed an organizational base, and here Gerrit Smith played a significant role. Before the 1830s, there was very little organized activity. Smith's early ideas about abolition, whether they centered on colonization or emancipation, focused on action at the local or state level. When he decided on immediate abolition as the best course, he saw the Constitution as an antislavery document; as a result, he came to view state and national political action as a legitimate means of pursuing abolition.

Others, mainly in Garrison's camp, maintained that the Constitution *supported* slavery, and they would not back political action, which they felt legitimated a corrupt Constitution. Smith's position was best stated in a resolution that he presented at the National Convention of the Liberty Party in Buffalo on October 20, 1847:

"Whereas the pro-slavery obligations of the Federal Constitution are found solely in the abundant speculations on the intentions of that instrument: and whereas its anti-slavery obligations are palpable from its plain declarations: Resolved, therefore, that, relying on these declarations, and refusing to be misled by those speculations, we hold, that slavery, whether in the District of Columbia, or in any other part of the Nation, is clearly and utterly unconstitutional."[93]

The National Congress had sole jurisdiction over Washington, D.C., and could abolish slavery there without state interference. In that slavery was an embarrassing institution to display in the capital of a republic, abolitionists called for immediate action. Interpreting the Constitution in this way justified immediate, radical action in the fight for abolition.

Smith was not alone; many abolitionists in the early 1830s had pushed for immediate action. Some sent antislavery petitions to state legislatures, but they were unsuccessful in bringing about any legislative action. And Congress, with heavy southern influence, refused to accept public petitions as issues for debate. Wendell Phillips, William Lloyd Garrison, and Theodore Dwight Weld were calling for radical action, and they were discouraged by the wait-and-see attitudes of other abolitionists. Said Weld, "The great body of Abolitionists seem to be mere passengers on a pleasure sail. They can't endure the drudgery of [work]. They are willing to take the helm… but [not] shipwork."[94]

Abolitionists generally believed in one of two major strategies for the implementation of immediate abolition: persuasion or political action. Not surprisingly, the adherents to each strategy became antagonistic to each other. Garrison in Boston led the persuasion enthusiasts, and Gerrit Smith in Peterboro became a recognized leader of those in favor of political action. Garrison believed gradual abolition to be "a sentiment… full of timidity, injustice and absurdity." He claimed that moral pressure would reshape the feelings and opinion of the public to the extent that democratic leaders would eventually have to respond to it.

Those who opposed Garrison's "moral suasion" approach to changing the public attitude referred to it as a process of screaming at deaf people.[95]

Garrison had burst onto the scene in 1831 with *The Liberator*, a radical abolitionist paper through which he demanded to be heard—regardless of what others thought of his ideas. Garrisonians regarded slavery as a sin, and believed that religion could convert enough people to anti-slavery to bring about social change. They moralized about slavery until their moralizations resembled an addictive obsession; they had set themselves up as God's spokespersons and executors, and alienated many other abolitionists.[96]

As with most abolitionists, Garrison opposed the use of violence. He established the Nonresistance Society in Boston in 1838 as a sign of protest against other abolitionists who did advocate violence. Garrison viewed political action advocates merely as reformers who were interested in using an institutional system that had proved itself incapable of bringing about change. Frederick Douglass was an early supporter of Garrison—until he was convinced otherwise by Gerrit Smith. Maria Chapman of Boston supported Garrison and opposed political action, believing it sapped strength out of the moral principle approach to abolition.

But others opposed his caustic writing and oratory. Abby Kelley saw Garrison as a tyrant trying to control the efforts of all abolition-ists.[97] Amos Phelps was aggravated by him, writing to Smith that "as a characteristic habit [Garrison] could not or would not see anything but sinister motive in the action of those who differed from him.... [He is] a thoroughly selfish, self-willed + self-seeking man."[98] R. R. Gurley of the Colonization Society expressed to Smith his fear that *The Liberator* would cause people to pull away from support of colonization. He opposed Garrison's "uncompromising + reckless spirit, which will excite the worst passions among all classes...."[99]

Garrison was probably not bothered by such opposition; he had, after all, intended to stir the public into action. He moralized, persuaded, and avoided politics. He was well known because he was one of the first vocal abolitionists, he edited *The Liberator*, and he was in Boston. Peterboro was not quite the hub of activity that Boston was. In spite of that, Smith's reputation for support of politi-cal action spread, and he did not tend to alienate others as Garrison did. In fact, even though Smith disagreed with Garrison's tactics, he respected both the differences and the man.

Garrison had assailed Smith as being morally unprincipled,[100] yet Smith was strong enough in self-respect to absorb the shot, saying,

"My opinions of the mental and moral worth of

our friend and brother WL Garrison are very high. Many of my wise friends think he is ambitious and selfish. But they have not succeeded in bringing me over to their views. Much, however, as I admire him, I am not blind to his faults. There must be something wrong in his temper. I have seen nothing from the pen of Brother Garrison, that savors so much of disingenuousness as his attempt to show my inconsistency on the subject of political action."[101]

Despite Smith's opposition to Garrison's tactics, Smith contributed money to *The Liberator* to keep it solvent during difficult economic times.[102] As the rift between abolitionist camps in the United States grew, Smith attempted to quell the fears of foreign abolitionists that the cause would be lost here. To a British Member of Parliament he wrote,

"How greatly do I lament [the] ignorance of William Lloyd Garrison.... But whatever [his beliefs] are, ...he is certainly a true hearted abolitionist.... I do not know how any can deny, that he is a man of great intellectual power, of invincible moral courage, and of unsurpassed sympathy with the poor + oppressed."[103]

John Greenleaf Whittier summed up the concern over a division among abolitionists with the simple question, "Dear Gerrit, why is it that this... bitter spirit of reproach... has come among us?"[104] Although all abolitionists worked toward the same goal, each of them believed they knew the right way to do it.

"Poor abolitionists!" lamented Gerrit. "What ill-tempered fellows they are! How we love to devour one another!"[105] While Smith's support shifted from colonization to antislavery, he made no apologies to his colleagues, thereby angering them. In Lewis Tappan's letter

to Smith inviting him to the New York State Anti-Slavery Society
in Utica, he reminded Smith,

> "Some of us think, dear sir, that before your public
> profession of Anti-Slavery doctrines you did
> your present associates injustice, and they have
> been disappointed that you have not made any
> confession of having done this injury."[106]

In a letter written a few days after that, Tappan wrote,

> "The accusations you brought against the Anti-S.
> Soc. and the prominent men in it, served as an
> opiate upon the consciences of many who might
> have united with us…. It does appear to me,
> my dear Sir, that…[you] should rejoice in an
> opportunity to recant."[107]

The first hint of Smith's interest in a political approach to abolition came as early as 1836, in a speech that he delivered at the third
annual meeting of the American Anti-Slavery Society. In the speech,
he advised northerners to defend themselves through political action against the ill effects of slavery.[108] James G. Birney, the future
presidential nominee of the Liberty Party, had been advising Smith
by letter that moral suasion was a waste of time, saying that "repen-
tance [of the slave owner] is far off, if at all to be expected."[109] Being
a former slave owner, Birney knew that a more practical approach
to change was necessary.

The irony is that the two approaches to achieving the abolition
of slavery—persuasion and politics—were each, in their own way,
inadequate and incomplete: successful politics through votes might
be able to change the rules (laws), but not people's minds. Attitudes
toward discrimination would need to change before racial equality
could ever be achieved, but moral suasion did not succeed against
entrenched vested interests. This made Garrison abstractly correct
but practically wrong, and it doomed his efforts to achieve equal-

ity. At the same time, all that political activists could achieve was a change in the social *rules*, but not in the *score*. And the negative results of that achievement are still with us.

A formal division between the moral persuasion and political action factions occurred at the seventh anniversary meeting of the American Anti-Slavery Society in May of 1840, when those advocating political action split off to organize the American and Foreign Anti-Slavery Society. That faction included the Tappans, Birney, Stanton, Whittier, and Smith; the apolitical Garrisonians stayed with the older Society.[110] The original American Anti-Slavery Society's view was that abolition could not be achieved short of changing the proslavery "heart" of the people nationwide by means of persuasion. Political efforts that might win a few votes, a purchased slave, or an aided fugitive could gain little, and they wasted resources. Gerrit Smith could see value in both strategies, supporting voters *and* speakers. While Garrison focused on a missionary type of preaching in the hope of converting minds, Smith concentrated on local community change by the dual means of helping individuals and soliciting votes. By encouraging local political awareness and activity, Smith alienated the urban Garrison group, which maintained a central headquarters of moral crusaders.

Because he could see value in both persuasive and political strategies, Smith worked to reconcile feuding abolitionists. "Moral suasion," he said three years later, "is ... indispensable to the antislavery cause: but it is so, mainly because of the political action, which is its legitimate result."[111] Smith thought the two groups' techniques were mutually supportive, and he disliked the battle among abolitionists because their goals were the same. As he told Garrison, "Their grand point of agreement... is, that slavery is... a diabolical, mean, shameless outlaw,"[112] and disagreement among them over tactics only weakened their power. To the *Liberty Gazette,* Smith said this:

> "Abolitionists must respect each other, if they would have their opponents respect them. We are quite low enough in the public esteem without

setting ourselves at work to degrade each other."[113]

Smith refused to fight with Garrison, even though Garrison, writing in *The Liberator*, seemed to beg for it. Smith received support for his conciliatory stand from powerful friends. Both Lewis Tappan and Senator Charles Sumner sent notes of approval,[114] and Beriah Green agreed that abolitionists drew strength from one another. [115] But even Green and Tappan eventually had public disagreements with Smith. Abolition was so controversial that it produced a hotbed of emotions whenever it surfaced. As level-headed men like Gerrit Smith and Frederick Douglass worked together to unite factions of the antislavery movement for the purpose of producing more political power, Garrison was having nothing to do with the effort. He thought his strategy, working outside of the evil, proslavery Constitution, was the right way.[116]

Although he tried hard, Smith never did succeed in uniting the abolitionist factions. The fact that he kept trying in the face of early and continuing frustration was a sign of his optimism and dedication. He wrote to John T. Norton, a colleague who was also trying for abolitionist unity,

"My whole heart rejoices, that you have
undertaken the good work of reuniting the divided
friends of the slave. That it will be a successful
work, I have not great hope…. During the whole
time of this unhappy + injurious division, I
have lamented it, and labored to heal it. But my
lamentations and labors have been in vain."[117]

The enduring split among abolitionists was geographical as well as philosophical. The east coast from Boston to New York City harbored those who clung in some degree to religiously based moralism and persuasion, while inland central and western New Yorkers advocated political action. William Lloyd Garrison led the "Boston clique" that exhibited a liberal, anti-Calvinistic religious orientation, embracing mainly Unitarian and Quaker beliefs. Adherents were professionals with an urban outlook that led them to feel and act in an independent, self-assured manner.[118] Lewis Tappan led a corollary clique to the Garrisonians, with mainly Presbyterian and Congregationalist leanings. In style, they were somewhat more temperate in their persuasive approach to the public, but they still pursued evangelical immediatism.[119]

Gerrit Smith's circle of mostly upstate New Yorkers avoided religious affiliations because of the popular perception that organized religious denominations tended to favor slavery. Their political activity centered on either voting for major-party candidates who opposed slavery, or working for antislavery third parties. Most adherents to the Smith faction were well-educated, respected professionals with experience in reform movements who tried to build coalitions and networks for a power base to produce change. They were older and more practical than those who identified with the Garrison/Tappan cliques, and they depended on Smith's money to fuel their reform efforts.[120]

Before the advent of the Liberty Party, the American Anti-Slavery Society placed heavy emphasis on how one voted, encouraging people "to vote, irrespective of party, for those only who will advocate the principles of Universal Liberty...." The Society also opposed the formation of an antislavery third party because of the potential for such a move to neutralize its influence on the political scene.[121] Smith, at this time, was not encouraging the formation of a third party. He was focused on "our main concern... that abolitionists do not practice the gross inconsistency and incur the great guilt of voting for proslavery candidates."[122] He even proposed that antislavery organizations place in their constitutions the requirement that members vote only for antislavery candidates.[123] He insisted that if no such candidates were nominated, that abolitionists should abstain from voting.[124]

Smith saw the existing major political parties—Democrats and Whigs—as being equally supportive of slavery; but the Democratic Party received his most heated criticism. Democrats, he said, were "stone blind, both morally and politically."[125] Smith's friend, James Caleb Jackson, lamented over abolitionists who identified with political parties—even third parties—for their own gain.

"Such miserable tools of Party. My soul loaths them. I want to act with them no more. I cannot trust them in an emergency. They are the slaves of Expediency."[126]

This anti-party attitude extended to what Smith called "ecclesiastical parties," or Christian denominations. He even warned blacks to avoid them.

"So long as the free colored people of this country continue to run after + to hang + fawn upon our great men in Church + State, they will be degraded.... For know they not that all our National parties are...proslavery?"[127]

Smith howled about the inequitable treatment of black people in this supposedly republican and Christian country.

"This is a land of the most horrible despotism and of the deepest religious hypocrisy. True republicanism and true Christianity count 'all men as created equal.' But our sham republicanism and our sham Christianity declare that one man is born to oppress, and another to be oppressed."[128]

The oppression he saw in slavery was a type of imprisonment that eliminated all human rights of those in chains. He found similar enslavement in the religious groups' rigidity. As he wrote to John Scoble of the British and Foreign Antislavery Society in 1843,

"American abolitionists are still hard at work. But, whether we shall ever succeed in breaking the iron bands of our proslavery ecclesiastical and political parties is uncertain.... They are the keepers of the

American Bastile."[129]

This 'slave prison', Smith claimed, existed because religious institutions with the power to destroy it instead condoned it. "The cause of humanity is bleeding and dying for the lack of the testimony of our ecclesiastical bodies against the wickedness of slavery...."[130] This characteristic of the established churches had angered Smith so much that he had stopped participating in them and formed his own Free Church of Peterboro, which was actually a hybrid religious/political institution. Free Churches throughout central New York became a base of support for the Liberty Party.

By the early 1840s, Smith had moved away from all brands of moral persuasion and into political activity in support of the newly created Liberty Party. In retrospect, the Garrisonians had the right idea that politics and law would never eliminate discrimination against and oppression of blacks; but Smith, in his typically practical way, gravitated toward political action as a means to achieve emancipation quickly. This practical approach to change left the Garrisonians out completely, and it left Lewis Tappan and his followers hanging somewhere between persuasion and political effort. By 1843, Tappan worried, "I have seen that a very large proportion of abolitionists, who are not of the Garrison School, are members of the Liberty Party."[131]

Gerrit Smith was the respected founder and leader of the Liberty Party, and twice would be its presidential nominee. Myron Holley exhibited the respect typical of many of Smith's colleagues. When Smith was ill, Holley said, "I have some apprehension that it may disable you at a crisis requiring high measures of comprehensive wisdom, prudence, decision and influence—and at which, with health, you can do more to give the right direction than any man living."[132]

A Peterboro resident also admired Smith's political efforts. Henry Campbell wrote to his sister in 1848, "I wish you and I could keep the Sabbath and every other commandment like Mr. S[mith]. It will not do to follow the interpretations that Slaveholders...have put on the Bible and [make] politicks taboo because they conflict with the villany of oppressor and his apologist."[133]

Smith's greatest influence was in his home base of Madison County—especially in Smithfield and Peterboro. Believing that antislavery public sentiment was necessary for political activity to succeed, he challenged the township of Smithfield to set an example for the nation.[134] He feared civil war if no governmental unit in the country could exhibit a clear opposition to slavery; so, he set himself the task of building a local coalition that could guide a whole township of voters.

Neighbors in Peterboro, highly influenced by Smith's views, became the foundation for this task. They included James Barnett, Horace Brown, William Martindale, Abishai Schofield, George Klinck, Hiram Hadden, and James Caleb Jackson. Outside of Peterboro, Smith received support from Beriah Green, William Chaplin, William Goodell, Alvan Stewart, Myron Holley, and others.[135] This is an impressive list of men who had at least statewide influence, and there is one more name that needs to be added to it: Frederick Douglass.

By the late 1840s, Douglass was dissatisfied with the progress of the Garrisonian tactics of persuasion. Smith had been trying to convince Douglass to support political action, and because of Douglass' growing understanding that blacks needed political power, he was beginning to listen. His switch from Garrisonian "moral suasion" to the more radical stand of immediatism combined with political action signaled a shift from the white paternalism of his former employer (Garrison) to independence as a black abolitionist leader. Douglass accentuated this shift by moving from Boston to Rochester, New York in 1847 and inaugurating his editorship of *The North Star*, a radical abolitionist newspaper. He had established himself as a political activist.[136] Accepting Smith as a mentor, Douglass became convinced that the Constitution of the United States was an antislavery document.[137]

The influence that Gerrit Smith and Frederick Douglass had on one another was profound. They were bound together by their common self-perceptions as persons who battled the traditional markers of class and caste. Slavery blocked the achievement of their dreams of a noble country built on principles of equity and justice for all. They had to redefine themselves in an attempt to counteract the dead weight of social inertia that was so resistant to change. Rather than give up on their dreams of a moral America, they plunged into its structure to purify it.

But while they succeeded in breaking down the dualism of race in their relationships with each other, they could not dissolve the social machinery of discrimination. There was deep mutual respect; each viewed the other as someone from whom he could learn a great deal. Douglass offered Smith the perspective of a former runaway slave who had become a self-educated national leader. Smith offered Douglass the perspective of a rich white male who modeled equitable treatment for all. Smith needed Douglass in his political action group as an indication of black support, and Douglass needed Smith to finance the merger of *The North Star* and *The Liberty Party Paper* in 1851, resulting in *Frederick Douglass' Paper*.

Both men advocated "manual labor" schools for young blacks, and Douglass' "growlry," a small building built near his home in which he sought solace when under stress, might have been modeled after Smith's Land Office.[138] As public speakers, they were both able to grab the attention of the public and move people to action.

Upon Douglass' death, Elizabeth Cady Stanton would remark about his previous influence over audiences that "laughed and wept by turns, completely carried away by the wondrous gifts of his pathos and humor. [Douglass] stood there like an African prince, majestic in his wrath."[139]

The commitment of both men to abolition was legendary. They both were worrying over a peaceful solution to the issue of slavery when, in 1852, some abolitionists abandoned the Liberty Party in favor of the Free Soil Party. Douglass and Smith viewed the Free Soil Party as not nearly radical enough, because although it opposed the extension of slavery, it did not demand abolition.[140] This bothered Smith throughout the 1850s. In 1860 he wrote of the party to Douglass, "The calculating policy of non-extension has taken the place of the uncompromising principle of abolition."[141]

One peculiar feature of the abolition movement was the way it perceived and treated women. They were an untapped source of grace and eloquence of speech, and they had experienced first-hand the effects of a lesser—if still considerable—form of discrimination. Still, women were, for the most part, ignored as abolitionists. The accompanying engraving of a dozen "Eminent Opponents of the Slave Power," [142] produced in 1864, illustrates the point: The nucleus of abolitionists was perceived as a 'white boys' club'.

Where are Harriet Tubman, Sojourner Truth, Frederick Douglass, Jermain Loguen, James McCune Smith, Angelina Grimké Weld, and many more? Even as late as 1956, scholars of history were still looking at abolition as a white men's club; yet, as early as the 1820s, there were black antislavery societies in the Northern states, and many underground railroad supporters were black and/or female.[143] The fact is that black abolitionists and women abolitionists were treated as relatively unimportant in the struggle. At first, even Gerrit Smith opposed women as public speakers. But by 1837, he had changed his mind, and he accompanied the Grimké sisters on speaking engagements in eastern New York.[144] With Gerrit Smith as chair of the American Anti-Slavery Society's annual convention held in New York City in May 1839, the Society voted for the seating of women. The vote was close—184 in favor, 141 opposed—with the victory for women probably influenced by the fact that Gerrit Smith was the presiding officer.[145]

A year later, at the World's Anti-Slavery Convention in London, England, women delegates from the United States were not even allowed to be seated. After a cross-ocean voyage of 20 days, American Anti-Slavery Society delegate Lucretia Coffin Mott had to sit in the spectator gallery as a non-voting observer. In protest, the other three American delegates, William Lloyd Garrison, Charles Remond, and Nathaniel P. Rogers, sat with her.[146] An ironic result was that the convention in London became a catalyst for the women's rights movement in the United States. Mott and her friend, Elizabeth Cady Stanton—also in mute attendance in London—committed themselves to holding a women's rights convention in the United States when they returned. That was the genesis of the 1848 Seneca Falls, New York convention.

When women did speak on abolition, they melded the themes of slavery and women's rights—and often faced heckling and discrimination from men. Angelina Grimké was the first woman to speak before a state legislature on the subject of abolition. It was in Massachusetts on February 21, 1838 when she claimed, "We abolition women are turning the world upside down." The press sometimes called her "Devil-ina," because she blamed northerners for the intense discrimination against both blacks and women. Even some men in the abolition movement tried to gag Grimké, because they feared that juxtaposition of the subjects of women's rights and abolition would detract from the success of the abolition message. When they were warned to allow male abolitionists and ministers to instruct women before speaking, Angelina's sister and fellow travelling speaker Sarah responded, "This I utterly defy. I have suffered too keenly from the teaching of man to lead anyone to him for instruction."[147]

Smith liked and helped the Grimké sisters, and he was disappointed when they stopped their speaking tours.[148] Lucy Stone was once introduced in Massachusetts as "a hen who will attempt to crow." Abby Kelley received death threats, and nearly all female abolitionists were heckled at the rostrum.[149]

One technique at which women abolitionists were successful in the 1830s and 1840s was in the use of petitions. Because women were considered to be outside of the political power structure, petitions to be delivered to legislative bodies became an effective tool for antislavery activity because they gave citizens a sense of participation in democracy and served as aids to organization

"Eminent Opponents of the Slave Power." Engraved by J.C. Buttre, New York. This amazing image was purchased by the author at an antiques fair in nearby Bouckville, NY. See opposite page for identifying caption.

and agitation.[150] The American Anti-Slavery Society reported that 414,471 antislavery petitions were delivered to Congress between May 1837 and May 1838.[151]

Generally, women favored the persuasive approach of Garrison to the political strategy of Smith. Realizing this, Garrison opened a "ladies department" in *The Liberator* in which he allowed women to submit articles for publication. One of their efforts was the establishment of female anti-slavery societies, which by 1834, existed in Massachusetts, Michigan, New York, Rhode Island, Maine, New Hampshire, and Ohio.[152]

That females should have to establish their own organizations in order to have an impact on abolition seems somewhat antithetical, and some women refused to participate. Lydia Maria Child of Wayland, Massachusetts, near Boston, refused to organize such a segregated group or to attend other women's groups' conventions, because she believed their existence repudiated the notion of equal rights. At a young age, Child was a novelist whose writings appalled Boston businessmen but had some influence in turning Wendell Phillips, Charles Sumner, and T. W. Higginson toward favoring abolition.[153] In 1841 she became the editor of *The National Anti-slavery Standard*, the journal of the American Anti-Slavery Society. She followed Garrison's teachings, writing, "It is the misfortune of our country that nearly all its teachings tend to give undue importance to politics, so that men tend to trust in management rather than in principles and calculate contingencies instead of relying on truth."[154]

Child held on to this attitude, which opposed Gerrit Smith's ideol-

---

The engraving on the opposite page includes images of the following (starting clockwise on the outside from the top photo): John Quincy Adams, William Lloyd Garrison, Joshua R. Giddings, Cassius M. Clay, Benjamin Lundy, Owen Lovejoy, Gerrit Smith, William Cullen Bryant, Henry Ward Beecher; (center, second from top) John Greenleaf Whittier; (center, bottom two photos, left to right) Wendell Phillips, Charles Sumner. Tiny text ringing the bottom two photos reads: "Entered according to act of Congress in the year 1864 by O.D. Case & Co. in the Clerks Office of the District Court of the United States for the District of Connecticut."

ogy, for a long time. Almost 20 years later Edwin Morton, a former employee and colleague of Smith who had visited Child in Boston, commented, "Her husband is a great help to her…. He being all fact + logic, while she is all imagination…." He then quipped, "being so long with Child it was strange she should have no children."[155]

Also on the apolitical side was Abby Kelley of Connecticut. Smith, who did not oppose women speakers or persuasive measures, offered Kelley $1,100 to speak for two months in central New York while staying with his family in Peterboro. She feared that he was trying to recruit her for the Liberty Party, so she refused his offer.[156] Kelley was amazed that Smith's desire for immediate abolition, which had caused him to drop out of the Colonization Society, had not kept him from the slow progress of politics. "I… have mourned over the position you have occupied in the warfare for freedom," she wrote him in 1843.[157] In a November 5, 1843 letter to Garrison, she said regarding upstate New York, "There is an inclination among almost all abolitionists to go from us, for they have a strong belief that slavery can be abolished by getting abolitionists in office."[158] In spite of her differences with Smith, Kelley did respect his opinions. Ann Smith wrote to her daughter later that year, "Stephen Foster + Abby Kelley wrote us that they would be here today to discuss antislavery matters with your father."[159]

Elizabeth Margaret Chandler, a Quaker poet and friend of Lucretia Coffin Mott, was also an abolitionist and a Garrison supporter. In 1829 she had edited the "Ladies Repository" section of *The Genius of Universal Emancipation*, an early paper published by Benjamin Lundy and Garrison in Baltimore, Maryland. Because she died in 1834 at age 27, she did not have much contact with Smith, but she faced criticism for encouraging women to become abolitionists. She was one of the first to support the boycott of the products of slave labor, a policy of which Smith approved.[160]

Overall, Smith did not treat the female Garrisonians harshly. He was supportive of their work and thankful for their help in spite of their perception of "a hot conflict with the political demon."[161]

Probably the most fascinating female abolitionist of the persuasion variety to visit Smith in Peterboro was Sojourner Truth. Born Isabella Baumfra, she traveled widely telling people the truth about slavery; hence, her name. In response to a heckler's sexist suggestion that she bare her breasts during a speech, she is reputed to have said, "These breasts have suckled many white children, and the shame is not mine, but yours."[162] Smith liked Truth's direct approach and her ability to get people to listen even though they were tired of hearing political lessons or aristocratic snobs. He supported her work.

There were two female abolitionists heavily influenced by Gerrit Smith who championed the strategy of political action: Susan B. Anthony and Smith's cousin, Elizabeth Cady Stanton. Anthony and Stanton became friends and co-workers in the women's rights movement in the 1850s. One of the biggest contributions of Anthony and Stanton to abolition was their effort through the Women's National Loyal League to gather two million signatures in support of the 13th amendment to the Constitution abolishing slavery.[163]

When it came to women abolitionists, Gerrit Smith supported them no matter what strategy they preferred to use—and in the face of powerful institutional opposition to women's participation in politics or social events. This coincided with his intense, long-term commitment to the abolition of slavery.

- 17 -

Commitment to Abolition

"I love slavery," Gerrit Smith wrote sarcastically to Julia Griffiths in 1857. "It is so useful in revealing character."[1]

This cynical comment accented Gerrit Smith's dedication to the abolition of the "peculiar institution" of slavery. Early in his life—even before his commitment to immediatism—he knew he had to do *something* for the "unhappy children" who had been taken from Africa. One of his first ideas was to establish "a seminary in which to prepare young Africans for the Gospel Ministry."[2] As Smith's ideas matured from the education of blacks, to colonization, and eventually to immediate abolition, he continued to see slavery as a heinous act of one person against another. "Even murder is less a crime than slavery," he wrote to his cousin, Elizabeth Cady Stanton.[3] And death, he thought, would be preferable to slavery.[4]

Abolition was more to him than just a policy for the liberation of slaves. It demanded a deep empathy that went beyond simple pity for slaves and embraced not just charity, but benevolence, a loving kindness toward one's brothers, a generous sharing of whatever bounty filled one's resources. It was a liberal and gracious altruism—or, as Smith might put it, a humane quality of heart and head. He embraced these feelings to the point that at times he felt himself to be "colored."[5]

Smith was not interested in the argument that referred to slavery in terms of states' rights versus federal power. He was more concerned with the moral aspects of slavery—good versus evil, justice versus injustice. Divinely given natural rights, he reasoned, had to be universal, so he based his opinions on principles that appeared to him to be perfectly clear. In the case of slavery, he said, "there are certainties, gracious certainties, on which it is my privilege to rely."[6]

One of the weaknesses of Smith's thinking was that he believed everyone should—or at least *could*—see things the same way he did. People needed only to use the power of reason to see natural truths. In an early letter to John Quincy Adams, Smith described the likely result if Congress should abolish slavery in the District of Columbia.

> "Is Southern conscience so petrified, that it would be entirely unmoved by the solemn declaration of Congress, that the relation of slaveholder and slave is so repugnant to all relationships + so wicked that, at whatever hazard of consequences, it must be immediately broken up? I cannot think it."[7]

Believing this, Smith, in his early days, still believed in a peaceful end to slavery, and he committed himself to helping its achievement. He said to Adams, "I feel [it] my duty to labor to avert a vengeful, and to secure a merciful, removal of the great curse of my country...."[8] His subsequent actions gained for Gerrit Smith a national reputation.

As early as 1835, just after Smith had adopted immediate abolition as his philosophy of action, he was developing a widespread reputation as an important abolitionist. Ray Potter, a relatively unknown abolitionist, wrote from Pawtucket, Rhode Island, "It is not likely that you have much knowledge of me, but I have of you; so you need not be surprised that I write you.... You are known, sir, extensively—and how great is your responsibility."[9] Smith took this responsibility so seriously that it obsessed him to the point that he wondered if his commitment was too high.

> "I am by no means sure, that my own breast had not had some experience of fanaticism on the

subject of slavery. I have felt very strongly and sometimes perhaps fanatically + wildly, in view of the measureless wrongs to which slavery subjects its victims."[10]

In a dispute with Hamilton College over its stand on slavery, he asked that the college elders not consider him slanderous, but to attribute his words to

"antislavery fanaticism…. Say, if you please, 'Gerrit Smith is not an intentional wrong doer: —but on the subject of slavery, he is crazy:' Say so— + I'll be content—for perhaps my intense and long continued interest in the cause of the slave has given a noise of insanity to my poor brain."[11]

Unfortunately for Smith, the public believed his own assertion that he was "crazy." Reporting on an antislavery convention in Cazenovia, New York in 1850, *The Chittenango Phenix* noted, "A business committee was appointed consisting of crazy Gerrit Smith, two males and two females."[12] The reporter considered him so contrary that he differentiated him from the "males" and "females." Smith's annotation on this clipping reads: "Even in my own County I am regarded as crazy."

Smith's friend, Boston abolitionist Thomas Wentworth Higginson, recognized that true reformers were nonconformists who raised the ire of society. "Thus it is that the insane cling to those who, though really sane, are content to be called crazy…." Wendell Phillips also acknowledged that the reformers were persecuted not "because they were crazy, but because they were known not to be."[13]

Not surprisingly, Smith considered this public perception of him as crazy to be a liability. When Syracuse abolitionist Samuel J. May requested his membership on an antislavery committee, he declined, claiming that he would "be an unwelcome co-worker. They look upon me to be fanatical, intolerant, visionary. They expect evil, and only evil, from my efforts."[14] Years earlier, When Smith was scheduled to speak at an antislavery meeting in Ithaca in April of 1837, the following poster appeared in the city:

"DOWN WITH ABOLITION
Fellow citizens, A foul Abolitionist; a
'Child of the Devil,' will hold forth
today at the Presbyterian Church,
at 11o'clock A.M. Let every good
citizen attend to KEEP ORDER. April 27."[15]

Smith annotated his own copy of this poster: "Many copies of this were stuck up in Ithaca the morning of the day I spoke there in Apl 1837." Clearly, abolition was not a popular subject. "To be an abolitionist in America is to be hated and persecuted 'for righteousness sake,'" Smith wrote to The Right Honorable Daniel O'Connell, MP, Lord Mayor of Dublin, Ireland.[16] O'Connell had written to Smith regarding reports he had read of the bad habits of American abolitionists, so Smith reassured him that all abolitionists were not to be judged by a few.

He was often upset with newspaper reports of his endeavors; he once wrote to Lewis Tappan with a touch of humor, "What a world of reports this is! I find two of a curious character on my return home—One is, that I have quit the abolitionists! The other is that I am about to join the Baptists!!"[17] But probably the most frequent— and perhaps the most accurate—reports of his public behavior had to do with his intense empathy.

Smith had a reputation for being empathic. He considered it one of his grandest compliments, receiving messages to its effect even from those who opposed him. William Lloyd Garrison called him "the tried friend, generous and eloquent advocate, and...intrepid supporter of the colored race universally."[18] John McDougall, a New Orleans resident, wrote Smith that he had always viewed abolitionists "as the embodiment of offensive Puritanism characterized by... the Garrisonian view...instead of the milder...judicious + really humane light in which you do view it." McDougall had seen Smith speak in Chicago, and he went on:

> "Instead of the [odious abolitionist], I was
> agreeably reminded of (pardon me) our good, old,
> wholesouled, portly, manly + generous looking
> country gentleman.... In a word, I liked you,
> + like you the more, + thousands of our poor
> unfortunates join with me a heartfelt praise of one
> of nature's noblemen who is not afraid nor ashamed
> to speak kindly of + for an unfortunate people."[19]

Smith thought well of all people—even slaveholders—and when others realized this, they had a greater tendency to listen to what he had to say. His empathy ran deep, and his hope was that his example would teach others of the value of good feelings instead of vengeful ones. One person close to him who had difficulty overcoming prejudice was his wife, Ann. While in Philadelphia in the winter of 1836, she wrote to Gerrit about her black friend:

> "Miss Fortin was here yesterday, and I found
> myself in a perfect tremor for the fear that some of
> my aristocratic friends would call before she left.
> This feeling makes me despise myself, and I trust
> that it may soon be conquered...."[20]

Evidently she did conquer it, as she became a gracious host to reformers at Peterboro for four decades, and there is evidence that both Ann and Elizabeth contributed to the support of antislavery work.[21]

One source of support for Smith that was delicious to him came from Frederick Douglass, who liked Smith's ideas and frequently printed Smith's writings in his paper. "My readers love the slave, love the truth, and love Gerrit Smith, the friend of both," Douglass wrote to Smith.[22] When Smith became ill in 1857, Douglass was afraid that he might die, and he expressed elation at his eventual recovery.

"In behalf of my woe smitten people and the
thousands to whom your life is precious I thank
God that you have been raised up from your recent
illness…. Your life has been a blessing to all classes
and conditions of men, but to none more than
those who are now meted out and trodden down
in slavery."[23]

Douglass dedicated his autobiography to Smith in order "to
couple my poor name with a name I love and honor."[24] Perhaps Julia
Griffiths best noted Smith's empathy.
"He possesses all the virtue and high… principle of
an uncompromising abolitionist…. Every despised,
oppressed and injured son of Africa finds in Gerrit
Smith a kind and sympathizing brother."[25]

Another staple of Gerrit Smith's life was his reputation for persistence. Even in the face of harrowing frustrations, he plodded on in
agreement with the popular proverb, "Persistence and determination
alone are all powerful." Had he heard Winston Churchill say "Never
give in, never give in, never, never, never, never,"[26] he would have
applauded. He was dismayed with the internal rivalry among abolitionists, but he did not give up, attempting several times to unify
them. He was disappointed with the poor showing of the Liberty
Party, but he did not give up, plugging for its major goals through
the Liberty League. The proslavery stand of churches disheartened
him, but he did not give up on the potential for Christianity to effect
abolition, even starting the non-sectarian Church of Peterboro. He
abhorred the action of political parties for nominating and of voters
for electing proslavery candidates, but he did not give up, allowing
himself to be drafted as an independent candidate and elected to
Congress in 1852. He was disheartened that opposition to abolition
was strong in the North, but he did not give up, contributing morally and financially to abolition until the Civil War.

In his own words, "Let us ever remember, that our power consists in our principles—and that our persevering adherence to those principles—to every hair's breadth of them—will alone assure us success."[27]

Titus Gilbert, a former neighbor and colleague, wrote from Ohio that reform movements "might not have been commenced… and… might not in any other person find so strong, and so determined an advocate."[28]

Gerrit Smith's commitment to reform—especially abolition—was uncompromising. He would not deter from or dilute a goal that he perceived as being right and just, even in the face of entrenched prejudice and public opposition. One example of this was his determined support for the formal education of blacks.

Smith was motivated to support education for two reasons. First, as far as he was concerned, state supported schools were producing infidels. And second, blacks needed to be educated in order to have an equal chance to succeed.

George Washington Gale, a former Presbyterian pastor who supported the religious revivals sweeping through central New York, established the Oneida Institute in Whitesboro, New York in 1827. Gale organized the institution to educate new ministers quickly, and when Beriah Green became its president in 1833, he made it an interracial educational institution.

Smith approved of this daring move toward equality, and he gave financial support to Green's efforts.[29] The school for black males that Smith started in Peterboro only operated for a couple of years in the mid-1830s, and even after it had closed, Smith received letters from reformers offering to help provide students for it.[30] In 1839, Oberlin College was interracial and had begun teaching radical reform principles, but it was in financial trouble when Smith donated $2,000 and 21,000 acres of land.[31]

Smith's commitment to abolition and education was the reason for his withdrawal of support from his alma mater, Hamilton College. Personnel there refused in 1839 to sanction student antislavery activities, an action Smith perceived as "insensible to the sin and miseries of slavery."[32] A few years later, when Dartmouth College decided to admit black students, Smith sent them a $100 donation to show his approval.[33]

His reputation supporting the education of blacks spread, so institutions in need appealed to him. Angelina and Theodore Weld operated the Eagleswood School, a small liberal arts school in New Jersey that was open to all. They asked Smith to help pay their bills and to support some needy students. He did so.[34] A school for blacks in New York City had already received donations of $100 each from Frederick Douglass and Jermain Loguen when its administrator, Bob Hamilton, solicited a similar donation from Smith.[35]

In 1863, Smith was asked if he would support the establishment of a "seminary for educating Colored Teachers" in the Peterboro building that had previously housed Smith's school for black men.[36] Finally, in the spring of 1874, just months before his death, he was supporting two colleges for free blacks in Virginia (one of which was the Hampton Institute, a school established in 1867 by the American Missionary Association), and had planned a trip to visit them.[37]

Smith's commitment to black education reflects his conviction that free blacks could not simply be let go into American society and be treated with equality without some training.

Smith regarded himself as an advisor on abolition, and he seldom missed a chance to enlighten both the public and the elite. On a packet boat trip from Utica to Schenectady in 1836, he noted, "The boat was so crowded that no berths were made…. We had to sit or stand all night. When the evening was far spent it was proposed to discuss abolition the remainder of the night…." A fair speculation is that this was Smith's proposal. "When daylight broke upon us… the vote was taken, + [was] gloriously for abolition—49 fanatics to 20 some."[38]

He took it as his responsibility to inform those whom he perceived as mistaken in their views on abolition. When a wealthy resident of Cazenovia appeared to be backsliding regarding abolition, Smith advised him, "If… you have been led in an evil hour, to take a single step in that crooked way which results in open apostasy from the cause of the perishing slave, let me beseech you to pause, and to look up to God for wisdom…."[39] To Kentucky abolitionist Cassius Clay, Smith advised, "there are some defects in… the type of your abolition…. We much desire that your abolition should be more prompted by pity for the slave + less by your love of Kentucky…."[40]

Smith's proslavery relative, George Fitzhugh, asked for advice on slavery in a series of letters to Smith written between 1850 and1852. Fitzhugh thought slavery was a benevolent institution, as he was prejudiced against the blacks' innate ability to become citizens. His sociology was not just a defense of slavery, but an attack on democratic institutions and human rights.

Through proscription and cruelty, the South's 'Slave Power' conspired to rule the Union via a two-class system of oppression, and the abolitionists would have nothing to do with it. Fitzhugh wanted to learn about the abolitionist perspective, saying to Smith, "I am sincerely anxious to retain your good opinion—at least that you should still think, my heart if not my head, right."[41] By July 29, 1852, it appeared that Smith's advice had had some influence on Fitzhugh, who said, "I learned some important truths… that the [proslavery people] wish to keep the sufferings of the Blacks from their sight."[42]

Perhaps Smith's most daring bit of advice was to the black people themselves. "Friendly whites" he said,

> "may help diminish the obstacles in the way of the
> redemption of the colored people of this country;
> —but the colored people must themselves work out
> their own redemption.... The free colored people
> of this country have lost their self-respect…. The
> oppressors of my colored brethren… will never…
> relax their oppressions, and restore the rights they
> have plundered until they have come to respect

those brethren; —and this will never be, until
the free portion of those brethren have come to
respect themselves…. Could I but get the ear of my
Northern colored brethren… I would say to them:
'Cultivate self-respect—cultivate self-respect—
cultivate self-respect.'"[43]

Frederick Douglass voiced agreement with Smith on this point.
He wrote to Smith in 1851,

"I have often felt that what the colored people want
most in this country is… self reliance, and this
we must have or be like all other worthless things
swept away before the march of events."[44]

The scores of invitations to antislavery meetings that Smith received underscored the value of Smith's opinions on abolition.

Smith enjoyed speaking in public, and often called the meetings
himself. His commitment to abolition kept the issue before the
public—especially locally. His young daughter once referred happily
to her father's return from an antislavery address that he delivered
in Binghamton,[45] and Betsey Kelty spoke of Gerrit as having "had a
hard Abolition Campaign. He was almost worn out with speaking
outdoors + riding at night…."[46]

In December 1841 he called an antislavery meeting at which
he would speak in Peterboro, and another in nearby Clockville on
February 3, 1842. He held these meetings "to arouse our friends
in the County to greater efforts to sustain the Mad. Co. Abolitionist…."[47] Also in 1842, the Executive Committee of the American
and Foreign Anti-Slavery Society appointed him as a delegate to
the World's Anti-Slavery Convention in London, to be held June
13, 1843.[48] He declined the honor, claiming "that the state of my
property concerns will not allow me to leave the country."[49]

Smith's oratory was in such demand that when he turned down
an invitation, people got very upset with him. Having refused a

speaking invitation in Boston, Smith received a terse reply from abolitionist Senator Charles Sumner of Massachusetts:

"Pardon me, but I do not see on what grounds
you can be excused from a public lecture…. Your
presence would give character and weight to our
cause…. You excuse yourself on account of your
many engagements…but we have a right to expect
you to make the necessary sacrifice. You are rich +
can afford it."[50]

But Smith felt that he had the *right* to refuse, and the criticisms did not seem to bother him. His antislavery speaking schedule was still considerable; he relayed his itinerary for one week of January 1865 to his daughter. "I am to leave early tomorrow + to be gone for a week speaking in Rome, Utica, Oswego + Syracuse."[51]

An example of the whole Smith family's commitment to abolition was their "abstinence from the products of slave labor." He wrote to Lewis Tappan in 1836, "Mrs. Smith and I have for the past year been convinced, that such abstinence was our duty, and have practiced accordingly."[52] New Jersey Quaker John Woolman first introduced abstinence as a policy in the 1770s. Soon after the American Revolution, the Pennsylvania Society for Promoting the Abolition of Slavery, with Benjamin Franklin as its first president, encouraged abstinence from products made by slaves.

Gerrit Smith agreed that the boycott would be a way to extricate one from participating in slavery, while at the same time putting economic pressure on slave holders. He wrote in 1836 that there was probably nothing

"which abolitionists could do that would contribute
so far to the abolition of slavery as their abstinence
from the products of slave labor. Let 100,000 men
and women in this nation avow and adhere to their
noble determination never to pollute their lips or
their persons with that which is wet with the tears

and stained with the blood of the 'innocents,' and I
believe, that the testimony of such self-denial would
carry more conviction to the minds of slaveholders
of the truth and power of antislavery doctrines and
of the sincerity with which they are held, than all
the testimony of types and pens."[53]

Slave labor yielded products such as cotton, sugar, rice, and
tobacco. Abstaining from the latter two probably posed little inconvenience for the Smiths, but shunning cotton and sugar took
a bit of creativity. Even when away from home, Elizabeth would
proudly write of how she managed to avoid "slave sugar." While in
Rochester, she told how "Aunt Rebecca has been very kind to me,
and has got me some other sugar." And again, "We had a very nice
tea…with free sugar."[54] While in Philadelphia, she wrote "Papa" of
patronizing an antislavery bakery. "They have some of the candy
in small pieces put in paper and a motto wrapped up with them. I
will copy some of the mottos.
  'Roast your slave coffee as you will,
  It smells and tastes of slavery still.'
  'I like to buy Sharpler's good candies and cakes,
  For free is the sugar of which he them makes.' "[55]

Abstaining from the use of slave-produced cotton posed a greater
problem for the Smith family. Their expense records of the late 1820s
show frequent purchases of muslin, a cotton cloth used by many
families in large amounts for the making of bed sheets, petticoats,
curtain linings, and dresses.
  Lewis Tappan thought the 'abstinence' idea was such a good one
that he proposed that Smith, with Tappan and William Goodell's
cooperation, "commence an association whose motto shall be 'total
abstinence from the products of slave labor'…."[56]
  Smith tried to make the boycott international. In 1839 he wrote
to Thomas Howell Buxton, who had worked with William Wilber-

force to achieve the 1833 abolition of slavery in England and its colonies:

> "If Great Britain will do what she can to
> discountenance the consumption of the products
> of slave labor,… she will strike fatal blows at
> American slavery."[57]

Cotton produced entirely by non-slave labor was difficult to find, so most sympathizers to the abolitionist cause probably ignored abstinence. Even Smith did not push very hard for it, and he showed little interest in the American Free Produce Association when it was established in 1838. When the American Anti-Slavery Society failed to endorse abstinence, the policy faded away.[58]

Smith expressed his sincere commitment to abolition most effectively with the way he financed the movement, focusing mainly on two areas. First, he financed the people who supported abolition. The majority of his money went directly to abolitionists, who he saw as the leading crusaders in the cause. Second, Smith financed the purchase of slaves. His primary tactic to influence the course of events was gifts of money. By the mid-1840s, according to his own estimate, he had already contributed over $50,000 to the antislavery movement.[59]

He said of the abolitionists to whom he sent money,

> "The large landed estate which my father left me, it
> has ever been my purpose to use in benefiting and
> blessing my fellow men…. I recognize no stronger
> claim on the property in my stewardship than is
> theirs, who are seized, imprisoned, tortured…
> for the offense of endeavoring by peaceful means
> to deliver their fellow men from the horrors of
> slavery."[60]

Smith wrote checks to defray the travelling expenses of abolitionists William Goodell and John Thomas,[61] and he sent Elizur Wright of the American Anti-Slavery Society $100 as a "loan."[62] He annotated a letter to Wright with, "Keep this as evidence that he owes me $100.00—for which, however, he is never to be pressed. He is a noble man." William Lloyd Garrison wrote in approval of Smith's donation of $100 to William Powell, "a true and clear-sighted abolitionist" who was starting a business in New York City as a druggist.[63]

One abolitionist who consistently received large gifts of money from Smith was Frederick Douglass. Having escaped from slavery in 1838, Douglass became self-educated with superb literary skills. When his paper, *The North Star,* merged with the *Liberty Party Paper* in 1851 to become *Frederick Douglass' Paper,* Smith agreed to fund it at the rate of $100 per month.[64] Douglass described it as "a paper devoted to the cause of Human Rights," which "holds Slavery to be a sin and crime, to be abolished...."[65] As the only journal in the country owned and edited by a black person, it supported immediatism and radical views, often publishing material written by Smith.

Douglass, however, refused to publicize Smith's monetary contributions for fear that the revelation would offend potential subscribers.[66] In his list of credits for the paper, Douglass named several contributing authors and "Philanthropic white persons," but did not name Smith. As the new Republican Party emerged in the mid-1850s, it attracted former Liberty Party people who had drifted away from Douglass' radicalism. As his paper struggled, he sought Smith's advice concerning what to do. And into the 1860s, Smith kept sending money to support his effort.[67] Smith's gifts of money in support of abolition included a range of recipients, from large organizations to single individuals. He donated over $16,000 in the mid-1850s to agencies that sought to produce a free state in Kansas. He gave $50 to a freed man in North Carolina to help him establish a new life.[68]

In 1821, New York State had passed legislation requiring a black man to own property worth $250 in order to be able to vote.[69] In the mid-1840s, Smith chose a few of the top representatives of the black community to help him pick 3,000 poor black males to receive gifts of 40 to 60 acres of land each, with the understanding that if each developed his land as a farm, it would be worth over $250. The people he chose as his "land agents" were Henry Highland Garnet of Troy, an early advocate of rebellion; Dr. James McCune Smith of New York City, the first black physician in the country; Jermain Wesley Loguen of Syracuse, a fugitive slave who aided over 1,000 other fugitives; Theodore S. Wright, the first black graduate of a theological seminary; and Charles Bennett Ray, editor of *The Colored American* and a stationmaster on the Underground Railroad.

Smith chose these men to lend credibility to his effort to enfranchise blacks. "Since they must become landholders," he wrote to his agents, "that they may be entitled to vote, they will become landholders. Vote they will, for… it is before the vote only, that the tyrants and dastards, who oppress them, will quail."[70] While Smith worked to acquire the vote for a number of free blacks, he was also busy with a more radical move: purchasing slaves from southern slaveholders.

He spoke of "the great delight I take in purchasing the Liberty of slaves…. None of my expenditures of money have brought me more gladness of heart."[71] Smith often spent thousands of dollars to purchase the freedom of slaves, whom he had sent to Peterboro where he could feed them, clothe them, and help them train for and find work. He expected nothing in return from them. "I have not a moral right to receive it," he wrote to slave owner John Thomson Mason of Maryland in 1846. "I am rich, + they are poor and that is reason enough, why I decline to receive it."[72]

Smith continued to help slaves buy their freedom while he was a Congressman in Washington, D.C. In an 1854 account book, he notes: "March 8, 1854—I give Basil Hall to help him buy wife + children—$15.00. March 15, 1854—I give Ellen Lee to help her purchase her liberty—$10.00"[73] In all, there are 26 entries in the account book, totaling $380.

Smith's commitment to the purchase of freedom includes these examples, some even paid for during the depression:

$450 paid to Mr. Woodbin for one slave. "My heart yearns toward him. I want to comfort him—and I want to see him usefully employed at the North."[74]

During 1841, "I have paid the present year between four + five thousand dollars in the purchase of the liberty of slaves."[75]

September 28, 1842, a note in Smith's handwriting: "I buy 9 slaves at $750.00 per slave—$6,750.00."[76]

Five hundred dollars paid to Mr. Davis to purchase one slave called "the captain."[77]

One thousand dollars paid to John T. Mason for the purchase of his slaves.[78]

By 1847, Smith was running low on funds for the purchase of slaves. In response to a request for money to free a slave named Phil, Smith wrote,

"Poor Phil! I should love to be instrumental in effecting his discharge from slavery. But, so loaded am I with similar applications, and so much have I paid recently, in purchasing the liberty of slaves, that I cannot do much toward making a free man of Phil."[79]

Still, he sent $100 to help Phil. And when abolitionist Wendell Phillips requested Smith's help in supporting the fugitive slave George Thompson, he sent Phillips $200.[80]

Smith's most well-known purchase of slaves occurred in 1841. Ann Smith's parents, William and Ann Fitzhugh, had sold their Maryland plantation and moved with some of their family to

Rochester, New York in about 1816. Young Ann's nursemaid, a slave named Harriet Sims, was given to her older brother, James Fitzhugh, as a slave. Harriet married another Fitzhugh family slave named Samuel Russell, with whom she had a family of several children.

When Ann's father, William Fitzhugh, died in 1839, Ann remembered her former nursemaid. She felt guilty about Harriet's status as a slave, and she asked if Gerrit, with his newly developed abolitionist perspective, would find Harriet and purchase her freedom. James Fitzhugh had sold Harriet and Samuel Russell, who were eventually located as the property of slave owner Samuel Worthington in Kentucky. Smith sent an agent, James C. Fuller (an abolitionist from Skaneateles, New York), to Kentucky to transact the business of purchase. The two parties agreed on the price of $3,500.[81] The letter sent by the Smiths to the Russells informing them of their freedom is quoted in full:

> "Dear friends, We have purchased your liberty and
> that of your five children, and paid therefor $3500.
> In addition, we have paid several hundred dollars
> to defray your travelling expenses and those of
> the dear friend James C. Fuller who went for you.
> We now consent to let you occupy until 1st April
> next without rent the small white house opposite
> Mr. Scofield's. The few articles of clothing which
> we let you have and of furniture which consist of
> beds, bedding, table, chairs, etc. etc.—we give you.
> We also give you ten dollars in money. And now
> we say to you that this little outfit is all in the way
> of property, which you are to expect from us. For
> the means of your subsistence hereafter you are to
> look under God to your own industry + frugality +
> prudence. Our advice is, that Samuel should seek
> employment immediately in one of the large towns
> in this vicinity—and that the two oldest girls be
> put into families where they will be fed + clothed

+ educated without any expense to yourselves. We
beg you to be very industrious—and to lay up as
much as you can of your earnings, so that you may
in the course of four or five years be able to buy
a little home for yourselves. But above all, we beg
you to seek the salvation of your own and your
childrens' souls, and to lay up treasure in Heaven.

Your friends,
Gerrit Smith
Ann C. Smith"[82]

Five months later, Smith notified James C. Fuller, "Samuel and his family are well—and they are highly esteemed by us and our neighbors."[83] Descendents of the Russells live in Peterboro today.

Some challenged Smith's purchase of slaves, as an overly expensive way to further the cause. Ezekiel Birdseye said, "The sum is large, probably the same amount expended in some other way might do more good."[84] The antislavery movement could have used financing in other areas: speaking tours for renowned abolitionists who might influence the opinions of many, budgets of antislavery organizations that lobbied legislators, schools that educated whites against racism, or blacks for marketable trades. Lucretia Mott criticized the tactic of purchasing slaves because she believed it to be a pernicious policy that only provided resources to slave holders, who could then buy more slaves.[85]

Actually, the purchase of individual slaves fit Smith's philosophy quite well. He believed in philanthropy on the local level and in directly helping oppressed people. Buying a single slave and bringing that person to Peterboro provided immediate, tangible, visible evidence of success. Smith could see and feel the effects of his money. He always felt a bit guilty about his wealth; giving money directly to people who needed it assuaged some of that guilt and made him feel good.

One can view his purchase of slaves as a move that, although it did not aid the antislavery movement as a whole very much, did

Malvina "Vinny" Russell was the youngest of five Russell children and the last former slave to live in Peterboro, NY. She is seated on the back steps of the Cottage Across the Brook, former home to Gerrit Smith Miller, where the author lives today.

Photo courtesy of the Madison County Historical Society

serve to keep his mind balanced. That is, he was not excessively depressed over unjust social conditions, or excessively anxious over his wealth. His philanthropy was his way of taking care of himself and staying balanced in a chaotic world that was in the process of tearing itself apart.

In addition to the purchase of slaves, Smith also gave money to efforts aimed at helping slaves. In 1846, he offered Josiah Spaulding $250 to help him develop a petition to present to a state governor for the release of men imprisoned for promoting the escape of slaves. When Spaulding refused the money, Smith assured him, "I know you will spend the money judiciously, and I therefore wish you to spend it freely. I love to part with money in such a cause."[86]

A Georgia slave holder, S. W. Magill, had heard that Smith was offering to support slaves if owners would free them and send them to Peterboro. Magill was moving to Ohio, and he needed such aid, so he appealed to Smith.[87] Smith was elated:

"I seldom receive a letter, that produces so much joy in my heart as does your letter.... Could I receive a dozen such letters in the present year, I should be confident that the days of American slavery were well nigh numbered.... Can you not prevail on other masters to send me their servants?"[88]

This was similar to an offer Smith received from a North Carolina slave holder in 1838. He wanted Smith to take his 12 slaves, "give them liberty in your state, grant them some means of education, full religious privileges, superintend their moral habits + keep them from Southern kidnappers + such other villains as may claim them for run-away slaves."[89] Smith usually helped in these cases by setting up the former slaves in situations where they could, in time, provide for themselves. In 1852 he invited 51 freed slaves to Peterboro, offered them his mansion to live in until he could find suitable homes for them, and guaranteed them jobs on local farms or on the wharves in Oswego.[90]

Probably one of Smith's most ambitious ideas was his gift of $50 to S.P. Andrews to develop a plan for raising $100,000 to $200,000 to free 2,000 slaves in Delaware, hoping to make Delaware a free state.[91]

Gerrit Smith was committed to the immediate abolition of slavery no matter what the motives or the techniques, and his tactics were so unconventional that they were bound to draw criticism. Some *slaves* even questioned his intent by refusing the freedom that he had offered to purchase for them, fearing that he was "some cruel slave trader."[92] The riskiest tactic he engaged in during the antislavery movement was his unwavering determination to aid fugitive slaves.

No one will ever know the full extent of Gerrit Smith's activities in aiding fugitive slaves. Runaways kept few diaries and station-masters on the Underground Railroad kept few records, so there is no way to know the total number of fugitive slaves whose hunger for food and freedom was met through Smith's resources. Agents of the Underground Railroad worked quietly close to their homes, so their individual efforts gained little attention in history books. Still, those of us who have always been free can scarcely imagine the importance of those efforts to any one fugitive.

Having escaped his own chains, Frederick Douglass gave us a glimpse of the terror that accompanied the slaves' travels north.

"The motto which I adopted when I started from slavery was this—'Trust no man!' I saw in every white man an enemy, and in almost every colored man cause for distrust: It was a most painful situation; and, to understand it, one must need experience it, or imagine himself in similar circumstances... without home or friends— without money or credit—wanting shelter, and no one to give it—wanting bread, and no money to buy it, ... pursued by merciless men-hunters, and in total darkness as to what to do, where to go, or

where to stay,—perfectly helpless both as to the
means of defense and means of escape,—in the
midst of plenty, yet suffering the terrible gnawings
of hunger,—in the midst of houses, yet having no
home,—among fellow men, yet feeling as if in the
midst of wild beasts...."[93]

Gerrit Smith's empathy allowed him to *feel* these indignities and
to respond as a friend. What Douglass called the "soul-killing effects
of slavery" weighed heavily on Smith, who knew that slaves sang
because they were *un*happy, and that, although he would receive
no renown for being their friend, it was his destiny to help them.
In 1842 he delivered an address to the New York State Abolition
Convention that may have been the first address of an abolitionist
aimed directly at the slaves. In it he encouraged abolitionists to

"use [their] intelligence to promote the escape of
ignorant and imbruted slaves from their prison-
house.... We call on every slave who has the
reasonable prospect of being able to run away from
slavery, to make the experiment."[94]

Fugitives wandered into Peterboro with thinning muscles, broken
spirits, and scarred backs. Their conditions testified so clearly to the
brutality of the institution of slavery that Smith could not watch
idly; he had to help them gain freedom. He told Douglass, "There
is nothing that is in my eye more unequivocally the work of Satan
than casting back into the pit of slavery the poor brother or sister
who has escaped from it."[95]

If it was not enough for Smith to feel the slaves' anguish; his
abolitionist friend in Tennessee, Ezekiel Birdseye, sent him long
accounts of his own experiences. Birdseye wrote of a slave whose
owner "thought him extremely unreasonable" for having run away
because he had "always endeavored to treat him kindly...." The slave
was "ungrateful for it," and was probably suffering more for having

run away, according to the owner. Birdseye closed the letter by noting of the slave, "He reasoned, no doubt, differently."[96]

Freedom was such a powerful force that it drew people to it in the face of death. Birdseye wrote about an escaped slave,

> "I had… conversation with him about his winter
> residence in the mountains and said to him,
> 'I suppose you must have suffered much.' He
> said, 'I did… but it was but a trifle to the idea of
> [slavery].'"[97]

And of a slave who had spoken with two visitors from New York, he said, "The Negro gave the best attention and a few days after was off… direct to the free states."[98] Such stories drove Smith onward. He often bought the freedom of fugitive slaves. He also requested papers of manumission from owners for slaves who had arrived at Peterboro. When these were received, he would offer the owner monetary compensation.[99]

In one celebrated fugitive slave case, Smith traveled to Canada in mid-winter to act as a lawyer in defense of a runaway accused of murder in the United States. William Anderson had escaped from slavery in Kentucky and was headed for Canada when his owner captured him. Anderson killed him and fled to Canada. When Kentucky attempted to extradite Anderson to the United States under the provisions of the 1842 Ashburton Treaty, Smith objected and took up Anderson's defense. He argued that because neither the U.S. Constitution nor the Ashburton Treaty (which had settled a boundary dispute between the two countries) recognized the legitimacy of slavery, authorities could not demand the surrender of a fugitive slave. His argument won.

Loring Fowler, a lawyer and a friend of Smith, wrote after Smith's successful defense, "[Your defense] is a close, well reasoned + powerful argument. It is not only well reasoned, but unanswerable…. It will inaugurate a great change in the public opinion as to the rights of slaves…."[100]

Smith realized the gravity of his argument, which defied his own government's laws against aiding fugitive slaves. He said in his speech in defense of Anderson, "And the slaves' friends, the abolitionists of my country... may yet need Canada for a retreat.... For we know not what is in store for us."[101]

> "We may all, in less than a year, be in a dungeon
> for assisting a fugitive slave. I for one am ready to
> go. I shall do my duty. Let the end be what it may, I
> am ready to meet it."[102]

Another risky move for Smith involved his participation in the Jerry Rescue, which occurred in Syracuse on October 1, 1851. It has become a well-known and celebrated case of private citizens—black and white—resisting the enforcement of the federal Fugitive Slave Law of 1850.

The real significance of the rescue of fugitive slave Jerry Henry, however, is more political than social: although the abolitionists involved were concerned about the individual civil rights of Jerry, they were more concerned with sending a message to all that civil disobedience of a law perceived to be unjustified and unconstitutional was legitimate.

Before the rescue of Jerry Henry took place, Smith set the tone at a planning meeting. He supposed that a local commissioner appointed to enforce the 1850 law might release Jerry following the initial hearing of his case. Smith worried that

> "the moral effect of such an acquittal will be as
> nothing to a bold and forcible rescue. A forcible
> rescue will demonstrate the strength of public
> opinion against the possible legality of slavery, and
> this Fugitive Slave Law in particular. It will honor
> Syracuse and be a powerful example everywhere."[103]

Evidently, Smith directed the rescue, which he and his men staged for dramatic effect. Several rescuers blackened their visible skin to take on the appearance of black men, then used a battering ram to gain forcible entry into the building where Syracuse police were holding Jerry. They intended that their makeup would create the illusion that blacks were the villains in the eyes of pro-slavery interests. This technique is reminiscent of the tactics used by those who perpetrated the Boston Tea Party; that is, in an effort to resist tyrannical authority, private citizens adopted a recognizably faulty disguise in order to humiliate those in power.

In order to provoke further humiliation of public authorities, some Syracuse women connected with the abolition movement sent thirty pieces of silver to James R. Lawrence, the government's prosecuting attorney in the Jerry Rescue case.

These classic accusative techniques cast those charged with law enforcement in the Judas-like role of traitors to a higher cause, thus molding public opinion in favor of abolition. The "rescuers" succeeded in splashing the issue of slavery all over the national press by resisting federal law with a flourish.

According to Smith, Jerry told him, "I will never go back into slavery—I will have every bone in my body broken first."[104] Smith, Samuel May, and Charles Wheaton were indicted for treason for participating in the event, but they were not convicted,[105] and for several years thereafter, Smith presided over and spoke at annual celebrations of the rescue.

The significance of the Jerry Rescue was huge for Smith: it demonstrated his open defiance of a Federal Law that he perceived to be unjust. This defiance also characterized the long-term use of Smith's Peterboro home as a station on the Underground Railroad. Contrary to popular belief, "stationmasters" were usually not clandestine about their operations. Smith issued "an open invitation to slaves to come to Peterboro," publicly stating his intent to aid their escape and making his house "an important station for runaway slaves."[106] He knew the risks, but he thought them to be worth taking.

Proslavery spies were sometimes sent to Peterboro to watch Smith's house for the arrival of runaways, and slave owners offered bounties as high as $2,500 for the assassination of "stationmasters" and "conductors," those who aided escaping slaves.[107] Although the Underground Railroad provided a successful escape to freedom for only a small number of slaves, its symbolic value became legendary. The quest for freedom was the main principle upon which the nation was built, and the Underground Railroad conveyed a moral message to all people. It mixed individual courage and loosely organized assistance into a form of guerrilla action that threatened the stability of southern culture.

In *Uncle Tom's Cabin*, Harriet Beecher Stowe eloquently portrayed the escape of the slave woman Eliza and her son. As did many slaves, they left behind everything they had known for the unknown, displaying not only courage, but also determination, persistence, and an intense desire for justice and freedom.[108] Hailed as the greatest book of its age, *Uncle Tom's Cabin* enraged slaveholders, as much as did the openly defiant attitude of northern stationmasters. Use of the Underground Railroad contradicted the slaveholders' claims that blacks were content with their lives on the plantation. And the success of former slaves at establishing new communities and finding productive work in the North and in Canada disproved southern racist claims of genetic inferiority.

A major impetus for the Underground Railroad was the prohibition of the international slave trade in 1807. This meant an increase in the domestic slave trade and in the breeding of slaves for sale. Because they were uncertain that they would spend their lives in the comparatively stable service of one owner, slaves had an added incentive to escape. Although the first Underground Railroad activity occurred in Pennsylvania during the opening decades of the nineteenth century, it did not become used extensively until the 1830s. Pennsylvania in the early 1800s offered runaways proximity to the slave states and the presence of Quakers willing to help escapees. Then in the 1830s, William Lloyd Garrison's *The Liberator* appeared, antislavery societies sprang up at all levels, and speakers traveled the northern circuit, demanding immediate abolition.

Gerrit Smith responded to the call with an enthusiasm that persisted for over three decades.

> "If I refuse to unite with my neighbors in concealing a poor innocent brother from the monsters, who would plunge him into the pit of slavery: —if I withhold my horse, or carriage, or driver, and refuse to unite with my neighbors in aiding his flight from these monsters—then, most certainly do I trample on my manhood, and deny my God."[109]

He wrote to William Seward, "For many years I have regarded the helping of slaves to liberty, especially at the great peril of the helper, as among the most beautiful expressions and among the most decisive evidences of disinterested benevolence and genuine piety."[110] For Smith, being an Underground Railroad station master was a way to transform individual moral duty into action. It allowed him to put faith and prayer to practical use in the tangible accomplishment of a moral goal. He was an effective station master for two reasons: his wealth and the geography of New York State.

In the early 1800s, most of the United States population lived in New England, the Ohio Valley, and the Central Piedmont area of New Jersey, Delaware, Maryland, and Virginia. New York State was heavily populated in the western and southeastern regions, but only sparsely so in its central area. This was due in part to the natural geographic features of the state: the Catskill Mountains cover much of the south-central portion of New York, while the Adirondack Mountains occupy the north-central territory. Travel through these areas was difficult 200 years ago, so travelers followed the Hudson River Valley north from the coast, and then westward through the central corridor of flat, arable land that separates the Catskill and Adirondack Mountains.

The other major route north led from Binghamton in south-central New York State up the plateau area west of the Catskills to the Syracuse/Utica area, where it intersected the east-west central corridor. At this juncture, halfway between the cities of Syracuse and Utica, were Peterboro and Gerrit Smith.

The southeastern Pennsylvania area developed more routes on the Underground Railroad than any other area of the United States,[111] with three routes coming from the Maryland border and converging at the Phoenixville home of stationmaster Elijah F. Pennypacker. From there, two routes went north, one east of the Catskills and one west of the Catskills "to Gerrit Smith at Peterboro in Central New York." The station at Peterboro was particularly important, as the more western route north from Elmira was not established until 1844.[112]

Western New York State had many routes leading to the Niagara area, but only two major routes traversed the central area of the state, coming from Albany and from Binghamton and converging at Peterboro. From Peterboro, three overland routes led north. One led west to Syracuse, then on to Niagara and Canada. A second went northwest to the Mexico/Oswego area, and then across Lake Ontario by boat. The third led north to Cape Vincent at the junction of Lake Ontario and the St. Lawrence River, and then to Kingston by boat.[113]

At Oswego, Smith's business agent John B. Edwards, also an abolitionist, was charged by Smith to aid fugitive slaves sent to him from Peterboro. In one case Edwards wrote to Smith, "The Fugitive Slave Dorsey came to me today with your letter. I have just put him aboard of a vessel bound for Canada + gave him $1.00"[114]

Fugitive slaves found upstate New York to be a hospitable place. Few of the established transportation routes were very well known, and that made it hard for pursuers to follow. The extensive woodlands offered many hiding places. Relatively flat land west and north of the Catskill Mountains offered easy travel, and the Erie Canal provided both travel and job opportunities. Resident Native Americans also offered some help, and station masters were present in most areas.[115]

Gerrit Smith's "station" was especially attractive to fugitives not only geographically, but also psychologically. His attitude toward fugitives was more than just accommodating; he defended their right to escape from unjust oppression by whatever means necessary. He welcomed them into his village not as criminals, but as equal brothers and sisters. He wrote Frederick Douglass in 1860,

> "I would have every slave run away from his
> master; and I would afford him every facility for
> his peaceful escape. I would tell him, as I have
> been telling him these twenty years, to 'take the
> horse, the boat, the food, the clothing;' and to
> believe in no rights of property any where in the
> South as against his needs...."[116]

In return for his aid, Smith imposed some moral conditions on the fugitives in an attempt to ensure that they would be industrious, frugal, and temperate.

Help in Peterboro usually started with the unannounced arrival of a fugitive slave. Fugitives were guided to Peterboro through their earlier stops on the route north. According to one report, "During the years devoted to the running of this [underground rail] road, it was a frequent spectacle to see a negro in the street inquiring the way to Mr. Smith's residence. No matter how pressing his business, Mr. Smith left everything to help these fugitives from bondage to a land of freedom."[117] His daughter Elizabeth, in writing about the "millennial peace and beauty" of a winter frost scene, added, "When our pageant was at its height a poor fugitive, scarred from head to foot, found his way to our doors. A few weeks previous, another had come maimed and branded! No Millennium yet to these poor souls...."[118]

And Gerrit wrote,

> "Yesterday morning a very interesting fugitive
> slave made his appearance at our door.... I had
> an hour's conversation with him. He ate a hearty

breakfast—and having given him what he needed,
money, directions, letters, …I sent him on his way
to Oswego for Canada."[119]

Smith enjoyed his position as an Underground Railroad station
master at the end of the line; that is, the fugitive slave's next stop
was often Canada. This feature fit Smith's *practical* needs very well,
because he could see and feel the immediate results of his efforts and
he believed that he was doing something that was directly effective
in destabilizing the southern slave-holding culture.

Smith took very good care to meet all of the needs of the escapees.
Slaves were comforted mentally and reassured of the rightness of
their decisions. They received counseling on morals and virtues for
a stable, prosperous life, and were given materials they would need
for the continued trip. They received rest and lodging, new clothes,
nutritious food, free transportation to Canada, and enough money
to sustain them until they acquired work there.[120]

A letter from Smith to John Thomson Mason, a slave holder who
had inquired of Smith as to the status of slaves who were fugitives
from his Maryland plantation, illustrated the escape process.

"The slaves called themselves Jack Johnson (the
father), Daniel, Abraham + Franklin (the sons).
They spent a day at my house…. [They said] that
nothing but the fear of their being sold prompted
them to run away…. The slaves represented,
that, on a Saturday morning, they obtained
permission to go to Hagerstown to Church—+
that, instead of going to Hagerstown, they reached
Chambersburgh the next morning. From that
place they came to Harrisburgh, Wilksbarre, +
Binghamton…. They… had… $4.00 when they
reached my house…. I added a few dollars to their
scanty funds, + sent them in my wagon to the Erie
Canal, with directions on whom to call at Syracuse

+ Oswego…. I learnt from Mr. Henry Fitzhugh, a
brother of Mrs. Smith, that they had spent a few
hours at his house [in Oswego], + were very well.
They left Oswego in a Steam Boat for Toronto…. I
obtained strong promises from the slaves, that they
would totally abstain from intoxicating liquors,
would be industrious, frugal, and virtuous…. I
trust, that you need not <u>see</u> their new born liberty
to increase your sense of its value + to increase
your abhorrence of slavery."[121]

Gerrit Smith had so much of this type of direct experience with
fugitive slaves that Harriet Beecher Stowe wrote to him, seeking
data to support the pictures of slavery that she had drawn in *Uncle
Tom's Cabin*. She asked for any statistical support Smith could provide regarding numbers of runaways, separation of black families,
reasons for escape, and numbers of slaves reaching Canada. She also
asked if Smith knew what proportion of slaves escaped for "love of
liberty" as opposed to escaping suffering.[122]

The experience of other station masters in the upstate New York
area was similar. In Rochester, Frederick Douglass and Julia Griffiths
did their part, and in Syracuse, Jermain Loguen and Samuel J. May
served the cause. Griffiths wrote to Smith about one incident.

"On Saturday, three Fugitives… came… to ask
aid…. We secreted them for 8 or 9 hours—clothed
them partially—I fed them…. Mr. Loguen + I
drove to the Landing to make necessary inquiries
concerning Canada Boats…."

Because spies were suspected in the area, "I left him with the
understanding to make a <u>signal</u> if, in the interim, any suspicious
persons appeared…."[123]

One of the most notable persons in the Underground Railroad
with whom Smith had frequent contact was Harriet Tubman. The

number of times that Tubman traveled through Peterboro conducting fugitive slaves to freedom is a matter for speculation, and is probably irrelevant. Her route north usually ran from Maryland or Delaware through Philadelphia and into eastern New York State. From the Albany area she traveled west to the Peterboro/Syracuse area, probably stopping at Smith's residence often. Her presence there can be documented on at least two occasions,[124] and her biographer refers to another: on one of her trips through Peterboro she had no shoes when she arrived at "The Big House." Gerrit's son Greene postponed a hunting trip in order to go to the village and buy her a pair of shoes.[124] She liked the route through the center of the state because it was relatively safe. Her "friends" there were well-financed, experienced, and organized, and the Anti-Slavery Society of New York was strong, so she knew that she could depend on extensive support in this area.[125]

In Peterboro, Harriet Tubman viewed the Smith mansion as "an important station on the Underground. The barn and the kitchen floor were utilized as chambers for the fugitives."[126]

"Maybe so," said Mildred Tucker, a recent African-American resident of Peterboro who worked as a servant in the Smith mansion before it burned on March 2, 1936. "There was," she said, "an area of one of the kitchens where 'the help' was not allowed to go."[127]

Tubman was committed to freedom for slaves to the point that she knowingly risked her own freedom and her life to achieve it. Smith said that she exhibited "a deep and sublime philanthropy."[128] He and Tubman were alike in that they both appreciated practical, individually targeted efforts that led to quick and visible results.

After the Civil War, when Tubman was having difficulty supporting herself financially, Smith underwrote the cost of printing her memoirs so that she would have a source of income. Tubman's book was published in January of 1869.[129] In fact, anyone offering aid to a fugitive slave faced a $500 fine by the federal government, and the laws of some southern states included jail time.[130] One of Tubman's stationmasters, Thomas Garrett, a Quaker in Wilmington,

Delaware, was arrested and fined repeatedly for aiding fugitives who were in the care of Tubman. Garrett said to the judge,

> "Thee hasn't left me a dollar, but I wish to say…
> that if anyone knows of a fugitive who wants a
> shelter and a friend, send him to Thomas Garrett,
> and he will befriend him."[131]

The event that galvanized this level of commitment in the face of legal risk was the passage by the national government of the Fugitive Slave Act of 1850. The territories of New Mexico, Utah, and California had come under U.S. rule following the Mexican War in 1847. Abolitionists worried that these new territories would become slave states, and while the House of Representatives passed the Wilmot Proviso blocking slavery in the territories, the Senate refused to act on the matter. It was obvious there must be an agreement that would satisfy northerners while tightening penalties for fugitive slaves from southern states. The result was the Compromise of 1850, which included the Fugitive Slave Act. It was debated on the legislative floor for 10 months. It held that most of the new territory would be slave-free, while keeping the southerners happy by strengthening the fugitive slave law. The legislature at the time held 112 Democrats (mostly pro-slavery), 105 Whigs (mostly anti-slavery), and thirteen Free Soilers, who held the balance of power.[132]

If signed into law, the Compromise of 1850 would allow federal law enforcement agents to pursue fugitive slaves and those who aided them. This bill was actually an extension to the Fugitive Slave Act of 1793, which legitimized the capture and return to slavery of fugitive slaves and had been declared constitutional twice in state Supreme Court tests.[133]

The threat of prosecution for upholding the national promise of "liberty to all" enraged northern abolitionists, who became convinced that they should oppose with violence if necessary not only the bill, but the law itself should the bill be passed. In spite of the danger of publicizing his views, Smith used the sponsorship of the

New York State Vigilance Committee of which he was president to organize a two-day convention of abolitionists in August in order to protest Congressional debate of the bill.[134]

Cazenovia, New York was chosen as the site for the convention. Located between Syracuse and Utica, both hotbeds of antislavery activity, Cazenovia had a resident population of about 2,000. A previous antislavery convention there in 1842 had attracted "at least two thousand persons."[135] Smith encouraged all northern abolitionists to attend, especially those from New York State.

Held on August 21 and 22, 1850, the convention featured attendees such as Frederick Douglass, Samuel J. May, James Caleb Jackson, Charles B. Ray, and others. One local, long-term abolitionist who did not attend, in spite of Smith's insistent prodding, was Beriah Green of Whitesboro, New York, near Utica. He had had some recent disagreements with Smith and preferred not to attend.[136]

The Cazenovia Anti-Fugitive Slave Law Convention drew about 2,000 persons, overflowing the small Free Congregational Church where it met. Smith invited the conventioneers to continue in Peterboro on the following day, but the suggestion proved to be unnecessary when Grace Wilson, a Cazenovia resident, offered her apple orchard (now on the west side of Sullivan Street, across from Cazenovia College) as a meeting place.[137] Daguerreotypist Ezra Greenleaf Weld (Theodore Weld's brother) produced an enduring record of the convention in the orchard. In attendance were about 50 former slaves, a tribute to the success of the local Underground Railroad network.[138]

Much of the debate at the convention was radical in nature, declaring the U.S. Constitution to be an antislavery document and issuing a "Fugitive Slave Letter," a message to those still in bondage. Smith composed the letter, and he used the same terminology advocating escape by any means necessary that he had used before. Following the convention, local newspapers blasted the participants. The *Madison County Whig* called them "political enthusiasts" and derided them as being too few in number and too insignificant

The Cazenovia Convention picture includes Frederick Douglass (to left of table with elbow on table); Theodosia Gilbert (lady keeping notes at center of table; also identified as Abby Kelley Foster, but Foster may have been in Ohio at the time); Theodore Weld (seated in front of Douglass, to the left of table); Joseph Hathaway (at right end of table taking notes); Mary Edmonson (black woman in shawl behind Gilbert); Gerrit Smith (standing at center, arm out); Emily Edmonson (black woman in shawl to right of Gerrit Smith); George W. Clark (standing just over the right side of Emily Edmonson's shoulder); Samuel J. May (just behind Joseph Hathaway); Charles B. Ray (to the right of May); and James Caleb Jackson (to the right of Ray). Identifications by historian Daniel Weiskotten.   *Photo used with the permission of the Madison County Historical Society*

in influence to have any real power. They were, instead, "simply mischievous"—and a hindrance to responsible discussion of the issue of slavery.

The *Utica Daily Observer* labeled Smith as a bigoted fanatic. The *Buffalo Morning Express* called him "insane," a "madman and knave." The *Syracuse Daily Journal* summed up the convention as "making too much of nothing," and deserving of "oblivion."[139] The protest convention did not prevent the bill from becoming law. And when it did, it triggered radical reactions.

Under the Compromise of 1850, northern citizens were required to assist in the capture and return of runaways, thereby acting as property agents for southern slaveholders. Some northern states passed "personal liberty laws" in an attempt to counteract the effect of the Federal Law. Jermain Loguen howled, "The time has come to change the tones of submission into tones of defiance...."[140] The 1850 law piqued attitudes of resistance and aggression among the abolitionists. As a condemnation of abolitionist activities, the law fostered pro-revolutionary thinking. It was an attempt to silence by government authority the right to free speech, and to settle by means of legal discrimination what was essentially a conflict not otherwise solvable. It sparked a confrontation between authority and ethics that prompted those attending an anti-fugitive slave law conference in Syracuse on January 9, 1851 to state: "It is our duty to peril life, liberty, and property, in behalf of the fugitive slave, to as great an extent, as we would peril them in behalf of ourselves."[141]

The most immediate and profound consequence of the law was its incendiary effect on northern abolitionists. Many people in the North now viewed federal policy as despotic, unnecessary, and reversible. The law temporarily cooled the question of slavery in the expanding territories, but it certainly did not settle the issue. Because it ignored individual rights and elevated property rights, it had the ironic effect of causing more slaves to seek freedom in Canada, a land administered by a government against which the American colonies had themselves fought for freedom.

More Underground Railroad stations opened, and lawyers defended captured fugitives and those who aided them. More money was committed to aiding escapes, black churches and Free Churches formed, and people of the North felt more empathy with blacks. As this activity heated up, slave owners in the northernmost slave states were frightened into selling some slaves deeper into the South.[142] Gerrit Smith became incensed at the new law, but he believed that the intensity of the anger it stirred up would hasten the end of slavery. Shortly after the law was enacted, he wrote to Samuel J. May,

> "This law is but a natural and legitimate trial of slavery—just the occasion for denouncing slavery, …proslavery parties, …proslavery churches, [and] proslavery schools."[143]

In October of 1851 he wrote to the Liberty Party members of Madison County,

> "It was not until after the enactment of the 'Fugitive Slave Law' that I suspected, that the abolition of American slavery is an event near at hand…. Its enforcement serves to increase and intensify the feeling, which… will… break forth irresistibly and overwhelmingly against slavery…. How much short of a pack of hypocritical devils would this Nation prove itself to be, if, after having begun its existence with the declaration that 'all men are created equal,' it should be found hanging some of its subjects for no other reason than their opposing the enslavement of others of its subjects?"[144]

Smith saw more clearly what he perceived to be a problem of social class. "Why… are the American people so ready to give up a black man…? It is because the spirit of caste… is in their hearts…."[145] This spirit, he felt, justified not only the escape of slaves, but also violent slave insurrections. The slaves' cause was a moral one founded in their natural right to equity and justice; therefore, he argued, anyone who thought a proslavery law was fair should be resisted.

After Daniel Webster's May 1851 speech in Syracuse warning anti-slavery radicals that the 1850 law would be enforced, abolitionists reacted defiantly by planning the aforementioned "Jerry Rescue."

The law spawned a series of conventions calling for resistance to it. One such gathering was held for two days in Peterboro in late August of 1850. Julia Griffiths attended, and wrote that the participants met the first day at the Baptist Church, where Frederick Douglass "addressed the assembly for an hour and a half, in his own peculiarly earnest, eloquent, felicitous manner." The second day's meetings were held "in a fine grove, adjacent to 'the old home' of Gerrit Smith in Peterboro."[146]

On October 10, 1850, it was probably Gerrit Smith who had printed an announcement of antislavery meetings to be held in Canastota, Cazenovia, Hamilton, and Peterboro: "None but real men and women are wanted. The sham men and women who can stick to the Whig and Democratic parties are not wanted.... There is no hope of good from persons who can stick to those Devil-prompted parties."[147]

Smith also attended the Liberty Party convention in Syracuse in October 1850, at which the following resolution of resistance was passed:

"Resolved that having been compelled by our manhood and our religion to identify ourselves with these helpless poor, and to defend them even as we would defend ourselves, however imminent the danger of the dungeon or death, we have no other determination but to resist the execution of this diabolical law, cost what the resistance may of property, or liberty or life."[148]

As time passed, the aggressive intent of Anti-Fugitive Slave Law resolutions became more obvious. The January 7-9, 1851 Syracuse convention of the New York State Anti-Slavery Society included this declaration:

> "Resolved, that we pour out upon the Fugitive
> Slave Law the fullest measure of our contempt
> and hate and execration; and pledge ourselves to
> resist it actively, as well as passively, and by all such
> means, as shall, in our esteem, promise the most
> effectual resistance."[149]

An example of this resistance, and an embarrassment to the abolitionists and to the Anti-Fugitive Slave Law Convention of 1850 at Cazenovia, was the "Chaplin Affair." William L. Chaplin was an abolitionist in upstate New York, a friend of Gerrit Smith, and a member of the New York State Anti-Slavery Society. By 1848, he had moved to the Washington, D.C. area to continue his antislavery work, and stayed in contact with Smith who aided his work there. Smith had probably started planning the Cazenovia convention in July of 1850, and against Smith's recommendations, Chaplin signed on by offering to conduct some fugitive slaves to Cazenovia, arriving with them in the midst of the proceedings.[150] This was designed to emphasize the abolitionists' resistance to the Fugitive Slave Law and to give the convention an emotional boost and lots of publicity.

Chaplin aided the escape of two slaves owned by two Georgia Congressmen, Robert Toombs and Alexander Stephens. As he attempted to escort them out of Maryland, District of Columbia police arrested him on August 8 in Rockville, Maryland, and put him in jail with bail set at $25,000.[151] According to one report, he and the two slaves resisted the arrest, and two of the three men were injured.[152] Chaplin was indicted on seven counts—three for assault with intent to murder, two for the larceny of slaves, and two for assisting the escape of slaves.[153]

Smith wrote to Chaplin at the jail, lamenting his arrest and informing him of progress being made toward holding the Cazenovia convention.[154] On the same day, Smith started making plans for collecting bail money for Chaplin. He offered $5,000 toward bail,[155] and claimed that it was all he could afford due to his high debts at the time.[156] He eventually contributed ten thousand dollars to the bail fund.[157]

Smith acted as "treasurer" for the Chaplin bail fund, collecting money for it, and probably contributed even more himself, a fact that his business agent realized when he wrote, "I am sorry it takes such a great sum to bail him from his imprisonment for acts of mercy. The great part of this burden will devolve on you."[158]

In the fall of 1850, Smith received $228 through the efforts of William Goodell.[159] Of the bail fee, Goodell exclaimed, "That villainous demand!... Can it ever be raised!"[160]

Even poor persons sympathetic to the antislavery cause contributed. I. S. Mann, a Potter County, Pennsylvania resident, sent one dollar for Chaplin, saying, "May God give him health + strength to proclaim the sin of slavery through the length + breadth of the land."[161] As of the spring of 1852, Smith was still receiving funds to apply toward Chaplin's bail.

While in jail, Chaplin received visitors who helped him keep a positive attitude. His fiancée, Theodosia Gilbert (seated at the table in the Caz Convention daguerreotype), went to the Maryland jail to see him. "If there is no hope of Mr. Chaplin's immediate release, ...I must be by him," she wrote.[162]

Shortly after the convention, James Caleb Jackson went "to his [Chaplin's] aid and assistance," to stay with him and work to raise bail money.[163] While there, he learned that the Maryland marshals holding Chaplin were delighted with their catch, and hoped it would stem the tide of slaves escaping from Montgomery and Prince George's counties. But Jackson remarked,

> "...dear fellows [slaves], they keep going in droves,
> so that the excitement is kept up.... There are
> persons who... swear without compunction to add
> to the difficulties of his bail."[164]

The "Chaplin Affair" is significant in that it illustrates the commitment of abolitionists to their goal. The hunger for liberty motivated not only those who were oppressed, but those who empathized with them. Smith risked public disapproval, the loss of business connections, arrest, and imprisonment for openly breaking Federal law, capture or death by bounty hunters seeking rewards, family or property damage at his home by proslavery interests, and his wealth. When Chaplin did not return to Washington, D.C. for trial, Smith lost all the bail money he had donated.[165] Still, Smith thought that the potential benefits to society were worth the personal risks. If one took the Declaration of Independence, the Constitution, and Christian doctrine seriously, slavery was an obvious moral and legal infringement on human rights.

By the late 1850s, the intent of Northern states to resist the 1850 Fugitive Slave Law became manifest. In a Wisconsin case in 1859, Sherman Booth was charged with violating the Fugitive Slave Law by helping a slave named Joshua Glover to escape from a Milwaukee jail. Glover had escaped slavery in St. Louis six years earlier and had been living and working in Wisconsin when a federal marshall named Stephen Ableman arrested him. Booth and other abolitionists had stormed the jail in much the same fashion as Smith and others had in Syracuse during the Jerry Rescue.

When the case went to trial, the Wisconsin Supreme Court declared the federal law unconstitutional. And when the U.S. Supreme Court issued to the Wisconsin state court a writ of error, ruling that state courts had no jurisdiction in federal matters, Wisconsin defiantly ignored it. Booth was captured in 1860 and spent the better part of a year in custody in Milwaukee, being set free only after the Civil War had begun.

Even before Wisconsin, states had begun to assert themselves into the debate over the Fugitive Slave Law. The Vermont Freedom Act of 1858 defied the federal law by declaring every person living in or migrating to Vermont to be free.[166] Smith had gone to Congress in 1853 with the hope of having some influence on efforts to

PRACTICAL DREAMER

repeal the Fugitive Slave Law. As his level of disappointment grew in Washington, D.C., he wrote to Frederick Douglass:

> "You ask, if the antislavery cause has anything
> to hope for from the present Congress. It has
> not. What can Liberty hope from a… House of
> Representatives, not fifty members of which dared
> to say, that they were in favor of repealing the
> Fugitive Slave Act?"[167]

Should we consider as radical or eccentric a pattern of behavior that opposes people owning other people as property? The abolitionists' opposition to the Fugitive Slave Law was valid: they were upset with a culture that placed the value of private property and profit above those of justice and freedom, and they were willing to stake their social and economic fortunes on the process of reform. This was a group of secure and optimistic people willing to face the consequences of their actions if it meant they would accomplish their goals. For Smith, the commitment was less a symptom of personal disturbance than of personal security and health.

Another illustration of the level of Gerrit Smith's commitment to securing freedom for his black brothers and sisters was his relationship with and dedication to the activities of fellow abolitionist John Brown.

From John Brown to the Civil War

"I am going to be indicted, sir, indicted! You must not talk to me about it...." Smith said to a *New York Herald* reporter in late October 1859.

The events leading to John Brown's raid on Harpers Ferry and Gerrit Smith's alarmed retort to the *Herald* reporter in 1859 began a decade earlier. By the mid-1850s, tensions between the North and the South were escalating to the point that some even feared that a conspiracy in the South would force slavery on the rest of the country. Congress designed the Kansas-Nebraska Bill of 1854 to allow the new voters of those two territories to decide via popular vote whether their newly proposed states should enter the Union as slave states or free states.

Although the proposal was intended to solve the issue of the expansion of slavery, it actually voided the Missouri Compromise of 1820, which had designated which areas of the western territory could be slave or free states. The new bill represented a collective moral indifference regarding racism.

A major effect of the bill was to activate abolitionists—especially those who had been quiet for a while. William Lloyd Garrison, in a February 14, 1854 speech in New York City, challenged the logic of the extension of slavery by asking if stopping the spread of a cancer would cure it.[1] Angelina Grimké Weld welcomed violence in Kansas as a precursor to the end of slavery. Lydia Maria Child worked to help send free-soil families to Kansas. Theodore Parker and Gerrit

Smith financed Kansas-bound people, weapons, and ammunition. Thomas Wentworth Higginson advocated forming a Kansas militia, and even Henry Ward Beecher—a minister—promoted an armed solution to the Kansas issue.

In all, the struggle in Kansas Territory became a bloody symbol of the ideological divisions in the nation—and a prelude to civil war. What Garrison had called the "parchment lies" of the Constitution were now exposed, as a hypocritical nation denied freedom to some of its citizens—with governmental sanction.[2]

President Franklin Pierce signed the Kansas-Nebraska Bill into law on May 30, 1854, empowering voters in each state to decide their own slave or free status. Abolitionists worried that pro-slavery interests would capture the developing West. They could see several signs of this: The Fugitive Slave Law encouraged incursions of proslavery sympathizers into the North, and the Dred Scott decision of the U.S. Supreme Court denied rights of citizenship to blacks. The country was electing proslavery presidents. Congressman Preston Brooks of South Carolina used a cane to severely beat Senator Charles Sumner of Massachusetts in the Senate chamber after Sumner spoke out against slavery on the Senate floor. Fighting in Kansas for slave-or-free status seemed contradictory to the democratic goals of the Kansas-Nebraska Act, and the Biblical justification of slavery as preached in many churches in both the North and the South helped to activate abolitionists in a growing passion for action and quick results.

Gerrit Smith agonized over any means used to expand slave territory. He argued and voted in Congress against the Kansas-Nebraska Bill, claiming in a later speech that if slavery had a legal right to exist *anywhere*, it had that right to exist *everywhere*.[3] As he searched for a way to oppose slavery in the South—and especially the extension of slavery into new territories—he began to focus on Kansas as the place where slavery might meet its end. He felt that in grasping for more territory, the proponents of slavery might exhaust its welcome and cause it to die—especially if he could marshal resources against

it in Kansas. For Smith, those resources included his own money—
and a radical agent who was willing to carry the fight against slavery
into the field in Kansas. That agent was John Brown.

The relationship between Gerrit Smith and John Brown was an
unlikely one. Because in social life like usually attracts like, it is
a wonder that the two men ever forged a bond. Smith was a successful and wealthy businessman; Brown had failed at most of his
attempts at business and was perpetually poor. Smith was a tall,
baronial figure with a college degree; Brown was small, unremark-
able, and unlettered. Smith, for most of his life, advocated political
action and peaceful solutions to issues; Brown was apolitical and
aggressive, and opted for violent solutions. As Smith matured, he
became more empathetic with blacks, and like them, he saw slavery
as a state of war. Blacks, of course, always knew this and understood
that it would take war to eliminate their bondage. Smith came to
agree and to see the use of violence as a necessary weapon in the
abolition of slavery.

For Brown and Smith, their common ground rested in their vision
of a free, just, and equitable society. As Smith became increasingly
frustrated with politics and persuasion as effective agents of social
change, he turned toward the support of one who was willing to
install a growing radicalism in an aggressive manner.

Their first meeting occurred in 1848. Brown's father, Owen, was a
trustee at Oberlin College. He told John, who was in need of money
and ideas for his crusade against slavery, of a wealthy abolitionist in
Peterboro, New York who had donated land to the college.[4]

On April 8, 1848 Brown arrived in Peterboro, intent on persuading Smith that he could mentor the blacks in the skills of farming
on land that Smith had donated to free blacks near Lake Placid.
Brown later commented that he found Smith to be "a little naïve, a
somewhat open and pleasant country gentleman who could afford
to subsidize his own opinions."[5]

Smith's clerk, Caleb Calkins, penned an account of that meeting:
"The result of their interview was the removal of Brown + his family

to Essex Co. He became there the father + friend of [Smith's] little colored colony.... Brown + [Smith] became bosom friends—strongly attached to each other + continued until Brown's death."[6]

Having grown up in the Calvinist tradition, John Brown thought in absolutes, one of which—consistent with Smith's thinking—was inalienable, natural human rights. Franklin Sanborn, a Boston educator and abolitionist who was a friend of Smith, saw Brown as one of "a small and fast-dwindling band of men and women who... years ago resolved that other persons ought to be as free as ourselves. Many of this band made sacrifices for the cause of freedom—the freedom of others, not their own." Sanborn described Brown with a superb analogy: Brown, he said, saw the cancer that was destroying the nation, understood the surgery necessary to remove it, and "had the force and nerve to make the first incision."[7]

Brown's search for the resources to make that "incision" landed him in Smith's office. But if Smith had not been willing to offer his support, it is not likely that Brown would have been deterred. He considered his course to be right and destined for success, and he blamed his past failures on others who either had conspired against him or did not have enough confidence in his ideas.[8] One of his followers remembered him exhibiting "imperial egotism," and another claimed that he "always acted upon his own impulses—he would not listen to anybody."[9] Smith admired this decisiveness and was ready to support Brown's radical ideas.

John Brown had a plan for the action he wanted to take as early as 1848, and he may have seen Smith's Adirondack community as a step toward its achievement. If Brown were successful in freeing a large number of slaves, he would need a safe haven in the north for them, and a black community near Lake Placid would provide that. After a visit with Brown in Kansas, his son Salmon wrote, "I feel more like fight now, than I ever did before.... I have no doubt of the success of the plan."

Brown's biographer added, "Surely Salmon knew about Brown's secret plot to send a small guerrilla force into the mountains of the Deep South to run off slaves and was referring to that plan."[10] Eventually, his plan led to the incident at Harpers Ferry. But in the mid-1850s, Brown's focus was in Kansas.

Abolitionists worked to make Kansas a free state by supporting the immigration of "free-soil" people. Brown went to Kansas to help the new free-soilers defend themselves against those from the neighboring state of Missouri who were proslavery. He advocated violence toward them, and carried out some brutal acts against the "border ruffians" from Missouri, probably using money that came, in part, from Gerrit Smith. Kansas met Brown's needs for instigating violence; the stage already was set there for mutual distrust and aggression based on sectional differences.

Southerners saw themselves as law-abiding patriots resisting the incursion of "nigger stealing" outlaws from the North. Northerners saw themselves as a moral, freedom-loving people trying to save the whole country from war. In Kansas, these opposing sides found themselves in constant contact with each other, a fact that often led to acts of violence. Smith supported this through John Brown, but apparently, most of the money Smith sent to Kansas did not go directly to Brown. Caleb Calkins counted only $400 to $500 sent directly to Brown, but he knew that as much as $16,000 to $17,000 had been spent to send free-soil families to Kansas.[11]

For a time in 1856, Smith was spending as much as $1,000 each month to finance the relocations of people to Kansas. "I am using all the money I can lay hold of to send good families to Kansas, and help secure that Territory to Freedom," Smith wrote.[12] This large expenditure probably had little influence on making Kansas a free state, though, as most of the people who voted for that designation had moved from Iowa and Illinois instead of from the East.[13]

William Goodell sent to Smith a couple of very critical letters regarding his use of money for the free Kansas effort. Goodell argued that abolitionists needed to focus their efforts in "the midst of the slave states" instead of wasting resources on new territory. "If I had $10,000.00 to give," he wrote, "I would give it to certain presses and lecturers against slavery. I should have <u>no</u> <u>doubt</u> that <u>this</u> would do good...."[14]

Smith's focus on Kansas as the possible site of the end of slavery in America was typical, perhaps part of a lifelong pattern of misplaced resources. As Goodell had indicated, there were more effective ways to mobilize the nation for change.

During his early opposition to slavery, Smith had employed relatively peaceful means—donations of money, speech-making, and grass-roots outreach—to build an antislavery political party. He informed one correspondent who inquired about slavery, "It is proper for me to apprise you," he wrote in 1840, "that I am of the number of those who believe slavery to be sinful, and who desire its bloodless + peaceful termination."[15] The British had shown that slavery could be eliminated peacefully by paying off owners and instituting job training for former slaves.[16] Although it was an unpopular position in the North, Smith advocated that the end of American slavery be similarly accompanied by monetary compensation for slave owners.[17] But in spite of his efforts to bring slavery down peacefully, he was not optimistic.

As early as 1845, Smith said,

> "I confess that I have not great confidence that American Slavery will die a peaceful death. The strong probability is, that this infatuated Nation will go on in its proslavery wickedness, until her slavery has come to a violent and bloody end."[18]

As the 1840s ended, Smith was frustrated with peaceful, political attempts to overrule slavery and was ready for action. By 1851, he had concluded that only violence could overthrow slavery.[19] Still, he dreaded that, because it "would constitute one of the bloodiest chapters in all the book of time. It would be such a reckoning for deep and damning wrongs—such an outbursting of smothered and pent-up revenge, as living man has never seen."[20]

Gilbert Haven's proposal to form a "Manumission Aid Society" that might induce slaveholders to free their slaves came too late for Smith's interest. He told Haven that he would have joined such an organization years ago, but now, he was sure that "There is not virtue enough in the American people to accomplish this object. American slavery is to die a bloody death."[21]

Kansas galvanized Smith's resolve for violence. "Hitherto," he wrote to the *Syracuse Daily Journal* in 1856, "I have opposed the bloody abolition of slavery. But now, when it begins to march its conquering bands into the Free states, I [am] ready to have it repulsed with violence...."[22] And, of course, the agent for action in Kansas was John Brown. His daughter, Ruth, had written to him that "Gerrit Smith has had his name put down for $10,000 toward starting a company of one thousand men to [send to] Kansas."[23]

Smith's new attitude toward fighting slavery brought him into contact with Thomas Wentworth Higginson, a belligerent, militaristic man who had become a preacher in the Free Church of Worcester, Massachusetts. Higginson badgered other abolitionists to become more violent because he believed the South would respond to nothing less. He wrote to Smith, "The people of Kansas are...ready to fight...." And he asked Smith to support their effort.[24] Together, they agreed to organize a militia "of picked men, who shall be ready to go to Kansas in case of need, to aid the people against any opponent...."[25] At the same time, Smith was contributing to a fund to arm Brown in Kansas.[26]

In the spring of 1857, antislavery action in Kansas cooled off after Governor John W. Geary called on Federal troops to help establish peace there. The abolitionists were disappointed that their efforts to ferment opposition to slavery had been quelled, and it was after this pacification of Kansas that John Brown turned toward Virginia to find more fertile ground for sowing the seeds of war.[27] It was probably around mid-1857 that Brown solidified his plan to attack the South at Harpers Ferry. Having made up his mind, his new task was to convince his backers to continue their support.

Gerrit Smith was convinced by this time that violence was necessary to end slavery, but he would deny until his death that he knew of Brown's treasonous Harpers Ferry plan. Smith's claim of ignorance of Brown's plan could have been a ploy to prevent his indictment; he wrote on July 27, 1857, "We must not shrink from fighting for Liberty—and if Federal troops fight against her, we must fight against them."[28] Smith believed that Brown's plan to capture arms and rally slaves for an insurrection could succeed—even though the possibility for success ran counter to Brown's well-established reputation for failure.

Smith's optimism and frustration combined to produce the hope for this last resort. Perhaps he did not see the futility of attacking the South because in his desperation to end slavery, he was eager to try anything. Perhaps his wealth and his isolation in the Peterboro hills lulled him into a false sense of optimism that such a radical move would work. Perhaps he was just growing so old that he feared he would not live to see the liberation of the slaves if he did not support Brown's plan. Whatever the combination of forces may have been, Smith did concede, and he continued to send money to Brown.

Support for the Harpers Ferry invasion did not come only from Smith. Brown developed backing from five other men, and the group became known as the "Secret Six."

Thomas W. Higginson of Worcester was one of the most hawkish of the six.

Franklin Benjamin Sanborn was a young man of 25 in 1857, a school teacher in Concord, and secretary of the Massachusetts State Kansas Committee, which had been formed to make Kansas a free state. A graduate of Harvard, he was a budding intellectual, a romantic idealist, and an immediate abolitionist. He liked John Brown and Gerrit Smith, and introduced them to others of the Secret Six.

Theodore Parker met Brown through Sanborn and liked his radical stand. Also a member of the Kansas Committee, he was a Unitarian minister in Boston who advocated a scientific approach to religion by seeing God in nature. An intellectual who spoke several languages, he was dogmatic in his advocacy of temperance and human rights. He had preached against the Fugitive Slave Law.

George Luther Stearns was a Boston merchant, chair of the Kansas Committee, and a philanthropist who aided fugitive slaves. He supplied arms to Brown by paying for them himself.

Samuel Gridley Howe, also of Boston and a member of the Kansas Committee, was an adventurous risk-taker with a passion for human-rights causes. He had fought in foreign wars he thought were morally justified, and he worked on educational reform for the blind and psychologically ill. A militant abolitionist, he had aided fugitive slaves and Kansas free-soilers.[29]

This group of six, including Smith, conspired to raise funds for and offer moral support to John Brown as he hatched his plan for liberating slaves. They believed that Brown's plan was worthwhile because it would hasten war.[30] These six became self-appointed heroes. Obsessed with the rightness of their own ideas, they embarked on a brand of Christianized anarchy that justified their clandestine support of violence. Having found an outlet for their obsession, they decided to support terror in order to foment war. John Brown, in turn, brilliantly manipulated the guilt of these middle- and upper-class white males. He met with them each separately, letting each think himself to be the most important member of the group—and the closest to Brown. He instilled in them a sense that they were almost "black" themselves.

Although Frederick Douglass did not support Brown, other prominent Northern blacks did—Jermain Loguen of Syracuse, and Dr. J. N. Gloucester of New York City among them—thus lending more support to his effort.[31]

In early February of 1858, Brown wrote to his son, John Brown, Jr., that Gerrit Smith was in such enthusiastic agreement with his Virginia plan that he was "ready to go in for a share in the whole trade."[32] Because Smith denied knowledge of the Harpers Ferry raid, a fair question to ask is, 'What did he know, and when did he know it?' The answer to this question is unclear.

This brings us to the incident with which this book opened: the February 23, 1858 meeting in Peterboro attended by John Brown,

Gerrit Smith, Franklin Sanborn, and Edwin Morton. (Morton was a resident of Smith's household, hired as a pre-college tutor for his son, Greene. He was a college roommate of Sanborn.) In early 1858, John Brown visited Frederick Douglass in Rochester and told Douglass of his plan to invade the southern mountains in an effort to free the slaves. Douglass, being an escaped slave, saw flaws in Brown's plan and advised him not to pursue it. But "Brown characteristically did more talking than listening," and wrote to each of the Secret Six, soliciting funds to support his plan.[33]

Smith responded by inviting Brown to Peterboro for discussions. Brown invited the others to join them in Peterboro, but Sanborn was the only one who came.[34] Brown arrived on February 18 and Sanborn on February 22. For parts of two days, February 22 and 23, the four men discussed Brown's plan of invasion. Sanborn and Morton objected to his tactics, but Brown refused to listen to them, saying he would go ahead with his plan with or without their support. Sanborn later offered that Brown left them "only the alternatives of betrayal, desertion, or support."[35]

Smith and Sanborn had the responsibility of disbursing the money, so after the "conference of four" in Smith's house, Brown and Morton stayed inside while on the afternoon of February 23, Smith and Sanborn went outside for a walk in the snowy hills and fields surrounding the mansion. There, without other ears to hear, they agreed to finance Brown's plan, realizing that even if it failed, it would likely stimulate a greater war against slavery.[36] There is no record of what occurred when Sanborn and Smith went back to the house and informed Brown of their decision. It was a decision of great significance, however: it later became clear that the Peterboro meeting of February 23, 1858 was a pivotal moment in the march toward civil war.

A few days later, on March 4, 1858, John Brown traveled to Boston and rented a room at the American House on Hanover Street. There, he had a series of meetings with each of the other five members of the Secret Six, all of whom agreed that it was time to instigate violence in order to end slavery.[37] Gerrit Smith was thrilled that Brown's meetings with the Boston five had resulted in their approval of the plan; it diluted his sense of guilt at having bought into a scheme to attack the South. With a touch of elation, Smith wrote to Joshua Giddings, "The slave will be delivered by the shedding of blood, and the signs are multiplying that his deliverance is at hand."[38]

The group of five at Boston concurred with Smith and Sanborn, largely because of the influence of Sanborn. He had been at Peterboro with Brown and Smith, and had been infected with the optimism of both. Besides, they all had a seemingly unwavering faith in Brown to deliver on his promises. As Sanborn said, "Without accepting Brown's plans as reasonable, we were prepared to second them merely because they were his."[39]

Brown also solicited support from other abolitionists. He met with Frederick Douglass in Philadelphia and in Chambersburg, Pennsylvania, with Jermain Loguen in Syracuse, and with Harriet Tubman in St. Catharines, Canada.[40] He especially wanted Tubman's approval for two reasons: She might be able to recruit soldiers for his mission, and she knew the intricacies of the operation of the Underground Railroad and could help slaves who might escape because of the coming insurrection.

Brown traveled to St. Catharines in the spring of 1858 after having stopped in Peterboro for a visit with Smith to get money for his trip and for Tubman.[41] With all this work on Brown's invasion plan, it was unlikely that Gerrit Smith would not have known the specifics of it. Yet he would claim for the rest of his life that he had not known or endorsed the plan or its details. This dubious claim deserves more attention.

First, consider the claim that Smith did not know what John Brown's plans were. Brown and Caleb Calkins, Smith's Peterboro business clerk, were well acquainted with one another. All of Brown's letters to Gerrit Smith were addressed through Calkins "because of the…known identification [of Mr. Smith] with the cause of Kansas." Calkins wrote in his personal report,

"Brown recd. from [Smith] in 1859 $400.00—vis
Dft. of $200.00—+ $100.00 in May + $100.00
in August.... So as far as [I know, Smith] never
let Brown have moneys for any specific purpose
whatever. He had great confidence in Brown's
wisdom + benevolence + let him have moneys to
do good with—to help the poor and deliver the
oppressed.... [I] never heard him speak of Harpers
Ferry until the raid.... [I] knew Brown well—
Brown told [me] of his plans—[I] never heard him
speak of Harpers Ferry."[42]

Although Calkins was not privy to all the conversations between
Smith and Brown—including the February 23, 1858 one—he was
intimately connected with Smith's activities, so this is an important
report. Franklin Sanborn, who was present on February 23, also
claimed that Brown withheld the details of the Harpers Ferry plan.
Sanborn wrote,

"The choice of Harpers Ferry as the point of attack
made what was before desperate enough, now
practically impossible. Brown's men saw this, and
remonstrated; so did Douglass when informed of
the place, and so should we all have done, had the
place been seriously suggested to us, as it certainly
was not, unless possibly to Mr. Smith."[43]

Smith wrote years later, "I had no knowledge of John Brown's designs upon Harpers Ferry, until I heard that he was a prisoner."[44]
Sanborn commented,

"[We] knew he meant to fortify himself
somewhere in the mountains of Virginia or
Tennessee, and from that fastness with his band of
soldiers, sally out and liberate slaves by force. His
plan to this extent was known, early in 1858, by

Frederick Douglass, Gerrit Smith (at whose house
and in whose presence I first heard Brown declare
it), Theodore Parker, Dr. S. G. Howe, George L.
Stearns, T. W. Higginson, and myself...."[45]

Frederick Douglass conferred with Brown in Chambersburg,
Pennsylvania, shortly before the attack. He later wrote to Smith, "He
told me that he had given you a general idea of his plan—but that
he had not given you the full particulars, lest you might turn from
him.... At Chambersburg... he informed me that he had determined
upon that [Harpers Ferry] invasion."[46]

A few days later, Smith claimed,

"I learned... that... he meant to go into [the]
mountains of a Slave State, and invite slaves to
flee to him, and give them arms to resist attempts
at their recapture.... But that Brown intended a
general insurrection, ...there is not the slightest
reason to believe.... I cast no blame on any one for
supposing that I had a full knowledge of Brown's
plans.... Nevertheless, ...I had but a partial
knowledge of these plans...."[47]

Perhaps all they knew was that Brown's attack would take place
somewhere in Virginia. Higginson, the most bloodthirsty of the Secret Six, did say of the others that Brown did not want them to hear
what he had told Higginson: "[Brown] had appeared to acquiesce
far more than he really did. It was essential that [the others of the
Secret Six] should not think him reckless. But he wished me not
to tell them what he had said to me."[48] Brown perceived Smith to
be a very practical person; perhaps it was this perception that kept
him from telling Smith exactly what he intended to do. The *New
York Herald* reported that when Brown was captured in Virginia,
he claimed, "There was no one connected with the movement but
those who came with me."[49]

Whatever the case, Smith's defenders make a credible argument
that Smith was unaware of the specifics of Brown's invasion plan.
There is an equally credible argument, however, that Smith *did*
know the details.

In early February 1858, Edwin Morton, Smith's resident tutor,
wrote to his former Harvard roommate, Sanborn, "with word that a
letter from Brown to Smith left little to the imagination."[50] It is likely
Smith had discussed Brown's letter with Morton. A significant point
here is that, after the Harpers Ferry invasion, Smith destroyed all his
correspondences with John Brown in order to eliminate evidence
of treason. Why do this had he not known of the plan?

Sanborn's first-hand report of the February 23 meeting indicated
that he, Morton, and Smith knew what Brown was going to do.

> "On the evening of... the 22nd, I reached
> Peterboro.... Brown had been there since the
> preceding Thursday, and had unfolded much of his
> plans to the Smiths. After dinner, ...I went with
> Mr. Smith, John Brown, and my classmate Morton,
> to the room of Mr. Morton in the third story. Here,
> in the long winter evening that followed, Brown
> unfolded for the first time to me his plans for a
> campaign somewhere in slave territory east of the
> Alleghenies.... It was an amazing proposition—
> desperate in its character, wholly inadequate in its
> provision of means, and of most uncertain result.
> Such as it was, Brown had set his heart on it...."

The discussion continued on the following day. "As the sun was
setting over the snowy hills of the region where we met, I walked for
an hour with Gerrit Smith among the woods and fields...." Smith,
in desperation bred of frustration, said to Sanborn, "You see how
it is; our dear old friend has made up his mind to this course, and
cannot be turned from it. We cannot give him up to die alone; we
must support him."[51]

Then, to the horror of those involved, Brown's plan was divulged to public authorities by Hugh Forbes, one of Brown's accomplices. Hugh Forbes had an aggressive mentality. He had fought in military campaigns in Italy, and, through Higginson, had become an ally of John Brown. In late 1857, Brown hired him at $100 per month as a military instructor for his volunteer guerrillas.[52] According to Sanborn,

> "Forbes was… to publish a manual for irregular
> soldiers, such as he had commanded in Italy,
> and to write appeals to the soldiers of the United
> States Army, inviting them to join in an attempt
> to abolish slavery by force…. This part of Brown's
> plan was not communicated to his Boston friends,
> but was known to Gerrit Smith, at whose house
> Forbes had visited on his way to join Brown in
> 1857."[53]

Using Forbes was probably a bad decision by Brown, who needed secrecy for his endeavor. An impetuous, revolutionary radical, Forbes operated too independently, drawing out the ire of those with whom he worked. He sent some of the money for support of Brown to his family in Europe, and was deceitful in his soliciting of money for the raid. Frederick Douglass commented of Forbes, "When he could make no more money by professing to advance the project, he threatened to expose it and all connected with it."[54]

Brown and Forbes quarreled over who should lead the small military band of revolutionaries, and they discussed the issue with Sanborn and Smith. Sanborn wrote, "It was probably Forbes's quarrel with Brown that hastened his disclosure to us of the Virginia plan, in the end of February, 1858, at Gerrit Smith's house."[55] Forbes' vindictive nature led him to expose Brown's Virginia invasion plan in Washington, D.C. to Horace Greeley and others, probably in early May of 1858. The public disclosure of the plan disturbed its planners deeply. Smith immediately wrote to Sanborn, "I never was convinced of the wisdom of this scheme… but as things now stand, it seems to me it would be madness to attempt to execute it."[56]

On May 24, 1858, while Smith was in Boston for the delivery of an address to the American Peace Society, he met in the Revere House with four of the other five members of the Secret Six to discuss the public disclosure of the plan.[57] Higginson, already upset over the lack of aggression exhibited by the others, did not attend. Brown sided with Higginson and wanted to attack anyway, but without the backing of his financial supporters, he could not. Brown called Smith "a timid man" for recommending that action be postponed until the fervor over possible treason had passed.[58]

The group decided to put off the invasion for at least a year. Sanborn noted, "It was hoped that by this delay the story of Forbes would be discredited; and this was correct—for nobody believed the scoundrel, though he told the truth."[59] Later, on July 6, Sanborn tried to calm Higginson by telling him that the plans for the invasion "hold good, and it is to be put in action next spring…."[60] In the meantime, the group of six recommended to Brown that he return to Kansas for a year and continue his abolition work there.[61]

Brown did return to Kansas with his band of rebels to fight against slavery. In the winter of 1859, when news reached Gerrit Smith of what Brown was doing, he wrote to his wife, "Do you hear the news from Kansas? Our dear John Brown is…pursuing the policy which he intended to pursue <u>elsewhere</u>."[62] Brown had marched into Missouri, liberated slaves, and brought them back to Kansas.

Smith seemed pleased, and because the turmoil over the disclosure of Brown's plan had subsided, he was eager to see Brown come back to the East to carry it out. On April 11, 1859, John Brown arrived in Peterboro on his way back from having taken some rescued Missouri slaves to Canada.[63] He stayed in Peterboro until April 14, addressing an antislavery gathering at the Free Church and discussing the Virginia plan with Smith and Harriet Tubman, who was also visiting.[64]

Tubman recommended striking at Harpers Ferry on July 4 to emphasize the freedom and independence issue, but the plans and recruits could not be secured until a later date.[65] As the time for the invasion drew nearer, Edwin Morton wrote to Brown in August of 1859 that Gerrit Smith "had 'his whole soule absorbed in' the Virginia invasion."[66] By that time, Smith was obsessed with the plan and probably very worried about its outcome; yet he had surrendered himself to it whatever the cost.

In late August, Smith wrote to John Thomas that blacks had become so disillusioned with the

> "policy of white men [that]… they are brought to the conclusion that no resource is left to them but in God and insurrections…. For insurrections then we may look any year, any month, any day. A terrible remedy for a terrible wrong! But come it must…."[67]

And come, it did. On October 16, 1859, Brown captured the United States arsenal at Harpers Ferry and was in turn captured by Robert E. Lee and a contingent of troops. So many people knew of Brown's plan in advance of October 16 that it is a wonder that it was not thwarted. Forbes had tried, but found unreceptive ears. David J. Gue, a Quaker friend of Brown in Iowa, also tried by writing to Secretary of War John B. Floyd, exposing Brown's plan as a means of saving his friend from certain defeat. Floyd ignored Gue's August 1859 letter.[68] Just before the attack, Brown had become disgusted with his supporters and with abolitionists in general. He had attended the New England Anti-Slavery Society convention in 1859 and said of Garrison and others, "These men are all talk. What is needed is action."[69]

Brown realized that his plan to attack had a high probability of failure in the short term, but he did not mind. He had written to Sanborn in 1858, "God has honored but comparatively a very small part of mankind with any possible chance for such mighty + soul satisfying rewards."[70]

Brown maintained a high regard for Gerrit Smith until the end, even though he considered Smith to be too timid. Brown said,

> "I agree with Mr. Smith that moral suasion is
> hopeless. I don't think the people of the slave states
> will ever consider the subject of slavery in its true
> light till some other argument is resorted to than
> moral suasion."[71]

A June 4, 1859 letter from Smith found with Brown when he was captured supports the belief that Smith knew the specifics about the Harpers Ferry plan. In it, Smith referred to helping Brown continue his "Kansas Work."[72] Smith obviously knew Brown had left Kansas in April of 1859; Smith had even spent time with him in Peterboro.

As Sanborn put it, "The phrase 'Kansas work' misled none of [us], who all knew that Brown had finally left Kansas and was to operate henceforth in the slave States."[73] "Kansas work" had become a code phrase to refer to the Harpers Ferry plan, thereby misleading folks who might intercept communications about Brown.

One letter from John Brown to "one of his sons" dated April 16, 1859, told of Brown's April 11-14 visit with Smith in Peterboro, and documented the receipt from Smith of $180 and a note for $200 more.[74] Further evidence that Smith knew of the Harpers Ferry plan is the fact that he purged his own files of all correspondence with Brown, and had others do the same with their own collections of papers.

Reactions to Brown's invasion and capture ran the full spectrum. Slavery's supporters were thrilled that the crazed, northern abolitionist fanatic was finally caught; antislavery folks mourned. William Lloyd Garrison drew an apt analogy: "Let no one who glories in the revolutionary struggle of 1776 deny the right of the slaves to imitate the example of our fathers."[75]

Lydia Maria Child wrote for Brown a touching poem, prefacing it with the note that "when he passed from the Jail to the Gallows, he stooped to kiss a little colored child." The poem reflected the attitude of Gerrit Smith also:

> "A winter sunshine, still and bright,
> The Blue Hills bathed with golden light,

And earth was smiling to the sky,
When calmly he went forth to die.

The old man met no friendly eye,
When last he looked on earth and sky;
But one small child, with timid air,
Was gazing on his silver hair.

As that dark brow to his upturned,
The tender heart within him yearned;
And, fondly stooping o'er her face,
He kissed her, <u>for</u> <u>her</u> <u>injured</u> <u>race</u>.

But Jesus smiled that sight to see,
And said, "He did it unto <u>me</u>".
The golden harps then sweetly rung,
And this the song the Angels sung:

'Who loves the <u>poor</u> doth love the Lord!
Earth can not dim thy bright reward.
We hover o'er yon gallows high,
And wait to bear thee to the sky.'"[76]

Whether or not Brown actually kissed a black child as he went to the gallows is immaterial to the point—that Brown, like Smith, had a strong sense of the feelings induced by oppression and intended to do something serious about it.

Whatever the actual state of knowledge that Gerrit Smith had concerning Brown's Harpers Ferry raid before it occurred, in its aftermath, the effect on Smith was devastating. He was a man of words and money; Brown was a man of action. Smith envied this, and even felt a fair amount of guilt over not being a part of the action. Over their brief decade-long relationship, they became friends as well as colleagues in abolition. But the friendship was an elusive, fair-weather type. Smith grudgingly accepted Brown's extreme radicalism, and Brown only vaguely trusted Smith's loyalty. Yet Smith admired Brown as a Christian and an abolitionist willing to risk all to accomplish what appeared to both of them to be the goal of the century.

While in prison in Charlestown, Virginia after his capture, John Brown exhibited a peaceful acceptance of his fate. One visitor remarked, "[He] was calm and at peace, and earnestly desired to maintain that mind, with unshaken self-control to the end."[77]

While others prepared a vengeful trial, Brown relaxed and recuperated from his wounds. He wanted no counsel and told his captors, "I am ready for my fate.... I have now little further to ask, other than that I may not be foolishly insulted only as cowardly barbarians insult those who fall into their power."[78] Governor Henry A. Wise of Virginia was advised to summon Hugh Forbes to testify at Brown's trial because Forbes was believed to be a vengeful man who would probably be willing to compromise the freedom of his former associates. But Forbes had returned to Europe.[79]

From his cell, Brown wrote to those close to him. To his former teacher H. L. Vaill, he reported feeling "joyful in all my tribulations.... I do not feel condemned of Him whose judgment is just; nor of my own conscience." He felt good that injustice had been redressed, even though his own full plan had not been carried out. He told Vaill, "I felt assured that in the worst event, it would certainly PAY...."

He wrote to his sisters about his comfort with death:
"The scaffold has no terrors for your own poor,
old, unworthy brother.... I am now shedding tears:
but they are no longer tears of grief or sorrow....
I am weeping for joy ± gratitude that I can in no
other way express."

Brown felt glorified that God had provided him an opportunity to die for such a worthy cause, and he stated that he wished to have slave children attend to him at the gallows. To his brother he wrote,

"I have fought the good fight [and] finished my course." In his last letter to his family written on December 1, 1859, he said, "I have now no doubt that our seeming <u>disaster</u>: will ultimately result in the most <u>glorious</u> <u>success</u>." Brown was sure that he had lighted the fuse that would lead to an explosion of civil war and the eventual emancipation of the slaves. He felt no remorse for his acts.[80]

Brown's hanging on December 2, 1859 brought a profound response across the North. The bells of Syracuse City Hall clanged 59 times to honor each of the years Brown had lived.[81] Albany "town officials" honored him with a 100-gun salute. Akron, Ohio businesses closed. In Cleveland, they honored Brown in a public meeting. At Lawrence, Kansas, antislavery settlers passed resolutions praising Brown's efforts for liberating slaves, and the local *Republican* editorialized: "The death of no man in America has ever produced so profound a sensation. A feeling of deep and sorrowful indignation seems to possess the masses."

Rochester and Syracuse, New York witnessed public prayer meetings and church services honoring Brown. In Concord, Massachusetts, Henry David Thoreau spoke in his honor, and William Lloyd Garrison spoke for the first time in favor of violence as the only technique that could end slavery.[82]

Frederick Douglass, although he had opposed Brown's plan, acknowledged in late October of 1859, "Posterity will owe everlasting thanks to John Brown [who] has attacked slavery with the weapons precisely adapted to bring it to the death…. Like Sampson, he has laid his hands upon the pillars of this great national temple of cruelty and blood, and when he falls, that temple, will speedily crumble to its final doom, burying its denizens in its ruins."[83]

At Brown's funeral in North Elba, New York, on December 8 in Brown's farmhouse, Wendell Phillips delivered a eulogy calling Brown "a marvelous old man [who] has loosened the roots of the slave system; it only breathes—it does not live—hereafter."[84]

Smith's business clerks, deeply concerned over their boss' involvement in Brown's raid, wrote to one another about it. "John Brown is making a great jar to this wicked nation. The Blind Eyes

+ Deaf ears of the North are being opened + fearfulness is seizing the South."[85]

John Brown's violence helped speed up the death of slavery, but it agonized Gerrit Smith. The biggest disappointment of Smith's life was the need to abandon peaceful means to accomplish his dreams of abolition. His decision drove him to temporary emotional and psychological imbalance. His complicity in the plan nourished his sense of guilt to the point that he began to question what was real. This may have been why he denied that he knew about Brown's plan. Those who claimed he had known and those who claimed he had not were, in a sense, both correct.

Smith had known that Brown intended to invade a slave state with his band of soldiers and arm some slaves for the purpose of self-defense against capture. He may *not* have known that Brown's specific target was the Federal arsenal at Harpers Ferry, but it is likely that if Smith did not realize he was supporting treason, he certainly knew that he was sanctioning violence. The one indication that Smith may have known Brown was about to commit treason rested in Smith's previously quoted letter to Thaddeus Hyatt, in which he stated his willingness to fight against Federal troops.

One certainty following the Harpers Ferry event is that Smith was scared. His post-raid denial of any connection with John Brown was akin to Christ's disciples' denial of Him. When one's leader got into trouble, it was time to hide. And if physical invisibility was impossible, social invisibility was not.

Smith's colleague, Frothingham, believed that Smith knew all the details of the Harpers Ferry raid beforehand—and later lied about it. "Biography was to him more important than history," Frothingham wrote. "He chose to set aside the literal details of history, which did violence to his sober judgment…." His lying, according to Frothingham, was his technique of balancing dissonance, yet "The eagerness of his denial was a confession of his secret."[86]

Sanborn was puzzled as to why Smith continued until his death to deny knowledge of Brown's plan, and Higginson, in his characteristically insensitive way, referred to Smith's denial as "the extreme of baseness."[87]

The raid at Harpers Ferry spread fear throughout the South. Local militias patrolled streets, people armed themselves against suspected invading armies, and southerners began to express openly their hatred of abolitionists. Northerners were refused entry into the South. Some who already were there were murdered, and hundreds were "violently expelled." In Augusta, Georgia, *The Chronicle* suggested that the punishment for any abolitionist should be instant death.[88]

Paranoia eliminated peaceful communication between North and South, and a mutual sense of trepidation increased. War seemed inevitable, and Smith became worried that he would be blamed for it. The image of John Brown as a trophy of southern slave masters made even northerners angry over Harpers Ferry, and Smith grew more and more certain that he was vulnerable. There can be little doubt that the aftermath of the raid caused in Smith a stress-induced illness.

Smith's reputation as a role model for his family was important to him, so the fact that his nephew, Claggett Fitzhugh, was one of the captors at Harpers Ferry weighed heavily on him.[89] Newspaper reports on the Secret Six portrayed them as vile conspirators, further upsetting Smith.[90] Also, evidence implicating Smith in the plot was found among Brown's possessions after his capture.

As he prepared for the raid, Brown had stashed his documents in a carpetbag and left it at the Kennedy farmhouse just outside of Harpers Ferry, where he and his followers had been staying. J. E. B. Stewart, leading a few U.S. troops, confiscated the bag, which contained a letter from Gerrit Smith to Brown in which Smith supported Brown's "Kansas work"—and a bank draft from Smith to Brown for $100.[91]

Smith had written to John B. Edwards about having been involved in planning the raid, and received Edwards' reply, "I have your letter of this day. It gives me some fear that your life may be in peril...."[92] Newspapers reported Smith's connection to the raid, even telling of the physical evidence found with Brown.[93]

Smith feared that he might be indicted for a crime. A *New York Herald* reporter who had received copies of the letters found in Brown's bag visited Smith in Peterboro for an interview. His report, printed on November 2, 1859, reflected Smith's state of anxiety. "I am going to be indicted, sir, indicted! You must not talk to me about it…. If any man in the Union is taken, it will be me."[94] Extradition to Virginia was also a possibility.

The *New York Herald* reported on October 29, 1859 that Virginia Governor Wise would seek Smith's extradition.[95] To protect Smith, "a military company was organized at Peterboro and another at Oneida," and his house was put under guard against capture or assassination.[96]

The threat was short-lived. As early as November 2, 1859, in an apparent move to allay some of Smith's fears, he received a letter from W. W. Gitt informing him that a "gentleman from VA.," perhaps an emissary of Governor Wise, "desires to assure you that you are in no danger from any impending indictment or prosecution. The democracy, and most certainly the South, have made as much of the Harpers Ferry affair as they desire."[97]

Smith's fear, however, did not subside. In an action that betrayed his lifelong obsession with record keeping, he destroyed all correspondences in his possession that connected him to John Brown. He sent his son-in-law, Charles Dudley Miller, on a mission to do the same to the papers of the Brown family in Ohio and those of the members of the Secret Six in Boston. According to Smith's wife, Ann, "Mr. Smith himself directed the destruction of papers relating to Brown, and supposed others had taken the same precaution…."[98]

One letter from Higginson to Smith written in 1867 referred to others he had sent Smith "about antislavery matters," but those others have been purged from Smith's papers.[99] This destruction of records clearly does not support Smith's innocence in the Harpers Ferry incident.

Adding to Smith's stress after the raid was the fact that he did not flee to avoid prosecution as did his colleagues. While he remained conspicuous, others vanished. Frederick Douglass, having met with Brown shortly before the raid, fled to Canada, as did Samuel Gridley Howe and George Luther Stearns. Edwin Morton, who had been present at the February 23, 1858 "Peterboro Conference," went to England. Theodore Parker escaped to Rome, Italy. Franklin Benjamin Sanborn destroyed all relevant papers, as Smith had, then fled to Canada.

Only Thomas Wentworth Higginson, in his obstinate and self-assured manner, stayed healthy and free in Boston—and criticized the others for being timid.[100]

Sanborn wrote to Higginson from Canada, pleading with him to be silent on the Harpers Ferry matter.[101] Parker wrote to Smith from Italy, "When I saw you last I did not think my next letter would be from such a place or for such a purpose."[102]

For as much as a year before the Harpers Ferry incident, Smith's close associates had noticed in him an unusual pattern of excitement and depression. Following Brown's capture, Smith's symptoms grew worse. He stopped writing, could not sleep or eat, hallucinated, and had delusions of betrayal and persecution by friends and family. His psychological tailspin resulted from the conflict between his public role as a moral guide and his participation in a felonious act against the government.

By early November of 1859, Smith's own guilt had convinced him that he should go to Charlestown, Virginia, where John Brown was being tried, and turn himself in to be tried as well. He planned a trip to Charlestown and left Peterboro with family members on November 7. Caleb Calkins observed, "Determined to suffer…with Brown, [Smith] went off with the undoubting expectation of going to Virginia."[103] En-route, he "was persuaded to call on Dr. J. P. Gray at Utica…and he became at once a patient in the State Hospital for the Insane, of which Dr. Gray was superintendent."[104]

Smith's family had preplanned this course, and they brought him to the New York State Lunatic Asylum at Utica under the ruse of going to Virginia. To add to his woes, newspapers now reported that he was insane, that his physical health was destroyed, and that his ancestors had also been mad.[105]

John Perdue Gray was well respected in the medical community. As a psychiatrist, he subscribed to a new theory that suggested environmental stress could bring on mental illness. Smith had received a previous opinion on his mental condition from Dr. John McCall of Utica, who advised him that his confusion of mind was a result of constipation. McCall had prescribed diet, exercise, and cheerfulness.[106]

Fortunately, Smith now had expert advice. Gray saw Smith's problems as having started long before November. He said,

> "The fact is the cause or causes of his present attack
> go back beyond the Harpers Ferry affair. That shock
> was but 'the last straw'.... For months before he
> came here he had periods of depression...."[107]

Gray believed that Smith's instability was a result of stress over a long period of time that would have eventually caused a psychotic episode—even if the raid on Harpers Ferry had not occurred. Gray's diagnosis was that Smith was suffering from a bipolar disorder, which he labeled "acute mania," with alternating manic and depressive episodes.[108]

Some have suggested that Smith faked his psychotic episode to avoid prosecution,[109] but such claims result from an incomplete reading of the case. There was no doubt that Smith's symptoms were real and not feigned.

Treatment for Smith at the hospital involved a combination of chemicals, diet, and rest. Because he had not been eating well for some time, Gray designed a special, high-nutrition diet for him. In order to calm his acute anxiety, the regimen also called for cannabis and morphine.[110]

The treatment worked quickly. Gray had described Smith as a ship that "seemed to be drifting away, without sail or rudder or helmsman, through the night and storm!"[111] He attributed his patient's quick recovery to his faith in God and his constant ritual of prayer. It seems more likely that the drugs altered both his physical and his mental condition so quickly that he was able to shed his delusions. As if morphine and cannabis were not sufficient treatment, anodyne was also added to the prescription list. Anodyne was a general term that referred to any medicine designed to relieve pain or distress. In the mid-19th century, anodynes were usually a solution high in alcohol content. To quote one labeled bottle:

"Lafayette Pain Anodyne
contains 63% of alcohol
Kills your pain Internally
And Externally

For the relief of Rheumatism, Sore
Throat, Coughs, Colds, Chills, Cramps,
Diarrhoea, Colic, Cholera Morbus,
Painful Menstruation, Stiff
Joints, Sprains, Bruises, Toothache,
Neuralgia, Stings, Cuts, Burns,
Backache and Chilblains.
Will relieve pain of any kind. Is
Perfectly harmless and can be
Used without danger. Contains
No Opiates nor Anaesthetics."

At 63-percent alcohol, one would not have needed opiates or anesthetics to calm the nerves.

While at the hospital, Smith found that visits from his family and friends were restricted under the assumption that they had been part of the cause of his illness. During Smith's nearly two-month stay in Utica, Ann was allowed to take Thanksgiving dinner with him, and he was attended daily by one of the servants from his home. When his patient had improved somewhat, Gray allowed Smith to stay with him in his home on the grounds of the hospital.[112]

Gray's attention to Smith's health continued after Smith had been sent home to Peterboro. Gray wrote to Smith's daughter on January 13, 1860, "He will occasionally have a poor night... and he will at times be nervous—(say somewhat hysterical)—at times depressed. Do not be alarmed at either of these conditions...." Again on January 16, he advised Elizabeth, "As it is, his brain wants rest + restriction. It will act on its own responsibility quite enough to give it reasonable exercise. It does not now require for its best health systematic direction or to be put in line with the current events of the times.... Tell him what is going on in a general way but don't seek to <u>trust</u> him beyond the surface." [113]

In April of 1860 Smith, feeling much better, visited Gray in Utica and gave him and his staff a gift of $500. Gray later wrote of his gratitude for the gift and commented,

"You looked remarkably well... which rejoiced
me.... I treasure those words [about my treatment
of you] in days of darkness + distress.... Those
were only days and yet how long they were to the
heart of the sufferer and to those dear ones who
waited for their ending."[114]

As Smith steadily improved at home, Gray stayed in contact and gave advice.

"Continue your outdoor exercise; mingle with
others; <u>do not</u>—<u>do not</u> study; secure a large amount
of sleep, at least 7 or 8 hours in 24; rest always
for an hour before dinner; If you continue to be
nervous take a teaspoonful of the anodyne in a half
a glass of wine at ten (10) oclock every day...."[115]

Lewis Tappan, happy to see Smith back at home, also chimed in with his advice: "Don't plunge into business again as heretofore."[116]

Smith's recovery from the psychotic episode was so quick that it led to speculation that he had faked the illness from the start. Not so, according to the clinical records, and he did have very high-quality medical care. Although Ann did not visit him often at the hospital, she kept up a stream of letters to him, reassuring him of her love and prayers, and looking forward to his return home.[117]

Even Dr. Gray was surprised at his rapid recovery. He wrote to Ann, "I am happy to say that your husband…is doing quite well if not better than…anticipated."[118]

Smith's rapid recovery was a testament to his overall lifelong health. This one problem in 1859 occurred when he was sixty-two years old. Had he been chronically imbalanced, such symptoms would have appeared years earlier. By 1859, he had dealt well for 24 years with stresses attendant to his chosen position as an abolitionist. He was likely pushed over the edge toward imbalance by the unusually severe stresses accompanying the Harpers Ferry affair.

Upon Smith's return to Peterboro, two important days—his anniversary and Ann's birthday—were approaching. He did his best to write his traditional rhymes to Ann, and he annotated his anniversary poem to her: "He was then recovering from his protraction of body + brain."

"Dear treasure of my bleeding breast!
Excuse my lack of rhymes today:
My smitten brain must now have rest—
It yet may have its usual play."[119]

And a week later on her birthday:
"Though mind is broken, heart is whole—
Though reason fails me, true's my soul.
Though intellect be in eclipse
Love still inspires my pen + lips."[120]

As the controversy surrounding Harpers Ferry subsided and Smith recovered, his friends who had fled resumed contact with him. Sanborn had returned to Boston in the spring of 1860. He was once again teaching school and was happy to hear of Smith's recovery.[121]

Edwin Morton returned from England to New York City and was
planning a visit to Peterboro. "I am...glad to be once more safely in
America, + at the near prospect of meeting you + all, again, + hoping
to find you all well.... I shall leave tomorrow I think by the day boat
in time to reach Peterboro by the Saturday evening stage...."[122]

Wendell Phillips wrote to Smith's grandson, "Please tell him how
tenderly we have all watched his illness, + with what hearty delight
we have welcomed every assurance of his returning strength."[123]

M. Pinner, editor of the antislavery Kansas City, Missouri *Post*,
expressed joy at Smith's recovery and lauded his achievements in
abolition.

> "The cause of freedom is constantly and surely...
> progressing, and...in your wake, thousands upon
> thousands follow. Missouri will be free, and all
> other States, too."[124]

Looking back, Gerrit Smith described his own illness as "prostrat-
ing," with much of the past year seeming "hazy and uncertain."[125] As
Dr. Gray had noted, the Harpers Ferry incident was only the precipi-
tating factor in the progression of an illness that had been building for
some time. Gerrit acknowledged in a May 1860 letter to his cousin,
Elizabeth Cady Stanton, that accumulating stressors had been influencing his perceptions and behavior for over two years.[126]

In March, when Smith had recovered enough to care for himself,
Ann characteristically escaped to New York City for her "retreat."
She wrote to him in mid-March,

> "Six nights without an anodyne. How good that is.
> Your nerves must be in a much better state. When
> you can do entirely without anodynes you will
> approach more rapidly your full health of brain
> and body."[127]

One stressful issue Smith had to deal with while at home was the
work of the Senate investigation committee for the Harpers Ferry

affair. The U.S. Senate appointed the Mason Committee on December 14, 1859, charging it with the investigation of all aspects of the Harpers Ferry raid. The subject of the investigation was to be not only those present at the raid, but also all others implicated through contributions of arms, money, or other kinds of support. Smith again had good reason to be worried about his own indictment.

The committee consisted of James M. Mason of Virginia as chairman, with chief investigator Jefferson Davis of Mississippi and committee members G. N. Fitch, J. Collamer, and J. R. Doolittle.[128] After the Civil War, Jefferson Davis and Gerrit Smith would connect with one another again.

On January 11, 1860, the Committee authorized the chairman to summon witnesses to testify. Gerrit Smith was among those on his list. Being concerned about Smith's health, Charles Dudley Miller, Smith's son-in-law, wrote to Dr. Gray to question the wisdom of having Smith travel to Washington, D.C. to appear before the Mason Committee. Gray responded,

> "I must advise against it. I cannot think his health is
> sufficiently restored to justify… the visit to Washington.
> The fatigue of such a journey—the necessary excitement
> + brain labor attending…such an effort would incur
> trouble, not only arrest his improving health but subject
> him to the great danger of a relapse."[129]

At this time, John Cochrane, Smith's nephew, was a member of Congress. He engaged in personal consultations with members of the Mason Committee.[130] He also received a letter from Governor Henry Alexander Wise of Virginia, who indicated that he considered Smith's illness to be evidence of his innocence.[131]

It appears that these three connections—Gray, Cochrane, and Wise—influenced the Mason Committee's decisions, and Smith was never summoned. The other members of the Secret Six were relieved that Smith would not have to talk with the committee; they were afraid Smith's ultra-moral mind might see fit to confess.[132]

Sanborn's attitude was "to give these enemies of man as little information as possible…. Let them grope in the dark…."[133] When Sanborn refused to go to Washington, D.C. to testify, the Mason Committee attempted to have him arrested in Massachusetts. State authorities there, however, perceived the effort as an inquisition by the backers of southern slavery and refused to arrest him, thereby undermining the legal authority of the committee.[134]

George L. Stearns and Samuel G. Howe did testify before the Mason Committee, but they were surprised by how easy it was. Howe reported that the questioning was very superficial, and that it "failed to get out of me some information which they might have been glad to have."[135]

In the end, the Mason Committee was passive in pursuing the conspirators in the Harpers Ferry raid. Speculations vary as to why this was so. Perhaps they did not wish to add fuel to the sectional fires. Perhaps the committee members did not want to embarrass the upper-class members of the Secret Six. Or perhaps they did not want to make any more martyrs for the antislavery cause. Whatever the reasons, the Mason Committee simply let everyone off the hook. Its report, released on June 15, 1860, said that it found no evidence of subversive activity of individuals or organizations outside of those who had been with John Brown at Harpers Ferry.[136]

Benign as it may have seemed, the report did succeed in spreading fear in the South that southern culture was in danger from fanatical northern abolitionists who could get away with criminal activity. This fear was undoubtedly a factor in the secession of southern states from the Union. The Mason Committee absolved Smith of legal responsibility for the raid.

An unfortunate result of the Harpers Ferry affair for Smith was the publication of an article by Horace White, editor of the *Chicago Tribune*. The article appeared on June 13, 1865, and, according to Smith, accused him of feigning mental illness in order to avoid prosecution. He sued the *Chicago Tribune* for $50,000 for libel, only to have the defiant White reprint the entire article twice, in

November 1865 and July 1867.[137] Perhaps not wishing to have his relationship with John Brown examined by a jury, Smith retained two lawyers and sought an out-of-court settlement. The *Tribune* did settle out of court, but it sought some revenge by printing the claim of John Brown, Jr. that Smith had known of the raid before it took place.[138]

The significance of this lawsuit against the *Tribune* lies not in the facts of the case, but in its illustration of a pattern in Gerrit Smith's life. He did not embark on the suit to polish up his reputation as much as to protect those less well-off than himself. Newspapers frequently attacked abolitionists, most of whom were not rich. As he wrote to fellow abolitionist Samuel J. May,

> "Were I to let this Chicago newspaper go unpunished, it might next fall upon one of my friends—say upon yourself, who could not very conveniently spare a few thousand dollars to carry on a suit against this very wealthy and influential Corporation. I could not be faithful to the human brotherhood, and leave unresisted this emphatically infernal endeavor to destroy my reputation."[139]

The same can be said of Smith's relationship with John Brown: there was little in it for Smith, but only to help 3.5 million slaves. In his printed circular titled "John Brown," written as a response to the *Chicago Tribune* suit, Smith asked, "Was it wrong in me to give Brown money to help the oppressed with?… Was it wrong because my oppressed countrymen were black men?"[140] Smith regarded Brown as a sensitive person who was trying to help oppressed people with whatever resources he had.

Abolitionists tended to regard each other as brothers doing what they could to help their oppressed brothers and sisters. They were not fanatics trying to destabilize the world with terrorism, but humanitarians trying to balance the world with justice. Their personal interests were broad and complex. Brown, for instance, loved classical music, and while Sanborn and Smith walked in the "snowy hills" around Smith's estate deciding on funding for Brown on February 23, 1858, Edwin Morton—also a musician—played Schubert's "Serenade" for Brown on a piano in Smith's drawing room.[141]

To impugn the lives of abolitionists by interpreting their activities in only one area—abolition—is absurd, because it ignores patterns that characterized their entire lifestyles. So it was with Gerrit Smith. He was not psychotic, a fanatic, or a hypochondriac, or selfish. He was doing the best he knew how—with what he had—to help oppressed people. And the pattern held true whether he was dealing with a poor neighbor in Peterboro or slaves in Mississippi.

Edwin Morton understood the charge Smith and his friends took on:

"If History shall remember of us that at anywhere
or at anytime, we helped John Brown in anything,
it will [remember] us as great humanists....
Ascending to my small means and small talent I
did for him all I could...."[142]

Smith probably did not know that Brown was going to attack a federal facility, and he certainly did not anticipate Brown's death by hanging. These factors temporarily upset Smith's emotional balance, which got much publicity, thereby tainting public opinion about him.

Smith's unexpected breech of moral behavior bothered him for the rest of his life. Near the end, in the early 1870s, Franklin Sanborn approached Smith with the urgent suggestion that they cooperate in an effort to publish accurate details of their connection with John Brown. "May I ask if there is any reason in your opinion, why the whole truth should not now be told...."[143]

Smith replied on October 20, saying, "If you could defer your contemplated work until after my death... you would lay me under great obligations to your kindness." Even Ann asked Sanborn to leave her husband alone regarding this issue, as it threatened to reignite his fears and anxiety. [144]

Sanborn's response to Smith on November 18, 1872 was respectful. He agreed not to mention Smith's name in his work, and claimed that he had "no other wish in the matter than that the whole and exact truth shall be eventually known to the world...."[145]

Sanborn believed that Smith should have known from what he learned in Peterboro in February of 1858 that John Brown was intending to attack the Federal arsenal at Harpers Ferry. This is paradoxical, as Sanborn had previously denied that he and Smith could have known all the facts from what Brown told them. Yet four years after Smith's death, Sanborn wrote,

> "The same plans [Brown] afterwards attempted to execute in Virginia, was obtained from Brown in Gerrit Smith's house at Peterboro, NY, February 22, 1858, and in the presence of Mr. Smith himself, with whom I discussed them fully on that day, the following day, and again on the 24th of May, 1858 at the Revere House in Boston."[146]

The exact story detailing who knew what, and when they knew it, may never be known. Smith, Sanborn, Morton, Brown, and others sacrificed personal gain for public benefit in accordance with plans they perceived to be reasonable. These plans certainly led to, or at least contributed to, the outbreak of civil war. By the time it started, many abolitionists saw it as not only inevitable, but welcome. They had become convinced that only war could destroy the institution of slavery.

The Constitution, The Churches, and the Civil War

"What a wonder, what a shame, what a crime, that, in the midst of the light and progress of the middle of the nineteenth century, such an abomination and outrage as slavery, should be acknowledged to be a legal institution!"

Gerrit Smith said this in a speech at the New York State Capitol in March of 1850.[1] During the mid-1850s in the United States, debate raged over whether new states carved from Western territory should allow slavery. Smith saw the effort to make new territory into slave states as an opportunity not only to challenge the legality of slavery in new areas, but also to challenge slavery where it already existed. In an 1854 speech before Congress on the Nebraska Bill, his position regarding the fundamental law of the Constitution was clear:

> "I hold, that the Constitution, not only authorizes no slavery but permits no slavery; not only creates no slavery in any part of the land, but abolishes slavery in every part of the land. In other words, I hold, that there is no law for American slavery."[2]

While Smith was still serving in Congress in 1854, the Nebraska Bill came up for debate. The bill would allow voters in new states to decide whether or not their states would allow slavery. Smith's letters reflect a deep interest in seeing the bill defeated,[3] and he wanted a chance to speak against it. "I hope to be permitted to take part in the discussion. I am, of course, ready to do so any day, any hour, any minute."[4] Smith's speech in Congress on the Nebraska Bill was a masterfully thought-out document. He logically made point after point regarding the meaning of the Constitution's words by expounding on the significance of the Constitution's meaning to its *adopters* rather than its *framers*.

Frederick Douglass told Smith that his speech was "the mightiest and grandest production—ever before delivered in the House or Senate of this nation."[5] Repeatedly, Smith emphasized Constitutional support of liberty and human rights. He manifested a fine grasp of history by setting the Constitution's meaning in the context of the time at which it was composed and adopted. For instance, he denounced the "three-fifths clause" as one that, instead of recognizing slavery, as the proslavery people claimed, "diminishes the power of a State in the national councils in proportion to the extent of its slavery."[6] Then he noted that if the rule had been applied to drunkards or illiterates, it would have been interpreted as a call for sobriety or for education instead of a recognition of the value of either.

Smith believed that the Declaration of Independence established liberty and human rights to be the foundation of American government. The Constitution, then, was adopted only "in order to form a more perfect union."

> "I understand the Declaration of Independence to say, that men are born with an equal right to use what is respectively theirs…. The enunciation of this great centre truth… would have justified every American slave, at the time of that enunciation, in claiming his liberty…. [This] centre truth [is] human equality and [the] inalienable right to liberty…. No human Government… has the authority to reduce man to a chattel—to transfer [people] into merchandise."[7]

Had the Constitution been clear in its allowance for slavery, Smith claimed, it would not have been adopted; no people would willingly and knowingly adopt human injustice as a characteristic of their culture. The Constitution's framers left the issue of the legality of slavery vague intentionally in order not to upset those who were profiting from it; that is, it was so important to the *adopters* of the Constitution that if slavery were clearly legal or illegal, the document would not have been ratified.

Because of his own bias, however, Smith did not consider the document to be vague. The validity of laws, Smith said, "is to be decided, not according to [one's] view of them, when applied to others, but according to [one's] sense of them when brought home to himself. Self application is the testing crucible in all such cases."[8] In his "Final Letter to His Constituents" from Washington, he hammered home that point:

> "My anti-slavery creed recognizes no law, anywhere,
> for the highest possible crime against the interests,
> and rights, and nature of man.... I care not what
> Statute-books, or even Constitutions, may say to the
> contrary. To every man, who has a soul in him—to
> every man, that is a man—truth and honesty are
> infinitely more authoritative than Statute-books
> and Constitutions.... And, ...I will never enforce...
> against another, that which, if applied to myself [I]
> would scorn...."[9]

Smith's argument that one discovered "natural law" through self-application challenged the legal existence of slavery, because it was unlikely that anyone would sanction rules for making oneself a slave. Yet Gerrit Smith did not exercise a pancultural view of the world. He simply did not embrace the notion that what is perceived as "natural law" can differ among cultures, and if it did, he would have said it should not. It was '*natural*' for southerners to perceive a divinely ordained hierarchy of human usefulness, amid which slave owners felt righteous in carrying out 'natural law'. But in Smith's opinion, that did not make it *right* for them to do so.

It is difficult to criticize Smith's moral stand on injustice, but one must see the 'rightness' of both sides before one can understand the Civil War. The fact that the Constitution could be interpreted either to legally uphold or to prevent slavery only contributed to feelings of righteousness on both sides of the debate. Smith saw slavery as the cause of war. He wrote to President Lincoln in 1861,

> "I do not forget that there are persons who look
> (wholly in vain, I think) for other causes of it....
> The South would never have made war had not
> Slavery first made her mad."[10]

Government and its legal systems, however, were not the only forces contributing support to the institution of slavery; institutions of religion did likewise. By the late 1830s, Gerrit Smith had come to regard the Christian church as a hindrance to abolition. His friend Lewis Tappan wrote to him, claiming Christianity to be a proslavery obstacle and wondering what could be done about it.[11]

When his opponents consulted the Bible as a source for legitimizing slavery, Smith reacted by saying, "to prove slavery to be right by the bible would not be to prove slavery right—but the bible wrong."[12] The Biblical verses usually referred to are Genesis 9: 20-26, in which a drunken Noah delegates his son Ham's descendants to be servants. Smith fumed,

> "A few words in the Bible respecting a curse
> belched forth by a drunken man may have been
> the justification of large portions of Christendom
> for sinking tens of millions of Africans in the pit of
> slavery...."[13]

Prejudice against black people, Smith thought, was the basis of Christianity's proslavery stand. "[Christianity's] murderous prejudice against the colored races proves it to be a spurious and satanic religion," he wrote in 1858.[14] No prejudice, he said, was as dangerous "as the mean and senseless prejudice against complexion.

Under the promptings of this prejudice, white Americans enslave black Americans."[15]

As evidence of the church's institutionalized prejudice, Smith cited the negro pew.

> "Would Jesus Christ... build negro pews? ...Vain is it to hope that the prejudice against our colored brother will give way, so long as it finds this authoritative recognition and this vital support in the sanctuary."[16]

One of Smith's allies in striking out against proslavery Christianity was Frederick Douglass. Both men believed that the Christian Church was engaged in an effort to keep black people in an inferior social position. In his autobiography, Douglass agreed with Smith, who condemned "a bastard christianity" that endorsed slavery—a "sham christianity [which] markets men as beasts, ...draws down its stupid face, and pronounces the shuffling of the feet to music to be a great sin."[17]

To quote Douglass at length:

> "The slave auctioneer's bell and the church-going bell chime in with each other, and the bitter cries of the heart-broken slave are drowned in the religious shouts of his pious master. Revivals of religion and revivals in the slave-trade go hand in hand together. The slave prison and the church stand near each other. The clanking of the fetters and the rattling of chains in the prison, and the pious psalm and solemn prayer in the church, may be heard at the same time. The dealers in the bodies and souls of men erect their stand in the presence of the pulpit, and they mutually help each other.... Here we have religion and robbery the allies of each other—devils dressed in angels' robes, and hell presenting the semblance

of paradise. [Christians] are... represented as professing to love God whom they have not seen, whilst they hate their brother whom they have seen."[18]

Gerrit Smith's approval of this incisive rhetoric was total. He wrote to black minister Charles B. Ray in 1848, "It does, indeed, rejoice my whole heart to see with what energy [Frederick Douglass] endeavors to kick back American Christianity into the pit, whence it sprung...."[19]

It was not so much individual Christians that bothered Gerrit Smith; it was the formal, organized, institutional support of slavery that drove him to speak out against Christianity. Of his own Presbyterian denomination, he noted, "the members [as individuals] were ready to ascribe to slavery its own awfully and transcendently wicked character; nevertheless as Presbyterians, they were not."[20]

The difficulty that Smith saw was not with people, but with organizations. While individual people could understand human rights and opt for justice, organizations were too concerned with their own maintenance, and in order to ensure it, they often refused to upset the status quo. Whereas the average person had enough common sense to see slavery as wrong, the conservative, hierarchical organization trying to perpetuate its own existence could not. As Smith put it,

> "Common sense revolts at the attachment of authority or the manifestation of respect to any of the opinions of an ecclesiastical assembly that refuses to pronounce as sinful the system...which... markets men, women and children as beasts."[21]

Smith's solution to this proslavery Christianity problem was to found his own church—free of all denominational links. When the Free Church of Peterboro was established in 1843, abolitionists adopted its pulpit as their forum. Smith, Douglass, May, and others traveled around central New York State delivering anti-slavery messages in local Free Churches. As early as 1840, Smith had vowed to use the pulpit as an antislavery forum.[22] Years later he said, "I cheerfully admit, that I warmly hope + fully intend, that my Sunday meetings shall aid the Liberty Party...."[23]

He won the approval of those who also saw the traditional denominations as obstacles to abolition,[24] but traditional churches did not welcome his abolition message. Having made an effort to acquire invitations to speak in churches in Watertown, Smith found them all closed to him. "I feel sure that, notwithstanding my peculiar odiousness, there was not a church in Watertown, the doors of which being under the control of an antislavery spirit, would have been closed against me."[25]

When Smith did get his chance to speak against proslavery Christianity, antislavery folks loved it. After he spoke at a convention in Chelsea, Massachusetts, nearby Wayland resident Joseph A. Robie wrote him,

> "I was present at Chelsea + heard from your lips
> more sound sense—more practical truth—more
> food for my soul in 15 min's than I have heard
> from the Orthodox pulpit in this place for 12
> months."[26]

As a public speaker, Smith exhibited an unbridled liberalism that inspired many to see him as a noble giant. Yet he did have critics who claimed that his liberal views were a cover for latent racism.

The claim was that, after the Harpers Ferry incident and Smith's illness of 1859, he felt betrayed and exhibited more openly a racist attitude that he had always harbored. Whereas this might appear to be the case, a careful reading and analysis of his positions both before and after 1859 does not support these charges of racism. This is not to say that Smith had no prejudices, but the important question is, did he carry them out in acts of discrimination? If one needs to dig for symptoms of prejudice in Smith, they are there;

but finding examples of how they limited the life-chances of black people is impossible. Smith criticized himself regarding the failure of his efforts to bring about a just and equal society, but that result should not impugn his efforts.

Social reform pitted sinners who thought they were righteous against the righteous who thought they were sinners. Smith was trapped by this 'sinner' mentality, and he took the failure of moral reform personally. Still, his retreat from reform activity after 1859 need not be taken as evidence of latent racism.

Part of the professional prescription for Smith's recovery from his late 1859 mental illness was a retreat from both private business and public reform. He did withdraw from close and active relationships with other abolitionists such as James McCune Smith and Frederick Douglass, but this did not reflect prejudice against the progress of blacks. He perceived that the foundation for slavery was in discrimination against Africans, but that it had been perpetuated by distinctions of caste.[27] These caste divisions were what needed to be changed by extending equal rights to all Americans. Smith's naïve belief that any reasonable person could understand this led him to believe that implementing equal rights would eventually eliminate social distinctions based on skin color.

Smith did see the differences in colors, and he appears to have had some tendency to match the color black with evil and white with good. Today, we may see this tendency to be an exaggerated symptom of our sensitivity to political correctness, but we cannot negate the effects of recognizing social value in various colors. Yet Smith demonstrated no implementation of such values in his behavior. In "The Religion of Reason," Smith referred to "the selling of intoxicating drinks as the blackest crime...."[28] In "The One Test of Character," he spoke of the process of looking to the Bible for a justification of slavery as leaving "a big black blot upon the Bible."[29] He referred to his brief stay at the mental hospital as a "black dream."[30] He considered people who were libeled as having been "blackened."[31]

During a speech at a "Young Men's Mass Convention" in Syracuse, he scolded the Democratic Party, saying that "The boldest and most unprincipled portion of its leaders will stamp its character [upon the public]; and necessarily, therefore, it would be a very black one—so black as to reflect not a little disgrace upon every man who belongs to the party."[32]

Of John Brown's memory, Smith said, "If this nation shall ever be truly saved, it will no longer regard John Brown as worthy of the fate of a felon; but it will build the whitest monuments to his memory...."[33] When asked if he would allow his daughter to marry a Negro, he responded that he did not consider interracial marriage to be a sin, and had no right to control her decision-making by coercion, but would be concerned about an interracial relationship decreasing Elizabeth's influence in the social world.[34]

One has to dig to find these references, but they are there. Smith had long recognized the observable differences between races and had made group references based on color, but such thoughts and references did not lead him to overt acts of discrimination against blacks. Some have claimed that Smith's postwar emphasis on human adaptation of different skin colors in different climates was evidence of his belief in the innate inferiority of black people.[35] If inferiority in abilities did develop as a result of natural selection, its accurate measurement has never been detected, and Smith made no claim of knowledge of it.

Sometimes what looked like Smith's action against blacks turned out to be an effort to help them. He opposed President Grant's proposal to annex San Domingo (now the Dominican Republic) to the United States on what appeared to be racial grounds, but Smith actually wanted blacks to retain their power of self-rule there.[36]

When the Republican Party refused to extend equal rights to blacks because of their supposed ignorance, Smith agreed with their point, but claimed it to be no reason for discrimination by those "who enslaved and therefore darkened and debased this ignorant race."[37] He believed the ignorance of blacks had a cultural and not a biological cause, resulting from the policy of making "their instruction a crime."[38] When Smith referred to the "superior intelligence of the white man," his reference was not to innate differences in potential, but to the cultural experience of whites in having learned more due to their greater opportunities.[39]

In an 1856 speech to the New York State Legislature in Albany, Smith attempted to deflate white assumptions of superiority:

> "Although it is by our own hands that [blacks] have
> been cast down, we are nevertheless unreasonable
> and wicked and cruel enough to scorn them
> because they are down, and to justify our scorn by
> the fact, that they are down...."[40]

Smith carried the argument for many years, writing in 1862,

> "that one portion of the human family is essentially
> inferior to another is probably nothing better
> than a prejudice.... Changes of circumstances...
> alternately lift up and depress a people. But their
> inherent, inborn faculties are neither multiplied
> nor diminished because developed in one age and
> undeveloped in another."[41]

Smith considered all people to be equal in their potential for intelligence—subject to the forces of cultural development. He lamented what he saw as a postwar Reconstruction Bill that did not recognize that fact. He wrote to Ohio Congressman James Ashley that the bill "makes no provision that any black men, not even such of them as are eminent for...intelligence [can] vote."[42] Years earlier, Smith had used as an example of this point the historical fact that "few people have ever made as rapid progress as [British] emancipated slaves in knowledge...."[43] There was no presumption here of innate differences between races that might indicate that Smith had racist tendencies.

Regarding his antebellum work, Smith's founding and support of antislavery organizations worked for the benefit of blacks, as did his effort to enfranchise some of them through gifts of land. The expenses he incurred in purchasing the freedom of slaves, and in aiding fugitive slaves in their escape to freedom, does not reflect racist intent; nor does his founding of the Liberty Party or his opposition to pro-slavery churches. When the Liberty Party merged with Free Soilers in opposing the extension of slavery, Smith helped found the Liberty League to emphasize its total abolition. His founding of a school for blacks and his support of interracial education do not speak of racism, nor does his defense of our fundamental law, the U.S. Constitution, as an antislavery document.

Following the shock of Harpers Ferry, Smith did pull back from abolition work, but his behavior toward blacks was still nondiscriminatory. In fact, he worried over what racial discrimination would do to the future of his country. Blacks, he said, "are not yet a formidable foe, nevertheless, unless we prevent [their discontent] they will become such to our posterity." He argued that whites must not let the black man "wear <u>One</u> link of all his former chain."[44] He even cautioned President Andrew Johnson that if the black man did experience prejudice after the fall of slavery, "a guerilla warfare would ensue, which…might run through many years…."[45]

Smith feared that the Civil War might result only in emancipation, not in the liberation of blacks from "infernal contempt."[46] The freedmen, he claimed, were socially and biologically ready to learn and work to build an integrated nation—as long as discrimination did not hold them down.[47]

Post-war discrimination was what convinced Smith that he had been a failure. His dream of a land of equality and justice had not been brought about by either persuasion, politics, or violence. Shortly before his death he still wondered,

> "...how can a black man enjoy [the benefits of citizenship] if he [is] to walk and not ride, to carry bread and cheese in his pocket instead of sitting at the well-furnished table, and instead of a comfortable bed, to steal away like a fugitive slave into the woods?"[48]

If Smith discriminated against anyone, it was against those who used religion to deprive blacks. He worked against political parties and religious denominations that, to him, were pro-slavery. He displayed some anti-Semitism for the same reason, viewing Jewish self-pride as a pernicious social force. He wrote to President Grant in 1868,

> "The Pride of race... has ever stood in the way of
> realizing... true Peace, [and] never was there a
> people in whom, so much as in the Jews, the pride
> of race was controlling, contemptuous and cruel....
> The Jewish part of our religion [authorizes] a
> murderous caste-spirit toward the black man."[49]

Although Smith's prejudice cannot be defended, it was not racially based in a biological sense, but ethnically based in a cultural sense, and emerged from his concern for justice toward blacks.

Given all of Smith's thoughts and actions about justice for all Americans and the abolition of slavery, it is interesting that he viewed the Civil War as a war of moralities. To him, the war was to be fought not for national union or for the Constitution, but against rebels and slavery.

"Nothing less satanic than the spirit of slavery could have been sufficient to prompt men to so satanic a rebellion," he wrote. With the war, Smith said, the United States found itself in "a state of moral helplessness."[50]

White oppressors in both the North and the South had stolen human rights from blacks, and the Civil War was payment for that sin. Said Smith,

> "The slaves are getting their freedom without
> fighting for it. The blood of their oppressors
> Northern and Southern instead of their own
> blood is purchasing it.... And was there ever
> a punishment more justly alloted?—more
> righteously retributive?"[51]

He also was not beyond saying 'I told you so'. He saw abolition-ists—including himself—as "faithful prophets" who should have been consulted for advice concerning the conduct of the Civil War; after all, they could see the issues more clearly than could the na-tional political leaders. "Faithful were the abolitionists," said Smith, "all through a quarter of a century, to warn their countrymen of this day of blood."[52]

As an indicator of how committed the abolitionists were to their cause, Horace Greeley, near death in 1860, wrote to Smith, "The skies are very dark. I must work while strength lasts…. God will yet make my weakness humbly instrumental to the overthrow of American slavery."[53] The abolitionists saw the moral injustice to a portion of humanity to be so great that any sacrifice of resources they possessed was worthwhile, even if it led to war and the pos-sibility of losing national unification.

When abolitionists were blamed for causing the war, Smith agreed with Garrison, who reminded the public that without slaveholders, there would be no abolitionists.[54] As Smith said to New York Gov-ernor Horatio Seymour in 1863,

> "Every nation prepares its own cup. We have made
> ours very bitter. Nevertheless we must drink it. As a
> part of the punishment for our unsurpassed crimes
> against humanity we may have to witness the failure
> of all endeavors to save our beloved country…."[55]

Smith viewed the dissolution of the union as a horrible conse-quence of slavery and war, but he did not fear it or oppose it. Only patriots, he thought, could advocate maintaining the union intact. He wrote to Samuel J. May in 1857, "I have none of that wretched stuff in me called 'Patriotism'—and hence I have no patriotic horror of disunion."[56] If breaking apart the union was required to kill slavery, then so be it. As the abolitionists came to realize that disunion and war offered the road to emancipation that moral persuasion had not, they began to advocate it.

Smith was committed to effective pursuit of the war because he wanted to see it vigorously carried forward to a swift northern victory. He saw his philanthropy at the local level as his contribution to the success of the war effort, and he declared,

> "I may be of some service in the present crisis.
> I can... care for the families of my brave...
> neighbors who go forth to peril their lives for
> their country. Let this be my work. It falls in not
> with my principles only, but also with my habits of
> feeling and acting."[57]

Part of his support for the war involved raising troops to fight in it. As early as December of 1861 he was advocating the use of blacks to fight for the North,[58] and he suggested to Frederick Douglass that a black regiment should be established and sent off to fight. After some hesitation, Douglass agreed. The regiment was to be organized in Massachusetts, and when Douglass agreed to recruit 100 men for the regiment from New York State, his youngest son, Charles, was the first on his list. Smith offered Douglass $200 to support the costs of recruiting the company,[59] and he claimed that "Liberty won by white men would lack half its lustre."

Smith praised blacks who joined the regiment for their ability to rise above "our persistent ridicule, loathing, and murderous hate of a people, who have done not one wrong in return for the mountains of wrong under which we have buried them."[60] Smith also supported the local recruitment of soldiers. He encouraged people to invest in the future of their country by loaning money to the federal government in support of the war effort and signing up for military duty if eligible. In 1863, he offered every drafted citizen from the Town of Smithfield an incentive of $300. By the end of the year, 129 had joined the army.[61]

The next year, Smith printed a public appeal "To the People of the Town of Smithfield" to recruit "between thirty and forty men" for a Madison County regiment.[62] And at a meeting of Smithfield citizens held at Peterboro, he offered to pay one half of the $300 incentive offered to each recruit.[63]

In one interesting incident, a New York City resident, Erath von Salleri, claiming to be a "german... born abolitionist," offered to recruit for the war a regiment of slaves and call it "Gerrit Smith's Guard" or the "Gerrit Smith Legion" in honor of Smith's abolition work. The writer added a request of Smith to "be so kind to have to say nothing against it."[64] There is no record of Smith's reply—or of the existence of this regiment.

One thing certain about Gerrit Smith's opinion of the Civil War was his disapproval with the way in which it was conducted. Abraham Lincoln appeared to Smith to be a weak leader because he cared about too many issues rather than focusing on fighting the war viciously and ending it quickly. Smith criticized Lincoln's stance on racial issues as being too lukewarm for him to be able to lead the country to success in the war. In Washington, D.C., for example, Lincoln saw slavery as legitimate if the residents chose it, and he supported the enforcement of the Fugitive Slave Law. During the Lincoln/Douglas debates, he had even expressed the opinion that if blacks were to stay in the United States, they should remain subordinate to whites.[65]

He did, however, believe in a moral "higher law," and it was this point that made him an acceptable antislavery candidate for abolitionists, who "held their noses" and voted for him.[66]

By August 1861, Smith was dismayed that the war was not over already, and he wrote to Lincoln to offer advice. He criticized Lincoln's conduct of the war on two grounds. First, he accused the president of "Overrating the importance of Constitutional action in time of War." The legal rights protected by a constitution, Smith argued, could not be validly applied to an enemy. Lincoln was, Smith believed, catering to the needs of slave states that had not seceded—and to slaveholders who still claimed loyalty to the country.

Smith's objection was that an enemy should be treated as such as a whole, not in part, so his second criticism of Lincoln was his "overrating the importance of conciliating loyal slaveholders." Rules of civility that characterize peacetime politics, said Smith, should not be used when confronting an enemy. Lincoln should have worried less about the property of slaveholders, and should have called for blacks to sign up in the military to aid the North. This move, according to Smith, would have made many more troops available, would have presented an opportunity to foster racial integration, and would have denied the South the labor of slaves in its war effort.[67]

Throughout 1862, Smith's dismay only intensified. He charged that Lincoln supported weak military generals who seemed not to want to pursue war aggressively. He wrote to his wife, "No battles—indecision in Cabinet.... I still fear that our Nation is lost. Well, I have been a faithful witness."[68] In an open letter, "Gerrit Smith to his Townsmen," he encouraged people to support their government and not to worry over the legal implications of the Constitution relative to the South, for the rebellion must be put down by conquest.[69]

With no military experience and limited legal or political experience (his one partial term in Congress was his only elected office), Smith took on the role of advisor to politicians, armies, and voters. In hindsight, many of his instincts appear to have been right. He wrote to New York Governor Seymour about his disgust with the "shrinking and delay" displayed by the North.

> "At once should the President have brought out
> the Big Emancipation Gun: and he should have
> so charged it, and so aimed it, as not to spare one
> shred of slavery in all the land."[70]

As the war went on, Smith's friends wrote to him, supporting his position. His cousin, Elizabeth Cady Stanton, had spoken with Lincoln.

> "Henry [Stanton] and I had a long talk with
> Abraham.... He impressed me as a stronger
> and better man than I had from his official acts
> supposed him to be.... [But] it is enough to chill
> the soul to hear fat, sleek officials balance the

chances of success + failure, of life + death with as
much coldness + indifference as they speak of the
rates of exchange…."

She also wrote of Lincoln's personal situation:
"They say Abraham's shriveled appearance + poor
health is owing to being underfed…. In front of
the mansion [Mrs. Lincoln] has fenced off a place
where she pastures her cow. Thus she sacrifices
taste to thrift. But the cow is happy."[71]

Frederick Douglass, also hoping for a swift conclusion to the war,
wrote to Smith in 1862 regarding its mismanagement:
"Your gloomiest predictions have been even now
more than realized and I shudder at what the
future may still have in store for us."[72]

Horace Greeley also wrote to Smith of his discouragement:
"I… hope that the [disease] that has paralyzed our
gallant hosts on the Potomac will soon be removed,
and that our heroes will press on to victory—a
victory that leaves no Slave in its path."[73]

One of Smith's most intense disappointments during the Civil
War was disunity in the North, which he saw as the country's greatest
enemy. "It is not by the rebels that we can be conquered, but only
by ourselves. Nothing is truer than that the life of the Rebellion is
in disunion at the North."[74] He regarded as traitors anyone who was
not loyal to the cause of putting down the Southern rebellion. He
even claimed that those who were not usually acceptable to him,
such as "drunkards" and "pro-slavery" people, were colleagues in
battle if they wished to end the war.[75]

Smith's misgivings with the slow progress of the war did not
paralyze his better nature. He was glad that slavery would die soon;

still, he felt some responsibility for the war, and he aided those whose loved ones had gone to serve. "The war + the support of so many families of soldiers + of friends + relatives press hard upon my means," he wrote to his son, Greene.[76] Perhaps still hoping to aid a more peaceful solution, he donated $200 to the American Anti-Slavery Society in October of 1863, inspiring Garrison to write of "a fresh moral agitation of the slavery question…."[77] This was a strange mid-war donation; Smith certainly realized that the moral persuasion of proslavery interests had done little good—even though Garrison, by that time, had come grudgingly to support the achievement of political liberty by means of the practicality of war.[78]

If Smith's donation made him feel better, there were bad feelings, too. When local soldier Captain James R. Barnett was killed at Antietam on September 17, 1862, there was much grieving in Peterboro. His body was returned to Peterboro, and a memorial service was held at which was read a long poem by George W. Putnam honoring Barnett. The boiling mix of emotions can be felt:

"Amidst our gloom, with joy we see
Unrolled a brighter destiny,
Stretched forth Jehovah's hand;
The glorious word at last is spoken;
The bondmen's heavy chains are broken;
Hope lights the stricken land!"[79]

That "hope" was, of course, for emancipation, which Gerrit Smith had pursued with his actions for four decades. Early in the war, Smith was optimistic about the chances for the quick emancipation of the slaves. In the fall of 1861, he noted that General Fremont had granted freedom to all the slaves in Missouri.

"I hope the good news is true. About 120,000
slaves in that state. All…slavery must soon pass
away. The Rebellion will I think be quelled by
Spring. Your dear country will yet become a
glorious land of Universal Liberty."[80]

Then in May 1862, Union General David Hunter proclaimed that all slaves in his command (South Carolina, Georgia, and Florida) were free. To Smith's great displeasure, Lincoln nullified both orders of his generals; during wartime, only the president, as commander-in-chief, had the power to emancipate slaves.[81]

Even when Lincoln finally issued his Emancipation Proclamation on January 1, 1863, Smith was not impressed. He saw the Proclamation as a timid step compared to Lincoln's immediate and decisive reversal of Generals Fremont and Hunter and their efforts to emancipate slaves in their commands. Because the proclamation only liberated slaves who lived in states that were at war with the North, it was merely a partial move toward equality. Smith felt that it should have been issued much earlier, and he chastised the president for timing its release for political purposes instead of making "justice to the negroes the motive and ground of his... Proclamation."[82]

Smith regarded the written document of emancipation in Lincoln's hand not as a historical treasure, but as a practical way to make money to support the soldiers fighting the war. When a draft of the Proclamation was put up for sale in a fund-raising lottery sponsored by the Albany Army Relief Bazaar, Smith purchased tickets and won it, then put it up for auction—with the proceeds to go to the soldiers and their families.

> "My purpose when I purchased the tickets... was to let it go to the individual or association, who should pay the largest price for it.... As I believe the putting down of this infernal Rebellion to be our highest and holiest work, so I recognize no other claim upon my possessions to be as strong as that of the Soldiers, who are prosecuting this work."[83]

The document never came to Peterboro, as it was auctioned from William Barnes' Albany office. Smith's purchase of the draft fit into his lifelong pattern of benevolence toward the oppressed and to those who did the stressful work of reform or war. The pattern also flowed into his perceptions of what should be done to, or with, the South after the war.

Smith's attitude toward the conquered South was conciliatory, as it had been from the beginning. He viewed Northern acquiescence to slavery as an encouragement to the South, and he therefore saw equal responsibility for slavery in both regions. Just after the Civil War had started, he told his neighbors at a "War Meeting in Peterboro" that when the war was over, the North should "be restrained from dealing revengefully with Southern leaders."[84]

He repeated the theme in 1863, believing that concessions to the South would benefit the welfare of the entire country. "Notwithstanding their enormous crimes against their country," he said in a speech, "…we shall gladly look upon our sorrowful Southern brethren as our brethren still."[85]

Northern revenge, Smith felt, would only make national post-war recovery more difficult. Perhaps more importantly, it would ignore the humane point that the South only did the same thing that the North had done in trying to preserve its values. To treat southerners as traitors would deny the basic tenet that citizens of a republic have the right to rebel. Besides, he reasoned, because the South was treated during the war as a belligerent nation, treason was not an appropriate charge anyway.

Smith believed that the South had suffered enough. The North, he felt, should be a role model of kindness to the world by treating the South

> "mildly and humanely! Thereby would we gain the respect and gratitude and love of the whole South…. Moreover, a reasonable and humane Peace, following this horrid war, would not only honor us in the sight of other nations, but it would contribute largely to advance the cause of civilization, and to elevate mankind, the earth over."[86]

One of Smith's fears regarding the post-war treatment of the South hinged on the untimely death of Abraham Lincoln. Where Lincoln had been conciliatory toward the South, his successor, Andrew Johnson, was not. Smith wrote to Johnson, warning against "a vigorous and bloody policy toward the conquered rebels," adding, "it is apprehended that there may be qualities in yourself to which such a policy… would be entirely welcome."[87] His advice to Johnson was to be gentle, and not vengeful, toward the South.

Smith did receive some rewards for his post-war kindness. Ann wrote to Elizabeth, "Father continues to receive many letters from Virginia thanking him for his spirit of kindness to the South."[88]

Smith's empathy toward the South was, perhaps, best demonstrated in his posting of bail for Jefferson Davis, the war-time president of the Confederacy. In his printed circular "On the Bailing of Jefferson Davis," he summarized his post-war thoughts: "The work, now, of the conquering North should not be to punish but to comfort; not to open wounds afresh but to perfect their healing; not to repel the Southern heart, but to win it…."[89] Given this attitude of conciliation toward former enemies, Smith was horrified to observe the continued discrimination against blacks following emancipation.

After the Civil War, as the passions of enemies continued to burn, Smith tried to use what influence he had to cool off heads and to warm up hearts. He disagreed with William Lloyd Garrison, who was vengeful toward the South.[90] A writer from Macon, Georgia expressed gratitude for Smith's generosity toward his southern countrymen. Maurice Robertson wrote to Smith, "May we all unite to dethrone Passion, + establish the rule of Love."[91]

Smith believed the rules of "reconstruction policy" ignored the rights of blacks, and he predicted that this discrimination would lead to racial tension. He saw it as the responsibility of the public—not of statesmen—to harbor high expectations and high regard for all citizens, including slaves.[92]

Discrimination against natural rights was, for Smith, the basest of all sins. When his daughter was fourteen, he wrote to Ann, "I hope that our Dear Libby, if she has one particle of that… thing in her heart called prejudice against people of color, will make haste to get rid of it. This prejudice is a quarrel with God."[93] Discrimination, he believed, divided people who "instead of being enabled with the soul of manhood [are] shrivelled with the spirit of caste, [and] humanity has nothing to hope for from [this] miserable counterfeit."[94]

Abraham Lincoln held similar beliefs about forgiveness, and during the war he spoke against persecutions, revenge, and torture of Southern political or military leaders. He asked for acts of aggression from both sides to cease. Lincoln and Smith alike wanted to give the South and the nation a *second chance*.

In building a policy to actuate that chance, the peacemakers considered the rights of black people to be an issue of paramount importance. To Gerrit Smith, the key indicator of justice toward blacks was the extension to them of the right to vote. If that was withheld, he told Garrison and Phillips, it would be a symptom of national hatred of blacks and would result in a "race war" based on vengeance.[95] He sought allies in his fight for suffrage for blacks. And he criticized those who would not support it.

When General Ambrose Burnside wrote to Smith, complimenting "the gallantry and efficiency of your son…," Smith wrote back, "Whilst I rejoice that the fighting is over, I do not feel sure that we shall very soon reach a sound peace." Then he advised Burnside to call for "Negro suffrage + for mercy for the South."[96]

Franklin Sanborn, Smith's old ally in his dealings with John Brown, wrote in support of Smith's endeavors: "The danger of neglecting the colored man in plans of Reconstruction is still great. I was glad to see by your recent letter that you felt how important is the suffrage for the Negro. We must strive for that in the coming year."[97] Smith opposed the Reconstruction Bill because it did not provide for the enfranchisement of blacks.[98]

When the 13th Amendment to the Constitution was ratified on December 18, 1865, outlawing slavery, Gerrit Smith welcomed it—but only as the beginning of change. He knew that the legality of emancipation did not change the racial attitudes of people nationwide, especially in the South. Only voting power in the hands of blacks could really emancipate them, he said, and he viewed the antislavery victory celebration in 1865 as premature. Writing to Senator Charles Sumner, he argued that denying the vote to freed slaves was an unveiled attempt to maintain racial superiority through political power.[99] When he noted that Robert E. Lee was advocating no franchise for freed slaves, Smith told him that the racial relationships that would develop would represent "a type of slavery, more cruel and crushing than the former one…."[100]

Smith pressured newly elected President U.S. Grant to work toward eradicating racial hatred by implementing equal rights as the only basis of "true Peace."[101] His concern over suffrage for blacks presaged the 14th Amendment to the Constitution. Fearing continued discrimination, he foresaw the need for a Federal guarantee of "equal protection of the laws;" yet the 14th Amendment was not ratified until late July 1868.

Smith was not alone in believing that it would take more than legal emancipation to put an end to racism; some abolitionists recognized early that a northern victory in the war might, in itself, bring a strong and sudden racist backlash. Lydia Maria Child warned Smith less than two years into the war, "Even should they be emancipated,… everything must go wrong, if there is no heart or conscience on the subject."[102]

As early as 1861, Smith recognized a long-term threat stemming from a victory in the war. He stated his position well in a letter to John A. Gurley, who had introduced a bill in the House of Representatives proposing that if the slaves were liberated, they should be colonized in Florida under white rule. "The great sin of our country," Smith said, "is the assumption of special powers by her white race over her other races…."

He asked Congress to recognize the rights of blacks "and withhold from them no civil or political rights which it accords to others." To do otherwise would be a "perilous incongruity," and would make of blacks "a formidable foe...to our posterity." Smith recognized the classic sociological point that the more one has, the more one wants. As he put it, "the more rights they get, provided they get not all of them, the more they are discontented."[103]

The French economist Alexis De Tocqueville had encountered this phenomenon during the French Revolution. Tocqueville wondered why the French revolted against aristocratic rule while people who were worse off in other countries did not. His answer, verified now by other research, was that improvements in the lives of French peasants stimulated their appetites for more, in turn sparking an upheaval in the social structure.[104]

Today, this phenomenon is recognized: if someone feels deprived relative to someone else, they will be ready to cause social agitation for change.[105] When their lives get a little better, people take rising fortunes as a sign that they should receive more and receive it quickly, and their expectations continue to rise exponentially.[106] As oppressed people make gains, those in power feel threatened and react in a way that limits those gains. Gerrit Smith saw this happening following emancipation. Indeed, after the Civil War, whites who felt threatened by the rising status of blacks formed the Ku Klux Klan and passed Jim Crow laws designed to enforce segregation and retard the progress of blacks.[107]

What Smith and other abolitionists had feared became manifest, as racist whites imposed prejudiced rule in place of slavery, thereby sustaining oppression. As the ethic of equality ebbed, the moral reformers lost out to economic promoters who seemed obsessed with the need for racial caste. As a response to this white terrorism, some abolitionists and many blacks considered a variety of colonization schemes as a means of escape from an abusive culture.[108]

Smith's awareness of post-war discrimination symbolizes an important perception among abolitionists: they felt that the abolition movement had been a failure. But how could that be? Emancipation was a fact, blacks had been enfranchised, and slavery was declared unconstitutional. The abolitionists' perception of failure grew from their realization that although the legal goals of the movement had been achieved, its moral goals remained unfulfilled. The early "moral suasion" goal had been to achieve the latter first, with the legal aspects of freedom coming later. Obviously, that had not happened: former slaves were legally free and, after 1868, could vote. But nationwide attitudes of prejudice and acts of discrimination still oppressed them. Thus the abolitionists felt defeated, and they feared for the future social health of the nation.

The philosopher John Stuart Mill, living in Avignon, France, warned Americans one month after the war had ended, "One thing I hope will be considered absolutely necessary; to break altogether the power of the slaveholding caste. Unless this is done, the abolition of slavery will be merely nominal."[109]

Frederick Douglass noted, "A mightier work than the abolition of slavery now looms up before the Abolitionist." He felt that rising levels of discrimination could rob blacks of justice. "The South, by unfriendly legislation, could make our liberty...a delusion...."

And Charles L. Remond, a free black speaking at an American Anti-Slavery Society meeting in May of 1865, remarked, "Put the question...to the American people today, whether they are prepared for the entire and full recognition of the colored man's equality in this country, and you would be voted down ten to one."[110]

In like fashion, Henry B. Stanton wrote to Smith, "I am at times indignant, sad, discouraged, disgusted, at the wicked + deplorable turn which events are taking toward the Negro. Can it be possible that we have learnt so little by this war?"[111]

Smith agreed regarding the increasing tendency among whites to discriminate against blacks. In his important essay titled "The Lesson Not Learned," Smith wrote in 1868,

> "The lesson taught by our horrid War is <u>Justice to the Negro</u>. A lesson costlier in treasure, tears and blood, was never taught. And, yet, it remains unlearned."

He blamed long-term prejudice and threats to white status for preventing that learning.

> "After all [that this country] has done against the
> negro, outraging and crushing him through the
> whole period of her existence,…what is there left
> on which to base the reasonable expectation that
> she will be just…? Nothing."[112]

Smith saw that free blacks were even being mistreated in the North. An 1864 convention of blacks in Syracuse, New York hosted by Jermain W. Loguen, a local black abolitionist, had as its agenda the economic, political, and educational improvements needed in order to "lift the burden of institutional and personal racism that [makes] elevation of African Americans so difficult." Loguen commented to Frederick Douglass, "Had I not been wronged…I think I should have been a very still, quiet man. [But] oppression has made me mad."[113]

Long before the most prescient Americans predicted civil war, Smith recognized the high probability that racial discrimination would outlive the institution of slavery. In 1844 he had written to Cassius M. Clay, a former slaveholder-turned-abolitionist, "There will be multiplied + well nigh insuperable obstacles in the way of the success + improvement of the… emancipated slaves. Such obstacles are in the way of the free colored people of the North."[114]

> "Even those [blacks] who are called free, are
> pursued by cruel, unrelenting prejudice. The
> avenues to honor and happiness and usefulness are
> studiously closed against them. They are vilified,
> scorned, hated. They are outcasts from the public
> sympathy."[115]

Smith and his abolitionist friends recognized the perils of freedom gained through force. Beriah Green commented on the success of war by noting that "Freedom, in any proper sense of the inspiring

word, is not a child of violence."[116] William Wells Brown chimed in
with a song on the same theme:

> "Slaves may yet see their masters cowering,
> While whole plantations smoke and blaze!
> Yet free them not by sword or shield,
> For with men's hearts they're unavailing."[117]

Frederick Douglass claimed that freedom won by military means
could only lead to future anger and discrimination.[118] In fact, Smith
and others knew too well that the Civil War as an effort to end the oppression of blacks was tragically doomed. They knew that the abiding
enemy to equality was a prejudice that was so deeply ingrained that
legal emancipation would be little more than a cruel joke to blacks
who went from being legally oppressed to being freely lynched.

Acquaintances also wrote of their fears of postwar discrimination. His housekeeper, Betsey Kelty, wrote in her journal on July 4,
1865 that before she died she wanted to "hear the sound of universal
Emancipation, that as a nation we may no longer claim to be free +
independent with our foot on our Brother's Neck." She also recorded
a few lines from a poem by abolitionist John Greenleaf Whittier:

> "In vain the bells of war shall ring
> Of triumphs and revenges,
> While still is spared the evil thing
> That severs and estranges."

Chloe Merrick, a North Carolina teacher with whom Smith had
traveled, wrote to him in 1868 of her observations of continuing
discrimination against blacks resulting from "the demoralizing
influences of slavery."[119] John C. Underwood remarked of northerners, "They will require as many plagues as visited Egypt before
they will consent to treat the colored people kindly or in any true
sense 'let them go.'"[120]

Smith found these supportive remarks reassuring to his own
position. As New York Congressman Clinton Merriam wrote to

Smith, "The responsibility of our civilization did not terminate with the unloosening of the shackles."[121]

Those in power gave only weak acceptance to their ongoing responsibility after the war; as the Jim Crow/Ku Klux Klan mentality spread, the nation faced increasing threats of racial violence. Frederick Douglass, a giant in the struggle against slavery, was disgusted to see the institution replaced by blatant discrimination. He and Smith agreed that all of the political wrangling over interpretation of the Constitution, non-taxation of the South as a recovery measure after the war, the trying of Jefferson Davis, the enfranchisement of blacks, and reparation payments to the South only served to convince blacks that whites wanted to maintain control.[122]

Smith saw this white domination as a "dishonorable and treacherous spirit which…throws off the sense of moral obligation, when tempted to it by the prospect of advantage."[123] In the post-war era, this "advantage" that was accruing to whites was, at the same time, setting the stage for future violence.

Smith wrote to President Ulysses S. Grant, calling his attention to the continued denial of "equal civil rights" for blacks. "To cease from this injustice… is the nation's first duty. The nation cannot be safe… if the discharge of this duty shall be delayed much longer."[124] Smith had a prophetic vision of what might happen if civil rights legislation at the national level did not follow closely on the heels of the northern victory and legal emancipation. "[Blacks] may be driven by the sense of their wrongs to fearful and widespread violence."[125]

Douglass agreed. In "An Appeal to Congress for Impartial Suffrage" published in the *Atlantic Monthly,* he warned,

> "If black men have no rights in the eyes of white
> men, of course the white have none in the eyes
> of blacks. The result, is a war of roses, and the
> annihilation of all proper human relations."[126]

Douglass remained optimistic, however. He told Smith of his own experience with post-war discrimination,

"I am so used to being snubbed, and receiving insults
because of my color, and so confident of the ultimate
improvement in the civilization of my countrymen that
I succeed in making a pleasant thing of life after all."[127]

To give some validity to Douglass' and Smith's perceptions, H. W.
Johnson, Jr., a black man and a former United States resident who
had moved to Liberia in 1866 to escape post war discrimination,
informed Smith,

"Tired of the struggle against Hope, I abandoned
the contest and sought refuge in my 'fatherland'....
The load of oppression immediately rolled off my
weary shoulders, and I felt—for the first time in
my life—that I was a man and a Brother and a
freeman in the land of Freedom!"[128]

Some activists attempted to work out new social arrangements
to counteract racial prejudice. In Oswego, they formed the Independent Lecture Association to advance the social acceptance of
blacks. The association invited speakers such as Frederick Douglass
to address the public in an adaptive effort to motivate change in
racist attitudes.[129]

Abolitionists called for conventions to oppose continuing racism. Smith was asked to sign the call for a National Convention of
the Friends of Equal Civil and Political Rights.[130] Douglass commented,

"Unless the call can be influentially signed...
I think it better not be held. The names of
prominent abolitionists such as yourself Garrison
and Phillips would be at once an assurance of
character and earnestness in the movement."[131]

Douglass chose public conventions because he was dissatisfied, as
was Smith, with politics as a means of social or moral progress. As if

to accent their disgust, the Democrats in 1874 once again resumed control in the United States House of Representatives.[132]

From Washington, D.C., Douglass told Smith,

"The moral atmosphere here is more than twisted, it is rotten. Avarice, duplicity, falsehood, corruption, servility, fawning and trickery of all kinds, confronts us at every turn. There is little here but distrust and suspicion."[133]

Another initiative to alleviate post war discrimination against blacks was education. Some localities started schools for blacks to help them adjust to their new status,[134] while others wrote books to advise them of new needs. Lydia Maria Child received a $50 donation from Smith toward her effort to write a book aimed at teaching freedmen black cultural pride.[135]

Abolitionists still traveled the speaking circuit to rally the public for equal rights. Sojourner Truth, combining the women's and blacks' rights themes, connected with Smith as she pursued the equal rights movement, saying,

"I am now in Sericuse will have a metting here friday night i would like to come out to Peterboro and have a metting there and see you and would then go out west."[136]

Smith also received invitations to speak, but he did not accept many of them. Following the war he had withdrawn from vigorous public activity, and even though he was in demand as a speaker, he spent most of his time at home.[137]

To his credit, one of Gerrit Smith's visionary ideas for future peace was conveyed in a post-war letter to President Johnson. After pleading with Johnson for leniency toward the South, Smith proposed the establishment of an "International Congress" for the prevention of future wars.[138] Smith's idea would be realized 54 years later, with the birth of the League of Nations following World War I.

Probably the one act that best summarized Smith's attitude toward the South, toward blacks, and toward the future of the country—the act that best reflected his lifelong pattern of providing both philanthropy and justice—was his act of posting bail for Jefferson Davis.

While Davis was jailed at Fortress Monroe in Hampton, Virginia, his physician was John J. Craven. He came to know Davis personally and wrote an extensive account of Davis' attitudes and experiences while in prison. Smith owned a copy of Craven's book,[139] and it is likely that its contents greatly influenced his philanthropic move to free Davis. Craven commented in his book,

"Is it not true that the chief... prejudices of public
opinion come from our not understanding...
the true motives... of the men to whom we are
opposed....? History [will not] consent to regard
Mr. Davis in the odious, monstrous, or contemptible
light which has been...the only one in which the
necessities and passions of our recent struggle would
permit him to be presented to our age."

Davis, shackled in chains during the early part of his post-war imprisonment, claimed that

"...the laws guarantee certain privileges to persons
held for trial. To hold me here for trial, under
all the rigors of a condemned convict, is not
warranted by law [and] is revolting to the spirit of
justice. In the political history of the world, there is
no parallel to my treatment."

Davis felt humiliated and believed "that the South should be restored its full rights in the Union and that it should be done quickly in order to avoid hatred developing out of vengeance." He added that "'Quarrels' between friends are best healed when they are healed most promptly...." As Smith read about Jefferson Davis' imprisonment, he certainly agreed with Craven's main point:

"Make him a martyr and his memory is dangerous;
treat him with the generosity of liberation and
he...will be a power for good in the future of peace
and restored prosperity which we hope for the
Southern States."[140]

While many in the North called for revenge and for Davis' head, Gerrit Smith saw the need for humaneness. Noting that northern newspapers were upset with his signing of Davis' bail bond, Smith printed a circular outlining his reasons for having done so. First, Smith wrote, it was cruel and unfair to hold a person in prison for two years without offering a trial. Second, he felt a moral obligation to sign it, given his previously published positions on the war. The charge under which Davis was being held was treason. This, said Smith, was illogical, because the war was not fought under the rules of a constitution, but under the "law of war." To try Davis for treason would be to admit that the South had remained part of the nation throughout the war. Smith warned Supreme Court Chief Justice Salmon Chase not to be trapped by this inconsistency.[141]

Smith viewed the North's tendency toward vengeance as a heady abuse of victory.

"The shame of defeat is as nothing compared with
the shame of abusing the power of success....
We may not recover so far from our passion and
prejudice, as to be ashamed of this perfidy—but
our children will be ashamed of it."[142]

Perhaps Elizabeth Cady Stanton, who had written to him in 1865 just after the war had ended, had influenced Smith:

"I feel for Lee + Davis very much...profound
sympathy and respect.... I feel sorry to have
Lincoln take possession of his house.... It seems so
like trumpeting over a fallen foe."[143]

Horace Greeley, Cornelius Vanderbilt, and Gerrit Smith each put up $25,000 while a group of others supplied the remaining $25,000 for Davis' bail.[144] Smith was confident that the act would lead to the healing of wounds that remained open due to the failure of political action to reunify the country.

At the same time, Smith's act did not suggest he had forgiven Davis for his crime of rebellion. The signing of Jefferson Davis' bail bond epitomized Smith's lifelong pattern of compassion for the oppressed. In this case, the oppressed included not just Davis, but also the slaveholders who were a continuing target of Northern vengeance, the former slaves who looked forward to at least ungrudging if not loving acceptance, the South which needed its leader restored to dignity, and the whole country, which Smith felt needed the divisive court issue resolved.

Perhaps Smith left himself open to charges that he used his money to bribe his way into national policy. But one cannot avoid the conclusion that in pursuing his own values, he did use his resources altruistically. With this particular act—in spite of the public criticism it brought him—he was quite satisfied. In his poem to Ann on their forty-sixth anniversary, he wrote whimsically:

> "My only feat in all the year
> Is signing Davis' Bail Bond
> And fearing not that he'd abscond...
> And...have all the folks
> O'er the whole land at me crack jokes."[145]

Although Smith was convinced of the importance of the abolition movement in hastening the end of slavery, it is likely that in the long run, slavery would have died of a combination of economic and moral forces. There are some still who claim that the "holier-than-thou" attitude taken by northern abolitionists only infuriated southerners, causing them to become more defensive. One critic wrote,

> "Abolitionists had done more to rivet the chains of
> the slave, and to fasten the curse of slavery upon

the country 'than all the pro-slavery men in the
world had done, or could do, in half a century.'"[146]

There can be little doubt, however, that the incessant work of
the abolitionists in writing and speaking out kept the issue in vivid
colors before the eyes of the public, continually irritating nerves of
guilt. The effect of the Harpers Ferry raid in accelerating the process
of abolition is also undeniable. Slaves were grateful that there were
at least a few people like Smith and Brown who simply would not
sit back and do nothing in the face of such monumental injustice.
Years before the raid, Smith bemoaned the fact that the world's new
democracy—"the moral and political lighthouse of the world"—had
disgraced itself with the institution of slavery. "In the house of her
friends," he said in opposition to the Nebraska Bill in 1854, "Liberty
has received her deepest stabs."[147]

In his own mind, one of Smith's most satisfying triumphs regarding abolition and the public's attitude toward blacks involved
Peterboro. An 1837 petition signed by Peterboro residents and
sent to the state legislature called for New York State to allow free
blacks to vote, and called for the right to trial by jury for fugitive
slaves.[148] Writing to a Virginia slaveholder in 1840, Smith boasted
in proprietary fashion about his "village:"

> "In the village in which I live, a vigorous
> application of gospel principles was made a few
> years ago to the overthrow of the wicked prejudice
> in question… and now colored persons sit where
> they please in our sanctuaries—and I know not
> the family in our village, that would reject a decent
> colored person from their table…. How I should
> love to have you see the state of heart in my little
> village toward the colored man. You are waiting for
> the South to move forward with you in the work of
> emancipation. This little village did not wait for the
> North to take right ground in this matter."[149]

Smith's pride seemed justified to Franklin Sanborn, who, late in his life, wrote of having visited "Gerrit Smith's villa at Peterboro, where, amid inherited acres which he managed with noble generosity, that baronial democrat lived and bore his part in our struggle for liberty...."[150]

Others shared admiration for Smith's lifelong effort at abolition. When New York City was making arrangements to celebrate the ratification of the 15th Amendment to the Constitution, which gave black males the right to vote, Smith received an invitation to speak there. In the invitation, former escaped slave and Garrisonian William P. Powell noted,

> "Your name stands side by side with the earliest
> tried soldiers of that noble army of fanatics, who
> dared to 'cry aloud and spare not,' against the
> iniquitous, gigantic, monstrous, atrocious system
> of American slavery...."[151]

Smith saw slavery as a long-lasting trauma that had alternately shaped and shattered the United States, and had played a large part in creating the social structure of America. He would probably be dismayed anew if he could see that since his death, the focus of American history has been on the Civil War instead of on the institution that caused it. The shelves of contemporary bookstores are crammed with volumes about the war—but only a few about slavery. There is more fascination with battles and violence than with the institutionalized cruelty suffered by slaves over a far longer period of time.

We admire battlefields with parks and monuments for their beauty instead of recognizing them as symbols of moral defeat. Southern plantation estates with gorgeous gardens and fawning tourists appear as peaceful places of natural wonder, inspiring admiration because they look more like Eden than like former prisons for black slaves.

Gerrit Smith's recurring dream was that the nation he loved would fulfill its promise to its people. He believed freedom was the most powerful force in world history, and he was convinced of its eventual triumph:

"The antislavery cause has moved the depths of the soul," he wrote in 1851, "and the tumult will never be stilled, until the cause has triumphed…. Nay, the human soul must first turn traitor toward all its instincts, and disown its nature."[152]

In the cause of abolition, Smith's goal was noble, his motives unselfish, and his resolve complete. With others like himself, he worked tirelessly for almost a lifetime, expending what resources he had for the benefit of others whom he did not know—in a cause he could not resist. His commitment to abolition dominated his life. He fought it with his voice, his pen, his money, and his heart—right up until his death.

In early December of 1874, at age 77, Smith felt quite well. He had written a couple of letters to abolitionist G.C. Sampson regarding political party policies and loyalty, and Sampson responded on December 6, "I trust I may accept your last 2 letters as ample proof of your bodily health as they are that of your mind."[153]

Because Ann had been away since mid-October, Gerrit was alone in the Peterboro house, tended by his housekeeper, Betsey Kelty. Concerning these last months of his life, Betsey commented,

"Always gentle, kind + pure minded, he was feeble,
his upright form was bowed and his firm, elastic
step had given place to shoving his feet along for
fear of falling, but his brain… urged him on to
keep up his correspondence + his reading, writing,
and thinking but it had become hard for him."[154]

In late December, Smith traveled to New York City to visit Ann, who had been undergoing eye treatment while staying with her niece, Ellen Walter. On Christmas day, he composed four letters. One was to Aunt Betsey in Peterboro, "charging her not to neglect the poor in the village, to see that the children of the orphan asylum had their holiday supplies, and that papers were sent to the free reading room, which he maintained."[155] His last meal on that day was at four o'clock in the afternoon. He was jovial, told stories of his early life, and even sang "a snatch of an Irish air."[156]

On the following morning of December 26 he rose from bed at 7:30 am after chatting with Ann "pleasantly for nearly an hour." He pulled a chair up in front of a newly lighted fire and attempted to dress himself. Betsey Kelty noted later, "While dressing, his wife looked at him, he was so pale + she thought his voice unnatural. She took hold of his arm and led him to the bed. As he laid down he said, 'weak, very weak,' and those were his last words [as he] went into an unconscious state."[157]

The *New York Herald* finished the tale: "From that moment he never spoke or appeared to return to consciousness."[158]

After this sudden stroke hit, Ann tried to communicate with Gerrit, but succeeded only in getting him to raise one hand in recognition of her voice. When the family physician, Dr. Bayard, arrived, he diagnosed a stroke that had paralyzed the entire right side of Smith's body. Gerrit lingered in this condition until he drew his last breath shortly after 1 o'clock on the afternoon of December 28.

It is fortunate for Gerrit Smith that his death came suddenly; but the hole it left in the lives of others was gigantic. When his body arrived at his Peterboro home on New Year's Eve, his daughter had decorated with only a few flowers. Gerrit had not wanted an ostentatious funeral.

> "In the hallway hung the motto, 'Equal rights to all.' Over Mr. Smith's picture in the parlor were the words, 'Human rights are above all laws and constitutions'...."

The undertaker was Thomas Dugan from New York City, and Reverend E. T. Hawthen, a Syracuse friend of Gerrit's, conducted the ceremony. The casket was made of black walnut with solid silver handles, and lined with lead first and then with white satin. A bouquet of white roses adorned it "in behalf of the Colored Orphan Asylum in Brooklyn, N.Y." The people of Peterboro filled the mansion, but Ann and Greene did not attend "on account of sickness." They were probably consumed by grief.

Elizabeth Cady Stanton and Betsey Kelty were present, along with the 30 residents of the local orphan asylum that Gerrit had founded and supported. They "peered sadly over the sides of the casket at their dead benefactor." They sang his favorite hymn, reflecting his lifelong optimism.

"Let us gather up the sunbeams
　　Lying all around our path;
Let us keep the wheat and roses
　　Casting out the thorns and chaff.

Let us find our sweetest comforts
　　In the blessings of today,
With a patient hand removing
　　All the briars from the way."

Just before his casket was closed, his daughter cut four locks of his hair to keep as mementos. A procession of over 500 people walked in 20-degrees-below-zero temperatures about one half-mile to the cemetery. Tears must have frozen as warm hearts expressed love for a fallen idol.[159] The obituaries were many and long. The *New York Times* stated,

"The history of the most important half century
of our national life will be imperfectly written
if it fails to place Gerrit Smith in the front rank
of the men whose influence was most felt in the
accomplishment of its results."[160]

The Evening Mail offered, "...a mind... more vigorous in the unselfish service of the race has not been known in this century...."[161]

The Gerrit Smith Mansion in winter, looking east from the area near the Land Office. At the time of Gerrit Smith's death, more than 500 people braved weather like this to stand in line and view his body inside the mansion, before walking a half-mile to the cemetery in temperatures that reached 20 degrees below zero.

From the author's collection

Smith's will reflected his lifelong attitude of benevolence. He left many thousands of dollars to his children, grandchildren, in-laws, and other relatives. He provided for lifetime support of his family's surviving servants and forgave the outstanding debts of former clerks. Whatever remained of his estate or property was to be divided—one half to Ann, one quarter to Elizabeth, and one quarter to Greene.

Perhaps more significant than the obituaries were the testimonials written by Gerrit's friends. His pastor at the Methodist Church in Peterboro, David Koeppel, wrote:

> "Gerrit Smith is dead! The great world will be
> lonely without him, but how much more the circle
> of his friends and neighbors. No cottage around
> his home was so humble that he was not often
> there. Sickness, poverty and death were calls which
> his great heart could not resist."[162]

Gerrit Smith, as photographed six months before his death, at the age of 77. This portrait was taken on May 1, 1874 by Newell J. Miller of Excelsior Photograph Palace, Morrisville, NY. When Smith died on December 28 of that year, this photo was used in his death notice.

From the author's collection

On the first Sunday after his death, Gerrit Smith's pew in the Methodist Church was draped, and then covered with wreaths, flowers, and a photograph of him.[163] An interesting letter came to Elizabeth Smith Miller from a woman in Norwich, Connecticut who had met Smith briefly at conventions in 1852 and 1864.

> "I never loved another with whom I was so slightly acquainted as I loved him. He has been my...
> ideal of a great and good man for the past thirty-five years.... I feel that I have suffered a personal loss—and it seems to me strange."[164]

Betsey Kelty had known Gerrit for sixty years. On February 15, 1875, she wrote in her journal:

> "I had known him from a youth in his 15th year, always gentle, kind, tender hearted, and <u>fine minded</u>...." I thank God that he left him so long to labor for the right...."

Even his former antagonist praised him. Probably the best summary of Smith's legacy, preserved in the *Gerrit Smith Papers* from an unknown newspaper, is the memorial written by William Lloyd Garrison:

> "Today, December 28th, [an] impressive record is completed by the telegraphic announcement of the decease of one who, by reason of his intellectual and moral force, his munificent liberality, his rare self-abnegation, his stirring eloquence, his courageous and resplendent example, his personal gifts and graces, his all-embracing philanthropy, made himself pre-eminent in the tremendous struggle for the abolition of slavery. To whom can I refer but that great and good man, Gerrit Smith? His case is hardly to be paralleled among the benefactors of mankind in this or any other

country. The language of eulogy, often so absurdly
or so timidly applied, may in this instance be
used in its strongest form without danger of
exaggeration. No description of sublime deeds can
match their performance. Truly, in the Peterboro
philanthropist and reformer was seen
'A combination and a form, indeed
Where every god did seem to set his seal,
To give the world assurance of a man' –
of a man not only remarkable for the beauty
and stateliness of his person, the suavity of his
manners, and the charm of his social intercourse;
but exceptional among millions in what he
achieved in the matter of self-conquest over
the strongest temptations and the most ample
opportunities to lead a luxurious and purely
worldly life."[165]

Epilogue

As I write this epilogue, I sit in Gerrit Smith's land office on a cool, rainy night in late November. He may have died 135 years ago, but as the rain patters softly on the wood shingle roof, I can hear the scratching of his pen writing a note to forgive the debt of a poor person who could not meet his payments.

Inside this small, brick building is a single room measuring 25 by 20 feet, with a brick floor laid on top of a wood frame. Split lath shows through the hair plaster in one spot on the ceiling as the light from two kerosene lanterns dances in the rippled glass windows. A six-inch round hole in the chimney wall shows where the wood stove stood. Gerrit's desk was on a raised platform across the room from the stove. Smith spent 55 years doing the work of his land business in this room, and as I listen carefully through the soft rain, I can hear voices.

In cascading scenes, I can see Harriet Tubman in her tattered shoes sitting by the south window, quietly asking for aid and advice on helping 12 fugitive slaves reach safety in Canada. One of them, a young, very dark male, sits next to her. He looks frightened and happy at the same time.

There, by the warm stove, stands John Brown, his eyes sparkling as he reveals to Gerrit his latest plans for a free Kansas and asks for money to buy supplies for his next trip west.

Frederick Douglass gazes dreamily through the east window toward the Smith mansion. He speaks over his shoulder to Gerrit of his own glorious feeling of freedom and his satisfaction in aiding the cause of abolition through his newspaper, *The North Star*. His stature, with arms folded and muscles tense, elicits the determination of an obsessed man, a national leader, a black Abraham Lincoln destined to succeed.

In the wooden chair beside Gerrit's desk sits a middle-aged man, hat in hand, who has just walked five miles from Clockville to negotiate a postponement of his payments. In front of the desk stands a defiant Kentucky slave owner who has traveled north searching for his fugitive property. After his shouts have filled the small room with harsh threats, Gerrit calmly invites him to stay for dinner.

Over a half-million acres of land changed ownership in this room. Yet the most important symbol of this land office is its humility. Smith could have sat in golden chairs and had others do all his work for him, but he chose to work 12-hour days in a plain, unpretentious building. He did not live or work or think in an ivory tower, nor did he wish to be alienated from other people because of his wealth.

By idolizing or criticizing him, his admirers and detractors made him either more or less than he deserved to be. Smith was a poorly read man with such faith in the wisdom and reasonableness of the masses that he believed he could guide them to a better life. He envisioned a world in which there was no prejudice, no greed, no palaces, no beggars—a world in which liberty was every person's inherent right.

A self-appointed moral leader, he based his recommendations on what he saw as "common sense" coming from his own parochial experience. He lived precariously on the edge of acceptance and disapproval, full of innocent hope in the face of the unjust public bias that produced social inequality. Always working for and expecting the best as he saw it, Smith realized that he was in a tiny minority.

Some of us prefer to play the safe game of pleasing everyone and using the acceptance of others to help us feel good. Gerrit Smith's self-assurance was stable; he felt good even when others criticized him intensely. Frederick Douglass said of Smith that he was "as safe on the floor of the House of Representatives, as when listening with crazy awe to the gibberish of rapping spirits in Peterboro, or preaching to a Syracuse mob."[1]

The reform that Gerrit Smith supported, he pursued unselfishly. He neither sought nor expected personal gain. In some ways, he was a pathetic figure doomed to frustration; in other ways, he was an heroic figure leading the popular imagination toward visions of an ideal community. He believed in the power of benevolence to win minds for the moral right, and his public habit of kindness was both cathartic for him and therapeutic for the public.

His high level of optimism helped him to avoid the traps that ensnared many of his fellow reformers. Reform itself is an iconoclastic venture in which social rebels risk developing a cynical spirit that does not forgive, a skepticism that breeds negativism and pessimism. Smith stayed positive and worked with the system he wanted to change by building institutions such as schools, churches, and political parties. He wanted to effect social change while loving people and living simply.

To Gerrit, living as simply as possible meant enjoying Peterboro mornings, observing nature, reading the Bible, writing bad rhymes, recognizing the value of little things, and believing the world could be fair. But he was brought closer to reality by his wealth, by family tragedies, travel, politics, and ill health, all of which he tolerated but did not enjoy. Requests for his aid and influence in national issues drew him into complex problems that he could not escape.

Gerrit Smith spent much of his life trying to make the effects of oppression real to people who had never seen or felt it, urging them to care about something that did not affect them directly. He probably accomplished more than he ever realized; he helped to change the way that future generations would think about the less fortunate. He stood with the giants who fought for the rights of those who had no power: blacks, women, the poor. He stands with us still as we carry on the same fight. In his battle against slavery, he helped awaken the nation to its greatest sin. The promise of freedom, legally secure but socially elusive, rests with us to fulfill.

Smith's most intense disappointment in life was that he never witnessed the moral victory of emancipation and the achievement of equality to which he dedicated his life and much of his fortune. The effort to achieve abolition through moral conversion of the masses proved futile, defeated time and again by timid politics, repressive economics, and rabid selfishness. Yet despite the institutional failures, Gerrit Smith did not let defeat rule his emotions.

Douglass said of him,

> "Gerrit Smith is one of the most remarkable men that ever lived in this age, or in any age: remarkable for his intellect, remarkable for his purity of heart, remarkable for his child-like simplicity, and for that majesty of soul which accepts to the full that sublime doctrine of Christian faith—'Do unto others as ye would that others should do unto you.' "[2]

If Gerrit Smith were alive today, what issues would draw his attention? Obviously, one would be racism. Ten years after the Civil War, in the last year of his life, Smith recognized the long road blacks still had before them as they traveled toward true freedom.

> "Alas, how many a colored brother and colored sister have felt their hearts die within them, whilst travelling, or attempting to travel, through this still caste-cursed and still Satan-swayed land!"[3]

It is caste-cursed still; almost any adult black person can tell personal stories of discrimination—not only in the United States, but the world over. On January 7, 2003, the school board of the city of Auburn, New York rejected a proposal to name an elementary school in honor of the legendary Underground Railroad conductor Harriet Tubman, who had made her home in Auburn after the Civil War. In classic racist style, white residents who attended the public meetings to discuss the renaming of the building claimed that if it were not a black school, the new name would stigmatize students who attended it. They asked why more local black residents did not attend the meetings, implying that any topic dealing with Harriet Tubman was a black issue instead of an American issue.[4]

More recently, the election of Barack Obama as the first black president of the United States of America brought with it a backlash of racially motivated anger, with white supremacist groups expecting to see a swelling of their ranks—even before Obama's inauguration.[5]

Gerrit Smith identified closely with and aided the efforts of black women such as Harriet Tubman and Sojourner Truth, even while other abolitionists avoided their "radicalism." Recently, the reputations of both of these black women have been resurrected, and they have been transformed into heroes who epitomized the old and continuing fight against racism and sexism. Smith's focus on them symbolized his accurate perception of the long-term effects of a discriminatory culture. Today, these women focus the contemporary eye on a shameful part of American history; they are essential components in the war against discrimination that they waged along with Gerrit Smith a century and a half ago.

Our craving for symbols like Tubman, Truth, and Smith highlights a contemporary concern for the justice and equality for which they fought. But the war is not over; even slavery is not dead. According to one recent international survey, "more people were sold into bondage around the world in the 20th century than were shipped as slaves to the cotton fields of America…. Slavery continues for many of the same reasons it did hundreds of years ago: greed, exploitation and power."[6] Today, the American Anti-Slavery Group fights against institutions of slavery wherever they exist, much as did the American Anti-Slavery Society prior to the Civil War.

One of Smith's last fights was against human rights violations in Cuba, where slavery was well entrenched. In April 2001, more than a century after Smith's last speech on the matter, "Cuba was again condemned by the United Nations [for] human rights problems and political oppression…."[7] Smith would be disappointed to see such lack of progress in human rights issues.

Temperance would also attract Smith's attention today. The continuing battle for women's rights would as well. And given that Smith believed that nature was the one true teacher of lessons for stability in life, he would likely be concerned about environmental issues. In short, things have not changed so much that Gerrit Smith would not know where to start his work.

A recent sociological study has noted the development of people who are called "Cultural Creatives." In a complex social world with a mosaic of values, these people are college-educated, optimistic, sensitive persons who focus on the development of caring relationships and a sense of community. They have a new sense of the sacred "that combines personal growth, service to others, and spirituality...." They attempt to create balance and harmony among diverse forces in an effort to produce a more humane, equitable, and just society.[8]

This sounds like a contemporary version of Gerrit Smith. As a man who was ahead of his time, he presaged the "salad bowl" philosophy of society that recognizes and legitimates diversity amid unity. Perhaps his greatest accomplishment in life was his way of thinking, which integrated culturally accepted dichotomies—a rare accomplishment in *any* era. He helped people see interconnections between segments of life that they had traditionally perceived as separated.

Regarding racial issues, his "black heart" encouraged perceptions of equality among all humans. He melded class divisions through his philanthropy and brought together politics and religion through the Liberty Party. He viewed gender distinctions as social constructs, and he encouraged people to defy the traditional male and female roles society was trying to force upon them.

His ecology-based way of thinking led him to see a world in which everything is hitched to everything else, where people are a part of nature instead of apart from it. He supposed people to be responsible for and to each other. In breaking down thought patterns that produced opposites and separated people from one another as well as from their natural environment, Smith presaged the modern integrative discipline of ecology in his lifelong attempts to reform selfishness.

It seems fitting that Smith died in New York City, a place that exposed the paradoxes of life for which he sought and envisioned solutions. On a large scale, the city reflected the global community of balance amid diversity in the pursuit of societal goals. On a smaller scale, this complexity led to perversity, immorality, injustice, and inequality for many individuals.

A nature lover, Smith died in an unnatural setting that symbolized much of what he had attempted to change. His final act was to raise his arm in recognition of Ann's presence, symbolizing a partnership of the sort we all crave with one another—and with the world. Although he never succeeded in implementing the global fraternity he had envisioned, he influenced the ideas of many people and actually improved the lives of many more—especially in his local area.

Gerrit Smith had a major impact on a small scale. He loved "his neighbors" in "his village," and counseled them toward what he perceived as a better life. He exhibited his emotional health through several traits. Empathy ran so deep within him that he understood the perspectives of others to be as logical as his own. Not only did the oppressed receive his favor; so did the slave owner. Smith was so magnanimous with his enemies that he held no grudges or petty resentfulness toward them; in the midst of fundamental disagreements, he could see and compliment their best qualities.

While opposing his enemies' beliefs, he could still develop friendships and alliances with them. His sense of personal balance was strong enough to ignore others' claims that he was a fanatic. Instead, his optimism drove him to try to leave the world better for having lived in it by helping others to think better of themselves.

It can be said that his large-scale efforts at reform were futile. He wasted time, effort, and money on the cause of temperance.

He wavered in his commitment to women's rights. In spite of his gargantuan efforts at abolition, the emancipation of slaves would have happened eventually without him—on legal terms, but not moral ones. Smith lacked the glitter and fame of public figures who attract a lot of attention. He was not a successful politician, statesman, theologian, clergyman, editor, poet, or author. But should the small-scale achievements of his charitable and unselfish lifestyle count any less because they did not reach very far?

I am reminded of the story of the clam digger who was labeled a fool because he threw back only one misshapen clam. How, the critic asked, could such a modest effort possibly matter? The clam digger's response: "It matters to *that* one."

Smith's example of kindness toward individuals can aid all of us in moving a step closer to dignity. He shed tears for a humanity that did not elevate every person to his or her highest possible status. He believed that any act that limited one person injured *all* people, so he worked to minimize oppression. He agreed with his close friend and fellow reformer, Beriah Green, that they should work hard to demonstrate "compassion for the least, the last, and the lost."[9]

Smith's vision of a better world clashed with worldly realities, thereby frustrating his dreams and goals. But his commitment stayed high. If he met with some success at reform in his beloved Peterboro, which Henry Highland Garnet referred to as "Heaven," he felt disappointed when the rest of the world would not follow suit. To some extent, life in Peterboro for half a century in the mid-1800s begged the questions raised a century later by folk singers Peter, Paul, and Mary:

> "How many years can some people exist
> before they're allowed to be free?
> How many times can a man turn his head
> and pretend that he just doesn't see?
> …How many ears must one man have
> before he can hear people cry?"

In Peterboro, at least, Gerrit Smith saw, and heard, and cried, and acted. He pledged his time, his thought, his money, and his life to the welfare of his American brothers and sisters in an honorable and noble attempt to achieve 'Liberty and Justice for All'. Although his efforts may have been at times misguided and futile, one can never say that he did not try. As a practical dreamer, he viewed the world as a place where one should give more than one takes.

His legacy has been recognized at least physically by the United States Government's designation of his Peterboro home site as a National Historic Landmark, and by the listing of his Land Office on the National Register of Historic Places. His social legacy remains in the 'dry' township of Smithfield and in the social example he set. His life was characterized by empathy. He showed us all what is possible: a socially integrated Peterboro, education of oppressed minorities, and the power in the grassroots reason of common people to change social systems.

Gerrit Smith's courage to take radical stands made everyone reconsider what they were thinking and doing; it may even have made people with more moderate positions on slavery—like Abraham Lincoln—more electable. He did not shake the world into recognition of a new age of humaneness, or lend his name to a city or a college.

His beloved Peterboro achieved the status as home to the National Abolition Hall of Fame and Museum in 2004. Yet no monument stands to commemorate his efforts to free slaves or to help poor people. Probably his most significant act on a national scale—the aiding of John Brown—was the one about which he was most embarrassed. What made him feel best was the comforting of an individual.

Gerrit Smith's body rests in a modestly appointed grave in the Peterboro Cemetery, on a knoll overlooking the hamlet to which he dedicated his life. His headstone there reads only, "Gerrit Smith;" there follows no glorious epitaph chipped in stone, no elegant marble carvings.

The aura that emanates from that spot evokes the best human qualities to which we all can aspire: a combination of liberalism and parochialism, wisdom and foolishness, profundity and shallowness; but always, *always*, an abundance of innocent hope.

Acknowledgements

Many people deserve thanks for their help during the process of research. The staff of the Department of Special Collections at the Ernest Stevenson Bird Library of Syracuse University were especially helpful in guiding my access to and handling of original source material in the Gerrit Smith Papers, as was also the staff of the Madison County Historical Society at Cottage Lawn in Oneida, New York, and the Geneva Historical Society in Geneva, New York. I also appreciated the professional help of personnel at the Daniel Burke Library of Hamilton College in Clinton, New York, the Cazenovia Public Library in Cazenovia, New York, and the Morrisville Public Library in Morrisville, New York.

A special personal thanks is extended to the staff of the Donald G. Butcher Library of the State University of New York at Morrisville for their cheerful endurance of my constant presence and questioning, and for the use of their equipment.

On a personal level, special recognition is due to Robert and Joyce Clark, long term residents in the Peterboro, New York area, who generously allowed me to photo-copy their bound volume of Gerrit Smith's printed speeches, letters, and circulars. Mary DeLorme aided in the research on medical issues.

Because the original manuscript was written in longhand by the author, the expert help of professional typists Jill Yorton and Beverly Patchin was dearly appreciated.

The expertise of first readers of the manuscript was indispensable in checking for accuracy of data and clarity of ideas, and in catching errors that would have marred the quality of the final product. I express sincere and deep appreciation for the time and the attention to detail of Milton C. Sernett, Ph.D., Professor Emeritus of African American Studies and History, and Adjunct Professor of Religion in the College of Arts and Sciences at Syracuse University; and of Donna Dorrance Burdick, retired Whitney Point Central School teacher and Town of Smithfield historian.

Finally, with intense accolades and praise, I thank my life-partner, Dorothy H. Willsey-Dann, for her original inspiration to research a biography of Gerrit Smith, and for her tolerance of an obsessed and preoccupied husband.

Bibliographic Note

One of the difficulties in documenting this research involves the huge number of original sources. To list each one in a bibliography is prohibitive, yet the reader deserves knowledge of the source of a point made, and where to find it. Books, magazines, newspapers and journal articles will appear in the bibliography, but the many hundreds of letters will not be so listed. When a letter is quoted or referred to, its reference will appear in the end notes. The writer and the recipient of the letter will be referred to with initials where appropriate as follows:

GS – Gerrit Smith
ACS – Ann Carroll Smith
ESM – Elizabeth Smith Miller
GrS – Greene Smith
ECS – Elizabeth Cady Stanton
FD – Frederick Douglass
PS – Peter Smith

The letters are located in various collections and will be referenced in the documentation as follows:

MCHS – Madison County Historical Society
PHS – Peterboro Historical Society
SU – Syracuse University, Bird Library
GHS – Geneva Historical Society
HCL – Hamilton College Library
NYPL – New York Public Library
SLC – bound volume of speeches, letters, and circulars in possession of the author. This volume will be donated to the Peterboro Historical Society.

An example might be GS to ACS, Dec. 22, 1851, SU. This reference gives the writer, the recipient, the date, and the location of the letter.

Throughout the book, I will not attempt to cover material chronologically. In searching for feelings and patterns, it makes more sense to match these at different time periods than to segregate them.

Notes

Introduction
1. Address at the erection of the Asa Wing Monument, Sept. 11, 1855, SU.

Chapter 1
1. GS to Elizabeth L. Smith, Nov. 20, 1815, SU.
2. Rutger B. Miller to ESM, Feb. 18, 1877, SU.
3. GS to President Brown and Professor North of Hamilton College, Nov. 16, 1874, HCL.
4. GS to GrS, Sept. 1, 1861, MCHS.
5. Harlow, p. 4.
6. Bill of Sale of slaves, Peter Smith to Jesse Ives, August 17, 1801, SU.
7. George W. Putnam to the National Anti-Slavery Standard. Jan. 28, 1860. Letter dated Jan. 14, 1860; U.S. Census, 1810; newspaper clip, "Gerrit Smith Miller," Blandina Miller, no date, but probably about 1900.
8. Frothingham, 1st ed., 10-12.
9. Frothingham, 1st ed., 20.
10. New York Herald. Dec. 29, 1874, 4.
11. Henry A. Foster to GS, March 20, SU.
12. C.N. to Peter Smith, May 3, 1810, NYPL.

13. GS to Elizabeth L. Smith, July 16, 1815, SU.
14. GS to PS, Nov. 3, 1816; GS to Elizabeth L. Smith, Nov. 20, 1815; Nov. 30, 1816, SU.
15. GS to PS, April 7, 1817, SU.
16. Rutger B. Miller to ESM, Feb. 18, 1877, SU.
17. Frothingham, 1st ed., 24.
18. Oren Cothin to GS, Jan. 21, 1819, SU.
19. Dodge, 31.
20. Encyclopedia Britannica, 15th edition, 1976, vol. 2 406; vol. 7, 694; vol. 6, 1019, 1020; vol. 8, 1017-1021, 1071-1073; vol. 3, 4; vol. 17, 982-985.
21. Autobiographical sketch, SU.
22. Jan. 5, 1817, SU.
23. GS to Joseph Noyes, Oct. 18, 1819, HCL.
24. Thomas, Jan. 5, 1875.
25. Edward Ludlow to GS, Feb. 8, 1819, SU.
26. President McEldowney to GS, July 10, 1865, SU.
27. *The Oneida Dispatch*, Jan. 8, 1875.
28. GS to Judge Barlow, Dec. 10, 1857, HCL.
29. Bartlett.
30. Bartlett, 22.
31. Higginson, 10,12.
32. GS, "The Religion of Reason," Jan. 23, 1859, in *Sermons and*

Speeches.
33. Koeppel, MCHS.
34. Thomas, MCHS.

Chapter 2
1. Diary entry, June 22, 1842 in Frothingham, 1st ed., 130.
2. Aug. 15, 1873, MCHS.
3. GS, "Speech for Human Rights," Feb. 6, 1861, in *Sermons and Speeches*, 160.
4. GS to James McCune Smith, et. al. Nov. 14, 1846, SU.
5. GS to Nellie W. Dyer, March 30, 1874, MCHS.
6. GS to Right Hon. Daniel O'Connell, MP, July 28, 1843, SU.
7. GS to W. L. Garrison and Wendell Phillips, Sept. 12, 1865, SLC.
8. 1863, SU.
9. Circular, "Andersonville," March 20, 1865, SLC.
10. Feb. 28, 1856, SLC.
11. GS to Miss Mason, Jan. 7, 1849, SU.
12. Eulogy to Myron Holley, Rochester, NY, June 13, 1844, SU.
13. Harlow, 373.
14. Circular, GS to his Peterboro neighbors, Feb. 24, 1864, SLC.
15. Cross, 79.
16. GS, "Final Letter to his Constituents," Aug. 7, 1854, in Speeches, 376.
17. March 6, 1831, SU.
18. ACS to ESM, Aug. 15, 1836, SU.
19. Eulogy to Myron Holley, June 13, 1844, SU.
20. GS, Speech at the inauguration of the New York State Anti-Slavery Society, Oct. 22, 1835, SU.
21. GS, "Speech on the Bill to Aid Minnesota," March 7, 1854, in *Speeches,* 102.
22. Frothingham, 1st ed., 370.
23. GS to ACS, Jan 23, 1830, SU.
24. GS to Cornelia Rossiter, June 2, 1834, SU.
25. GS to GrS, March 26, 1851, SU.
26. Mary H. C. Booth to GS, March, 1862, SU.
27. GS, "Speech on War," Jan 18, 1854, in *Speeches*, 54.
28. GS to GrS, March 26, 1851, SU.
29. Harlow, 272.
30. GS to Dr. Fitzhugh, May 1, 1873, SLC.
31. GS to Daniel Dickey and George Ellinwood, March 21, 1845, SU.
32. "Letter No. II," *The North Star*, Sept. 5, 1850.
33. GS, Speech: "Let Crushed Cuba Arise," July 4, 1873, SLC.
34. Newspaper clipping, Recollections of Carlton Rice, no

date, SU.

35. GS to ACS, May 29, 1873, SU.
36. Smith, M.T.
37. GS to Stephen Willard, Dec. 29, 1845, SU.
38. Marvin Bovee to GS, July 1, 1867, SU.
39. GS to Elder Raymond, Feb. 15, 1851, SU.
40. GS to Abby Kelley, Aug. 1, 1843, SU.
41. Frothingham, 1st ed., 363-364.
42. Harlow, 234.
43. GS to Col. Young, Dec. 6, 1841, SU.
44. GS to John S. Hay, Feb. 28, 1872, SU.
45. Harlow, 382.

Chapter 3
1. "Gerrit Smith," Dec. 29, 1874, 4.
2. 1856, SU.
3. 22.
4. Jan. 14, 1875, MCHS.
5. McKivigan, John, 19.
6. Harlow, 11,12.
7. Frothingham, 1st ed., 356.
8. GS, "The Religion of Reason," Jan. 23, 1859, in *Sermons and Speeches.*
9. GS, Discourse in Peterboro, Nov. 20, 1864, MCHS.
10. Hearn, 1, 2.
11. Lewis Tappan to GS quoting GS, July 9, 1866, SU.
12. Written one month before his death; quoted in Koeppel's Memories, Jan. 14, 1875, MCHS.
13. Verse Book, Oct. 23, 1860, SU; Gerrit called Ann "Nancy".
14. GS to Warner Clemens, Nov. 23, 1846, SU.
15. GS to John T. Mason, Nov. 18, 1846, SU.
16. GS to Marius Robinson, April 3, 1846, SU.
17. Frothingham, 1st ed., 139-143.
18. Luce, 5.
19. Frothingham, 1st ed., 349.
20. GS to C.S. Renolaw, April 18, 1842, SU.
21. Frothingham, 1st ed., 361.
22. GS to ECS, Dec. 1, 1855, SU.
23. June 19, 1838, SU.
24. Johnson to GS, April 5, 1860, SU.
25. GS to Mr. + Mrs. T. C. Leonard, March 15, 1844, SU.
26. GS to Gilbert, Jan. 9, 1843, SU.
27. Hearn, 70.
28. Franklin.
29. GS to Rich, March 29, SU.
30. GS to Raymond, Nov. 2, 1847, SU.
31. GS to Perry G. Palmer, Nov. 24, 1846, SU.
32. A.V. Bentley to GS, July 23, 1860, SU.

33. GS, "The True Office of Civil Government," speech in Troy, 1851, SU.
34. Harriet C. Sykes to GS, Oct. 26, 1853, SU.
35. to GS, March 6, 1874, SU.
36. C.J. Talbot to GS, April 26, 1859, SU.
37. William Jenks to GS July 25, 1850, SU.
38. Anne Adams to GS May 28, 1871, SU.
39. To GS, May 28, 1864, SU.
40. Bull, 246.
41. To GS, May, 1856, SU.
42. To GS Dec. 28, 1874, SU.
43. Smith and Barnes, 11.
44. To GS, SU.
45. GS to C. G. Finney, April 25, 1839, SU.
46. C. G. Finney to GS, May 7, 1839, SU.
47. Harlow, 224-226.
48. Blackett, 39, 46.
49. Wright 11, 64-67, 104.
50. S. E. Dwight to GS, Jan. 2, 1829, SU.
51. GS to Pres. Lord, Nov. 2, 1845, SU.
52. John G. Fee to GS, July 15, 1858, SU.
53. John G. Fee to GS, Aug. 18, 1874; Feb. 7, 1873; Jan. 28, 1874, SU.
54. White to GS, Sept. 1, 1862, SU.
55 GS to James Barnett, Caleb Calkins, C. D. Miller, Nov. 28, 1850, SU.
56. GS to GrS, June 21, 1851, SU.
57. GS to GrS, Dec. 4, 1851, SU.
58. Henry Campbell to his sister, Oct. 24, 1851, Henry Campbell letters.
59. Newspaper clipping, Dec. 30, 1874, SU.
60. *Fredrick Douglass' Paper*, Aug. 24, 1855.
61. FD to GS, Aug 25, 1874, SU., and E. W. Robinson to GS, Oct. 19, 1868, SU.
62. Pres. Whipple to GS, July 12, 1873, SU.
63. J. Marshall to GS, Dec. 14, 1874, SU.
64. S. S. Howe to GS, May 15, 1836, SU.
65. Thatcher Adams to GS, June 9, 1869, SU.
66. Letters of thanks from A. H. Malcolm to GS, Sept. 26, 1831, SU; John W. Adams to GS, June 17, 1837, SU.
67. John W. Adams to GS, Oct. 16, 1837, SU.
68. Yellin, 289.
69. Patrick Ford, editor of *Irish World,* to GS, Nov. 13, 1873, SU.
70. Alvin Bronson, et. al. to GS, Aug. 11, 1853, SU.
71. John B. Edwards to GS, May 26, 1855; Oct. 30, 1855; June 12, 1856, SU.

72. Alvin Bronson to GS, Oct. 8, 1856, SU.

73. Alvin Bronson to GS, June 20, 1862, SU.; Edwin Marke to GS, March 3, 1868, SU.

74. A. S. Post to GS, Nov. 24, 1856, SU.

75. Gov. Carpenter of Iowa to GS, Aug. 5, 1874, SU.

76. John Hizt, Consul General of Switzerland to GS, Nov. 9, 1868, SU.

77. *Friend of Man,* June 1836, 3.

78. Sam G. Ward, treasurer to GS, 1869, SU.

79. S. P. Russell to GS, July 29, 1872, SU.

80. GS to Warner Clemens, Dec. 2, 1846, SU.

81. Galpin.

82. Henry B. Stanton, *Syracuse Journal,* Dec. 30, 1874.

83. *People's Rights,* July 7, 1844.

84. GS to Wright, Ray, Smith, Nov. 14, 1846, SU.

85. GS to John H. Cooke, Dec. 11, 1840, SU.

86. Donaldson, Vol. II 6.

87. Feb. 26, 1850, SU.

88. Hunter, 179, 180.

89. Marble to GS, Sept. 6, 1850, SU.

90. Circular to County magistrates, May 1, 1849, SU.

91. SU.

92. GS to Duplissis Nash, Dec. 2, 1846, SU.

93. GS to Eastman, Feb. 6, 1847, SU.

94. Feb. 27, 1847, SU.

95. GS to George Evans, Dec. 2, 1846, SU.

96. GS to Elizabeth M. Torry, Nov. 30, 1846, SU.

97. Annotation on letter A. Raymond to GS, Aug. 4, 1848, SU.

98. GS to E. Jacobs, Oct. 23, 1840, SU.

99. Sept. 25, 1847, SU.

100. To GS, May 11, 1874, SU.

101. Connolly to GS, Aug. 11, 1855, SU.

102. GS to Henry, Oct 24, 1846, SU.

103. GS to ESM and GrS, March 6, 1847, SU.

104. John Stauffer, *GIANTS: The Parallel Lives of Frederick Douglass and Abraham Lincoln*; page 331, note 24.

Chapter 4

1. GS to several newspapers, May 12, 1851, SU.

2. Fitzhugh, 91.

3. Fitzhugh, 90.

4. McKivigan and McKivigan, 191.

5. WEB.SYR.EDU.

6. Ward, 55.

7. Frothingham, 1st ed., 72.

8. Notes of Sopherina A. C. Lloyd, Cazenovia, March 1849, PHS.

9. *The National Era*, Dec. 2, 1847, 3.

10. Dec. 29, 1874.

11. James Richards to GS, Dec. 28, 1863, SU.

12. *Frederick Douglass's Paper*, May 19, 1854.

13. *Frederick Douglass's Paper*, Jan 27, 1854.

14. *The North Star*, July 20, 1849.

15. To GS, Oct. 14, 1843, SU.

16. GS to Asa Rand, Oct. 25, 1845, SU.

17. M.A. Rioter to GS, early 1859, SU.

18. *The Democratic Volunteer*, April 7, 1875.

19. To GS, Feb. 9, no year, SU.

20. ESM to GS, Feb. 2, 1861, SU.

21. Henry S. Randall to GS, Sept. 10, 1849, SU.

22. SU.

23. SU.

24. For example, "The One Test of Character," in *Sermons and Speeches*, SU.

25. K. Graves to GS, April 6, 1866, SU.

26. *Speeches*, April 6, 1854.

27. See "Be Natural," Nov. 20, 1864, MCHS.; or GS to ECS, Dec. 1, 1855, SU.

28. GS, "Speech on the Nebraska Bill," April 6, 1854, in *Speeches*, 176.

29. GS to FD, July 13, 1860, SU.

30. GS to Hon. Preston King, Jan.

29, 1864, in *Smith, Speeches, and Letters*, 70; MCHS.

31. GS, "The Religion of Reason," Feb. 21, 1858, in *Sermons and Speeches*, 9.

32. Dec. 29, 1874.

33. Harlow, 297.

34. GS to Vice Pres. Colfax, May 14, 1870, SLC.

35. Quoted in Frothingham, 1st ed., 196-200.

36. GS to Greene C. Bronson, Oct. 18, 1854, MCHS.

37. GS, "Final Letter to his Constituents," Aug. 7, 1854, in *Speeches*, 382.

38. Lewis Tappan to GS, Dec. 17, 1848, SU.

39. GS to J. P. Mendum of the *Boston Investigator*, Oct. 26, 1866, quoted in Frothingham, 1st ed., 88, 89.

40. Feb. 6, 1861, in *Sermons and Speeches*, 178.

41. GS, "Speech on the Reference of the President's Message," Dec. 20, 1853, in *Speeches*, 13.

42. to GS, Oct. 19, 1869, SU.

43. GS to Edmund Quincy, Nov. 23, 1846, quoted in full in Frothingham, 1st ed., 201-208.

44. GS, "Final Letter to his Constituents," Aug. 7, 1854, in *Speeches*, 376.

45. GS, "Speech on the Homestead Bill," Feb. 21, 1854, in *Speeches*,

73.

46. GS, "Speech on the Reference of the President's Message," Dec. 2, 1853, in *Speeches,* 14.

47. GS to the editor of *The Emancipator*, Aug. 23, 1847, MCHS.

48. GS to John W. North, Jan. 9, 1849, SU.

49. GS "The Religion of Reason," June 19, 1859, in *Sermons and Speeches,* 51.

50. GS to the faculty of the Theological Seminary at Hamilton College, Oct. 3, 1843, SU.

51. April 28, 1843, SU.

52. To the editor, *National Anti-Slavery Standard*, Jan. 28, 1860.

53. Verse Book, SU.

54. GS to N. Huntington, F. Dana, and D. Dorrance, Nov. 9, 1843, SU.

55. GS to A. Rand, Sept. 23, 1845, SU.

56. GS to A. Rand, Sept. 25, 1845, SU.

57. Nov. 12, 1841, SU.

58. March 5, 1842, SU.

59. Oct. 6, 1862, SLC.

60. Some letters printed in full in Frothingham, 1st ed., 196-208.

61. Aug. 15, 1873, SLC.

62. SU.

63. To GS, July 22, 1840, SU.

64. July 17, 1869, SU.

65. GS to Crozier, April 5, 1850, SU.

66. GS to Postmaster, March 4, 1852, SU.

67. Sept. 10, 1865, SU.

68. GS to ACS, Aug. 13, 1843, SU.

69. *Republican Monitor*, Nov. 27, 1838, SU.

70. GS to Rev. Mills, April 2, 1840, SU.

71. Sept. 24, 1847, SU.

72. GS to the local public, "Thoughts to the People," April 14, 1865, SLC.

73. GS to Oliver Johnson, July 6, 1840, SU.

74. April 28, 1843, SU.

75. GS to E.S. Barrows, June 16, 1840, SU.

76. Aug. 28, 1840, SU.

77. Jan 7, 1848, SU.

78. GS to John Hill, Sept. 10, 1841, SU.

79. GS to E. C. Hyde, Dec. 16, 1847, SU.

80. Aug. 12, 1847, SU.

81. GS to Greene C. Bronson, Oct. 18, 1854, PHS.

82. GS to Mrs. N. Huntington, April 20, 1843, SU.

83. Oct. 29, 1841, SU.

84. Oct. 17, 1857, SU.

85. Harlow, 450-454.

86. Gray.

87. Verse Book, Sept. 21, 1860, SU.

88. Nov. 9, 1871, SU.

89. GS to Brother Johnson, Feb. 2, 1842, SU.

90. To GS, Nov. 3, 1849, SU.

91. Smith and Barnes, 77, 78.

92. NYHS to GS, March 27, 1827, SU.

93. Marvin Bovee to GS, Nov. 13, 1867, SU.

94. Nov. 11, 1852, SU.

Chapter 5

1. GS to ACS, June 19, 1873, SU.,

2. *Historical and Statistical Gazetteer*, 393; *Madison County Times*, Oct. 19, 1878.

3. *Republican Monitor*, Nov. 27, 1838.

4. *Oneida Community Journal*, March 2000 15-16.

5. June 25, 1845, SU.

6. to ACS, April 3, 1832, SU.

7. GS to ACS, early June, 1836, SU.

8. GS to ACS, June 9, 1836, SU.

9. N.V. Hull to GS, Jan 16, 1856, SU.

10. GS, "Letter Announcing His Purpose to Resign His Seat in Congress," June 27, 1854, in *Speeches*, 305.

11. Bishop.

12. GS to ACS, July 12, 1873, SU.

13. J. Playfair to GS, July 19, 1837, SU.

14. Tribute, 38, 39.

15. July 25, 1851 clipping, SU.

16. Edwards to GS, April 19, 1845.

17. John B. Edwards to Caleb Calkins, Sept. 18, 1855, SU.

18. Edwards to GS, July 19, 25, 1859, SU.

19. Verse Book, SU.

20. Bull, 245.

21. Bull, 246.

22. GS to ACS, Dec. 30, 1840, SU.

23. GS to ACS, Jan. 6, 1859, SU.

24. July 27, 1832, SU.

25. GS to ACS, Dec. 28, 1836, SU.

26. Household expense account book, SU.

27. Burdick, vol. 3, 7.

28. Burdick, vol. 3, 6.

29. Nov. 13, 1839, SU.

30. GS to ACS, March 16, SU.

31. SU.

32. Miller, 433.

33. Account sheets, SU.

34. Edwards to GS, Feb. 28, June 2, 1855; Aug. 2, Sept. 27, 1856; Jan. 28, Sept. 8, 1857, SU.

35. Stanton 454.

36. SU.

37. Henry Campbell to his brother, May 1, 1843, Henry Campbell letters.

38. SU.

39. Verse Book, SU.

40. GS to GrS, Sept. 1, 1861, SU.

41. ACS to ESM, March 3, 1840, SU.

42. June 26, 1851, SU.

43. June 11, 1851, SU.
44. Charles Stuart to GS, Aug. 15, 1841, SU.
45. Feb. 21, 1858.
46. GS to ACS, May 11, 1836, SU.
47. Verse Book, July 5, 1861, SU.
48. GS to ACS, April 20, 1850, SU.
49. GS to ACS, Dec. 15, 1845, SU.
50. ACS to ESM, June 4, 1869, SU.
51. May 2, 1873, SU.
52. June 1, 1873, SU.
53. June 2, SU.
54. Verse Book, Aug. 15, 1861, SU.
55. GS to GrS and GS Miller, Jan. 24, 1852, SU.
56. To GS, Aug. 30, 1861, SU.
57. Galpin.
58. 1st ed., no dates, 140-141.
59. SU.
60. ACS to ESM, no date, SU.
61. ACS to Bess, Oct. 26, 1873, SU.
62. Griffiths to Mrs. Howitt, Oct. 6, 1852, in *Frederick Douglass' Paper*, Oct. 15, 1852.
63. Jan. 17, 1844, SU.
64. Aug. 5, 1870, SU.
65. to GS, Nov. 18, 1861, SU.
66. FD to GS, Sept. 2, 1871, SU.
67. GS to ACS, Sept. 11, 1842, SU.
68. GS to ACS, Sept. 12, 1842, SU.
69. Fladeland, 158, 165.
70. To GS, June 15, 1842, SU.
71. Frothingham, 143.
72. Thomas, MCHS.
73. March 24, 1868, SU.
74. Nov. 13, 1839, SU.
75. Verse Book, SU.
76. ACS to GS, from New York City, April 4, 1870, SU.
77. Bull, 246.
78. Frothingham, 1st ed., 137.
79. GS to Brother Johnson, Feb. 2, 1842, SU.
80. GS to Fuller, Nov. 16, 1841, SU.
81. GS to ACS, March 18, 1831, SU.
82. ACS to GS, May 17, 1862, SU.
83. ESM to GS, Aug. 11, 1841, SU.
84. Jan. 18, 1840, SU.
85. ACS to ESM, Dec. 1, 1843, SU.
86. ACS to ESM, March 3, 1840, SU.
87. No date, probably 1857, SU.
88. No date, probably 1860, SU.
89. Verse Book, Nov. 21, 1860, SU.

Chaper 6
1. ACS to GS, Dec. 2, 1824, SU.
2. Jan. 9, 1823, SU.
3. ACS to GS, Dec. 2, 1824, SU.
4. ACS to GS, June 3, 1829, SU.

5. Jan. 23, 1836, SU.
6. Dec. 24, 1839, SU.
7. GS to ACS, Dec. 22, 1836, SU.
8. To ACS, Feb. 17, 1836, SU.
9. Sept. 6, 1871, SU.
10. To ACS, Aug 20, 1843, SU.
11. Elizabeth H. Kelty to Caroline F. King, Nov. 25, 1843, PHS.
12. Nov. 14, 1843, SU.
13. Verse Book, April 14, 1866, SU.
14. March 20, 1860, SU.
15. To GS, April 6, 1862, SU.
16. Miller, 17.
17. Miller, 17, 18.
18. Miller, 17.
19. Miller, 21.
20. Verse Book, Oct. 19, 1866, SU.
21. Miller, 19.
22. Miller, 23.
23. Ibid.
24. Miller, 282, 283.
25. Verse Book, "Lillie" refers to Elizabeth, Dec. 31, 1852, SU.
26. Verse Book, SU.
27. Verse Book, March 17, 1862, SU.
28. No date, SU.
29. GS to ESM, Dec. 13, 1864, SU.
30. ESM to GS, Aug. 31, 1871, SU.
31. GS to ESM, July 16, 1869 SU.
32. Sept. 30, 1869, SU.
33. ESM to GS, July 21, 1869, SU.
34. Early Nov., 1874, SU.
35. To GS, Nov. 13, 1874, SU.
36. SU.
37. March 6, 1868, SU.
38. March 7, 1872, SU.
39. Elizabeth H. Kelty to Caroline F. King, Nov 25, 1843, PHS.
40. Verse Book, Jan. 4, 1847, SU.
41. May 12, 1850, SU.
42. GS to GrS, April 14, 1851, SU.
43. Perry 197, 198.
44. GS to GrS, April 10, 1851, SU.
45. GS to GrS, June 2, 1851, SU.
46. Lerner, 251.
47. Angelina Grimké Weld to GS, May 1, 1852, SU.
48. Welds to GS, Aug. 14, 1852, SU.
49. To GrS, Dec. 4, 1852, SU.
50. GS to GrS, Jan. 26, 1853, SU.
51. Jan. 22, 1853, SU.
52. Nov. 29, 1852, SU.
53. Jan. 29, 1853, SU.
54. Feb. 5, 1853, SU.
55. Theodore Weld to GS, Feb. 5, 1853, SU.
56. GrS to GS, May 1, 1853, SU.
57. May 29, 1853, SU.
58. Feb. 7, 1855, SU.
59. April 6, 1855, SU.
60. April 24, 1855, SU.
61. Verse Book, Feb. 15, 1859, SU.
62. Verse Book, April 14, 1859, SU.
63. To GS, Sept. 12, 1860, SU.

64. to GS, Jan. 29, 1861, SU.

65. Sept. 1, 1861, MCHS.

66. Nov. 23, 1861, MCHS.

67. March 7, 1862, MCHS.

68. GS to ACS, Dec. 28, 1861, SU.

69. June 1, 1863, SU.

70. SU.

71. ACS to GS, Jan. 9, 1861, SU.

72. ACS to GS, Jan., no day, 1861, SU.

73. ACS to GS, Oct. 30, 1861, SU.

74. Feb. no day, 1862 from Rome, Italy, MCHS.

75. ACS to GS, April 27, 1862, from Lucerne, Switzerland, MCHS.

76. GS to ACS, Jan 10. 1862, MCHS.

77. ACS to GS, Jan. 3, 1866, SU.

78. ACS to GS, Jan. 8, 1866, SU.

79. ACS to GS, Feb. 29, 1866, SU.

80. ACS to GS, June 13, 1870, SU.

81. Jan. 2, SU.

82. Verse Book, Feb. 4, 1857, SU.

83. Feb. 23, 1857, SU. 84. Theodore Dwight Weld to GS, March 4, 1852, SU.

85. Feb. 5, 1860, SU.

86. John P. Gray to GS, May 6, 1860, SU.

87. To GS, May 11, 1860, SU.

88. Sept. 8, 1861, SU.

89. *Madison Observer*, July 14, 1914.

90. Note in Caleb Calkins account book, SU.

91. ESM to Bessie, Aug., 1862, SU.

92. GrS to GS and ACS, July 30, 31, Aug. 1, 7, 9, 14, 19, 1864, PHS. For other similar first-hand descriptions of the Battle of the Crater, see Trudeau, 109–127.

93. GrS to ACS, Nov. 18, 1864, SU.

94. Nov. 14, 1864, SU.

95. Nov. 29, 1864, SU.

96. Dec. 1, 1864, SU.

97. GS to ESM, Dec. 11, 1864, SU.

98. ACS to ESM, SU.

99. Historical Data Systems, Inc. www.civilwardata.com.

100. ACS to ESM, Feb. 3, 1865, SU.

101. Diary of unkown Peterboro resident, May 26, 1863 entry; GrS to GS, Feb. 3, 1869, SU.

102. GS to ACS, April 16, 1844, SU.

103. Kelty.

104. July 20, 1865, SU.

105. GrS to GS, Dec. 5, 1866, SU.

106. GrS to GS, Oct. 27, SU.

107. GrS to GS, April 17, 1870, SU.

108. GrS to GS, April 24, 1870, SU.

109. White to GS, Feb. 28, 1869, SU.

110. Kelty.
111. April 14, 1863, SU.
112. *Cazenovia Republican*, July 29, 1880.

Chaper 7
1. GS to ACS, Dec. 18, 1861, MCHS.
2. March 6, 1868, SU.
3. Dec. 12, 1869, SU.
4. Quoted in ESM to GS, Sept. 6, 1871, SU.
5. C.D. Miller, Jr. to GS, Jan. 21, 1872, SU.
6. Feb. 10, 1872, SU.
7. C.D. Miller to GS, June 25, 1874, SU.
8. March 1, 1872, SU.
9. June 1, 1863, SU.
10. SU.
11. Verse Book, July 24, 1857, SU.
12. GS to ACS, Dec. 24, 1861, MCHS.
13. GS to ACS, Dec. 25, 1861, MCHS.
14. GS to ACS, Jan. 2 and Jan. 4, 1862, MCHS.
15. Ann F. Miller to GS, April 27, 1868, SU.
16. Verse Book, Nov. 28, 1867, SU.
17. GS to GrS, Oct. 29, 1873, SU.
18. C.D.Miller, Jr. to GS, Jan. 21, 1872, SU.
19. Verse Book, Dec. 25, 1848, SU.

20. Edwin Morton to GS, May 25, 1855, SU.
21. Kelty.
22. Verse Book, GS to Betsey, Dec. 25, 1848, SU.
23. ACS to ESM Jan. 22, 1865, SU.
24. Kelty.
25. Kelty. The bookmark itself is preserved in the Gerrit Smith Papers, SU.
26. Kelty.
27. Kelty.
28. Kelty, Jan. 20, 1871.
29. Kelty, Jan. 20, 1873.
30. Kelty, Jan. 20, 1859.
31. ESM, quoted in Kelty.
32. ESM, quoted in Kelty, Jan. 20, 1857.
33. ESM, quoted in Kelty, Jan. 20, 1864.
34. ESM to Betsey, quoted in Kelty, Jan. 20, 1874.
35. Kelty, June 26, 1874.
36. GrS, in Kelty, Jan. 20, 1864.
37. Kelty, Oct. 1849.
38. Quoted in Kelty.
39. Aug. 12, 1826, SU.
40. April 27, 1829, SU.
41. Sept. 9, 1870, SU.
42. W. Walter to GS, Sept. 5, 1837, SU.
43. Oct. 20, 1862; April 18, 1866, SU.
44. SU.
45. Fitzhugh to GS, Aug. 30, 1827 SU.

46. Verse Book, Aug. 19, SU.
47. Verse Book Nov. 25, 1862, SU.
48. Verse Book, Dec. 7, 1866, SU.
49. Verse Book, Feb. 4, 1867, SU.
50. SU.
51. ACS to ESM and Charles, Dec. 7, 1843, SU.
52. e.g., C. D. Miller to GS, Dec. 23, 1846, SU.
53. Verse Book, Dec. 25, 1848, SU.
54. ESM to GS, March 24, 1871, SU.
55. GS to ACS, March 18, 1831, SU.
56. GS to Elder Whitcher, May 7, 1842, SU.
57. GS to Peter S. Smith, April 1, 1843, SU.
58. GS to PS, June 16, 1836, SU.
59. GS to James Glover, Jan.5, 1835, HCL.
60. GS to ACS, Sept. 11, 1842, SU.
61. March 17, 1848, SU.
62. Nov. 29, 1848, SU.
63. Dec. 7, 1849, SU.
64. Peter Skenandoah to GS, July 9, 1848, SU.
65. Peter Skenandoah to GS, Sept. 16, 1848, SU.
66. Peter Skenandoah to GS, June 2, 1848, SU.
67. April 11, 1848; May 5, 1848, SU.
68. Oct. 24, 1850, SU.
69. April 20, 1851, SU.
70. April 27, 1851, SU.
71. June 19, 1851, SU.
72. Aug. 26, 1851, SU.
73. March 14, 1858, SU.
74. April 29, 1832, SU.
75. ACS to GS, Feb. 14, 1834, SU.
76. Henry Fitzhugh to GS, April 28, 1835, SU.
77. GS to ACS, Sept. 12, 1825, SU.
78. GS to ACS, March 6, 1831, SU.
79. GS to ACS, April 14, 1831, SU.
80. Tribute, 266-268.
81. Dec. 15, 1835, SU.
82. Lewis Bailey to GS, March 12, 1836, SU.
83. Tribute, 269-272.
84. GS to PS, June 22, 1836, SU.
85. GS to PS, July 27, 1836, SU.
86. Dec. 28, 1836, SU.
87. Sept. 5, 1836, SU.
88. to GS, July 14, 1836, SU.
89. to GS, Jan. 12, 1837, SU.
90. GS to Ann, April 21, 1845, SU.
91. Theodore Gold to GS, Nov. 10, 1823, SU.

Chapter 8
1. William Lloyd Garrison to ESM, 1875, in Bull, 247, 248.
2. F.M. Haight to GS, June 6, 1819, SU.
3. Verse Book, SU.

4. Thomas, Beekman to GS, Aug. 17, 1819, SU.
5. Verse Book, SU.
6. GS to ACS, Aug. 15, 1843; GS to ACS, Aug. 15, 1870, SU.
7. Verse Book, Jan. 3, 1866, SU.
8. To GS, Feb. 5, 1867, SU.
9. Dec. 11, 1864, SU.
10. ACS to GS, Dec. 19, 1836, SU.
11. ACS to GS, 1868, SU.
12. Jan. 9, 1859, SU.
13. 1st ed., 140.
14. SU.san B. Anthony quoted in Stanton, 1853, 71.
15. Verse Book, Jan 11, 1859, SU.
16. GS to Elizur Wright, Jan. 10, 1852, HCL.
17. GS to S. I. Wilkinson, June 4, 1846, SU.
18. Verse Book, SU.
19. Dec. 29, 1844, SU.
20. Verse Book, March 20, 1845, SU.
21. Verse Book, SU.
22. Sept. 1, 1861, MCHS.
23. GS to GrS, April 5, 1851, SU.
24. GS to ACS, Oct. 20, 1874, SU.
25. ACS to ESM, Jan. 31, 1869, SU.
26. Dec. 29, 1865, SU.
27. Feb. 6, 1866, SU.
28. Dec. 1, 1874, SU.
29. Verse Book, Oct. 7, 1871, SU.
30. Nov. 16, 1841, SU.
31. Verse Book, Jan. 3, 1863, SU.
32. GS to ACS, Jan. 22, 1862, MCHS.
33. GS to ACS, March 20, 1831, SU.
34. SU.
35. May 14, 1836, SU.
36. May 17, 1836, SU.
37. June 15, 1836, SU.
38. Frothingham, 1st ed., 39; Harlow, 35; Renehan, 16.
39. Richardson, 904.
40. The Liberator, Vol. XIX, no. 986, Nov. 30, 1849, 192.
41. March 30, 1831, SU.
42. GS to ACS, Dec. 30, 1840, SU.
43. Sept. 1, 1871, SU.
44. GS to ACS, Jan. 25, 1870, SU.
45. GS to ACS, Dec. 27, 1871, SU.
46. GS to ACS, March 16, 1873, SU.
47. GS to ACS, June 6, 1873, SU.
48. Nov. 7, 1874, SU.
49. June 16, 1873, SU.
50. GS to ACS, Nov. 9, 1839, SU.
51. GS to GrS, Dec. 4, 1851, SU.
52. Jan. 31, 1861, SU.
53. Jan. 29, 1861, SU.
54. Jan. 6, 1867, SU.
55. March 19, 1831, SU.
56. March 5, 1857, SU.
57. E. H. Kelty to Horace Corydon, March 23, 1873, PHS.
58. Nov. 30, 1824, SU.
59. Dec. 26, 1836, SU.

60. ACS to GS, April 7, 1857, SU.
61. March 6, 1826, SU.
62. Feb. 11, 1838, SU.
63. ACS to GS, Aug. 29, 1854, SU; Aug. 27, 1854, SU; Jan. 22, 1825, SU.
64. GS to ACS, March 7, 1843, SU.
65. ACS to GS, Feb. 5, 1835, SU.
66. ACS to GS, Jan. 11, 1837, SU.
67. ACS to GS, Jan. 20, 1867, SU.
68. ACS to Mrs. N. Huntington, no date, SU.
69. Ellen Walter to GS, Feb. 10, 1862, MCHS.
70. April 3, SU.
71. ACS to GS, April 15, 1873, SU.
72. July 12, 1874, SU.
73. June 20, 1873, SU.
74. March 15, 1867, SU.
75. Dec. 2, 1824, SU.
76. ACS to GS, Dec. 17, 1836; Feb. 8, 1837; Oct. 21, 1850, SU.
77. ACS to GS, April 20, 1873, SU.
78. ACS to GS, March 18, 1860, SU.
79. ACS to GS, no day, 1872.
80. ACS to GS, March 15, 1860, SU.
81. McFeely 154.
82. June 6, 1869, SU.
83. ACS to GS, May 12, 1858; ACS to ESM, Nov. 10, 1872, SU.
84. Verse Book, Jan. 11, 1858, SU.
85. ACS to PS, April 25, 1834, SU.
86. Aug. 2, 1860, SU.
87. Verse Book, SU.
88. MCHS.
89. Verse Book, Jan. 3, 1855, SU.
90. Verse Book, SU.
91. Verse Book, Jan. 11, 1855, SU.
92. Verse Book, Sept. 18, 1860, SU.
93. Verse Book, Jan. 11, 1855, SU.
94. Verse Book, Nov. 9, 1867, SU.
95. March 3, 1848, SU.
96. Verse Book, Jan. 23, 1851, SU.
97. Verse Book, Jan. 11, 1852, SU.
98. Verse Book, Aug. 24, 1852, SU.
99. Verse Book, SU.
100. Verse Book, SU.
101. Verse Book, Jan. 3, 1853, SU.
102. Jan. 3, 1854, MCHS.
103. Verse Book, March 6, 1854, SU.
104. Verse Book, March 6, 1854, SU.
105. Verse Book, Jan. 3, 1859, SU.
106. Verse Book, Oct. 31, 1862, SU.
107. Verse Book, May 17, 1865,

SU.
108. Dec. 8, 1863, SU.
109. Verse Book, Oct. 12, 1862, SU.
110. Verse Book, SU.
111. Verse Book, Aug. 24, 1857, SU.
112. Verse Book, May 28, 1864, SU.
113. Verse Book, May 1, 1866, SU.
114. ACS to GS, Dec. 23, 1836, SU.
115. March 5, 1857, SU.
116. May 11, 1858, SU.
117. ACS to GS, May 15, 1858, SU.
118. ACS to GS, Feb. 27, 1861, SU.
119. May 6, 1862, MCHS.
120. Jan. 11, 1867, SU.
121. SU.
122. ACS to GS, June 3, 1869, SU.
123. Jan. 8, 1866, SU.
124. ACS to GS, Jan. 6, 1867, SU.
125. GS to ACS, Feb. 15, 1868, SU.
126. June 6, 1869, SU.
127. ESM to GS, April 21, 1873, SU.
128. Elizabeth Birney [Ann's sister] to GS, Sept. 18, 1850, SU.
129. ACS to GS, Aug. 19, 1833, SU., Tumors of the rectum, ESM to GS, March 20, 1873, SU.

130. ESM to GS, Aug. 24, 1874, SU.
131. ESM to GS, March 21, 1861, SU.
132. Cooley 571.
133. ESM to GS, March 5, 1861, SU.
134. Ellen Walter to GS, March 27, 1861, SU.
135. March 23, 1873, SU.
136. Ellen Walter to GS, Oct. 17, 1874, SU.
137. Oct. 29, 1874, SU.
138. ACS to GS, Nov., no day, 1874, SU.
139. GS to ACS, Nov. 7, 1874, SU.; GS to ACS, Dec. 4, 1874, SU.
140. Dec. 10, 1874, SU.
141. The *Oneida Democratic Union*, March 11, 1987, 2.
142. Verse Book, March 6, 1845, SU.
143. Verse Book, Jan. 11, 1855, SU.
144. GS to ACS, Jan. 3, 1848, SU.
145. Verse Book, Jan. 3, 1847, SU.
146. Verse Book, Jan. 3, 1857, SU.
147. Verse Book, Jan. 3, 1865, SU.
148. Verse Book, GS, Oct. 17, 1871, SU.
149. Verse Book, GS, Oct. 17, 1871, SU.
150. Verse Book, GS, May 1,

1866, SU.
151. to ACS, Feb. 18, 19, SU.
152. John Cochrane to ACS, Feb. 22, 1875, SU.
153. EdWard, North, Hamilton College to ACS, March 1, 1875, SU.
154. SU.
155. West, 41.
156. Shryock, 301.
157. Kay.
158. Richardson, 774.
159. *Friend of Man*, July 28, 1836, 23.
160. Wang, 164.
161. Caillé.
162. Facklemann, 239.
163. West, 41.
164. Hau, 482.
165. Hau, 482; 477.
166. Hau, 478.
167. Steeb, et. al., Docline copy, 7.
168. Steeb, et.al., Docline copy, 8.
169. Bull, 247, 248.

Chapter 9
1. Feb. 18, 1861, SU.
2. Dec. 15, SU.
3. Jan. 21, 1869, SU.
4. Morton to GS, March 3, 1866, SU.
5. March 10, 1843, SU.
6. GS to B. B. Stewart, Feb. 13, 1844, SU.
7. Green to GS, March 17. 1835,
SU.
8. Beriah Green to GS, Feb. 26, 1840, SU.
9.Jan. 5, 1850, SU.
10. Feb. 23, 1850, SU.
11. Aug. 4, 1850, SU.
12. GS to ACS, July 2, 1832, SU.
13. GS to Marcus Smith, Dec. 9, 1839, SU.
14. ESM to GS, Feb. 2, 1861, SU.
15. GS to ACS, Aug. 15, 1843, SU.
16. GS to ACS, March 6, 1856, SU.
17. GS to ACS, May 26, 1854, SU.
18. Putnam, 1860.
19. John B. Edwards to GS, Nov. 7, 1855, SU.
20. Nannie and Gatty were ESM's children. GS to ACS, Aug. 29, 1868, SU.
21. GS to ESM, Dec. 13, 1862, SU.
22. T.S.
23.GS to ACS, June 16, 1836, SU.
24. GS to ACS, June 15, 1836, SU.
25. ACS to ESM, Nov. 29, 1864, SU.
26. GS to ACS, Nov 22, 1839, SU.
27. GS to ACS, Nov. 15, 1839, SU.
28. GS to ACS, Dec. 16, 1839, SU.
29. GS to ACS, Aug. 9, 1842, SU.
30. GS to ACS, Oct. 20, 1874,

SU.
31. Dec. 28, SU.
32. GS to ACS, Nov. 10, SU.
33. Jan. 29, SU.
34. Edwards to GS, Aug. 5, 1852, SU.
35. Feb. 16, 1852, Henry Campbell letters; Diary of an unknown Peterboro resident between March and October, 1863.
36. GS to GrS, June 21, 1851, SU.
37. John B. Edwards to GS, Oct. 26, 1857, SU.
38. Edwards to Caleb Calkins, Nov. 20, Dec. 1, Dec. 7, 1857; Edwards to GS, Dec. 21, 1857, SU.
39. Putnam; Cady; Edwards to GS, Nov. 28, 1853; Dec. 20, 1854; Jan. 3, 12, 1855, SU.
40. Edwards to GS, March 13, 1852, SU.
41. GS to GrS, March 14, 1853, SU.
42. GS to ACS, March 26, 1868, SU.
43. John B. Edwards to GS, Aug. 11, 1854, SU.
44. ACS to ESM, Nov. 3, 1870; ACS to ESM, no day, 1869, SU.
45. GS to ACS, Nov. 19, 1839, SU.
46. SU.
47. Jan. 1, 1858, SU.
48. GS to ESM, May 6, 1835, SU.

49. ACS to PS, Feb. 18, 1836, SU.
50. Edwards to GS, Sept. 11, 1846; Dec. 29, 1847; Aug. 31, 1858, SU.
51. C. Collins to GS, May 11, 1840, SU.
52. John Bayley to GS, Feb. 27, 1840, SU.
53. GS to H. Fuller, Jan. 9, 1845, SU.
54. GS to ESM, July 11, 1845; GS to ACS, Jan. 2, 1848; GS to Elihu Burritt, June 11, 1849; GS to Julia Griffiths, July 25, 1857; GS to ACS, March 5, 1861, SU.
55. to GS, June 22, 27, 1853, SU.
56. to GS, Aug. 19, SU.
57. Nov. 20, 1862, SU.
58. GS to Wake, Peterson, and Crummell, July 8, 1845, SU.
59. GS to Dr. Walter, Aug. 6, 1842, SU.
60. GS to ACS, Sept. 3, 1842, SU.
61. GS to ACS, SU.
62. GS to ACS, Aug. 12, 1843, SU.
63. GS to ACS, Sept. 5, 1842, SU.
64. GS to Wake, Peterson, and Crummell, July 8, 1845, SU.
65. Frothingham, 42.
66. GS to Lewis Tappan, March 14, 1840, SU.
67. ACS to ESM, March 3, 1840, SU.
68. GS to Alvan Stewart, July 20, 1840, SU.

69. GS to D.L. Jones, Oct. 6, 1840, SU.
70. GS to Tubbell and Cuna, Jan. 30, 1841, SU.
71. GS to Edmund Quincy, Dec. 30, 1846; GS to A. Becker, Feb. 1, 1847, SU.
72. to ACS, Sept. 5, 1842, SU.
73. March 20, 1869, SU.
74. John Gray to Mrs. Brent for the Smiths, Nov. 20, 1873, SU.
75. May 24, 1874; Nov. 2, 1874, SU.
76. GS to ACS, March 16, 1873, SU.
77. ACS to Bessie, Greene's wife, Oct. 26, SU.
78. David Plumb to GS, May 7, SU.
79. SLC.
80. Address to the Anti-Dram-shop Party, Peterboro, Nov. 6, 1872, SLC.
81. ECS to GS, Dec. 24, 1873, SU.
82. The North Star, Aug. 25, 1848.
83. GS to Abby Kelley, Aug. 1, 1843, SU.
84. June 26, 1843, SU.
85. C. Underwood to GS, May 2, 1863, SU.
86. GS to Rev. Johnson, Dec. 12, 1852, SU.
87. Undated, probably about 1870, MCHS.

Chapter 10

1. Schramm, 58.
2. Cross, 202.
3. Gilbert Barnes, 11.
4. Harlow, 47.
5. A. Gilbert to GS, Oct. 18, SU.
6. ACS to Betty, June 14, 1825, SU.
7. GS to ACS, Sept. 12, 1825, SU.
8. March 6, 1826, SU.
9. McKivigan, 24.
10. Perry, 57.
11. Frothingham, 1st ed., 44.
12. Frothingham, 1st ed., 47.
13. ACS to ESM, May 6, 1835, SU.
14. GS to ACS, Dec 28, 1836; GS to ACS, April 8, 1831, SU.
15. Frothingham, 1st ed., 45, 54, 46.
16. GS to ACS, Nov. 22, SU.
17. Betsey Kelty to unknown, no date, probably early 1875, PHS.
18. In footnote, 53.
19. Verse Book, SU.
20. GS to ACS, Aug. 7, 1842, SU.
21. Kelty, composed Dec. 29, 1860, NYPL.
22. Smith and Barnes, 107. Hereafter referred to as S+B.
23. S+B, 16.
24. S+B, 125.
25. Speech in Canastota, NY, Oct. 27, 1869, SLC.
26. GS, "Miracles," April 14, 1861, in *Sermons and Speech-*

es, 124.

27. GS, Speech on the Nebraska Bill, April 6, 1854, in *Speeches,* 114.

28. S+B, 7.

29. S+B, 127.

30. S+B, 128.

31. GS, "Miracles," April 14, 1861, in *Sermons and Speeches,* 126.

32. GS, "Miracles," April 14, 1861, in *Sermons and Speeches,* 128.

33. S+B, 121.

34. Frothingham, 67, 68, 75.

35. GS to H.W. Beecher, May 20, 1863, SLC.

36. GS, "Limiting Grants of Land to White Persons," May 3, 1854, in *Speeches,* 226.

37. GS, "Be Natural," Nov. 20, 1864, MCHS.

38. GS to W. Beechman, Nov. 26, 1839, SU.

39. Patrick Ford, editor of *Irish World,* to GS, Nov. 13, 1873; I. Huntington, secretary of Young Catholic's Friend Society to GS, Dec. 17, 1873, SU.

40. GS, "The One Test of Character," July 22, 1860, in *Sermons and Speeches,* 91.

41. Verse Book, July 17, 1864, SU.

42. ACS to ESM, Nov. 24, 1864; William Mills to GS, Dec. 22, 1864, SU.

43. GS to H.V. Johnson, April 24, 1865, SU.

44. GS to President Grant, Nov. 4, 1868, SLC.

45. GS, "The One Test of Character," July 22, 1860, in *Sermons and Speeches,* 85.

46. address to "Christian Union Convention," Aug. 21, 1838.

47. McKivigan, 167-168.

48. GS to The Minister and Elders of the Presbyterian Church at Peterboro, Jan. 14, 1841, SU.

49. GS to E. G. Messinger, March 4, 1848, SU.

50. GS, "The Religion of Reason," June 10, 1859, in *Sermons and Speeches,* 63, 64.

51. GS to W.E. Channing, Aug. 17, 1841, SU.

52. GS to B.B. Stewart, Feb. 13, 1844, SU.

53. Frothingham, 1st ed., 85.

54. GS to Marcus Smith, Dec. 9, 1839, SU.

55. GS to Edwin M. Clarke, Sept. 5, 1839, SU.

56. Printed circular, MCHS.

57. Friedman, 107.

58. Proceedings of the Church of Peterboro meeting, Nov. 27, 1849, MCHS.

59. Cross 280; GS to Silas Hawley, Dec.11, 1840, SU.

60. GS to William J. Potter, Sept. 30, 1873, SU.

61. Strong, 45-57.
62. *The Democratic Volunteer,* April 15, 1875.
63. SU.
64. May 14, 1844, MCHS.
65. May 17, 1844, SU.
66. Watchman and Reflector, Nov. 7, 1867, SU.
67. "Discussions of Christian Union on the reports of the majority + minority of the committee on plan — Argument of the minority, Peterboro, April 1841."
68. Spelling not corrected from the original.
69. GS, "Religion of Reason," Jan. 23, 1859 in *Sermons and Speeches,* 16, 17.
70. Henry Campbell to his sister, Feb. 23, 1850, Henry Campbell letters.
71. GS, April 8, 1861, SU.
72. GS to Hiram P. Crozier, May 17, 1849, SU.
73. GS to ACS, Sept. 29, 1861, SU.
74. SU.
75. Asa Rand to *The Patriot*, Oct. 13, 1845, SU.
76. GS to Asa Rand, Sept. 24, 1845, SU.
77. SU.
78. Oct. 24, 1845, SU.
79. Aug. 10, 1845, SU.
80. Sept. 24, 1845, SU.
81. Rand to GS, Sept. 24, 1845, SU.
82. Rand to GS, Sept. 24, 1845, SU.
83. Preparatory notes for a speech, June 16, 1847, SU.
84. July 13, 1847, SU.
85. July 20, 1847, SU.
86. Rand to GS, July 31, 1847, SU.
87. SU.
88. Rand to GS, Sept. 22, 1847, SU.
89. Sept. 9, 1847, SU.
90. GS to Mrs. Huntington, April 26, 1843, SU.
91. GS to Warner Clemens, Nov. 25, 1846, SU.
92. GS to Lewis Tappan, Dec. 22, 1848, SU.
93. GS, Speech at the National Liberty Party Convention, Buffalo, NY, Sept. 17, 1851, SU.
94. GS to Judge Gridley, Dec. 3, 1845; GS to Beriah Green, March 5, 1850, SU.
95. GS personal notes, SU.
96. to GS, May 28, 1849, SU.
97. July 26, 1849, SU.
98. Crozier to GS, printed in *Frederick Douglass' Paper,* Aug. 31, 1849.
99. printed circular, Aug. 31, 1849, SU.
100. GS to Crozier, April 9, 1852, SU.
101. April 15, 1852, SU.

102. GS to Julia Griffiths, April 24, 1852, SU.

103. GS to Calkins, Oct. 2, 1849, SU.

104. April 8, 1852, SU.

105. Quoted in H. P. Crozier to GS, May 27, 1850, SU.

106. GS to J. P .Mendum, Oct. 26, 1866, SU.

107. Cross, 76.

108. GS to James Smith, Dec. 9, 1839, SU.

109. GS to Elder Kingsley, Sept. 1, 1845, SU.

110. GS to John G. Curtis, May 19, 1841, SU.

111. GS to James R. Willson, Professor at Allegheny Theological Institute, Dec. 22, 1840, SU.

112. Nov. 1843, in Frothingham, 1st ed., 58.

113. GS to the President of the National Convention of the Liberty Party, Aug. 10, 1843, SU.

114. Harlow, 100-102.

115. GS to Hiram H. Petrie, Oct. 19, SU.

116. ACS diary, July 23, MCHS.

117. ACS diary, July 27, 1843, MCHS.

118. Edwards to GS, July 17, 1845, SU.

119. GS to ACS, Oct. 21, 1844, SU.

120. 22.

121. 235.

122. Circa 1852, SU.

123. GS to Elizabeth Cady Stanton, Dec. l, 1855, SU.

124. GS, Speech to the NY State Legislature, Feb. 28, 1856, SU.

125. S+B, Aug. 15, 1868, 76.

126. S+B, Dec. 25, 1867, 13.

127. S+B, Aug. 15, 1868, 65.

128. S+B, Dec. 25, 1867, 4.

129. GS, Discourse in Peterboro, Feb. 21, 1858, SLC.

130. GS, Sermon in Peterboro, Feb. 21, 1858, SLC.

131. GS, "Religion of Reason," Feb. 21, 1858, in *Sermons and Speeches,* 6.

132. GS, "Religion of Reason," Jan. 23, 1859, in *Sermons and Speeches,* 36.

133. GS, "Be Natural," Nov. 20, 1864, MCHS.

134. GS, "Religion of Reason," Jan. 23, 1859, in *Sermons and Speeches,* 26.

135. GS, "Be Natural," Nov. 20, 1864 7, MCHS.

136. GS, "Be Natural," Nov. 20, 1864 8, MCHS.

137. S+B 72, 73.

138. George E. Isbell to GS, July 29, 1859, SU.

139. e.g., Charles Collins to GS, May 17, 1859, SU.

140. Oct. 7, 1861, SU.

141. SU.

142. To GS, Aug. 10, 1859, SU.

143. Nov. 5, 1868, SU.
144. Olney Place to GS, June 22, 1859, SU.
145. GS, "Bible Civil Government," Nov. 18, 1860, in *Sermons and Speeches,* 116, 120.
146. S+B, 120.
147. S+B, 101.
148. S+B, 132.
149. S+B, 99, 100.
150. S+B, 11.
151. GS, Discourse in Peterboro, Feb. 21, 1858, SLC.
152. S+B, 107.
153. S+B, 82, 83.
154. S+B, 5.
155. S+B, 80.
156. S+B, 106.
157. S+B, 93.
158. S+B, 114.
159. S+B, 115.
160. S+B, 94.
161. S+B, 82.
162. S+B, 121.
163. Aug. 6, 1859, SU.
164. A.V. Bentley to GS, 1858, SU.
165. Mary Quiney to GS, Jan. 15, 1868; March 8, 1869, SU.
166. S+B, 8.
167. GS, "Miracles," April 14, 1861, in *Sermons and Speeches,* 126.
168. GS, "Religion of Reason" Jan. 23, 1859, in *Sermons and Speeches,* 47.
169. GS, "Be Natural," Nov. 20,

1864 13, MCHS.

Chapter 11
1. GS to David Jones, Oct. 27, 1835, SU.
2. GS to D. S. Jones, Oct. 17, 1835, SU.
3. 159, 160.
4. 166, 167.
5. Dec. 29, 1874.
6. Campisi, 56.
7. Campisi, 51, 52.
8. Shattuck, 62.
9. Shattuck, 12.
10. Campisi, 59.
11. Luce.
12. Campisi, 59.
13. *Speeches,* 167.
14. John Haddock to GS, April 5, 1871; Dec. 1, 1873, SU.
15. GS to Charles B. Ray, Nov. 16, 1848, SU.
16. Lists of payments appear in the business records, SU.
17. Griffith, 5; GS to PS, March 23, 1821, SU.; Harlow, 14–27.
18. William Henderson to GS, Jan. 5, Sept. 23, 1819; Jane Denwick to GS, Nov. 24, 1821, SU.
19. SU.
20. All in letters, Federal Dana to GS, SU.
21. GS to Dana, June 30, 1843, SU.
22. Dana to GS, June 15, 1843, SU.

23. John B. Edwards to GS, Dec. 4, 7, 1854; April 30, 1855; Feb. 15, 1856, SU.
24. GS to Dr. Corliss, April 1, 1840, SU.
25. GS to Leander Cadwell, Oct. 30, 1844, SU.
26. GS, "Speech on the Homestead Bill," Feb. 7, 1854, in *Speeches*, 73.
27. *Speeches*, 72.
28. GS, "Speech on the Bill to Aid the Territory of Minnesota," March 7, 1854, in *Speeches*, 103.
29. Faust 41, 43; inSU.rance receipt, July 14, 1829, SU.
30. Feb. 17, 1831 agreement, SU.
31. June 26, 1860, SU.
32. April 10, 1852, SU.
33. SU.
34. GS to Joseph Witcomb and John Clark, Feb. 15, 1820; GS to Francis Galligher, Nov. 23, 1819; GS to Stephen Bosworth, Nov. 23, 1819, SU.
35. Aug. 3, 1820, SU.
36. GS to William B. Astor, May 12, 1843, SU.
37. Edwards to GS, July 5, 1853, SU.
38. John B. Edwards to GS, Jan. 4, 1855, SU.
39. Faust 40, 41.
40. Sands Higenbotham to GS, March 29, 1866, SU.
41. T. V. Russell to GS, May 14, 1846, SU.
42. SU.
43. Post to GS, June 30, 1869, SU.; GS to Scovell, Wilson, and Fowler, Directors of the Lake Ontario Shore Railroad, April 13, 1870, SLC.
44. Note by Calkins, no date, SU.
45. To GS, Jan. 29, 1846, SU.
46. Astor to GS, July 28, 1837; Astor to GS, Nov. 8, 1837, SU.
47. Frothingham, 1st ed., 33.
48. GS to D. Kendrick, Dec. 7, 1839, SU.
49. Dec. 2, 1839, SU.
50. May 1, 1843, SU.
51. Harlow, 26, 27.
52. GS to Israel Smith, Nov. 21, 1839, SU.
53. Frothingham, 1st ed., 136.
54. Jonathan Norwood to GS, June 12, 1837, SU.
55. Lemuel Knapp to GS, April 3, 1837, SU.
56. Rufus Blakslee and John Youngs to GS, April 24, 1837, SU.
57. Dec. 1, 1837, SU.
58. GS to Thos. Buckman, Dec. 10, 1841, SU.
59. to Jeanette DeForest, April 23, 1845, SU.
60. Dana to GS, Feb. 23, 1843, SU.
61. GS to Federal Dana, June 26, 1843, SU.
62. SU.

63. Dana to GS, June 30, 1843, SU.
64. ACS to ESM, Feb. 20, 1844; Feb. 22, 1844, SU.
65. Elizabeth H. Kelty to Caroline F. King, Nov. 25, 1843, PHS.
66. GS to Peter Skenandoah Smith, May 23, 1842, SU.
67. GS to ACS, Aug. 9, 1842, SU.
68. GS to ESM, March 1, 1845, SU.
69. GS to Judge Jones, July 13, 1843, SU.
70. GS to John Cochrane, April 23, 1842, SU.
71. Henry Campbell to his brother, May 1, 1843, Henry Campbell letters.
72. GS to Lewis H. Sanford, Jan. 31, 1842, SU.
73. GS to Mr. Tyler, Nov. 4, 1841; GS to Mason Whiting, Jan. 13, 1840, SU.
74. GS to C. S. Renolaw, April 18, 1842, SU.
75. GS to administrators at Hamilton College, July 3, 1840; Nov. 9, 1840; Dec 5, 1840, HCL.
76. GS to Genl. Ostrum, June 11, 1840, SU.
77. GS to Amarancy Paine, Dec. 24, 1841, SU.
78. GS to Abraham Ming and Cyrus Burnham, Jan. 13, 1845; GS to M. M. Ellis, June 3, 1846, SU.
79. ACS to ESM, April 10, 1845; GS to C. D. Miller and ESM, March 1, 1845; Loring Fowler to GS, Dec. 22, 1845, SU.
80. GS to Caleb Calkins, Aug. 1, 1846, SU. The clerks were Calkins, Fowler, Dana, Edwards, and Huntington.
81. Aug. 19, 1846, SU.
82. GS to William B. Astor, April 6, 1848, SU.
83. GS to Br. Leavitt, Nov. 8, 1847, SU.
84. GS to D. Jones, March 7, 1840, SU.
85. GS to Henry Bandals, Sept. 12, 1849.
86. GS to J. B. Edwards, May 4, 1866, SU.
87. GS to Abm Becker, Feb. 3, 1845, SU.
88. GS to John F. Seymour, March 23, 1847, SU.
89. e.g., GS to Arnold Nelson, Sept. 18, 1841, SU.
90. J. Brinkerhoff to GS, April 10, 1847, SU.
91. EdWard, Maynard to GS, Aug. 18, 1849; GS to EdWard, Maynard, Aug. 27, 1849, SU.
92. Client to GS, June 12, 1859; GS to client, June 14, 1859, SU.
93. July 22, 1858; March 15, 1847, SU.
94. John Cook to GS, June 5,

1837, SU.

95. John Hart to Caleb Calkins, March 11, 1862, SU.

96. GS to T. S. Fairchild, May 11, 1847, SU.

97. Jan. 16, 1843, SU.

98. Philo Murray to GS, Dec. 10, 1819, SU.

99. GS to M. Sanford, Feb. 14, 1840; June 8, 1840, SU.

100. GS to Professor Eaton of Hamilton Baptist Seminary, Jan. 2, 1841, SU.

101. Feb. 2, 1858, SU.

102. SU.

103. SU.

104. GS to D. S. Jones, Feb. 22, 1841, SU.

105. April 27, 1847, SU.

106. Dec. 4, 1843, SU.

107. Jan. 3, 7, 1843, SU.

108. GS to W. Campbell, May 16, 1837, SU.

109. GS to Seymour Scovell, Feb. 26, 1842, SU.

110. Oct. 29, 1841, SU.

111. GS to Treadway, Nov. 11, 1841, SU.

112. July 6, 1858, SU.

113. GS to ACS, Dec. 29, 1865, SU.

114. Johnson to GS, Feb. 7, 1849, SU.

115. SU.

116. SU.

117. Faust, 59.

118. Edwards to GS, Jan. 10, 1855; Aug. 3, 1857, SU.

119. SU.

120. SU.

121. Henry B. Stanton to GS, May 20, 1861, SU.; GS to Ellen Walter, June 15, 1842, SU.

122. SU.

123. GS to Abram Becker, Feb. 28, 1846, SU.

124. Nov. 14, 1843, SU.

125. Dec. 19, SU.

126. To George Thomas, Dec. 31, SU.

127. GS to ACS, Feb. 3, 1866, SU.

128. Dec. 23, SU.

129. GS to ACS, Dec. 27, SU.

130. GS to ACS, Feb. 3, 1866, SU.

131. GS to John T. Mason, Nov. 30, 1846, SU.

132. Thomas, 7.

133. April 29, 1832; Dec. 16, 1839; Dec. 28, 1861, SU.

134. Feb. 23, 1850, SU.

135. Oct. 14, 1843, SU.

136. Nov. 14, SU.

137. To Hon. O. Robinson, Nov. 23, SU.

138. GS to ACS, Feb. 22, 1861, SU.

139. GS to ACS, March 20, 1868, SU.

140. GS to Luther Wright, Oct. 1, 1841, SU.

141. Harlow, 24, 40, 314.

142. Business records, SU.

143. April 2, 1838, SU.

144. Burdick, vol. 2, 5.

145. Caleb Calkins to GS, July 9, 1838, SU.

146. Calkins to GS, Oct. 10, 1838, SU.

147. Calkins to GS, Feb. 25, 1843, SU.

148. Calkins to GS, Feb. 22, 1848, SU.

149. GS to Calkins, April 30, 1862, SU.

150. SU.

151. Burdick, Vol. 6, 10.

152. Dana to GS, June 19, 1832, SU.

153. Dana to GS, June 30, 1843, SU.

154. Dana to GS, Feb. 8, 1869, SU.

155. Nehemiah Huntington to GS, March 10, 1828, SU.

156. Huntington to GS, May 6, 1843, SU.

157. Fowler to GS, April 16, 1847.

158. GS to Bissel, June 25, 1868, SU.

159. e.g., see Calkins' account ledgers, May 1, 1848; Nov. 14, 1850, SU.

Chapter 12

1. GS to Josiah Spalding, Jan. 5, 1846, SU.

2. Aug. 4, 5, 1858, NYPL.

3. GS to the editor of *The Emancipator*, Aug. 23, 1847, MCHS.

4. GS to Hamilton College, June 20, 1847, HCL.

5. GS to Seth M. Gates, Nov. 19, 1841, SU.

6. GS to the *Albany Patriot*, May 8, 1847, SU.; see also GS to Alvan Stewart, July 20, 1840, SU.

7. GS to Judge Nye, July 27, 1848, SU.

8. GS to The Rank and File of the Democratic Party, Oct. 20, 1864, SLC.

9. GS to George T. Downing, March 6, 1874, SU.

10. GS, speech in Milwaukee, June 17, 1857, SU.

11. Wiecek, 219-221.

12. GS, Speech on the Nebraska Bill, April 6, 1854, in *Speeches,* 171.

13. GS, Speech on Temperance, July 22, 1854, in *Speeches*, 343.

14. GS, open letter, "Will the American People Never Cease to Oppress and Torture the Helpless Poor?" Dec. 12, 1874, SLC.

15. GS to Asa Rand, Sept. 23, 1845, SU.

16. GS, Speech in Milwaukee, June 17, 1857, SU.

17. GS, "Bible Civil Government," Nov. 18, 1860, in *Sermons and Speeches*, 108, 109.

18. GS, "Final Letter to His

Constituents," Aug. 7, 1854, in *Speeches*, 394.

19. William C. Cotting to GS, Nov. 10, 1861, SU.

20. *Canastota Bee-Journal*, Jan. 28, 1876, 6.

21. Address to the State Temperance Convention at Syracuse, NY, Jan. 19, 1848, PHS.

22. Friedman, 103-110.

23. GS, "Speech for the Harbor of Oswego," July 12, 1854, in *Speeches*, 313, 314.

24. GS, "Speech on Supplying the city of Washington with water," June 24, 1854, in *Speeches*, 284.

25. GS to Madison County politicians, Oct. 8, 1839; GS to E. Crosswell, April 9, 1840, SU.

26. D. H. Frost to GS, Feb. 2, 1840, SU.

27. GS to Charles Stebbins, Nov. 5, 1873, SU.

28. GS to Henry Bandals, Sept. 12, 1849; GS to Beriah Green, Jan. 5, 1850; GS to W. L. Crandall, April 28, 1850, SU.

29. GS, "Speech on the Abolition of the Postal System," June 15, 1854, in *Speeches*, 270.

30. GS to Rev. Dr. Kendrick, March 22, 1848, SU.

31. GS, "The Common School Compromise," Dec. 14, 1869, SLC.

32. GS, "Government Bound to Protect from the Dramshop," July 22, 1854, MCHS.

33. GS, Diary entry, June 22, 1842, in Frothingham, 1st ed., 130.

34. Diary, June 22, 1842.

35. Frothingham, 1st ed., 134.

36. GS to Albert Barnes, Aug. 15, 1868, SU.

37. GS to Charles G. Finney, Sept. 18, 1852, SU.

38. Notes of David Keppel, 1874, SU.

39. GS to The Liberty Party, May 7, 1846, SU.

40. GS, "Final Letter to his Constituents," Aug. 7, 1854, in *Speeches*, 394.

41. GS to L. H. Rousseau, Dec. 31, 1851, SU.

42. GS, "Speech on the Pacific Railroad," May 30, 1854, in *Speeches*, 253, 254.

43. GS, "Speech on the Mexican Treaty and Monroe Doctrine," June 27, 1854, in *Speeches*, 294.

44. GS to Senator Hamlin, July 17, 1854, in *Speeches*.

45. GS to The Electors of the County of Madison, Winter, 1823-24, SU.

46. GS, Speech in Syracuse, Sept. 3, 1863, MCHS.

47. GS to the *Friend of Man*, Nov. 8, 1838, SU.

48. Aug. 12, 1840, SU.

49. Aug. 28, 1854, SU.
50. GS to C. P. Kirkland, Sept. 24, SU.
51. GS to Everett Brown, Aug. 9, 1872, SLC.
52. Nov. 23, 1874, SLC.
53. Gerrit Smith and the Vigilant Association of New York, John A. Gray, printer, 104.
54. GS, "Speech on the Second Deficiency Bill," March 16, 1854 in *Speeches,* 109.
55. May 26, MCHS.
56. GS to Dr. Cuyler, Jan. 1, 1868, SLC.
57. J. D. Hammond to GS, Feb. 5, SU.
58. to GS, Nov. SU.
59. Wellman, 152.
60. GS to William Goodell, *Friend of Man*, Feb. 8, 1840.
61. Fladeland, 185.
62. Harlow, 146, 147.
63. GS to Lewis Tappan, March 14, 1840, SU.
64. Finney to GS, July 22, 1840, SU.
65. Friend of Man, Aug. 15, 1838.
66. GS to Beriah Green, March 29, 1840, SU.
67. June 19, 1840, SU; Mayer, 40.
68. *Madison Observer*, Nov. 29, 1843; Kraut 74, 82, 83.
69. Dumond, 358-359.
70. Bretz, 94.
71. April 15, 1840, SU.
72. ECS to GS, Aug. 3, 1840, SU.; Hesseltine, 33, 34.
73. Nov. 13, 1843, MCHS.
74. Kraut, 126-127.
75. Kruczek-Aaron, 270.
76. *Liberty Herald*, Dec. 7, 1843, 1.
77. Kelley to GS, July 28, 1843, SU.
78. GS to Alfred Wilkinson, Oct. 19, 1840, SU.
79. GS to E. S. Bailey, et. al., April 10, 1846, SU.
80. Salmon P. Chase to GS, July 31, 1845, SU.
81. GS to the Right Hon. Daniel O'Connell, MP, July 28, 1843, SU.
82. Written in Smith's hand to "The Members of the Liberty Party," c. 1840, SU.
83. GS to The Liberty Party, Nov. 28, 1850, MCHS.
84. Strong, 7.
85. Kraut, 81.
86. GS to The Liberty Party, May 7, 1846, MCHS.
87. GS to the National Liberty Party Convention at Buffalo, Sept, 17, 1851, MCHS.
88. GS to The Liberty Party, Nov. 28, 1850, MCHS.
89. Blassingame, 234.
90. GS to W. Kinney and E. Dodge, Aug. 30, 1843, SU.
91. Ransom F. Wake, et. al. to

GS, June 13, 1845; GS to E. S. Bailey, A. Raymond, and F. Rice, April 10, 1846, SU.

92. GS to Warner Clemens, Nov. 25, 1846, SU.
93. Friedman, 122.
94. Friedman, 120, 121.
95. Friedman, 120.
96. Friedman, 119.
97. Oates, 91.
98. Perkal 76; Sewell, 287.
99. Hunter, 183.
100. Perkal, 67, 106.
101. Field, 128, 136.
102. Conrad, 88.
103. John B. Edwards to GS, Aug. 20, 1856, SU.
104. GS to ECS, June 6, 1864, MCHS.
105. Kelty.
106. GS to The Rank and File of the Democratic Party, Oct. 20, 1864, SLC.
107. Mayer, 472, 567.
108. Harlow, 467.
109. GS to FD, June 27, 1874, SU.
110. E. Williams to GS, Nov. 19, 1825, SU.
111. Frothingham, 1st ed., 145.
112. July 7, 1858, SU.
113. Hesseltine; Frothingham, 1st ed., 194.
114. Friedman, 118.
115. Nash, 56.
116. GS to the *Albany Patriot*, May 8, 1847, SU.
117. Dec. 15, 1847, SU.

118. GS to Elias Gilbert, July 9, 1847, SU.
119. Harlow, 363; Frothingham, 1st ed., 194.
120. Harlow, 427; W. H. Holt to GS, April 8, 1862 in GS annotation; Hunter 187; John B. Edwards to GS, June 2, 1856, SU.
121. Henry Campbell to his sister, Oct. 24, 1851, Henry Campbell letters.
122. John B. Edwards to GS, June 2, 1856, SU.
123. Harlow, 149, 377; Edwards to GS, Aug. 5, 1858, SU.
124. GS to Samuel J. May, July 7, 1858, SU.
125. Frothingham, 1st ed., 194; Edwards to GS, Nov. 16, 1858, SU.
126. Putnam.
127. In Letterbook II, SU.
128. GS, "Bible Civil Government," Nov. 18, 1860, in *Sermons and Speeches,* 103.
129. note in Verse Book, Nov. 7, 1866, SU.
130. J. B. Edwards to GS, Dec. 28, 1850, SU.
131. Edwards to GS, Sept. 28, 1852, SU.
132. Snow to GS, Oct. 11, 1852, SU.
133. FD to GS, Oct. 8, 1852, SU.
134. Wilson to GS, Oct. 11, 1852, SU.

135. Frothingham, 1st ed., 212.
136. 13.
137. Frederick Douglass to GS, Nov. 6, 1852, SU.
138. Hawley to GS, Nov. 5, 1852, SU.
139. Bentley to GS, Nov. 8, 1852, SU.
140. Nov. 12, 1852.
141. Jay to GS, Nov. 9, 1852, SU.
142. 1st ed., 213.
143. Harlow, 318.
144. GS to John Pratt, Sept, 7, 1853, SU.
145. Cash Book, Nov. 1853—Aug. 1854, SU.
146. GS to D. H. Frost, Nov. 29, 1853 from Philadelphia, SU.
147. John B. Edwards to GS, Dec. 13, 1853, SU.
148. Jan. 1, 1853 in Harlow, 316, 317.
149. Nov. 5, 1852 in Frothingham, 1st ed., 216.
150. Harlow, 317, 318.
151. Waugh, 1.
152. GS to FD, Aug. 24, 1854, in *Speeches*, 408, 404, 411.
153. GS, "Final Letter to his Constituents," Aug. 7, 1854, in *Speeches,* 380.
154. GS, "Resolutions of Thanks to Capt. Ingraham," Jan. 5, 1854, in *Speeches*, 36.
155. In *Speeches,* 13-32.
156. John B. Edwards to GS, Jan. 17, March 2, 1854, SU.
157. Stanton, H. B., Dec. 30, 1874.
158. GS to H. C. Goodwin, Jan. 5, 1855, SU.
159. Edwards to GS, July 4, 1854; Edwards to Caleb Calkins, July 18, 1854, SU.
160. S. G. Haven to GS, Nov. 27, 1854, SU.
161. Abzug, 271.
162. May to GS, Aug. 31, 1854, SU.
163. FD to GS, Aug. 22, 1854, SU.
164. to GS, June 5, 1854, SU.
165. April 14, 1862, SU.

Chapter 13
1. GS to Silas W. Tyler, March 5, 1845, SU.
2. Bartlett, 76, 77.
3. Thomas, 8.
4. Wellman, 204, 205.
5. GS to Silas W. Tyler, March 5, 1845, SU.
6. Wells, 102.
7. GS to Judge Gridley, Dec. 3, 1845, SU.
8. GS to John Stuart Mill, Feb. 5, 1869, SU.
9. GS, "Government Bound to Protect from the Dramshop," July 22, 1854, in *Speeches,* 351.
10. GS to Edwin Heale, June 26, 1841, SU.
11. GS to EdWard, C. Delevan,

July 20, 1839, SLC.

12. GS to Benjamin Stewart, Dec. 3, 1841, SU.

13. Sept. 12, 1865, SLC.

14. GS to E. C. Delevan, Sept. 11, 1833, SU.

15. GS, Autobiographical Sketch, 1856 SU.

16. Harlow, 68, 69.

17. Hewit to GS, Aug. 3, 1829; Sept. 8, 1829, SU.

18. GS to Hewit, no day, 1829, SU.

19. GS to John Tappan, Aug. 11, 1834, SU.

20. J. B. Edwards to GS, May 16, 1832, SU.

21. GS to Justin Edwards, Nov. 26, 1833, SU.

22. GS to Rev. E. D. Willis, July 1, 1837, SU.

23. GS to E. C. Delevan, Nov. 6, 1837, SU.

24. GS to E. C. Delevan, July 9, 1838, SU.

25. GS to L. Fowler, Feb. 6, 1843, HCL.

26. July 13, 1860, SU.

27. Reviewed in the *Oneida Daily Dispatch*, July 4, 2008, 7.

28. GS to B. B. Stewart, Feb. 10, 1844, SU.

29. Morton to GS, April 13, 1867, SU.

30. GS to Bisell, July 13, 1868; July 27, 1868, SU.

31. Hooker to GS, Jan. 22, 1869; G. C. Sampson, et. al., to GS, Aug. 10, 1869, SU.

32. J. H. Abbott to GS, Sept. 7, 1870, SU.

33. GS, "Address to the Convention of the New York Anti-Dramshop Party," Aug. 17, 1870, SLC.

34. GS, "The Dramshop" March 2, 1870, SLC.

35. GS to Daniel Dickey, Aug. 27, 1841, SU.

36. GS to E. C. Delevan, May 3, 1841, SU.

37. GS, "To the People of the Town of Smithfield," March 15, 1843, MCHS.

38. Pledge of Duplissis North, Nov. 1, 1842; GS to David Coe, Dec. 12, 1842; GS to Hiram Petrie re his brother Peter, Oct. 19, 1842, SU.

39. GS to N. Sanford, Feb. 14, 1840, SU.

40. GS, "Vindication of the Chicago Temperance Convention," Oct. 9, 1869, SLC.

41. GrS to GS, Nov. 26, 1869, SU.

42. GrS to GS, Dec. 9, 1869, SU.

43. GS to Vice President Colfax, May 14, 1870, SLC.

44. GS to "his Colored Brethren," Oct. 26, 1870, SLC.

45. GS, quoted in Frothingham, 1st ed., 150.

46. GS, "No Legislating for Tem-

perance!" Letter to legislators, July 10, 1873, SLC.

47. Sept. 12, SU.

48. Joseph Speed to GS, Jan. 25, 1832, SU.

49. To GS, March 22, 1861, SU.

50. Verse Book, Oct. 23, 1866, SU.

51. ESM to GS, April 1, 1873, SU.

52. GrS to GS, Jan. 4, 1862, MCHS.

53. GS to John H. Cocke, Dec. 11, 1840; GS to Genl. Messinger, April 26, 1841; GS. to Edwin Heale, June 26, 1841, SU.

54. GS, "Stand by the Government," Feb. 27, 1863, SLC.

55. GS, open letter to Madison County voters, Jan. 20, 1871, SLC.

56. Campbell to his sister, June 20, 1851, Henry Campbell letters.

57. GS to Woodworth, May 17, 1841, SU.

58. GS to Woodworth, May 4, 1841, SU.

59. GS to Stower, Dec. 27, 1841, SU.

60. A. V. Bentley to GS, Dec. 29, 1845, SU.

61. GS to John Thomas, Aug. 27, 1859; GS to Frederick Douglass, July 13, 1860, SU.

62. GS, "Temperance," Aug. 18, 1865, SLC.

63. Handbill, May 23, 1870, SLC.

64. David Plumb to GS, April 6, 1871, SU.

65. GS to The Thoughtful and Candid of the County of Madison, March 8, 1871, SLC.

66. GS to E. C. Delevan, July 29, 1839, SLC.

67. GS, "Government Bound to Protect from the Dramshop," July 22, 1854, in *Speeches*, 344, 361.

68. Verse Book, Jan. 21, 1851, SU.

69. GS to GrS and Gatty, Dec. 4, 1851, SU.

70. John Elmore to GS, Jan. 7, 1842, SU.

71. Peter Skenandoah Smith to GS, June 9, 1855, SU.

72. GS to Elder Hitchcock, Nov. 1, 1842, SU.

73. GS to Hawley, Jan. 9, 1846, SU.

74. GS, "No Legislating for Temperance," July 10, 1873, SLC.

75. GS, Speech at a meeting of Christians in Canastota, Frothingham, 1st ed., 79.

76. Ellen Walter to GS, Oct. 30, 1874, SU.

77. Frothingham, 1st ed., 152.

78. GS to E. C. Delevan, Sept. 11, 1833, SU.

79. Rev. Henry Dwight of Geneva to GS, March 4, 1830, SU.

80. Benjamin F. Butler to GS, May 24, 1830, SU.

81. GS to Harvey, May 24, 1841; GS to Harvey, June 26, 1841; GS to Harvey, July 9, 1841, SU.

82. GS to Gen. Messinger, Jan. 3, 1845, SU.; *The Democratic Volunteer*, Feb. 17, 1875.

83. GS to Hyde, April 11, 1845; April 15, 1845, SU.

84. SU.

85. *The Democratic Volunteer*, Feb. 17, 1875.

86. GS to E. Holmes, Aug. 18, 1846, SU.

87. Wurst, 167–170.

Chapter 14

1. Nov. 26, SU.

2. Wagner, 15.

3. Griffith, 58.

4. Griffith, 25.

5. *The Lily*, Aug. 26.

6. Anthony to GS, Sept. 5, 1856, MCHS.

7. GS to the Liberty Party, May 7, 1846, SU.

8. GS to ECS, Dec. 1, 1855, SU.

9. GS to Miss Pellet, Oct. 25, 1852, SU.

10. GS to ECS, Dec. 1, 1855, SU.

11. GS to Miss Pellet, Oct. 25, 1852, SU.

12. Feb. 5, 1873, SLC.

13. Dec. 1, 1855, SU.

14. GS to ECS, 1869, Frothingham, 1st ed., 124.

15. GS to Nellie W. Dyes, March 30, 1874, MCHS.

16. Wagner, 1996, 26.

17. Wagner, 1996, 1.

18. Address of Welcome to the International Council of Women, March 25, 1888, Dubois, 209, 210.

19. Address of Welcome to the International Council of Women, March 25, 1888, Dubois, 209, 210.

20. Smith and Barnes, Dec. 25, 1867, 11.

21. Wagner, 1998, 44, 57.

22. Wagner, 1998, 55.

23. DuBois, 229.

24. GS to James G. Birney, May 11, 1839; GS to John T. Norton, Dec. 20, 1842, SU.

25. Mary Grew to GS, April 3, 1873, SU.

26. GS to Anthony, Feb. 5, 1873, SLC.

27. GS to Anthony, Aug. 15, 1873 MCHS.

28. Anthony to GS, Aug. 20, 1873, SU.

29. March 6, 1867; also SBA to GS, July 1, 1863; Aug. 20, 1872; Dec. 25, 1872, SU.

30. Stone to May, Aug. 20, 1852, on a letter May to GS, Aug. 25, 1852, SU.

31. ECS to GS, Nov. 26, 1856, SU.

32. ECS to GS, April 10, 1865, SU.
33. Gage to GS, June 24, 1869, SU.
34. Stone to GS, Sept. 30; and March 19, 1870, SU.
35. Nov. 6, SU.
36. Charles Hammond to GS, March 6, 1869; Julia Ward, Howe to GS, Sept, 27, 1869; Mary L. Corner to GS, May 15, 1871, SU.
37. GS to SU.san B. Anthony, Dec. 30, 1868 quoted in DuBois, 119.
38. GS to Everett Brown, Aug. 9, 1872, PHS.
39. Oct. 10, 1846, SU.
40. Nebraska, April 6, 1854, in *Speeches*, 115, 116, 119.
41. Mayer, 610.
42. ECS to GS, Dec. 21, 1854, SU; Mayer, 610.
43. Verse Book, Dec. 13, 1860, SU.
44. ECS to GS, Dec. 16, 1861, SU.
45. ACS to GS, March 31, 1831; Feb. 12, 1834; Aug. 13, 1838, SU.
46. GrS to ACS, Dec. 9, 1863, SU.
47. Verse Book, Sept. 20, 1865, SU.
48. Oct. 10, 1839, SU.
49. GS to ECS, Dec. 1, 1855, SLC.
50. ECS speech, Aug. 2, 1848, Griffith, 61.
51. Speech to the American Anti-Slavery Society, 1860, Dubois, 83.
52. Ward, 95, 103.
53. GS, "Bible Civil Government," Nov. 18, 1860, in *Sermons and Speeches*, 103.
54. To GS, Aug. 6, 1866, SU.
55. GS to John Cochrane, et. al., Jan. 4, 1850, SU.
56. GS, "Speech on the Pacific Railroad," May 30, 1854, in *Sermons and Speeches*, 243.
57. GS, S+B, 111, 112.
58. "Gerrit Smith on 'The Index,'" May 1, 1873; "Woman's War Upon the Dramshops," March 24, 1874; "The Bible for 'Total Abstinence,'" May 14, 1874, SLC.
59. GS, "The Religion of Reason," Jan. 23, 1859, in *Sermons and Speeches*, 72, 73.
60. Griffith, 133.
61. Child to GS, July 23, 1864, SU.
62. GS to ECS, Dec. 1, 1855, SLC.
63. GS to ACS, Oct. 5, 1869, SU.
64. Dec. 25, 1855, Messinger, 48.
65. Aug 31, 1854, 140.
66. GS to ECS, Dec. 1, 1855, SLC.
67. Griffith, 92.
68. GS to ECS, Dec. 1, 1855, SLC.

69. ECS to GS, Dec. 21, 1854, SU.
70. Dec. 24, 1855.
71. ACS to GS, May 18, 1851, SU.
72. Address to the Founding Convention of the National American Woman Suffrage Association, Feb. 1890, Dubois, 223.
73. Anthony to GS, Dec. 25, 1855, SU.
74. Verse Book, April 1, 1860, SU.
75. Conrad, 216, 217.

Chapter 15
1. Harrold, 18, 19.
2. *Frederick Douglass' Paper*, May 27, 1853.
3. Henry Campbell to his sister, Jan. 10, 1842, Henry Campbell letters.
4. Ratner, 188,189.
5. Dec. 11, 1840, SU.
6. Rose, 446.
7. Phelan, , 69.
8. Oates, 334.
9. Lutz, 19, 20, 91.
10. Paraphrased from a broadside by Gerrit Smith, Aug. 27, 1841, SU.
11. GS, Speech in Albany, March 13, 1856, SLC.
12. Jan. 31, 1864, recorded in Kelty.
13. Schor 100; Road Records, Town of Smithfield, 1819-1855, PHS.
14. GS to John C. Spencer, Nov. 12, 1851, SU.
15. GS, Speech in Peterboro, April 27, 1861, in *Sermons and Speeches*, 189, 190.
16. GS to Horatio Seymour, Jan. 12, 1863, MCHS.
17. Lewis Tappan to GS, Sept. 5, 1839 from New York City, SU.
18. Ezekiel Birdseye to GS, Oct. 11, 1841, SU.
19. Fladeland, 103.
20. Jordan, 13.
21. Phallen, 38, 65.
22. Ellis, 93-102.
23. Ellis, 81.
24. Ellis, 92.
25. GS, "Speech on the Nebraska Bill," April 6, 1854, in *Speeches*, 125.
26. GS to Hon. Mr. Worden, April 13, 1841, SU.
27. Thomas, 5.
28. "Speech against Limiting Grants of Land to White Persons," May 3, 1854, in *Speeches*, 228.
29. "Speech for Human Rights," Feb. 6, 1861, in *Sermons and Speeches*, 160.
30. Nov. 14, 1846, SU.
31. Feb. 7, 1842, SU.
32. June 18, 1842, SU.
33. Feb. 5, 1844, SU.
34. "Speech on the Nebraska

Bill," April 6, 1854, in *Speeches*, 191.

35. "Speech on the Mexican Treaty and Monroe Doctrine," June 27, 1854, in *Speeches*, 296.

36. GS, "Speech on the Nebraska Bill," April 6, 1854, in *Speeches*, 171.

37. GS to John Thomas, Aug. 27, 1859, SU.

38. Gerrit Smith and the Vigilant Association of New York, 16, 17.

39. Oct. 28, 1835, MPL.

40. GS to John Spencer, Nov. 12, 1851, SU.

41. GS to John H. Cocke, Dec. 11, 1840, SU.

42. GS, "Speech on the Nebraska Bill," Aug. 6, 1854, in *Speeches*, 115.

43. GS, "Final Letter to his Constituents," Aug. 8, 1854, in *Speeches*, 379.

44. GS to Montgomery Blair, April 5, 1862, SU.

45. GS to Grant, Nov. 4, 1868, SLC.

46. Friedman, 194.

47. GS to C. B. Ray, T. S. Wright, and J. M. Smith, Sept. 9, 1846, SU.

48. "Speech on the Nebraska Bill," Aug. 6, 1854, in *Speeches*, 191.

49. Mayer, 344.

50. Jan. 12, 1839, SU.

51. May 127, 128.

52. Campbell, 74, 75.

53. Aug. 18, 1854, in *Speeches*, 402.

54. GS to S. Phillips, et. al., July 9, 1845, SU.

55. GS to FD, June 27, 1874, MCHS.

56. March 16, 1847, SU.

57. GS to FD, July 13, 1860, SU.

58. Aug. 31, 1861, SLC.

59. *Friend of Man*, May 24, 1837, 195.

60. Dec. 18, 1860, SU.

61. Antihypocrite to GS, Nov. 9, 1838, in Harlow, 144.

62. Scott, 27.

63. Ripley, 68.

64. Lutz, 56, 58.

65. May 11, 1839, SU.

66. ACS to ESM, May 21, 1839, SU.

67. Fladeland, 140, 141; Lutz, 72, 141.

68. Edmonston.

Chapter 16

1. GS to S. P. Chase, Nov. 1, 1847, SU.

2. "American Colonization Society", no date, SU.

3. Mayer, 135.

4. Friedman, 15.

5. John B. Edwards to GS, July 25, 1852, SU.

6. Ralph R. Gurley to GS, Jan. 5,

1828, SU.

7. Frothingham, 1st ed., 169.

8. Gurley to GS, Nov. 21, 1827, SU.

9. Gurley to GS, June 18, 1830, SU.

10. GS to Leonard Bacon, July 23, 1834, SU.

11. GS to Leonard Bacon, March 31, 1834, SU.

12. Nye, 52, 62-64.

13. April 25, 1832, SU.

14. GS to Leonard Bacon, July 23, 1834, SU.

15. Green to GS, March 25, 1834, SU.

16. *New Haven Journal of Freedom*, Aug. 20, 1834.

17. *The Liberator*, Feb. 15, 1834; Nov. 8, 1834.

18. Ripley 72; Klees, 3.

19. Kashatus, 41.

20. Sorin, 81, 82; Quarles, 4.

21. Quarles, 6,8.

22. Friedman, 18-20; Harlow, 113, 114.

23. letters dated Nov. 14, Dec. 30, 1834; Fladeland, 102.

24. Sernett, *North Star Country* 29, 32.

25. 16.

26. Dumond 204.

27. Smith, William 19.

28. GS, "Essay on Colonization" 105.

29. Oct. 5, 1833, SU.

30. GS to Elizur Wright, Aug. 13, 1834, SU.

31. Friedman, 34.

32. GS to *Friend of Man*, Jan 26, 1839, 23, SU.

33. *The Colored American*, Dec. 15, 1838.

34. Today, equivalent to $750,000.

35. John B. Edwards to GS, July 25, 1852, SU.

36. GS to Abby Kelley, Aug. 1, 1843, SU.

37. Fifth Annual Report of the Executive Committee of the American Anti-Slavery Society, 38.

38. Aug. 18, 1835, SU.

39. Pittman.

40. SU.

41. 1838, quoted in Frothingham, 1st ed., 169.

42. GS to Abby Kelley, Aug. 1, 1843, SU.

43. Feb. 28, 1856, SLC.

44. GS to the Anti-Dramshop Party, Nov. 6, 1872, SLC.

45. J. M. Smith to GS, Dec. 17, 1846, SU.

46. Channing to GS, Aug. 20, 1841, SU.

47. W. L. Hartwell to GS, Dec. 16, 1866, SU.

48. Friedman, 181, 182.

49. Davis.

50. Wiecek, 84, 85.

51. Dumond 139.

52. Wiecek, ,152, 153.

53. Wiecek, 21, 39, 160, 285.
54. Weicek 161, 171.
55. Quoted in Wiecek, 253.
56. Wiecek, 218, 254, 255.
57. Wiecek, 267.
58. Frothingham, 1ˢᵗ ed., 164.
59. Ripley, 62.
60. Harlow, 120, 121.
61. Green to GS, Aug. 19, 1835, SU.
62. SU.
63. J. C. Jackson memoirs transcribed by J. E. Jackson, 1998.
64. Jackson.
65. No author, *Ziyara Bugle,* 14.
66. Jackson; Sernett, *Abolition's Axe,* 43.
67. *Oneida Whig*, Oct. 27, 1835.
68. Dumond, 221.
69. *Oneida Whig*, Oct. 27, 1835.
70. Probably paraphrased by Jackson.
71. Jackson.
72. Oct. 27, 1835.
73. Jackson.
74. Speech in Peterboro, Oct. 22, 1835, SLC.
75. GS to Leonard Bacon, Oct 24, 1835, SU.
76. To GS, Oct. 14, 1872, SU.
77. Sernett, *Abolition's Axe* 43.
78. To GS, Nov. 30, 1835, SU.
79. March 18, 1838, SU.
80. To GS, Dec. 14, 1835, SU.
81. To GS, Dec. 11, 1835, SU.
82. GS to Hon. H. Hunt, Feb. 14, 1840, SU.
83. SU.
84. *Friend of Man*, Oct. 27, 1836, 73, 74.
85. Loguen, 358.
86. GS to ACS, May 14, 1836, SU; Elizur Wright, Jr., corr. sec. to GS, July 16, 1836, SU.
87. Nov. 10, 1837 181.
88. March 21, 1838, SU.; See letters: Simeon Jocelyn and Charles B. Ray to W.W. Chapman, Nov. 6, 1850, and William Goodell to W.W. Chapman, March 24, 1857, HCL.
89. T. Weld to GS, July 12, 1839; GS to the Madison County Anti-Slavery Society, May 30, 1840, SU.
90. Phelan, 71.
91. Friedman, 101.
92. Aug. 10, 1841, SU.
93. GS to S. P. Chase, Nov. 1, 1847, PHS.
94. Weld to GS, Sept. 16, 1839, SU.
95. Mayer, 112, 129, 355.
96. Scott 78, 251.
97. Lutz, 268.
98. Phelps to GS, March 9, 1840, SU.
99. Gurley to GS, Sept. 7, 1831, SU.
100. GS to H. C. Wright, March 14, 1840, SU.
101. GS to Oliver Johnson, July 6, 1840, SU.
102. Mayer, 569.

103. GS to The Right Honorable Daniel O'Connell, MP Lord Mayor of Dublin, July 2, 1842, SU.

104. GS, March 8, 1840, SU.

105. GS to Lewis Tappan, March 14, 1840, SU.

106. April 1, 1836, SU.

107. To GS, April 8, 1836, SU.

108. Third Annual Report of the American Anti-Slavery Society, 17.

109. Sept. 13, 1835, SU.

110. Harlow, 158.

111. GS to the People of the Town of Smithfield, March 15, 1843, MCHS.

112. May 6, 1852, SU.

113. GS to the editor of the *Liberty Gazette*, Aug. 30, 1847, SU.

114. Tappan to GS, July 5, 1836; Sumner to GS, July 31, 1860, SU.

115. Green to GS, Aug. 24, 1841, SU.

116. McFeely, 175.

117. GS to John T. Norton, Dec. 20, 1842, SU.

118. Friedman, 45-47.

119. Friedman, 68-70.

120. Friedman, 96-102.

121. James G. Birney, Elizur Wright, and Henry B. Stanton to GS, July, 1838, SU.

122. GS to the Secretary of the Madison County Anti-Slavery Society, Dec. 23, 1839, SU.

123. GS to A. A. Phelps, Dec. 28, 1838, SU.

124. GS to the editor of the *Union Herald*, Cazenovia, NY, Oct. 18, 1838, SU.

125. GS to Governor Seymour, Jan. 12, 1863, in *Speeches, and Letters*.

126. Jackson to GS, Nov., 1838; W. O. Duvall to GS, March 13, 1841, SU.

127. GS to Henry Highland Garnet, June 10, 1843, SU.

128. GS to Daniel Dickey and George Ellinwood, March 21, 1845, SU.

129. Feb. 1, 1843, SU.

130. GS to Luther Myrick, June 22, 1839, SU.

131. To GS, Sept. 9, SU.

132. Holley to GS, March 9, 1840, SU.

133. Henry Campbell to his sister, May 11, 1848, Henry Campbell letters.

134. GS to S. Phillips, et. al., July 9, 1845; GS to Daniel Dickey and George Ellinwood, March 21, 1845, SU.

135. Friedman, 97.

136. Stauffer, 160, 161.

137. FD to GS, Jan. 25, 1851, SU.

138. Discussions with Fred Morsell, professional actor portraying Douglass, April, 2000.

139. McFeely, 383.

140. FD to GS, Feb. 13, 1852.

141. GS to FD, July 13, 1860, SU.

142. J. C. Buttre, 1864.

143. Levesque, 188, 189.

144. Lutz, 98, 100.

145. Sterling, 83.

146. Lutz, 163, 168.

147. Lerner, 3-8, 142-154.

148. Lutz, 86-88, 104.

149. Lutz, 233, 207-210.

150. Lerner, 203.

151. Dillon, 102.

152. Lutz, 18, 53.

153. Lutz, 143, 26.

154. Lutz, 176, 179.

155. Morton to GS, Jan. 22, 1862, SU.

156. Lutz, 214.

157. Abby Kelley to GS, Aug. 7, 1843, SU.

158. Quoted in Lutz, 219.

159. ACS to ESM, Oct. 26, 1843, SU.

160. Lutz, 6, 9, 11.

161. Maria Chapman in Lutz, 154.

162. Speech by Margaret Washington, Feb. 21, 2001.

163. Anthony to GS, July 1, 1863, SU.

Chapter 17

1. GS to Julia Griffiths, July 25, 1857, SU.

2. GS to the editor of *Freedom's Journal*, March 31, 1827, SU.

3. GS to ECS, Dec. 1, 1855, SLC.

4. GS to Wright, et. al., Sept. 9, 1846, SU.

5. GS, "Speech Against Limiting Grants of Land to White Persons," May 3, 1854 in *Speeches*, 228

6. GS, "Speech on the Nebraska Bill," April 6, 1854, in *Speeches*, 214

7. Aug. 15, 1839, SU.

8. GS to John Quincy Adams, July 16, 1839, SU.

9. Nov. 16, 1835, SU.

10. GS to Hon. K. Rayner, July 8, 1841, SU.

11. GS to Professor Eaton, Jan, 2, 1841, SU.

12. Aug. 28, 1850.

13. Higginson, 329, 331.

14. GS to May, Jan. 15, 1851, SU.

15. SU.

16. July 2, 1842, SU.

17. Oct. 6, 1840, SU.

18. To GS, Sept., 1851, SU.

19. Nov. 26, 1866, SU.

20. Dec. 17, 1836, SU.

21. *Friend of Man*, June 12, 1839, 201; January 11, 1842, 42.

22. FD to GS, Dec. 23, 1853, SU.

23. FD to GS, Dec. 14, 1857, SU.

24. FD to GS, April 14, 1855, SU.

25. *North Star*, Sept. 5, 1850.

26. Oct. 29, 1941.

27. GS to W. M. Clark and Chas. Wheaton, April 7, 1842, SU.

28. Titus Gilbert to GS, July 9,

1853, SU.

29. GS to Beriah Green, Aug. 14, 1837, SU.

30. Wm. Watkins, et. al. to GS, Aug. 15, 1836, SU.

31. GS to C. G. Finney, April 25, 1839, SU.

32. GS to George Eaton, July 24, 1839, SU.

33. GS to Nathaniel Lord, President, Nov. 2, 1845, SU.

34. Welds to GS, Sept. 26, 1860, SU.

35. Hamilton to GS, June 9, 1863, SU.

36. L. James to GS, Aug. 20, 1863, SU.

37. T. S. "Gerrit Smith at Home," *Cazenovia Republican*, May 21, 1874.

38. GS to ACS, May 1, 1836, SU.

39. GS to Dr. Rice, Dec. 28, 1838, SU.

40. GS to Clay, Feb. 28, 1845, SU.

41. April 17, 1851, SU.

42. SU.

43. GS to Charles B. Ray, Nov. 16, 1848, SU.

44. FD to GS, Jan. 21, 1851, SU.

45. Elizabeth Smith to Caroline F. King, Jan. 6, 1838, PHS.

46. Elizabeth H. Kelty to Caroline G. King, Nov. 25, 1843, PHS.

47. GS to Mr. Myrick, Nov. 10, 1841; GS circular to the public, Jan. 22, 1842, SU.

48. Lewis Tappan to GS, July 11, 1842, SU.

49. GS to Lewis Tappan, July 16, 1842, SU.

50. Oct. 16, 1855, SU.

51. Jan. 17, 1865, SU.

52. GS to Lewis Tappan, April 1, 1836, SU.

53. *The Liberator*, July 2, 1836, 106.

54. ESM to GS, May 16, 1836; Aug. 11, 1841, SU.

55. ESM to GS, Dec. 23, 1836.

56. To GS, July 5, 1836, SU.

57. GS to Hon. Thomas, Howell Buxton, June 13, 1839, SU.

58. Joseph Sturge to GS, June 13, 1839; William Jay to GS, July 12, 1836, SU.

59. Hearn, 22.

60. GS to Joshua Giddings, March 21, 1852, SU.

61. Account book, 1847, SU.

62. GS to Wright, Sept. 5, 1845, SU.

63. Garrison to GS, Sept. 5, 1861, SU.

64. Julia Griffiths to GS, Nov. 24, 1851; FD to GS, May 1, 1851, SU.

65. *Frederick Douglass' Paper*, March 27, 1855.

66. FD to GS, May 1, 1851, SU.

67. FD to GS, April 12, 1856; May 23, 1856; Aug. 31, 1856; Dec. 16, 1856; Aug. 18, 1857; July 2, 1860; Sept. 8, 1862, SU.

68. J. H. Harris to GS, Aug. 6, 1867, SU.
69. Jones, 29.
70. GS to Wright, et. al., Nov. 14, 1846, SU.
71. GS to Ezekiel Birdseye, July 8, 1845, SU.
72. GS to John Thomas, Mason, Nov. 21, 1846, SU.
73. SU.
74. GS to E. Birdseye, Dec. 21, 1840, SU.
75. GS to Nathaniel Crenshaw, Dec. 30, 1841, SU.
76. SU.
77. GS to E. Birdseye, July 8, 1845, SU.
78. GS to Mason, Oct. 19, 1846, SU.
79. GS to H. L. Stanley, July 3, 1847, SU.
80. Wendell Phillips to GS, March 23, 1851, SU.
81. GS to Worthington, April 15, 1841, SU.
82. Oct. 1, 1841, SU.
83. March 5, 1842, SU.
84. To GS, June 21, 1841, SU.
85. Lutz, 201.
86. Feb. 10, 1846, SU.
87. Magill to GS, Dec. 27, 1839, SU.
88. Jan. 16, 1840, SU.
89. G. C. Sampson to GS, Jan. 16, 1838, SU.
90. GS to L. E. Simonds, Feb. 24, 1852, SU.
91. GS to Andrews, July 1, 1847, SU.
92. GS to John T. Mason, Nov. 21, 1846, SU.
93. Douglass, 109, 110.
94. Gerrit Smith and the Vigilant Association of New York, 21, 24.
95. GS to FD, July 13, 1860, SLC.
96. To GS, June 18, 1842, SU.
97. To GS, Oct. 17, 1842, SU.
98. Birdseye to GS, June 18, 1842, SU.
99. GS to John Price and Daniel Sullivan, March 9, 1842, SU.
100. Fowler to GS, Jan. 2, 1861, SU.
101. In *Sermons and Speeches*, 136.
102. *State Gazette*, Oct. 4, 1850.
103. Sperry.
104. GS to the Members of the Liberty Party in the County of Madison, Oct. 10, 1851, SU.
105. Buckmaster 213.
106. Siebert, 127.
107. Blockson, *Escape from Slavery*, 19.
108. 40-50.
109. GS to the Members of the Liberty Party in the County of Madison, Oct. 10, 1851, SU.
110. GS to William H. Seward, Aug. 11, 1850, SU.
111. Siebert, 120, 121.

112. Siebert, 122; 128.
113. Siebert, 126, 127.
114. JE to GS, April 29, 1852, SU.
115. Hardin, 1.
116. GS to FD, July 13, 1860, SLC.
117. *The Democratic Volunteer*, Feb. 24, 1875.
118. Verse Book, Dec. 31, 1860, SU.
119. GS to ACS, Aug. 8, 1836, SU.
120. Thomas, 12.
121. June 25, 1842, SU.
122. Stowe to GS, Oct. 25, 1852, SU.
123. Sept. 24, 1851, SU.
124. GS to ACS, Jan. 29, 1861; ACS to ESM, Nov. 29, 1864, SU.
124. Conrad, 69.
125. Conrad, 59.
126. Ibid.
127. Interview, June 16, 1995.
128. Siebert, 185.
129. Clinton 195; E.G. Stoke to G.S., Aug. 22, 1868, SU.
130. Ripley, 51.
131. Breyfogle, 178.
132. Waugh, 3, 4, 44.
133. Wiecek, "Latimer," 225.
134. Quarles, 154; Humphreys, 6.
135. GS to Right Honorable Daniel O'Connell, MP Lord Mayor of Dublin, July 11, 1842, SU.
136. GS to Green, Aug. 4, 1850; Green to GS, Aug. 8, 1850, SU.
137. Humphreys, 24.
138. Humphreys, 32, 33.
139. all quoted in Humphreys 12, 13, 31.
140. *The Rev. J. W. Loguen as a Freeman,* 29.
141. Phelan, 173.
142. *The New York Weekly Tribune*, Aug. 17, 1850, 2.
143. Jan. 15, 1851, SU.
144. Oct. 10, 1851, SU.
145. GS, "Speech for Human Rights," Feb. 6, 1861, in Sermons and Speeches, 172.
146. Letter no. II, North Star, Sept. 5, 1850.
147. Frothingham, 1st ed., 212.
148. Hunter, 116.
149. Quoted in Phelan, 173.
150. GS to D. A. Hall, June 11, 1852, SU.
151. Humphreys, 11.
152. *The New York Weekly Tribune*, Aug. 17, 1850, 2.
153. Lewis Tappan to GS, Nov. 18, 1850, SU.
154. Aug. 11, 1850, SU.
155. GS to Governor Seward, Aug. 14, 1850, SU.
156. GS to Lewis Tappan, Nov. 29, 1850, SU.
157. GS to Joshua Giddings, March 21, 1852, SU.
158. John B. Edwards to GS,

Nov. 22, 1840, SU.

159. Goodell to GS, Oct. 6; Oct. 18; Oct. 29; Nov. 26, 1850, SU.

160. Nov. 26.

161. Mann to GS, Jan. 27, 1851, SU.

162. Gilbert to GS, Oct. 7, 1850, SU.

163. Jackson to GS, Sept. 1; Sept. 2, 1850, SU.

164. Jackson to GS, Sept. 8, 1850, SU.

165. Friedman, 36.

166. Wiecek, 286, 287.

167. Aug. 28, 1854, SU.

Chapter 18

1. Mayer, 439.

2. Mayer, 445, 447, 448.

3. Kansas Meeting in Albany, March 13, 1856, SLC.

4. Oates, 45, 46.

5. Hearn, 18.

6. SU.

7. Sanborn, 81, 82.

8. Oates, 66, 67.

9. Sanborn, 109.

10. Oates, 88,89.

11. Sis personal account, SU.

12. GS to R. B. Miller, April 10, 1856, SU.

13. Harlow, 359, 360.

14. June 5 and 10, 1856, SU.

15. To Stephen Graves, Dec. 21, 1840, SU.

16. Scott, 73.

17. William Goodell to GS, Feb. 13, 1856, SU.

18. GS to Daniel Dickey and George Ellinwood, March 21, 1845, SU.

19. GS to John C. Vaughan, July 28, 1851, SU.

20. GS, "Speech on the Nebraska Bill," April 6, 1854, in *Speeches*, 201, 202.

21. Dec. 19, 1854, SU.

22. GS to *Syracuse Daily Journal*, May 31, 1856, quoted in Frothingham, 1st ed., 233.

23. July 20, 1855, quoted in Oates, 167.

24. Nov. 1, 1856, SU.

25. Higginson to GS, Nov. 22, 1856, SU.

26. Brown to George Stearns, April 27, 1857, letter written at Smith's house and signed by Caleb Calkins, SU; Oates, 91, 183; Sanborn, 119.

27. Scott 216-223, 28. GS to Thaddeus Hyatt, in Hyatt papers, Kansas Historical Society, quoted in Hearn, 49.

29. Oates, 181-190.

30. Renehan, 7.

31. Oates, 232, 233.

32. Feb. 9, 1858, quoted in Renehan, 142.

33. Oates, 224, 225.

34. Oates, 227.

35. Oates, 230.

36. Oates, 229; Hearn 53; Harlow, "Gerrit Smith and the

John Brown Raid," 40; Renehan, 144; Scott, 260.
37. Oates, 233.
38. March 25, 1858, Ohio Historical Society, quoted in Oates, 238.
39. Oates, 238.
40. Oates, 240-242.
41. Conrad, 114, 115.
42. SU.
43. 155.
44. GS to Henry Wilson, March 20, 1866, SLC.
45. Sanborn, "Comment by a Radical Abolitionist," 412.
46. Aug. 9, 1867, SU.
47. "John Brown," Aug. 15, 1867, MCHS.
48. Quoted in Oates, 250.
49. *New York Herald*, Oct. 19, 1859, 3.
50. Renehan, 140, 141.
51. 144-147.
52. Oates, 248.
53. 134, 135.
54. Sanborn, 138.
55. Ibid.
56. Renehan, 153.
57. Oates, 250.
58. Oates, 250.
59. Sanborn, 139.
60. Renehan, 170.
61. Sanborn, 155.
62. GS to ACS, Jan. 10, 1859, SU.
63. Putnam.
64. GS Diary, April 11, 14, 1859 in Frothingham, 1st ed., 237;
Conrad, 121; Sanborn, 237.
65. Conrad, 122.
66. Renehan, 182.
67. Aug. 27, 1859, SU.
68. Oates, 284, 285.
69. Lutz, 272.
70. Oates, 289.
71. Oates, 306.
72. GS to John Brown, June 4, 1859, quoted in full in Sanborn, 165, 166.
73. 166.
74. *New York Herald*, Oct. 28, 1859, 1.
75. *The Liberator*, Oct. 21, 1859.
76. Jan. 25, 1860, SU.
77. Oates, 343.
78. Oates, 308.
79. Sanborn, 141.
80. Oates, 340-341, 346-348.
81. Ramsey 18.
82. Sanborn, 354-356.
83. Oates, 315.
84. Sanborn, 357.
85. John B. Edwards to Caleb Calkins, Nov. 30, 1859, SU.
86. 1st ed., 251, 260, 266.
87. Harlow, "Gerrit Smith and the John Brown Raid," 47.
88. Mabee, 327, 33.
89. *New York Herald*, Dec. 29, 1874, 4.
90. *Utica Herald*, Oct. 24, 1859; Sanborn, 353; Oates, 312.
91. Oates, 301.
92. Oct. 22, 1859, SU.
93. *New York Herald*, Oct. 20 3,

Oct. 21 4, Oct. 28 1, 1859.

94. McKivigan and Leveille, 61.

95. Harlow, "Gerrit Smith and the John Brown Raid," 46.

96. Hammond, 71.

97. SU.

98. ACS to Sanborn, Jan. 3, 1874 in Sanborn, 239.

99. March 27, 1867, SU.

100. Sanborn, 224; Oates, 313-315.

101. Harlow, "Gerrit Smith and the John Brown Raid," 46.

102. Feb 16, 1860, from Rome, Italy, SU.

103. Caleb Calkins' personal account SU.

104. Hammond, 74.

105. *New York Herald*, Nov. 11 1,4, Nov. 16 5, 1859.

106. Harlow, "Gerrit Smith and the John Brown Raid" 49, 50.

107. Gray to John Cochrane, Smith's nephew, Dec. 16, 1859, SU.

108. McKivigan and Leveille, 71.

109. Bull; Benet.

110. McKivigan and Leveille, 71.

111. Gray to GS, April 16, 1860, SU.

112. McKivigan and Leveille 69, 70.

113. SU.

114. Gray to GS, April 16, 1860, SU.

115. Gray to GS, May 6, 1860, SU.

116. To GS, May 16, 1860, SU.

117. ACS to GS, Nov. 20; Dec. 9; Dec. 14; Dec. 16; Dec. 22, 1859, SU.

118. Gray to ACS, Dec. 19, 1859, SU.

119. Verse Book, Jan. 3, 1860, SU.

120. Verse Book, Jan. 11, 1860, SU.

121. Sanborn, to GS, April 25, 1860, SU.

122. Morton to GS, no day, 1860, SU.

123. To Gerrit Smith Miller, April 5, 1860, SU.

124. Pinner to GS, Feb. 12, 1860, SU.

125. GS to Charles Sumner, June 7, 1860, SU.

126. May 3, 1860, PHS.

127. March 15, 1860, SU.

128. Sanborn, 359, 360.

129. Gray to Miller, April 9, 1860, SU.

130. Cochrane to GS, Mar. 17, 1860, SU.

131. Nov. 16, 1859, SU.

132. Renehan, 256, 257.

133. Sanborn, to GS, May 10, 1860, SU.

134. Mayer, 506.

135. Howe, *Letters and Journals*, II 441, in Harlow, "Gerrit Smith and the John Brown Raid," 54.

136. Sanborn, 360; McKivigan,

"His Soul..." 287, 288.

137. *Chicago Tribune,* Nov. 29, 1865; July 22, 1867.

138. Harlow, 450-454.

139. Jan. 8, 1866, SU.

140. Aug. 15, 1867, MCHS.

141. Edwin Morton to Franklin Sanborn, April 13, 1859 in Sanborn, 161.

142. Morton to GS, Jan. 26, 1874, SU.

143. Sanborn, to GS, Oct. 13, 1872 in Sanborn, 231.

144. Sanborn, 232; 233.

145. SU.

146. Sanborn, 226, 227.

Chapter 19

1. GS, Speech in the New York State Capitol, March 11, 1850, MCHS.

2. "Speech on the Nebraska Bill," April 6, 1854, in *Speeches,* 127.

3. GS to D.W. Fort, March 21, 1854, HCL.

4. GS to Luke Hitchcock, et. al., March 12, 1854, Hamilton College Archives.

5. FD to GS, May 6, 1854, SU.

6. Nebraska, 143.

7. Nebraska, 131, 132, 169.

8. Nebraska, 181.

9. Aug. 7, 1854, in *Speeches,* 392.

10. GS to Abraham Lincoln, Aug. 31, 1861, SU.

11. Sept. 5, 1839; Jan. 19, 1842, SU.

12. GS to B. F. Chapman, Feb. 5, 1842, SU.

13. S+B,101.

14. GS, "Discourse in Peterboro," Feb. 21, 1858, SLC.

15. GS to John C. Spencer, Nov. 12, 1851, SU.

16. GS to the New York State Legislature, Feb. 28, 1856, SLC.

17. Nebraska, 188, 189.

18. Douglass, 120, 121.

19. GS to Charles B. Ray, Nov. 16, 1848, SU.

20. GS to Luther Myrick, June 22, 1839, SU.

21. GS to Luther Myrick, June 22, 1839, SU.

22. GS to F. P. Tracy, June 9, 1840, SU.

23. GS to Asa Rand, Sept. 23, 1845, SU.

24. Lewis Tappan to GS, Sept. 9, 1843, SU.

25. GS to Elder Houck, Watertown Wesleyan Church, Dec. 6, 1845, SU.

26. Oct., no date, 1845, SU.

27. GS to William Jay, Feb. 23, 1849, SU.

28. Jan. 23, 1859, in *Sermons and Speeches,* 79.

29. July 22, 1860, in *Sermons and Speeches,* 97.

30. GS to Charles Sumner, June 7, 1860, SU.

31. GS to William Lloyd Garrison, Feb. 22, 1865, SLC.
32. Sept. 3, 1863, MCHS.
33. GS "On the Fort Pillow and Plymouth Massacres," April 26, 1864, SLC.
34. *The Liberator*, March 30, 1858, 52.
35. See John Stauffer, *The Black Hearts of Men*, 265, 266. For Smith's comments on this, see GS to Hon. Mr. Churchill, Dec. 22, 1870, SLC.; GS to J. A. Gurley, Dec. 16, 1861, SLC.
36. GS to Hon. Mr. Churchill, Dec. 22, 1870, SLC.
37. "Equal Rights for Blacks and Whites," March 6, 1874, SLC.
38. GS to Herschel V. Johnson, Oct. 22, 1867, SLC.
39. GS to William Lloyd Garrison, Sept. 12, 1865, SLC.
40. Feb. 28, 1856, SLC.
41. GS to Montgomery Blair, April 5, 1862, SLC.
42. GS to General Ashley, Feb. 6, 1865, SU.
43. GS to J. A. Gurley, Dec. 16, 1861, SLC.
44. GS to J. A. Gurley, Dec. 16, 1861, SLC.
45. GS to Pres. Andrew Johnson, April 24, 1865, SLC.
46. GS to General Ashley, Feb. 6, 1865, SLC.
47. GS to William Lloyd Garrison and Wendell Phillips, Sept. 12, 1865, SLC.
48. GS to George T. Downing, March 6, 1874, SLC.
49. GS to President Grant, Nov. 4, 1868, SLC.
50. GS to George Thompson, Jan. 25, 1862, SU.
51. GS to Montgomery Blair, April 5, 1862, SLC.
52. GS to Governor Seymour, Jan. 12, 1863, in *Speeches and Letters*, 12.
53. Aug. 14, 1860, SU.
54. Mayer, 523.
55. Jan. 12, 1863, in *Speeches and Letters*, 12.
56. GS to S. J. May, Jan. 24, 1857, SU.
57. *The Christian Recorder*, May 11, 1861.
58. Harlow, 436.
59. FD to GS, March 5, 1863, SU.
60. Rochester, NY, news clip of March 2, 1863, in Kelty; GS, "Stand by the Government," Feb. 27, 1863, in *Speeches and Letters*, 22.
61. Harlow, 437.
62. July 2, 1864, SLC.
63. *Madison Observer*, July 20, 1864.
64. von Salleri to GS, April 24, 1863, SU.
65. Lincoln/Douglas debates Sept. 1858. Oaks, 122.
66. Mayer, 510, 512.

67. Aug. 31, 1861, SLC.
68. GS to ACS, Jan. 2, 1862, SU.
69. Oct. 6, 1862, SLC.
70. Jan. 12, 1863, in *Speeches and Letters*, 8.
71. May 6, 1863, SU.
72. FD to GS, Sept. 8, 1862, SU.
73. Greeley to GS, Oct. 21, 1862, SU.
74. GS, "Stand by the Government," Feb. 27, 1863, in *Speeches and Letters*, 24.
75. GS, "Speech on the Rebellion and the Draft in Oswego," July 29, 1863, in *Speeches, and Letters*, 39.
76. GS to GrS, Sept. 1, 1861, SU.
77. Garrison to GS, Oct. 31, 1863, SU.
78. Mayer, 520.
79. SU.
80. GS to GrS, Sept. 1, 1861, MCHS.
81. Clinton, 154, 155.
82. GS, "Gerrit Smith to his Townsmen," Oct. 6, 1862, SLC.
83. GS to William Barnes, March 12, 1864, SU.
84. April 27, 1861, in *Sermons and Speeches*, 190.
85. GS, "Speech on the Rebellion and the Draft," July 29, 1863, SLC.
86. GS, "No Treason in Civil War," June 8, 1865, MCHS.
87. April 24, 1865, SLC.
88. ACS to ESM, no month or day, 1867, SU.
89. July 6, 1867, SLC.
90. GS to Garrison, March 20, 1867, SLC.
91. Maurice Robertson to GS, July 23, 1867, SU.
92. GS to W. L. Garrison, Sept. 12, 1865, SLC.; GS to Hershel V. Johnson, Oct. 22, 1867, SLC.
93. Dec. 22, 1836, SU.
94. GS to Montgomery Blair, April 5, 1862, SLC.
95. GS to W. L. Garrison and W. Phillips, Sept. 12, 1865, SLC.
96. May 15, 1865, SU.; and July 20, 1865, SU.
97. April 10, 1856, SU.
98. GS to General J. M. Ashley, Feb. 6, 1865, SLC.
99. Feb. 5, 1866, SLC.
100. GS to Lee, Sept. 25, 1868, SLC.
101. GS to Grant, Nov. 4, 1868, SLC.
102. Lydia Maria Child to GS, Jan. 7, 1862, SU.
103. GS to Gurley, Dec. 16, 1861, SLC.
104. Tocqueville, 1856.
105. Merton, 1968.
106. Davies, 1962.
107. Dollard, 1939.
108. Painter, 222.
109. *The Liberator*, XXXV, no. 26, June 30, 1865 101; Mill's

letter written on May 13, 1865.

110. Ratner 199, 212, 220-221, quoted from *The Liberator*, May 26—June 2, 1865.

111. Sept. 22, 1865, SU.

112. GS, "The Lesson Not Learned," March 25, 1868, MCHS.

113. Hunter, 80 and 4.

114. Feb. 20, 1844, SU.

115. GS to Daniel Dickey and George Ellinwood, March 21, 1845, SU.

116. *The Liberator*, May 17, 1861, 79.

117. Mabee, 65.

118. Dillon, 264.

119. Nov. 20, SU.

120. To GS, Oct. 18, 1868, SU.

121. Clinton Merriam to GS, Sept. 15, 1873, SU.

122. GS, "Juggelry," Dec. 20, 1867, SLC.

123. GS, "No Treason in Civil War," June 8, 1865, 24.

124. March 6, 1873, SU.

125. GS, "To Thyself Be True," Nov. 23, 1874, SLC.

126. *The Atlantic Monthly*, Jan. 1867.

127. Sept. 11, 1872, SU.

128. Oct. 15, 1866, SU.

129. A. G. Comstock to GS, Jan. 15, 1866, SU.

130. Thomas, W. Conway to GS, Oct. 21, 1874, SU.

131. FD to GS, Oct. 8, 1874, SU.

132. Mayer, 616.

133. Sept. 24, 1874, SU.

134. Ebenezer D. Bassett to GS, Oct. 30, 1863, SU.; Ratner, 202.

135. Child to GS, April 4, 1864, SU.

136. Truth to GS, March 23, 1871, SU.

137. William P. Powells, Chas. L. Reason, Peter S. Porter, Committee on Invitations to GS, May 1, 1873, SU.

138. GS to Johnson, April 24, 1865, SU.

139. Signed "Gerrit Smith, June 16, 1866."

140. 195–198, 80, 248, 374–375.

141. GS to Chase, May 28, 1866, SLC.

142. GS, "On the Bailing of Jefferson Davis," June 6, 1867, SLC.

143. April 10, 1865, SU.

144. Strode 305, 309.

145. Verse Book, Jan. 3, 1868, SU.

146. William Smith, 41.

147. Nebraska, April 6, 1854, 191.

148. *Friend of Man*, Jan. 12, 1837

149. GS to John H. Cocke, Dec. 11, 1840, SU.

150. Sanborn, 145.

151. William P. Powell to GS, July 5, 1870, SU.

152. GS to John C. Spencer, Nov. 12, 1851, SU.

153. GS to ACS, Dec. 4 and Dec. 6, 1874, SU.

154. Betsey Kelty to unknown, no date, probably early 1875, PHS.

155. Smith, M. T., 76.

156. *The Sun*, Dec. 29, 1874.

157. Betsey Kelty to Horace C. Young, Feb. 1, 1875, PHS.

158. *New York Herald*, Dec. 29, 1874, 4.

159. Funeral account from *The Sun*, Dec. 31, 1874.

160. *New York Times*, Dec. 29, 1874.

161. quoted in Ringle, 24.

162. *Memories*, Jan. 14, 1875, MCHS.

163. Unidentified clipping, Jan. 4, 1875, SU.

164. S. Higgins to ESM, Jan. 1, 1875, SU.

165. SU.

5. "White Supremacists hope Obama win prompts backlash," *San Francisco Chronicle*, August 8, 2008.

6. Gadova, D1, D7.

7. Romeu, 1, 4.

8. Nesbitt, D9.

9. Sernett, *Abolition's Axe,* 152.

Epilogue

1. *Frederick Douglass' Paper*, July 29, 1853.

2. *Frederick Douglass' Paper*, Oct. 22, 1852.

3. GS to FD, June 27, 1874, MCHS.

4. "Tubman School Debate's Wounds Still Hurt." *The Post Standard*, March 16, 2003, B3.

Bibliography

Books

"A Rhetorical Analysis of Gerrit Smith's Speeches and Broadsides." http://web. syr.edu/~mdlattim/gs rhetor.html

A Tribute to the Memory of Fitzhugh Smith, the Son of Gerrit Smith, recorded by Josiah T. Marshall New York: Wiley and Putnam, 1840.

Abzug, Robert H. *Passionate Liberator: Theodore Dwight Weld and the Dilemma of Reform*, New York: Oxford University Press, 1980.

Barnes, Gilbert Hobbs. *The Anti-Slavery Impulse: 1830-1844*, New York: Harcourt, Brace & World, 1933.

Bartlett, Irving H. *The American Mind in the Mid-Nineteenth Century*. New York: Thomas Y. Crowell Company, 1967.

Benét, Stephen Vincent. *John Brown's Body*. New York: Rinehart and Company, 1927.

Bentley, Judith. *Harriet Tubman*. New York: Franklin Watts, 1990.

Blassingame, John W., ed. *The Frederick Douglass Papers*, vol. 2: 1847-1853, New Haven: Yale University Press, 1982.

Blockson, Charles L. *The Underground Railroad*. New York: Prentice-Hall, 1987.

Boskoff, Alvin. *The Mosaic of Sociological Theory*. New York: Thomas Y. Crowell Company, 1972.

Bretz, Julian P. "The Economic Background of the Liberty Party," John R. McKivigan, ed., *Abolitionism and American Politics and Government*, New York: Garland Publishing, 1999.

Breyfogle, William. *Make Free: The Story of the Underground Railroad*. New York: Lippincott, 1958.

Brownson, Simeon. *Diary*, PHS.

Buckmaster, Henrietta. *Let My People Go: The Story of the Underground Railroad and the Growth of the Abolition Movement*. Boston: Beacon Press, 1941.

Burdick, Donna Dorrance. *Snipets from the Hills of Smithfield*. Vol. 1-6, 1994-1999.

Caillé, Augustus. *Postgraduate Medicine*. New York: D. Appleton and Company, 1922.

Campbell, Stanley W. *The Slave Catchers: Enforcement of the Fugitive Slave Law, 1850-1860*, New York: W.W. Norton and Company, 1968.

Campisi, Jack. "The Oneida Treaty Period, 1783-1838." in *The Oneida Experience*. Jack Campisi and Laurence M. Hauptman, eds. Syracuse: Syracuse University Press, 1988.

Conrad, Earl. *Harriet Tubman*. Washington, D.C.: The Associated Publishers, Inc., 1943.

Cooley, Donald G. and Paul Zuckerman, eds. *Family Medical Guide*. New York: Better Homes and Gardens Books, 1973.

Craven, John J. *Prison Life of Jefferson Davis*, New York: Carleton, 1866.

Cross, Whitney R. *The Burned Over District*. Ithaca: Cornell University Press, 1950.

Davis, David Brion. "The Emergence of Immediatism in British and American Antislavery Thought" in David Brion Davis, ed., *Ante-Bellum Reform*. New York: Harper + Row, 1967.

Davis, Hugh. *Joshua Leavitt: Evangelical Abolitionist*, Baton Rouge: Louisiana State University Press, 1990.

Diary of an unknown Peterboro resident, March through October, 1863.

Dillon, Merton L. *The Abolitionists*, New York: W.W. Norton, 1974.

Dodge, Melvin Gilbert, ed. *Fifty Years Ago: The Half-Century Annalists' Letters to The Hamilton College Alumni Association, 1865 to 1900*. Kirkland: Hamilton College, 1900.

Dollard, John et. al. *Frustration and Aggression*. New Haven: Yale University Press, 1939.

Donaldson, Alfred L. *A History of the Adirondacks*. II, Port Washington: Ira J. Freedman, Inc., 1963.

Douglass Frederick. *Narrative of the Life of Frederick Douglass*. England: Penguin, 1997, first published in 1845.

DuBois, Ellen Carol, ed. *Elizabeth Cady Stanton, Susan B. Anthony, Correspondence, Writings, Speeches*. New York: Shocken Books, 1981.

Dumond, Dwight Lowell. *Antislavery: The Crusade for Freedom in America*. New York: W.W. Norton, 1961.

— "The Abolition Indictment of Slavery," in Hugh Hawkins, ed., *The Abolitionists*. 2nd ed., Lexington, MA: D. C. Heath, 1972.

Edelstein, Tilden G. "John Brown and his Friends," in Hugh Hawkins, ed., *The Abolitionists*. 2nd ed., Lexington, MA: D. C. Heath, 1972.

Ellis, Joseph J. *Founding Brothers*. New York: Alfred A. Knopf, 2001.

Encyclopedia Britannica. 15th edition, 1976.

Evans, Sara M. *Born for Liberty: A History of Women in America*, New York: The Free Press, 1989.

Faust, Ralph M. *The Story of Oswego County*. Oswego, NY: no publisher, 1954.

Field, Phyllis F. "Party Politics and Antislavery Idealism: The Republican Approach to Radical Change in New York, 1855-1860," Allan M. Kraut, ed., *Crusaders and Compromisers*, Westport: Greenwood Press, 1983.

Fifth Annual Report of the Executive Committee of the American Anti-Slavery Society. New York: William S. Dorr, 1838.

Fitzhugh, George. *Cannibals All! or Slaves Without Masters*, edited by C. Vann Woodward, Cambridge: Harvard University Press, 1960. Originally published in 1857.

Fladeland, Betty. *James Gillespie Birney: Slaveholder to Abolitionist*. Ithaca: Cornell University Press, 1955.

Franklin, Benjamin. *Autobiography*. Printed in *The Life and Letters of Benjamin Franklin*. No ed., WI: E. M. Hale + Company, no date.

Friedman, Lawrence J. *Gregarious Saints: Self and Community in American Abolitionism, 1830-1870*. London: Cambridge University Press, 1982.

Frothingham, Octavius Brooks. *Gerrit Smith: A Biography*. 1st ed. New York: G .P. Putnam + Sons, 1878.

Galpin, W. F. *Souvenir Program. New York State Holstein Field Day and Picnic*. August 17, 1929.

Gara, Larry. *The Liberty Line: The Legend of the Underground Railroad*. Lexington: University of Kentucky Press, 1961.

Garrison, William Lloyd. "To the Public," in Hugh Hawkins, ed., *The Abolitionists*. 2nd ed., Lexington, MA: D. C. Heath, 1972.

Gerrit Smith and the Vigilant Association of the City of New York. New York: John A. Gray, printer, 1860.

Glickstein, Jonathan A. "Poverty is Not Slavery" in Lewis Perry and Michael Fellman, *Antislavery Reconsidered: New Perspectives on the Abolitionists*, Baton Rouge: Louisiana State University Press, 1979.

Goodheart, Lawrence B. *Abolitionist, Actuary, Atheist: Elizur Wright and the Reform Impulse*, Ohio: Kent State University Press, 1990.

Gray, John A., printer. "Controversy Between *New York Tribune* and Gerrit Smith." 1855.

Griffith, Elizabeth. *In Her Own Right: The Life of Elizabeth Cady Stanton*. New York: Oxford University Press, 1984.

Grimké, Angelina to Catherine E. Bucher, letter, June 12, 1837, in Hugh Hawkins, ed., *The Abolitionists*. 2nd ed., Lexington, MA: D. C. Heath, 1972.

Hammond, Charles A. *Gerrit Smith: The Story of a Noble Life*. Geneva, NY: W. F. Humphry, 1908.

Harlow, Ralph Volney. *Gerrit Smith: Philanthropist and Reformer*. New York: Holt and Co., 1939.

Hardin, Evamaria. "Syracuse and the Underground Railroad." Syracuse: Erie Canal Museum, 1989.

Harrold, Stanley. <u>*American Abolitionists*</u>, Essex, England: Pearson Education Limited, 2001.

Haskins, James. *Get on Board: The Story of the Underground Railroad*. New York: Scholastic, Inc., 1993.

Hearn, Chester G. *Companions in Conspiracy: John Brown + Gerrit Smith*. Gettysburg: Thomas Publications, 1996.

Henry Campbell letters, 1842-1864, in the possession of Stuart Grant, Zurich,

Switzerland, e-mail: stuartgrant@swissonline.ch.

Hesseltine, William B. *Third Party Movements in the United States*. New York: D. Van Nostrand, 1962.

Higginson, Thomas Wentworth. *Contemporaries*, Boston: Houghton, Mifflin and Company, 1899.

Historical and Statistical Gazetteer of New York State, 1860. Syracuse: R. P. Smith, 1860.

Historical Data Systems, Inc., civilwardata.com.

Humphreys, Hugh C. " 'Agitate, Agitate, Agitate!' The Great Fugitive Slave Law Convention and its Rare Daguerreotype." *Madison County Heritage*, No. 19, 1994.

Hunter, Carol M. *To Set the Captives Free: Reverend Jermain Wesley Loguen and the Struggle for Freedom in Central New York 1835-1872*. New York: Garland, 1993.

Jackson, James Caleb. *Memoirs of the Formation of the New York Antislavery Society*. Transcribed by J. Edward Jackson, Rochester, NY, 1998.

Jordan, Robert Raul, ed. The Civil War. *National Geographic* Special Publications Division, 1969.

Kay, Moss. *Southern Folk Medicine*, 1750-1820. Columbia: University of South Carolina, 1999

Kelty, Elizabeth Hebbard. *Notebook. Peterboro, 1863-1880*.

Klees, Emerson. *Underground Railroad Tales*. Rochester, NY: Friends of Finger Lakes Publishing, 1997.

Kraut, Alan M. "The Forgotten Reformers: A Profile of Third Party Abolitionists in Antebellum New York" in Lewis Perry and Michael Fellman, *Antislavery Reconsidered: New Perspectives on the Abolitionists*, Baton Rouge: Louisiana State University Press, 1979.

— "Partnership and Principles: The Liberty Party in Antebellum Political Culture," Allan M. Kraut, ed., *Crusaders and Compromisers*, Westport: Greenwood press, 1983.

Kruczek-Aaron, Hadley. *Historical Archaeology at the Gerrit Smith Estate: Understanding the Everyday Practice of Reform in 19th Century New York*. Dissertation proposal. Dept. of   Anthropology, Syracuse University, 2000.

— *Struggling with Moral Authority: Religion, Reform, and Everyday Life in Nineteenth-Century Smithfield, New York*, Ph.D. dissertation, Graduate School of Syracuse University, 2007.

Leakey, Richard F. and Roger Lewin. *Origins*. New York: E. P. Dutton, 1977.

Lerner, Gerda. *The Grimké Sisters from South Carolina: Pioneers for Woman's Rights and Abolition*, New York: Oxford University Press reprint, 1998.

Loguen, Jermain Wesley. *The Rev. J. W. Loguen as a Slave and as a Freeman: A Narrative of Real Life*, Syracuse: J.G.K. Truair, 1859.

Luce, G. V. *Benefaction of William Evans and the Evans Festival*. 1858.

Lutz, Alma. *Crusade for Freedom: Women of the Antislavery Movement*. Boston:

Beacon Press, 1968.

Mabee, Carleton. *Black Freedom: The nonviolent Abolitionists From 1830 Through the Civil War*, London: Collier-Macmillan, 1970.

Maddock, R. "Discussions of Christian Union on the reports of the majority + minority of the Committee on plan – Argument of the minority, Peterboro, April, 1841."

Maslow, A.H. *Motivation and Personality*, New York: Harper and Row, 1954.

May, Samuel Joseph. *Some Recollections of our Antislavery Conflict*, Boston: Fields, Osgood, and Co., 1869.

Mayer, Henry. *All On Fire: William Lloyd Garrison and the Abolition of Slavery*, New York: St. Martin's Press, 1998.

McFeely, William S. *Frederick Douglass*. New York: W. W. Norton, 1955.

McKivigan, John R. "The Frederick Douglass – Gerrit Smith Friendship and Political Abolitionism in the 1850s" in Eric J. Sundquist, ed. *Frederick Douglass: New Literary and Historical Essays*. Cambridge: Cambridge University Press, 1990.

McKivigan, John R. "His Soul Goes Marching On: The Story of John Brown's Followers After the Harpers Ferry Raid," John R. McKivigan and Stanley Harrold, eds., *Antislavery Violence*, Knoxville: The University of Tennessee Press, 1999.

McKivigan, John R. *The War Against Proslavery Religion: Abolitionism and the Northern Churches, 1830-1865*, Ithaca: Cornell University Press, 1984.

McLoughlin, William G. "Charles Grandison Finney," in David Brion Davis, ed., *Ante-Bellum Reform*. New York: Harper + Row, 1967.

Merton, Robert K. *Social Theory and Social Structure*. New York: Free Press, 1968.

Miller, Elizabeth Smith. *In the Kitchen*. New York: Henry Holt and Company, 1903.

Mosby Year Book, 1998. "Arsenic Poisoning."

Nash, Howard P., Jr. *Third Parties in American Politics*. Washington, D.C., Public Affairs Press, 1959.

Nye, Russel B. *William Lloyd Garrison and the Humanitarian Reformers*. Boston: Little, Brown and Company, 1955.

Oates, Stephen B. *To Purge This Land With Blood: A Biography of John Brown*. Amherst: University of Massachusetts Press, 1984.

Oberschall, Anthony. *Social Conflict and Social Movements*. NJ: Prentice-Hall, 1973.

Painter, Nell Irvin. *Sojourner Truth: A Life, A Symbol*, New York: W.W. Norton, 1996.

Perkal, M. Leon. "American Abolition Society: A Viable Alternative to the

Republican Party?" John R. McKivigan, ed., *Abolitionism and American Politics and Government*, New York: Garland Publishing, 1999.

Perry, Mark. *Lift Up Thy Voice: The Grimke Family's Journey from Slaveholders to Civil Rights Leaders*, New York: Penguin Books, 2001.

Phelan, Helene C. *And Why Not Every Man? An Account of Slavery, the Underground Railroad, and the Road to Freedom in New York's Southern Tier*, Interlaken, NY: Heart of the Lakes Publishing, 1987.

Phillips, Wendell. "Philosophy of the Abolition Movement," in Hugh Hawkins, ed., *The Abolitionists*. Lexington, MA: D. C. Heath, 1972.

Pilkington, Walter. *Hamilton College: 1812 - 1962*. Clinton, NY: Hamilton College, 1962.

Quarles, Benjamin. *Black Abolitionists*. New York: Oxford University Press, 1969.

Ratner, Lorman. "Powder Keg," 1968, in Hugh Hawkins, ed., *The Abolitionists*. 2nd ed., Lexington, MA: D. C. Heath, 1972.

Renehan, Edward J., Jr. *The Secret Six*. New York: Crown Publishers, 1995.

Richards, Leonard L. *"Gentlemen of Property and Standing": Anti-Abolition Mobs in Jacksonian America*, New York: Oxford University Press, 1970.

Richardson, Joseph G. *Medicology*. New York: University Medical Society, 1905.

Ripley, C. Peter. "The Underground Railroad," in *Underground Railroad*. Washington, D.C.: Division of Publications, National Park Service, no date, c 1998.

Road Records. Town of Smithfield, 1819-1855.

Rose, Willie Lee. *A Documentary History of Slavery in North America*. London: Oxford University Press, 1976.

— *Life and Letters of John Brown: Liberator of Kansas, and Martyr of Virginia*. Boston: Roberts Brothers, 1891.

— *Recollections of Seventy Years*. I and II, Boston: The Gorham Press, 1909.

Schor, Joel. *Henry Highland Garnet: A Voice of Black Radicalism in the Nineteenth Century*. Westport: Greenwood Press, 1977.

Schramm, Henry W. *Central New York: A Pictorial History*. Norfolk: The Donning Company, 1987.

Scott, Otto. *The Secret Six: John Brown and the Abolitionist Movement*. Murphys, CA: Uncommon Books, 1979.

Sernett, Milton C. *Abolition's Axe*. Syracuse: Syracuse University Press, 1986.

— *North Star Country: Upstate New York and the Crusade for African American Freedom*. Syracuse: Syracuse University Press, 2002.

Sewell, Richard H. Ballots for Freedom: *Antislavery Politics in the United States 1837-1860*. New York: Oxford University Press, 1976.

Shattuck, George C. *The Oneida Land Claims: A Legal History*. Syracuse: Syracuse University Press, 1991.

Shryock, Richard Harrison. *The Development of Modern Medicine.* New York: Alfred A. Knopf, 1947.

Siebert, Wilbur H. *The Underground Railroad: From Slavery to Freedom.* New York: Russell + Russell, 1898.

Smith, Gerrit and Albert Barnes. *Correspondence of Gerrit Smith with Albert Barnes.* New York: American News Company, 1868.

— "Autobiographical Sketch of the Life of Gerrit Smith." Smith Papers, Ernest Stevenson Bird Library, Syracuse University, no date, c 1856.

— "Be Natural." Speech in Peterboro, Nov. 20, 1864. New York: The American News Company, 1864.

— "No Treason in Civil War." Speech at Cooper Institute, June 8, 1865. New York: The American News Company, 1865.

— *Sermons and Speeches.* New York: Ross + Tousey, 1861.

— *Speeches and Letters of Gerrit Smith (from January, 1863 to January, 1864) on the Rebellion.* New York: John A. Gray + Green Printers, Stereotypers, and Binders, 1864.

— *Speeches, Letters and Circulars, 1835-1874.* Copy in possession of the author to be donated to the Peterboro Area Historical Society. Copy also at the Madison County Historical Society.

Smith, Margaret T. *Genealogy and Reminiscences of William Smith and Family.* New York: Syracuse, 1874.

Speeches of Gerrit Smith in Congress. New York: Mason Brothers, 1855.

Sperry, Earl E. *Jerry Rescue,* Onondaga Historical Society, 1924.

Stanton, Elizabeth Cady. *Eighty Years and More: Reminiscences 1815-1897.* New York: Schocken Books, 1971. Reprinted from T. Fisher Unwin edition of 1898.

Stauffer, John. *The Black Hearts of Men: Race, Religion, and Radical Reform in Nineteenth Century America.* Cambridge: Harvard University Press, 2002.

— *GIANTS: The Parallel Lives of Frederick Dougless and Abraham Lincoln.* New York: Twelve, 2008.

Stewart, James Brewer. *Wendell Phillips: Liberty's Hero.* Baton Rouge: Louisiana State University Press, 1986.

Stowe, Harriet Beecher. *Uncle Tom's Cabin.* New York: Coward-McCann, 1930. First published in 1852.

Strode, Hudson. *Jefferson Davis: Tragic Hero, The Last Twenty-five Years, 1864-1899,* New York: Harcourt, Brace and World, 1964.

Strong, Douglas M. *Perfectionist Politics: Abolitionism and the Religious Tensions of American Democracy,* Syracuse: Syracuse University Press, 1999.

— "The Application of Perfectionism to Politics: Political and Ecclesiastical Abolitionism in the Burned Over District," unpublished manuscript, Wesley

Center for Applied Theology, Northwest Nazarene University, 2000.

Sydnor, Charles S. "Prologue to the End of Slavery," in Hugh Hawkins, ed., *The Abolitionists*. 2nd ed., Lexington, MA: D. C. Heath, 1972.

Third Annual Report of the American Anti-Slavery Society. New York, 1836.

Thomas, George. "Personal Recollections of Gerrit Smith." Jan. 5, 1875.

Toqueville, Alexis de. *The Old Regime and the French Revolution*. Stuart Gilbert, translator, New York: Anchor/Doubleday, 1955. First published in 1856.

Trudeau, Noah Andre. *The Last Citadel: Petersburg, Virginia, June 1864-April 1865*, Baton Rouge: Louisiana State University Press, 1991.

Wagner, Sally Roesch. *The Untold Story of the Iroquois Influence on Early Feminists*. Aberdeen, SD: Sky Carrier Press, 1996.

— *Matilda Joslyn Gage: She Who Holds the Sky*. SD: Sky Carrier Press, 1998.

Walker, David. *David Walker's Appeal*. Charles M. Wiltse, ed. New York: Hill and Wang, Originally published in 1829.

Ward, Geoffery C. *Not For Ourselves Alone: The Story of Elizabeth Cady Stanton and Susan B. Anthony*. New York: Alfred A. Knopf, 1999.

Ward, Samuel Ringgold. *Autobiography of a Fugitive Negro*. New York: Arno Press, 1968. First published, 1855.

Waugh, John C. *On the Brink of Civic War: The Compromise of 1850 and How it Changed the Course of American History,* Wilmington: SR Books, 2003.

Wells, Anna Mary. *Dear Preceptor: The Life and Times of Thomas Wentworth Higginson*. Cambridge: The Riverside Press, 1963.

Wellman, Judith. *Grass Roots Reform in the Burned-Over District of Upstate New York,* New York: Garland Publishing, 2000.

West, Geoffrey P. ed. *Blocks Veterinary Dictionary*. NJ: Barnes + Noble, 1985.

Wiecek, William M. *The Sources of Antislavery Constitutionalism in America, 1760-1848*. Ithaca: Cornell University Press, 1977.

— "Latimer: Lawyer's, Abolitionists, and the Problem of Unjust Laws." In Lewis Perry and Michael Fellman, *Antislavery Reconsidered: New Perspectives on the Abolitionists*, Baton Rouge: Louisiana State University Press, 1979.

Yellin, Jean Fagan, ed. *Incidents in the Life of a Slave Girl, Written by Herself,* originally edited by Lydia Maria Child, 1861, Cambridge, MA: Harvard University Press, 1987.

Periodicals

"Abolition Convention." *The Chittenango Phenix*. Aug. 28, 1850.

"A Man Ahead of his Time: Gerrit Smith of Peterboro." *Canastota Bee-Journal*, Jan. 28, 1976 6.

"An Exciting Slave Case." *The New York Weekly Tribune*. Aug. 17, 1850 2.

Blockson, Charles L. "Escape from Slavery: The Underground Railroad." *National Geographic*, 166, July, 1984 2-39.

Bishop, Jean Rausch. "He Was for the Birds." *Syracuse Herald American* May 3, 1970 9,10.

Blackett, R.J.M. "William G. Allen: The Forgotten Professor" in *Civil War History*, Vol XXVI, No. 1, March, 1980 39-52.

Buchwald, Alan L. "Intentional Overdose of Dimercaptosuccinic Acid in the Course of Treatment for Arsenic Poisoning." *Journal of Toxicology: Clinical Toxicology*. Jan. 2001 29 113.

Bull, Mary S. "Gerrit Smith." *Good Company*. 6, No.15, Nov.1880 241-248.

Davies James C. "Toward a Theory of Revolution." *American Sociological Review*. 27, No.1 5-19.

"Death of Gerrit Smith." *Daily Palladium* (Oswego). Dec. 29, 1874.

"Death of Greene Smith," Cazenovia Republican, July 29, 1880.

Description of Peterboro. *Madison County Times*, Chittenango, NY, Oct. 19, 1878.

Douglass, Frederick. "An Appeal to Congress for Impartial Suffrage." *The Atlantic Monthly*. Jan., 1867.

Dyson, Zita. "Gerrit Smith's Efforts in Behalf of the Negroes in New York." *The Journal of Negro History*. 3, 1918 354-359.

Edmonston, Nellie K. "Anti-Slavery Activist in Hamilton." *Chenango Valley News*. March 3, 1995, 9.

Evans, George Henry. "To Gerrit Smith," *People's Rights*, July 7, 1844.

Facklemann, Kathleen. "Arsenic: A Novel Cancer Remedy? *Science News*. April 11, 1998 153, 239.

Frederick Douglass' Paper, Aug. 24, 1855; May 19, 1854; Jan. 27, 1854; May 27, 1853; July 29, 1853; Oct. 22, 1852.

Friedman, Lawrence J. "The Gerrit Smith Circle: Abolitionism in the Burned-Over District," *Civil War History*, XXVI 1, 1980. 18-38.

Friend of Man, Jan. 12, 1837; Aug. 15, 1838; Nov. 7, 1839; Feb. 8, 1840.

Gadoua, Renee K. "The Modern Face of Slavery." Syracuse Herald American. May 13, 2001 D1, 7.

"Gerrit Smith." *New York Herald*. Dec. 29, 1874 4.

"Gerrit Smith: The Last of New York's Old Baronial Chieftans." *The Oneida Dispatch*. Jan. 8, 1875.

"Gerrit Smith's Funeral." *The Sun*. Dec. 31, 1874.

"Gerrit Smith's Last Hours." *The Sun*. Dec. 29, 1874.

"Gerritt [sic] Smith: Reformer, Philanthropist, Abolitionist: His Home a Famous Station on the Underground Railroad." *Ziyara Bugle*, 28, No. 8, Dec., 1958 14-17.

Griffiths, Julia. "Letter No. II," *The North Star*. Sept. 5, 1850.

Harlow, Ralph Volney. "Gerrit Smith and the John Brown Raid." *American Historical Review* 38, No. 1, October, 1932 32-60.

Hau, T. "Biology and Treatment of Peritonitis: The Historic Development of Current Concepts." *Journal of the American College of Surgeons.* 186, No. 4, April, 1998 475-484.

Jones, Katherine Butler. "They called it Timbucto." *Orion*, Winter, 1998 27-33.

Jones, William. "Meeting of the Colored People of Troy." *Albany Patriot*, Oct. 28, 1846.

Koeppel, David. "The Religious Experience of Hon. Gerrit Smith." *The Northern Christian Advocate.* Jan. 14, 1875.

Kruczek-Aaron, Hadley. "Choice Flowers ad Well-Ordered Tables: Struggling Over Gender in a Nineteenth Century Household," *International Journal of Historic Archaeology*, vol. 6, no. 3, September, 2002. 173-185.

Levesque, George A. "Black Abolitionists in the Age of Jackson." *Journal of Black Studies.* Dec., 1970, 187-201.

The Madison Observer, Nov. 29, 1843; July 20, 1864; July 28, 1880; July 14, 1914.

McKivigan, John R. and Madeleine Leveille. "The 'Black Dream' of Gerrit Smith, New York Abolitionist." *Syracuse University Library Associates Courier.* 20, No. 2, Fall, 1985.

— " 'He Stands Like Jupiter': The Autobiography of Gerrit Smith." *New York History.* April, 1984 189-200.

Mesinger, Judith. "The Feminist Movement as Reflected in the Gerrit Smith Papers," in *The Courier*, Syracuse University Press, Fall, 1973.

New Haven Journal of Freedom. Aug. 20, 1834.

New York Herald, Oct. 18-21, 28, 29, Nov. 2, 5, 6, 11-13, 16, 1859.

"Obituary. Gerrit Smith." *New York Times.* Dec. 29, 1874.

Oneida Community Journal, vol. 22, no. 1, March, 2008.

Oneida Whig, Oct. 27, 1835.

Putnam, George W. Letter to the editor. *National Anti-Slavery Standard.* Jan. 28, 1860.

Ramsey, David. "Misguided, Wild and Apparently Insane." *Syracuse Herald American.* Sept. 6, 1998, "Stars" 16-18.

Republican Monitor. Nov. 27, 1838.

Ringle, William M. "An Encounter in a Courtroom: Irony and the Evanescence of Fame." *Hamilton Alumni Review.* 28, Summer, 1999 22-25.

Romeu, Jorge L. "Tolerating Cuba." *Herald American.* May 20, 2001 D1, 4.

Sanborn, F. B. "Comment by a Radical Abolitionist." *Century Magazine*, July, 1883 411-415.

San Franciso Chronicle, "White supremacists hope Obama win prompts backlash." August 8, 2008.

Sernett, Milton C. "Common Cause: The Antislavery Alliance of Gerrit Smith and Beriah Green." *Syracuse University Library Associates Courier*. 21, No. 2, Fall, 1986.

Smith, Gerrit. "Essay on Colonization." *The African Repository and Colonial Journal*, March, 1835, ol. XI, No. 3 64-76, 105-119.

Stanton, Henry B. "An Estimate of the Life of Gerrit Smith at Time of His Death," *Syracuse Journal*, Dec. 30, 1874.

State Gazette. Vol. IV, No. 1142, Oct. 4, 1850.

Stauffer, John. "Beyond Social Control: The Example of Gerrit Smith, Romantic Radical." *ATQ*, 11, No. 3, Sept. 1997 233-259.

Steeb, Glen, et. al. "Infections Within the Peritoneal Cavity: A Historical Perspective." *The American Surgeon*. 66, No. 2, Feb. 2000 98-104.

T. S. "Gerrit Smith at Home." *Cazenovia Republican*. May 21, 1874.

The Christian Recorder, May 11, 1861.

The Colored American, Dec. 15, 1838.

The Democratic Volunteer. Feb. 17, 24, 1875; April 7, 15, 1875.

The Liberator, Feb. 15, 1834; Nov. 8, 1834; July 2, 1836; Dec. 7, 1843; Nov. 30, 1849; March 30,1858; May 17, 1861; Oct. 15, 1858; June 13, 1865.

The National Era, Aug. 31, 1854.

The North Star, Aug. 25, 1848; July 20, 1849.

"Tubman School Debate's Wounds Still Hurt," *The Post Standard* (Syracuse), March 16, 2003 B3.

Van Wagenen Jared. "The Story of Gerrit Smith: Reflections from a Visit to a Home Where History Was Made," *American Agriculturist*, Dec. 3, 1927 3, 22.

Wang, J. "Arsenic Pollution Disrupts Hormones." *Science News*, 159, March 17, 2001 164.

Watchman and Reflector, Nov. 7, 1867.

"William Chaplin in Prison." *The New York Weekly Tribune*. Aug. 17, 1850 2.

Wright, Albert Hazen. "Cornell's Three Precursors." *Studies in History*, No. 23, 1960.

Wurst, LouAnn. "For The Means of Your Subsistence… Look Under God to Your Own Industry and Frugality: Life and Labor in Gerrit Smith's Peterboro," in *International Journal of Historic Archaeology*, vol. 6, no. 3, September, 2002, 159-172.

Index

About The Author

Norman K. Dann was born in Providence, RI in 1940. After high school, he spent three years in the U.S. Navy as an aviation electronics technician.

He earned a B.A. degree in psychology from Alderson-Broaddus College in Philippi, WV and an M.A. in Political Science at the University of Rhode Island. He was graduated from Syracuse University in 1974 with a Ph.D. in Interdisciplinary Social Sciences.

He taught for 33 years on the faculty of the Social Sciences Department at Morrisville State College in Central New York.

In retirement, Norm has specialized in research and writing on the abolition movement, with several articles and book reviews for publication. His first book, *When We Get to Heaven: Runaway Slaves On the Road to Peterboro*, was published in 2008.

Norm has dedicated his retirement to sharing the story of local history regarding abolition. He is a member of the Peterboro-based Smithfield Community Association and helps manage the group's annual fund-raiser, Civil War Weekend. He is a founding member of the National Abolition Hall of Fame & Museum and serves on its Cabinet of Freedom.